During the 1920s a wave of postwar ebullience exploded into the Jazz Age, bringing a new and unprecedented accent on youth and a generation that cast off the vestiges of Victorian culture and embraced new trends in art, music, dance, poetry, fiction, and drama. The way was open for an actor who could recapture and redefine the glamour, skill, and galvanizing presence of an earlier day.

John Barrymore is such an actor, and his Richard III and Hamlet, first seen in New York during the 1919–20 and 1922–3 seasons, stand as high-water marks of twentieth-century Shakespearean interpretation. Barrymore was an original, capable of electrifying audiences with the subtle force and brilliance of his acting. His dynamic portrayals and the groundbreaking innovations of his production team, the director Arthur Hopkins and the designer Robert Edmond Jones, helped to revitalize Shakespearean acting and production in America and Great Britain and changed the direction of subsequent revivals.

In this meticulously researched and richly illustrated book, Michael A. Morrison draws upon newly uncovered sources and firsthand interviews with witnesses who knew the actor or saw him perform. Barrymore's historic performances are brought to life through accounts of the preparations, the productions themselves, and the responses of audiences and critics. This fascinating look at one of the more revered and tragic actors of the twentieth century sheds new light on his distinctive contributions in view of past and ensuing theatre traditions.

John Barrymore, Shakespearean Actor

John Barrymore, Shakespearean Actor

MICHAEL A. MORRISON

PUBLISHED BY THE PRESS SYNDICATE OF THE UNIVERSITY OF CAMBRIDGE
The Pitt Building, Trumpington Street, Cambridge CB2 1RP, United Kingdom

CAMBRIDGE UNIVERSITY PRESS
The Edinburgh Building, Cambridge CB2 1RU, United Kingdom
40 West 20th Street, New York, NY 10011-4211, USA
10 Stamford Road, Oakleigh, Melbourne 3166, Australia

First published 1997

Printed in the United States of America

Typeset in New Baskerville

Library of Congress Cataloging-in-Publication Data
Morrison, Michael A., 1953–
John Barrymore, Shakespearean actor / Michael A. Morrison.
p.   cm. – (Cambridge studies in American theatre and drama)
Includes bibliographical references.
ISBN 0-521-62028-7 (hb)
1. Barrymore, John, 1882–1942.
2. Shakespeare, William, 1564–1616 – Stage history – 1800–1950.
3. Shakespeare, William, 1564–1616 – Stage history – United States.
4. Shakespeare, William, 1564–1616 – Stage history – Great Britain.
5. Shakespeare, William, 1564–1616 – Film and video adaptations.
6. Theater – United States – History – 20th century.
7. Theater – Great Britain – History – 20th century.
8. Actors – United States – Biography.
9. Acting – History – 20th century.
I. Title.   II. Series
PR3112.M67   1997
792´.028´092 – DC21   97-12163
CIP

A *catalog record for this book is available from the British Library*

ISBN 0 521 62028 7 hardback

John Barrymore,
Shakespearean Actor

MICHAEL A. MORRISON

CAMBRIDGE
UNIVERSITY PRESS

PUBLISHED BY THE PRESS SYNDICATE OF THE UNIVERSITY OF CAMBRIDGE
The Pitt Building, Trumpington Street, Cambridge CB2 1RP, United Kingdom

CAMBRIDGE UNIVERSITY PRESS
The Edinburgh Building, Cambridge CB2 1RU, United Kingdom
40 West 20th Street, New York, NY 10011-4211, USA
10 Stamford Road, Oakleigh, Melbourne 3166, Australia

First published 1997

Printed in the United States of America

Typeset in New Baskerville

Library of Congress Cataloging-in-Publication Data
Morrison, Michael A., 1953–
John Barrymore, Shakespearean actor / Michael A. Morrison.
p. cm. – (Cambridge studies in American theatre and drama)
Includes bibliographical references.
ISBN 0-521-62028-7 (hb)
1. Barrymore, John, 1882–1942.
2. Shakespeare, William, 1564–1616 – Stage history – 1800–1950.
3. Shakespeare, William, 1564–1616 – Stage history – United States.
4. Shakespeare, William, 1564–1616 – Stage history – Great Britain.
5. Shakespeare, William, 1564–1616 – Film and video adaptations.
6. Theater – United States – History – 20th century.
7. Theater – Great Britain – History – 20th century.
8. Actors – United States – Biography.
9. Acting – History – 20th century.
I. Title.   II. Series
PR3112.M67   1997
792´.028´092 – DC21   97-12163
CIP

A catalog record for this book is available from the British Library

ISBN 0 521 62028 7 hardback

For my parents

Contents

Illustrations

Featured on the part-title pages: John Barrymore as Hamlet

Preface

JOHN BARRYMORE'S RICHARD III AND HAMLET, first seen in New York during the 1919–20 and 1922–3 seasons, stand as high-water marks of twentieth-century Shakespearean interpretation. Many of the conventions of modern practice can be traced to Barrymore's performances: He was the first actor to bring the vocal and physical manner of a postwar gentleman to Shakespeare's tragic protagonists; he was the first to reinterpret time-honored roles in light of modern psychological theory. In New York and London, he was greeted as a tragedian of the first rank. His dynamic portrayals and the ground-breaking innovations of his production team, the director Arthur Hopkins and the designer Robert Edmond Jones, helped to revitalize Shakespearean acting and production in America and Great Britain and changed the direction of subsequent revivals.

Barrymore's *Richard III* and *Hamlet* are generally acknowledged to be two of the most significant Shakespearean events in the history of the modern stage, yet surprisingly little effort has been made to situate his distinctive contributions to the acting of these characters and the innovations of his artistic associates within the broader context of nineteenth- and twentieth-century Shakespearean production. Biographical studies of the actor and his family have appeared steadily over the years, and the revivals have merited chapters in production histories of the plays in which he achieved distinction,[1] but their accounts of his performances are invariably brief and utilize only a small fraction of the available information. An in-depth study of Barrymore's interpretations has yet to appear. This book aims to remedy that oversight by offering a detailed examination of Barrymore's accomplishments in Shakespeare in light of past and ensuing tradition, and by providing a more complete account than has heretofore been available of the circumstances surrounding his portrayals, the details of his performances, and the meaning the productions held for the playgoers of his time.

To understand the formidable impact *Richard III* and *Hamlet* made on the post–First World War generation it is essential to understand the theatrical conditions to which Barrymore and his associates responded. Like Harley Granville Barker's famed Savoy revivals, the Barrymore–Hopkins–Jones productions can be viewed in retrospect as a revolutionary bridge between Victorian and modern methods of acting, direction, and design. The productions should thus be considered in light of the bravura acting of Edwin Booth and Henry Irving, the festive glamour of Augustin Daly's productions, the scenography of Herbert Tree, the neo-Victorian performances of E. H. Sothern and Robert B. Mantell, and the innovative Shakespearean revivals directed by Barker and Max Reinhardt. Consequently the Prologue is devoted to the many Shakespearean legacies Barrymore and his associates inherited. Chapter 1 looks at Barrymore's family background and formative influences and discusses his years on the stage between 1903 and 1919 while examining the forces that shaped him as an actor: Syndicate commercialism; his friendship with the playwright Edward Sheldon, at whose urging he abandoned the ephemeral comedies in which he had won popular stardom; and his early collaborations with Arthur Hopkins and Robert Edmond Jones, pioneering American practitioners of the New Stagecraft.

The second and third chapters examine in detail the 1920 Barrymore–Hopkins–Jones *Richard III* and the 1922–4 *Hamlet*. Both chapters include documentation of the preparation for these productions, performance reconstructions based on promptbooks, reviews, memoirs, and other evidence, and an analysis of the critical response. Chapter 4 documents Barrymore's 1925 production of *Hamlet* at the Haymarket Theatre in London – a noteworthy triumph for an American, and a seminal influence on a younger generation of English actor-practitioners. Chapter 5 features a discussion of the many attempts at Shakespeare, some successful, others not, made by Barrymore during the seventeen-year period (1925–42) he devoted mainly to motion pictures. The Epilogue examines the far-reaching impact of *Richard III* and *Hamlet* on subsequent generations of actors, directors, and designers.

Throughout, my focus is also on Barrymore and his production team's accomplishments in the context of the cultural revolution that swept across Western society after the First World War. Barrymore was emblematic of the theatrical changes that accompanied the postwar rebellion against Victorian and Edwardian values in much the same way that Edmund Kean had symbolized the Romantic revolution of a century earlier. Barrymore's efforts, and those of his associates, were a response not only to Shakespearean tradition but also to the spirit of artistic reinvention that permeated postwar culture.

An issue central to this study bears explanation. At various times I refer to the "bravura" repertory. By this, I mean simply the body of Shakespeare's plays that had, over the course of several centuries, emerged first and foremost as vehicles for a leading actor's skill. Examining the repertories of the eminent Shakespeareans of the late seventeenth, eighteenth, and nineteenth centuries one sees these plays time and again: *Hamlet, Richard III, Macbeth, Othello, The Merchant of Venice, King Lear.* At times, of course, these were joined by *Romeo and Juliet, Julius Caesar, Coriolanus, Richard II, Henry V,* and one or two more. The latter grouping generally occupied a secondary place, however, and the plays were performed less frequently. It has become common to refer to the first group, the heart of the repertory, as "Shakespearean tragedy." In fact, the actors who performed these plays came to be known as "tragedians"; yet this grouping properly incorporates a history (*Richard III*) and a comedy (*The Merchant of Venice*), both integral parts of a repertory in which a leading actor's portrayal, rather than the play itself, was often the primary attraction.

The need for this designation is clear when considering *Richard III* and *Hamlet* in the context of the longstanding American tradition of dynamic, exciting Shakespearean performance. Barrymore's impersonations can in many ways be viewed as the final flourishing of a tradition that had prospered in America for more than a century, a tradition enriched by charismatic interpreters such as Edwin Forrest, Junius Brutus and Edwin Booth, and Richard Mansfield, and enhanced by the frequent visits of foreign Shakespeareans such as Henry Irving and Johnston Forbes-Robertson. Great Britain has subsequently claimed Laurence Olivier and John Gielgud, but the United States, although witnessing no shortage of Shakespeare in the years since Barrymore's portrayals, has yet to produce an actor whose performances merit favorable comparison.

Although Barrymore attempted only two Shakespearean roles on stage – far fewer than the number attempted by the theatrical "greats" of an earlier era and the eminent British actor-knights to come – he achieved phenomenal success in parts that for centuries had been proving grounds for a tragedian's ability. His performances and the productions with which he was associated made an extraordinary impact on playgoers of his era. If the opinions of the critics, theatre artists, and other witnesses to his portrayals are to be trusted – and I have given them ample room to speak in the pages that follow – he stands as an original, an innovator among actors of Shakespeare, a tragedian capable, at his best, of electrifying audiences with the subtle force and brilliance of his acting. His impersonations created a furor in the theatrical capitals of the English-speaking world, and the influence of his portrayals, particularly his Hamlet, reverberated in the theatre for decades to come. To his contemporaries, his Shakespearean performances were among the modern theatre's towering achievements.

It is not my intention here to dwell on the details of Barrymore's complex and colorful private life except as they affected his development as an actor, and particularly his attempts at Shakespeare. Similarly, I make only brief mention of Barrymore's substantial film career, a fascinating realm but one that lies beyond the scope of this work. Rather, the main focus of this study is the manner in which Barrymore and his confreres revolutionized Shakespeare in performance during the 1920s and, in doing so, set the stage for much to follow.

Acknowledgments

I N   T H E   N I N E   Y E A R S I worked on this book I received valuable assistance from many institutions and individuals. I am grateful to the
staff of the Billy Rose Theatre Collection and the Hammerstein Collection
of Recorded Sound, New York Public Library, Lincoln Center; to the 42nd
Street branch of the New York Public Library and its Manuscript and Newspaper Library divisions; to Louis Rachow and Raymond Wemmlinger of the
Hampden–Booth Library at The Players; to Lynn Doherty, Kathy Mets, and
Marty Jacobs of the Theatre Collection, Museum of the City of New York; to
the Harvard Theatre Collection; to the Houghton Library, Harvard; to the
Manuscript Division, Muggar Memorial Library, Boston University; to the
Beinecke Rare Book and Manuscript Library, Yale University; to the Museum
of Television & Radio; to the Film Division, Museum of Modern Art; to the
Shubert Archive; to the Library of Congress; to Sam Gill of the Margaret Her-
rick Library, Academy of Motion Picture Arts and Sciences; to Jenni Inman
of the University of Colorado at Boulder Special Collections; to Melissa Miller of the Harry Ransom Humanities Research Center, University of Texas at
Austin; to the Special Collections, Jean and Alexander Heard Library, Vanderbilt University; to the Folger Shakespeare Library; to the Huntington Library; to Georgianna Ziegler and Nancy Shawcross of the Van Pelt Library,
University of Pennnsylvania; to Lorraine Brown of the Federal Theatre Archive, George Mason University; to Nena Couch of the Lawrence and Lee
Theatre Collection, Ohio State University; to Jon Reynolds, Georgetown University Archivist; to Nelson Maurice of Wesleyan University; to Geraldine
Duclow of the Philadelphia Free Library Theatre Collection; to the Philadelphia Public Library; to the Buffalo and Erie County Public Library; to the
Metro Toronto Central Reference Library; to the Emgee Film Library; and
to the Minna Rees Library of the City University of New York and its inter-
library loan division.

In England, I am indebted to the staff of the Theatre Museum, London;
to Joe Mitchenson and Richard Mangan of the Mander and Mitchenson Col-

lection, Beckenham, Kent; to the British Library and the British Newspaper Library, Colindale; to Steve Atkinson of the Haymarket Theatre archive; to F. R. Miles, Archivist, King's College School, Wimbledon; to Stephen Chaplin, Archivist, Slade School of Fine Art–University College, London; to the Shakespeare Library, Birmingham Central Library; to the library at the Garrick Club; to the BBC Sound Archive; to the British Sound Archive; and to Jonathan Barnes and Jessica Wood and Patrick Newley and Diana Galvin, who provided hospitality and encouragement while I was in London.

There were many people who shared their recollections of John Barrymore as an actor and individual and helped to provide cultural and theatrical context through in-person and telephone interviews and correspondence. Regrettably, a number of these witnesses to theatrical history have died since I began this book. I am grateful to Dame Judith Anderson, Wilva Davis Breen, Alexander Clark, Claudette Colbert, Joe De Santis, Dorothy Dickson, Honor Earl, Maurice Evans, Douglas Fairbanks Jr., Dame Gwen Ffrangcon-Davies, Robert Flemyng, Sir John Gielgud, Robert Harris, Helen Hayes, Katharine Hepburn, Evelyn Laye, Alison Leggatt, Robert Morley, Matthew Norgate, Elliot Norton, Philip Rhodes, Sybil Rosenfeld, Margaretta Scott, Athene Seyler, Louis M. Simon, Rosamund and A. C. Sprague, J. C. Trewin, Maurice Valency, Edward Wagenknecht, and Margaret Huston Walters.

I must also thank, for their pioneering contributions, the authors of the many biographies, studies, and articles about Barrymore and his family that have come earlier – several of whom have offered counsel and assistance – along with the authors of a number of valuable works on Shakespeare in performance. I have tried to acknowledge my debts to these sources in the notes and bibliography.

Finally, John Barrymore was assisted in his ascent to Shakespearean distinction by a "Board of Regents," consisting of Edward Sheldon, Arthur Hopkins, Robert Edmond Jones, and Margaret Carrington. Their wise and generous advice contributed much to his accomplishments. I have been equally fortunate. I am particularly grateful to James Kotsilibas-Davis for his hospitality, encouragement, editorial guidance, and advice, and for introducing me to the joys of collecting theatrical memorabilia. Stanley Kauffmann gave me the benefit of his considerable wisdom and provided helpful comments on the manuscript on many occasions. Marvin Carlson and Judith Milhous read this work in a number of its early drafts and offered valuable suggestions for improvement. Special thanks are due to Hollis Alpert, John C. Burnham, Anna Kay France, Michael Gnat, John Istel, Rosamund Krueger, Karl Levett, William Luce, Dana Sue McDermott, Martin F. Norden, Margot Peters, Joan Pollock, Lawrence J. Quirk, Jean Rawett, Loren Ruff, Charles H. Shattuck, Rakesh Solomon, Peggy Stewart, and Simon Trussler. Don B. Wilmeth and

Anne Sanow, my editors at Cambridge University Press, believed in this project from the first and helped to guide this book from manuscript to finished volume.

I am grateful to the Research Foundation of the City University of New York for providing travel and research grants, and to Vera M. Roberts for endowing a fellowship that enabled me to spend a year of uninterrupted writing. To my wife, Jeri E. Bullock, who has lived with this project for practically as long as we have known each other, my love and gratitude.

For permission to quote from published and unpublished material acknowledgments are due to the following: to Antony John Barrymore Fairbanks for published and unpublished writings of John Barrymore; to Fred W. Hall Jr. for unpublished writings by Robert Edmond Jones; to Margaret Huston Walters for unpublished writings by Margaret Carrington; to Phyllis Wilbourne for Constance Collier's unpublished essay on John Barrymore's acting; to the University of Pennsylvania Special Collections for John Jay Chapman's 24 November 1922 letter to H. H. Furness Jr.; to the Vanderbilt University Special Collections for unpublished writings by Lark Taylor; and to the Society of Authors for Bernard Shaw's 22 February 1925 letter to John Barrymore. The chapter dealing with John Barrymore's London *Hamlet* appeared in earlier form in *New Theatre Quarterly*.

PART ONE

SETTING THE STAGE

Prologue: Legacies

This young artist, profiting by the lessons of tradition . . . casts it boldly aside and emerges into the rarified atmosphere of a new art, greater because it is new, stronger because it is built upon an old foundation.
– *Brooklyn Times* (9 March 1920)

ON 6 MARCH 1920, the Plymouth Theatre in New York was filled to capacity with more than a thousand spectators eager to witness John Barrymore's Shakespearean debut in *Richard III*. Many in the audience that night were skeptical of Barrymore's ability to succeed. Although he had achieved noteworthy triumphs in dramatic roles beginning with his appearance in Galsworthy's *Justice* four years earlier, he was only half a decade removed from a career devoted almost exclusively to light comedy. His limitations – particularly his restricted vocal range – were widely known. Many in the audience, too, could recall the bravura Shakespearean performances of Edwin Booth, Sir Henry Irving, and Richard Mansfield. Barrymore, in effect, was challenging those great names.

By the end of the evening, however, it was apparent to most in attendance that Barrymore's skills compared favorably with those of his eminent predecessors. His repressed, psychological portrayal, coupled with a newly developed vocal technique and with ground-breaking direction and design by Arthur Hopkins and Robert Edmond Jones, had created a theatrical landmark. Barrymore's performance was praised as a welcome departure from the "tragic elevation" and orchestral tones of the Victorian and Edwardian period; the production was hailed by the leading critics of the day as the beginning of a new era for Shakespeare on the American stage.

Two years later, Barrymore again joined forces with Hopkins and Jones to present *Hamlet*. The production opened on 16 November 1922 to near-unanimous critical acclaim: Barrymore's performance, Hopkins's direction, and Jones's mise-en-scène combined to create one of the American theatre's

3

most vital, exciting Shakespearean events. The production broke new ground with its Freudian approach to character; Barrymore's "intellectual" portrayal – colloquial, restrained, yet forceful and startlingly clear – electrified the audience and moved the critics to proclaim him as one of the greatest of the Hamlets seen in New York.

Barrymore won further laurels in 1925 when he brought his Hamlet to the Haymarket Theatre in London – a city where American tragedians had in the past achieved scant success. His performance was acclaimed by discerning critics such as James Agate and A. B. Walkley; many of their colleagues hailed the "modern note" of his interpretation and, like their American counterparts, opined that Barrymore's production made *Hamlet* seem like "a new play."[1]

The Barrymore revivals constituted a theatrical revolution, one that swept aside the modified version of the nineteenth-century "grand manner" that a number of leading actors had kept before the public through the years of the First World War and beyond. Swept aside, too, were the colorful, interpolated pageantry and crowds of supernumeraries of tradition, along with the magnificent palaces, panoramic battlefields, and other tributes to the scene painter's art that had typified Shakespearean production during the Victorian era and its aftermath. Barrymore, Hopkins, and Jones played a major role in restoring the tradition of dynamic Shakespearean production to Broadway and the West End, but their most significant contribution – often overlooked by biographers and historians – was to introduce innovative methods of acting, direction, and design that radically transformed the style and interpretive techniques of nineteenth- and early twentieth-century Shakespeare and pointed the way toward modern practice.

Like all revolutions, of course, the upheaval in Shakespearean interpretation led by Barrymore and his confreres was dependent upon a traditional, established order to dethrone. In order to understand Barrymore's "new art" and the no less vital contributions of Hopkins and Jones, we must first understand the theatrical and cultural conditions that prevailed during the years preceding their bold attempts to "revitalize" Shakespeare. For a proper evaluation of the Barrymore revivals it is necessary to consider three essential questions: Who were the actors to whom audiences and critics could look as a basis of comparison with Barrymore's portrayals? What were the theatrical forces that influenced the work of Barrymore and his associates? How did the general cultural environment affect the triumvirate's approach to the classics?

Therefore, before we turn to an examination of the forces that influenced Barrymore's development as an actor, and to accounts of the *Richard III* and *Hamlet* productions, it will be helpful to set the stage, so to speak, with an investigation of the Shakespearean traditions of the then-recent past. A number of key factors that directly influenced Barrymore and his artistic associates provide a historical background for their innovative practices: the performances of the eminent Shakespearean actor-managers who came of age during the mid-to-late Victorian era; the decline of their tradition in the late nineteenth century; the rebellion against traditional Victorian staging in Europe and Great Britain during the 1900s and early 1910s; and the unsettled state of Shakespearean acting and production in America during the first two decades of the twentieth century.

Whenever possible, both here and in the chapters that follow, I have attempted to view the Barrymore revivals from the perspective of the rapidly changing cultural life of their time. The end of the First World War brought a remarkable new beginning to American society and to the smaller world of the theatre within. The late teens and early twenties were a time when America rose rapidly to a position of cultural preeminence in the West, a time when social philosophers and psychologists predicted a "brave new world" and younger intellectuals cast off the traditions of their predecessors, rejecting what they considered to be a genteel, simplistic view of the human condition and its characteristic credos and art forms.[2]

Though the conclusion of the Great War is generally considered a point of demarcation for American society, the seeds of this new beginning were in fact much in evidence in the decade prior to the Armistice. The watershed 1909 Clark University Conference in Worcester, Massachusetts, attended by Sigmund Freud and a number of his European and American disciples, helped to establish the "new psychology" in America; the famed 1913 Armory Show introduced New York audiences to Duchamp's *Nude Descending a Staircase*, along with paintings by Cezanne, Matisse, Van Gogh, and Gauguin, Brancusi's sculptures, and works by American post-Impressionists; Nijinsky toured America twice during the mid-1910s, bringing a more sensual, uninhibited style of ballet; and during the 1911–12 season, Max Reinhardt's production of *Sumurun* gave Broadway its first glimpse of Gordon Craig's New Stagecraft. All of these events and many more helped to foster a rich period of cultural foment that burst upon the American scene, creating a climate in which new methods of Shakespearean interpretation would be welcomed.

In the postwar years, especially, there emerged a new and heady atmosphere – a rebellion against pomposity, formal Victorian manners, and prudery. Victorian notions of culture were challenged time and again by revolutionary new methods of expression: Picasso's paintings, Stravinsky's music, Freud's theories that sexuality, aggression, and subconscious longings were primary motivating factors in human behavior. At the same time, Americans began to evince a growing interest in artistic experimentation, along with a diminishing tolerance for traditional methods of Shakespearean acting and production. Although the years preceding the Barrymore revivals were large-

ly a period of interregnum for Shakespeare in America – years when the tradition of Edwin Booth was carried along in the main by conservative actor-
managers of limited skill, and the artistic innovations that had arisen in Europe were seldom seen on Broadway – this same period witnessed significant
changes in the theatre and in American society in general. By the early 1920s,
Shakespeare, ever the "form and pressure" of changing manners and aesthetic values, was ripe for reinterpretation.

The Victorian Shakespeareans, 1860–1900

For more than three centuries prior to the Barrymore revivals, succeeding
generations of actors had made the plays of Shakespeare their own, building
upon the foundations established by their predecessors while reinterpreting
the plays in light of shifting conceptions of "nature" and "art." At times, these
changes had taken place gradually; for example, the classic style of Thomas
Betterton, who had established the tradition of Shakespeare's bravura repertory as the measuring rod of a post-Restoration tragedian's ability, was carried
on in modified form during the early eighteenth century by Barton Booth
and, later, by James Quin. In many instances, however, change had arisen as
the result of sudden, revolutionary upheavals in the style of playing. David
Garrick's London debut as Richard III in 1741 in a new, more "natural" style
instantly established a standard for a generation. ("If this young fellow be
right, then *we* have all been all wrong," Quin is said to have remarked.) Edmund Kean's 1814 Drury Lane debut as Shylock similarly launched a coup
d'état against the reigning formalism of the John Philip Kemble school by
bringing to Shakespeare a more passionate, visceral mode of playing. ("We
wish we had never seen Mr. Kean," commented William Hazlitt. "He has destroyed the Kemble religion . . . in which we were brought up.")[3]

Like most of his predecessors, John Barrymore inherited elements of an
older acting style, many of which he incorporated into his own technique. Although many critical column inches would be devoted to his "contemporary"
portrayals – his Hamlet, wrote Ludwig Lewisohn, was "in the key of modern
poetry" and "the finest modern fiction" – the director and critic J. T. Grein
was entirely correct in assessing his style as "an amalgam of modernity and
tradition."[4] Yet Barrymore, like Garrick and Kean, broke with tradition to introduce a more "natural" method of performing the time-honored repertory. By the early 1920s, the refined, idealized characterizations and "tragic
elevation" of the "old guard" were looked upon by many American playgoers
– especially the younger intellectuals – as belonging to a bygone era. Barrymore, while borrowing and adapting selectively from the older style, particularly in his emphasis on vocal range and variety and finely nuanced
pantomime, reacted against tradition; he deliberately shunned many of the

conventions of the Shakespearean theatre of his youth: the vocal mannerisms, graceful poses, rhetorical gestures, and "big moments" climaxes. At the
same time, however, Barrymore's predecessors played a key role in shaping
his art, and their portrayals were cited frequently by contemporary reviewers
attempting to appraise his impersonations in the context of the great performances of the recent past.

The Shakespeareans who had achieved legendary status in Great Britain
and the United States before the American Civil War were far too remote, of
course, to be more than honored names in the pantheon. Not so their eminent late-Victorian and Edwardian successors, whose performances lingered
in the memories of many playgoers, and whose legacies influenced Barrymore's impersonations in several key respects. Four actors of this period, especially, indirectly and directly affected Barrymore's portrayals and the response of his audiences and critics: Edwin Booth, Henry Irving, Richard
Mansfield, and Johnston Forbes-Robertson.[5]

Barrymore was too young to have had more than childhood memories of
Booth, if in fact he saw him, and the younger generation of reviewers – the
Woollcotts, Brouns, and Macgowans – would have had no firsthand knowledge of his virtuosity. Nonetheless, critics of a certain age – John Corbin,
Burns Mantle, Alan Dale, Percy Hammond, and J. Ranken Towse, along with
a number of commentators in London – could look to Booth's by-then legendary Hamlet (and in a few cases, his Richard III) as a basis of comparison
with Barrymore's portrayal.

To American playgoers of the period between the early 1860s and his retirement in 1891, Booth's Hamlet (Fig. 1) – described by William Winter as
"like the dark, mad, dreamy, mysterious hero of a poem," and acted "in an
ideal manner, as far removed as possible from the plane of actual life" – was
the most renowned Shakespearean impersonation of their time. Booth's purity of elocution was unmatched among his contemporaries; his low, rich, musical (though not loud) voice was almost universally praised for its range and
beauty. Booth was gifted with brooding, poetic good looks and expressive eyes
and features; his characterizations were illuminated by penetrating intellectual and spiritual insights. A series of personal misfortunes – the death of his
wife in 1863, his brother's assassination of Abraham Lincoln in 1865, the loss
in 1873 of Booth's Theatre, his "great national temple" of dramatic art, due
to financial mismanagement – only deepened his awareness of the nature of
tragedy. His hundred consecutive nights of *Hamlet* at the Winter Garden
Theatre in New York during the 1864–5 season inaugurated the era of the
Shakespearean long run in America, and he played the role, in cities large
and small, for more than thirty years. He played other roles, of course, in
Shakespeare and in plays that passed as "near-classics" in those days – Edward
Bulwer-Lytton's *Richelieu*, Tom Taylor's *The Fool's Revenge*, and many more –

Figure 1. Edwin Booth as Hamlet. Author's collection.

but his Hamlet, as Charles H. Shattuck observed, was the part "with which he was most identified, in which the people loved him best."[6] Booth's impact still lingered in the American theatre of the 1920s, long after he had made his final bow. Barrymore later maintained (innocently or not) that he had no knowledge of Booth's "Hundred Nights" when his own Hamlet was nearing that mark; yet he was surely aware of the shadow Booth's accomplishments cast upon American actors who attempted his celebrated roles.

Of more direct impact on Barrymore and his audience were the performances of Henry Irving, who opened his first London *Hamlet* at the Lyceum in October 1874 to extraordinary critical acclaim and played for 200 performances. His Hamlet, noted for its haunted quality and absence of traditional "points," had last been seen in America during the season of 1884–5

Figure 2. Henry Irving as Shylock. Author's collection.

and would have been recalled during the early 1920s by relatively few play-goers, but he had offered his Shylock (Fig. 2), Macbeth, Wolsey, and a galaxy of roles in costume melodrama for two decades to come, both in London at the Lyceum and on his frequent American tours, the last of which had come during the 1903–4 season. Irving had a magnetic personality and a distin-guished appearance. Although hampered by a voice not noted for its music, he acted with a compelling intensity that had a mesmeric power on his audi-ences. Barrymore would not have had an opportunity to see Irving's Richard III – his later assertion to his biographer, Gene Fowler, notwithstanding – but he did see him in a number of roles. He was doubtless impressed by Irv-ing's intensity and intelligence, and particularly by his "between the lines" byplay – an element that would later become a hallmark of his own Shake-

Figure 3. Richard Mansfield as Richard III. Author's collection.

spearean method. Indeed, it seems likely that Barrymore emulated this facet of Irving's style; years later, he listed Irving as his favorite actor, and at the time of his London *Hamlet,* he called him "the most arresting and exciting figure in the history of the modern stage."[7]

The dynamic and versatile tragedian Richard Mansfield rose to prominence in America during the 1880s in contemporary plays. In 1889, however, he turned to Shakespeare, presenting *Richard III* at the Globe Theatre in London. After modest artistic success and significant financial loss, he brought his production to the United States, where it was greeted with mixed reviews; nevertheless, it proved popular enough to warrant three revivals in Mansfield's repertory. Mansfield was gifted with mimetic powers and a "deep and thrilling" voice of exceptional range; contemporary critics often said

Figure 4. Johnston Forbes-Robertson as Hamlet. Author's collection.

that his acting failed to reach "the loftier heights of tragic emotion," yet they also acknowledged that he possessed an "electric quality" which aroused excitement and enthusiasm. Barrymore, in all likelihood, saw Mansfield's Richard III (Fig. 3). Although he was critical of Mansfield's "exaggerated" walk, his formidable voice might well have influenced Barrymore's decision to undertake vocal training prior to his own Shakespearean debut. He was aware that Mansfield's impersonation, last seen in New York during the 1905–6 season, had set a high standard for a generation and would be recalled in comparison with his own portrayal.[8]

Another performance often recalled by reviewers and playgoers of the early 1920s was the Hamlet of Johnston Forbes-Robertson (Fig. 4), first seen in London during the 1897–8 season. To the author and critic Hesketh Pearson, Forbes-Robertson was "blessed with every possible quality for success as an actor: classical features, an engaging manner, a natural elegance of speech and movement, and a rich melodious voice with the tone of an organ." From first to last, wrote Pearson, his Hamlet was "perfectly natural, nobly well-bred, ideally graceful, flawlessly spoken, and so charming that one could see it again and again . . . yet never tire of it." Unlike Irving, Forbes-Robertson eschewed "between the lines" business; Bernard Shaw commended him for playing the role "on the line and to the line, with the utterance and acting simultaneous, inseparable and in fact identical." An apprenticeship with the eminent Shakespearean actor-manager Samuel Phelps and extensive experience in modern plays enabled Forbes-Robertson to combine the best attributes of the classic and naturalistic schools, although like Booth and Irving, he interpreted Hamlet as "a microcosm of ideal Victorian manhood: gentleman, scholar, friend, man of honor, lover, moralist, son – 'and the Prince in everything.'"[9] He made eight starring tours in the United States between 1904 and his retirement in 1916, in many of which he offered his Hamlet. Though Barrymore maintained that he did not see Forbes-Robertson's acclaimed portrayal,[10] it was one that was widely known and admired on both sides of the Atlantic. His impersonation, familiar even to the youngest of critics, was a criterion of excellence by which Barrymore's Hamlet would inevitably be judged.

THE BRAVURA TRADITION, led by Irving, Forbes-Robertson, and Herbert Beerbohm Tree – a tragedian of limited skills but a gifted producer of "grand spectacular" Shakespeare in the high-Victorian manner – remained strong in England through the end of the nineteenth century. By that time, however, the American branch of the tradition, then more than a century old, had fallen into sharp decline, due in part to a cultural shift and modification that radically altered the way in which Shakespeare's plays were perceived by the public.

As Lawrence W. Levine has demonstrated, Shakespeare, during the first two-thirds of the nineteenth century, had been perceived in America as a popular playwright whose works appealed to all classes of society.[11] Typically the plays were presented with contemporary songs between the acts and comic afterpieces, thus attracting popular as well as "cultivated" audiences. Nineteenth-century Americans prized oratorical eloquence; Shakespearean passages were taught as rhetoric and elocution at public schools across the country, becoming part of a shared national culture. The heroic style of Shakespearean acting that flourished through midcentury and beyond was in many ways similar to the style of popular melodrama, and thus attracted a broad spectrum of playgoers. The touring star system, which enabled celebrated actors to travel from one local stock company to the next, was facilitated by the existence of a well-known repertory, at the heart of which lay bravura Shakespeare. New York alone saw ten *Hamlets* during the 1857–8 season; it was common for even the smaller cities to witness half-a-dozen *Lears* and *Othellos* each year.

By the end of the Civil War, however, a number of tendencies had emerged that led ultimately to a new attitude toward Shakespeare. The advent of more rigid class distinctions and the gradual elimination of the comic afterpieces and popular songs resulted in a growing disparity between "refined" and "popular" entertainment. During this same period, the oral culture that had assisted Shakespeare's popularity – the delight in oratory, rhetoric, and debate – began to diminish as well. American society in general became more cerebral, less rhetorical; Shakespeare's appeal was perceived increasingly as to the mind, not the ear.

There are no easy explanations for this phenomenon, which over a relatively brief period of time would transform Shakespeare from a popular playwright to an author whose works were regarded as the domain of the "culturally elite." Tastes in entertainment invariably change from one generation to the next, yet the cultural hierarchies that began to appear in America during the high Victorian era – which also affected contemporary attitudes toward opera and symphonic music – were in many ways unprecedented. Arbitrary boundaries between "high" and "popular" culture became increasingly evident as the century progressed; more and more, Shakespeare came to be viewed as a sacred author of "revered classics," a playwright to whose works much of the populace did not – or could not – relate.

In keeping with this new emphasis, the plays began to be taught primarily as literature at schools and colleges across the country. In 1882, A. A. Lipscomb, writing in *Harper's New Monthly Magazine*, argued that Shakespeare could be a valuable tool in raising America's cultural standards to a higher level; but he cautioned that the plays required "rigid mechanical training" to be understood. Shakespeare, he concluded, had "ascended to a new and higher sphere in the firmament of intellect" and was "destined to become the Shakespeare of the college and university, and even more the Shakespeare of private and select culture. Nor will he ever be perfectly himself and perfectly at home anywhere else."[12] This by no means isolated commentary was repeated for decades to come. During the 1880s and 1890s, Americans were reminded time and again that a level of education and cultivation were required to appreciate the plays, an emphasis that soon came to affect their widespread popularity. Audiences, comprised increasingly of the burgeoning middle class, demanded less "challenging" fare: To a new generation of playgoers, raised on ephemeral comedies, melodramas, swashbuckling adventures, and musicals, Shakespeare and the "old style" acting and production methods seemed stuffy and outmoded.

At least one critic welcomed this change in the public outlook. In 1890, A. C. Wheeler published an article entitled "The Extinction of Shakespeare," in which he argued that the theatregoing public had "outgrown Shakespeare" – especially the traditional bravura repertory. While predicting that Shakespeare the poet would "live on in higher and rarer atmospheres," he argued that in the theatre, Shakespearean tragedy, with its violent passions and larger-than-life acting, had little to offer the present day. "Does anyone suppose that the theatre will ever be able to reawaken in the public the interest in Shakespeare's work that attended its earlier productions?" he asked. The answer, to Wheeler, was obvious: Tragedy was dead. He concluded,

> In half a score of contemporaneous plays we shall find somebody answering to the "crushed tragedian," who is only an exaggerated type of the serious player of yesterday and who has only to mouth and declaim, and assume the antic air, and strut in high-stepping pace to become instantly ridiculous. This personage is always crushed. By what? Simply by the indifference of the age in which he superfluously lags.[13]

Wheeler's assessment, though typically overstated and acerbic, was in many ways an accurate barometer of changing cultural attitudes. During the season of 1890–1, Edwin Booth, in the twilight of his career, was asked by a Boston manager to forfeit a two-week engagement so that he would not interrupt the flow of profits generated by a sensational melodrama. Productions of Shakespeare's comedies – which not coincidentally lent themselves more freely to the "naturalistic" acting then in vogue – continued to flourish for a time, a result, in part, of the directorial talent of Augustin Daly, America's first great *regisseur*, whose opulent revivals in the 1880s and 1890s were among the most fashionable and glamorous theatrical events presented at the height of the Gilded Age. By the mid-1890s, however, public favor had begun to turn away from Daly and the comedies as well. Shakespeare – in any form – had increasingly become a playwright to be "highly respected" and "respectfully avoided" by mainstream American audiences.

This shift in public taste was solidified in 1896 with the formation of the Theatrical Trust, which soon came to be known as the Syndicate – an organization that would determine the workings of the American theatre for the next two decades. In August of that year, the producer Charles Frohman, along with Al Hayman, Mark Klaw, Sam Nixon, Fred Zimmerman, and Abraham Lincoln Erlanger, who together owned or controlled numerous theatres and booking agencies across the country, met in New York to combine their interests. The decline of the resident stock company system and the advent in the 1880s of touring "combination companies," most emanating from New York and offering a single play, had initially resulted in confused conditions for local managers. The Theatrical Trust resolved to centralize booking in New York, to bring order (not to mention profit) to the chaos of the new system. A number of actors and producers rebelled against the Syndicate's increasing power, including, at one time or another, Minnie Maddern Fiske, Sarah Bernhardt, and David Belasco, yet their efforts proved unsuccessful. Within a few years, the Syndicate controlled more than five hundred theatres across the country, dominating the fields of booking and production in a decade when monopolies and trusts – U. S. Steel, Standard Oil, American Telephone and Telegraph – ruled American business. Recognizing the public's growing aversion to Shakespeare and its limited interest in the new "intellectual" drama that was emerging in Europe, the Syndicate provided a steady supply of modern entertainments to Broadway and the heartland.

The realization that American audiences would no longer enthusiastically patronize Shakespeare as they had in the past was not confined to the new breed of manager. Henry Irving and Richard Mansfield journeyed across the country frequently through the 1890s and beyond, but typically with only one or two Shakespeare plays per season. The remainder of their repertory of half a dozen plays or more consisted principally of costume melodrama – a wise choice, considering the tastes of their audiences.[14] By the turn of the century, the prevailing wisdom among most American managers was that Shakespeare had become the province of a "refined minority" of playgoers and thus held limited appeal to the ticket-buying public.

The Winds of Change: Europe and Great Britain, 1900–14

The history of staged Shakespeare in the years preceding the Barrymore revivals is a study in contrasts. While acting and production remained largely traditional and conservative in America – understandably so, since there was little to encourage talented practitioners to devote their skills to the Bard – across the ocean there emerged a new spirit of innovation. In Europe and Great Britain during the 1900s and early 1910s, the plays experienced a remarkable upsurge, the result, in part, of vital new methods of staging and design that challenged the conventions of traditional Victorian practice.

Through the final years of the nineteenth century and beyond, actors and managers had vied to surpass each other with "historically accurate" costumes and scenery, majestic pageantry, and spectacular effects. The splendors of Irving's Lyceum, the crowds of supernumeraries that animated the Duke of Saxe-Meiningen's famed production of *Julius Caesar*, the extravagant pageantry of Herbert Tree's *A Midsummer Night's Dream*, with its sumptuous palace, verdant woodlands, and live rabbits on stage, built upon and perfected the pictorial tradition that had existed through much of the Victorian era. The realistic scenery, which fed the passion of contemporary audiences for spectacular scenic illusion, required frequent intervals for scene changes, often adding forty-five minutes to a play's running time. Texts were frequently rearranged for the sake of scenic convenience, while most actor-managers cut passages and eliminated "superfluous" subplots to focus on the title character, or to end each act with an effective "curtain." It was necessary, of course, to bowdlerize the plays for "propriety's sake." Victorian audiences, for example, heard nothing of Hamlet's "secret parts of fortune" exchange with Rosencrantz and Guildenstern, nor his chiding reference to Ophelia regarding "country matters" in the play scene.

By the turn of the century, however, the first stirrings of rebellion against traditional Victorian methods became evident. In England in the 1880s and 1890s, William Poel, convinced that the extravagant stagings, reverential delivery, and actor-centered texts of Victorian Shakespeare were contrary to the playwright's rhythm and style, began mounting amateur productions on neo-Elizabethan platform stages.[15] Poel's revivals, featuring rapidly spoken verse and near-complete texts, were generally regarded as pedantic experiments and had little immediate effect on the commercial theatre of Irving and Tree. Nevertheless, he continued his crusade through the 1900s and beyond, and the early years of the century saw the increased utilization of his methods on the professional stage. English companies led by Frank Benson and Ben Greet began to feature fuller texts and (partially for economic reasons) minimal scenery.

At the same time, other theatrical visionaries emerged whose methods similarly foreshadowed revolution. In the late 1890s and early 1900s, the Swiss theorist Adolphe Appia and the Englishman Gordon Craig independently began formulating a theory of theatrical practice involving the harmonious blend of acting, scenery, costumes, lighting, and text, welded together by a master artist, the director. Rejecting the lavish realism and multiple set pieces of Victorian tradition, they espoused simple, permanent or semipermanent settings and subtle lighting effects that symbolically "suggested" the essence of a play. Craig, the better self-publicist, became the evangelist of the new movement in 1905 with the publication of his manifesto, *The Art of the Theatre*. His provocative ideas and drawings proved increasingly influential through the decade and beyond, affecting the work of a younger generation of avant-garde artists endeavoring toward a "new" theatre.

Foremost among these younger artists was the innovative German *regisseur* Max Reinhardt, who in 1905 took over the Deutsches Theater in Berlin. Between 1905 and 1914, he directed thirteen of Shakespeare's plays, many of which were kept in the repertory; he presented ten different plays during the 1913–14 season alone.[16] Although Reinhardt became noted for his eclecticism, producing a number of plays in the realistic manner, he was the first important director to achieve noteworthy success applying Craig's principles.

His *King Lear* in 1908 and his *Hamlet* in 1909 featured stark settings that employed color, line, and light to suggest the mood of the drama. Reinhardt's experimental productions achieved widespread public and critical success, and their fame spread far beyond the Continent. For idealistic American men of the theatre with leanings toward "art," a visit to the Deutsches Theater became a rite of passage. Among those who came, in the late 1900s and beyond, were Sheldon Cheney, H. K. Moderwell, Livingston Platt, Maurice Browne, Lee Simonson, and Barrymore's collaborators, Arthur Hopkins and Robert Edmond Jones.

An equally formidable assault upon Victorian practice was launched by the English director Harley Granville Barker, whose productions of *The Winter's Tale, Twelfth Night,* and *A Midsummer Night's Dream* at the Savoy Theatre between 1912 and 1914 presented audiences with a revolutionary synthesis of Poel's rapid verse speaking and Gordon Craig's suggestive, symbolic mise-en-scène. Barker's landmark productions were praised for their vitality, and they proved successful with both critics and the public. Writing in 1912 of Barker's *Twelfth Night,* John Palmer of the *Saturday Review* remarked that "The dead weight of silly tradition . . . has dropped away . . . Mr. Barker's company . . . bring us more nearly in touch with the spirit of their author than any yet seen in modern London."[17]

Within a few years, however, Barker abdicated his position as Britain's leading director to devote his energies to literature and lecturing, leaving the bravura repertory to other, less inventive hands. At the same time, a "new commercialism" emerged in England, brought about by wartime conditions, with the result that Shakespeare and other serious drama were presented in the West End less and less. Meanwhile, the Old Vic began a new policy of featuring competent, conservative productions of Shakespeare's plays, and soon established itself as the "official home" of Shakespeare in London. These developments served to curtail the growing spirit of innovation and change. Away from London, however, in the provinces, the influence of Poel, Craig, and Barker continued to affect the work of Barry Jackson at the Birmingham Repertory Company and the productions of W. Bridges-Adams at Stratford-upon-Avon.

During this same period of foment, Shakespearean acting and production in America continued to be dominated by traditional methods. Although these years saw the cautious introduction of "simplified" scenery and the occasional bold experiment, the mainstream consisted principally of earnest, conservative actor-managers who carried on the legacies of the preceding era's esteemed Shakespeareans though with lesser skill. The innovative practices that had emerged in Europe and Great Britain had only a modest effect on their productions. To understand the impact of the Barrymore revivals on the postwar generation, however, we must necessarily take into account the efforts of these practitioners, along with the fortunes of staged Shakespeare in America during the post-Victorian era.

Immediate Predecessors in America: 1900–19

The early years of the new century witnessed a continuation of the trends that had begun in the previous era. The classical repertory of the old stock companies yielded increasingly to long runs of popular plays dealing mainly with contemporary issues and manners. Tragedy and tragedians continued to lose ground, as audiences turned instead to romantic comedies, society dramas, and fashionable "entertainments." Although Shakespeare remained a presence in the American theatre, the first decade of the twentieth century, especially, saw a further loss of vitality for "literary drama" in general. Actors with leanings toward the classics – a James O'Neill or an Otis Skinner, for example – were discouraged from carrying on the tradition of Edwin Booth and the tragedians of the recent past by the commercial realities of their era. This same period saw the passing of many of the gifted interpreters of an earlier generation. Irving died in 1905; Richard Mansfield's death two years later marked the end of an American tradition that had flourished for more than a century – a tradition of dynamic, exciting performance in which Shakespeare had been featured at the heart of the repertory.

Nowhere was the decline of Shakespeare in the public favor more apparent than in the reception afforded the last of the great Victorian Shakespeareans, Johnston Forbes-Robertson. During the 1903–4 season, when Forbes-Robertson gave his Hamlet for the first time in New York, he was hailed by American critics as the Hamlet of his generation and a worthy heir to Irving. The following season, however, when Forbes-Robertson again featured *Hamlet* in his repertory, the Broadway public failed to respond; the play drew "pitifully small" audiences of only a few hundred spectators.[18] Having learned a hard lesson in commercial reality, Forbes-Robertson returned to New York three times during the next four seasons, but he did not offer *Hamlet*. The following season his repertory centered on Shaw's *Caesar and Cleopatra* (a commercially "safe" choice, since Arnold Daly had produced half a dozen of Shaw's plays during the past two years, to financial and artistic success); *The Merchant of Venice* held a lesser place in the repertory. For the 1908–9 and 1909–10 seasons, his mainstay was Jerome K. Jerome's sentimental morality play *The Passing of the Third Floor Back*. The public, which had stayed away from *Hamlet*, flocked to the box office.

In 1909, an anonymous writer for the *New York Times* contributed a lengthy analysis of this phenomenon. Shakespeare, he wrote, had by then come to attract a "comparatively limited audience" who regarded attendance at the plays as "a sacred duty," an audience consisting in the main of "students of

English literature, members of reading circles, teachers, and a few who, for the sake of their professions, are obliged to take account of every effort to place the poet on the stage." The primary reason for this attitude, he remarked, was that Shakespeare offered no "point of contact" for contemporary audiences. Even *Hamlet* had "grown stale and unprofitable" on a stage that thrived on more modern examples of "human evasiveness and weak will expressed in terms more readily adjusted to the common understanding and experience." In the days of the rhetorical theatre, he continued, "speech and utterance were of more importance than action and the progress of events." He added, however, that modern audiences did not want the stage to be "a platform for the speaker" but rather "a picture book" offering examples of "the life that people know." "It is hoped," he concluded, "that there will be a large enough audience of special patrons of poetic drama to make [Shakespeare] profitable. But, when all is said and done, the tide of modernity in drama is too strong to make the outlook hopeful" (14 March 1909).

These comments reflect the general attitude of American playgoers toward Shakespeare during the first decade of the twentieth century. Nevertheless, a small commercial niche still existed for "culture" and "tradition," and during this period there emerged a new generation of Shakespearean crusaders – competent actors who dedicated their energies and limited skills to the traditional repertory and earned a measure of success (and the gratitude of "refined" audiences who still held an interest in the Bard) by staging and playing Shakespeare in the time-honored style of their predecessors.[19]

Foremost among the American Shakespeareans of this era was Edward Hugh Sothern, the actor E. A. Sothern's son, who had established himself during the 1880s and 1890s as a popular leading man in comedy and cloak-and-sword melodrama. In 1900, to the surprise of many observers, he attempted Hamlet and was received politely, and in some quarters, enthusiastically. Critical commentary made it clear, however, that his Dane was far below the Booth standard. Sothern was praised for his thoughtful, intelligent interpretation, but his portrayal, according to the *Times*, lacked "the force, the thrill, the uplifting effect of great tragic acting."[20]

For several seasons thereafter, Sothern returned to cloak-and-sword plays, occasionally reviving *Hamlet* as a special attraction (Fig. 5). In 1904, however, he entered into a partnership with the actress Julia Marlowe that lasted for two decades, during the course of which they built and maintained a Shakespearean repertory. The first Sothern and Marlowe season featured *Hamlet, Romeo and Juliet,* and *Much Ado About Nothing;* the following season they added *The Taming of the Shrew, The Merchant of Venice,* and *Twelfth Night.* They continued to tour through the 1906–7 season, spent two seasons apart (mainly in commercial, non-Shakespearean plays after diminishing returns forced them to abandon the Bard), then reunited for a disastrous *Antony and Cleopatra* that inaugurated the New Theatre in 1909. In 1911 they were married, after Sothern obtained a divorce from his first wife, the actress Virginia Harned; they toured with their repertory (adding *As You Like It* and *Macbeth*) until 1914, when they entered into a period of temporary retirement, from which they emerged five years later. They continued to appear until 1924, when they bid their final farewell.

During their two decades of Shakespearean activity, Sothern and Marlowe earned respect as competent interpreters of the traditional bravura repertory; but even the most favorable critics often conceded that they possessed limited talents. Julia Marlowe was praised for her expressive voice and for the intelligence of her interpretations, yet to many observers she lacked the vitality and charisma of a Helena Modjeska, an Ellen Terry, or an Ada Rehan. Sothern's deficiencies were even more pronounced, especially when he attempted the great tragic roles. "Sothern lacks fluidity and flexibility of both speech and action," wrote one Broadway commentator, soon after the couple emerged from retirement. "It is indeed remarkable that with such a really limited number of notes in his voice that he is able to act long didactic roles with the effect that he does."[21]

Nevertheless, to a generation Southern and Marlowe *were* Shakespeare; they became, in the words of the historian Lloyd Morris, a "national institution."[22] They were praised – at least in their early years – for their grace and charm, especially in the comedies, and for the sumptuous magnificence of their productions. The passing of time, however, saw a sharply diminishing tolerance for their performance style. To postwar audiences they began to seem increasingly conservative and uninspired. Their acting was invariably characterized by a "sombre stateliness," according to one postwar critic, who noted that "[t]hroughout all their performances there runs the sense of ritual. In all sincerity and very beautifully they are repeating a ceremonial with the outcome of which both they and their audience are thoroughly familiar."[23]

Much was made of the fact that the veteran team, upon their emergence from retirement, had "modernized" their productions. During the early years of their partnership, they had utilized the elaborate scenery of Victorian tradition; yet when planning their return, limited finances and admiration for the pioneering innovations of the New Stagecraft persuaded them to adopt "simplified" scenery for their revivals. "The 'progressives' exhibited some satisfaction," Sothern later remembered, "that we of the despised Victorian era had surrendered to the enlightened present."[24] One thing they could not surrender, however, was their acting; in terms of performance they had come to represent the conservative status quo, and to their "sense of ritual" Barrymore and his production team would respond.

Figure 5. E. H. Sothern as Hamlet. Author's collection.

Similarly dedicated to Shakespeare during the first two decades of the twentieth century was the Scottish-born actor Robert Bruce Mantell, who had emigrated to America in 1882 and, like Sothern, established himself as a popular leading man in romantic melodrama. His career was sidetracked, however, when a judgment for unpaid alimony forced him to remain outside of New York State for more than a decade, during the course of which he toured the provinces and built up a Shakespearean repertory.

By 1904 his legal problems were resolved and he was able to return to New York, where he opened in December with the Colley Cibber version of *Richard III* (Fig. 6). A robust, muscular figure with a powerful voice, Mantell brought a modified version of the heroic Edwin Forrest–John McCullough acting style into the twentieth century, which greeted his "old school" methods with surprising enthusiasm. Between 1904 and 1919 he appeared in New York a total of nine times in engagements ranging from two weeks to two months. His Shakespearean repertory was in many ways a throwback to the era of the barnstorming nineteenth-century tragedians and included Richard III, Macbeth, Hamlet, Jaques, Lear, King John, Romeo, and Othello. For thirty years he toured the country, bringing Shakespeare to innumerable small cities and towns.

In the decade following his return to New York, Mantell earned public and critical respect for his competent craftsmanship; yet the passing of time saw both an erosion of his skills and – as was the case with Sothern and Marlowe – a decreasing tolerance for his performance style on the part of sophisticated audiences and critics. By the late teens, many who had greeted him with warmth and affection a decade earlier had come to regard his bold, powerful characterizations as the exaggerated, bombastic readings of an "old school ham." Unlike Sothern and Marlowe, Mantell made no attempt to "modernize" his productions. He clung tenaciously to his methods and, in doing so, met the same fate as Forrest in his later years: To a new generation of fashionable sophisticates he seemed a quaint relic of an earlier day. His last Broadway appearance came during the 1918–19 season; thereafter he kept to the provinces.

During their early appearances, the Sothern–Marlowe team and Mantell benefited from an almost total lack of competition; their efforts were thrust into bold relief by the relative paucity of classical drama on the American stage. The second decade of the twentieth century, however, saw the first stirrings of improvement in the climate for Shakespearean productions. The English actor Lewis Waller brought his *Henry V* to Broadway in 1912; William Faversham, a popular matinee idol, played an acclaimed Mark Antony in *Julius Caesar* that same year; Forbes-Robertson returned with his *Hamlet* after his English farewell season to inaugurate the newly constructed Shubert Theatre in 1913, and this time he played to full houses. During this same period, America witnessed the cautious debut of innovative British and Continental production methods, led by John Corbin's 1910 "Elizabethan" production of *The Winter's Tale* at the New Theatre and Margaret Anglin's 1913–14 season of Shakespearean repertory, which featured "simplified" scenery designed by Livingston Platt.

Caution was thrown to the winds, however, when Harley Granville Barker came to New York to revive his production of *A Midsummer Night's Dream* as part of his 1915 repertory season at Wallack's. Barker's revolutionary staging was praised by the anonymous critic for the *Times* for its vitality and for exposing New York audiences for the first time to "an unreserved application of some of the new art of the theatre to a Shakespearean text." The Poel-inspired rapid verse speaking, according to the critic, represented "an open

Figure 6. Robert B. Mantell as Richard III. Courtesy Billy Rose Theatre Collection, The New York Public Library for the Performing Arts.

and welcome rebellion against all the pomposities of Shakespearean decla-
mation" (17 February 1915). Still, the production was not to everybody's
taste. G. C. D. Odell, a historian of Shakespearean production in England
and America and a man to whom Tree's lavish, "historically accurate" revivals
represented the ultimate in stage investiture, found it to be silly and vulgar.
"It would require a brave man to predict the future manner of presenting
Shakespeare on the stage," he commented. "I suspect it will not be wholly
Tree's way. . . . I hope it will not be Mr. Granville Barker's. Meantime . . . on
one conviction we rest: Shakespeare is not dead, and the way will be devised
for presenting him so that he shall not spell ruin, but the fullest measure of
success."[25]

Even an archconservative like Odell, however, recognized that a cycle had run its course, that the old methods of acting and production were in need of revitalization and change. In compiling his two-volume history of major trends in English-language Shakespearean production from Betterton to Irving, he could not help but be aware of the long tradition of revolutionary upheavals in style, of the fact that new generations tended to reject tradition- al interpretations to enthusiastically embrace the fresh perspectives brought by a Garrick, a Kean, a Booth. "Perhaps," he concluded, "it will be on the wave of a great democratic impulse that the dramatist who knew most about all kinds of men and women will be carried to new life in the very near fu- ture."[26]

What kind of new life remained unclear. The tercentenary of Shake- speare's death in 1916 brought a flurry of activity, yet Alexander Woollcott, writing in the *Times,* predicted only a limited measure of success for the dozen or more productions that had been planned. "The great Elizabethan is now speaking to a polite but alien house," he commented. The primary reason for this remoteness, he explained, lay in the fact that audiences had been "trained away from Shakespeare" by the "playwrights, producers, and players of the naturalistic school." Poetry, he added, "comes strange from lips and to ears attuned to the most matter-of-fact prose." Quiet, suppressed play- ing and restraint seemed incompatable with "the majesty of blank verse and the lavish outpouring of sheer word music . . . pageantry and impassioned monologue" (12 March 1916).

Woollcott's commentary served to spotlight an enormous gap, increasing- ly in evidence for several decades, that had grown between "Shakespearean" and "natural" acting. The "stately ritual" of Sothern and Marlowe and the larger-than-life characterizations of Robert B. Mantell were in sharp contrast to the repressed, naturalistic style then in vogue. The aura of artificiality that characterized most productions, Woollcott argued, served as a barrier to the audience's ability to relate to universal characters and situations. "Shake- spearean productions we do have, to be sure," he wrote. "Scan the records of the last three seasons here and you find performances, good, bad, and in- different, of no less than fourteen of the plays. Few were greatly satisfying, few prospered." Of the fourteen plays, Woollcott found "but one great per- formance – Forbes-Robertson's Hamlet – and but one example of Shake- speare as a producer's contribution – the Barker production of *A Midsummer Night's Dream.*"

The tercentenary brought numerous productions, led by Herbert Tree's appearances (his first in New York in two decades) in *Henry VIII, The Mer- chant of Venice,* and *The Merry Wives of Windsor;* the highlight of the festivities, to many critics, was a John Corbin–Louis Calvert production of *The Tempest,* which featured minimal scenery and an uncut text. The celebratory wave quickly subsided, however, and within a few seasons the *Literary Digest* commented that "Shakespeare with us has become almost a faded memory."[27]

Nonetheless, the tercentenary year also witnessed the full-blown emergence in New York of a grass-roots revolution aimed at revitalizing the American theatre as a whole. For several years prior to the tercenterary, in fact, the movement had rapidly been gaining ground. Visits to New York during the 1911–12 season by the Irish Players and by Max Reinhardt's production of *Sumurun* introduced American playgoers to vital new perspectives from overseas. Within a year, a growing spirit of rebellion against "the old foes – commercialism and traditionalism" had manifested itself in the establishment of "little theatres" across the country, dedicated to the plays of Ibsen, Strindberg, Wedekind, Hauptmann, Shaw, and Maeterlinck and to new European staging methods. The year 1916 saw seminal productions in New York by the Washington Square Players and the Provincetown Players, as well as the founding of *Theatre Arts Magazine* to provide a voice for native practitioners determined to create an "art theatre" in America.

Although in their early years the proponents of a "non-commercial stage" devoted their efforts almost exclusively to modern European drama and new American plays, it seemed almost inevitable that the new movement, with its emphasis on artistic values, "serious" drama, and Continental innovations in stagecraft, would ultimately turn to Shakespeare. January 1918 saw the inauguration of the Shakespeare Playhouse, a series of special matinees under the direction of Frank McEntee, a young University of Toronto graduate and veteran of Ben Greet's company, whose goals were "a fresh and original conception of the text" and the use of "simplicity and imaginative artistry" to eliminate "all that is obsolete and merely traditional."[28]

The twice-weekly matinees were sponsored first by John Cort at the theatre bearing his name and provided the public with simple, high-quality productions at low prices. Many of the leading actors of the day, among them Cathleen Nesbitt, Tyrone Power, Gilda Varesi, and Edith Wynne Matthison, welcomed the opportunity to participate. "It is Shakespeare that the actors of the largest gifts love best to play," declared McEntee. "Shakespeare is the measure of the acting art. Shakespeare worthily interpreted is essential to the best things of the theatre and to the measuring up of the whole spirit of the drama in any season and any place."[29] In the autumn of 1918, sponsorship of this ambitious new venture was assumed by Arthur Hopkins at the Plymouth Theatre.

The productions, which initially played to small audiences of intellectuals and Shakespeare buffs, soon began to attract a broader segment of the public. The enthusiastic support of the trend-setting carriage trade contributed much to their success. "The Bard has become fashionable," wrote Ada Patterson, soon after Hopkins presented his initial matinees. "It is the smart thing to-day to go to the Plymouth Theatre at half-past ten on Saturday morning, as it is to attend an eleven o' clock musicale at the Waldorf-Astoria, or an Isadora Duncan dance festival at the Metropolitan Opera House." Society, she commented, had "taken up Shakespeare" just as it had taken up "woman suffrage" a few years earlier. Scholars, artists, and the educated elite had passed on "the Shakespearean torch" to a new and rapidly expanding audience.[30]

A good deal of the enthusiasm for the Shakespeare Playhouse productions was due to the emergence of a new Shakespearean star. Walter Hampden, born Walter Hampden Dougherty in Brooklyn, had learned his craft in England, where he served a term of Shakespearean apprenticeship in Frank Benson's company. He returned to America in 1907 where, for the better part of a decade, he appeared in commercial drama and comedy. In 1916, however, he established his New York credentials as a Shakespearean with a much-praised Caliban in the tercentenary production of *The Tempest*, and two years later he won further laurels by playing Mark Antony in *Julius Caesar*, Oberon in *A Midsummer Night's Dream*, and Hamlet and Macbeth in Shakespeare Playhouse matinees at the Cort.

In the autumn of 1918, Arthur Hopkins agreed to present the actor in *Hamlet* and *Macbeth* revivals at the Plymouth. The first *Hamlet* matinee came in mid-November, a few weeks after Hopkins had opened *Redemption* with John Barrymore, also at the Plymouth. Barrymore, in fact, attended many of Hampden's performances that autumn while contemplating his own initial attempt at Shakespeare. The critic Burns Mantle later recalled that Barrymore, leaning against the back rail of the orchestra during one matinee, turned to a friend and remarked his surprise that the play was so good a drama; he had thought of it previously as "one of those formal and high sounding classics which, for this generation, might as well be left in the library," and he later praised Hampden's performance (Fig. 7).[31]

As had been the case the previous spring, critics, too, found much to praise in Hampden's rich voice, graceful presence, and intelligent, restrained interpretation. Although most reviewers found Hampden's portrayal to be lacking in humor and satirical wit, they were cheered by the absence of affectation, exaggeration, and rhetorical pomp. They were equally enthusiastic about the "innovations" Hampden brought to his production: a fuller text, a swifter pace to the verse, "simplified" scenery.

Unstated, but understood and appreciated, was the fact that Hampden brought a much-needed touch of youth to the bravura repertory. As most critics and playgoers were aware, the Shakespeareans of the century's first two decades were an aging generation. Forbes-Robertson was 63 when he bid farewell to the stage in 1916; Mantell turned 60 in 1914 (but gave New York an ill-advised Romeo a year later); Sothern would celebrate his sixtieth birthday in December 1919, a month after his comeback. The paucity of youth-

Figure 7. Walter Hampden as Hamlet. Courtesy The Players.

ful interpreters of the bravura tradition thrust Hampden's efforts into bold relief. "In a generation so nearly void of competent Shakespearean performances [Hampden's Hamlet] affords an opportunity not lightly to be missed," commented the *Times* (23 November 1918).

To many observers, Hampden initially seemed destined to be the "new Forbes-Robertson" (to whom he bore a slight physical resemblance), or even the "new Booth." In one sense, the comparisons were apt, for like his Victorian predecessors, Hampden presented audiences with an idealized, gentlemanly Prince of Denmark. His youth, skill, and the new "fashionability" of Shakespearean productions enabled him to succeed, at least at first, with a conservative, traditional interpretation of Shakespeare's character. His May 1919 revival at the Thirty-ninth Street Theatre, a commercial Broadway run, brought further critical plaudits.

Posterity rendered a harsher verdict on Hampden's skills. Over the course of the next four decades, he dedicated his energies to Shakespeare and other poetic drama whenever possible. In addition to Hamlet and Macbeth, his repertory included Romeo, Othello, Shylock, and many more; he achieved distinction as Richelieu and Cyrano. However, the initial burst of enthusiasm for Hampden's performances within a few years underwent a sharp reappraisal. Although he was admired and praised throughout his career, recurring criticisms soon emerged: He recited rather than fully assuming a character, he "lacked spontaneity," he made Shakespeare "sound not like poetry, but like verse."[32]

All this, however, would come later. To New York audiences during the 1918–19 season, Hampden was clearly the new Shakespearean champion, a youthful interpreter who offered a welcome alternative to the old-school characterizations of Mantell and the "stately ritual" of Sothern and Marlowe. To Barrymore and Hopkins, he represented a fresh, new standard against which their Shakespearean efforts would inevitably be measured.

The critical acclaim and audience support for Hampden's performances undoubtedly helped to convince Sothern and Marlowe that the time was right for a comeback. In November 1919, they opened at the Shubert, presenting *Hamlet, Twelfth Night,* and *The Taming of the Shrew* in repertory. Broadway welcomed them after a five-year absence, and the celebratory nature of their return, along with the "new fashionability" of Shakespeare and serious drama in general, were reflected at the box office. "Shakespeare Spells Ruin No Longer," proclaimed *Theatre Magazine,* noting that the receipts for Sothern and Marlowe's four-week engagement totaled more than $100,000.[33] To many observers, it seemed clear that Shakespeare could go beyond special matinees and "occasional" productions and was again ready to take its place in the Broadway mainstream. By the autumn of 1919, Hampden had made plans to return for another commercial engagement with three Shakespeare plays in repertory, and numerous other productions were in the planning stages.

These, then, were the legacies that Barrymore, Hopkins, and Jones inherited as they contemplated their initial Shakespearean venture. The first two decades of the twentieth century had seen a number of important transitions in the ways that Shakespeare was produced in America. "Simplified" scenery had become an accepted convention, even to Shakespearean conservatives. In retrospect, however, they accepted "simplification" with a cautious embrace: Economic advantages, reduced scene-shifting time, and the desire to be "modern" were primary considerations, rather than the aesthetic values championed by Gordon Craig and Max Reinhardt.

The trend toward "modernization" extended in more limited measures to performance style, which for the most part remained elevated and formal, in keeping with Shakespeare's half-century-long ascent to the realm of "high culture." Hampden earned justifiable praise for stripping away some of the artificiality and ritual that typified many productions of the preceding decades, but he made only tentative departures from the idealized notions of Shakespearean character passed on by his Victorian and Edwardian predecessors.

As Hopkins and Jones knew, no such conservatism was evident in Europe, where Shakespeare, especially in Germany, had been revitalized by the use of innovative new directorial concepts and production methods. They were familiar with the methods employed by Max Reinhardt at the Deutsches Theater in Berlin, Jones from firsthand observation.[34] Reinhardt's productions were to prove a seminal influence on their attempts to bring a modern, European style of direction and design to the traditional repertory in America.

The American theatre, in turn, was more than ready for a wholehearted application of Continental theory and practice. The second decade of the twentieth century had seen visits to New York by Barker and Jacques Copeau, whose innovative Shakespearean methods had been greeted warmly by audiences and critics. At the same time, the new movement to raise the American theatre to a higher artistic level had gathered momentum, bringing with it a rapidly expanding audience for "serious" drama and European-inspired acting and production styles.

By 1920, Shakespeare in America was ready to burst forth from two decades of residual Victorianism and artistic transition. A wave of postwar ebullience exploded into the Jazz Age, bringing new vitality to American society as a whole. With it came a new and unprecedented accent on youth and a generation that was ready to cast off the vestiges of Victorian culture to embrace new trends in art, music, dance, poetry, fiction, and drama and accept them into the mainstream. The moment was right for the imaginative application of new European staging methods to the traditional bravura repertory in America; and the way was open for an actor who could recapture and redefine the glamour, skill, and galvanizing presence of an earlier day.

1

The Education of an Actor, 1882–1919

There isn't any romance about how I went on the stage. I did it for just the same reason that a clerk gets a job in a store. I needed the money. I worked just like any clerk. I minded the "boss" – in my case the stage manager – and learned my trade . . . by slow hard stages.

– John Barrymore[1]

IN 1910 JOHN BARRYMORE concluded a brief essay on the current state of the American stage with an optimistic prediction. "In the present day," he wrote, "when the public will not pay to see Shakespeare's plays, few managers present them, but if there was a demand for them, be assured that there would be many actors found to play them, and play them as well as in the days of yore, but in a more quiet vein."[2]

It is unlikely, however, that Barrymore envisioned at the time his own Shakespearean accomplishments of a decade later. When he wrote those words, he had no ambitions, as he confessed a few years afterward, "of playing Mercutio or Benedick or Petruchio" or any of the great tragic roles. Indeed, few contemporary observers would have considered "the young vagabond of the Drew–Barrymore clan" a candidate for histrionic laurels. To audiences of the day, John Barrymore usually meant animation, joy of living, a certain rakish charm; as a "clever player of comedy parts," a matinee idol and colorful figure in New York's nightlife, his star was set and seemed destined to rise no further.[3] For half a decade to come, in fact, Barrymore would continue to devote his skills almost exclusively to romantic comedy, farce, and melodrama. Nevertheless, the years between 1916 and 1919 saw a remarkable transformation: Barrymore entered a new phase of his career, one in which he was to create four memorable serious characterizations – Falder in Galsworthy's *Justice,* the title role in Du Maurier's *Peter Ibbetson,* Fedya in Tolstoy's *Redemption,* and Giannetto in Benelli's *The Jest* – establishing himself in the process as a major force on the American stage.

Contemporary critics were often at a loss to account for Barrymore's "two careers." Why, as Alexander Woollcott wondered, would an actor of "resourceful mind, winged imagination, and a genius for the theatre" wait until he was in his midthirties before turning to dramatic roles? Of the many possible answers, two seem obvious. When Barrymore entered the theatrical arena in 1903, there was little to encourage actors with leanings toward "literary drama." As Brooks Atkinson observed, most plays "were not inquiries into the nature of life or discussions of ideas but vehicles designed to present the stars triumphantly." Ambivalent about his craft, which he adopted as "the easiest means to earn a decent living" after failing as a commercial illustrator, he fell easily into the theatrical status quo: comedies, musical comedies, sentimental farces.[4] By the mid-1910s, however, the growing vitality of the New Stagecraft, along with the burgeoning Little Theatre and Art Theatre movements, had brought theatre in America to a significant turning point; it was most likely not a coincidence that Barrymore's creative urgings stirred his will to action and prompted him to seek perfection in his art at the same moment the American stage began its own rapid surge to maturity.

A more compelling reason for his transformation, and a catalyst for many of his later accomplishments, were his meetings with three gifted men of the theatre: the playwright Edward Sheldon, the director Arthur Hopkins, and the designer Robert Edmond Jones. Barrymore, blithe and mercurial by nature, had been reluctant during his early years on the stage to take either himself or acting seriously; it took those outside himself to awaken his potential and set him on a course that would lead to his fulfilment as an artist. Sheldon, beginning in the 1911–12 season, discerned Barrymore's possibilities and over a period of time persuaded him to attempt "serious" roles, all the while seeking plays that would enable him to prove himself as an actor. It remained for Hopkins and Jones, however, to guide Barrymore on the final steps of his ascent. Their partnership, commencing in 1918 with *Redemption,* culminated within a few years in their landmark Shakespearean revivals.

The legend of the clown who longs to play Hamlet is an old one in the theatre; yet the annals of the stage reveal no more remarkable instance of this transmutation than Barrymore's reinvention of himself as a tragedian. The "evolution of Jack Barrymore, comedian, into John Barrymore, the artist" was a long and difficult one; it is only against the background of his early career that his accomplishments in Shakespeare can be fully understood. His journey to distinction began in a theatrical family in Philadelphia, was grounded in the ephemeral entertainments of the turn-of-the-century stage, and reached its zenith in the late teens and early twenties, when he abandoned the trivial amusements of his youth to test his "winged imagination" with a series of challenging dramatic roles.

Overture: 1875–82

When John Barrymore made his Shakespearean debut in 1920, he could look back not only to a performance tradition extending from Richard Burbage in Shakespeare's time, but also to a family acting tradition more than a century old. His forebears had appeared in support of many of the nineteenth century's celebrated tragedians, and his father and uncle were among the most highly regarded Shakespearean leading men of their generation. Much of this rich, colorful history lies beyond the scope of this volume, but one engagement in particular seems worthy of note: Rarely have the theatrical past, present, and future been juxtaposed as clearly as they were on a memorable evening toward the end of the third quarter of the nineteenth century.

On 25 October 1875, Edwin Booth opened as Hamlet at Augustin Daly's Fifth Avenue Theatre in New York. More than fifteen hundred spectators eagerly welcomed the great tragedian back to the metropolis for his first appearance there since he had declared bankruptcy and relinquished Booth's Theatre, his grand temple of the arts, two years earlier. Almost predictably, his Dane was greeted by the majority of reviewers as an esteemed institution. "Edwin Booth's impersonation of this part is as much a part of our time as Talma's or Garrick's impersonation was of his," wrote the critic for the *World*. "It is the flower of the eclecticism and culture of our age" (26 October 1875).

Nevertheless, there was dissent. Among the few unfavorable notices was a two-part review written by O. B. Bunce and published in *Appleton's Journal*.[5] Although Bunce found Booth's Hamlet to be "the best on the American if not on the whole English-speaking stage," he faulted the performance on a number of grounds. One of his principal objections was that Booth's conception failed to illuminate Hamlet's "fever of the brain" and "abnormal" behavior. "The psychological *Hamlet*," he concluded presciently, "is yet to arise."

Bunce's comments, clearly a minority view, are ironic in retrospect, for supporting Booth in *Hamlet* and in the nine other plays in which he acted during his four-week engagement at Daly's were two young and promising newcomers to the theatrical profession. The friendship they began that season would lead ultimately to the birth of an actor whose landmark characterization nearly half a century later would introduce to the stage the "psychological Hamlet" Bunce had prophesied.

The Rosencrantz, John Drew, had been a member of Daly's company for two years and could claim a formidable theatrical heritage. His maternal grandparents, Thomas Frederick and Eliza Lane, were versatile English provincial players who had appeared in Shakespeare opposite William Charles Macready at the Theatre Royal, Bristol, during the 1820–1 and 1823–4 seasons. His mother, Louisa Lane Drew (Fig. 8), had appeared as a child prodi-

Figure 8. Daguerrotype of Louisa Lane Drew as Ophelia. Courtesy Harvard Theatre Collection.

gy and as an adult leading lady opposite Macready, Edwin Forrest, Junius Brutus Booth, and Booth's sons, Edwin and John Wilkes; since 1861 she had been the highly regarded actress-manager of the Arch Street Theatre in Philadelphia. His father, also named John Drew, had been a popular Irish comedian noted for his Andrew Aguecheek, and for his portrayal of one of the Dromios in *The Comedy of Errors*.[6]

The Laertes, Maurice Barrymore, came from a different background entirely. Born in Amritsar, India, where his father was a commissioner in the Indian Civil Service, he had been christened Herbert Blyth. At 11, he was sent to England for a public school education; he subsequently spent a year at Oxford and studied for the bar. His true interests, however, lay elsewhere. On 21 March 1872 he won the middleweight boxing championship of England as a gentleman amateur and shortly thereafter abandoned law to become an actor, to the dismay of his conservative family. After several seasons of acting in the provinces, during the course of which he adopted his *nom de théâtre*, he journeyed to America, where in January 1875 he made his American debut in Boston as the hero of Daly's melodrama *Under the Gaslight*. Daly, impressed with the newcomer, offered him a position in his New York company soon afterward.

According to Barrymore family legend, it was shortly after the conclusion of Booth's engagement at Daly's that John Drew invited Maurice Barrymore to visit his mother's home in Philadelphia. There the dashing young Englishman began a Benedick and Beatrice courtship of Drew's sister, 20-year-old Georgiana, a talented actress in the Arch Street company and by all accounts his match in looks, wit, and charm. When Georgie joined Daly's company in 1876, they appeared together in numerous classic and contemporary plays, and on 31 December of that year they were married at Louisa Lane Drew's residence in Philadelphia.

In the years that followed, Maurice graduated to Shakespearean leads under Daly's auspices, playing Orlando and Orsino opposite Fanny Davenport's Rosalind and Viola. When financial difficulties forced Daly to disband his company temporarily, Maurice ventured into management and subsequently spent seasons at Wallack's and on tour in support of his mother-in-law's Mrs. Malaprop and Joseph Jefferson's Bob Acres in *The Rivals*. Georgie continued to act during this same period, at the Arch Street Theatre and elsewhere, but her career was frequently interrupted by pregnancy. On 28 April 1878, a son, Lionel, made his debut; on 15 August of the following year, a daughter, Ethel, was born. Two and a half years later, Georgiana Drew Barrymore gave birth to her third child. The entry in the family Bible states simply, "John Sidney son of Maurice H. & Georgiana Blyth Philadelphia Feb. 15 1882."[7]

Beginnings: 1882–1903

The early years of John Barrymore's life were the proverbial "years in a trunk" of theatrical legend. In October 1882, Maurice and Georgie, along with their three children, began a season's tour with the Polish actress Helena Modjeska, a coast-to-coast journey in which Maurice's dashing manner served him well as leading man in *As You Like It* (Fig. 9), *Romeo and Juliet*, *Twelfth Night*, and a number of popular French and German dramas. Maurice and his wife again toured with Modjeska during the 1883–4 season, and their children were left with Mrs. Drew in Philadelphia. In the summer of 1884, however, Barrymore and his brother and sister journeyed with their parents to England when Maurice accepted an offer from Squire and Marie Bancroft to

Figure 9. Maurice Barrymore as Orlando. Author's collection.

join their company at the Haymarket for their farewell season, and Maurice returned to the Haymarket in the autumn of 1885 under a new management.

Between 1886 and 1892, Louisa Lane Drew's home in Philadelphia provided a base of stability for Barrymore and his brother and sister while their parents toured. Their grandmother ran her household with the same nononsense attitude she used to run her theatre, yet she never disguised the affection she felt for her young charges, especially for John. Occasionally, she allowed her grandchildren to visit the velvet and gold Arch for Saturday matinees, where they would sit in her private box.

Barrymore later claimed to have had little interest in the family profession during his childhood and young manhood, yet it is likely that the impressions of actors and acting he formed during his early years influenced his approach to the craft he later adopted. Maurice's flair and panache, his athletic grace and virile presence, whether acquired by inheritance or unconscious emulation, were to become hallmarks of his younger son's style, both as a light comedian and as the skilled tragedian he later became.

So, too, did he gain the ease of manner and "colloquial" delivery for which his uncle, John Drew, was famed. During Barrymore's childhood, Drew earned a reputation as one of the foremost Shakespearean comedians of his generation, playing opposite Ada Rehan in five revivals directed by Augustin Daly between 1886 and 1891 and scoring an unprecedented personal success as Petruchio in Daly's famed production of *The Taming of the Shrew* (Fig. 10). In 1892, however, he defected to Charles Frohman's management, where his offstage sophistication was exploited mainly in a series of contemporary society dramas, a genre to which he devoted his skills almost exclusively for the remainder of his career. Barrymore's recollections of his uncle's Shakespearean performances would have been distant childhood memories, at best, but he did see many of his later portrayals, and learned valuable lessons from his uncle's "stately mannerisms" and ease onstage.

A more subtle, though no less important formative influence, was Louisa Lane Drew. Barrymore "worshipped and adored" his grandmother, and they shared a close relationship during his childhood and teens. He was aware of her disciplined professionalism and total dedication to her craft. In all likelihood, he heard her stories of playing Shakespearean heroines opposite the leading tragedians of the nineteenth century, and of her disdain for the American theatre's shift toward "personalities" and vehicles. "What is called the legitimate drama is disappearing with tragedians," she lamented to a reporter in 1896, "and that it is the case is to be regretted."[8] Although Mrs. Drew's Shakespearean legacy was to have little impact on her grandson's early career, and the irresponsibility he manifested during those same years was the antithesis of everything his grandmother represented, her rich heritage as an actress and her regret at the decline of classic drama may later have spurred his ambitions.

During his younger years, however, Barrymore's ambitions ranged far from the theatre. While attending an elementary school at the Convent of Notre Dame in Philadelphia, he was punished for misbehavior by being ordered to contemplate a copy of Dante's *Inferno* featuring Gustave Doré's macabre illustrations. This encounter awakened his creative imagination, and soon he was sketching devils and monsters on every available scrap of paper. "My interest was aroused," he remembered, "and a new urge was born within me. I wanted to be an artist."[9]

His artistic ambitions continued as the family fortunes shifted. Mrs. Drew was forced by diminishing business to relinquish control of her theatre in 1892, and the following year Georgiana Drew Barrymore's death from tuber-

Figure 10. John Drew as Petruchio. Author's collection.

culosis further disrupted the family. Economic necessity soon directed that Lionel and Ethel Barrymore join "the trade" under Mrs. Drew's auspices, while John continued his education at Mount Pleasant Military Academy in Ossining, New York, where his studies included memorized recitations from *The Merchant of Venice.* Nonetheless, he told acquaintances that he had no intention of becoming an actor (a result, perhaps, of witnessing his family's vicissitudes), and continued to devote every spare moment to sketching.[10]

In the autumn of 1895, Barrymore entered Georgetown Preparatory School in Rockville, Maryland, a Jesuit institution. Although he proved a capable, intellectually curious student and contributed imaginative drawings and poetry to the school magazine, his Georgetown years were also marked by smoking, drinking, and high-spirited hell-raising. At 15, or so his biographer Gene Fowler later claimed, he received his sexual initiation when he was seduced by Maurice Barrymore's second wife. This incident, and his grandmother's death on 31 August 1897, may have intensified Barrymore's habit of seeking refuge in drink, a habit that endured with only periodic interruptions throughout his life. It was in fact a drinking-related incident, and not the oft-told tale of being caught in a Washington bawdy house, that resulted in Barrymore's dismissal from Georgetown in November 1897. The Prefect of Discipline's diary for 27 November reveals that "One of the boys, suspended last Thursday, gave very evident signs on leaving Study Hall during regular studies tonight, that he was weak-kneed. Investigation showed that he belonged in the Infirmary, where he will wait until *Monday* morning & then he will take a train home. This is the first case of the kind this year." The entry does not specify the student's name, but a detailed record of Barrymore's financial disbursements ends at this time.[11]

A few months later, Barrymore accompanied his father to London, where in the autumn of 1898 he was enrolled at King's College School in Wimbledon Common. In November 1899, he registered for a dual course of English literature and art at University College and the Slade School in London, where his studies included readings of Macaulay, Addison, and Shakespeare and "drawing and painting from the antique and life." However, there is no evidence in the college fee books that he returned for a second term. He later claimed to have devoted much of his subsequent stay in London to bohemianism and nocturnal adventures, yet it is tempting to think that he attended the theatre frequently. His sister had acted with Irving at the Lyceum, and his father had performed with Forbes-Robertson and Tree at the Haymarket; the tradition of the great Shakespearean actor-managers was one with which he was undoubtedly familiar, even as an adventurous teenager.[12]

Barrymore returned to America in the summer of 1900, his formal academic education complete. Soon afterward, he made his stage debut with his father in Augustus Thomas's one-act comedy *A Man of the World* at a benefit performance in Coytesville, New Jersey. In October, he reprised his role opposite his father in a week-long vaudeville engagement at the Columbia Theatre in Cincinnati; among the other attractions on the bill was an "original, unique and eccentric juggler," W. C. Fields.[13] Still, he felt little inclination toward the theatre as a career, and he persuaded Maurice to finance lessons at the Art Students League and with the painter Carl Strunz. In November, he got a job as an illustrator for the *New York Evening Journal*.

Two events the following year were to have lasting repercussions on Barrymore's future. On 4 February 1901, Ethel Barrymore scored a stunning success at the Garrick as Madame Trentoni in Clyde Fitch's comedy, *Captain Jinks of the Horse Marines* – a Charles Frohman production – and found herself elevated overnight from ingenue to Broadway star. However, less than two months later, Maurice Barrymore suffered a complete mental breakdown as a result of tertiary syphilis and was institutionalized, first at Bellevue Hospital, then at a private sanitarium at Amityville, Long Island. Barrymore was shaken by his father's rapid descent into madness, and Fowler later observed that "the bleak overtone of this breaking of his parent's reason never quite died away" in his thoughts.[14] The immediate effect was entirely practical, however: There would be no more money from his father for art studies, and Barrymore was forced to subsist on his own modest salary, or, increasingly, on his sister's generosity.

In October 1901, Ethel Barrymore summoned her younger brother to Philadelphia as a short-notice replacement for an actor who had temporarily departed her *Captain Jinks* company. "I took the whole thing as a joke," he later admitted. "It was serious for my sister, but I didn't care. I was young and unimpressed by the situation." In the middle of the first act, his memory deserted him; both he and the cast were forced to improvise until the curtain. Charles Frohman, in the audience that night, was nevertheless impressed by his youthful flair. "With a better memory," he remarked, "you might make a comedian some day."[15]

Barrymore regarded the experience as little more than a whimsical adventure, and he returned to New York to continue his artistic career. While working for the *Journal,* he created a poster for Daniel Frohman's production of *If I Were King,* a starring vehicle for E. H. Sothern; he exhibited a grotesque sketch, "The Hangman," at a show sponsored by the Press Artists League, and was awarded a scholarship to study with the painter George Bridgeman; in January 1902, *Cosmopolitan* published four of his macabre drawings, along with an encouraging critique. That May, however, his tenure at the *Journal* came to an abrupt end when he arrived at the office minutes before his deadline one day and was assigned to provide a sketch to accompany an editorial about a sensational murder-suicide written by Arthur Brisbane, the *Journal's* editor. The resulting illustration was rushed to the photoengraving department, but there was little time for an adequate job of reproduction. Brisbane, seeing the blur that accompanied his article, promptly summoned the young illustrator into his office and fired him.

For the next year and a half, although he sold an occasional drawing, Barrymore subsisted largely on his sister's charity. By the autumn of 1903, however, Ethel Barrymore, aware of her brother's bohemian habits and at the same time paying a considerable portion of her salary toward her father's bills at the sanitarium, decided that it was time for the 21-year-old aspiring artist to fend for himself. The knowledge that family connections could provide work in the theatre led him inevitably to the family trade, though his first steps in that direction were without enthusiasm or inclination.

Apprenticeship to Stardom: 1903–10

The theatre that John Barrymore found when he decided reluctantly to abandon art and seek his livelihood on the stage was radically different from the theatre in which Maurice Barrymore and John Drew had trained and established themselves. A generation earlier, the stock company system had required actors to master a variety of dramatic styles; Shakespeare and classic drama lay at the heart of the repertory. By the time Barrymore made his debut, however, the acting profession had been thoroughly transformed by the public's attraction to "personalities" and modern "entertainments." Broadway runs were invariably followed by lengthy provincial tours, where the "direct from New York" label lured audiences to the box office. It was not unusual for actors to spend a season or more in the same play, often a vehicle for a popular star. However, vestiges of the old system remained, and it was in one such company that Barrymore made his formal stage debut.

The opportunity for Barrymore to join the family profession came in October 1903 in the person of his uncle Sidney Drew's father-in-law, McKee Rankin, manager of an itinerant stock company starring Nance O'Neil that was then touring the Midwest. Barrymore joined the company at W. S. Cleveland's Theatre in Chicago, where Sudermann's *Magda* had been chosen to inaugurate the run. Rankin, preoccupied with business matters, had little time to offer instruction; it was simply assumed that as a member of a theatrical family he possessed "a certain adaptability to the medium." On 31 October he made his Chicago debut in the minor role of Max von Wendlowski, the heroine's brother. Reviewing his performance, Amy Leslie, the *Daily News* critic, wrote dryly that "John Barrymore, handsome as a picture and uneasy as a bat at a wedding, wandered about through the little scenes as if he had been dressed up and forgotten. As the little blue soldier he had not much to do" (2 November 1903). His next role was equally insubstantial. In *The Jewess*, an adaptation of Augustin Daly's *Leah the Forsaken* that opened the following week, he spoke fewer than a dozen lines of dialogue. Soon afterward, the company's finances took a turn for the worse, and Barrymore, justifiably wary of their ability to stay afloat, returned to New York, having gained little from the experience other than a collection of colorful anecdotes and a heightened sense of insecurity regarding the vagaries of his new trade.[16]

In late November, Charles Frohman, no doubt at the prompting of Ethel or John Drew, arranged for Barrymore's Broadway debut in the small role of a Broadway press agent in Clyde Fitch's new comedy, *Glad of It*. The first appearance on a New York stage of the "last of the Barrymores" was anticipated eagerly by the press; when the play opened on 28 December, the critics who noticed him were generally kind. "His resemblance, in voice and manner, to his father of twenty years ago, walk and gesture, smile and look, was startling," remarked the *Dramatic Mirror*. "He was only in one act, the second, when he could, advantageously to himself and Mr. Fitch, have been in all four" (9 January 1904). Frohman rewarded Barrymore by shifting him to a larger role, but the play proved to be one of Fitch's rare failures, closing after thirty-two performances.

Frohman did not allow the young actor to remain out of work for long. Soon afterward, he cast Barrymore in the part of Charlie Hyne, a bibulous wireless telegrapher, in Richard Harding Davis's farce *The Dictator*. The play's star, William Collier – formerly a bit player with Augustin Daly's company and a comedy favorite with Weber and Fields – became a valuable mentor to the young actor, providing him with a solid education in the craft of comedy. "He had the quickest of minds," Collier recalled years later of his early association with the actor. "He assimilated direction easily, especially in the art of timing. . . . I thought then that he would be a fine comedian, which, indeed, he did become."[17]

On 4 April 1904 *The Dictator* opened on Broadway at the Criterion, earning praise for both star and apprentice. During a cross-country tour the following season, Barrymore gave an interview to Ashton Stevens of the *San Francisco Examiner*, in which he commented brashly on audiences (a "great hulking monster with four thousand eyes and forty thousand teeth . . . [that] makes or breaks men like me") and the lure of his craft ("Acting comes easy and pays well – that's the narcotic"). At the same time, though, he revealed to Stevens that beyond his glibness lay a thoughtful side:

> Acting is a great stunt, you know, if you can succeed at it, which is not hard at first, when you can reckon on that . . . elusive and nebulous thing called personality. . . . The actorial family tree with its prestige and immoderate share of the center of the stage will, for a time, make the young actor a point of attraction. But he's got to make good later on. He's got to justify the tremendous start in his favor. And he's got to take the thing seriously. (4 February 1905)

In practice, however, the reverse was often true. During his engagement with Collier, as indeed throughout much of his early career, the ambivalence Barrymore felt toward his craft often manifested itself in irresponsible behavior. Accounts of this period offer numerous examples of drunkenness, laziness, or arrival at the theatre with little time to spare before his first entrance;[18] but his abundant resources of charm, along with Collier's fondness for his protégé, allowed him to remain steadily employed in spite of a devil-may-care attitude that would have left other young actors looking for work.

During this period, Barrymore acquired the foundations of a technique that would serve him well in the future: He developed a sensitivity to audience response, learned how to "get his stuff over," and improved considerably as an actor. At the same time, however, he was far more interested in offstage distractions – drinking and womanizing – and devoted little earnestness to mastering a disciplined approach to his craft. To ease the tedium of the long run of *The Dictator*, which played more than three hundred performances during the 1904–5 season alone, he began to experiment and embroider on-stage. (Collier, a frequent improviser himself, set less than a sterling example.) The spontaneity he acquired in these early years was to serve him in good stead, yet his aversion to creating the same performance night after night was to leave its mark on much of his later work, even after acting became more than a congenial way to earn a living.

On 25 March 1905, Barrymore was playing *The Dictator* at the Star Theatre in Buffalo when his father died at the age of 55. Although Maurice had been a distant presence through much of his childhood, away on tour or preoccupied with offstage adventures, father and son had drawn closer after Barrymore's return from London. In the year prior to his father's breakdown, Barrymore had spent considerable time with Maurice, admiring his satiric wit and erudition; wondering, perhaps, at his restlessness and indifference to accomplishment; suffering through the days of his harrowing mental collapse. The trauma of witnessing his disintegration and his subsequent passing may have yielded insights into the nature of tragedy that would inform his later art; but for the moment, his father's death evoked no new sense of commitment.

For the next two years, Barrymore drifted between Collier's and his sister's orbits, continuing his irresponsible ways and, in all likelihood, playing the one against the other as each wearied of his capering. After a London engagement with Collier in *The Dictator*, he toured the West with Ethel's *Sunday* company; on 25 December 1905, he opened on Broadway in a James M. Barrie double bill, appearing with his brother Lionel as a cockney clown in *Pantaloon*, and playing an "amiable and gentlemanly young bachelor" opposite his sister in *Alice Sit-by-the-Fire*. His performances were critically praised, but his habitual recklessness and lack of discipline on stage aroused his sister's ire. On 20 March 1906, while the double bill was on tour, Alf Hayman, Charles Frohman's general manager (and brother to his Syndicate partner), wrote to Frohman in London, informing him that "Jack was drunk for two nights in Philadelphia and that worried Ethel terribly. She had me on the 'phone daily. At Ethel's suggestion I discharged him and at her request reinstated him. Couldn't do anything different."[19]

In April, Barrymore rejoined Collier for an Australian and North American tour of *The Dictator* and *On the Quiet*, which yielded a series of colorful tall tales to his already ample store but added little to his development. In December, however, he again enlisted in his sister's company, where he soon found an opportunity to test his skills in the most challenging role he had at-

tempted to date. On 31 January 1907, he appeared as Dr. Rank ("a deep, serious, psychological character in whom I became tremendously interested")
when Ethel Barrymore presented a special matinee of *A Doll's House* during
her engagement at Boston's Colonial Theatre.[20] His portrayal of the syphilit-
ic doctor – ironically, the same disease that had claimed his father, which was
perhaps a reason for his interest – was well received and indicated the rewards
to be found in creating a complex dramatic character. Dr. Rank produced no
epiphany, however, and Barrymore soon reverted to more ephemeral fare.
Ibsen, like Shakespeare, "didn't pay," and his single performance as Dr. Rank
proved a notable exception in a career which, at least in its early days, evolved
squarely within the commercial tradition.

Soon afterward, Barrymore's career was interrupted temporarily when he
was called to testify in a sensational murder trial. On 25 June 1906, while
Barrymore was touring Australia with the Collier company, Harry Thaw, a
wealthy socialite and the husband of Evelyn Nesbit, a Barrymore love interest
of a few years earlier, shot and killed the noted architect Stanford White, Nesbit's protector at the time she was involved with the actor. On 8 February
1907, Alf Hayman wrote to Charles Frohman: "Jack Barrymore is sick in Boston. I told him he had better get sick quick. He was subpoenaed as a witness
in the Thaw trial for today, and I knew it would mean a lot of notoriety, and
if he proved a bad witness it might ruin him. So he is sick, and I don't think
he will get well until after the trial." Citing "nervous exhaustion," Barrymore
withdrew to a sanitarium in Poland Springs, Maine, where he remained until
principal testimony was complete and the trial was adjourned for a special
hearing six weeks later. Upon leaving the sanitarium, Barrymore accepted
the role of Captain Carew in his sister's revival of Robert Marshall's comedy
His Excellency the Governor. The critical response to his performance was
mixed, however, and Alf Hayman wrote to Frohman soon after the opening
that Barrymore was "very bad" and should be replaced.[21]

Nevertheless, by the spring of 1907, Barrymore, after appearances in elev-
en plays, had progressed sufficiently as an actor to attract the attention of
Daniel Frohman, Charles's brother, who granted him his first leading role.[22]
On 23 May he took over the part of Tony Allen (originated six weeks earlier
by Arnold Daly), in Rida Johnson Young's comedy *The Boys of Company B.* The
few critics who took note of the event were generally favorable; the *Herald*
reported the next day that "The part of Tony well suited the breezy comedy
style of Mr. Barrymore, and he scored a success in the part."

The responsibilities of a leading man did little to assuage Barrymore's
temptation to cut capers and improvise. During the first act of a matinee at
which John Drew was in attendance, recalled Marie V. Wilde, who shared
Drew's box that day, he kidded his way through his role, "guying the other actors, queering and funning and upsetting everything to his heart's content."

After the first act curtain, Drew, livid at his nephew's lack of professionalism, scribbled a few lines on a program and sent it backstage. "What those brief lines contained the world will never know – but the result was nothing short of a miracle," Wilde remembered. "When the curtain went up on the second act Barrymore was another man. His whole personality seemed to have taken on earnestness and dignity."[23]

Chastened by his uncle's censure, Barrymore began to make at least a token effort to adopt a more disciplined approach to his craft. While on tour in Chicago in *The Boys of Company B*, Amy Leslie, his erstwhile critic, observed that "John Barrymore is not a good actor, but he is an enormous magnet. . . . As the hero of Miss Johnson's fanciful military squib [he] has the good taste to be himself, considerably amused by some of the lines and situations with which his vivid individuality is burdened" (*News*, 20 July 1907). Although there was much truth in her criticism – a caveat that was to be repeated by a number of reviewers throughout this phase of Barrymore's career – she granted that Barrymore's handsome young captain was "continuously engaging." Critics across the country generally agreed, and the tour established Barrymore as a popular leading man in the heartland.

After the tour, Daniel Frohman cast Barrymore as a docile, indecisive English lord in *Toddles*, a farce adapted from the French by Clyde Fitch, which opened in New York on 16 March 1908. The play was excoriated by the critics, but a number of reviewers praised Barrymore's comic flair and felt he had scored a personal success.[24] Other commentators disagreed, and his performance occasioned one devastatingly negative notice from Walter Prichard Eaton, critic for the *New York Sun*, who attributed the play's failure almost entirely to Barrymore's attempt to stamp his own brand of charm on the part. "It is the actor's business," he wrote, "to fit his part, not to make the part fit him . . . yet the idea seems to prevail that an actor can play any part, so long as it chances to 'fit' his personality." Barrymore, he concluded, although "the bearer of a distinguished and honorable name in the stage world, young, attractive, promising," had failed primarily because he had "not the trained resources of his art sufficiently at his command" (22 March 1908).

Barrymore, a faithful reader of his own reviews since his debut in *Magda*, was undoubtedly stung by Eaton's commentary, yet apparently he brushed it aside. Within a few months, he had drifted into musical comedy, opening on 1 June 1908 in *A Stubborn Cinderella* at the Princess Theatre in Chicago. His charm and ebullience helped carry the musical to success, and it went on to a seven-month run. In January 1909, the show moved to Broadway, where it failed to repeat its Chicago triumph. After touring in it briefly, Barrymore, on 24 May, took over the juvenile lead in a Broadway musical comedy, *The Candy Shop*, a part originated a month earlier by the English actor Leslie Gaze; but he failed to attract audiences, and the musical closed on 12 June.

Success had come easily in the heartland, but victory in New York proved more elusive.

Less than three months later, Barrymore arrived at the first of many turning points in his career. On 4 September 1909 he opened on Broadway in Winchell Smith's romantic comedy *The Fortune Hunter*. This time, critics acclaimed both vehicle and leading actor, and overnight Barrymore found himself catapulted from Broadway replacement and road-show leading man to Broadway stardom. As Nat Duncan, a young New Yorker who moves to a small Pennsylvania town in hope of finding and marrying a local heiress (but ends up falling for the druggist's daughter), he showed signs, according to the *Times,* of "grown and growing" powers. "He has lightness and ease, the happiest sort of frank assurance in playing, and a direct firm touch in making points which creates the impression of spontaneity," the reviewer remarked. "Moreover, as he played last night there was suggested a deeper note, a sort of undercurrent of sympathy and feeling, that gave tenderness to the laughter" (5 September 1909). The majority of reviews were equally favorable, and the play ran through the 1909–10 season.

In August 1910, Barrymore celebrated his newly won status as a star by contributing a perceptive essay on the current state of the stage to *The Spotlight,* in which he responded to Walter Prichard Eaton and other critics of the "personality and vehicle" school:

> Ever so often some dramatic writer or critic . . . will prepare an article for his paper in which he deplores the decline of legitimate acting and the commercialism of the stage. He will rant for a column about the evils of the "star system," and call for a return of the "palmy days of the drama," forgetting that the suit of clothes which he wears is cut in the latest fashion, his hat of the prevailing mode and everything surrounding him of the current style. Why does not such a man stop to think that the public sets a fashion in amusement – a fashion which the actor must live up to or be dropped by the wayside?[25]

Barrymore's remarks were an astute commentary on the craft of acting and the state of the theatre in general as they stood in America at the end of the first decade of the twentieth century. During the 1909–10 Broadway season, plays by Shakespeare, Ibsen, and serious-minded Continental and American dramatists had dotted the theatrical landscape, yet the majority of offerings were lightweight, contemporary plays designed to amuse the bourgeoisie. The modern comedies and melodramas that had replaced poetry and blank verse at the heart of the American repertory and the "lazy, stroll-about school of so-called repression,"[26] as Mrs. Drew had disparagingly called it, remained in vogue, abetted by popular demand and the continuing power of the Syndicate and the organization that, early in the century, had emerged as both rival and ally: the Shuberts. The 1909–10 season marked the low tide of Shakespeare and other "serious drama" in America; the exigencies of earning a steady living provided little incentive for actors to depart from the fashionable entertainments and engaging personas the public had come to expect.

Soon afterward, Eaton, writing in *Collier's Magazine*, fired back. He praised E. H. Sothern and David Warfield for a rare blend of charm, technique, and the power of impersonation, and he commended Ethel Barrymore for going beyond her "supremely attractive personality" and the "charm of youth and beauty" with her appearance in Pinero's incisive social drama, *Mid-Channel*, the previous season. However, he was skeptical that her brother might ever achieve a similar breakthrough:

> There is a small group of younger men players on our stage just now who are blessed with ingratiating personalities and sufficient skill to make them effective in the theater who will probably never scale the heights, but whose positions in the regard of the public are assured. John Barrymore is one of them. . . . The charm which he most exerts is not that of a carefully wrought and sustained impersonation, but of an ingratiating and fun-loving and physically attractive young man named Jack Barrymore. He is too skillful to oppose himself to the demands of the character; he makes the drama clear, as in *The Fortune Hunter;* but he does not make you forget him for the character. To be successful and popular he does not have to. That toilsome road of the player striving for technique he has short-cut. He has conquered by his charm.[27]

Eaton's remarks are tempered in part when we remember that he had been crusading zealously for several years to raise the standards of American drama and to put an end to the "school of self-impersonation." He was correct, however, in observing that Barrymore's performances to date offered little to suggest that he might one day "scale the heights." His apprenticeship with William Collier had taught him how to time a line; he was gifted with an amiable presence, a sparkling wit, and the requisite beauty and verve of a matinee idol. Five feet, eight inches and an athletically proportioned one hundred and forty pounds, his classic features set off by a debonair moustache, he cut a slight yet dashing figure onstage (Fig. 11). His raffish charisma projected over the footlights; audiences responded to his youthful high spirits, his extraordinary good looks. However, in three seasons as a leading man, the narrow range of parts in which he had appeared had made few demands on his abilities, and he had shown little inclination to depart from the rakish, insouciant persona that had made him a Broadway favorite. Although he possessed more of a technique than Eaton gave him credit for, and in fact had become an agile light comedian, few observers during the season of 1909–10

Figure 11. John Barrymore, c. 1909. Courtesy Billy Rose Theatre Collection, The New York Public Library for the Performing Arts.

would have foreseen that the star of *The Fortune Hunter* might one day develop into a tragic actor.

Edward Sheldon and the Years of Transition: 1911–15

For several seasons thereafter, Barrymore was content to follow the fashion by appearing in popular comedy. On 1 September 1910, newly prosperous and an established Broadway star, he married Katherine Harris, an attractive, stagestruck, 18-year-old debutante. Soon afterward he began a season-long tour of *The Fortune Hunter* with his new bride playing a small role.[28] His next vehicle was *Uncle Sam,* a collegiate comedy in which he costarred with the veteran comedian Thomas A. Wise. *Uncle Sam* failed to achieve the success of *The Fortune Hunter;* it opened in New York on 30 October 1911 and closed six weeks later.

At liberty once again, Barrymore accepted the lead in yet another romantic comedy. On the surface, *The Princess Zim-Zim* differed little from the light-comedy vehicles in which he had appeared for nearly a decade. In retrospect, however, his decision to accept the male lead marked the dawn of a new era, for the author of that play, Edward Sheldon (Fig. 12),[29] would ultimately have a profound effect on his career. Sheldon, four years Barrymore's junior, had been born into a wealthy Chicago family and was fascinated by the theatre from an early age. At 18, he enrolled at Harvard, where he attended George Pierce Baker's playwriting class, "The Technique of Drama," a precursor to the famous "47 Workshop." Soon after his graduation in 1907, he began work on *Salvation Nell,* a daring, realistic drama featuring a scrubwoman's triumph over her environment through membership in the Salvation Army. With Minnie Maddern Fiske in the title role, it opened in New York on 17 November 1908 and established Sheldon as a force to be reckoned with in an era dominated by Syndicate and Shubert confections. (Eugene O'Neill later wrote to him: "Your *Salvation Nell,* along with the work of the Irish players on their first trip over here, was what first opened my eyes to the existence of a real theatre as opposed to the unreal – and to me then, hateful – theatre of my father, in whose atmosphere I had been brought up.")[30] Two successful sociorealistic plays followed: *The Nigger* (1910) dramatized racial problems in the South; *The Boss* (1911) took machine politics as its theme.

To those who knew him, Sheldon's talent as a playwright was equaled by his personal charm and by his ability to offer sympathetic advice. Warm, open, incurably romantic, with patrician good looks and a probing intelligence, he became artistic advisor to numerous actors and actresses. Ironically, his concern for his friends in the theatre led him to turn away from social realism to devote his energies to a series of vehicle plays in many ways similar to the commercial comedies and romantic dramas that ruled Broadway at the time.

The Princess Zim-Zim, written in 1911 for Dorothy Donnelly, featured the actress as a Coney Island snake charmer with an Irish brogue; Barrymore was cast as Pete Milholland, a New York millionaire who falls in love with her. During a Boston tryout in December, Kenneth Macgowan, writing for the *Transcript,* acknowledged that the play provided "excellent acting material" for the leads and noted that although Barrymore played Pete "with his own mannerisms," it all fit into "an unusual study of a morose and troubled youth." Nevertheless, he found the play to be "a remarkable, a perplexing and a very much confused entertainment" (21 December 1911). Critical response in other cit-

Figure 12. Edward Sheldon. Courtesy Billy Rose Theatre Collection, The New York Public Library for the Performing Arts.

ies was much the same, and the play closed on the road. Its failure seems almost immaterial, however, for the friendship forged between Barrymore and Sheldon proved ultimately to be the most important of the actor's life. In succeeding years, Sheldon detected and nurtured the potential he saw in Jack Barrymore, the facile comedian. He recognized that Barrymore was far more intelligent than the average actor, sensed his capabilities as an artist, and began urging him to challenge his abilities in serious roles.

After *The Princess Zim-Zim* closed, Barrymore appeared in five comedies of little consequence between January and August 1912.[31] That autumn, however, saw his appearance in a vehicle that was a step up in quality, one he may have sought out at Sheldon's urging. On 14 October he opened in Barker's adaptation of Schnitzler's *The Affairs of Anatol* at the Little Theatre under the direction of Winthrop Ames, at the time one of a small minority of American producers interested in quality drama. In *Anatol,* a risqué Continental entertainment more sophisticated than his usual range of vehicles, Barrymore portrayed an "incurable Don Juan" who was called upon to make love to five different women. A number of reviewers were lukewarm in their praise for Barrymore's characterization, complaining that he played the part as a debonair American rather than as Schnitzler's Continental bon vivant, but the general consensus was that he had achieved a success second only to *The Fortune Hunter.*[32]

There was little for Sheldon to approve in Barrymore's next two engagements. After a limited Chicago run in *A Thief for a Night* the following spring (a role created on Broadway by Douglas Fairbanks a season earlier), Barrymore returned to New York, where on 19 August 1913 he opened in *Believe Me, Xantippe,* yet another farce-comedy, at the Thirty-ninth Street Theatre. Again, the critics found his "vivid individuality" to be far superior to his vehicle; the play closed after two months.[33]

By that time, however, Barrymore had begun to respond, tentatively and conservatively, to Sheldon's urgings to test his abilities. Eager to break free from the light-comedy straitjacket, he accepted the part of a flippant, aggressive American reporter in *The Yellow Ticket,* a lurid Russian melodrama produced by A. H. Woods and costarring Florence Reed. *The Yellow Ticket* opened on 20 January 1914 at the Eltinge to favorable reviews and ran through the spring. Barrymore's old irresponsibility emerged during the run, possibly because of his habitual inability to cope with repetition, but perhaps also a result of the character he had agreed to play: only a nominal departure from his light-comedy persona, albeit in serious surroundings. He made his initial entrance one night dead drunk, and Florence Reed, weary of his misbehavior, ordered the curtain rung down. Although he apologized to Woods and remained on his best behavior through the end of the run, *The Yellow Ticket* was far from the breakthrough he had hoped for.[34]

That summer, Barrymore, frustrated by the slow progress of his career and disheartened by the erosion of his marriage to Katherine Harris, made plans to join Sheldon in Italy, sailing on the *Olympic* on 26 June 1914. Feeling hopeless, he sought an escape from depression in Sheldon's comradeship. The time spent with Sheldon in Venice, Rome, and Florence had a revitalizing effect. Again, Sheldon urged his friend to challenge his abilities, and this time he found Barrymore listening intently.[35]

Soon after his return to America, Barrymore was offered the lead in another A. H. Woods production. *Kick In,* a "crook melodrama" by Willard Mack, was a thriller of little artistic value, with moments of comedy worked in for effect; but its leading role, Chick Hewes, a reformed ex-convict who finds himself inadvertently in trouble with the law, provided the opportunity to create a more serious and sympathetic character than any he had yet attempted. Accounts of this period of the actor's life are sketchy, yet is likely that he emerged from his Italian sojourn with Sheldon with a new seriousness of purpose. He doubtless recognized the opportunity the part presented and approached it as a make-or-break proposition. Anxious to prove himself as an actor, he devoted his formidable energies to his first bid for acceptance in a role that differed from "the usual type of Barrymore parts." He was undoubtedly aware, as well, that many observers were skeptical of his ability to bring it off:

> People thought Woods was crazy to trust me with the part. His friends – perhaps they thought they were my friends too . . . flourished the usual theatrical measuring stick of "personal limitations." According to them, mine were marked out by my previous parts: from the young good-for-nothing who gayly and facetiously wins out in *The Fortune Hunter* down to *Anatol* of the lively Parisian adventures. . . . That [Woods] did not yield to their protests showed a confidence in me for which I shall always be grateful."[36]

Woods's confidence was rewarded: When *Kick In* opened on 19 October 1914 at the Longacre it met with immediate success. Barrymore, wrote the *Journal of Commerce*, "made the most of his opportunity . . . played with force and feeling throughout, and made it apparent that no mistake was made when the role was entrusted to him" (20 October 1914). The public lined up at the box office, and the play ran into the spring of 1915.

Kick In marked an important transition for Barrymore, but Sheldon had even better things in mind. That spring, preliminary arrangements were made for Barrymore to appear the following season in Sheldon's *The Lonely Heart*, a sensitive drama that dealt almost exclusively with the inner life of a man confronted by a series of emotional and moral crises. Soon afterward, however, Sheldon, at 29, was stricken abruptly by the first symptoms of what would prove to be progressive and crippling rheumatoid arthritis. He underwent a variety of treatments, without improvement. The disease attacked his joints, making even the slightest movement painful, and left him with little strength for the duties the rehearsal period entailed. By early autumn the production had been postponed.[37] Barrymore, faced with an unexpected hiatus from the stage, instead devoted his efforts to a medium in which he was by then well established as a popular favorite: motion pictures.

Barrymore's career as a film actor had in all likelihood begun three years earlier, when he had entered the cinema as casually as he had gone on the stage, with supporting roles in four comedies produced by Lubin Studios in Philadelphia: *Dream of a Motion Picture Director, The Widow Casey's Return, A Prize Package,* and *One on Romance.* These films are now lost, presumably destroyed in a fire at Lubin Studios in 1914, and Barrymore never acknowledged them in accounts of his career, yet it is probable that he was the "Jack Barrymore" mentioned in cast lists issued to contemporary film periodicals – there is no record of another actor of that name. His reluctance to publicize his initial forays into the new medium may simply have been a result of the disreputability of the movies among "legitimate" actors and producers at that time.[38] In January 1914, his initial starring feature, *An American Citizen*, was released, the first in a series of farces made for Famous Players, a forerunner of Paramount Pictures. It was followed later in the year by *The Man from Mexico* (a William Collier vehicle on the stage), and in 1915 by *Are You a Mason?*, *The Dictator* (with Barrymore in the Collier part), and *The Incorrigible Dukane*. During the summer and fall of 1915, Barrymore made three films in rapid succession: *Nearly a King*, *The Lost Bridegroom*, and *The Red Widow*. The last of the three, adapted from a musical comedy, began filming in mid-October. It proved to be anything but art; Barrymore later recalled *The Red Widow* as "one of the worst films ever made."[39] He was aware of the negligible artistic quality of his vehicles, which provided lucrative compensation and a respite from the repetition of the stage but offered few artistic rewards. It is likely that he was besieged with offers to star in farce and melodrama, yet by the autumn of 1915, he clearly felt a desire for growth and change; he began listening more intently than ever to Sheldon's urgings to devote his skills to a challenging role in a quality play.

To attribute Barrymore's interest in becoming an artist entirely to Sheldon's influence is to oversimplify what was surely a more complex process of maturation. Sheldon himself claimed modestly that Barrymore was "completely responsible" for his own accomplishments; yet many who were close to the actor – Lionel Barrymore, Arthur Hopkins, Alexander Woollcott – credited Sheldon almost solely with sensing his true potentialities and pushing him toward their realization. His career became one of Sheldon's major preoccupations; he detected reserves of hidden dramatic power that lay untapped in Barrymore's abilities and gradually persuaded him to look beyond easy success and the trivial entertainments that for years had provided his livelihood. "His determination for Jack never wavered," Arthur Hopkins recalled. By the 1915–16 season, Barrymore, under Sheldon's guidance, was ready to begin a new and remarkable phase of his career.[40]

Mature Artistry and the Formation of the Triumvirate: 1916–19

In addition to Sheldon's influence, another significant factor was at work, for as we have seen, the mid-1910s witnessed the abrupt emergence of a new mood in the American theatre. The early teens had proven to be crucial years of transition both for Barrymore and the native stage in general; by the 1915–16 season, the insurgent spirit that had been gathering impetus since early in the decade was ready to emerge from the realm of the "little theatres" and assume a place in the Broadway mainstream.

No play, no performance would prove as symbolic of the revolution to come as John Barrymore's performance in the play Edward Sheldon brought to him that autumn: John Galsworthy's *Justice*, a searing drama, spare, simple, almost Aeschylean in its cumulative emotional power. The play centers on William Falder, a 23-year-old clerk for a London solicitors' firm who forges a check to rescue the woman he loves from her drunken, abusive husband. Apprehended before he can flee, he is placed on trial, found guilty, and sentenced to three years in prison, where he is subjected to dehumanizing conditions. On his release, the law firm offers him his old position but insists that he break all ties with Ruth, who had been forced to turn to prostitution after leaving her husband; crushed in spirit and hounded by the police, Falder commits suicide.

Sheldon brought *Justice* to the attention of his Harvard classmate John D. Williams, formerly a press agent for Charles Frohman, who had set himself up as an independent producer after Frohman's death on the *Lusitania* in August 1915. At the same time, he and Emilie Hapgood, wife of the critic Norman Hapgood and a close friend of Barrymore and Sheldon at the time, persuaded Barrymore to campaign for the role. Barrymore's decision to gamble his reputation was influenced by Sheldon and Hapgood's faith in his capabilities and by the response to the sympathetic ex-convict he had played in *Kick In*. Even so, the Galsworthy play was a daring leap forward. *Kick In*, although earnest in tone, was a melodrama cobbled together for dramatic effect; *Justice* was pure tragedy.

The director of the play, Ben Iden Payne, later remembered that in discussing the casting of *Justice*, Williams asked what he would think of John Barrymore in the leading part. Payne admitted he knew nothing about Barrymore's work or reputation, and Williams informed him that Barrymore had been associated almost entirely with comedy, but had aspirations toward serious work. Barrymore was perfectly willing, Williams assured him, to read for the part so that Payne might judge his suitability. Accordingly, Payne spent two afternoons with Barrymore in his apartment reading through the play. "Even at the first meeting," he remembered, "I came to the conclusion that he had all the qualities for the part and I so reported." To his surprise, Williams did not "look altogether happy" about his decision; he was worried about Barrymore's irresponsible behavior with other managers and feared that awarding him the role of Falder might jeopardize the entire production. He acceded, however, and rehearsals commenced with Barrymore in the leading role.[41]

The critic Clayton Hamilton later recalled how earnestly Barrymore grasped the opportunity to prove himself. "He went into training for the part, precisely as an athlete goes into training for a prize-fight or a race," Hamilton remarked – a pattern that was to be repeated with each serious role he attempted. Although in the past he had taken his work in "a careless and easy-going manner," there was nothing careless about his preparation for Falder. Driven by a desire to make good, he gave up drinking, switching to Bevo, a temperance "near beer."[42] He shaved his moustache, an emblem of the Broadway blade for more than a decade, and had his hair cropped close to his scalp. He developed a soft Cockney accent for the downtrodden clerk, a device he had used for comic effect in *Pantaloon* a decade earlier, and devoted long hours to the creation of his role, subduing his personality to the demands of Galsworthy's character.

On 3 March 1916 the play began a tryout in New Haven, moving on to Boston a few days later. The New York opening was scheduled for the Candler Theatre on 3 April. Though the play had received favorable reviews on the road, Barrymore felt uncertain of the reception that awaited him; but Galsworthy's play – and his harrowing portrayal of the leading role – were hailed as epochal Broadway events. The *Times* called the opening night "a great occasion," adding that Barrymore's performance was "extraordinary . . . in every detail of appearance and manner, in every note of deep feeling" (4 April 1916). Alexander Woollcott subsequently devoted several of his "Second Thoughts on First Nights" columns to the play and to Barrymore's performance. Barrymore's Falder, he commented, was "electrifying," noting that for the actor, "the first night of *Justice* was a milestone. . . . By his simple, eloquent, deeply touching performance as young Falder he arrested the attention of the city and gained overnight a prestige which is priceless in the theatre, a prestige all his work in trivial entertainment could not give him."[43]

Most critics agreed with Woollcott; the consensus was that a major new tragedian had arrived. Barrymore's Falder, vulnerable, inarticulate, and impressive in its restraint, was regarded as a performance of remarkable depth and power. To many observers, the climactic scene of Galsworthy's drama, in which Falder, his mind and spirit broken after the strain of solitary confinement, pounds helplessly on the door of his prison cell, was one of the great moments of the modern American stage.

Still, success as a tragedian did little to ameliorate Barrymore's old problem: his boredom and lack of discipline during a long run. Cathleen Nesbitt, who played Ruth Honeywell, Falder's love interest, recalled that

He loved to invent ways of teasing and trying to "throw" his fellow actors. At the final curtain of *Justice*, for instance, he had to lie dead for a moment with his back to the audience, while I threw myself down beside him weeping and Peter Heggie said gently, "No one'll touch him now! Never again! He's safe with gentle Jesus!" It was a difficult line to say and Heggie said it beautifully without any sentimentality. But Jack started playing tricks – telling rather obscene stories under his breath, sometimes pretending he saw a cockroach crawling towards him or that he was going to sneeze. . . . After warning Jack several times, [Heggie] walked out of the theatre without waiting for the curtain calls, only leaving a note to say that "unless Mr. Barrymore apologized for his behavior and gave a written oath to refrain from any more monkey business, Mr. Heggie would leave the company for good and not return." . . . He stayed away for three days till Jack, knowing how immensely valuable Peter was to the play, had his lawyer draw up a contract swearing on his solemn oath to refrain from any misbehavior.[44]

Justice ran for 103 performances and the following season began an extended tour. It attracted good notices but failed to achieve commercial success; provincial audiences, accustomed to lighter attractions, found it dreary and depressing. A member of the company that season, the veteran Irish actor Whitford Kane (later to play the First Gravedigger to Barrymore's Hamlet), recalled that during leisure hours Barrymore's fellow cast members urged him to attempt the great classical roles: Hamlet, Romeo, Iago. Barrymore took their interest in his future "kindly" but "with a little suspicion," replying noncommitally and finally admitting that he was more interested in Richard III than Hamlet.[45]

Barrymore returned to New York in January 1917, heartened by his personal success. Although he may not have felt ready to attempt Shakespeare as a follow-up to *Justice,* he was clearly determined to build on his triumph in the Galsworthy play by attempting other serious roles. Preliminary arrangements had again been made for a production of *The Lonely Heart,* but fate intervened in the person of the English actress Constance Collier, a friend of Barrymore's since his turn-of-the-century sojourn in England and one of many actresses who looked to Ned Sheldon as advisor and confidant. In 1915 she had organized a benefit matinee of John N. Raphael's adaptation of George Du Maurier's 1891 best-seller, *Peter Ibbetson.* The following year, en route to Hollywood to film *Macbeth* with Herbert Tree, she attempted to interest New York managers in a production but failed to arouse any enthusiasm. She confided her problems to Sheldon, presenting him with a copy of the Raphael script and suggesting that Barrymore would be ideal in the title role. Sheldon agreed, selflessly setting aside the problematic *Lonely Heart* to rewrite the Raphael play. Barrymore was inundated with offers, but gradually his affection for the Du Maurier tale – one of his father's favorite novels and a role Maurice Barrymore had longed to play – and Sheldon's faith that he was right for the part convinced him to attempt the role. His commitment was sealed when his brother Lionel agreed to play the villainous Colonel Ibbetson, ending a twelve-year sabbatical from Broadway devoted mainly to motion pictures.

Peter Ibbetson presented Barrymore with yet another challenge to his growing abilities. A romantic, cloyingly sentimental role in the Victorian tradition, it required a delicate, subtle handling. Du Maurier's character, refined, sensitive, and "inclined to be dreamy," finds himself reunited after years apart with the childhood sweetheart, now the Duchess of Towers, who urged him to "dream true." When Colonel Ibbetson, Peter's uncle, falsely claims that Peter is his illegitimate son, a struggle ensues and Peter kills him with a cane; he is sentenced to life imprisonment, made bearable by the fact that each night he is able to rejoin his beloved in his dreams. Forty years later, both die within a day, but their love transcends death and they are reunited in heaven. Constance Collier, who played the Duchess of Towers and directed much of the production, remembered that at times Barrymore was "hard to handle because he was ashamed of himself playing love scenes." Nevertheless, he was "avid for criticism." "I was very tentative in directing him," she recalled, "but he would say, 'Don't tell me if I am good, tell me where you feel I am bad.' If I did have to criticize him severely, he would take it wonderfully."[46]

On 18 April 1917, *Peter Ibbetson* opened at the Republic Theatre, where it captivated the audience; Barrymore's poetic, spiritual portrayal was greeted as both a personal triumph and a distinct step forward in his artistic development. Charles Darnton of the *Evening World* found that he "achieved heights and depths of sentiment never reached by him in other performances. . . . His vocal monotony was the only defect to be found in an otherwise admirable example of acting" (19 April 1917). The anonymous critic for the *Times* (probably Alexander Woollcott) praised his "tenderness and romantic charm" and the "riches of skill, eloquence and imagination" he brought to the part (19 April 1917). Lionel Barrymore was welcomed back to Broadway with critical raves for his villainous colonel.

Peter Ibbetson proved to be popular escapist fare in the early days of America's participation in the First World War. Although its sentimentality was distinctly Victorian, its theme of love transcending separation and death held poignant appeal for audiences with husbands, sons, and brothers who might soon be risking their lives. The play closed in June for a summer hiatus; it resumed in September to continuing box-office success and subsequently toured for six months. By the time the play reached Chicago, however, Barrymore was fatigued and weary of the role. As had often happened in the past, he became restless when he could no longer be "creative" in finding new shadings for his character; the endless repetition and the intense concentration his part required had by then taken their toll in missed performances and explosive outbursts of temperament when his concentration was shattered by distractions from the audience. "Jack came into my dressing room

and said, 'I just can't go on,'" Constance Collier remembered. "It was devastating and a great blow to me, but I understood. He was physically tired. He
was strung up to a point where he couldn't go on."[47]

In May 1918, Barrymore returned to New York, this time to a top-floor
studio apartment he had taken on West Fourth Street in Greenwich Village,
around the corner from the Provincetown Playhouse. He had been living
apart from his wife since the summer of 1916; in December of the following
year he was granted a divorce. Around the same time, he began courting
Blanche Oelrichs Thomas, the daughter of a Newport society family, who
wrote poetry under the masculine nom de plume Michael Strange. The fact
that she was married and the mother of two young sons limited their courtship at first, but the relationship intensified after her husband received a
commission in the army and was sent to Europe.

Far more important to Barrymore's artistic development, however, were
relationships formed during this period with two bold theatre practitioners
who stood in the vanguard of the American movement toward suggestive
staging and quality drama. Arthur M. Hopkins (Fig. 13),[48] modest, short, and
rotund, began his career as a reporter for the *Cleveland Press*, later becoming
a vaudeville press agent and a booking agent. In 1912 he entered the field
of theatrical directing and production; his initial effort, Eleanor Gates's *The
Poor Little Rich Girl*, was one of the first Broadway dramas to deal with psychological issues in a modern context. Soon afterward, Hopkins went to Europe
to investigate the English, French, and German theatre. He was especially
taken by the majesty and simplicity of Max Reinhardt's productions at the
Deutsches Theater and the Kammerspiele, the first works he had seen that
were influenced by the art and theories of Gordon Craig. "What struck me
most in the German theatre was its adult tone," he recalled years later. "It had
progressed far beyond being a place of amusement."[49] He returned to America determined to employ in his own work what he had seen. His first major
success came in 1914 with Elmer Rice's *On Trial;* two years later, he began
what would prove to be a long and artistically rewarding association with a
talented young scenic artist who had been similarly influenced by the German stage.

Robert Edmond Jones (Fig. 14),[50] the son of a New Hampshire farmer,
had shown an interest in drawing and painting at an early age. At Harvard,
he designed scenery for student productions and discovered the work of Gordon Craig. After postgraduate study and a year of teaching, he went to Europe, spending much of the 1913–14 season as a behind-the-scenes observer
at Reinhardt's Deutsches Theater. Soon after his return to America, he was
invited to design the scenery for the Stage Society's production of Anatole
France's *The Man Who Married a Dumb Wife*, directed by Barker as part of his
1915 repertory season at Wallack's. Jones's simple, boldly colored set created

Figure 13. Arthur Hopkins. Courtesy Billy Rose Theatre Collection, The New York Public Library for the Performing Arts.

an immediate sensation, and he quickly emerged as the leading designer of the New Stagecraft in America. A good scene, he later wrote, "is not a picture. It is something seen, but it is something conveyed as well: a feeling, an evocation."[51]

While in Germany, Hopkins had seen Reinhardt's production of Tolstoy's *The Living Corpse,* the story of wealthy and dissolute Fedya Vassilyevich Protosov, who abandons an unhappy marriage to seek comfort with a band of gypsies. When his wife renews her attraction for an old suitor, Protosov makes it seem as if he had drowned himself, freeing his wife to remarry. For a year he lives secretly among the gypsies, but finally the truth is revealed; to save his wife from a charge of bigamy, he kills himself. Hopkins found Reinhardt's Fedya, Alexander Moissi, to be the actor he had "always dreamed of" and re-

Figure 14. Robert Edmond Jones. Courtesy Culver Pictures.

solved that, if he could find the right actor, he would one day do the play in English. As it turned out, the actor found him.

Barrymore had seen and admired Jacob Adler's performance in *The Living Corpse* in Yiddish during the spring of 1916; Sheldon prepared an English-language adaptation soon afterward as a possible follow-up to *Justice.* Although Barrymore was announced to appear in the play in February 1917, he chose instead to do *Peter Ibbetson.* When Sheldon learned subsequently that Hopkins was contemplating a production, he told Barrymore, who approached Hopkins to express an interest in playing the lead. Hopkins assured him that he was willing to mount a production whenever Barrymore was ready, but later recalled that these "preliminaries were so brief and nebulous that I would not have been surprised at hearing no more from him."[52] When

Barrymore returned from the *Ibbetson* tour, however, he reiterated his desire to do the Tolstoy play. The role of Fedya – complex, spiritual, at times grotesque – presented risks, and Barrymore was then being courted for the lead in Barrie's *Dear Brutus*, a sophisticated tragicomedy and surefire hit; but again he decided to gamble.

At a luncheon meeting, Hopkins told Barrymore of his ambitious scheme to bring lasting prestige to the American stage. For three years, he proposed, they would build a repertory at the Plymouth Theatre (which Hopkins had leased through a generous arrangement with the Shuberts), followed by American and international tours. At least two plays of the highest artistic merit would be presented each season. Barrymore found the plan to be "rather overburdened with hope," yet he consented to participate, perhaps because Hopkins offered $1,000 per week and half the profits – an arrangement that was to continue through their subsequent collaborations. Hopkins listened to Barrymore's suggestions for future productions and agreed that they would be done. No formal agreements were entered into; either party was free to abandon the arrangement if he chose to do so.[53]

Rehearsals for *The Living Corpse*, by then retitled *Redemption*, began in September, using a translation arranged by Sheldon with assistance from Michael Strange. As rehearsals progressed, Hopkins came to know "the deeply earnest side" of Barrymore. "He was tireless in preparation," Hopkins recalled. "The myth of his laziness, frequently amusingly taunted by Uncle John Drew, had blown away. . . . Rehearsals for him were a ceaseless quest." He was at rehearsal first and was the first to know his part; each day's rehearsal "revealed the wider range of his exploration." To Hopkins, it was "like watching the working of a treasure mine and occasionally, as director, detecting and revealing to him treasure that he was overlooking." In the process, he added, "I never attempted to give Barrymore anything that was not his own. I was a weighing machine revealing to him when his delivery was short or overweight. It was rarely short, but frequently overweight" with "a residue of the old bombastic theatre, the theatre that Grandmother Drew had long made her own."[54]

Redemption opened at the Plymouth on 3 October 1918 and was greeted as a welcome addition to a Broadway scene still dominated by ephemeral fare. The response to Barrymore's Fedya was generally favorable, and in some cases his characterization was met by rapturous approval. Francis Hackett of the *New Republic* noted he had created a portrayal "that can be ranked with the best acting of our generation. . . . [He] simply soars out of all his limitations and gives a performance that is the performance of genius, from the inside out." John Corbin of the *Times* found that his Fedya was "divined with extraordinary psychologic subtlety . . . and expressed with a personal and artistic distinction so rare on our stage as to be virtually unique," adding, "Together with his Falder in *Justice* and his Peter Ibbetson, this Fedya places Mr.

Barrymore among the very few artists of creative imagination on the English-speaking stage." Several critics, however, raised objections to his "vocal monotony" in earlier scenes, and particularly to his flamboyant theatricality in the second act, where Hopkins, despite his best efforts, had failed to eradicate vestiges of the "old bombastic theatre." As one reviewer remarked dryly, "He is in this play more a male Bernhardt than he has ever been before." Nevertheless, the consensus was that Barrymore had added significantly to his laurels. Admired, as well, were Hopkins's spare direction and Jones's simple, evocative sets and subtle lighting. "If there has ever been a more completely atmospheric production on our stage it does not now come to mind," Corbin concluded.[55]

Even so, *Redemption* was not an immediate success. Most reviewers stressed the play's artistic merit, but they also emphasized the aura of Russian gloom; an influenza epidemic during the early weeks of the run further discouraged potential patrons. However, Hopkins's lease on the Plymouth enabled him to keep the play running for small but enthusiastic audiences. Within a few weeks word of mouth had spread, and soon the Plymouth was playing to capacity. A good deal of *Redemption*'s ultimate triumph at the box office stemmed from the improved artistic climate for serious drama, and the fact that its second month coincided with the end of the Great War. More and more, audiences began looking to "serious" literature and drama for insights into the human condition; the idealistic worldview of prewar culture began to seem inexplicable in light of a conflict that had yielded eighteen million dead and wounded. The play could easily have run through the end of the season, but Hopkins, in keeping with his plan to present a series of plays while building a repertory, withdrew it in April after 204 performances.

By then, the next play in the series was already well into rehearsal. A few years earlier, Barrymore, perhaps at Sheldon's urging but in all likelihood investing his own funds, had acquired the American rights to Sem Benelli's *La cena delle beffe* ("The Supper of the Jest"). A sensation at its 1909 Rome premiere, it had quickly become a mainstay of the Italian repertory and had been performed the following year by Sarah Bernhardt in a French adaptation. (Barrymore's role, in fact, was played in most European productions by a woman.) Sheldon had begun work on an English-language version in 1916, freely adapting Benelli's play into colorful, rhythmic prose. An early draft had then been sent by Barrymore to David Belasco in February 1917, but Belasco had declined the opportunity to produce the play, and Barrymore had chosen instead to act in *Peter Ibbetson* that season. Sheldon, undeterred, had continued to work on the script; he tailored the leading role, a hunchback in Benelli's original, to Barrymore's romantic image and abilities, persevering even after his arthritis required surgery to break up calcification in his knees, followed by months of painful stretching exercises.

The Jest, as Sheldon's adaptation was retitled, concerns Giannetto Malespi-
ni, a frail young Florentine painter in the time of Lorenzo the Magnificent
who is tormented for years by two brutish Pisan mercenaries, the brothers
Neri and Gabriello Chiaramantesi. When they steal Ginevra, his beloved, the
painter plots an elaborate revenge. He effects a quarrel between the brothers
and ultimately uses his cunning to trick Neri into fratricide and madness.

Stimulated by the challenge of creating yet another complex dramatic
character, and by the opportunity to again appear with his brother Lionel,
cast as the brutal Neri, Barrymore threw himself into rehearsals with his by-
then customary commitment. "Barrymore worked harder to perfect his gift
for the theatre than anyone I know," remarked Jones. "He was never satisfied.
He was discontented, troubled, impatient with his own imperfections."[56] In
an effort to overcome what both he and his critics perceived as a liability, a
lack of vocal flexibility and range, Barrymore took lessons (at $20 an hour)
from a voice coach, Robert Hosea, to whom he later wrote:

> My dear Mr. Hosea – I trust you will not be too surprised by this letter but
> I feel I must tell you in view of the unprecedented success of "the Jest" –
> how much I feel I owe you – for whatever small share I might have in it.
>
> Of all the many defects there might be in my acting – the salient one was
> my speaking voice – which in a long part was almost sure to be monotonous
> and unvaried in character – as I did not know how to use it properly – and
> in remedying that defect for me as you have done I feel I owe you a debt
> of gratitude that is impossible to repay – as it will naturally last for the rest
> of my theatrical career – I think your method is extraordinary in its simplic-
> ity and its almost immediate effect – Believe me – Yrs. most gratefully John
> Barrymore.[57]

The Jest opened at the Plymouth on 9 April 1919, causing an immediate
furor. To John Corbin of the *Times*, it seemed "destined to become one of the
sensational successes of the decade." Barrymore's portrayal evoked widespread praise; the *Sun* found it to be "remarkable for its grace and imagination, as well as for its unexpected power in certain scenes." His performance,
along with his brother's, wrote Alan Dale in the *American*, restored to Broadway "the enthralling quality of what used to be called 'romantic acting.'"[58]

A number of reviewers made it clear, however, that Barrymore, despite his
vocal training with Hosea, had failed to overcome his old faults. H. T. Parker,
veteran critic for the *Boston Transcript*, found that in long passages his speech
lacked "sufficient variety of modulation, pace, color"; the *New York Herald* noted his "monotonous sameness of intonation." Nonetheless, to the majority of
commentators, Barrymore's vocal deficiencies were of relatively minor concern; the *World* found that the flaws in his delivery seemed "insignificant compared with the beauty and finish of his general accomplishment." Most critics found much to admire in his portrayal: his sensuality, his psychological

illumination of the wounded spirit, his penetrating flashes of malevolent cunning. Also commended frequently were Hopkins's staging and Jones's richly colored costumes and scenery, which evoked an aura of Renaissance splendor and sensuality. "No play we can remember has afforded such remarkable stage pictures," wrote Heywood Broun, who praised Jones's settings as "a new mark for American scenic art."[59]

Still, few critics failed to notice that beyond the bravura performances, the sensuality (an irresistible lure to "sexually liberated" postwar audiences), and the atmospheric production, *The Jest* was a play of glittering surfaces and little substance. "Shallow, external, coarse and crude . . . a stage jewel if ever there was one," carped the *New Republic*.[60] Like the melodramas that Irving and Mansfield had made a central part of their repertories, it was exciting entertainment and an effective vehicle for star performance, but ultimately offered little in the way of depth and dimension.

The Jest closed for the summer in June, and reopened in September to continuing success, although Lionel Barrymore left the play in late 1919. It could have run indefinitely, but by early 1920, Barrymore, as had often happened in the past, found himself tiring of his character. When he experienced a bout of grippe (or so it was announced), Hopkins, following European precedent, replaced him with an actress, Gilda Varesi. Barrymore returned after a week, but *The Jest* played its final performance on 21 February.

Rehearsals, meanwhile, were already under way for the next play in the repertory. In reviewing *The Jest*, a number of critics had encouraged Barrymore to attempt what seemed to be the next logical step in his artistic development: Shakespeare. Although a Shakespearean role would mean yet another daring leap forward, and Barrymore's vocal limitations meant that success was far from certain, many observers felt that his rapid ascent to the height of his profession foreshadowed greater things to come. John Corbin, remarking on the performances of the brothers Barrymore, wrote, "To the future of such actors, it is impossible to set any limit. Some day we shall see them, perhaps, as Othello and Iago." Burns Mantle noted, "John could play Hamlet tomorrow and set the town by its ears." Alexander Woollcott commented that Barrymore's Giannetto, despite the "marked unevenness of his work from night to night," revealed "flashes of spiritual beauty and evidence both of a deep understanding and a soaring imagination that are beyond the reach of any other man now playing on the English speaking stage," adding, "he stands, in the minds of many, as the legitimate successor to Richard Mansfield in the American theatre."[61]

By this time, Barrymore, with the encouragement of Sheldon, Hopkins, and Jones, felt ready to accept the challenge. For his Shakespearean debut, he turned not to Othello, Iago, or Hamlet, but to a role that Mansfield had defined for a generation: Richard III.

PART TWO

THE PRODUCTIONS

2

Richard III, 1920

Richard III . . . is hardly the revelation described by the praising chorus who review plays for the New York newspapers. It is more nearly a revolution. It is this because it brings one era in the legitimate to an end and begins another.

Of this new era John Barrymore will undoubtedly be first lord.

– *Variety* (12 March 1920)

Few shakespearean impersonations in the annals of the American stage have been greeted with the critical acclaim bestowed upon John Barrymore's Richard III.[1] Barrymore's Shakespearean debut was welcomed with surprise and delight by a theatrical community that had admired his "bravery in storming the fortresses of Mansfield and Booth," yet in many cases had doubted his ability to succeed in a demanding classical role. His "intellectual, stealthy, crafty and subtly malevolent" portrayal was viewed by the critical fraternity as both "an amazing triumph" and a theatrical changing of the guard – an impression that extended to the groundbreaking contributions of Arthur Hopkins and Robert Edmond Jones, whose innovative European-inspired methods were regarded as milestones in Shakespearean staging and design.[2]

Richard III burst upon the theatrical season of 1919–20 and captured the imagination of a playgoing public that generally still regarded Shakespeare as "high culture"; yet in many ways the timing was right for a bold, experimental approach to the Bard by Broadway practitioners. As we have seen, the second decade of the twentieth century had witnessed a decreasing sympathy on the part of sophisticated playgoers for traditional methods of Shakespearean acting and production and a growing openness toward the artistic experiments and new theories of human nature, mainly European in origin, that had made themselves known since early in the decade. During the winter of 1918–19, when Barrymore and his artistic associates first contemplated

67

mounting a Shakespearean production, adventurous New Yorkers might have frequented an exhibition of paintings by American post-Impressionists, attended a "simplified" staging of *Twelfth Night* directed by Jacques Copeau, or read Freud's recently translated *Reflections on War and Death*.

Although Broadway retained its share of frothy comedies, melodramas, and musical entertainments, the prevailing mood in the theatre remained one of hope and promise. The movement toward quality drama and Continental staging methods had gained new impetus as the second decade of the twentieth century neared its end. In April 1919, the Bourgeois Galleries on Fifth Avenue exhibited stage designs by Robert Edmond Jones, Lee Simonson, and Norman Bel Geddes – "the first full-fledged recognition of the importance of the artist in the American theatre and 'the progress of the modern stagecraft' in this country."[3] The coming season would offer dramas by Gorki and Drinkwater, Theatre Guild productions of plays by Tolstoy, Masefield, and St. John Ervine, and the premiere of Eugene O'Neill's first full-length play, *Beyond the Horizon*. The celebratory revolt against "commercialism and traditionalism," in evidence since the midteens, continued to affect the aspirations of a group of idealistic younger practitioners who saw a magnificent theatrical future just around the corner.

It was in this spirit that Barrymore and his production team, buoyed by their success with *Redemption* and *The Jest*, recommenced their ambitious plan to bring lasting prestige to the American stage. As in their past collaborations, Jones remembered, "We all sat down and plotted like conspirators" to dream out a Shakespearean production "more vivid, newer, more audacious, with more imaginative resources" than any which had come before.[4]

The ensuing *Richard III* was by no means a complete departure from tradition. Barrymore's portrayal owed a considerable debt to the techniques of high-Victorian romantic realism, most notably in his emphasis upon vocal range and variety and between-the-lines byplay. The acting text centered as relentlessly on its protagonist as any nineteenth-century production: Despite the movement toward ensemble performances, exemplified by Barker's productions at the Court and Savoy during the 1900s and 1910s, Barrymore was pure star in the Booth–Irving–Mansfield manner. Nonetheless, most reviewers agreed with the critic for the *World* (8 March 1920) who cited admiringly the revival's "audacious scorn of precedent." It is this aspect of the production – its innovative and far-reaching approach to Shakespearean performance, staging, and design – that make it well worth investigating. From the first, *Richard III* was a daring attempt to reinvent the way in which the bravura repertory was acted and produced; its success with critics and the ticket-buying public marked a significant turning point for staged Shakespeare in America.

Plans for the Production

Barrymore later claimed that his first thought of playing Richard III came when he was at the Bronx Zoo with Edward Sheldon, looking at a "particularly sinister" red tarantula.

"He looks just like Richard the Third," he remarked.

"Why don't you play him," Sheldon suggested.

"All right, I will," Barrymore replied.[5]

A charming story, yet his decision to attempt Richard was not nearly that simple. As we have seen, Whitford Kane testified that Barrymore had expressed an interest in the part while on tour with *Justice* during the winter of 1916–17, and he may well have harbored ambitions of one day "perusing the iambics" during the 1917–18 season while he was appearing in *Peter Ibbetson*. It seems likely, however, that he first began to consider seriously an attempt at Shakespeare in November 1918, just after the opening of *Redemption* – and soon after Hopkins had assumed the sponsorship of the Shakespeare Playhouse. His ambitions were spurred, in part, by Walter Hampden's success as Hamlet. Clayton Hamilton later recalled that Barrymore saw Hampden play the role at the Plymouth several times; he admired his performance, praised it, and studied it carefully. He became aware of his lack of knowledge on matters Shakespearean and began to study earnestly, reading through the texts and consulting with noted scholars. Hamlet was the part that most attracted him, and he was urged by his friends to attempt it; but according to Hamilton, he "was not at all sure that he was ready to play Hamlet." An awareness of his vocal limitations and his lack of experience in reading blank verse persuaded him that Hamlet was a risky proposition – at least for the moment. Barrymore then began to consult his friends about the role of Romeo – a part in which his father had achieved noteworthy success. Hamilton later remembered "the conflict between difficulty and enthusiasm which took place within his mind, in the spring of 1919, while he was considering this part."[6] Thoughts of Romeo were soon abandoned, however, perhaps because of his growing aversion to "scented, bepuffed, bewigged and ringletted characters." After the sentimental excesses of *Peter Ibbetson* and the "mordantly beautiful young sensualist" he was called upon to play in *The Jest*, Romeo held limited appeal.[7]

Finally, after months of deliberation, Barrymore met with Hopkins to discuss the role toward which he was leaning. He later proclaimed to a reporter that "I played Richard III because it hadn't been done lately,"[8] and this statement, although not entirely accurate, in all probability contains a grain of truth; the scarcity of recent interpreters made comparisons far less inevitable than they would have been for Hamlet, for which Hampden, Sothern, and the recently retired Forbes-Robertson were fresh in playgoers' memories. Mansfield's Gloucester was by then more than a decade removed; Mantell still included the part in his repertory, but at 65 his skills were in decline, and his last Broadway appearance in the role during the autumn of 1918 had elicited scarcely a critical mention.

It seems likely, however, that a more significant factor in Barrymore's decision was the spiritual affinity he felt for Shakespeare's character. As a child he had drawn demons and monsters; as an adult, Robert Edmond Jones remembered, he continued to be captivated by "horror and cruelty and torture," by "artists like Doré and Fuseli, authors like Edgar Allan Poe . . . the macabre, the bizarre, the grotesque."[9] Richard's misshapen body and deformities of mind, his ironic humor and malevolent intensity undoubtedly fueled Barrymore's dramatic imagination and heightened his attraction to the part. Sheldon's confidence that he could succeed, and the enthusiasm of Hopkins and Jones for the proposed Shakespearean adventure, ultimately sealed his resolve.

By the spring of 1919, Barrymore, Hopkins, and Jones had made a firm commitment to present *Richard III* as the next play in their repertory. In April, soon after *The Jest* opened, plans began in earnest. The decision to begin preparations for *Richard III* was known, however, only to a select few. No public announcements were made, and for the next eight months plans proceeded under the strictest secrecy.

Arthur Hopkins later recalled that once the decision was made to attempt *Richard III*,

> I studied the play, made cuts, mulled over the variorum, and accumulated literature on the play and its various performances. None of this suited me. It seemed to me that the traditional treatment and interpretation of the play was a mass of personal imposition which in the desire to impress itself had left the author out of account. I felt I had found the reason for Shakespeare's apparent remoteness. His text was not dated, but its recognized treatment was that conceived by actors long dead. It was fair to assume that Shakespeare was more alive than his crumbled interpreters, so I dismissed authority, went back to the play itself. . . .[10]

Yet on one point he quickly sided with tradition: Radical alterations were necessary in order to make the play effective in the theatre. Cibber's blood-and-thunder adaptation, first produced in 1700, had held the stage for a century and three quarters, long after the rest of the Restoration and eighteenth-century "improvements" had been consigned to oblivion. During the 1876–7 and 1877–8 seasons, Irving (in London) and Booth (in New York) gave highly publicized restorations of "Shakespeare's text," but in both cases the play was greatly cut for performance.

Of more immediacy, however, was the acting text prepared by Richard Mansfield for his British and American productions in 1889. Mansfield's adaptation began, like the Booth and Irving "restorations," with Shakespeare's "Now is the winter of our discontent." What followed was a radically cut five-act version of *Richard III* with frequent interpolations, including the murder of King Henry VI from *3 Henry VI* (V.vi), twenty lines from Richard's soliloquy in that play (III.ii), and Cibber's sentimental scene in the Tower with the little princes and their mother. Mansfield's text contained one noteworthy innovation, however: the notion that the events of the play occur over a fourteen-year time period. The first act and first scene of the second took place in May 1471, when Richard was 19; twelve years elapsed between II.i and II.ii, followed by the upheaval of events leading to Bosworth Field.

It seems likely that all parties concerned were familiar with the Mansfield version. Barrymore, as we have seen, claimed to have witnessed Mansfield's portrayal, and Hopkins would have had ample opportunity to do so. The acting text of *Richard III* that Hopkins and Barrymore ultimately employed differed radically from Mansfield's, yet in dreaming out the production it is likely that a decision was made early on to borrow its most striking novelty: Richard's psychological progression over a period of time from callow fledgling to haunted, fitful tyrant.

The psychology of Barrymore's Richard emerged, however, as far more subtle and "modern" than that of Mansfield's creation, and here it is interesting to speculate on one possible influence on Hopkins's thought processes. In 1916, Sigmund Freud had published an essay entitled "Some Character-Types Met with in Psycho-Analytic Work," in which he detailed a category of human behavior "connected with experience and suffering." Certain individuals, he wrote, conscious since earliest childhood of an unfair and "unjust disadvantage," subsequently come to regard themselves as "exceptions," behave rebelliously, and claim privileges over others. As an example of this character type, he cited "a figure in whose character the claim to be an exception is closely bound up with and is motivated by the circumstance of congenital disadvantage": Richard III.[11]

Freud cited lines from Richard's opening soliloquy, wherein Richard decries his deformity and resolves that if he cannot "prove a lover" he will "prove a villain," as the key to his character. Nature, Freud's Richard argues, "has done me a grievous wrong in denying me the beauty of form which wins human love. Life owes me reparation for this, and I will see that I get it. I have a right to be an exception, to disregard the scruples by which others let themselves be held back. I may do wrong myself, since wrong has been done to me." At the same time, howerver, the soliloquy enables the audience to feel "a secret background of sympathy" for Richard by revealing "an enormous magnification of something we find in ourselves":

We all think we have reason to reproach Nature and our destiny for congenital and infantile disadvantages; we all demand reparation for early
wounds to our narcissism, our self-love. Why did not Nature give us the
golden curls of Balder or the strength of Siegfried or the lofty brow of genius or the noble profile of aristocracy? . . . We could carry off beauty and
distinction quite as well as any of those whom we are now obliged to envy
for those qualities.[12]

Although Hopkins never mentioned this essay directly, he later testified
that he had been introduced to Freud's writings and theories by Dr. Reginald
Allen of the University of Pennsylvania in 1912, was "immediately fascinated," and from then on read all he could find on the subject. "I have felt ever
since," he wrote, "that no one doing interpretive work in the theatre can really know just what materials he is translating without some understanding
of the Freudian principles."[13] It seems likely that one of Hopkins's primary
concerns was to present a "new" acting text that would go beyond the Mansfield version to illustrate Richard's psychological development in a more up-
to-date manner. To realize his aim, he turned again to the playwright whose
skillful adaptations of *Redemption* and *The Jest* had proven successful: Edward
Sheldon.[14]

During the summer and fall of 1919 the text for *Richard III* underwent a
number of drafts and revisions. Hopkins and Sheldon entered into a collaborative partnership (with Sheldon, in his sickroom, doing much of the arrangement); completed drafts were circulated to Barrymore, who made comments and returned the text for further revisions. An early draft from this
period survives among the Edward Sheldon papers in the Harvard Theatre
Collection. This version of the play, in four acts, was Barrymore's personal
copy. It features several handwritten notations by the actor: In I.iii he made
cuts to the Richard–Warwick exchange; in I.iv he wrote, "It is now night.
Torches illuminate the scene." Neither change is of particular importance,
but both reveal Barrymore's ongoing participation in the process of textual
refinement. Numerous alterations were to be made before opening night.
Among the additions were the "winter of our discontent" soliloquy and the
scene of Clarence's murder, omitted entirely in the draft; the four acts of the
draft were later arranged into three-act form for performance.[15] The promptbook reveals, however, that the structure of the play was intact from an early
stage. The primary innovation of the "new" version was to go beyond the Cibber and Mansfield acting texts (both included a scene of Henry VI's murder
based on *3 Henry VI*, V.vi and excerpts from Richard's soliloquy in *3 Henry VI*,
III.ii) to include five scenes from the last play in the *Henry VI* trilogy as prologue to the eleven scenes retained from *Richard III*.

Most scenes were compressed to half their length or less to keep the script
within a workable length (a duty to which Sheldon responded with a skillful

editorial eye and a keen sense of dramatic structure); many scenes contained brief interpolations from other scenes, and lines within scenes were freely reassigned. As in Mansfield's version, locations were shifted for the sake of scenic convenience. Mansfield wooed Lady Anne on a lavishly appointed road to Chertsey; many of Sheldon's scenes were set, with Jones's proposed unit setting in mind, before the Tower. The only vestige retained from Cibber was the hybrid line, "Chop off his head! [*Richard III*, III.i, 193] So much for Buckingham [Cibber, IV.iv, 188, which begins, "Off with his head"]." The result was a new and entirely unprecedented version of the story of Richard III.

Sheldon's efforts went beyond cutting and rearranging the text, however. The draft promptbook contains dozens of instances in which he rewrote lines, substituted words of his own choosing, or occasionally, for the sake of continuity, invented "Shakespearean" lines. In some cases the substitutions seem arbitrary – "scorn his course," for example, became "mock his course" (*Richard III*, II.i, 80). However, in most instances, Sheldon's aim is apparent: Lines were altered to tighten the plot by eliminating "baronial complications" or to clarify their meaning to a modern audience. Richard's "Would he were wasted, marrow, bones and all" (*3 Henry VI*, III.ii, 125), referring to his brother Edward, was changed to "Would they were wasted . . ." to include Clarence; in the tent scene, his "What, is my beaver easier than it was!/ And all my armour laid into my tent?" (*Richard III*, V.iii, 50–51) was altered to read "What, is my helmet easier than it was! And all my armour laid in readiness?"

These changes were accomplished, for the most part, with subtlety and a keen poetic ear. Although the new arrangement of the text and the relative paucity of Richards on the New York stage within recent memory were undoubtedly mitigating factors, it is worth noting that not one reviewer would comment on a specific instance of Sheldon's rephrasings.[16]

Preparations for *Richard III* continued through the autumn of 1919. Robert Edmond Jones had spent the summer in London gathering research material for his scenic and costume designs and had by then executed preliminary sketches. The actual date of production remained vague, however, and Barrymore's advance preparation was limited by his other commitments. In September, *The Jest* resumed, and soon afterward he began filming his most ambitious motion picture to date: an effort that would, in effect, be another challenge to the Richard Mansfield legacy.

For several years after his appearance in *Justice*, Barrymore had continued to make film farces at the rate of one per year: His light-comedy persona lived on in films long after its demise on the stage. *Raffles, the Amateur Cracksman* was released in 1917; *On the Quiet* in 1918; and *Here Comes the Bride* in early 1919. Later that year, however, Barrymore's first "serious" film was released: *The Test of Honor,* a melodrama with a *Justice*-like theme in which he played a man wrongfully imprisoned for manslaughter. In November 1919, he began work on another "serious" film: *Dr. Jekyll and Mr. Hyde* – like Richard III, a role that Mansfield had defined for a generation. A number of changes were made in the story line, the most notable of which was the depiction of Stevenson's Mr. Hyde, a rather ordinary-looking figure in the novel, as physically bizarre. The hunched posture, grotesque figure, and crabbed, angular movements Barrymore devised for Mr. Hyde proved an experimental foreshadowing of Richard's physicality. Once principal scenes were completed, Barrymore felt ready to turn his attentions to Shakespeare.

By mid-December, rumors were circulating in the theatrical community that Barrymore would appear as Richard. The first public acknowledgment of the pending production came soon afterward. "All hands now admit freely that John Barrymore will act *Richard III* before the season is over," commented the *Times* (21 December 1919). Many members of the theatrical profession initially gave Barrymore little chance at success, however. "When it was announced that he was to do *Richard III* . . . complete skepticism was the general opinion," recalled Arthur William Row, a Broadway veteran who would later appear in the production.[17]

A good deal of the skepticism arose from a widespread public knowledge of Barrymore's limited vocal prowess; his slipshod diction and "vocal monotony" had been much commented upon in the press. "Jack's chief handicap for the poetic classics was a furry voice," Arthur Hopkins recalled years later. "There was a rasp which one feared could only be removed by a surgical miracle." Barrymore later claimed that soon after the decision was made to attempt Richard, "I went out into the woods . . . and recited the entire play, and then threw the book away. It couldn't be done. My voice had a high, nasal tone and I recited 'A horse, a horse, my kingdom for a horse!' like a terrified tenor trying to escape from a couple of blondes."[18]

Criticism of his earlier performances and an awareness of his limited range convinced Barrymore that intense vocal training was necessary if he was to succeed in his first Shakespearean role. "It was characteristic of Jack to know that he had to find a new voice," Arthur Hopkins commented. "He never deceived himself about his handicaps, nor did he believe that by other compensations they could be got around."[19] Soon afterward, Barrymore began to take steps to remedy his deficiency. Arthur Row later recalled that he studied with three voice and diction teachers while preparing for the role.[20] The first was probably Robert Hosea; it seems likely that Barrymore began shaping his vocal powers during *The Jest* period with future Shakespeare in mind. For reasons unknown, however, he discontinued his studies with Hosea and attempted lessons with a second teacher, whose identity is not now recoverable, and whom he eventually abandoned as well. The third teacher, however, would prove a charm.

Margaret Huston Carrington (1877–1942) was born in Orangeville, Ontario, the third of four children of Robert Moore Huston and Elizabeth MacGibbon. Her parents were of Irish–Scots descent; her father was a provincial farmer who left his rocky patch of ground to set up a construction company in Toronto at around the time his youngest child (the actor Walter Huston) was born in 1884.[21] At an early age Margaret demonstrated a talent for singing; she began performing publicly as a child and subsequently earned a reputation throughout the Toronto area with a voice that matured into a rich mezzo-soprano. In October 1896, a number of "prominent patronesses of music" sponsored a benefit concert at Pavilion Music Hall, raising funds that enabled her to travel to Paris, London, Germany, and Italy, where she studied with many of the leading singers and teachers of the day including Jean de Reszke, Emma Calvé, and Nellie Melba.

In 1903, Margaret Huston began a career as a recitalist; she gave a "homecoming concert" in Toronto on 26 November of that year and, subsequently, a number of recitals in Paris, Berlin, London, and New York, earning a reputation as a skillful interpreter of the avant-garde art songs of Debussy and Hugo Wolf. After the outbreak of the First World War she returned to New York, where soon afterward she met William Carrington, a wealthy, Toledo-born retired grain merchant twenty-two years her senior. Following a whirlwind courtship, she and Carrington were married in 1915, and she gave up her career to devote herself to her husband.

In the mid-to-late teens, doubtless desiring an artistic outlet after her retirement, Margaret Carrington turned her formidable energies to teaching. Robert Edmond Jones (who, after the death of William Carrington, became her second husband) later remembered that

> Through long and exhaustive study and practice Mrs. Carrington had evolved an idea that was nothing short of tremendous. She had come to believe that it was possible to free the speaking voice to such an extent that one could hear, not the speaker's intention or his personality, but his inner essence, the self, the soul, speaking through him. Only a child or a saint or a genius could hold such a belief and Mrs. Carrington was all of these.

Her students included numerous opera singers and actors. (Among her later pupils were her brother Walter, Alfred Lunt, Orson Welles, and Lillian Gish.) She accepted no fees for lessons, tutoring only those in whom she took a personal interest. Of medium height, solidly built, with red-gold hair and compelling blue eyes, she projected physical vitality, psychic intensity, and an imperturbable air of authority (Fig. 15). "Jack always said she was a witch," Robert Edmond Jones remembered years later. "She was in a way, a white witch. Her intuitions were always uncanny. Many people were in awe of her."[22]

Her initial meeting with Barrymore came in December 1919, soon after the first public announcements of the production. Michael Strange had met her socially in Santa Barbara and, harboring ambitions for a theatrical career, become a pupil, continuing her lessons in New York. Aware of Barrymore's apprehensions, she suggested that he pay a call on Margaret Carrington and arranged a meeting at the conclusion of one of her lessons. Soon afterward, Barrymore presented himself in the blue-and-gold drawing room of the Carringtons' spacious apartment at 760 Park Avenue at 72nd Street.

Years later, yielding to the urging of Robert Edmond Jones to set down her recollections of working with Barrymore, Margaret Carrington began to compose a series of notes on their collaboration. At their first meeting, she recalled, Barrymore appeared in her drawing room

> tremulous, modest and shy . . . to tell me that he was going to act Shakespeare and that he was afraid of it. I could not believe that the most popular actor in America could be afraid of anything. Then, with that devastating Barrymore charm, he made me understand that he was asking me to help him. I felt reluctant to undertake the responsibility of piercing the outer shell of a sensitive high-powered theatre personality with new ideas which might or might not help him in his first step in Shakespeare, especially as the play of *Richard III* was announced to open in six weeks.

Barrymore's voice, moreover, was "tired, and in spite of its individual quality was of short range" due to a complete lack of breath control.[23]

Nevertheless, she agreed to accept the challenge. When Barrymore arrived for his initial session the next day, she asked him to explain his conception of the role. "Well, it's like this," he claimed to have replied. "I have a great entrance where I come in carrying the head of a man I've just killed. Like this! Look!" He strode in majestically, roaring his lines, boasting loudly about what he'd done. His exaggeration was met by withering sarcasm. "You think you're an actor?" Margaret Carrington asked. "You're just a damn fool. That's the hammiest Richard III that ever existed." She made him sit down. "Now tell *me*, not the whole world, about cutting this fellow's head off," she instructed. "Tell me the story of the play, what it's all about, in your own words."[24]

He did; and then he listened carefully as Margaret Carrington explained her method of vocal training. "The essence of the actor's craft," she later wrote

> is to reveal the exact meaning of the text and at the same time to project the emotional content of the drama through his own personal sound. Words should remain in the front of the mouth, where consonants are articulated, while sound should move with the emotion, in the vowel spaces. Few actors observe this balance in their reading. . . . An infallible rule in reading Shakespeare is that it must be read to the punctuation set down in

Figure 15. Margaret Carrington. Author's collection.

the texts. I do not know whether these punctuations [were] in Shake-speare's original manuscripts. In any case we cannot do better than to fol-low . . . the accredited editions in use today. We must read through the com-mas to the semicolons, which are suspended breath-pauses. It is only after the full stops that we can take a full breath. To do this demands the same breath support that singers and players of wind instruments must have when they phrase music. Actors who lack this power to breathe to the punc-tuations . . . break the continuity of the sense as well as the rhythm of the verse."[25]

"It is common knowledge that a voice cannot be built in a few weeks," she remarked. "I told [Barrymore] that I had no tricks up my sleeve – that it would mean the most intensive work and concentration on his part to even develop the necessary breath control in reading Shakespeare's verse." Yet she found Barrymore amenable to her methods.

> I had hoped to meet someone who would be receptive and responsive to one or two simple principles underlying speech control. I had worked for years on a kind of research in Nature's Laboratory on the spoken word in its relation to the Speech of Actors. After my first hour with Barrymore, I knew that here was an actor who was simple and obedient enough to understand what these principles would do, and then began the most exciting and constructive experience of my life.[26]

For the next six weeks, Barrymore worked intensively with Margaret Carrington; he returned the next day and nearly every day thereafter until opening night. He immersed himself totally in his vocal preparations for the role, working with "humility, patience and concentration" to "polish every phrase" of the play. He worked for five or six hours at a time; he sang, practiced breathing and diction, labored "unceasingly on intonations," and "learned to speak Shakespeare's lines understandingly, as though they had been spoken for the first time."[27]

"I asked him to do something which I believed would help him quickly," Carrington remembered.

> I told him there was a longer way around but that if he was willing to throw out everything he had ever done in the theatre for a few weeks, he might accomplish in a short time what generally took months or even years for people who lacked his prehensile intelligence. It seems difficult to focus all one's forces in acquiring the control of an art, yet anyone who has succeeded in any field had to do it this way. There is no royal road to expertness. It is a matter of concentration plus talent.[28]

Barrymore was quickly won over by her knowledgeable, no-nonsense approach. In turn, Margaret Carrington was impressed by her pupil's dedication, his desire to learn, his "dynamo energy." Barrymore "responded to every nuance and implication of meaning of the text," she recalled.

> [He] worked incessantly on gaining the necessary breath control to suspend and sustain the long unbroken phrases of Shakespeare's verse. He worked as he walked in the streets prolonging his vowel sounds until he acquired the muscular control required to read through to the end of a sentence on one breath. This was a veritable tour de force on his part in the use of will and imagination, and in my experience has never been done by any actor in so limited a time.[29]

Together Barrymore and Carrington worked on character analysis as well as vocal technique. "The role of Richard III was a challenge to Barrymore's mordant and rapier-like mentality," she remembered. "It is a superhuman test of an actor's ability to play a villain like Richard and project the beauty and significance of Shakespeare's text and not fall into a theatric or realistic interpretation of a role fraught with pitfalls for actors without creative or poetic imagination." In Richard's lines in the first scene they found a "complete key" to his character: "I that am curtail'd of this fair proportion,/ Cheated of feature by dissembling nature,/ Deform'd, unfinish'd, sent before my time/ Into this breathing world scarce half made up . . ." "There is more in this speech than mere villainy," Carrington remarked. "It is perhaps the greatest written revelation of human frustration."[30]

Another facet of the preparatory period involved creating a technique to deal effectively with Shakespeare's soliloquies. "This might be defined," wrote Carrington, "as the difference between thinking and talking. The soliloquy must have only the sound of thought – while dialogue is straightforward speech, but the real difficulty is that the audience is in on the soliloquy. How to bridge this seeming inconsistency depends on an actor's ability to project these two dimensions in sound." She suggested a novel reading for "Was ever woman in this humor wooed? Was ever woman in this humor won?" "In saying these lines to himself the scene was let down," she commented. "I suggested that he throw these lines into the auditorium. . . . The effect was startling. . . . It took bold courage to step aside from tradition and only an actor with Barrymore's impeccable theatre instincts could dare do it successfully."[31]

In retrospect, the analogy of bridging is appropriate, for the entire six-week preparatory period was devoted to one overriding aim that both Barrymore and Margaret Carrington understood instinctively: the development of a vocal technique that would bridge the much-commented-upon disparity between Shakespearean and "natural" acting. The "tragic elevation" and musical intonings common in early-twentieth-century revivals were looked on as cardinal sins; all efforts were focused on creating a technique that would convey the illusion of "natural" speech while at the same time retaining the meter of the verse and communicating the subtleties of Shakespeare's language.

Throughout the preparatory period, Barrymore was driven by the desire to make good, to prove the skeptics wrong. The fact that the opening had been announced, the costumes and scenery designed, served as a powerful incentive to accomplish a vocal miracle within a limited period of time. To this he dedicated an almost superhuman energy and discipline, devoting every available moment (while at the same time performing in *The Jest* and filming additional scenes for *Dr. Jekyll and Mr. Hyde*) to developing a technique that would effectively convey the Richard of his imagination. By the end of January, Barrymore – after six weeks of intensive study and practice – possessed an entirely new voice.

The Cast

For many years, the myth has been perpetuated that Arthur Hopkins cast *Richard III* with actors who had "no Shakespearean experience." The source for this myth was Hopkins himself, and it has been repeated in numerous accounts of the production.[32] It was not, however, true: The company included veterans of the Henry Irving, Forbes-Robertson, and Ben Greet companies, a fact of which Hopkins could hardly have been unaware. Nevertheless, it seems likely that Hopkins, in casting *Richard III*, did circulate the word that Shakespearean experience was neither necessary nor even desirable. What he was clearly seeking to avoid were actors with traditional and preconceived notions as to how Shakespeare should be played. The rumor may have been spread along Broadway that "Shakespearean actors needn't apply," but a classical background was no hindrance to employment if Hopkins sensed that an actor seemed capable of adapting to the repressed style of playing he sought to complement Barrymore's portrayal.

Auditions were held at the Plymouth in mid-to-late January and early February 1920. A few actors already known to Hopkins through past productions may have been precast, but the majority of roles were available, and dozens of actors turned out each day, lured by Hopkins's artistic track record and the glamour surrounding Barrymore's Shakespearean debut. As was his custom, Hopkins engaged actors based on the impression he got from talking to them individually rather than from readings or recitations; he sought a personal quality that was right for particular parts.[33]

The principals he engaged were, in the main, veteran English actors, most with noteworthy Shakespearean credits. Rosalind Ivan, the Queen Margaret (later to earn distinction as a character actress in films) had played Nerissa to the Portia of Ellen Terry and the Shylock of Henry Irving during the 1901–2 season; Burford Hampden, who played her son, Edward, Prince of Wales, had appeared as Puck in Beerbohm Tree's 1911 revival of *A Midsummer Night's Dream;* Walter Ringham, the Earl of Warwick, and Montague Rutherford, who doubled Bourchier and Ratcliff, had toured in *Hamlet* and *Othello* with Forbes-Robertson. As the company was an interesting and varied one, a more complete discussion of the cast (and the actors who performed with Barrymore in the New York and London productions of *Hamlet*) is included as Appendix A.

Arthur Row's testimony reveals that Barrymore had a crucial voice in the casting process. Row (1878–1961), a native of Montreal, had made his professional debut in 1899 with Maurice Barrymore and Mrs. Fiske in *Becky Sharp*. He subsequently established himself as an able journeyman; he supported Richard Mansfield during his final season, toured with Mantell, and appeared in minor roles in Barker's *Androcles and the Lion,* Herbert Tree's tercentenary

Henry VIII, and Ethel Barrymore's 1917 revival of *Camille*. He later set down a vivid account of his audition for the initial Barrymore–Hopkins Shakespearean production.

> The picture was lurid that Jack made the day he engaged me for *Richard III*. He revelled in looking like the worst of his legends – unkempt, unshaved, yellow skin, straggling hair. . . . He wore a disreputable old fur coat that seemed to have been slept in. Underneath it were probably only pajamas for it is certain this early hour appointment had rudely disturbed his slumbers. Jack sat all huddled up in a hard kitchen chair. . . . My hour had struck. This was the most critical moment of my whole career. I sat at a small prompt table facing Jack – behind Jack was standing Arthur Hopkins. Draped round our little scene was one of the enormous medieval screens used in *The Jest*, which shut us off completely from the view of a hundred anxious actors awaiting an audience. I told Jack at once of my playing with his father and also with Miss Barrymore, adding "It is a tradition with me to act only with the Barrymores." (A slight exaggeration but it served!) Then I timidly asked if there would be something for me in *Richard III*. Jack was quickly obviously touched by my reference to his father who he adored. Evidently I was not to escape a little kidding too for he asked me if he might have my address for his personal book, and proceeded to gravely write it in. Mr. Hopkins' eyes gleamed with amusement! I made a slight faux pas by admitting I had played before with Mantell in this play, but for the life of me could not remember what! Instantly Jack raised a forbidding hand and said "Don't" with absolute finality. With some excitement Jack whispered to Hopkins over his shoulder, "He is Henry VI – I can see him in that soliloquy!"[34]

Rehearsals

Rehearsals for *Richard III* began on Tuesday, 3 February, and the scheduled opening of the play was pushed back from the week of 15 February to 26 February. At the first read-through, Hopkins later recalled, he was determined to treat the work as a new play (which, in effect, it was). He gave the actors typewritten "sides" with their parts, and cautioned his cast to avoid reverence, explaining that the play was a melodrama and must be treated as such, not as cold verse to be intoned by dead tongues.[35]

For the first week, the cast sat in a semicircle of chairs set up on the stage of the Plymouth, reading through the play again and again, with few interruptions. Hopkins took individual actors aside to offer corrections only when a reading revealed a misconception of meaning or importance or an "unnatural" approach. The whole effort, he remembered, was to "become immersed in the rich flow of the play."[36] Rehearsals began at ten, and usually lasted five to six hours.

During the second week, blocking began. Hopkins had previously settled in his mind where the areas of action were to be and showed the actors their general positions and movement. His direction stressed a new, European trend in staging: Supporting actors were permitted to gesture only when speaking their own lines; for the most part they refrained from extraneous movement, with minimal reaction to what was said and done. When appropriate to the mood of a scene he instructed his actors to move "slowly and ominously around the stage."[37] The actors walked through their parts, without neglecting reading values, until Hopkins was satisfied that the blocking and motion approximated their final form. Traditional stage business was discarded; hints of expansive, "Shakespearean" gesture were nipped in the bud. Rehearsals were a simultaneous process of building and stripping away; Hopkins's ideal was for movement and stage business to grow easily and naturally.

Direction, as was Hopkins's custom, was usually low-key and inconspicuous; actors were given leeway to develop their individual characterizations. "The actor," Hopkins wrote years later, "has only one responsibility – to make the character honestly live."[38] Arthur Row testified subsequently to the director's insistence on "truth" in every line reading. "As Henry VI I had a line – 'I am your sovereign' – at rehearsal Arthur Hopkins was not satisfied – convinced! In fact he said right out loud, 'I don't believe you!' I repeated it. Silence from Arthur H. [I repeated it] again. Then Arthur H. said 'Now I believe you.'"[39]

Barrymore had come to rehearsals after six weeks of intensive study with Margaret Carrington. His new voice and conception of his character were firmly in place; one of Hopkins's primary duties as director was to "rein in" his performance when, as in rehearsals for *Redemption*, he began to show a "residue of the old bombastic theatre." This time, Hopkins was more successful. Barrymore had learned a valuable lesson from the criticism of his all-out flamboyance in the earlier play. The emphasis in *Richard III* was on subtlety and restraint; Hopkins and Margaret Carrington were quick to correct the actor when his readings and gestures became too broad, too showy.

William Keighley, who doubled Brackenbury and Rivers (and who, in ensuing decades, became a noted film director), later remembered "sitting at rehearsal after rehearsal enthralled by the magnetic personality of this great actor." Barrymore, he commented, was "the giant of my generation on the stage. To hear his beautiful rendition of the role of Richard was a privilege and I'd have gladly worked for nothing rather than miss it."[40]

Barrymore was almost unfailingly patient with members of the company as they developed their characterizations. "He was a great help to me, as was Mr. Arthur Hopkins, who kept me in the role when I felt too awful for words," recalled Arthur Row. "It was only the encouragement of the star and manager that kept me going." He later remembered that at rehearsal one day, "I, for some reason, forgot my death scene. Finally [Barrymore] strolled over to me with, 'Don't you want to act with me?' – this brought me to my senses." Barrymore's training with Margaret Carrington, moreover, had made him quick to notice even the slightest imperfections of speech. "One day at rehearsal he whispered in my ear . . . 'Peer – there are two e's.' I had blurred it in some way and he was kind enough to correct me," Row recalled.[41]

Throughout the rehearsal period, Barrymore continued to spend hours each day on vocal exercises. He was similarly dedicated to discovering an effective method to convey Richard's physicality. His intention from the first was to present audiences with a subtle handling of the character's impairment, stressing instead his deformity of mind. Years later he claimed to Gene Fowler that to develop the swift limp he would use in the role

> I merely turned my right foot inward, pointing it toward the instep of my left foot. I let it stay in that position and then forgot all about it. I did not try to walk badly, I walked as *well* as I could. You will find, I think, that a cripple does not try to walk with a worse gait than he has to employ. He endeavors to walk as well as he can. That's the mistake Robert Mantell made, I believe; he consciously exaggerated, and thus made of the part a roaring caricature. This was true of Mansfield's Richard [as well].

Yet the story was passed down in his family that he resorted to another, more discomforting method: putting stones in his shoe.[42]

Hopkins had originally scheduled three weeks of rehearsals before opening night. When this proved impractical, the opening was delayed, first to 1 March and finally to 6 March, a Saturday. The final two weeks (of a total of five) were spent on the "polishing and liberating process" – setting the play's rhythm and fine-tuning characterizations and movement. *The Jest* played its last performance on 21 February; for two weeks the Plymouth was dark while the set and lighting instruments were installed and rehearsals continued.

Several dress (technical) rehearsals were held during the week of 29 February. William Keighley later remembered that Barrymore's "eccentricity was evidenced at [one] dress rehearsal when he spent the evening trying on costumes and sitting in the orchestra pit watching Arthur Hurley the stage manager read the character of Richard."[43] At the final run-through, Arthur Row remembered, Ethel Barrymore "sat out in front, alone, in the center of the orchestra. On her face was an inscrutable smile. It is possible she feared that this would be only another adventure – an interesting, laudable one."[44]

The Scenery

While in London during the summer of 1919, Robert Edmond Jones made numerous sketches of the Tower, which he envisioned as a permanent symbolic background for the play. The resulting Craig- and Reinhardt-influenced unit rose forty-eight feet above the stage, an ominous-looking, dull gray half-hexagon with angled sides extending to the wings. The central portion, parallel to the lip of the stage, featured a massive portcullis with a practicable iron gate. Two doors on either side of the portcullis were used for entrances and exits; one led to "the chapel." In every scene, all or part of this setting could be seen; it provided a background for all street scenes and most exteriors (Fig. 16).[45]

For other locations, Jones designed easily moved set pieces – "mere scraps of background" – to suggest a sense of place. A rich-looking tapestry, approximately fifteen feet in height, corresponding to the angles of the Tower and crowned with heraldic shields, masked the bottom of the central unit during court scenes. Entrances could be made through a central vent. Before the tapestry was set a tall throne, its rectangular back portion decorated with three heraldic lions. Two broad steps, extending to the front and to both sides, led to the platform upon which the throne rested. The scenes in York's castle featured a gold rectangular arras, which was placed in front of the tapestry. A low platform stood before the arras, with three short steps to either side.

For the murder of Henry VI, an iron cage was placed in the center of the stage, masking the central opening. The scene of Clarence's murder featured a similar effect: An iron trellis was lowered from above, stretching across the entire proscenium. The various battle scenes were indicated by blotting out the Tower in darkness and placing large canvas rocks against the central opening and at different parts of the stage, against which could be seen the massive, towering shadows of combatants. For the final duel with Richmond, a grim gibbet was set in black silhouette against the red-lit walls of the permanent facade.

As was his custom, Jones spent many hours with George Schaff, the Plymouth's master electrician, who helped to design and perfect the subtle chiaroscuro lighting effects – accomplished exclusively with overhead illumination and side- and backlighting – that enhanced the mood of individual scenes and served to unite the disparate elements of the production.[46]

Scene changes were accomplished, for the most part, with uncommon speed; many observers later commented upon the revival's "cinematic" nature. Alexander Woollcott, virtually alone among his peers, carped that the production "called for more than a dozen illusion-dispelling intervals for the shifting of the scenery" (*Times*, 8 March 1920), yet it seems likely that most changes were effected quickly. When a shift in locale was necessary the house curtain was generally lowered; changes were probably made to the accompaniment of incidental music by Eugen Haile, much of it recycled from the score to *The Happy Ending*, a Hopkins failure of a few years earlier. When the locale remained the same, however (as in Sheldon's I.ii and I.iii), and in bat-

Figure 16. Robert Edmond Jones's drawing for the wooing of Lady Anne. Courtesy Billy Rose Theatre Collection, The New York Public Library for the Performing Arts.

tlefield scenes (as in Sheldon's I.iv, and in the concluding scenes at Tewkesbury), transitions were accomplished with lighting alone; the effect, wrote one observer, was that of "an episodic panorama . . . that opens, discloses and fades away."[47]

Variety (12 March 1920) noted an important theatrical advantage of this system; the production, wrote their critic, was "broken up into 16 short scenes, each of them fading in and out, which breaks the monotony and does away with the old-fashioned idea of concluding a long speech in the center of the stage and 'walking off cold' to the entrance." Spotlights and lighting localized on only a small segment of the stage, used in the scene in Richmond's camp and elsewhere, at times created an intimacy compared by one observer to cinematic "close-ups."[48]

To Heywood Broun, the mise-en-scène proved one of the most impressive aspects in the "breaking and bettering of traditions" that typified the production. Jones's scenery, he remarked, was "almost as simple as the most barren offering of Mr. Ben Greet," yet he succeeded in "creating gorgeous stage pictures," and at no time was depth "sacrificed to the exigencies of scene shifting." Broun concluded by reminding his readers that "in most of the Shakespearean productions of the last fifty years there was a regular alternation between shallow scenes played in front of a painted drop and scenes in which the full stage was employed. As a boy we remember being puzzled and troubled by the fact that Polonius always seemed to be living in a hallway" (*Tribune*, 14 March 1920).

The Costumes

In London Jones made sketches of pictures from the War of the Roses period and purchased fabrics for the realization of his designs. The armor for the soldiers, both royal and common, was rented from a Covent Garden supplier and was heavy and realistic, as opposed to the lightweight metal used in most theatrical productions. Each suit of armor included a visored helmet; the visors, on hinges, were worn up during nonbattle scenes. A band of chain mail was worn around the waist.

The courtiers, for the most part, were clothed in short, late-fifteenth-century tunics and hose. The costumes for the women were more elaborate: In the court scenes (which, according to Francis Bruguiere's production photographs, included half a dozen or more waiting gentlewomen) they wore individualized floor-length gowns with long, tight sleeves and low necklines, accompanied by an assortment of butterfly, conical, and other headdresses of the period. The dominant colors were cerise, purple, and emerald green. A stark touch was provided for the three queens; they were clad in austere black mourning gowns that resembled nuns' habits. Throughout, the costumes appeared "historically correct," yet there was a subtle departure from strict accuracy, for, as the *Christian Science Monitor* was to note, they featured "ever so slight grotesque exaggerations" (16 March 1920).

The greatest care was devoted to Richard's costumes, which were many and varied. Two suits of armor – one black and one coppery – were custom-tailored for Barrymore by Henry Fachs, a German-born, Newark-based metalsmith who frequently restored and repaired armor for museums. During the course of the preparatory period Barrymore made numerous trips across the river for fittings and adjustments. The black armor was worn during the first five scenes; the copper-colored armor was worn during the scene of Richard's mother's curse and in the troop-rallying and battle scenes thereafter. In all battle scenes, Barrymore carried a heavy broadsword of his own design, based on a weapon used during the War of the Roses.

During the last scene of the first act and much of the second act, Barrymore wore a colorful assortment of blood-red and red-orange short tunics with dark hose, in sharp contrast to the costumes worn by other members of the court. At his side he wore a short sword. For the coronation scene, he was clad in a stunning, floor-length violet and gold mantle lined with silver metallic cloth – a garment cited admiringly by a number of critics – from which, in a stunning coup de théâtre, he later emerged clothed entirely in black.

The *World* (8 March 1920) commented admiringly that "surely no monarch who ever sat upon a tyrant's throne in a play was ever so magnificently attired."

Throughout, Barrymore wore a lank, black wig, banged in the front and extending at the sides to his shoulders. His makeup sharpened and harshened his features while at the same time emphasizing a lean, pale appearance. It is likely that additional makeup was applied in later scenes to highlight his increasing years, for as Charles Darnton noted, "He aged before our eyes" (*Evening World*, 8 March 1920).

Opening Night

"Not since the best days – or nights – of Augustin Daly's Theatre has a stage door been guarded as zealously as the Plymouth Theatre during the last week, where John Barrymore and his company have been rehearsing *Richard III* in preparation for the first performance tonight," commented the *Evening Telegram* (6 March 1920). "It is said that Mr. Arthur Hopkins, the manager and producer, has been particularly anxious lest a dramatic critic or a historical anachronism should creep past the dragon at the door and spoil the little surprise party which is ready for the first nighters this evening."

Tickets for opening night, at an unprecedented scale of five dollars for the first ten rows of the orchestra, had been sold out for several weeks. More than a thousand spectators turned out, braving unusually inclement weather. On Friday, a drenching rain had changed to sleet, then hail, followed the next day by a blizzard, a thirty-degree drop in temperature, and a seventy-two-mile-an-hour gale. They were drawn, wrote Alan Dale in the *American*, by "curiosity, speculation, old-timery, Shakespeareomania, rubber neck-itis and a genuine sense of drama" (8 March 1920). Most commentators agreed that the audience was one of the most distinguished in recent memory. No account of the premiere would be complete, remarked Alexander Woollcott, "that did not speak of the electric atmosphere with which the house was charged – the sense of a great occasion. The combination of Arthur Hopkins, John Barrymore, and the Plymouth Theatre, with such precedents as *Redemption* and *The Jest* put into the mind of the playgoers . . . recaptured for the New York stage a certain festive glamour that has been missing since Augustin Daly died" (*Times*, 8 March 1920).

Hopkins and Jones, as was their custom, occupied seats in the high reaches of the second balcony. (Sheldon, in California in an attempt to recover his health, was destined never to see the Shakespearean debut he had encouraged, nor the onstage realization of the text he had arranged.)[49] Seated nearby was Michael Strange, whose entrance via the red carpet leading from the curb to the Plymouth foyer drew excited comments from the crowd of onlookers gathered behind police barricades. The performance was scheduled to begin at 8:30 P.M. There were numerous unexplained delays, however, and it was not until ten to nine that the house lights finally were dimmed.

More than four hours later – as the hour was approaching one o'clock – the final curtain descended. Barrymore, emerging to take his bow in the copper-colored armor he wore for his final duel with Richmond, was greeted by a standing ovation and was called before the curtain again and again. The audience, which as many observers would note, had distinguished itself by incessant coughing, was weary after the lengthy performance but had remained to cheer its conclusion. Only a handful of spectators had left the theatre. As the reviewer for *Town Topics* wryly commented, "Rarely has a New York premiere enjoyed such a blaze of glory or enjoyed that blaze for so many hours."[50]

The Performance

Compared to the surfeit of information available on Barrymore's *Hamlet* there is relatively little documentation of *Richard III*. Sheldon's draft promptbook is the only promptbook of the play to survive in an archival collection; much of the stage business is not now recoverable. Nevertheless it is possible to reconstruct many of the details of Barrymore's performance and Hopkins's direction. Contemporary newspapers and magazines devoted considerable space to the production, and in many cases cited examples of the acting and staging. To these can be added the recollections of Arthur Row, Margaret Carrington, and others. A wealth of additional evidence exists, including more than forty sketches for the costumes and mise-en-scène made by Robert Edmond Jones and the production photographs by Francis Bruguiere.

Two other sources cannot be overlooked: the recordings Barrymore made of Richard, years after the stage production, and his soliloquy from the Warner Brothers film *The Show of Shows*.[51] The sound documentation includes a 1928 RCA Victor record of Richard's soliloquy from *3 Henry VI* (III.ii), private recordings of Richard's soliloquies after the murder of King Henry VI and following the ghostly visitation, and a 1937 NBC radio broadcast of an abridged version of the play. In many cases, especially that of the radio broadcast (later released commercially as a long-playing album), Barrymore's vocal quality is darker, his readings less subtle and controlled than in earlier recordings. A comparison of earlier and later recorded evidence is revealing, however. In three versions of the soliloquy from *3 Henry VI* (III.ii), for example, Barrymore's scansion, tempo, and emotional tone remain essentially unchanged. No two performances, of course, were ever exactly alike, but the evidence clearly indicates that Barrymore's interpretation was carefully worked out on a line-by-line basis. Even in later years, when his technique had begun to erode, he tended to retain the patterns he had established while studying for the role. Thus, in a few cases recordings have been used – conservatively and with caution – to indicate volume, emphasis, and mood. All references to recorded material are indicated in the notes; stresses are shown by italics, or, in the case of strong emphasis, italic small capital letters. Throughout, I have used the symbol [/] to denote a slight hesitation. Sheldon's departures from the quarto and folio texts are indicated by brackets.

One crucial element to keep in mind when considering the performance is the element of surprise, upon which much of the production's impact depended. The opening night audience for *Richard III* was aware of Barrymore's vocal limitations. Before he attempted Richard, Arthur Row remembered, his diction was "atrocious," he had "about three notes to his voice," and "as they say in theatrical argot, no legato"; yet to Row, the result of his training with Carrington was "an English as near perfection as any human being can achieve." Barrymore's new vocal powers came as a revelation to audiences. His range had expanded considerably, his elocution was flawless, and the monotonous quality of *Redemption* and *The Jest* had been replaced by crisp, deep, rounded (though not loud) tones of unanticipated subtlety and expressiveness. "Those who heard his opening night in *Richard* were astonished at the change in his personal sound," Margaret Carrington recalled.[52]

Equally surprising to the audience was the overall performance style. Playgoers of 1920 were thoroughly accustomed to the conservative Shakespearean status quo of Sothern and Marlowe and Robert B. Mantell, to the "stately ritual" of the former and the old-school characterizations of the latter – especially the bloodthirsty Richard of the Cibber text and nineteenth-century tradition, which Mantell had kept before the public through much of the previous two decades. Barrymore's Richard, praised by the critical fraternity as more "realistic" and "psychologically truthful" than the portrayals of other contemporary interpreters, is best seen through the eyes of those accustomed to musical delivery, reverential productions, and neo-Victorian characterizations, audiences for whom the vitality of Barker's *A Midsummer Night's Dream* was a rare exception rather than the rule.

The element of the unforeseen extended to Hopkins's staging and Jones's mise-en-scène. Many in the audience were aware of Max Reinhardt's utilization of austere staging and Craig-inspired scenery in his German productions of Shakespeare, which had received ample coverage in the New York press and theatrical journals. Still, Hopkins's spare direction and Jones's imaginative settings, with their emphasis on minimalism, symbolic values, and rapid, "cinematic" scene changes, provided many spectators with their first exposure to a creative application of Craig's principles in a Shakespearean drama.

Taken as a whole, the production – and particularly Barrymore's performance therein – represented a new, forceful, and entirely welcome change in style. This, of course, was hardly unprecedented. The history of the stage reveals many similar debuts, in which a charismatic actor has emerged suddenly to restore "nature" to the bravura repertory, marking a sharp turnabout from an elevated, classical mode of acting Shakespeare that had held the stage for a generation or more. Garrick, Kean, and the Anglo–French tragedian Charles Fechter, whose "colloquial" Hamlet had caused a sensation in London during the 1860–1 season, were each extolled for introducing a method more "lifelike" than that of their immediate predecessors.

One caveat is very much in order when considering the performance, however. Critics and audiences of 1920 acclaimed Barrymore's Richard for bringing to Broadway an impersonation that had "less a sense of stage and more of reality than at any Shakespearean performance of recent years";[53] yet "nature" on the stage is a relative term, as even the most cursory study of the theatre's history quickly reveals. It is defined anew by each generation; performances that seem vital and "real" at any given time more often than not would be considered "theatrical" and artificial if witnessed by audiences removed from their cultural and historical context.

Nearly seventy years after the fact, Maurice Valency, for many years Brander Matthews Professor of Dramatic Literature at Columbia University, looked back upon Barrymore's Richard, which he had seen and admired while in his midteens. Viewed by contemporary audiences, he commented, Barrymore's portrayal would probably seem extravagant and mannered; the aura of glamour Barrymore brought to the role "probably wouldn't hold up anymore." No actor today, he remarked, "would dare to act so flamboyantly as Barrymore did in those days. He was able to put a lot more schmaltz into his acting than most actors permit themselves to do now." However, Valency was quick to add, "we enjoyed that."[54]

Act I

Act I, scene i. *Throne Room.* [*3 Henry VI,* I.i]

The house lights dim; the curtain rises on the throne room setting. A brightly colored tapestry covers the lower portion of the Tower, in sharp contrast to the austere, dimly lit gray walls that rise above the level of the proscenium. Before the tapestry sits a tall wooden throne emblazoned with three heraldic lions. Three steps lead to the low platform upon which the throne rests. The atmosphere is one of severe dignity and grandeur.

The Duke of York enters almost immediately, followed by the Earl of Warwick and the Duke's sons, Edward and George. All are dressed in chain mail armor and visored helmets with swords at their sides. Following slightly be-

Figure 17. Richard, Duke of Gloucester. Courtesy Billy Rose Theatre Collection, The New York Public Library for the Performing Arts.

hind them is Richard in dull black armor, draped with a black cloak. Chain mail is visible around his waist. He wears a black battle helmet; a long sword hangs in a scabbard at his side. He walks with a slight limp, yet his posture conveys an air of swaggering insolence. He is carrying a canvas bag.[55]

Warwick speaks the first line: "I wonder how the king escaped our hands." Edward boasts of his accomplishments in battle and holds forth his sword, stained with the blood of the Duke of Buckingham. George holds out his own sword: "And, brother, here's the Earl of Wiltshire's blood,/ Whom I encounter'd as the battles join'd." His line is followed by Richard's firm, sharp interjection, as he looks down at the bag: "*Speak thou* for *me* [/] and tell them what I *did*."[56] He opens the bag, lowers it to the ground, rolls out the severed head of the Duke of Somerset, grasps it, and holds it aloft (Fig. 17). "Richard hath best deserved of all my sons," comments the Duke of York. Warwick urges the Duke to claim the crown from the "cowardly" King Henry, promising his assistance. "Be resolute," York assures his lords. "I mean to take possession of my right."

A flourish. King Henry enters, in chain mail and a red battle doublet adorned with three black lions. He is accompanied by Lord Clifford, the Earl of Westmoreland, and Soldiers. Henry orders York to "descend my throne,/ And kneel for grace and mercy at my feet;/ I am thy sovereign." York responds, "I am thine."

Warwick disputes Henry's right to the throne; York calls for his abdication. Warwick stamps his foot and Soldiers enter, armed with bows and arrows. Henry pleads to retain the crown for his lifetime, agreeing to disinherit his son and honor York's claim if York and Warwick will end their hostilities. Clifford and Westmoreland rebuke him and leave to bear the news to the Queen. York agrees to his request and comes down from the throne to embrace King Henry.

York, his elder sons, Warwick, and the Soldiers exit left. Richard trails behind. He stops as he reaches the periphery of the stage; he then turns and silently observes the ensuing scene, a subtle, lingering presence. Queen Margaret, wearing a red and blue battle costume and boots to midcalf, and the Prince of Wales, wearing a similarly colored tunic, enter and angrily berate King Henry for yielding his son's claim to the throne. They resolve to continue the battle against York and Warwick.

After they exit, King Henry is left alone at center stage. He turns left to discover Richard on the stage extreme left. Richard says nothing – just looks at him with a cold evil glance that chills him to the marrow. Henry stands profile to the audience, and as realization grows in his consciousness of Richard's intention, he very slowly convulses the hand nearest the audience, then as slowly lets the fingers become normal. All this time – some seconds – Richard never takes his eyes off him, then very slowly, backs off the stage.[57] The lights fade to black with King Henry staring after him. The house curtain falls.

Alan Dale noted that Richard was "first seen as a decidedly intelligent, cynical, repressed, and interesting malefactor. Physically he was deformed. He had the hunchback prescribed, but he was not unsightly. He was lean and a bit cadaverous. His face was craftily expressive, but at times quite bland and agreeable. In fact, [he] might have deceived anybody accustomed to theatrical Richards" (*American*, 8 March 1920).

Barrymore's performance, recalled Arthur Row, "began with one splendid thing – decision." His initial line was delivered with "a blessed authority" and "from that first minute he proceeded to tell them who he was in no uncertain way."[58]

Act I, scene ii. *York's Castle.* [*3 Henry VI*, I.ii, concluding with Richard's soliloquy from III.ii, 124–195]

In place of the throne, a curtained gold rectangular arras is positioned in front of the tapestries. A low platform with three steps at either end is set in front of the arras. The house curtain rises.

Richard, Edward, and George are discovered in the midst of a heated discussion. The Duke of York enters and asks the reason for their quarrel. Richard explains that it is over "The crown of England, father, which is yours," and urges him to break his oath and claim the throne immediately by force. "Richard, enough," York responds. "I will be king, or die." News arrives that the Queen and an army led by the northern earls and lords intend to besiege York's castle. York sends George to alert Warwick. Drums are heard in the distance. Alarum. York and Edward exit to prepare for battle.

Richard, alone, contemplates his course in life. He begins his soliloquy slowly, thoughtfully: "*Would* [they] were *wasted, marrow, bones* and *all* (low tone, quietly),/ That from their *loins* no *hopeful branch* may *spring,*/ To *cross* me from the *golden time* I *look for!*"[59] He examines the obstacles that stand in his way to the throne: "And yet, *between* my *soul's desire* and *me* (higher tone) – / [Beside my father and his brace of sons] – Is [still King] *Henry,* and his [child] young *Edward,*/ And all the *unlook'd* for *issue* of their *bodies.* . . ." His introspection soon brings him to the realization that the crown might be too "far off," which leads to another train of thought: "Well, *say* there is no *kingdom* then for *Richard;*/ (low, contemplative tone) What other *pleasure* can the *world afford?*" A gleeful thought springs into mind: "I'll *make* my *heaven* [/] in a *lady's lap,*/ And *deck* my *body* in *gay ornaments,*/ And *witch* [/] *sweet ladies* with my *words* and *looks* (rising tone)." Yet his mood quickly shifts. He emits a sharp sigh of disgust as he realizes the futility of his last impulse: "O *miserable thought!* and *more* un*likely*/ Than to ac*com*plish *twenty golden crowns!*"

With bitter, self-mocking irony he catalogues his deficiencies. "Why, *love* [/] fore*swore* me in my *mother's womb;*/ She did *corrupt frail nature* with some *bribe,*/ To *shrink* mine *arm up* like a *wither'd shrub;*/ To make an *envious mountain* on my *back,*/ . . . To *shape* my *legs* of an *unequal size;*/ To *disproportion* me in *every part,*/ *Like* to a *CHAOS,* or an *unlick'd bear-whelp.*"

His tone again becomes soft, introspective. "And *am* I *then* a *man* to *be* (drawn out) *belov'd?*" He emits a gutteral laugh. "O *monstrous fault!* to *harbour* such a *thought.*" He pauses a moment to gather his thoughts, then quietly and firmly resolves his future: "Then, since this *earth* affords *no joy* to me,/ (his delivery speeds up) But to *command,* to *check,* to *o'erbear* such/ As are of *better person* than *myself,*/ (slower) I'll *make* my *heaven* [/] to *dream* upon the *crown!*" Yet he is quickly forced to admit that "I know not how to *get* the crown. . . ." An instant later, however, his course becomes clear. He speeds his delivery and the speech builds in momentum as he resolves to win the throne by cunning and deceit: "Why, I can *smile* [/], and *murder* [/] whiles I *smile/.* . ." He asks himself gleefully, "Can I *do this,* and *cannot* get a *crown?*/ *Tut* (sharp, gutteral exclamation – then quickly and triumphantly, with a rise in volume), were it *further off,* (fortissimo; he reaches upward with a grasping gesture) *I'LL PLUCK IT DOWN!*" Slight pause, followed by a diabolical, self-satisfied burst of cackling laughter. The lights fade.

Heywood Broun, writing in the *Tribune* (8 March 1920), found the first soliloquy to be one of the performance's high points:

> In particular, the soliloquy of Richard, in which he contemplates his course in life, serves to give John Barrymore one of his best opportunities of the evening. At that time he presents us with an intense, ambitious but still hesitant man who has as yet no fixed goal. In the speech he lays before himself his various inhibitions . . . and examines them critically.
>
> "My eye's too quick, my heart o'erweens too much, unless my hand and strength could equal them." Barrymore makes this contemplative. Richard is not making a sophistical case for himself, according to Barrymore's reading, but is actually taking stock of what possibilities life affords him. It is when he has seen the hopelessness of everything for such a marred and misshapen one that he decides that he must have supreme power by whatever means come to his hand.

Act I, scene iii. *York's Castle.* [*3 Henry VI,* II.i]

Alarum. The lights come up. The arras and platform from the previous scene remain on stage. Edward, Richard, and Soldiers are discovered; all are dressed for battle. The initial encounter with the Queen's forces has been fought; Richard wonders aloud "[what of our] valiant father is become." The news soon arrives that he has been slain by Lord Clifford in the skirmish. Richard is secretly delighted, yet vows publicly to avenge his death. Warwick and George enter with their army; Richard and Warwick rally the troops for the coming battle. The lights fade; the house curtain falls.

Act I, scene iv. *Tewkesbury.* [This scene represented Sheldon's boldest rearrangement of the text and in the draft contained material from eight scenes in *3 Henry VI:* V.ii, II.iii, II.iv, II.v, IV.vi, IV.viii, V.v, and II.vi. It is likely that most, if not all, of this material was retained in performance]

The tapestry and arras are withdrawn; a few canvas boulders are placed onstage. The house curtain rises. The lights come up, localized, on the stage area; the Tower is shrouded in darkness. During the course of the scene, individual battles and King Henry's soliloquy are isolated by lighting only part of the stage. The scene begins with the death of Warwick [V.ii, with a few lines interpolated from II.iii]. Richard urges the troops into battle [II.iii – lines Shakespeare assigned to Warwick]. Richard encounters Clifford and they skirmish [II.iv]. King Henry is discovered alone on another part of the field [II.v] and delivers his "Here on this molehill will I sit me down" soliloquy, which is followed by his encounter with Richmond [IV.vi]. The Prince of Wales enters [II.v; end] and urges his father to flee. Edward, Richard, and their Soldiers enter and capture the King [IV.viii]. Queen Margaret bids farewell to her husband; the captured Prince of Wales is brought in [V.v] and is stabbed to death by Edward, George, and Richard. Edward creates Richard Duke of Gloucester and George Duke of Clarence [II.vi]. Richard exits "to London on a serious matter" – to murder the King. Edward follows to prepare for his coronation [V.v]. The house curtain falls.

Act I, scene v. *A Cell in the Tower of London.* [*3 Henry VI,* V.vi]

The house curtain rises. The lights come up. King Henry VI is discovered in a large iron cage, center, that masks the central entrance to the Tower. The somber gray facade now seems the walls of a dungeon. Richard enters from a door in the wall (probably the stage right door; the left door served in other scenes as the entrance to the chapel) with Brackenbury. He bids him leave, then enters the cage. The brief exchange between Richard and King Henry is "weird, uncanny." Richard finally protests, "I'll hear no more: die, prophet, in thy speech," and stabs the King. Withdrawing his sword, he looks at the body, reaches down, and, taking one of the King's inert hands from his chest, flings it furiously away from him.[60]

Richard begins the soliloquy that follows with a guttural grunt. His tone is initially harsh yet quiet.[61] ". . . See how my sword *weeps* (slight pause) for the *poor king's death!*" His volume begins to rise on "If any *spark* of *life* be *yet remaining,*" and on the following line, "*DOWN, DOWN TO HELL; AND SAY I SENT THEE THITHER,*" he rises abruptly to fortissimo volume. Again he stabs the King. He becomes sardonically introspective as he reflects on the circumstances of his birth: ". . . I have often heard my *mother say/* I *came* into the *world* with my *legs forward* . . ./ The *midwife* (slight pause) *wonder'd,* and the *women cried/* O! *Jesus BLESS* us, he is *BORN* with *TEETH* (pause)./ (Softer) And *so* I *was;* which *plainly signified/* That I should *snarl* (drawn out) and *bite* (upward emphasis) and *play* the *dog* (downward emphasis)."

"Then, *since* [/] the *heavens* have *shaped* my *body* so,/ *Let hell make crook'd* my *mind* to *answer* it . . ." is delivered on a note of "tragic self-pity" – the "cry of a wounded spirit that would . . . build a protective armor [of ruthlessness] about its infirmity." On "I *am* [/] my*self alone,*" he rises to "a very modern cry of self-justification."[62] "*Clarence* (pause) *beware* (upward emphasis); thou *keep'st* me from the *light*" is spoken slowly and deliberately, as are the lines that follow: "But I will sort [/] a *pitchy day* for thee;/ For I will *buz abroad* such *prophecies/* That *Edward* (slight pause) shall be [/] *fearful* of his *life,/* And then, to *purge* his *fear,* [/] *I'll be thy death.*/ *King Henry* [/] and the *prince* his *son* are *gone:/* (louder) *Clarence* (pause), *thy turn is next* (a guttural laugh), and *then* the *rest* (matter of factly) . . ." His voice rises in volume and again assumes a harsh tone for the concluding couplet: "I'll *throw* thy *body* in *another room,/* And *triumph, Henry,* in thy *day* of *doom.*" The lights fade. The house curtain falls.

Barrymore, Row recalled, was particularly vehement in dispatching the King. "When [Barrymore] killed me as Henry VI," he remarked, "I never quite knew whether I'd really survive the performance. When he stabbed me, the sword was faked to slip down my upstage side, but one night, at least, it fell full on my chest and was pulled back just in time to keep from pinning me to the boards." On another occasion, when Barrymore flung the King's hand away from his chest after the murder, Row's hand "landed full on an upturned spike" in his prison cell. "The pain was awful," Row remembered, but when Barrymore asked him after the scene if he was hurt, Row graciously said no: "I did not want him to be worried during the performance."[63]

Act I, scene vi. *Outside the Tower.* [*Richard III,* I.i and I.ii]

After a brief interval, the house curtain rises. When the lights come up, Richard is discovered, wearing a scarlet doublet and cap and glossy sable hose. He is no longer the black-armored warrior; he has become "debonair and beguiling" in a costume "carefully calculated to emphasize the salient mood of the moment."[64] The Tower setting is for the first time unmasked.

The scene begins with the opening soliloquy from *Richard III.* The "winter of our discontent" speech is delivered with "leisurely tentativeness," and an "obvious search in the mind for the next thought." Through "sheer vocal finesse," Richard produces "the impression that the country has settled down, after a period of harsh warfare, to days of unruffled peace."[65]

At the conclusion of the soliloquy, Richard's brother George, now the Duke of Clarence, enters; he is escorted by four Guards and accompanied by Brackenbury. Richard is "hypocritically affectionate" with his brother, but he reveals his true feelings to the audience after his exit: "*Simple, plain* Clarence! I do *love* thee so,/ That I will shortly send thy *soul* to *heaven* . . ." Hastings enters and delivers the news that King Edward is gravely ill; Richard sends him off and contemplates this new turn of events: "He cannot live, I hope; and must not die,/ Till George be pack'd with post-horse up to heaven . . ." He then resolves to marry "Warwick's [fairest] daughter" Lady Anne, the widow of Henry VI's son Prince Edward, whom he stabbed to death at Tewkesbury.

Lady Anne enters in a long, rich-looking black and violet gown and high headpiece. Accompanying her are six Gentlemen in black robes with white crosses on the back, bearing the corpse of Henry VI. Five of the coffin bear-

ers withdraw to the shadowy periphery of the stage after they "set down the
corse"; one remains to guard the body of the murdered king during the ensuing encounter.[66]

The Lady Anne scene is played with subtlety and restraint. Throughout,
Richard is "smooth and ingratiating" and although he reveals flashes of "malignant humor" his wooing is generally low-key. He plays the scene as "a
straight and enormously ardent love scene," suppressing all display of apparent hypocrisy. He is "almost boyish," but "not without a definite romantic
charm." He engages in "earnest, gentle, persuasive pleading, as though he
enjoy[s] acting the role of a misunderstood saint for a change."[67]

After Anne's exit, Richard delivers his soliloquy directly to the audience.
His initial outburst, "Was *ever woman* in this *humor woo'd* (drawn out)?/ Was
ever woman in this *humor won?*" is an eruption of unrestrained glee and "sneering cynicism." For the first time he appreciates "the full height of success to
which evil may lead."[68] Then, quickly: "*I'll have* her; but I will not *keep* her
long." He retains his tone of glee and cynical irony, building in speed and momentum as the speech progresses: "*What! I,* that kill'd her *husband* and his *father,/* To TAKE her in her *heart's extremest hate,/* With *curses* in her *mouth, tears*
in her *eyes* . . . (he laughs gleefully) *Upon* my *life,* she *finds,* although *I* can *not,/*
Myself to be a *marvellous proper man. . . .*"

As he reaches the line, "*Shine out, fair sun,* till I have *bought* a *glass,* that I
may see my *shadow* as I *pass!*" he becomes "in bodily shape like some hideous
reptile," he cringes, he crawls, he squirms and sways "with dreadful passion
from side to side" until he reaches his exit. He is addressing the sun "with the
audacity of one to whom it was a minion." He exits with a "concluding burst
of ironic laughter."[69] The lights fade. The house curtain falls.

Burns Mantle found Barrymore's scene with Lady Anne to be admirably "free
of those smirks and grimaces with which many Richards decorate it for the
amusement of the crowd." He added that it was "the more convincing for its
lack of obvious byplay" (*Evening Mail,* 8 March 1920).

Clayton Hamilton also admired Barrymore's performance in this scene,
but voiced objections to his physical repression and Hopkins's staging:

> In the difficult scene of the wooing of Lady Anne, Mr. Barrymore is very in-
> teresting to watch, because of the sly and subtle handling of his face and of
> his voice; but, in my opinion, his performance of this passage is far inferior
> to Mansfield's, because Mr. Barrymore plays the entire scene flat-footed.
> His mental agility is marvellous; but he shows no physical agility at all. His
> steps and gestures reveal a sense of stricture that is still to be regretted; and
> his work is further handicapped by the fact that Lady Anne – who ought, of
> course, to run away from him, and to lead him a chase around the dumb,
> accusatory body of the murdered king – stands anchored in one spot upon

a large and empty stage, as if her fleeing feet had been caught in a rabbit-trap.[70]

The response to Barrymore's acting of this scene was generally favorable, however. Agnes Smith of the *Morning Telegraph* noted that "In the scenes of malignant humor, such as the encounter with Lady Anne, it seemed as if no one could have read the lines better. With the outburst, 'Was ever woman in this humor woo'd,' we got an electric shock" (8 March 1920).

First Intermission

Act II

Act II, scene i. *Throne Room.* [*Richard III,* I.iii]

The house curtain rises. The lights come up. Queen Elizabeth, the wife of Edward IV, is discovered upon the throne, wearing a green butterfly headdress and a long, green, low-bodiced gown (Fig. 18). She is attended by Gentlewomen and by Lord Rivers and Lord Grey. Speaking with repressed dignity, she expresses concern about her husband's health and the fact that Richard will be the protector of her sons if the King dies.[71] Buckingham enters in a rich-looking, ankle-length green and gold gown, accompanied by the Earl of Derby; they tell Elizabeth that the King "desires to make atonement/ Betwixt the Duke of Gloucester and [yourself]" and warn her of his impending arrival.

Richard enters in a scarlet doublet "of a cut the very opposite of that worn by other gentlemen of the court and royal group." At his side he wears a short sword.[72] He is accompanied by Hastings. He complains to the Queen that he has been falsely slandered to the King. Queen Margaret, Henry VI's widow, enters and curses Richard and the Queen for depriving her of the throne. Richard engages in "swift baiting" of the former Queen; after she exits he hypocritically expresses regret at his part in the murder of her husband, then crosses himself.[73] Catesby enters to summon the Queen and courtiers to the King. All exit except Richard, who confesses his duplicity to the audience. The two murderers enter, and he sends them brusquely to the Tower to kill Clarence. The lights fade. The house curtain falls.

Act II, scene ii. *Cell in the Tower.* [*Richard III,* I.iv]

The house curtain rises. An iron trellis has been lowered across the proscenium opening. The lights come up; the entire stage now seems a barred prison

Figure 18. Queen Elizabeth (Evelyn Walsh Hall) with her ladies-in-waiting. Courtesy Culver Pictures.

cell. Clarence is discovered. The First and Second Murderers enter, engage in "gruesome bantering," then stab Clarence to death.[74] The lights fade. The house curtain falls.

Act II, scene iii. *Throne Room.* [*Richard III,* II.i and II.ii]

The house curtain rises. The lights come up. King Edward IV, garbed in a long black and gray robe, and Queen Elizabeth, dressed as in her previous scene, are discovered seated on two thrones set upon the platform, center. The members of the court are grouped at either side. Edward, gravely ill, expresses pride that he has reconciled the warring factions of his family. Richard enters in an ebullient mood: "Good morrow to my sovereign king and queen;/ And princely peers, a happy time of day!" He reconciles himself to the Queen and courtiers, but the tone of the scene shifts abruptly when he announces that Clarence is dead. The King, overcome with remorse, exits with the Queen. Richard subtly attempts to pin the blame for Clarence's death on Elizabeth: "Mark'd you not/ How that the guilty [features] of the queen/ [Turned] pale when [she] did hear of Clarence' death?" All exit to comfort the King.

The old Duchess of York, Edward and Richard's mother, enters with Clarence's young son and daughter and attendants. Elizabeth enters soon afterward to announce the King's death. Richard, Buckingham, and members of the court reenter. Richard offers words of comfort to the Queen, kneels before his mother, and wins "hearty response" from the audience with his line, "Amen; and make me die a good old man!" which he "sarcastically tacks on to his mother's blessing."[75] He suggests that Prince Edward be brought from Ludlow to be crowned king; all exit except Richard and Buckingham. Buckingham suggests a close watch on the prince, and Richard agrees. He promises Buckingham the Earldom of Hereford when he is king [lines interpolated from III.i] and both exit for Ludlow. The lights fade. The house curtain falls.

Act II, scene iv. *Outside the Tower.* [*Richard III,* III.i]

The house curtain rises. The lights come up on the Tower. Richard is discovered center stage before the entrance seated on a tall white horse held by a servant. He is wearing a voluminous red cloak that drapes him from shoulder to stirrup, falling over the horse's purple blanket.[76] To one side stands Cardinal Bourchier, clad in dark clerical robes. Buckingham, Catesby, and others attend. Over all, a bright sunlight is diffused.

The young Prince Edward enters in a black tunic reaching to midthigh and black tights with green accents. Richard greets him [with a line originally assigned to Buckingham]: "Welcome, sweet prince, to London . . ." The Lord Mayor enters with attendants and is greeted by Richard, who soon afterward sends the Cardinal and Hastings to fetch the Prince's brother, the Duke of York. Seated upon his horse, Richard "converses with the boys in the guise of a kindly seeming uncle."[77] As the scene progresses, there is a subtle change in the lighting; by the time Richard persuades the princes enter the Tower it is dusk. They enter through the central portcullus. The lights fade.

Heywood Broun noted that Barrymore succeeded in making Richard "such an engaging figure that even when the little princes are trundled off into the Tower there comes from the audience no wave of protest, but a satisfied little chuckle to indicate that good old Richard has turned another neat stroke" (*Tribune,* 14 March 1920).

Act II, scene v. *The same.* [*Richard III,* III.vii]

The lights come up. Buckingham and Richard are discovered. They discuss the success of their plan to brand Edward's children as bastards and the pending arrival of the Lord Mayor. Richard exits through the stage-right door to the Tower ("the chapel"). After Buckingham confers with the Lord Mayor, Richard reenters through this door, prayer book in hand, accompanied by two clergymen in brown habits with large silver crosses hanging at their sides. He speaks quietly and with humble, winning sincerity through the scene of the proffer of the crown.[78]

Richard bids farewell to Buckingham, the Lord Mayor, and the others; they exit. Left alone on the stage, he slowly draws himself up to a kingly stature by standing on his toes; his right hand trembles upward in a triumphant gesture, as if it grasped already an imaginary scepter. He stands "rapt in exultant meditation, drawing deep breaths of anticipation" as he clutches the imaginary symbol of his newfound power.[79] The lights fade. The house curtain falls.

A good deal of commentary was devoted to the business that came at the end of this scene. Since the time of Garrick, the traditional business had been for Richard, alone on stage, to fling the prayer book away. Clayton Hamilton remembered that Mansfield employed his own variation: "He pretended to read his prayer-book sedulously until the delegation of citizens had left the stage. Watching their exit with the tail of his eye, he subsequently looked back at his breviary and discovered that he had been holding it upside down. He turned it about, with a sarcastic smile. Then he closed the scene by flinging the prayer-book triumphantly over his shoulder." Barrymore discarded the old business and, according to Hamilton, far surpassed his "great predecessor" at the close of this scene.[80]

Louis V. De Foe found Barrymore's business to be "electrical" and called it "the finest moment" in his performance. As his fingers involuntarily grasp for the scepter, De Foe commented, he realizes that "the goal of his infernal plotting and doubly infernal covetousness has been attained" (*World,* 14 March 1920).

Second Intermission

On opening night during the second intermission, Barrymore came before the curtain to make a brief speech, in which he referred to his "audacious initial plunge" into the realm of Shakespeare and commented that he had hoped for tolerance, but didn't expect enthusiasm. During the same interval, an additional element of glamour was added to the proceedings with the arrival of the other acting members of the Drew–Barrymore family, who had completed their labors at other theatres. "Before the third act commenced," commented the *Evening Telegram* (8 March 1920), ". . . Uncle John Drew with his son-in-law, sister Ethel with her hair dressed in the manner of the Venus of Milo, and brother Lionel with his wife, Miss Doris Rankin" entered their box to tumultuous applause.[81]

Act III

Act III, scene i. *Throne Room.* [*Richard III,* IV.ii and IV.iii]

The house curtain rises. The scene begins with an elaborate coronation pageant; at its conclusion, Richard is seated beside Queen Anne on the throne. Over the shoulders of the monarch, "setting off with striking effect the evil lines of his cruel features," is spread a long, brocaded violet and gold mantle lined with shimmering silver metallic cloth. Richard's draperies surge around him and his unhappy consort sits shivering by his side. They are attended by richly dressed Ladies and Lords.[82]

Anne and many of the courtiers exit after the coronation. Buckingham, Catesby, and others remain. In this scene, Richard first begins to reveal his insecurities. His exchanges become harsh, sharp, less assured; throughout the remainder of the third act he displays "a disintegration of the spirit that is expressed by a growing feebleness and feverishness of speech and bodily gesture." The harshness, insecurity, and quickened speech are first evident in the exchange with Buckingham as to the fate of Edward's young sons. Richard sits upon the throne "like an obscene condor meditating the death of the princes" (Fig. 19), while Buckingham grows "timid and virtuous at his feet."[83]

Richard's tone becomes calmer, less agitated, as he sends a Page to summon Tyrell. After the Page's exit, he is again the clear-thinking conspirator; he orders Catesby to "*Rumor* it *abroad/* That *Anne,* my *wife,* is *sick* and *like* to *die.*" After Catesby's exit, he casts aside his robes and emerges as a "bottled spider" garbed entirely in black. He walks down the steps of the platform and moves downstage very slowly and deliberately; he is again quiet and meditative: "I must be *married* to my *brother's daughter,/* Or else my *kingdom* stands on *brittle glass.*"[84]

Tyrell enters; Richard is "inhumanly pitiless," yet speaks quietly and firmly when from the throne, he instigates the murder of the children in the Tower.[85] His mood changes abruptly, however, with Tyrell's exit and Buckingham's reentry with his request to "claim your gift, my due by promise" – the Earldom of Hereford.

Figure 19. Richard as king. Courtesy Billy Rose Theatre Collection, The New York Public Library for the Performing Arts.

Richard is calmly sardonic when he remarks that "As *I* re*mem*ber, [/] *Henry* the *Sixth*/ Did *pro*phecy [/] that *Richmond* should be *king* (upward emphasis). . . . A *bard* of *Ireland* told me *once,*/ I should not *live long* [/] after I *saw* Richmond." Yet soon he begins to be "streaked with madness – a mental disintegration that is revealed at first as by flashes of fitful and distant lightning."[86] After Buckingham's "My Lord!" he screams out *"Ay, what's o'clock?"* He breaks with his former ally with "imperturbable insolence" and delivers "I am not in the *giving vein* today" with harsh, sharp sarcasm.[87]

After Tyrell's account of the murder of the princes in the Tower, Richard receives the news of their death calmly yet joyfully. He dismisses Tyrell; he is again slow and meditative as he plots aloud to marry "young Elizabeth, my brother's daughter." The lights fade. The house curtain falls.[88]

Act III, scene ii. *Outside the Tower.* [*Richard III,* IV.iv]

The house curtain rises. The lights come up on the Tower. Queen Margaret, then Queen Elizabeth and the Duchess of York enter. They are wearing black mourning gowns trimmed at the collar with white. Margaret and Elizabeth wear low headdresses with veils; the Duchess of York wears a black conical headdress with a veil trailing behind. They gather before the heavy wooden doors to the Tower and deliver their antiphonal lamentations quietly, deliberately underplaying the emotionalism of their words (Fig 20).[89]

A flourish, then Richard enters, wearing copper-colored armor and a gold skullcap. He is followed by Soldiers attired in chain mail, over which they wear white tunics with violet sleeves featuring large red crosses on the chest; they are wearing blue headpieces and tights and carry longbows. Again, the mood is restrained, subdued; the curses of the Duchess of York "do not echo in their tone the revulsion that the outraged mother feels against such an unnatural son."[90] Yet a crucial change in Richard's character is apparent: He no longer exhibits the brash confidence of earlier scenes. There is "a suggestion that fear has begun to haunt his mind when he nervously crosses his breast and cowers under his mother's curse."[91]

The Duchess of York exits, and Richard's "infamy soon reasserts itself as he turns to make dissembling love to the widow of his brother."[92] Again he becomes the skillful deceiver; he makes a subtle plea to Queen Elizabeth for her daughter's hand. After Elizabeth exits, Richard is quick and sharp with Catesby and Ratcliff, who bring news of gathering opposition led by Richmond and Buckingham; yet his tone, even in a mood of excitement, avoids melodramatic excess, and when he learns that his former ally has been captured he understates his command to "Chop off his head. So much for Buckingham."[93] A flourish; Richard and his supporters exit to meet their foe at Salisbury. The lights fade. The house curtain falls.

Barrymore's pleading with Elizabeth, according to the *Sun* (8 March 1920), was "among his subtlest moments." The critic noted that "When he woos Lady Anne Richard is on the rising crest of good fortune and is in the best of spirits. But when he interviews the widowed ex-Queen he is beset with fears and is fighting for his kingdom and his life. The contrast in his acting of these two scenes alone would mark him as one of our leading actors."

Figure 20. The three queens. Courtesy Billy Rose Theatre Collection, The New York Public Library for the Performing Arts.

Act III, scene iii. *Richmond's Camp.* [*Richard III*, V.iii]

The house curtain rises. The lights come up. The Tower is shrouded in shadows. Large, rough-hewn canvas boulders lean against it, covering the entrance. At one side of the stage, Richmond's soldiers, in chain mail, with red roses emblazoned on their white tunics, pitch his tent. Richmond, in silver-colored armor with a large, heraldic cross emblazoned on the front, prepares for bed and prays for a victory. The lights fade.

Act III, scene iv. *Richard's Tent.* [*Richard III*, V.iii]

The lights come up on the opposite side of the stage, where Richard's soldiers pitch his tent; they are wearing "elaborately realistic armor" which "clatters realistically as they move about." Richard's commands to Norfolk, Catesby, and Ratcliff are firm and direct; he is very much in control.[94]

After lying on the couch in his tent, Richard is depicted as "conscience-racked in sleep."[95] The ghosts of Prince Edward (son to Henry VI), King Henry, Clarence, the two young princes, Buckingham, and Lady Anne enter as a group rather than individually. They gather closely in a corner of the tent and quietly murmur their curses.[96]

After their exit, Richard awakens with a start, gets up, and in a panic, hurls nearby objects about the tent.[97] He emits a high, sharp cry – "*Oh – Oh –*" (a pause) – then a moan.[98] Then, in a high, tenor head tone: "*Give me* (pause) *another horse: bind* up my *wounds./ Have mercy,* Jesu! – Soft! I *did* but *dream.*" He continues, shaken: ". . . The lights *burn blue.* It is now *dead midnight./ Cold, fearful drops* stand on my *trembling flesh./* (then, with quickening pace) *What* do I *fear?* my*self?* There's *none else by* (rising emphasis)." His voice drops to a lower register on "Is there a *murderer* here? *No.* [/] *Yes, I* am." On "My con-science hath a *thousand several tongues . . .*" he quickens his pace; he is reflec-tive yet clearly troubled. "There is no *creature* [/] *loves* me; And if I *die,* no [man] will *pity* me . . ." is spoken with a woeful awareness of his situation.

Ratcliffe enters, and Richard soon recovers to rally his forces for the com-ing battle. The scene that follows is "explosive and boisterous, and frenzied." Richard's declaration, "A thousand hearts are great within my bosom!" is like "a trumpet call."[99] The lights fade.

Much critical commentary was bestowed upon the appearance of the ghosts, almost all of it overwhelmingly negative. The *Evening Telegram* (8 March 1920) noted that their entry "was lacking in supernatural quality," adding that a "darker stage might have helped the illusion at that point." According to the *Sun–Herald,* the ghosts, "apparently in the best of health, huddled in a corner of [Richard's] tent and mildly muttered their imprecations" (8 March 1920).

Most critics agreed that the final episodes lacked the conviction and im-pact of earlier scenes. The reviewer for the *World* (8 March 1920) noted that

> In the Dream Scene in the tent on the eve of the Battle of Bosworth Field, when the King's sleep is disturbed by visions of his murdered victims, the fine imagination with which Mr. Barrymore had played the preceding episodes seemed to desert him. Here his suggestion of conscience-stricken remorse and superstitious terror was neither startling nor convincing. The scene seemed to elude him, although the lessening of the play's tensity at this point may have been due to the ineffective stage management.

Act III, scene v. *Bosworth.* [*Richard III,* V.iv and V.v]

The lights come up. The sky and the walls of the Tower are streaked with red; a grim gibbet is silhouetted at the rear of the stage.

After several skirmishes between members of the warring armies ("No ef-fort was made to give it the illusion of a general engagement of great forces of men"), Richard enters wearing his copper-colored battle armor. He deliv-ers his opening line – "A *horse!* a *horse! my kingdom* for a horse!" – with quiet urgency.[100]

Richard meets Richmond and they savagely clash swords. Richard is final-ly driven to bay and disarmed; he "strikes impotently at his adversary with his mailed fists." When the fatal thrust comes, he staggers back and gasps for breath for a long moment like a drowning man. Then, with "a last infuriated scream of rage and pain" he "plunges backward to the ground" – "pell-mell, armour and all" – with a resounding crash. His hands "clutch the air pitiably in his dying agony" and at last lay still at his side.[101]

Richmond, standing over the body, proclaims, "God and your arms be praised, victorious friends!/ The day is ours; the bloody dog is dead." Derby hands him the crown and Richmond speaks the concluding couplet: "Now civil wounds are stopp'd, peace lives again;/ That she may [live here long], God say amen!"

On opening night, according to Charles Darnton of the *Evening World* (8 March 1920), Barrymore's "crashing fall full on the back" at the close of his duel with Richmond "unfortunately meant death to Richard's flying wig," a catastrophe which might have proven a disaster for a lesser actor; yet the audience remained spellbound and stayed to cheer him with a standing ovation after the final curtain. "Although under the tremendous strain of a performance that kept up till nearly 1 o'clock Sunday morning," wrote Darnton, "he gained rather than lost strength in the course of it, and at the end stood established as a Shakespearean actor capable of holding his own on the stage of any country."

The Critical Response

The first reviews appeared on Monday 8 March. Many more appeared over the next few weeks; the overwhelming majority were extravagant in their praise for Barrymore's portrayal. To Heywood Broun of the *Tribune* (8 March 1920), his Richard was "the most inspired performance which this generation has seen." "All in all, a magnificent achievement," wrote Alexander Woollcott in the *Times* (8 March 1920). "It ranks with Ada Rehan's Katherine and Forbes Robertson's Hamlet in this playgoer's Shakespearean experience."

Most reviewers were quick to note the vitality, freshness, and element of surprise in Barrymore's characterization. In an unsigned editorial, the *Globe* commented that "It is genuine dramatic history that John Barrymore is making with his remarkable portrayal of Richard III." The combination of Barrymore's acting and Sheldon's adaptation, the writer noted, suggested interesting possibilities for the future. Eventually, he concluded, "Shakespeare may thus be livened up – or is 'jazzed' the proper term? – to the point of real popularity on Broadway, even without the aid of Mr. Barrymore's really amazingly fine acting" (8 March 1920).

Woollcott, in his "Second Thoughts on First Nights" column, hailed the revival for its sharp departures from the reverential tradition of the past: "It is such a bully good show it will give a pleasantly tingling shock to all those who still go to Shakespeare conscientiously, like earnest Chatauquans filling pathetic notebooks with words of wisdom let fall by passing lecturers, a fine jolt for all those who take their Shakespeare with a wry face and a sense of rectitude, as one takes calomel" (*Times,* 21 March 1920). To most reviewers, the production and Barrymore's performance had clearly captured the temper of the times. *Current Opinion* noted that "This new version of *Richard III* suggests that each epoch of the theatre may reflect its own ideals in the vast universe of Shakespeare."[102]

Although Walter Prichard Eaton later chided the "younger critics" for their "strange ignorance of theatrical tradition," commenting that none of them pointed out that Garrick and Edwin Booth had also made their Shakespearean debuts as Richard III, most reviewers were quick to compare Barrymore's performance with those of the Shakespeareans of the recent past.[103] Moreover, in nearly all cases, comparisons were favorable. Commentators too young to have firsthand recollections of Booth and Irving could at least remember Mansfield, and many reviews featured an attempt to situate Barrymore's performance in a historical context. The consensus was that Barrymore had easily surpassed in skill the Shakespearean crusaders of the post-Mansfield interregnum and had restored to Shakespeare the vitality and glamour of an earlier day.

The *Brooklyn Times* (9 March 1920) commented admiringly that "The gap made in America's stage history by the death of Richard Mansfield at last has been closed. John Barrymore occupies and fills it. With his impersonation of Richard III . . . he has silenced the wailers and mourners who have said that there is no successor in this land to the long line of giant Shakespearean actors with which we were blessed many, many years ago."[104] James Metcalfe of *Life* – old enough to remember – found that "We have to go back to Booth to find so tolerable a Richard."[105]

A number of critics noted Barrymore's sharp departure from the "old school" of performance. "The reading is entirely wanting in those overtones, statuesque poses, declamatory finales and hissing sotto voce interpretations that until now have been earmarks of the acted character," commented the *Chicago Evening Post* (12 March 1920). "The old time monotony, pomposity, affectation, adulteration – all is missing; and in the stead are simple, straightforward, succinct readings that, somehow or other, seem to convey an impression of fact and realism and actual happenings that we did not get invariably from all the earlier interpreters."[106]

The most effusive praise, however, was devoted to Barrymore's newly acquired vocal skills. Several critics felt that he read the lines too deliberately, keeping too often to a single tempo, but most observers were impressed by his unexpected prowess. Woollcott noted that Barrymore's first performance in a Shakespearean role "marked a measurable advance in the gradual process of bringing his technical fluency abreast with his winged imagination and his real genius for the theatre. Surely it was the highest point yet reached in that rapid, unexpected ascent which began four years ago with the production of Galsworthy's *Justice,* and which has been unparalleled in the theatre of our time" (*Times,* 8 March 1920). "Not only is the voice greater in range than ever before," commented Heywood Broun, "but it has become one of the enchanting sounds of our theater, and it was not always so" (*Tribune,* 8 March 1920). Francis Hackett, writing in the *New Republic,* termed the production "Buffalo Bill Shakespeare," but nevertheless found Barrymore's performance to be "superb," noting that

> The nose, an excellent olfactory but a poor elocutionary contrivance, has at last been subordinated by Mr. Barrymore to its humbler uses. His voice is now beautifully placed, deep and sonorous and free. And his body, once a rather shiftless tenement, is now a mansion, or rather a house in which there are many mansions. He is so master of his craft today that he can give Richard III two lame legs, both the right and the left legs short at will, and he shifts from one to the other so subtly that only a shrew could detect him.[107]

A number of reviewers stressed, however, that Barrymore's success was more than a matter of technique. His emphasis on Richard's psychological development – in a thoroughly modern sense – came as a revelation to many observers. The critic for *Town & Country* noted that

> the last ten years has seen an enormous improvement in the intelligent handling of our classic dramatic masterpieces. We have, to a certain extent, begun the attempt to understand their psychology. Mr. Sothern, for instance, takes it for granted that the emotional progress of Shakespeare's characters needs no explanation beyond that afforded by the words he speaks. . . . Mr. Barrymore has gone far beyond that. Every moment he is before his spectators he is living, feeling, developing, justifying the emotional conduct of *Richard III.* For the first time in our memory it occurs to us that *Richard III* may actually have lived, have been a man of keen mind, prevented by a deformed body from using that mind in a normal way, have been led by opportunism into a criminal career which pyramided itself until the strain broke him and his fortunes. And it is because Mr. Barrymore has been able to do this that we repeat: his performance of *Richard III* is the surprise of this generation of theater goers. It unquestionably makes him our foremost American tragic actor.[108]

Despite the overwhelmingly favorable response, however, a number of objections were voiced. Virtually all the reviewers agreed that Barrymore's performance in the final scenes, when he was called upon to abandon restraint and act with "old-style flamboyancy," was far less satisfying than it was earlier in the play. His psychological interpretation of the character, although clear in terms of development, was, to some observers, contrary to Shakespeare's Richard, to medieval psychology, and to Renaissance psychology.

Furthermore, in several cases, critics found that Barrymore had chosen to overemphasize the cerebral facets of his character. J. Ranken Towse, writing in the *Post* (8 March 1920), commented that

> In all modern representations, from the days of Cooke down, there has been a tendency to emphasize the savage side of Richard at the expense of the intellectual. An exception, perhaps, ought to be noted in Edwin Booth. But nearly always Richard has been played in terms of that lurid melodrama for which he undeniably offers a ready excuse. But sardonic humor, cynical hypocrisy, inhesitant will and malignant craft are just as strongly marked characteristics of the part as its prompt ferocity, and it was upon these that Mr. Barrymore elected to lay his chief, and perhaps too much, stress.

Nevertheless, Towse found Barrymore's Richard to be "an impersonation of decided originality and merit, infinitely better than anything that he did in *The Jest* would have led one to expect." There was, Towse concluded, "a temptation to say that he imitated Henry Irving, who metamorphosed Macbeth to bring that character into accord with his own limitations. But that would scarely be fair."

Other critics had no such reservations. A small yet vocal minority, led by Ludwig Lewisohn of *The Nation,* again brought forth the caveat of a decade earlier: Barrymore relied on personality, rather than the power of impersonation, to make his effects. The performance, Lewisohn wrote,

> is an arresting and even fascinating one. But it is not really great. Mr. Barrymore has moments of the highest histrionic effectiveness; he allures and dazzles. But the word histrionic with all its connotations stands between him and the spirit from which greatness issues. He misses . . . the note of an ultimate sincerity. He does not lose himself; he is not consumed in the flame of his own creative imagination. We watch John Barrymore doing marvellous things, and he watches himself with an eager appreciation and applause. He permits himself to be surrounded, notably here, by large companies of very inferior actors who play in subdued tones, raise his personality into an immoderate relief, and shatter the drama which he feigns to interpret. . . . As acting [his performance] suffers from a display of personal idiosyncrasy and untempered power.[109]

Clayton Hamilton, although generally approving, found Mansfield to have been better equipped for the part in every area except facial expression. He missed Mansfield's physical agility; Barrymore, he commented, played the entire part "as quietly and carefully as if he were depicting a mainly meditative character, like Hamlet."[110] Dissenters were in the minority, however, and most commentators were effusive in their praise of Barrymore's characterization – and especially his newfound vocal ability. "The thing I was proudest of," he would later remember, "was that the critics said, 'He's found a voice.'"[111]

Hopkins's Direction, Jones's Mise-en-Scène, and the Text Criticized

Arthur Hopkins's direction was generally admired. "Mr. Hopkins' staging is as strikingly original as it is effective," wrote the critic for the *Dramatic Mirror* (13 March 1920). "The drama holds and grips you in its panoramic as well as its dramatic power. It moves with the majesty of a pageant, but also with the rapidity of a film." The majority of commentators felt, however, that in eliminating "Shakespearean" gesture and urging his actors to speak in quiet, "natural" tones, he had carried repression a step too far. Some of the sharpest criticism visited upon the production was reserved for the supporting cast, who had simply attempted to follow Hopkins's instructions. Asked the critic for the *Sun–Herald* (8 March 1920):

> How does Mr. Hopkins as director train his actors? The answer must be approximately to act Shakespeare in the mood of Henry Arthur Jones. The blood and fire, the torrential expressions of emotion, the storm and stress which constitute the existence of these abnormal folk of a barbaric day – these in his manner of acting the play, are never suggested . . . the words that these men and women speak are the denial of the manner in which they utter them. . . . The grand style, the sweep and swell of deep and elementary feeling – these are missing.

Most reviewers cited a few members of the cast approvingly, with Arthur Row's King Henry VI, Rosalind Ivan's Queen Margaret, and E. J. Ballantine's Clarence earning the bulk of their praise, but the company as a whole was regarded as "not particularly interesting," "colorless," and "in several cases decidedly inept." Woollcott pinned the blame for the supporting cast's deficiencies squarely on Hopkins, noting that it was "a rag-tag-and-bobtail company, of which half the players are intolerable and the other half are – well, tolerable." The company, he added, was scarcely comparable with the one supporting Sothern and Marlowe across town. "Perhaps," he concluded, "we haven't enough players for two Shakespearean companies" (*Times*, 8 March 1920).

Hopkins's decision to center the action of the play on his leading actor – at the expense of the supporting cast – was also subject to critical quibbling. Clayton Hamilton found the staging to be "manifestly bad," noting (in somewhat exaggerated fashion) that in "every scene, every actor – with the single exception of Mr. Barrymore – has apparently been ordered to stand still, upon a predetermined spot, and never, under any circumstances, to use his arms for the purposes of natural gesticulation. . . . The whole production looks very much like a revelation of the imaginative adventures of Mr. Barrymore among a group of wax figures."[112] Critical commentary made it clear that the supporting cast was far less skilled at effecting the "new" style of playing than was the star;[113] yet to many observers, Barrymore's repressed yet at the same time "superhuman" characterization served as a unifying factor. As the *Sun–Herald* noted (8 March 1920), "It was when the spectators observed the acting of Mr. Barrymore that the soft pedal which the manager had put on the performance was readily comprehensible."

One Hopkins novelty noted by several commentators was the absence of the picturesque crowds of extras that had filled the stage in most Shakespearean productions since the time of Charles Kean. William Seymour, who had acted with many of the nineteenth century's leading actor-managers, was quick to point out that "In the old arrangement of the funeral procession, for example, there were from 70 to 80 people, and they all remained on the stage during the scene of the wooing of Lady Anne. In the Barrymore production there are six men, and only one of these is in evidence during the scene."[114]

Although Hopkins's direction on the whole proved controversial, especially in terms of the "repressed" speech and movement of the supporting cast, it nevertheless found many defenders. Agnes Smith, writing in the *Morning Telegraph* (8 March 1920), concluded that

> Personally, we think that Mr. Hopkins's way of presenting Shakespeare needs no defense. Boldly to knock down traditions is better than compromising, better than making half-way attempts. . . . Mr. Hopkins frankly makes the performance a one-man affair. The limelight is thrown upon Mr. Barrymore. But he justifies it. . . . We have never seen the creation of a dramatist brought to life so vividly.

Robert Edmond Jones's scenery, costumes, and lighting effects were universally admired for their beauty and appropriateness, and every critic went out of his or her way to praise Jones's work. Ludwig Lewisohn commended the "dark and naked magnificence" of Jones's investiture, noting that "His tower of London blends the architectural reality with all one's imaginative visions of a harsh, bloody, and turbulent age. The throne room is rich and beautiful, but its very lines and patterns accord with the swift and cruel fate of these transitory kings."[115] Woollcott found all of the scenes to be "rich and right – the work of an unerring artist of the theatre," adding that "We are all always absurdly haunted by the fear that Mr. Jones is about to overstep himself, to import, for instance, a fantastic quality and an enervating prettiness into a Plantaganet play. But Mr. Jones's precision as an artist is as sure as his imagination is boundless" (*Times*, 8 March 1920).

The critic for *Town & Country* noted that "It is in this respect, perhaps, that the progress of intelligence on the American stage since the Victorian Era can be most clearly measured. It is one thing to be historically accurate and this gift is very highly to be commended; it is another thing to have historical imagination. And of that Robert Edmond Jones has shown himself unmistakably possessed." The scenes were "not dug out of a library on historical architecture but created by one with a feeling for the savageness, the vividness, the elemental gorgeousness of the England of the Wars of the Roses."[116]

Not lost among the chorus of praise for the production's "originality" was the fact that *Richard III* owed an enormous debt to Continental theory and practice. Almost predictably, Kenneth Macgowan led the accolades for the harmonious blend of production elements, which outdid "in value, expressiveness, and significance the sum of the individual playing." The production, he commented, was "welded into a single emotional whole by decorations and lights conceived and managed in a manner never equalled or even approached in our theatre" and achieved "in America, by Americans, and for Americans, the modern miracle of the theatre which we have only credited heretofore to some alien theatre of far Berlin or Moscow. Here among us is an art grown to both popular and absolute perfection." *Richard III*, he wrote, was an "almost perfect" experiment, "revolutionary in conception and of the very highest importance," and marked "the finest moment of the American theatre" (*Globe*, 8 March 1920).

Critics did not ignore the text itself. The play, commented Alan Dale, was "served up in sixteen scenes and a hundred and fifty liberties." Yet he quickly conceded that "Only fanatics will rebel at the liberties" (*American*, 8 March 1920). To Heywood Broun, Sheldon's addition of five scenes from *3 Henry VI* represented "a helpful fusion which serves to clarify the story and the character of Richard" (*Tribune*, 8 March 1920). Kenneth Macgowan commented that the new version "leaves out yards of baronial complications" and perhaps because of that "remains a much more entertaining tale for the audiences of another land and another day" (*Globe*, 8 March 1920).

A number of reviewers noted that the new acting version afforded Barrymore with an opportunity to illuminate with striking clarity the psychological change in Richard's character. Woollcott commented in the *Times* (8 March 1920) that

> Beginning, as the Plymouth version does, with the stirring, groping boyhood of Richard, when the lad, embittered by his wanton deformity, stands hesitant at the crossroads where part the paths to good and evil – this grouping of the material permits that visible growth and change to a poisonous, dank, sin-rotted soul, spinning his plans from the throne of England, like some black and incredibly malignant spider. It is the progressive

change which Mansfield so reveled in and which makes a living thing of Barrymore's Richard.

Several reviewers attempted a brief historical summary of the play's textual history, commenting upon the long reign of Cibber's adaptation and the new versions of the play brought to the stage by Booth and Mansfield; few failed to notice Sheldon's retention of the hybrid Cibberism, "Chop off his head! So much for Buckingham!" To one critic, his adaptation served much the same purpose as the acting text that had held the stage for nearly two centuries: Sheldon's version of the play, like Cibber's, was clearly designed for "exploiting the performer of singular gifts" (*Christian Science Monitor*, 16 March 1920).

On one point, the critics were in total agreement: Barrymore's "singular gifts" were exploited at too great a length. Nearly every reviewer voiced objections to the four-hour performance on opening night, and most agreed with Charles Darnton of the *Evening World* (8 March 1920), who advised Hopkins that "a long knife should be drawn and applied to the cutting process without delay."

The Run

On Monday 8 March, Hopkins met with his cast. The early reviews and post–opening night comments (one playgoer was overheard after the final curtain thanking his companion for "a lovely weekend") had persuaded the director that a prompt reduction of the revival's running time was in order. The third scene, at York's Castle, was eliminated, saving ten to twelve minutes, and a number of internal cuts were made. Subsequent performances were scheduled to begin at 8:10 rather than 8:30. The cast was urged to quicken the pace, and the second performance ended at 11:40. Additional cuts were made on Tuesday, and the final curtain fell by 11:30 thereafter.

The favorable reviews resulted in a considerable advance sale, which soon amounted to six figures. "Seats Eight Weeks in Advance," announced the posters outside the Plymouth. *Richard III* drew in the vicinity of $2,000 per night, and during the first full week took in $18,000 ($2,000 below capacity) leading all nonmusical attractions. Even the highest ticket scale in New York – $3.50 for the first ten rows, and $3.00 for the remainder of the orchestra and front row seats in the balcony – was no deterrent.[117] The ticket-buying public clearly believed that this was not "another Shakespearean performance to be sat through." Barrymore had made the play fervid, menacing, exciting.[118]

Arthur Row later remembered that "All the great qualities were there – all the ingredients for a complete composition – blazing passion . . . fiendish joy in inflicting pain, a very ecstasy in commiting murder. Scintillant comedy, irony and scathing sarcasm. Above all, distinction and great elegance. It was a royal performance." To Arthur Hopkins, Barrymore was unforgettable. "He had fire, beauty, humor, cajolery, chilling cruelty," Hopkins remembered. "Shakespeare tragedy, for the first time in our day, became vibrantly alive."[119]

Barrymore remained typically modest about the enthusiastic response to his Shakespearean debut, calling his Richard "a meticulous and not very inspired performance" and admitting that "I probably, with no intention of so doing, sang a great deal of the text." Later, however, he told Gene Fowler that it was "the first genuine acting I ever managed to achieve, and perhaps my own best. It was the first time I ever actually got *inside* the character I was playing. I mean I thought I *was* the character, and in my dreams I *knew* that I was he."[120]

As in his earlier roles, however, he was not averse to making subtle adjustments to his character in response to his audience. Among those in attendance at the first Thursday matinee was an 18-year-old actor, Alexander Clark, who had arrived toward the end of the first act on opening night after working all day in Mamaroneck on D. W. Griffith's *Way Down East*. Five days later, he returned to see the complete (albeit cut) performance. Clark (who later founded Friends of Richard III, Inc., dedicated to eradicating the Tudor propagandist view of Richard as inhuman monster) had seen *The Jest* four times, and was impressed by the technical strides Barrymore had made. His voice was "stronger, deeper, harsher," Clark remembered. "It made all the difference." He found Barrymore's Richard to be "intense, strong, evil, funny," adding that a good deal of the performance's impact came from the fact that he was "far more natural" than E. H. Sothern and other contemporary interpreters.

To Clark, one of the most memorable moments at the afternoon performance came in the third act, when Richard, learning that Richmond's forces have landed, rallies his troops with a cry of "Away towards Salisbury!" At the Thursday matinee, he remembered, Barrymore, spotting a friend, the elderly character actor James Bradbury, in the front row, rewrote the line for his benefit, proclaiming, "On to Bradbury!"[121] Gene Fowler later claimed that on another occasion, Barrymore, after hearing a guffaw from the balcony on his line, "A horse! A horse! My kingdom for a horse!" raised his sword toward the offender and called out: "Make haste, and saddle yonder braying ass!"[122]

Barrymore, however, had little tolerance for departures from the script and blocking by other members of the cast. "He was a wonderful person to work with on the stage, but quick to resent fancied or real actors' tricks," commented William Keighley, who later remembered that during the run, Barrymore "suspected a lady in the cast of moving during one of his important scenes" and changed his own blocking accordingly. "Ever after," Keighley recalled, "she was forced to play her entire scene with her back to the audience."[123]

It soon became obvious to Barrymore that Richard III was the most physically and emotionally demanding role of any he had attempted. After two eight-performance weeks, he convinced a reluctant Hopkins to eliminate the Thursday matinee beginning the week of 21 March, arguing that five performances bunched in the final three days of the week presented too heavy a strain.[124] Reducing the number of performances did little, however, to ameliorate Barrymore's growing physical and emotional exhaustion. On Wednesday, 31 March, the audience could not help but notice that Barrymore was fumbling his lines. On several occasions during the performance he almost collapsed, and he finished with great difficulty. The next night, Thursday, 1 April, it was announced that Barrymore was unable to appear. The audience was turned away from the theatre at curtain time; their money was refunded, and future ticket sales were halted. Ticketholders for the Friday night performance were advised to telephone the box office after 2 P.M. to see if there would be a performance, but Friday night the Plymouth was again dark. Barrymore was said by his friends to be suffering from a nervous breakdown; it was rumored on Broadway that he would be unable to act for a long period of time. Hopkins made brief announcements to the company and to the press, stating that he hoped Barrymore would be able to resume the role after a period of rest. *Variety* later reported that he refunded more than $35,000 to disappointed ticketholders.[125] "It was heartbreaking to the cast," William Keighley remembered, ". . . for such great performances are milestones in the theatre, and so few had been privileged to witness it."[126] *Richard III* had played three weeks and four days – 27 performances.

To most observers, it seemed clear that the major factor in Barrymore's nervous collapse was overwork. *Richard III* had opened a mere two weeks after the final performance of *The Jest*, and Barrymore had summoned up almost a superhuman energy for the rehearsal period and performances. From November 1919 through the end of February he had dedicated his energies to more than one project at a time. November and early December had been devoted to filming principal scenes for *Dr. Jekyll and Mr. Hyde* during the day while playing *The Jest* at night and at matinees. In January and February he would often arise early in the morning to be at Paramount Studios on 57th Street at eight o'clock to film additional scenes for the Stevenson classic; he would then journey to Margaret Carrington's apartment to work on *Richard III*, appearing that evening (or afternoon) in *The Jest*.

Once performances were under way, the part of Richard made strenuous physical demands on the slightly built actor. Barrymore was on stage for almost the entire performance; much of the time he wore heavy armor in which he was required to engage in several energetic scenes of stage combat.

On a number of occasions, the armor he wore in the final scenes grew so hot under the lights that it had to be hosed down before it could be removed; the spine-jarring, acrobatic fall at the close of his duel with Richmond often left him close to unconsciousness.[127]

Added to the strain of Barrymore's performance was his tempestuous relationship with Michael Strange. Their affair was characterized by mutual artistic encouragement, but also by an intense possessiveness and jealousy that intensified the stress brought on by months of overwork. Michael Strange remembered that the evening of his collapse, as Barrymore made up for Richard, he had engaged in "a brilliantly inquisitorial display . . . during which, unsavory facts had been unearthed about my conduct."[128] Almost inevitably, the cumulative effects of Barrymore's driving himself physically and emotionally over a period of time took their toll.

"If there was a tragedy in his short run of *Richard III*," Margaret Carrington commented years later, "it was because a man of his temperament and talent could not physically sustain so high a standard as he achieved in his performance under the pressure of influences surrounding him at that time. His performances were electrifying as well as being a demonstration of demoniac talent used at its highest pitch."[129]

Years later, Robert Edmond Jones looked back upon Barrymore's nervous collapse, commenting that

> It was the sheer energy of his mind that drove him to the edge of unreason. I remember seeing a performance of *Richard III* in which he gave so much, revealed so much, that I said to myself, this can't last! Something is going to happen! It's excessive. It's abnormal. It isn't human to drive yourself like that!
>
> And yet, do you know, when you are possessed by a thing, or by an idea, or by an emotion, while you are under the spell of it, you can live a life that is utterly abnormal quite simply, as if it were utterly normal. This heightened world can be your world for the time being and you exist in it and are fed by it, and you are under no strain at all.
>
> And then all at once, for no reason, the bottom drops out of it. Everything drops away. And nothing is left.[130]

Following his breakdown, Barrymore remained in seclusion at his home in the city through the weekend. On Tuesday, 6 April, he departed for a sanitarium near White Plains, run by his father's old friend William Muldoon, a former wrestling champion who had played Charles to Maurice Barrymore's Orlando in *As You Like It*. At Muldoon's, he was placed on a strict regimen. He was awakened at dawn, took a cold shower, then spent time in a gymnasium tossing a medicine ball with the ex-wrestler. After breakfast he was allowed a two-hour rest. A brisk, five-mile walk was the highlight of the afternoon program. Smoking and drinking were strictly prohibited, and Muldoon managed to foil all attempts to smuggle in bathtub liquor, finally placing the telephone off limits.[131]

A week after his arrival, Barrymore wrote to his friend John Jay Chapman, an essayist and Shakespeare scholar whose advice he had solicited while preparing for his Shakespearean debut:

> I know you must think me most damnably gauche – not to have answered your delightful letter sooner than this – but I have been in such a maelstrom of labor garnitured by exhaustion that I have put off everything – like some swimmer in the Atlantic Ocean might say – I'll put off telephoning till I land! I have landed at last more or less on my back – as playing that dynamically ruthless old buck – eight times a week for all one is worth – after being pretty much "all in" anyway was like trying to break 10 seconds flat in the hundred yard dash after walking up a long long hill!
>
> I loved every word of your letter and what is more it helped me like the devil as I believed firmly everything you said – Richard is a melodrama and all melodrama especially of the pageant-quality background ought to gallop along like a mad stallion – I was *new* at the Shakespearean game and was watching *myself* instead of the *sweep* of the thing. I wish you could have been on the side-lines before – to yell at them "You're all dieing on your feet!!" I'll do it again sometime. He is *enormous* fun – as he is so utterly unequivocal or sentimental or good-to-his-mother or noble – or sweet or sincere or *romantic* or any of the God-awful things actors have to be as a rule. I suppose that is the reason they are all potential murderers off the stage![132]

On 15 May, Barrymore, judged by Muldoon to be sufficiently recovered after six weeks of rest, returned to New York. Hopkins, still hopeful that he might resume the role, greeted his return optimistically; but Barrymore, pleading exhaustion, quickly dashed his hopes. Soon afterward, he left on an extended vacation with Michael Strange.

In subsequent years, *Richard III* tended to be overshadowed by the landmark *Hamlet* that followed, an impression assisted by the brevity of its run and the melodramatic nature of its plot and central character. In retrospect, however, it deserves to be considered in its own right as it was perceived by Charles Darnton in his opening-night review: as "an event that deserves a conspicuous place in the history of the American stage" (*Evening World*, 8 March 1920). Barrymore's portrayal, more colloquially spoken, less physically stylized, and more psychologically grounded than those of his immediate predecessors, and the innovative approaches to Shakespearean direction and design by Hopkins and Jones, fired a cannon volley against tradition that would resonate through the 1920s and beyond. Although Sothern and Marlowe were to offer their repertory a few seasons longer, and Belasco was soon to produce a picturesque *Merchant of Venice* as opulently mounted as any revival of Irving or Tree, the production introduced critics and the public to visionary methods of interpretation that foreshadowed much to come in the twentieth century.

In setting down his memories of *Richard III* years later, Arthur Row, fully aware of the revolutionary impact of the production, recalled that he had once asked Robert Edmond Jones if Barrymore, Hopkins, and Jones would ever revive it. "No," Jones replied. "It was all done too perfectly. It is finished. There is nothing more to do!"[133] Yet something did, in fact, remain to be done: Two years later the innovative methods of preparation, acting, design, and direction developed for *Richard III* were applied anew when Barrymore and his production team turned their attention to *Hamlet*.

3

Hamlet, 1922–1924

The clearest, the most interesting, intelligent and exciting Hamlet of our
generation.

    – Heywood Broun, *New York World* (17 November 1922)

JOHN BARRYMORE'S HAMLET stands as a landmark in the history of
the American theatre. His interpretation won enthusiastic praise
from nearly all quarters, and by the end of the initial New York run, in which
he eclipsed Edwin Booth's "record" of one hundred consecutive performances, it had attained the status of a legend. It mattered little that John E.
Kellerd had played Hamlet for one hundred and two consecutive performances a decade earlier, or that Henry Irving had given two hundred consecutive performances at the Lyceum in London during the 1874–5 season. For
those of his generation – and beyond – Barrymore's Hamlet was an epoch-
making interpretation that established his place in the pantheon along with
Booth, Irving, Forbes-Robertson, and the acclaimed Shakespeareans of the
more distant past.

    A good deal of the performance's impact arose from the fact that Barry-
more's Hamlet – like Booth's impersonation and the bravura characterizations of Garrick and Kean – broke with longstanding traditions and captured
the spirit and artistic sensibilities of a generation determined to sever its ties
with the past. By 1922, American society, transformed by the horrors of the
First World War and its aftermath, had set itself in eager rebellion against the
vestiges of Victorian and Edwardian culture. New methods of artistic expression were rapidly emerging: The year of Barrymore's debut as Hamlet also
saw the publication of Joyce's *Ulysses*, Fitzgerald's *The Beautiful and the Damned*,
and Eliot's *The Wasteland*. At the same time, Ezra Pound and e. e. cummings
were, along with Eliot, reinventing poetry, and John Dos Passos and Sinclair
Lewis were desentimentalizing the novel. In the theatre, Ibsen and Shaw, ex-
tremists two decades earlier, had been accepted into the mainstream. Their

position at the cutting edge had been assumed by a new wave of experimental movements from Europe: futurism, dada, and – most influential of all – expressionism, exemplified by the Broadway premieres during the 1921–2 and 1922–3 seasons of Eugene O'Neill's *The Hairy Ape* and Elmer Rice's *The Adding Machine.*

Within this context of artistic rebellion and change, Barrymore's Hamlet was widely viewed as having captured the essence of his time. His bearing and gestures, wrote Ludwig Lewisohn, had "the restrained but intense expressiveness of the bearing of modern men who live with their nerves and woes in narrow rooms," yet they seemed "utterly right – right in an unsought-for and unhoped-for measure. And this illustrates the truth that a supreme masterpiece is one that each successive age can interpret in the terms of its own moods and needs and special passions, if but the right interpreter can be found."[1]

As was the case with *Richard III,* however, the production and its central performance were by no means a complete break with the past. Barrymore's Hamlet, like his Richard III, was slow and reflective in the late-nineteenth-century manner; he employed frequent pauses and a good deal of pantomimed business in the tradition of Henry Irving. Hopkins, with criticism of the previous lengthy opening night no doubt in mind, presented audiences with a performance text that was cut as thoroughly as any given by Irving or Booth.

Yet for the most part Shakespearean custom was overlooked. Traditional stage business was ignored, as were the reverential approach and "school of recitation" that had typified many American and British Shakespearean offerings of the preceding decades. "Again we followed the plan that had been so rewarding in *Richard III,*" Arthur Hopkins recalled years later:

> All fustian and reverence were banished. Previous interpretations were ignored. We began with our own conception and developed it in all parts of the play. I doubt if Hamlet had ever been given a clearer course to sail. His bark was unencumbered by traditional barnacles that had long been accumulating. We spent no time charting the shoals. We struck at once for the deep, turbulent waters with what seemed to us Shakespeare's clear intent as our compass. We made ourselves completely servants of the play, untempted by any beckoning to leave our personal and peculiar imprint.[2]

The result was a production of power and authority that served the play well, in the view of most contemporary critics, but it was also one that did, in fact, benefit from their "personal and peculiar" imprints. Barrymore's repressed acting style, the innovative Continental production values, and the triumvirate's psychological approach to the text bridged the interpretive

methods of the old century and the new and in doing so, brought new life
to a time-honored classic. "It is *Hamlet* thought out anew, *Hamlet* freshly
dreamed and freshly played . . . [,] the realest *Hamlet* we have known," remarked Alexander Woollcott (*Herald*, 17 November 1922).

This chapter's examination of the preparations for *Hamlet*, their realization, and the critical response focuses specifically on the ways in which Barrymore, Hopkins, Jones, and Margaret Carrington "preserved the best traditions" of the play and yet "breathed into it an utterly modern spirit."[3] By
viewing this *Hamlet* from the vantage point of audiences accustomed on one
hand to the genteel characterizations and realistic investiture of Victorian
tradition, and on the other to the atmosphere of cultural reinvention that
permeated American society during the early 1920s, we can more easily appreciate the production's extraordinary impact on the post–First World War
generation and its repercussions for generations to come.

Transition: 1920–2

The two years following *Richard III* were a period of transition for Barrymore,
privately and professionally. After his breakdown he was understandably reluctant to attempt an immediate return to the stage or to marry Michael
Strange, given their frequently tempestuous relationship. The latter issue was
decided, however, when she became pregnant with his child early in the
summer of 1920. After she obtained a hasty divorce from her husband, she
and Barrymore were married in New York on 5 August.

That autumn, there was much speculation as to when Barrymore would return to the theatre. Finally, it was announced that his physicians had advised
him to rest for at least a year to regain his strength. Hopkins notified the
press that he would recuperate until the 1921–2 season, when, after reviving
Richard III and *Redemption*, he would attempt the long-awaited *Hamlet*.[4] Soon
afterward, however, Barrymore returned to professional activity, long before
the recommended period of convalescence. In November, he journeyed to
Miami to film First National's *The Lotus Eater*, a romantic fantasy in which he
starred as a man who flees civilization by sailing in a balloon to a remote Pa-
cific Island. Once exteriors were completed, he returned to New York, where
plans were underway for another Hopkins–Jones Shakespearean production:
Macbeth, featuring Lionel Barrymore.

Less than a year had passed since the first performance of *Richard III*, and
many of the same rehearsal and production techniques were again employed.
One crucial difference, however, was the decision by Hopkins and Jones to
forgo Gordon Craig's suggestive scenery and harmonious blend of elements.
Instead, they embraced one of the latest avant-garde movements to emerge
from Europe: expressionism. In preparing for *Macbeth*, Hopkins found rele-

vance, no doubt, in the expressionists' primary philosophical concerns: extreme despair, human relationships at the point of highest tension, dreams and visions. Similarly, Robert Edmond Jones, obsessed with the new science of psychoanalysis, found fertile ground in expressionist scenic values, which often were manifested in visual distortion and exaggeration meant to reflect a protagonist's emotional state. In designing *Macbeth*, he turned away from the graceful, geometric, Craig-inspired scenery of his earlier work to embrace the harsh, jagged lines of the new movement.[5]

Clearly, Hopkins and Jones intended to bring Shakespeare even further into the realms of modern psychology and experimental staging than they had with *Richard III*. On 6 February 1921, they announced to the press that the aim of their new production was to "release the radium of Shakespeare from its vessel of tradition," and indeed, a week later, playgoers were informed that the new *Macbeth* would be "several steps in advance of anything that even the continental theatrical radicals have attempted."[6] The revival opened at the Apollo Theatre on 17 February, with John Barrymore in the audience to cheer his brother on. A few minutes before midnight, the audience dispersed, shocked, wrote Woollcott in the *Times* (18 February 1921), "that Lionel Barrymore, while often good, and occasionally very good, should never once have brushed greatness." Shocked may be an understatement of the critical reaction to Jones's settings. The mise-en-scène included three giant silver masks appearing above the heath, disturbingly slanted and distorted arches, and an Inverness that to Woollcott resembled "a giant molar tooth pitched rakishly in space" and made him long for "the battered backdrops of Robert Mantell." It was, he concluded, a production that "will be talked of until the cows come home – as an oddity." Kenneth Macgowan, virtually alone among his peers, defended Jones's abstract set pieces as epoch-making for suggesting psychological and emotional ideas rather than locale. Like most of his colleagues, however, he found fault with Lionel Barrymore's "tedious and unimaginative" Thane. "The acting center of the play failed to glow with the luminosity which this extraordinary production demanded," he wrote, concluding that had John Barrymore or Jacob Ben-Ami acted the role against Jones's backgrounds the production would have been "an occasion of the very highest significance in the calendar of the American Theatre."[7]

Many of the production's problems, however, clearly arose from Hopkins and Jones, who in their eagerness to embrace modern psychological values and expressionist staging and design abandoned the theoretical tenets that had served them well in the past. They did not make themselves "servants of the play," nor did they achieve the harmonious blend of elements that had characterized many of their previous efforts. The production, a failure with both critics and the public, closed on 12 March after 28 performances. In subsequent years, John Barrymore championed Lionel's Thane. ("You've done everything but paint your scrotum green," he told his brother by way of explanation.)[8] It seems likely, however, that he learned two valuable lessons from his brother's failure. In preparing for *Macbeth,* Lionel Barrymore had not undertaken vocal training, perhaps because both he and Hopkins had found his voice to be adequate; he was then widely criticized for vocal monotony. Equally important was the fact that the production instilled in John Barrymore a deeply felt suspicion of Hopkins's and Jones's more radical production concepts. The need for intense vocal preparation and a desire for scenic and conceptual conservatism (at least, relatively speaking) would be among his primary concerns a year later when the triumvirate turned its attentions to *Hamlet.*

Before returning to Shakespeare, however, Barrymore would make an ill-starred Broadway appearance during the spring of 1921. On 3 March, a daughter, Diana, was born to Michael Strange, and soon afterward Barrymore began rehearsals for the play his wife had been working on for several years: *Clair de Lune,* adapted from Victor Hugo's novel *L'Homme qui rit* (The Man Who Laughs). After reading the script, Arthur Hopkins wisely turned down the opportunity to produce and direct. Barrymore, however, chose to ignore Hopkins's comments regarding the quality of the material. His decision was based, no doubt, on the intense devotion to his wife that came about during her pregnancy, and the allure of the character she called upon him to play: Gwymplane, a facially deformed mountebank, noble and pure in spirit, romantic yet grotesque – a role that held much the same appeal as Mr. Hyde and Richard III. Barrymore persuaded his sister to undertake the Queen – their first joint appearance in nearly a decade. He designed many of the costumes and much of the scenery, and plunged into rehearsals with his customary energy.

On 18 April 1921 the play opened at the Empire to a sold-out house. At the final curtain, however, it was evident to most in the audience that *Clair de Lune,* like the Hopkins–Jones–Lionel Barrymore *Macbeth,* was a theatrical disaster. Moments of Barrymore's performance were praised, but the play itself was excoriated for its murky plot, its awkward and pretentious style (an attempt to blend Hugo's characters and story line with Maeterlinck-inspired symbolism), and especially its dialogue. "What chiefly characterizes Michael Strange as a playwright," wrote Woollcott, "is a certain gloating magniloquence of language, a resolutely poetic speech. It is speech which is every now and again shot through with the color of real imagination, but more often it is merely stilted, effortful and self-important" (*Times,* 19 April 1921).

Barrymore was irate at the critical response to his wife's creation and fired off letters of protest – never published – to the *Times* and the *Tribune.*[9] Despite the reviews, *Clair de Lune* managed a respectable showing at the box office; the glamour of two Barrymores, even in a critically panned vehicle, kept audi-

ences coming for eight weeks. By the end of the run, however, Barrymore was
surely aware that he was virtually alone in his estimation of the play's merit.
His first artistic failure in nearly a decade – and his first as a serious actor –
doubtless strengthened his determination to succeed when he turned his attention to *Hamlet.*

After *Clair de Lune,* a full year was to pass before Barrymore again made
plans to return to the stage. On 7 July 1921 he and Michael Strange sailed for
Europe, where they spent the summer. Barrymore then proceeded to London, alone, to film exteriors for *Sherlock Holmes,* adapted from William Gil-
lette's stage vehicle. On 22 October 1921, his English scenes completed, he
departed for New York, where he filmed interior scenes through January
1922. Late winter and early spring of 1922 brought a period of artistic inac-
tivity – much of it spent on vacation in the Bahamas – during which Barrymore began to consider an attempt at Hamlet, a role he had wanted to play
for nearly four years. Accounts of this period are often contradictory, yet a
picture emerges of an actor who, after a notable failure on the stage and two
films with which he was less than satisfied, clearly craved artistic success and
recognition. He later wrote that when he returned to New York he found that
"John Barrymore had been practically forgotten" and "knew that it would
take something terrific" to bring him back into public notice. "The logical
thing for me to do," he remarked, "was to suppress no longer my desire to do
Hamlet."[10] He had hardly been forgotten, of course, but the aura of artistic triumph that had surrounded him since *Justice* had been somewhat diminished.
In personal life he was dissatisfied as well; he had quarreled tumultuously
with Michael Strange and was again drinking heavily.[11]

Ethel Barrymore later recalled that her brother, "very unhappy and at a
loose end," came to stay with her for a while at her estate in Mamaroneck. "So
I literally took him by the hand to French Lick, Indiana [a popular spa], with
a little red Temple *Hamlet* in my pocket," she remembered. "At French Lick,
Jack was bored, and I gave him the little red *Hamlet* and told him to learn
one of the soliloquies and he did. When he read it to me, neither one of us
was quite happy about it, but I still knew that the spark was there."[12] Barrymore claimed that he then went down to White Sulphur Springs, West Virginia, and pored over the play for weeks, then went out into the woods and
rehearsed himself in parts of it. As he was to remark a few years later:

> I was amazed to find how simple *Hamlet* seemed to be, and I was no little be-
> wildered that anything of such infinite beauty and simplicity should have
> acquired centuries of comment. It seems to me that all the explanation, all
> the comment that is necessary upon *Hamlet* Goethe wrote in *Wilhelm Meis-
> ter.* These simple words in short sentences, with which the editor of the
> Temple edition has had the wit to preface the text, are more illuminating
> than all the commentaries: "And to me it is clear that Shakespere [*sic*]

sought to depict a great deed laid upon a soul unequal to the performance of it. In this view I find the piece composed throughout. Here is an oak tree planted in a costly vase, which should have received into its bosom only lovely flowers; the roots spread out, the vase is shivered to pieces."[13]

Arthur Hopkins later remembered that "Jack appeared at the office one day, said he was ready for *Hamlet* and wanted to begin at once," and it seems likely that a decision had been made by late spring of 1922 to begin preparations for a production both men had contemplated for a number of years.[14] *Hamlet* was no longer the formidable obstacle it had seemed four years earlier; *Richard III* had served as an important stepping-stone, and the passing of time had made the inevitability of comparisons seem less imposing. Forbes-Robertson had been in retirement for more than half a decade; Sothern's interpretation was respectable though hardly great, and at sixty-two he could not look the part; Mantell had exiled himself to the provinces; Fritz Leiber, for many years Mantell's leading man, had met with only modest success when he had attempted *Hamlet* during his 1921–2 season of Shakespearean repertory. More important, Walter Hampden's status as the new Shakespearean champion had eroded; his Hamlet no longer seemed as fresh and vital as it had four years earlier. When he revived his production in New York, little more than a week after the opening of Barrymore's *Richard III*, Woollcott had damned him with faint praise, finding him to be "unquestionably the best [Hamlet] we have – but not quite the best we might have." Four days later, Woollcott ventured the opinion that if John Barrymore "be minded to take the last step of his ascent, he could be the finest Hamlet of our time."[15] Such encouragement surely played a part in Barrymore and Hopkins's decision to proceed, as did a confidence that with dedication and effort they could create a production that would recapture the theatrical magic of *Richard III*, with the failed *Macbeth* serving as a lesson in what not to do.

In late May or early June, Barrymore, aware of the need for intense study and vocal preparation, asked Hopkins to approach Margaret Carrington to see if she would again work with him. Her response was affirmative yet pragmatic. She had accepted Barrymore as a pupil after the opening date of *Richard III* had been announced, and was aware that the intensity of their efforts and the pressure to remake his voice in a limited time had been contributing factors to his breakdown. She later remembered that when Hopkins asked her to help Barrymore with *Hamlet*, "I said I would on one condition. That there would be no fixed date for the opening until we had worked for a month, and that the play would be produced when I thought he was ready."[16] Hopkins agreed, and soon afterward turned his attention to shaping the text and making preliminary cuts. On 26 June 1922, Michael Strange sailed for

Europe on the *Mauritania,* with Barrymore on the dock to bid her farewell; a day or two later he journeyed to the Carringtons' farm in Connecticut, where work on *Hamlet* would begin in earnest.[17]

A Summer of Preparation

Denbigh, the Carringtons' North Greenwich estate, was a comfortable country home. The remodeled two-story farmhouse, white with green shutters, had five or six bedrooms in addition to the servants' quarters; the grounds featured an ample expanse of lawn, rose and heliotrope gardens, and an orchard. When Barrymore arrived, he discovered an already crowded household. In addition to William and Margaret Carrington there were five servants; also in residence that summer were Margaret Carrington's niece and nephew, 14-year-old Margaret Huston and her 11-year-old brother William "Bud" Huston, the children of her older brother, Alexander.

Years later, Margaret Huston (by then Margaret Huston Walters) remembered the day of Barrymore's arrival. "The first time I met him was in the garden," she commented. "They'd been strolling around looking at the flowers and my aunt called me over. I'll never forget the first time I saw him. He had really marvellous eyes. He wasn't tall – he was slight – small boned." Although Barrymore seemed "very handsome," he struck Margaret Huston as "a very nervous sort of man – not a comfortable type at all."[18]

Life at the Carrington household followed a routine. In the morning, Margaret Carrington directed plays featuring Margaret and Bud Huston and children from the neighborhood. Barrymore usually arose around noon. After breakfast in bed, he presented himself downstairs to begin work on *Hamlet.* Most sessions were held in the living room; three steps led up to the library, where for most of the summer, Margaret Huston sat reading – at Carrington's request – while her aunt worked with Barrymore. ("After all, he does have a reputation as a ladies' man," Carrington jokingly told her niece. "I want somebody close by – just in case.") "She wasn't terribly serious about it," Margaret Walters recalled, "but she wasn't about to give the neighbors a chance to chatter." For propriety's sake, the door separating living room and library was always left slightly ajar.

Margaret Carrington later recalled her impressions of working with Barrymore on the role. "The day he arrived," she wrote, "he was carrying an armful of books. The *Hamlet* variorum, histories of the play as interpreted by the actors of the past. I suggested that we put the books away and find out for ourselves what the play was about." Together they began to study the play as they would "a modern script that had never been performed." Carrington remarked that

I think this accounted for his spontaneous reading and acting throughout the various scenes and helped to banish any natural fear he might have had in appearing for the first time in a part that has been the high spot in every actor's experience. To face the potential Hamlet "back seat" actors, those kibitzers of the theatre – the critics who seem sure that there can be nothing original in a contemporary Hamlet – the elderly Shakespearean first-nighters whispering to their neighbors how Booth, Barrett and Mantell interpreted the part in their day! Surely this is enough to intimidate any actor.

"I can truthfully say that we had a good time discovering Hamlet by ourselves," she continued. Barrymore had agreed not to attempt to memorize the role until they had explored every shade of meaning in the unfolding of the play. As one of the keys to the drama, they looked to Hamlet's line, "O my prophetic soul! / My uncle!" This line, Margaret Carrington commented, "reveals that Hamlet had intuitively known all the time that his uncle had murdered his father. From that moment every act and circumstance in Hamlet's life was influenced by that knowledge. He had sworn to avenge his father's murder. He was bound to secrecy to protect his mother. His love for Ophelia was doomed. . . . He carried the burden of his responsibility alone."[19]

Their efforts, however, were devoted primarily to vocal exercises that enabled Barrymore to communicate effectively their interpretation of the text. "Not only did they rehearse *Hamlet* extensively but my aunt first 'put him through his paces' with language in general," Margaret Walters recalled. "She drilled him for days on the usual singer's practical polishing of consonants and vowels. . . . I, listening in the adjoining room, marvelled to hear his tones becoming deeper, purer and more musical."[20]

When working with the play itself, Walters remembered, "they stood, they walked," passing Barrymore's small red Temple edition back and forth as needed. Margaret Carrington would read a line and say, "Now try it like this." Barrymore would then repeat his line or speech as many times as was necessary, pacing with his book, until his reading met with her approval. Barrymore was "a bit stilted at first," and her aunt's efforts were devoted primarily to "making him be more natural." At times she used withering sarcasm to make her aim clear. "Make it more relaxed, John," she would tell her pupil. "Don't be so pompous." "She wasn't a bit shy with him," her niece attested. Barrymore would start a speech, and time and again she would stop him abruptly and instruct him – sternly yet patiently – on "proper diction, breathing, and the vowel sounds." Margaret Walters recalled Barrymore's recalcitrance:

> He wasn't an easy pupil. He sort of fought. He had to be made to do things. I could hear her saying, "Oh, no, no, no, no, no, no, Jack. Not like that – like this." And she'd show him how. She'd say, "Now I want you to breathe. And I want you to give that full value." So he'd keep trying and she'd say, "well

that's better," but she wasn't easily satisfied. They went on for a long time – she made him work. She took quite a little trouble with him. He was quite stubborn. But he was anxious to learn.

Most evenings Barrymore headed upstairs around nine. In his bedroom, he studied his part, chain-smoked, and drank coffee until the wee hours. "What a happy summer that was – we worked six, eight hours a day – sometimes into the night," Margaret Carrington remembered. Sessions were occasionally held during afternoon walks "in the garden – and the woods." For two and a half months he remained at Denbigh, working on *Hamlet* every day, through dampish, oppressive summer weather. Years later, she remarked that

> I have often been asked why we worked so long on *Hamlet*. My answer has always been that Barrymore is the only actor I have ever known in America who was willing to polish every phrase of a play until he was satisfied that the deepest meaning of Shakespeare's texts were completely revealed and understood. . . . This process is not so easy as it may appear. It demands the most intense study of every sentence in a play.[21]

Barrymore's studybook, now in the library at The Players, testifies to the intensity of their efforts. Its inscription reads: "To Margaret Carrington – with love & gratitude for her very great helpfulness & kindness. This is the copy we worked from. It's a small copy – but God – how we worked!!"[22]

A Psychological Approach

In early September, Barrymore returned to New York, where the impending *Hamlet* production was by then public knowledge. Soon afterward, he met with Arthur Hopkins and Robert Edmond Jones to discuss production concepts. Jones's initial suggestions evoked Barrymore's sharp disapproval. "At times his ideas frightened Jack, who in some ways was strangely tradition-bound," Hopkins remembered. Barrymore's desire for scenic conservatism was understandable, however, in light of his brother's failure the previous season; he naturally wished to avoid the much-criticized motifs of Jones's *Macbeth*. "We argued for four days," Barrymore remembered. "At last I won. . . . Jones came down to earth."[23]

Another issue likely to have been discussed at this time was the Freudian interpretation of the play. Hopkins's knowledge of Freud's specific comments on *Richard III* can only be speculated upon, but in the case of *Hamlet* there can be no doubt. Freud's discussion of the Oedipus complex and its applications in *Hamlet* had first appeared more than two decades earlier, and had been expanded upon in Ernest Jones's 1910 article, "The Oedipus Complex as an Explanation of Hamlet's Mystery."[24] By 1922, the Oedipus complex and suppressed desires were common currency in American society. Many observers would note the "incestuous" handling of the Queen's closet scene, yet it was apparent to others that the use of modern psychology extended even further, to the interpretation of Ophelia and to an overall view of the play.

In later years, the implications of this reading would arouse a good deal of controversy. In *Good Night, Sweet Prince,* Gene Fowler argued that "Perhaps Barrymore did not actually insert these stark values into the play. Possibly he merely recognized, and then projected the suggestions which already were present, though long-hidden, in the tragedy." He suggested that Barrymore's alleged sexual initiation with Maurice Barrymore's second wife may have been the source of his conception of Hamlet as an incestuous prince and noted that Barrymore did not adhere to a strict Freudian party line: He had clearly shown affection for the ghost, rather than jealousy.[25] Fowler's remarks prompted a letter from Dr. Harold Thomas Hyman, a New York physician and the author of many medical books, who argued that not the least of Barrymore's accomplishments in his *Hamlet* was his "psychoanalytic concept of many of the incidents." Part of this, he commented, "was his extraordinary intuition, but part, which you fail to mention . . . were his many conferences with Pearce Bailey or [Edwin] Zabriskie, I cannot remember which."[26] Fowler, justly irate at Hyman's statement that Barrymore had viewed the Ghost as "a father image and a villain," fired back in a letter, stating his view that

> It was apparent that the incestuous motif . . . was solidly lodged within the Barrymore *Hamlet.* Still, I ruled out his pre-play conferences with psycho-analysts. I had to do so for two principal reasons: first, all the competent testimony . . . pointed to the fact that Margaret Carrington was his principal and only *real* adviser in regard to this role. And even she merely dispelled the smoke-screen and opened the channel through which he moved into navigable waters by virtue of his own intuitions and first-hand experience with situations.[27]

What Fowler and subsequent commentators overlooked, however, was the fact that Barrymore was not alone in conceptualizing the production, that the contributions of Arthur Hopkins and Robert Edmond Jones went far beyond simple staging and design, and that both Hopkins and Jones had held an intense and well-documented interest in modern psychology for more than a decade. There is also evidence to indicate that Barrymore may have consulted a psychiatrist around this time. During the preparatory period for *Hamlet,* both Hopkins and Jones were being psychoanalyzed by Dr. Smith Ely Jelliffe, whose wife Belinda later remembered that Barrymore knew her husband socially and professionally. (Jelliffe, in fact, had published psycho-analytic critiques of Barrymore's Peter Ibbetson, Fedya, and Giannetto in the *New York Medical Journal* several years earlier, and his daughter Helena was cast as one of the "extra ladies" in *Hamlet* court scenes; she later recalled that her father had advised Hopkins on "how Ophelia should sing her mad song.")[28]

Whether Barrymore and Jelliffe saw each other professionally during the period of preparation or discussed *Hamlet* is unknown. It seems likely, however, that if he did consult with Jelliffe it was due to the influence of Hopkins and Jones, and that much of the psychological content emanated from them, although Barrymore was aware of psychoanalytical theories regarding the play and his character; an actress in his company later recalled that he was "literally fascinated with Freud." No doubt there was much spirited discussion as to the degree this element would be included (with Barrymore, perhaps, citing the disastrous *Macbeth* as a cautionary tale). The final interpretation can only be seen as selective in its incorporation of Freudian (or Jonesian) elements, yet the influence was clearly present in the Queen's closet, in Ophelia's abrupt emergence from sensual repression to the opposite pole in her mad scene, and in Hamlet's bitter resentment of Claudius's presence in his mother's bed. Barrymore later told Gene Fowler of the image he held in mind while speaking the "rogue and peasant slave" soliloquy: "That dirty, red-whiskered son-of-a-bitch! That bastard puts his prick in my mother's cunt every night!"[29]

Overlooked as well was the fact that the "psychological Hamlet" was also a response to the "sweet prince" of Victorian and Edwardian tradition. Barrymore, perhaps recalling his ethereal Peter Ibbetson and Giannetto, told Hopkins that "I want him to be so male that when I come out on the stage they can hear my balls clank,"[30] and the character he presented, in keeping with the emerging sensibilities and psychological theory of the time, was more sexual and menacing than the idealized figure of nineteenth-century convention. This shift in emphasis was made possible, in part, by landmark restorations to the traditional acting text. Since the time of Garrick, it had been customary to eliminate the play's many sexual references, a tradition to which Booth, Irving, and their successors (and even that champion of textual restoration, William Poel) had willingly adhered. By the early 1920s, however, American society no longer deemed it necessary or even appropriate to bowdlerize the Bard. Some observers saw the production's sexuality as pure sensationalism, but to others it was very much in tune with a new and welcome tendency to view Shakespeare's characters as psychological, fully rounded human beings rather than the poetic, idealized figures of Victorian and Edwardian tradition. However, here too the triumvirate was selective. Hamlet could be bawdy with Rosencrantz and Guildenstern in the restored "secret parts of fortune" exchange, but with Ophelia he adopted as gentlemanly an approach as any of his Victorian predecessors; his references to "country matters" and "a groaning" were deleted.

The interpretation may seem selective when viewed in retrospect, and the triumvirate was not unaware of the value of striking theatrical effects. It is clear, however, that a bold and conscious effort was made to view *Hamlet* in terms of the modern psychological ideas and more open sexuality that had emerged during the previous two decades, and it is likely that the decision to reinterpret parts of the play in this light was jointly agreed upon by Barrymore, Hopkins, and Jones.

The Cast

After his return to New York, Barrymore continued to work privately with Margaret Carrington on vocal technique and interpretation.[31] In mid-September Hopkins began rehearsing alone with his star; at the same time, he turned his attention to casting the play. A number of roles were awarded to actors whose work he had supervised or admired in the past. Whitford Kane, a Shakespearean veteran who had played a Jewish grandfather in Hopkins's production of *The Idle Inn* a few years earlier, remembered that upon hearing of the impending *Hamlet*, "I immediately wrote Mr. Hopkins asking him to let me play my old part of the Gravedigger, and he indulged my wish and engaged me." Soon afterward, however, he began to hear strange rumors about the production. "It was said that trained Shakespearean actors were not going to be used in the cast; that actors with preconceived notions about Hamlet weren't wanted," he remembered. "Everything seemed shrouded in secrecy." He began to wonder why he had been engaged.[32]

The aura of mystery surrounding the production hardly deterred actors from seeking positions in the company. As was the case with *Richard III*, the majority of roles were available, and hundreds of actors sought to fill them when open auditions for *Hamlet* were held in early October. John Lark Taylor, a veteran of the Sothern and Marlowe company, later remembered that

> Arthur Hopkins was preparing a magnificent production of *Hamlet* for John Barrymore, and with much confidence I went to see him. He was not to be seen and the office-boy curtly told me to come back the next day. At the Plymouth Theater the following morning there was a line of actors from the stage-door to the end of the block, like a run on a bank. There were many old friends and a great number I knew only by sight and reputation, all ages, sizes and types, laughing and chatting gayly. Hopkins and stage manager Hurley were seated at a table with a screen back of them, briefly glancing at each actor who filed past. The gentleman ahead of me, a tall, handsome, gray haired popular actor of enviable reputation, walked by without a word being spoken. Hopkins looked at me indifferently, and hardly moving his lips, murmured, "No, I don't think so." And I proceeded on and out.[33]

After several days of looking at actors, however, Hopkins had not been able to find the cast he sought. Soon afterward, he contacted William P. Adams, formerly a stage manager with the Sothern and Marlowe company, who agreed to provide assistance. Adams got in touch with many of the actors he had worked with in the past, several of whom had already auditioned, and invited them to the Plymouth for a second look.[34] A few days later, Taylor, summoned by Adams, again presented himself at the Plymouth. "Margaret Carrington came out of the theater with Barrymore as I went in," he recalled. "She was exceedingly cordial and the three of us chatted for a few minutes and they introduced me to Hopkins." Taylor's testimony reveals that the second series of auditions featured a change in Hopkins's customary method of choosing actors. This time, he asked auditioners to read from the play and was openly willing to consider actors with extensive Shakespearean experience if they seemed flexible enough to adapt to the repressed style of playing he sought. "From the stage I read a bit of Polonius and a little of the First Player," recalled Taylor. "Because of a too resonant voice I was given the First Player instead of Polonius, the part I had hoped to get."[35] Also hired from the Sothern and Marlowe company were Sidney Mather and Frederick Lewis, the Laertes and Horatio; Tyrone Power, a veteran of numerous Shakespearean productions, including several of Augustin Daly's revivals during the 1890s and the 1918 Shakespeare Playhouse production of *Julius Caesar,* was engaged as the King. Within a few days, most of the cast was set, and Hopkins asked Adams to stay on as production stage manager.

Several crucial parts remained to be cast, however. On 17 October, Barrymore wrote to Michael Strange in Paris, informing her that

> Yesterday Hopkins and Margaret and I tried out people in the theatre. . . . Miss [Rosalinde] Fuller who is a folk-song singer went through the part [of Ophelia]. She is a strange unprepossessing little English woman but has a detached rather zany quality – which Margaret says might be developed. She sings infinitely better than she speaks. . . . She is *very* English and has a queer lack of vitality – or humanity – but something very effective might be gotten there perhaps – particularly in the mad scenes.[36]

Blanche Yurka, who was to play Gertrude (although she was in fact five years younger than Barrymore), recalled returning home to find a message from Hopkins awaiting her:

> My family informed me that one day a voice over the telephone had asked for me. When told that I was away on my honeymoon the voice simply said, "This is Arthur Hopkins. When she gets back have her call me." I did. The office interview took about three minutes. A greeting, then, "Would you like to play the Queen to John Barrymore's Hamlet?" . . . I answered, "Maybe." He added, "We want her played rather younger than has been

customary. They are having a reading rehearsal down on the stage. Why not go down and see how you feel about it?" . . . Down I went. The stage of the Plymouth Theatre was bare except for a semi-circle of ordinary wooden chairs on which sat the actors already engaged; a table and a work light completed the picture. Tyrone Power, Sr. had a dark moodiness and a glorious voice – both perfect for the King. Rosalinde Fuller's Tanagra-like figure was lovely for the mad little Ophelia. Only John Barrymore, the Hamlet, was missing; Bill Adams, the stage manager, read his lines. . . . When the rehearsal ended I went upstairs to the little cubicle which was Mr. Hopkins' office. "If you think I can give it what you want," I said, "I would like to do it." "Good," he said. That was all.[37]

Rehearsals

Full rehearsals for *Hamlet* began on Wednesday, 18 October. A total of four weeks were scheduled, with rehearsals beginning at 11 A.M. and lasting until 5 P.M. At the first read-through, Lark Taylor remembered, "We waited expectant and self-conscious. Hopkins, a short, rotund, baby-faced man, made me think of a small boy caught stealing apples. He greeted us shyly, sat near the footlights and also waited expectantly. After an awkward interval John Barrymore nonchalantly strolled in. He and Hopkins shook hands and conferred quietly for a few moments." The actors were then told to draw their chairs into a semicircle, given Temple editions of the play, and told to make cuts as they read. "The first pop out of the box, Hopkins asked me to play Bernardo," Taylor remembered. He had been engaged as the First Player, but Hopkins explained that he wanted his voice for the first line. At the subsequent read-through, recalled Taylor, Barrymore was "letter perfect" in his lines, yet he read quietly, making no attempt to act.[38]

For nearly two weeks thereafter, the company sat and read. "When we really began to rehearse we practically knew our lines from the constant reading," Taylor remembered. He later confessed that he had "rather dreaded rehearsing with [Barrymore], having been told he was a 'perfect fiend,' absolutely impossible at rehearsals and to act with when playing." Yet Barrymore soon proved to be quite the contrary. "Never was there a more considerate or kinder person at rehearsals or on the stage," Taylor commented. "At times he went far out of the way to be kind and courteous. He rarely directed anyone, but occasionally offered a suggestion that was always good. He and Hopkins puzzled us by harping on the company not being Shakespearean. But we soon realized they meant the old style ranting usually associated with Shakespeare."[39]

"I've never known rehearsals to go so smoothly, so easily, before we quite realized it, we were all of us rehearsing without our books," Taylor recalled.[40] Many of the Shakespearean veterans in the cast, however, had difficulty with the new version of the text. "In cutting the play Hopkins carefully retained all lines generally cut and eliminated lines usually spoken," Taylor commented. "The First Player was almost a new part and it was difficult not to say the old lines of the Sothern–Marlowe version. Mather and Lewis had the same trouble with Horatio and Laertes, and John O'Brien never did say all of his lines correctly, though he had less excuse than the rest of us for he had played Polonius with Ben Greet with none of the play cut. One day Hopkins held the book, stopping [O'Brien] almost every line. Finally he smiled and said, 'You had better look those lines over carefully, we want them just as Mr. Shakespeare wrote them."[41]

Hopkins was also faced with the problem of finding a theatre to house his production. The Plymouth was already occupied by Don Marquis's long-running comedy *The Old Soak*, which was still playing to profitable houses. The Cort was considered briefly, but was claimed by Kaufman and Connelly for their new comedy, *Merton of the Movies*. After two weeks of rehearsals Hopkins announced that *Hamlet* would open at the Sam H. Harris Theatre on 42nd Street on Thursday, 16 November – a provident omen, for six years earlier Barrymore had launched his career as a serious actor at the same theatre (then called the Candler) in *Justice*.

Blocking began during the week of 30 October. Soon Whitford Kane began to feel that perhaps some of the strange rumors he had heard about the production were true. Rehearsals, he remembered, "were all conducted with a mysterious air. Standing on an empty stage, I would boldly ask if I were in the correct spot for the grave trap and three or four assistant stage managers would come running and whisper slyly that I was. Then one of them would stealthily propel me a few steps stage right, and say in a low voice, 'Now you stand there for a moment.'"[42] Another unsettling element to many cast members was the production's frank sexuality – a sharp contrast to the bowdlerized, genteel *Hamlet* to which most were accustomed. In an early talk Barrymore told Blanche Yurka of his vision of the first court scene: "'A hunt dinner is in progress; it's a drunken orgy . . . tankards roll off the table . . . slabs of meat are thrown to great hunting dogs . . . court ladies loll with their shoulders and bosoms half bare . . . it is to be a sensuous, dissolute court, dominated by a lecherous king. In the midst of it Hamlet sits, a mute black figure, bathed in firelight.'"[43] More obvious in rehearsal was the lewd quality Rosalinde Fuller brought to her mad scene. Many cast members considered this offensive, but Hopkins and Barrymore were delighted.[44]

"Of rehearsing in the usual manner, of experimenting with the scenes, there was almost none," Blanche Yurka later recalled. Barrymore "obviously had planned his own performance down to the smallest movement; it soon became apparent that our job was to be found in places where his movements required us to be."[45] He could be irate when colleagues were careless with previously determined positions. "I very soon realized that Barrymore expected one to keep to the same business," commented Lark Taylor. "He and Hopkins both left most of us to our own devices. I've never received so little direction at rehearsals, but Barrymore always remembered bits of business or expressions, and would recall them to you if you happened to forget." At times, director and star differed on matters of interpretation. Taylor recalled that on one occasion he was

> placed in something of a quandary by Hopkins and Barrymore being of differing opinions regarding the first line of the play – "Who's there?" Hopkins wanted it without any consciousness of the ghost. Barrymore wanted it the other way – and rightly. Both had advised me privately to do it his way. I settled it by doing it Hopkins' way while he and Barrymore were standing together watching the rehearsal. Instantly, Barrymore called out – "Are you going to do it that way?" I waited for Hopkins to explain, which he did, and, after a few moments of undertone discussion, I was told to do it the way Barrymore wanted it – but not "too loud."[46]

Throughout much of the rehearsal period, Taylor remembered, Barrymore rehearsed very quietly, skipping the longer soliloquies. One day he let himself go in a big speech. "He made us all jump – it was positively electric – and I think made some of the company realize for the first time that this *Hamlet* was going to be something quite unusual," he recalled. "Tyrone Power came over to me, during the rehearsal, and said 'By God! He's going to be great. He's going to make the hit of his life in this part.'" By then, Taylor realized that Barrymore was going to give "a remarkable and sensational" performance, and that he would have Margaret Carrington to thank for a great part of it. "I could see her work in every line he spoke," he remembered.[47]

As rehearsals progressed, one of Hopkins's primary duties, as was the case in earlier collaborations, was to serve as "a weighing machine," revealing to his star when his performance was "short or overweight." "Occasionally," Taylor continued, "Barrymore would say to Hopkins: 'Watch this Arthur.' Then he would do a scene or a long speech, and Hopkins would say: 'No, I don't think so, Jack,' or, 'Yes, that's good,' as the case might be, and generally with an unerring instinct for the most effective way."[48]

Several important developments took place during the week of 6 November – the last full week of rehearsals. Hopkins cut the scene where Claudius questions Hamlet about Polonius's body [IV.iii], which the company had worked on until that point, perhaps because he was worried about the play's length. A good deal of time was spent on improving the dueling scene. "Barrymore had considerable trouble with the fight with Laertes in the last act," Taylor remembered. "He and Mather worked diligently with a fencing-

master, and one day Douglas Fairbanks gave him almost the entire day, trying out stunts that might be effective."[49]

Much time was devoted, as well, to the play scene, which had been almost
completely overlooked until that point. "At every rehearsal," Taylor remembered, "Hopkins said, 'Cut the play scene.' Naturally we were all curious.
Hamlet without the play scene was unthinkable, and we all wondered how it
was to be done. Jack told me that he wanted to do something unique with
it. As he phrased it, 'Something to make them sit up and take notice.'" The
first hint of anything different came early in the week, when a 15-year-old boy,
Frank Hearn, came in to rehearse the Second Player (a part generally played
by an actress), and three mime players began to act the play scene in pantomime while Hearn and Taylor "intoned – or sort of chanted" the lines. Soon
afterward, Barrymore summoned Taylor, Hearn, and the mime players to
Margaret Carrington's suite at the Ambassador Hotel. "We tried out the play
scene in various ways," Taylor remembered, "finally settling that Hearn and
I should kneel on either side of the stage – speaking all the lines of the play,
King, Queen and Lucianus, while the three boys enacted the play in a sort of
exaggerated, conventional manner."[50]

On Monday, 13 November, the cast moved from the Plymouth to the Sam
H. Harris Theatre for dress rehearsals. "We had all dreaded the dress rehearsals, but they were nothing," Taylor commented. "The first meant merely trying on costumes and makeup."[51] The second dress rehearsal, held on Tuesday, 14 November, was a complete run-through featuring numerous pauses,
stops, and starts for technical adjustments. Whitford Kane was excited by his
initial glimpse at the staging of the first court scene; he later remembered
that "I don't think I ever saw a more wonderful looking Hamlet or one so
young." He was dismayed, however, by Barrymore's low-key approach, by the
use of a wavering light for the ghost ("Here my mid-Victorianism rose in
rage"), and by the Oedipal ramifications of the Queen's closet.[52] A prop-
master's oversight that day resulted in a novel bit of business. "When Ophelia came on in the mad-scene," recalled Taylor, "Barrymore looked at her a
moment, then called out: 'Arthur, isn't she going to have any flowers?' Hopkins replied: 'Oh, God! No!' And that was the end of that."[53]

The final dress-rehearsal was, to many observers, the most memorable.
Blanche Yurka recalled:

> One day just before we were to open, word was passed around that [Barry-
> more's] sister, Ethel, was coming to rehearsal. Jack was excited. It was to be
> our first uninterrupted run-through of the play. The thrill of creativity illu-
> minated everyone's performance; in my opinion no later performance we
> gave ever quite equalled it. All through the closet scene I scarcely moved,
> so paralyzing was the intensity of the wild-eyed Hamlet, so compelling his

biting scorn, so poignant his pathos. I could not have moved had I wished to. As the scene ended he whispered to me, "That was perfect. Now for Christ's sake don't let anyone change you one iota."[54]

"Jack didn't dress for it," recalled Ethel Barrymore. "He was just in his ordinary street clothes, and I suppose it was the greatest experience I ever had in a theater. He was superb, magnificent, unforgettable, and had in some mysterious way acquired that magical ease, as if he really were Hamlet. It was for me the fulfilment of all I had ever hoped for him and more."[55]

The Scenery

In April, May, and June 1922, Robert Edmond Jones and Kenneth Macgowan had journeyed to Europe, where for ten weeks they visited the theatres of France, Sweden, Germany, Czechoslovakia, and Austria, seeing close to sixty productions.[56] Among the productions that made a lasting impression were those directed by the innovative German *regisseur* Leopold Jessner and designed by Emil Pirchan at the Prussian State Theater, the Schauspielhaus, in Berlin. The dominant visual element in Jessner's stagings was massive flights of steps – *Jessnertreppen* – for which he had become famous in Europe. The platforms and levels he employed, wrote Macgowan, "are to him what screens, towering shapes, great curtains are to Gordon Craig." The *Jessnertreppen*, he continued, "are the key to the physical things in this director's productions. They give the stage one general shape for each play. They establish a formal quality. . . . And – their main purpose – they provide the director with most interesting opportunities for maneuvering his actors."[57] It was to Jessner's massive flights of steps, which he had seen utilized in the director's productions of *Richard III, Othello,* and Grabbe's *Napoleon oder die Hundert Tage* (*Napoleon; or, The Hundred Days*), that Jones turned in September 1922 after Barrymore had rejected his more radical design concepts.

The resulting unit setting was unabashedly derivative – a fact that went unnoticed by the critics in New York and London. A note of originality, however, lay in Jones's decision to combine the ideas of Jessner and Gordon Craig, for beyond the steps rose an enormous Craig-inspired Romanesque arch. The simple, austere setting represented a return to simplicity after the extravagance and heavy-handed symbolism of *Macbeth.* The five stairs, tapering upward, were nineteen feet wide at the bottom and rose approximately five feet to a platform ten and a half feet wide and five feet deep, upon which Francisco, Bernardo, and Marcellus made their initial entrances via small flights of steps situated left and right. Above the arch, a wall of dull grayish-brown rose beyond the level of the proscenium to a height of approximately fifty-two feet. Angled wings, each with two high windows that mirrored the shape of

Figure 21. Robert Edmond Jones's drawing of the foreground tableau curtains. Reproduced with permission of the estate of Elizabeth Jones.

the arch, extended outward in a half-hexagon. A low platform at the foot of the stairs, fronted by a single low step, extended to the wings, following the angles of the castle walls. The mainstage, fifteen feet deep from the lip to the small step leading to the lower platform, featured a grave trap, center; a semi-circular apron extended four feet into the audience.[58]

Several scenes were played in front of tableau curtains – another common Jessner practice. These served to mask the unit set and were pale green in color; they featured six massive, mystic-looking human figures robed in purple and gold, all identical and resembling to one observer the "illuminations in an ancient Bible." The figures lacked hands and arms, and their faces were blank and surrounded by a halo of pale blue – an effect achieved by shining small spotlights on the heads of the figures whenever the curtain was used (Fig. 21). In general outline, they suggested the representation of the Ghost in the first act.[59]

A cyclorama beyond the arch could be lit to indicate time of day or mood; most scenes took place at night, before a deep blue sky. The same light could be seen through the windows piercing the walls of the castle. Three tableau curtains, black and gold, black, and white, were situated beyond the arch and were closed to mask the cyclorama or brought on one or two feet to create a "window" effect.

At least one company member was taken aback by his initial glimpse of Jones's arch and stairway. "Then I knew," recalled Whitford Kane, "that this was not . . . to be an ordinary *Hamlet* like that of [Forbes-Robertson]; this was to be an up-to-date, modern *Hamlet* of the year [1922]. I felt suddenly very old and mid-Victorian."[60]

Jones was assisted in his efforts by two figures worthy of note. George Schaff, Hopkins's master electrician (c. 1885–1981) was an integral part of the production team, as he had been for *Redemption*, *The Jest*, and *Richard III*. His major contributions were to help Jones realize the revolutionary lighting effects he envisioned and to supervise the technical elements during the run, but his duties went beyond the realm of technical direction. By 1922, one of Hopkins's stage managers later remembered, Schaff "was such an essential component in the Hopkins–Jones–Barrymore combination that Hopkins relied on him to maintain the sort of discipline over Barrymore that was necessary to ensure continuity and consistently high-quality performances by this brilliant, but extremely erratic actor."[61] Just how Schaff did that is not specified. Equally valuable to the Hopkins–Jones–Barrymore productions was Adam Tait (fl. 1918–25), Hopkins's master carpenter, who supervised the construction of Jones's scenic designs.

Jones spent innumerable hours with Schaff to perfect the complex lighting scheme. Spotlight gels in varying shades of pink, rose, purple, green, violet, and blue were used to emphasize the mood of individual scenes and the beauty of the costumes.[62] Five overhead spotlights and two spotlights behind the arch were used to create the effect for the Ghost, who was represented in several scenes by a pale green wavering light. Like Jones's *Jessnertreppen*, however, this was clearly a derivative device and had been used in German and Austrian productions for many years – a fact of which Jones could hardly have been unaware.[63] This, however, was in keeping with Jones's purpose and that of the New Stagecraft in general: the creative application of new European ideas in the American theatre.

The production featured only minimal onstage properties.[64] Hamlet was discovered in the second scene seated in an oak chair. A simple, gold-draped throne served as Claudius's seat of power. The play-within-a-play was enacted in front of a large screen set before the Romanesque arch; a small gold-draped table was brought on for the dueling scene. Hand properties were also kept to a minimum. Hamlet wore a small notebook tablet around his neck, which he used for his business after the "host of heaven" and "rogue and peasant slave" soliloquies. In the closet scene he drew a locket from his blouse and compared it to a similar locket worn by his mother. Whitford

Kane's duties as the First Clown (Gravedigger) were "exceedingly light," he remembered. He had "a spade, but no pickaxe or ropes, and of course there was no earth to shovel." At various intervals he would duck into the grave trap, lay a skull or a bone on his spade, and cast it forth, yet the absence of customary props made him feel as if he were "a backsliding member of the Shakespearean Gravediggers' Union and had betrayed its traditional rulings."[65]

The Costumes

Robert Edmond Jones's costumes, conservative and "historically correct," were based on designs of the late Italian Renaissance rather than a tenth- or eleventh-century Northern European motif. Only a few details – the cloak worn by Hamlet in several scenes and the fur trim on one of the Queen's mantles – suggested Denmark's harsh climate. The designs were executed under the supervision of Lulu Fralick, who for many years had been wardrobe mistress for the Sothern and Marlowe company.

Lark Taylor noted that many of Jones's *Hamlet* costumes were recycled from the disastrous Hopkins–Jones–Lionel Barrymore *Macbeth* and were made of "the cheapest materials" – denim, burlap, flannel, and cotton rep – as opposed to "the rich brocades, damasks and heavy velvets of the Sothern–Marlowe production." Nevertheless, they possessed an undeniable visual impact. Jones used extravagant reds and strong blues and greens, which "against the somber, massive set . . . made the scenes like a series of beautiful old tapestries."[66] Much use was made of color symbolism. The Queen wore red for nearly the entire play, as did several of the court Ladies. For the burial of Ophelia, the entire funeral procession was swathed in flowing white robes, lending the effect of churchly dignity.

Through much of the play, the Queen was costumed in a floor-length gown and fur-trimmed mantle along with a thin headband. Her hair was arranged in youthful blonde ringlets. Ophelia's dress during her early scenes was of similar length and featured a low neckline and gold trim at the sleeves; she wore a mesh Juliet cap with a veil, pinned back and trailing to her waist. In her mad scene, she wore a clinging white gown that enhanced the sensuality of her interpretation. Polonius was costumed in a simple floor-length robe and wore a shoulder-length gray wig and gray beard. The King wore a variation on this design befitting his age and status. His gown featured gold braided circlets around the collar; he wore a salt-and-pepper wig extending to just above the shoulder and a moustache and short beard.

The men of the court wore short tunics extending to midthigh; each featured individualizing details. Horatio wore a thick gold chain around his neck; Laertes's collar was trimmed in eye-catching white. Marcellus, Bernardo, and Francisco wore conical helmets and chain-mail armor, with long swords bucked at their sides. The Gravediggers wore rustic, burlap-based garments; the Second Gravedigger appeared in a cloth headcovering.

According to Taylor, there was much experimentation with costumes during the first dress rehearsal. He found Jones's sketches in some cases to be "rather grotesque," and voiced objections to his initial ideas for the First Player: a "stiff, bristling wig, Chaplin moustache and small goatee." Taylor substituted his own wig, which Jones agreed was better, and reduced his facial hair to a pencil-line moustache and a bit of crepe hair on his chin, which, he claimed, made him look like Shakespeare.[67] The players wore loose, light-colored tunics with dark mantles and shoulder accents; Taylor's mantle, befitting his status as the leader of an otherwise youngish troupe, was longer than the rest. In the play scene, the Players were arrayed in stiff, rich-looking gold robes; the Mime King and Queen wore stylized crowns.

The dress rehearsal experimentation extended to Hamlet's costume. Barrymore "had much difficulty getting just the costume he wanted," Taylor remembered. After many trials he decided on "a plain, simple costume of black silk duveteen," a material "resembling velvet, but with a very close nap, and without the sheen of velvet." His doublet, which reached to midthigh, was slit at the left to reveal a white shirt beneath. Around his neck he wore a simple, three-stranded gold chain. He wore two belts during the production: a sword-belt comprised of metal squares and a leather cincture, studded with jeweled ornaments with an oval buckle to the left, from which hung a dagger. On the ramparts and for Ophelia's burial he wore a floor-length black cloak; when appropriate – on the ramparts and in the King's chapel and Queen's closet – he wore a long sword in a scabbard at his left side. He wore no wig, but rather "used a piece of hair in the back, to give more fullness." His own hair was brushed back and completely concealed the rubber band to which the false hair was attached. His tights contained greaves – padded "symmetricals" used by ballet dancers – to enlarge his thin calves. According to Taylor, he used "a makeup he had used in the movies – pale, and quite dark shadows about his eyes."[68]

Opening Night

"Tonight's the night!" announced the *Evening Mail* on Thursday, 16 November 1922. "At 8 o'clock sharp (due notice having been served by Arthur Hopkins that first nighters will not be seated after that hour until the end of the first scene), the curtain will rise at the Sam H. Harris Theatre and reveal John Barrymore as the melancholy Dane in Mr. Hopkins' production of *Hamlet*." Among the competing attractions playing that evening were George S. Kaufman and Marc Connelly's comedy *Merton of the Movies* at the Cort and Ina

Claire in *The Awful Truth* at Henry Miller's; *Abie's Irish Rose* at the Republic and Somerset Maugham's *Rain,* starring Jeanne Eagels, would go on to establish long and profitable runs. George M. Cohan's *Little Nellie Kelly* was among the musical comedies; Ziegfeld's sixteenth *Follies* was thriving at the New Amsterdam. Significantly, there were also a number of serious dramas. Karl Capek's *R.U.R.* was playing at the Liberty; the premiere American production of Pirandello's *Six Characters in Search of an Author* was at the Princess; Galsworthy's *Loyalties* was at the Gaiety; and Ethel Barrymore was appearing at the Longacre in Hopkins's production of Hauptmann's *Rose Bernd.*

On a cool, clear evening, with temperatures in the low forties and gusting winds, more than a thousand ticketholders – many of the men in formal dress, and many of the women in ermine wraps and evening gowns – entered the Harris Theatre, passing through police barricades beyond which hundreds of gawkers and onlookers had crowded.[69] The most expensive seats were priced at $5.50, fifty cents more than the high end of the scale for *Richard III*, with tickets for the upper balcony priced at $2.20. It was, without question, a glamorous occasion; but as more than one observer noted, the brilliant first-night audience seemed to be in attendance because it was interested in John Barrymore and the innovations of Arthur Hopkins and Robert Edmond Jones and "cared not a picayune about Shakespeare."[70]

Amid the glamour and expectation, however, there was a note of uncertainty. The Hopkins–Jones–Lionel Barrymore *Macbeth* and the Barrymore–Strange *Clair de Lune* had proven to be noteworthy failures, and the aura of artistic triumph and invincibility that had surrounded the earlier efforts of the triumvirate had been shaken. Unlike *Macbeth*, there had been little pre-opening publicity or advance statements by director, designer, or star, merely a simple announcement in the entertainment pages of the metropolitan dailies, stating that "Arthur Hopkins announces the opening performance of John Barrymore in *Hamlet.*"

At 8 P.M, the curtain rose on the Robert Edmond Jones set. Dozens of latecomers were forced to stand at the back of the theatre until the first scene had ended; they surged forward en masse at the beginning of the first court scene. Late arrivals continued to take their seats through the ensuing scene with Polonius, Laertes, and Ophelia, ignoring the ushers' whispered instructions to wait for a suitable interval. "The large, wealthy, and distinguished audience at *Hamlet* the first night acted like restless, unruly, and ill-mannered schoolboys," carped one observer. "They herded up and down the aisles while the scene was on, they rushed, they whispered, and . . . coughed in solos, in duets, in ensembles, and in insidious little undertones which crept up in the pauses on the stage."[71]

It soon became obvious, however, that this evening they would not be disappointed. The audience, wrote Percy Hammond in the *Tribune* (17 November 1922), "was the most excited, at several points, that we have ever seen in a theater." "First nighters who are still on the sunny side of life can recall somewhere between twenty-five and thirty Hamlets, interpreted by the most famous actors of several decades," noted the *Evening Mail* (17 November 1922). "It may be safely doubted, however, that any of them can remember a previous performance which more certainly gripped the heart of a New York audience." A fervor of applause greeted the principals as they took their choreographed bows after the first act. A similarly noisy tribute occurred after the second act, when again the principals appeared before the curtain; for the first time in his managerial career Arthur Hopkins appeared onstage to take a bow. Barrymore responded to an insistent demand by making a brief curtain speech at the end of the second intermission, in which he said that all the members of the company who had played with other Hamlets had been "monuments of tact and hopefulness" and wished the author could have been there to express his appreciation.[72] No curtain calls were taken after the third act – an odd note to modern audiences, yet appropriate to the spirit of the play, for as the *Sun*'s reviewer noted, "after the body of Hamlet was carried away with Fortinbras's soldiers as pallbearers, Hamlet remained dead and Mr. Barrymore did not spoil the reality of his beautiful performance by taking any additional bows" (17 November 1922).

The next day, John Corbin, writing in the *Times*, summed up the impact of the initial performance.

> The atmosphere of historic happening surrounded John Barrymore's appearance last night as the Prince of Denmark; it was unmistakable as it was indefinable. It sprang from the quality and intensity of the applause, from the hushed murmurs that swept the audience at the most unexpected moments, from the silent crowds that all evening long swarmed about the theatre entrance. It was nowhere – and everywhere. In all likelihood we have a new and a lasting Hamlet.

The Performance

Hamlet played for 101 performances during its initial New York season, closing on 9 February 1923. Nine months later Hopkins revived the play at the Manhattan Opera House for a three-week run, and a brief road tour ensued, closing in Cleveland on 26 January 1924. A London engagement followed the next year. During this time Barrymore presented audiences with not one but many Hamlets. "As always," commented Arthur Hopkins, "his first performance was his best. Some of his later were embarrassingly bombastic. He did not have the gift of knowing when he was right. . . . Once he had successfully created a part he was given to embroidering, and his embroidering was not good. . . . It was as though once he had made the mold he proceeded to break it."[73] Barrymore was given to altering his stage business and line readings to suit the mood of the moment, and his onstage eccentricities became the stuff of theatrical legend. Other changes were directorial in nature. Many of the entrances and exits were altered during the initial run, and several scenes were reblocked in their entirety. The majority of these alterations are well-documented, however, and most emerge as only minor variations in the staging and its central performance. A study of the evidence reveals that Barrymore's blocking and scansion remained fairly constant throughout. There were numerous exceptions, of course, given his penchant for spontaneity and experimentation. During the initial New York run, for example, he began trying to get in a word edgewise during Polonius's lengthy cataloguing of the Players' versatility [II.ii, 415–421], a comic bit of scene stealing that was ultimately abandoned. The blocking of this same scene called for Hamlet to lean against the back of his chair at several points, which more often than not came several lines earlier or later than in the original scheme. Still, for the most part Barrymore adhered to the Hopkins staging and the scansion he had carefully worked out with Margaret Carrington. The original blocking and business, significant variations, and many of the line readings can be reconstructed in detail by examining the wealth of evidence that exists.

Documentation of the Production

Barrymore's Hamlet is among the most fully documented stage performances of the twentieth century. In the weeks following the New York opening, dozens of newspaper and magazine reviews were published, many of which captured for posterity significant details of the production. In addition, there were critical columns, related articles, and letters from playgoers. Indeed, throughout much of the initial run *Hamlet*-mania (and Barrymore-mania) swept New York. The media flurry decreased during the second season, when relatively little column space was devoted to the revival – the production was by then taken for granted by many of the critics. In London, however, the excitement began anew; more than forty reviewers and columnists were granted seats for the British premiere. To these sources may be added written accounts by Arthur Hopkins, Lark Taylor, Blanche Yurka, Whitford Kane, and others, along with the written and oral recollections of witnesses who retained vivid memories of Barrymore's *Hamlet* many years after the fact.

There is a wealth of audiovisual evidence. The official production photographs by Francis Bruguiere preserve details of many of the costumes, and Jones's drawings capture his sets for posterity.[74] There are a number of sound recordings of excerpts.[75] Several of these were made during the 1930s and bear only a faint resemblance to Barrymore's original performance; his weary, exaggerated readings reveal the extent to which his skills had eroded in the years since he had performed Hamlet on stage. As in *Richard III*, however, comparisons with earlier recordings and written documentation can be revealing, for even in decline Barrymore's scansion retained much of the interpretation worked out for the original production. Perhaps the most intriguing audiovisual source is the *Hamlet* screen test Barrymore made for John Hay Whitney's Pioneer Pictures in 1933.[76] This test, directed by Robert Edmond Jones (with assistance from Margaret Carrington, who again coached Barrymore for the role), features Hamlet's first encounter with the Ghost [I.iv] and the scene with the King at prayer [III.iii], and retains the staging of the original New York production. Barrymore was 51 at the time, as the occasional closeup is quick to reveal, yet his voice retains a youthful timbre and his readings are subtle and powerful – in sharp contrast to his radio broadcast of the play a mere four years later.

The most detailed documentation of the stage business of Barrymore's Hamlet is contained in promptbook records of the production. Four promptbooks were made during the initial run, second season, and tour by Lark Taylor, who functioned as the production's unofficial historian. Taylor (1881–1946), who in addition to Bernardo and the First Player took over the role of Fortinbras when the actor who originated the part was dismissed by Hopkins after opening night, was a Tennessee native and a graduate of Vanderbilt University. Early in his career he appeared in Daly's last revival of *The Taming of the Shrew;* for many years he was a mainstay of the Sothern and Marlowe company, playing Polonius, Capulet, Ross in *Macbeth,* and Frederick in *As You Like It.* Taylor had developed the habit of making souvenir promptbooks while a member of the Sothern and Marlowe company; over the course of nearly two decades he made more than twenty promptbooks of their Shakespearean revivals. From the first, Taylor was aware that with Barrymore he was taking part in a historic production. On the day of the initial rehearsal he began making notes in both a personal copy of the play and the Temple edition provided by Hopkins, and he continued to add material through the rehearsal period and first and second seasons. Taylor's efforts were encouraged by Barrymore and the cast, whose signatures he solicited for each of the four volumes. Significant changes in stage business occurring during the run were recorded and often dated. Ironically, Taylor much preferred Sothern's interpretation of the role. He later commented that "I do not think Barrymore's Hamlet is as fine or as big as [Sothern's], nor could the production in any way be compared with the Sothern and Marlowe production for beauty and impressiveness." He granted that "parts of Barrymore's performance were more effective – a little more electric and thrilling," but concluded that "never once did he approach the princely bearing, the scholarly dignity, of Sothern."[77] These and similar comments reflect both a conservative nature and loyalty to the actor-manager who had employed Taylor steadily for much of his adult life. He was aware, however, of the profound impact Barrymore's impersonation made on the public consciousness and dutifully recorded the stage business and two anecdotal accounts of the production.

An equally detailed (and at times complementary) account of the blocking and stage business is contained in William P. Adams's stage manager's promptbook, donated by his widow to the theatre collection at Lincoln Center in 1976. This was made between the first and second seasons from an earlier working promptbook, and was used during second-season rehearsals as well as during the second season and tour. Adams's typescript contains a number of details not included by Taylor, yet they corroborate each other on most significant points. Changes during the second season and tour – the inclusion of an actor on stage portraying the Ghost, for example – are indicated by notes in pencil and in pen. In addition, the Adams promptbook contains cuts and stets of several dozen lines to which Taylor does not refer; these are discussed in the Notes and in Appendix B.

The major promptbook records of Barrymore's *Hamlet* are as follows:[78]

1. Lark Taylor's First-Season Promptbook
(Folger Shakespeare Library, Washington, D.C.)[79]

A Roycroft edition, this was Taylor's souvenir promptbook started at the first reading of the play on 18 October 1922. It contains autographs of the first-season cast, drawings and approximate dimensions of the scenery, music for the production, and detailed stage business, including Hamlet's duel with Laertes. It was finished on 10 February 1923, the day after the original run ended.

2. Lark Taylor's First- and Second-Season Promptbook
(Vanderbilt University Library, Nashville)[80]

This is the Temple edition Taylor received at the first rehearsal on 18 October 1922, and contains first-season cuts, an account of the Moscow Art Theatre's visit on 1 February 1923, changes in the cast for the second season, a preliminary tour itinerary, and notations from the second season, including the cutting of the recorder scene.

3. Lark Taylor's Second-Season Promptbook
(Folger Shakespeare Library)[81]

Another Roycroft edition, which Taylor began to prepare in Philadelphia on 1 January 1924; it was completed in New York on 12 February 1924 and contains notes on second-season cast changes, a curtain plot, drawings of the set, and autographs with accompanying Hamlet quotes from the second-season cast, as well as much stage business and an account of closing night in Cleveland.

4. Lark Taylor's Overall Production Record Promptbook
(Vanderbilt University Library)[82]

A third Roycroft edition dated November 1922, but including material from both seasons and the tour (Fig. 22). It contains a reproduction of a J. S. Sargent drawing of Barrymore, self-portraits in character by Frank Hearn, E. J. Ballantine, and Cecil Clovelly, a light plot, and a property plot. This promptbook features transcriptions of stage business from earlier Taylor promptbooks and contains the signatures of the first season cast and second season replacements.

5. William P. Adams's Stage Manager's Promptbook
(Lincoln Center)[83]

Adams's working copy of the text, made between the first and second seasons for second-season rehearsals. Typewritten on onionskin paper, with three holes punched for insertion into a notebook; later bound. Much typewritten stage business as it stood at the end of the first season, with stage manager's cues in parentheses; additional pen and pencil notes on second-season stage business and cuts and restorations to the text. Also includes property, lighting, and scenery plots, which Taylor copied into his own promptbooks.

6. Barrymore's Studybook (The Players, New York)[84]

A Temple edition that contains partial cuts to the text (other parts are cut minimally if at all, and cuts to Hamlet's lines are incomplete), occasional word emphases and notes on interpretation by Barrymore, and several drawings, including a self-portrait as Hamlet lying dead at the end of the play.

The Taylor and Adams promptbooks contain a host of contradictions, yet most are relatively minor, involving Hamlet moving, sitting, or leaning a few lines earlier or later than in other promptbook sources. The majority of these differences arise from the business being noted at different times during the run. (Significant differences in stage business are cited in the Notes.) Promptbook notations of alterations made during the initial run (the addition of an iron gateway in the graveyard scene, for example) and during the second season and tour (most notably the physical appearance of the Ghost

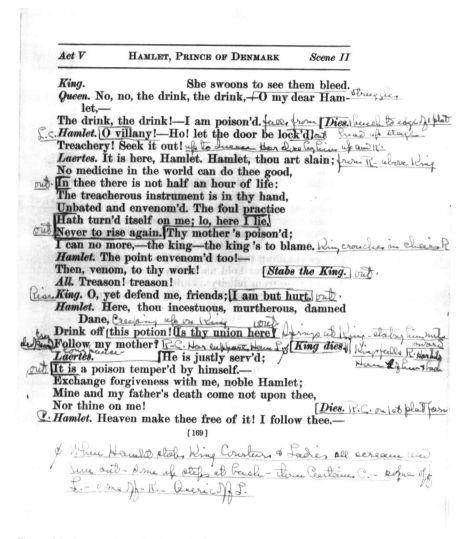

Figure 22. A page from Lark Taylor's 1922–4 production record promptbook for *Hamlet.* Courtesy Jean and Alexander Heard Library, Vanderbilt University.

and the elimination of the apron) are described in the Notes and in ensuing sections of this chapter.

The majority of the stage business in the promptbooks and most of the review evidence concerns the initial New York season. Occasionally in the reconstruction of the production that follows, I have drawn upon critical comments from the second season and tour and the London staging to provide a more complete record. All stage directions are given from the actors' perspective. Word emphases are taken mainly from the recordings, although occasionally they are indicated elsewhere. The full pauses in Hamlet's speech are, for the most part, from Taylor; as in the reconstruction of *Richard III,* I have used the symbol [/] to indicate a slight hesitation, taken in nearly all cases from the recordings but occasionally from other sources. All sources for these readings are cited in the Notes. As in Chapter 2, emphases are indicated in the text by italics, and, in the case of strong emphasis, small capital letters.

The Text

The Barrymore–Hopkins–Jones *Hamlet* was given in three acts, with ten-minute intervals after the "rogue and peasant slave" soliloquy and the Queen's closet scene. The text, in retrospect, seems as traditionally actor-centered as any presented by a nineteenth-century actor-manager; yet it did not differ radically from most Shakespearean acting versions presented by commercial managers in the 1920s. Here it is important to remember that in 1922 complete or near-complete texts and rapid verse speaking were still a novelty (as, for example, with Poel's amateurs or Ben Greet's company) and were more easily presented with the shorter plays, as was the case with Barker's Savoy productions. In 1919, William Archer and George Bernard Shaw had engaged in a lively debate about cutting the plays, conducted in the pages of the *Fortnightly Review,* but they left the issue far from resolved.[85]

It seems likely that one of Hopkins's primary concerns was to present the play at a length his audience would accept without protest. He deleted many of the subplots and cut what he considered to be obscure and overly rhetorical passages; his aim, in all probability, was to clarify the main story line. This decision was also pragmatic, for much of the psychological impact of the production would arise from Barrymore's slow, "conversational" delivery of the text; the production ran three and a half to four hours, even with one-third of the lines deleted. In New York, little exception would be taken to the much-abridged acting version. A few critics expressed minor reservations on the excision of the recorder scene, but most found the text to be adequately full. This is surprising in light of Walter Hampden's 1919–20 production, which featured the retention of Cornelius, Voltimand, and Reynaldo, and a relatively full Fortinbras subplot, but underscores the fact that the early 1920s were still a time of textual transition. The movement toward fuller texts had made significant inroads, but in America, at least, the tradition of cutting Shakespeare for the sake of convenience and to emphasize the leading performer was accepted with only minor quibbling. (The response of the London critics, discussed in Chapter 4, was altogether different.)

The most notable restorations were many of the play's sexual references, traditionally deleted and excluded in the acting versions used at the time by

Hampden and E. H. Sothern. These are discussed in Appendix B, as are deletions, interpolations, and occasional inconsistencies in the promptbooks. All line numberings refer to the Temple edition.[86]

Barrymore's Conception of the Role

During the last month of the initial New York run, Barrymore discussed his conception of the character in an interview given to Beauvais Fox of the *New York Tribune* (14 January 1923).[87] He described Hamlet as "every man with a fine spirit," yet his overall view of the character was that of an intellectually gifted aristocrat with a highly strung, artistic nature, a compulsive thinker and rationalizer whose tragedy lay in his "inability to compromise with life." Hamlet, he commented, was "super-sane," an "artist in spirit and intelligence" who happened to "be born a gentleman." A man "so sensitive, so artistic, so fine, has a prophetic sense," he added, and would know the truth "without the halting aid of the evidential process"; yet at the same time "a vision and a touch so sensitive would make for procrastination in action." Hamlet's intellectual nature, the actor remarked, made him "inordinately just" and hesitant to act until he was absolutely certain of the truthfulness of the ghostly disclosures.

The decision to highlight Hamlet's wit and irony, along with his aristocratic nature, was a deliberate one. Hamlet, Barrymore continued,

> is a great gentleman and has all the attributes of one. . . . [He] is full of consideration for others; his history before his soul-shattering cataclysm is that of an enemy of restraint, suspicion, gloom or resentment. He has a sense of humor, is intensely human and, even when dreadfully wounded in spirit, he cloaks his feelings, as is inevitable with people of finer instinct and breeding. Tortured and outraged from the very opening of the action, he has his hysterical outbursts, but he has too much charm, too much humanity, to be gloomy or lugubrious when he is in control. In his parting with Ophelia, with whom he is very deeply in love, he spares her the truth, and indeed his knowledge of her and his knowledge of most human beings, as is the case with every finely tuned spirit, is too deep for any explanation!

The character, he commented,

> has irony, which every wise person must have whose soul rebels against conditions instead of accepting them. I believe he had the vibrant, highly sensitized and beautiful nature of an artist, without the cosmic energy to make his own conditions as another artist, Whitman, did, for instance. The slings and arrows of outrageous fortune bounded off Whitman as they would off the Rocky Mountains. But Hamlet was a shriller and more highly attenuated instrument.

"And isn't it extraordinary," he concluded, "that the most popular character ever written should apparently be defeated by life instead of transcending it?"

THE FOLLOWING IS A RECONSTRUCTION of what the audience might have witnessed during a "typical" performance of Barrymore's Hamlet. It is made, of course, with full knowledge that no such thing ever existed.[88]

Act I

Act I, scene i. *Elsinore. A platform before the castle.* [Temple edition I.i, 175 lines cut to 92]

The house lights dim. When the curtain rises on the Robert Edmond Jones set (Fig. 23), the stage is faintly lit; the deep blue night sky can be seen through the central arch. A short silence; a few seconds later we hear a drum roll, then a flourish of trumpets from offstage left, followed by four drum beats. As the music concludes, Francisco, on guard, enters from the right on the upper platform. He is wearing a conical helmet and chain-mail armor; a long sword hangs in a scabbard at his side and he carries a spear. He paces slowly down the short flight of steps at the right, crosses the platform, and goes up the steps at the opposite side and off. He returns and goes up the right-hand steps, again disappearing out of sight. He goes down the steps again. As he reaches the third step from the bottom, Bernardo – fearful and anxious – calls from offstage, left of the platform: "Who's there?"[89]

Francisco halts, holds his spear at arms, and replies, "Nay, answer me: stand and unfold yourself." Bernardo calls out, "Long live the king!" and enters from the left down the short flight of steps to the platform. The blue light on the backdrop throws the figures of the watchmen into bold relief. "Bernardo?" asks Francisco. "He," Bernardo replies, crossing to the center of the platform. Bernardo pauses an instant, fearfully, as he asks, "Have you had [/] quiet guard?"[90] "Not a mouse stirring," Francisco replies. Bernardo's "Well, good night," is an expression of relief. After "If you do meet Horatio and Marcellus,/ The rivals of my watch, bid them make haste," he crosses to the right in back of Francisco and exits up the steps.

As soon as he is off, Horatio and Marcellus are heard in ad-lib conversation off the top platform. After Francisco's "I think I hear them. Stand, ho! Who is there?" Horatio and Marcellus enter down the left steps. They salute Francisco by raising their right hands above their heads, palm out. Francisco returns their salutes.[91] "Friends to this ground," Horatio replies, crossing to left center. "And liegemen to the Dane," Marcellus adds, crossing above and

Figure 23. The Robert Edmond Jones *Hamlet* set. Courtesy Mander & Mitchenson Collection.

to the right of Horatio. After Francisco bids them good night, he exits up the right-hand stairs.

Bernardo reenters down the steps at the right when called by Marcellus. He crosses to right center. Horatio salutes him; Bernardo returns the salute. Marcellus makes first mention of the Ghost: "What, has this thing appear'd again to-night?" After Bernardo's "I have seen nothing," Horatio laughs. Marcellus comments that he has brought the skeptical Horatio to confirm what he has seen, and Horatio, after his reply – "Tush, tush, 'twill not appear" – laughs slightly. At Bernardo's bidding to sit and hear the story of what he has seen the past two nights, Horatio reclines on the steps at the left and laughingly agrees. Bernardo takes a step toward Horatio and begins his story, only to be interrupted by Marcellus, who suddenly looks off right; he clutches Bernardo's arm and exclaims, "Peace, break thee off; look, where it comes again!" A strong spotlight comes up from offstage right, spilling over onto the right platform area and distorting the faces of the watchers.[92] Bernardo quickly looks off right, crowds back against Marcellus in terror, and adds, "In the same figure, like the king that's dead" (he points off right). Horatio sits up, staring offstage, on Marcellus's "Thou art a scholar; speak to it, Horatio." Bernardo exclaims, "Looks it not like the king? (he points offstage) mark it, Horatio." After "It would be spoke to" he shrinks back.[93]

Horatio attempts to question the offstage apparition; he rises on "by heaven I charge thee, speak!" and crosses right on "Stay! speak, speak! I charge thee, speak! Stay, illusion!/ If thou hast any sound, or use of voice,/ Speak to me . . ."[94] The light fades. "'Tis gone, and will not answer," Marcellus comments. Bernardo, close to Horatio and behind him, clutches his waist and tells him, looking into his face, ". . . Is not this something more than fantasy?/ What think you on't?" He looks off right. Horatio marvels at what he has seen.

Marcellus reiterates that the Ghost has appeared the past two nights, which to Horatio "bodes some strange eruption to our state." "It was about to speak, when the cock crew," Bernardo comments.[95] After Horatio's ensuing line, Marcellus draws a bit to the left; Horatio draws to the right and turns to Marcellus; Bernardo stands behind them to listen to Marcellus's speech about the season "Wherein our Savior's birth is celebrated" (all bow their heads and cross themselves on "Savior's").[96] Horatio, standing right center, indicates off left that "the morn, in russet mantle clad,/Walks o'er the dew of yon high eastward hill." As dawn comes to the guards on the battlements of Elsinore a faint pink tinge strikes their helmets.[97] Horatio invites the watchmen to impart the news of what they had seen to Hamlet, "for, upon my life/ This spirit, dumb to us, will speak to him." Marcellus agrees; they exit up the stairs at the left, Marcellus first, followed by Bernardo and Horatio. The house curtain is lowered.

This scene featured one rather than two "entrances" by the Ghost, who is "seen" offstage by the watchmen and Horatio. No lighting effect is mentioned in any of the promptbooks. It is likely, however, that a strong radiance was seen at the right entrance to the top platform, for no mention is made in any of the promptbooks of the midnight-to-dawn progression noted by a reviewer. It seems equally probable that no sound effects accompanied the Ghost's "appearance" as they did in later scenes, for these are clearly noted in Adams and Taylor.

The evidence indicates that Hopkins cast the actors in this scene for their vocal ability to bring off the ghostly effect. Taylor's "too resonant voice" was the primary reason he was asked to play Bernardo; during the second season Alexander Woollcott remarked that "the [casting] change we most regret is that which has taken place in the little role of Marcellus. Somehow something is lost when the clear, curiously thrilling voice of E. J. Ballantine no longer sounds out on the nipping and the eager air, filling the scene with the prophecy of drama down the road" (*Herald,* 1 December 1923).

Act I, scene ii. *A room of state in the castle.* [Temple edition, I.ii, 258 lines cut to 216]

The scene is changed behind the house curtain. The gold and black curtains are closed behind the central arch. A throne-bench, with gold drapery, is placed on the lower platform at the left. The Hamlet chair, with a black cloak draped over the left arm, is placed right center, about three feet below the break in the steps.[98]

As the house curtain rises we hear a long roll of drums and a flourish of trumpets from the offstage orchestra. The stage lights start to come on during the last measure of curtain music. The music ceases, and we hear the hushed sound of whispered conversation.[99] Hamlet is discovered seated in his chair, tense and "listless with grief," a "thing entirely apart from the life and movement of the court." His right arm is draped over the right arm of the chair, and his left elbow rests on the chair's opposite arm. He supports his head with his left hand; his head is bent slightly forward and to the right and his eyes are downcast. The Queen sits on the throne-bench. The King stands left center, talking to the group above the Queen. Polonius stands center stage just below the lower platform. Laertes stands to the left of Polonius. Six Ladies and four Lords of the court are grouped on the platform and steps above the Queen. They are "lolling in amorous groups." All the courtiers wear flaring reds and greens and blues, with touches of gold in the robes of the King, Queen, and attendants (Fig. 24).[100]

When the lights are fully up, the King turns to the front; the whispering ceases abruptly. The King begins: "Though yet of Hamlet our dear brother's death . . ." Hamlet lifts his eyes at the King's first words; throughout the address to the court, he is "silent, morose, suspicious," yet reveals "with commendable economy of effect" his deep interest in the King's speech.[101] After ". . . we with wisest sorrow think on him,/ Together with remembrance of ourselves," the King crosses to below the Queen and stands with one foot on the step leading to the first platform. On "Therefore our sometime sister," he takes the Queen's hand; after "now our Queen" he kisses it. On "For all, our thanks," he rests his right hand on the throne; all bow except Hamlet and the Queen.[102]

The King addresses Laertes regarding a request he has made. Laertes takes a step toward the King, kneels before him, and asks permission to return to France. After the King's "What says Polonius?" Laertes rises and Polonius crosses to downstage right of his son; Laertes steps back to him.[103] Polonius gives his approval and the King grants the request; Laertes exits left.

On "But now, my cousin Hamlet, and my son –" the King "looks at Hamlet smilingly." Hamlet looks him in the eyes for a moment, then looks away. Slight pause.[104] And then, aside, "A little more than kin, and less than kind." After the King asks, "How is it that the clouds still hang on you?" Hamlet looks back at the King and replies, "Not so, my lord; I am too much i' the sun." He is "taciturn and cryptic" in his exchange with his mother. After she tells him that death is "common," he replies "Ay, madam (pause), it is common."[105] When the Queen asks, "Why seems it so particular with thee?" he replies, "Seems, madam! *nay it is;* (quickly) I *know* (rising tone) not 'seems.'[106]/ 'Tis not alone my inky cloak, *good mother,*/ (he fingers his "inky cloak" as it is mentioned)[107] Nor customary suits of solemn black,/ . . . Together with all forms, moods, *shapes* of grief,/ That can denote me truly: these indeed *seem,*/ For they are actions that a man might (slight pause) *play:/ But I have that within which passeth show* (slowly);/ *These* (slight pause) but the trappings and the suits of woe."[108]

"'Tis sweet and commendable in your nature, Hamlet,/ To give these mourning duties to your father," the King replies, but he grows increasingly stern as he tells him that "to persevere/ In obstinate condolement is a course/ Of impious stubbornness; 'tis unmanly grief." Hamlet looks at the King; the Queen puts her left hand out and touches the King's right hand, gesturing him to be calm.[109] He starts, and again "becomes smiling" as he urges Hamlet to "throw to earth/ This unprevailing woe, and think of us/ As of a father"; he urges him to remain at court rather than return to Wittenberg. The Queen's "I pray thee, stay with us; go not to Wittenberg" is followed by a long pause of about ten seconds. Hamlet looks at the Queen and then looks away before replying, "I shall in all my best obey you, madam." On the King's "Madam, come," he takes the Queen's left hand; she rises from the throne and comes to his right. Hamlet rises. On the King's "Come away," the tympani and trumpet flourish that introduced the scene is reprised; the King, Queen, and Polonius, followed by the court, exit left.[110]

Hamlet looks after the King, then sits in his chair, his right arm, with fist clenched, resting on his right knee, his left hand clutching the arm of the chair. He begins his soliloquy slowly, quietly, and in a low voice: "O, that this

Figure 24. The first court scene in London – a variation on the American staging. Courtesy Hulton Getty Picture Collection.

too too solid flesh would melt,/ Thaw and resolve itself into a dew! (high pitch)/[111] Or that the Everlasting had not fix'd/ His canon 'gainst self-slaughter!"[112] Throughout, he speaks "with the calm deliberation of a person moodily thinking out loud." His delivery is "full of hesitations" and reveals "a mind so full that he [has] to pause and find exactly the thought he [wishes] to express and the words to clothe that thought."[113] His "O God! God!/ How weary, stale, flat and unprofitable/ Seem to me all the uses of this world! (gesture) Fie on't! ah fie! 'tis an unweeded garden,/ That grows to seed; things rank and gross in nature/ Possess it *merely*" is "a withering declaration . . . replete with the significant uncertainty of the suspicion troubling and perplexing him."[114] He is "almost in tears" as he remembers how his father was "so loving to my mother,/ That he might not beteem the winds of heaven/ Visit her face too roughly."[115] On "why she would *hang* on him," he puts heavy stress on "hang" and almost lets the "him" disappear.[116] "Let me not think on't – " is drawn out, and on "Frailty, thy name is woman! –" he indicates surprise; his delivery becomes firmer and more regular thereafter.[117] He laments his mother's hasty marriage, concluding, "O, most wicked speed, to post/ With such [/] *dexterity* [/] to incestuous sheets!/ It is not, (he rises from his chair) nor it cannot come to good:/ But break (facing left, he pauses about five seconds), my heart (he crosses up to the first platform, left center), for I must hold my tongue!"[118]

Horatio, followed by Bernardo and Marcellus, enters at the right. Horatio crosses to below and left of the Hamlet chair. Marcellus, with Bernardo above him, stands at the right. Horatio greets Hamlet with "Hail to your lordship!" Hamlet turns to him as he speaks: "I am glad to see you well:/ *Horatio,* (he springs downstage center and takes Horatio's hands; he is again the "boyish comrade of happier hours") – or I do *forget* myself." On "Sir, my good friend," he clasps Horatio's shoulders and asks him joyously, ". . . And what make you from Wittenburg, Horatio?" He looks at Marcellus then addresses him cordially: "*Marcellus?* . . . I am very *glad* to see *you.*" Bernardo bows after Hamlet greets him with "Good *even*, sir."[119]

Hamlet again asks Horatio why he left Wittenberg, and after Horatio replies, "A truant disposition, good my lord," he tells him jovially: "I would not hear your enemy say so." On "I know you are no truant" he laughs slightly and again grasps Horatio's shoulders. After he asks, "But what is your *affair* in Elsinore?" there is a burst of ribald laughter from offstage left. Hamlet looks left. A pause, and then: "We'll teach you to drink deep ere you depart." Horatio replies, "My lord, I came to see your father's funeral." Pause. Hamlet tells him, "I pray thee, do not *mock* me, fellow-*student;* (slight pause)/ I *think* it was to *see* my *mother's wedding*/ . . . Thrift, *thrift,* Horatio!/ the *funeral baked*-meats/ Did [/] *coldly* [/] furnish forth the *marriage tables.*"[120]

Long pause. Hamlet turns to Horatio, draws close, and earnestly delivers a partial aside: (confidentially) "Would I had met my *dearest foe* in *heaven*/ Or ever I had *seen* that *day*, Horatio!" Long pause. Hamlet looks out straight ahead. His voice becomes husky and tremulous and he is close to tears: "My *father!* – methinks I see my *father* (tenderly)."[121] Horatio, a bit agitated, replies, "O where, my lord?" Hamlet looks outward with a half-smile: "In my *mind's* eye, Horatio/. . . . He was *a man,* (pause) take him for *all* in *all*/ (long pause – overcome by emotion – then sadly) I shall not look upon his *like again.*" He walks slowly a few steps toward left center to hide his emotions. Pause. Horatio waits until Hamlet is center stage before offering, "My lord, I think I saw him yesternight." Hamlet, still turned away trying to regain self-control, replies, uncomprehendingly, "*Saw?* [/] *who?*" Pause. He turns and stares wonderingly at Horatio, who tells him, "My lord, the king your father." "The *king* (pause) my *father!*" Horatio asks him to listen to his story. A pause, and then Hamlet replies hesitatingly, "For *God's love,* (he takes a step right, then quickly) *let me hear.*"

Horatio recounts the events of the previous evening. There is a tense pause, followed by Hamlet's "*But* (pause) where *was* this?" Marcellus interjects, "My lord, upon the platform where we watch'd." Pause, then Hamlet asks, "Did you not *speak* to it?" After Horatio's reply Hamlet pauses wonderingly; he looks out and speaks with effort: "'Tis very strange."[122] Horatio swears to the truth of his story. Slight pause, then Hamlet responds, ". . . *Hold* you the *watch* to-*night?*" Marcellus and Bernardo reply that they do.

Pause. They tell him the Ghost was "Arm'd . . . from head to foot" and Hamlet asks (intently to Horatio) "Then (pause) saw you not his face?" Horatio tells him of the pale, sorrowful countenance. Pause, then Hamlet asks Horatio, "And fix'd his eyes upon you?" Horatio replies, "Most constantly." Pause. Hamlet looks toward the front: "I would I had been there." Horatio replies, "It would have much amazed you," and Hamlet, astonished, tells him "Very like, very like."[123] Pause. Hamlet looks at Horatio, then asks, "Stay'd it long?" He pauses and glances at Horatio before "His beard was grizzled? no?" and again pauses after Horatio describes it as "a sable silver'd." Looking outward, he continues quietly, "I will *watch* to-*night;/* Perchance 'twill *walk again.*" Horatio, at the front of the stage, replies "I warrant it will." After Hamlet, still looking outward, resolves to speak to the apparition, he pauses, then turns to the others and requests their silence about what they have seen and may see again that night. After "I will requite your loves" he steps upstage left: "*So* [/] *fare* you *well:/* Upon the *platform,* 'twixt *eleven* and *twelve,/* I'll *visit* you." Horatio, Marcellus, and Bernardo reply, "Our duty to your honor." They bow and start to go. Hamlet stops them with "Your *loves*" (all stop; he crosses to Horatio and places his hands on his shoulders) "Your *loves,* as *mine* to *you: farewell.*"[124] Bernardo bows out to the right; Marcellus and Horatio follow.

Hamlet, alone, stands at the left and comments on what he has heard: "My *father's spirit* [/] in *arms!* (high) all is not *well;/* I doubt some *foul play:* (he crosses downstage right) would the *night* were *come!*" (quite emotional, almost a sob) He crosses upstage center: "Till then [/] sit *still,* my *soul:* (then, harshly) *foul deeds* will *rise,* (breath)/ Though all the *earth* [/] *o'erwhelm them,* [/] (quietly, low tone) "to *men's eyes.*" After a short pause he starts to exit right. He hesitates, glares at the throne, then departs. As he exits the lights dim out. The house curtain is lowered.[125]

The initial tone of sensuality in this scene was mentioned by Barrymore in his 14 January 1923 interview in the *Tribune.* "In *Hamlet* you feel the voluptuous atmosphere of the Danish court. The whole palace knows about the royal liaison prior to the murder of the old King. All the characters are gossiping about it, though the scandal is muffled in courtly robes. I felt that the carousing and sensuous atmosphere, like a great purple waterfall, ought to run throughout the whole piece." He added, however, that "we were baffled when we undertook to indicate it on the stage." The whispering at the beginning of the scene, described by Margaret Webster in her accounts of the London *Hamlet,* was an innovation of the 1925 production, but since it proved an effective piece of business I have included it here.[126]

In the same interview, Barrymore commented upon Hamlet's instinctive distrust of the King, and on his fondness for Horatio. The Prince, he stated, "clearly divines the quality of his associates in the court of Denmark. He knows that Horatio's isn't a brilliant mind. But he loves him because he is real. He discerns in Horatio something that is lacking in either the King, Queen, Rosencrantz or the others, and that is character in the noblest sense."

Act I, scene iii. *A room in Polonius's house.* [Temple edition, I.iii, 136 lines cut to 87 $^1/_2$]

Behind the house curtain, the tableau curtains with their six massive figures are drawn on from either side of the stage, just below the first platform. The house curtain rises; the lights come up after the curtain is fully raised and everything is set. Six "baby spots" from above focus on the heads of the tableau curtain figures, creating the illusion of halos. Ophelia (right center) and Laertes (left center) are discovered.

Laertes prepares to embark; he cautions his sister about Hamlet's obligations to the state and urges her to resist his efforts to capture her heart or her "chaste treasure." Ophelia acknowledges his concern and cautions him slyly to resist similar temptations in France. Polonius enters through the vent in the curtains. Laertes kneels for his father's blessing and lecture ("Neither a borrower nor a lender be"). Afterward he rises: "Most humbly do I take my leave, my lord." He crosses to Ophelia and takes her hands to bid her farewell, then exits through the curtains.

Polonius crosses to the left of Ophelia and inquires about what Laertes had told her and her relations with Hamlet. After his "Do not believe his vows," Ophelia starts to protest but he quickly cuts her off before she can speak: "I would not, in plain terms, from this time forth,/ Have you so slander any moment leisure,/ As to give words or talk with the Lord Hamlet./ Look to't I charge you: (he crosses up to the opening of the curtains, turns to Ophelia, then speaks in a more gentle manner) come your ways." Ophelia replies, "I shall obey, my lord" and exits through the curtains, followed by Polonius. The lights dim out as they exit.[127]

Polonius was played "entirely for comedy," according to Lark Taylor, who thought his portrayal to be almost "the worst performance in the play." John S. O'Brien's performance was generally admired, however, despite being played along broader lines than usual; according to the *Sun* he "succeeded in being genuinely comic, and yet never stepped out of the part" (17 November 1922).[128]

Act I, scene iv. *The platform.* [Temple edition, I.iv, 91 lines cut to 64, and I.v. 191 lines cut to 168 ¹/₂; scenes played continuously]

The tableau curtains are pulled off in darkness. The lights come up on the bare stage; the archway is lit to suggest soft moonlight and a deep blue night sky. After a short pause, Hamlet enters stage left on the upper platform, followed by Horatio and Marcellus. He is wearing a black cloak over his shoulders; a long sword is in a scabbard at his side. The others are cloaked as well. Hamlet crosses to the right of the platform and speaks his first line quietly and firmly: "The air bites *shrewdly;* (slight pause) it is very *cold.*"[129] Horatio, left of Hamlet, replies, "It is a nipping and an eager air." Hamlet turns his back to the audience, looks at the sky, and asks (sharply) *"What hour now?"* Horatio replies, "I think it lacks of twelve." On Marcellus's "No, it is struck," Hamlet turns to face him. After Horatio's "it then draws near the season/ Wherein the spirit held his wont to walk," we hear distant laughter and a flourish of trumpets offstage left. Horatio asks, "What doth this mean, my lord?" Hamlet, pacing nervously up and down the platform, answers with an undertone of agitation and bitterness: "The king doth *wake* to-night and takes his *rouse,*/ . . . And as he *drains* his *draughts* of *Rhenish down*/ The kettle-drum and *trum*pet thus *bray out*/ The *tri*umph of his *pledge.*" "Is it a custom?" asks Horatio." Hamlet, still pacing, replies, "Ay, marry, is't:/ . . . it is a custom/ More honor'd in the *breach* than the *observance.*/ . . . and indeed it tak –"

Suddenly he stops, sensing some unusual presence. Wind effects and whistle and saw are heard off right. A second's pause. Horatio turns his head and sees the Ghost offstage right. A cold white light comes on slowly, striking Hamlet as Horatio speaks: "Look, my lord, it comes!" Hamlet stands rigid – as if turned to stone – staring off right. Horatio and Marcellus stare in the same direction; Marcellus clutches Horatio's arm. Hamlet turns slowly and looks off right with an expression of awe and wonder. His face is brilliantly lighted. His cloak slips off his shoulders (Fig. 25). He speaks in a very high, thin, penetrating head tone:[130] *"ANGELS* and *MINISTERS* of grace (lower) *defend* us!" (quick, with a quavering tone; slight pause) "Be thou a *spirit* of *health* or *goblin damn'd,*/ Bring with thee *airs* from *heaven* or *blasts* from *hell,*/ Be thy *intents wicked* or *charitable,*/ Thou *comest* in such a *questionable shape* (upward emphasis on the last word, which is drawn out; slight pause)/ That I will *speak* to thee: (slight pause) I'll *call thee* (slight pause) *Ham*let, (approaches a step right; slight pause)/ *King,* (rising tone; slight pause) *FA*ther, (higher, in a quavering voice; he sinks to his knees and claps his hands as if in prayer) *royal* Dane: O, answer me! (descending tone)/ . . . What may this *mean* (downward emphasis) / That thou, *dead corse,* again, in *com*plete *steel,*/ Revisit'st thus the *glimpses* of the *moon,*/ Making *night hideous* (quavering voice, but firmer; slight pause) . . . / Say, why *is* this? (slight pause; descending tone) *wherefore?* (slight pause; lower descending tone) what should we *do?*" (short pause). The light dims off Hamlet. Then, in a low tone: "It will not *speak;* (he rises, and with his left hand reaches for his sword; slight pause) then I will *follow* it."[131]

Horatio (left of him) urges, "Do not, my lord" and seizes Hamlet by the shoulders. Hamlet replies in a low tone, "Why, what should be the *fear?* (downward emphasis) / I do not *set* my *life* at a *pin's fee* (low tone);/[132] And for my *soul,* (last word drawn out with upward emphasis), what can it *do* to that (quickly and forcefully),/ Being a thing *immortal* as *itself?*/ (slight pause; then, in a low tone) It waves me *forth* again: I'll *follow* it."

Horatio argues, "What if it tempt you toward the flood, my lord,/ Or to the dreadful summit of the cliff/ . . . And draw you into madness?" He uses force to restrain Hamlet, maintaining his grip on his shoulders. "It *waves* me *still,*" Hamlet replies quickly, his arms outstretched.[133] "*Go on* (low tone); I'll *follow thee.*" Marcellus crosses right to above Horatio and seizes Hamlet by the shoulders: "You shall not go, my lord." "My *FATE* cries *OUT* (loud),/ . . . UN-HAND me gentlemen." Hamlet struggles with Horatio and Marcellus. "By *HEAVEN,* (quick, with rising volume) I'll make a *ghost* of him that *LETS ME* (he throws them off to the left)/ I say *AWAY!*" (loud crescendo). Hamlet turns right. He is seized by a tremendous paroxysm of anger then stands in rigid stillness for a long moment. At last, he moves the little finger of his right hand to indicate his decision. Then, in a low, drawn-out tone: "Go on; I'll *follow* thee."[134] He draws his sword and inverts it so that the hilt forms a cross. Holding it before him, he exits slowly up the stairs of the top right platform.[135]

A long pause, then Horatio says, "He waxes desperate with imagination." Marcellus suggests that they follow, adding, "Something is rotten in the state of Denmark." Horatio, picking up Hamlet's cloak, replies, "Heaven will direct it." After Marcellus's "Nay, let's follow him," both exit right via the steps of the upper platform.[136]

The blue lights on the cyclorama slowly dim to half-magnitude. As Horatio and Marcellus come off the platform, the ghostly effects of wind machine and saw begin offstage right and are kept up until Hamlet is on the stage again and well up on the lower platform.

Hamlet enters right on the mainstage. As he enters, the body of the Ghost appears as a greenish, wavering, diffused light, ten feet high, against the midnight blue of the backdrop; the figure of the armored king can be faintly made out. The sound effects continue. Hamlet steps up to the lower platform, still holding his sword ahead of him as a cross. He moves slowly to center, below the steps leading to the archway. The stage is dimly lit. As he starts to speak, a whistle effect is blown twice in long, wailing notes.[137]

Figure 25. Hamlet, Marcellus (E. J. Ballantine), and Horatio (Frederick Lewis) confront the Ghost. Courtesy Billy Rose Theatre Collection, The New York Public Library for the Performing Arts.

"Whither wilt thou *lead* me?" is spoken quietly, in a low, apprehensive tone. Slight pause. "*Speak;* [/] I'll go no *further* (low tone). The head of the Ghost appears on the backdrop. The image "flickers and fades and forms" throughout the scene.[138] The Ghost's "Mark me" is spoken in a high tenor voice from left center. Hamlet's "I will" in response is delivered in a low, quiet monotone. The Ghost tells him, "My hour is almost come,/ When I to sulphurous and tormenting flames (whistle and saw sounds)/ must render up myself." Hamlet's "*Alas,* poor ghost!" is low, practically a whisper. On his "Speak; I am bound to hear," the lights go up a little through the window at the left; a white light strikes Hamlet. The Ghost tells him, "I am thy father's spirit," and Hamlet, groaning, sinks to his knees right center, facing the arch. He listens as the ghostly voice says he is forbidden to reveal the secrets of hell (whistle and saw sounds).[139] Hamlet's "*O God!*" in reply is a low moan. After the Ghost commands, "Revenge his foul and most unnatural murder," Hamlet pauses, and his "Murder!" in reply is a whispered exclamation. He pledges revenge and listens as the Ghost tells him that "The serpent that did sting thy father's life/ Now wears his crown." His "*O my prophetic soul!* (short pause)/ My *uncle!*" is spoken in a low whisper.[140] He listens attentively as the Ghost tells the story of his murder. After the Ghost laments that he was cut off "With all my imperfections on my head," Hamlet groans, and following the Ghost's "O horrible! O horrible! (whistle and saw effect) most horrible!"/ (whistle and saw effect) he groans again.[141] He listens intently to the Ghost's admonition to "Let not the royal bed of Denmark be/ A couch for luxury (whistle and saw effect) and damned incest"/ and the advice to "Taint not thy mind, nor let thy soul contrive/ Against thy mother aught: leave her to heaven." After the Ghost's "Fare thee well at once," the blue lights on the cyclorama begin to come back to full, and the Ghost body and head lights dim out gradually, reaching a blackout on "Adieu, adieu, adieu! remember me."[142] The light on Hamlet from the window dims out slowly at the same time. He falls face down to the stage – prone and groaning – and the window light reaches a blackout. A spotlight and the blue lights beyond the arch come on immediately and rise gradually as soon as the window light is black.

Hamlet begins his soliloquy prone on the stage, in a shadow so deep that his form is almost invisible.[143] "O (pause) all you *host* of *heaven!* [/] O *earth!* (rises up a bit) *what else?*/ And shall I *couple hell?* O, fie! (starts to rise – up on hands) *Hold,* [/] *hold,* my *heart;*/ And you, my sinews, grow not instant old, (supporting himself with right hand)/ But bear me stiffly up. Re*mem*ber thee! (he sits up, then speaks upstage)/ Ay, thou *poor ghost,* while *memory holds* a *seat* (sadly, almost in tears)/ In this *distracted globe.* Re*mem*ber thee!" (pause; he gets up on his knees, then crawls to the lower platform). On "O most *pernicious woman!*" he starts to rise excitedly, and by the end of "O *villain, villain, smiling, DAMNED villain,*" he has jumped up, shrieking in rage; he delivers the line with the sharpness of a knife thrust.[144] Pause. On "My tables," he reaches into his blouse and withdraws a small notebook with pencil attached and starts to write (with "perfect good sense"): "– meet it is I set it down,/ (writing) That one may smile, and smile, and be a villain;/ (pauses, and then cautiously adds) At least I'm sure it may be so in Denmark."[145] He finishes writing: "So uncle, there you are." He closes the book and grasps it in his right hand: "Now to my word;/ It is, 'A*dieu,* a*dieu!* re*mem*ber me.'/ I have sworn't."

Horatio and Marcellus are heard calling off right. Hamlet crosses to the right and calls out to them. Marcellus, then Horatio, enter on the mainstage. They ask Hamlet for news of what he has seen. After his reply he crosses quickly to their left. With a conspiratorial air he places his arms around their shoulders: "But you'll be secret?" They promise, and Hamlet pauses to play up the suspense of what he then reveals to them (politely and sensibly): "There's ne'er a villain dwelling in *all* Denmark/ (whistle and saw effect; Hamlet pauses at this evident warning to be secret – and then, almost as if it were a joke) But he's an arrant knave."[146] He crosses to the left with an airy wave of his hand. Horatio tells him, "There needs no ghost, my lord, come from the grave/ To tell us this." Hamlet replies, ". . . You are i' the right," and crosses to right center. He suggests they shake hands and go their separate ways, adding, "for my own poor part,/ (he crosses to Horatio) Look you, I'll go pray." He crosses upstage left on the platform, agitated, then paces back to center.[147]

"These are but wild and whirling words, my lord," Horatio comments. He takes a step toward Hamlet, who continues to pace nervously. On Hamlet's "Touching this vision here,/ It is an honest ghost, that let me tell you," Horatio and Marcellus move to him. He swears them to secrecy about what they have seen, then picks up his sword and crosses to them: "Upon my sword." (holds the hilt toward the audience) Marcellus protests that they have sworn already, but Hamlet insists. The Ghost, behind the right of the steps, cries out "Swear." All start affrighted.[148]

Hamlet calls in response (hysterically, almost gaily), "Ah, ha, boy! say'st thou so?" And then lightly, trying to control his hysteria: "art thou there, true-penny?" He holds out his sword hilt, then crosses to Horatio and Marcellus and tells them "Never . . . speak of this that you have seen,/ Swear by my sword." The Ghost again cries "Swear." All start. Hamlet replies lightly, "Hic et ubique? then we'll shift our ground." He crosses left. "Come hither, gentlemen,/ (Horatio and Marcellus cross to right of Hamlet) And lay your hands again upon my sword:/ (he holds out his sword; Horatio and Marcellus obey his order) Never to speak of this that you have heard,/ Swear by my sword."

The Ghost (now behind the center of the steps) again calls out "Swear." All start; Hamlet crosses to center stage. Looking at the floor, he speaks to the voice in the cellarage; his words are not so much "wild and whirling" as inwardly ecstatic: "Well said, old mole! canst work i' the earth so fast?/ A worthy pioner! Once more remove, (he crosses right) good friends."[149] Horatio comments that "this is wondrous strange" and Hamlet tells him, "There are more things in heaven and earth, Horatio,/ Than are [/] *dreamt of* [/] in your philosophy./ But come."[150] He crosses to between Horatio and Marcellus, Horatio and Marcellus put their hands on his sword; Hamlet places his on top. He tells them he may "put an antic disposition on" and asks them to swear they will not reveal the reason. The Ghost (now behind the left of the steps) again intones "Swear."

All start. Hamlet sinks to his knees, left center, addressing the Ghost: "Rest, rest, perturbed spirit!" (sincere and touching).[151] He rises and sheathes his sword. "So, gentlemen,/ (he places his hands on their shoulders) . . . Let us go in together;/ (he takes his cloak from Horatio and crosses to right center; Horatio takes a step toward Marcellus) And still your fingers on your lips, I pray./ The *time* is *out* of *joint:* [/] O *cursed spite* (sadly),/ That ever *I* was *born* [/] to *set* it *right!*"[152] He throws the skirt of his cloak over his left shoulder.[153] He holds Horatio at arm's length with a gesture and then says, "Nay, come, let's go together (boyishly)." He exits first on the mainstage left, followed by Horatio and Marcellus. The lights dim out.[154]

Years later, Barrymore told Gene Fowler of his feelings for the Ghost. Hamlet, he commented, "is fond of the old boy who was once his father. . . . The play . . . depends on this bond of sympathy to promote the revenge. Ergo, when the ghost of the father appears, I am a bit startled, and for the moment confused, yet I actually am glad to be with him once again. So I don't rant or scream. I listen attentively to the old man, hear his gossip, then engineer the appropriate murders."[155]

This, however, like many of Barrymore's later comments, should be taken with a grain of salt. In his *Tribune* interview two months after the opening, Barrymore revealed that between Hamlet's meeting with the Ghost and the "appropriate murders" a good deal of intellectual skepticism and soul searching had taken place. He described Hamlet as "inordinately just," and commented that

> In an early soliloquy matching up his suspicion of the King with the ghostly disclosures, he says, "The spirit I have seen may be of the devil." [*sic*] Previously, at the meeting with Horatio and his friends, Hamlet in a flaming outburst had cried: "As touching this vision here, it's an honest ghost, that let me tell you!" [*sic*] Yet, not trusting its sanction, he later admits that the spirit might be a malevolent agent. The inaction is not due to weakness of character. Again, he questions whether he is "thinking too precisely on the event." Not that he is "three-quarters coward," but because of his inordinate desire to be certain of the event.

Act I, scene v. *A room in Polonius's house.* [Temple edition, II.i, 120 lines cut to 39]

The tableau curtains are brought on during the blackout. After a wait of about fifteen seconds the lights come on, including the baby spots on the curtain figures. The scene is played on the apron.[156]

As the lights come up, Polonius is discovered on the apron right center. Ophelia rushes through the curtains and comes down to the center of the apron.[157] Polonius greets her, and she tells him she has been "affrighted" by Hamlet's appearance in her closet with his "doublet all unbraced . . . to speak of horrors." "Mad for thy love?" Polonius asks. Ophelia turns away a little and replies, "My lord I do not know,/ (she turns back and crosses to Polonius) But truly I do fear it." She tells her father the story of Hamlet's disturbing visitation. Polonius commands, "Come, go with me: (he turns left and starts up to center) I will go seek the king/ (he stops, facing front) This is the very ecstasy of love;/ Whose violent property fordoes itself/ And leads the will to desperate undertakings./ (he turns back to his daughter) What, have you given him any hard words of late?" Ophelia pauses before replying that she did "repel his letters and denied/ His access to me."[158] Polonius fears "he did but trifle" and concludes, "Come, go we to the king:/ This must be known." He takes Ophelia's hand then places his arm around her shoulder and leads her through the curtains as the lights dim out.[159]

Act I, scene vi. *A room in the castle.* [Temple edition, II.ii, 634 lines cut to 411]

The tableau curtains are pulled off during the blackout. The gold and black curtains behind the arch come on full. The throne-bench with gold drapery is placed center on the lower platform. The Hamlet chair, its back to the audience, is placed directly below the break in the steps right center. Music: a trumpet flourish with accompanying tympani. The lights come on gradually during the last measure.[160]

Rosencrantz and Guildenstern are discovered kneeling left center, facing the King and Queen. The Queen sits on the right side of the throne. The King stands in front of the left side of the throne with one foot on the step.[161] Polonius stands right center on the mainstage, left of the Hamlet chair.

The King welcomes Rosencrantz and Guildenstern and entreats them to learn, if possible, the cause of Hamlet's transformation. They agree, bow after the King's "Thanks, Rosencrantz and gentle Guildenstern," and bow again after the Queen's "Thanks, Guildenstern and gentle Rosencrantz." The Queen asks them "instantly to visit/ My too much changed son." They rise, bow, back three steps left, then turn and exit. Polonius assures the King that he has discovered the cause of "Hamlet's lunacy." The King starts eagerly and replies, "O, speak of that; that do I long to hear." The Queen puts her hand on the King's arm on her ensuing lines, "I doubt it is no other but the main;/ His father's death and our o'er hasty marriage."[162]

Polonius takes a step toward the throne and removes a scroll from the pocket of his cloak; he holds it out, opens it, turns a little toward the front, then reads: "'To the celestial, and my soul's idol, the most beautified Ophelia, – '" He looks up at the King and Queen, comments that it is "an ill phrase, a vile phrase," and continues reading. After the King's "But how hath she/ Received his love?" he launches into his lengthy explanation. Toward the end of his speech, the Queen, bored, looks at the King.[163] Following Polonius's explanation of Hamlet's "madness," the King turns to the Queen: "Do you think this?" The Queen replies, "It may be, very like" and nods her head thoughtfully. After Polonius instigates the plan to "loose my daughter" and then hide behind the arras with the King to observe Hamlet, the King replies, "We will try it" and rises. The Queen rises and looks off left, starts, and directs the King's attention: "But look (Polonius and the King look off left; Polonius crosses to left center) where sadly the poor wretch comes reading." Polonius urges, "Away, I do beseech you, both away:/ (the King takes the Queen's hand, leading her; they start to cross right) I'll board him presently (the Queen looks back). O, give me leave." The King and Queen exit right on the mainstage, the Queen first. Polonius remains right center.[164]

After the King and Queen are well off, Hamlet enters left on the mainstage, reading a book; he crosses to right center and pauses. Polonius looks after him, then speaks: "How does my good lord Hamlet?" He crosses three steps downstage toward him. Hamlet hesitates in his walk, looks up a second, looks back at his book, then speaks as he continues to the chair at right center: "Well, God-a-mercy." A short pause. Polonius asks, "Do you know me, my lord?" Hamlet replies "Excellent well; (he looks at Polonius) you are a fishmonger." Pause. He turns away and crosses upstage right a little, then looks down at his book and continues reading. After Polonius's protest, "Not I, my lord," Hamlet turns and faces him: "Then I would you were so honest a man." A pause; Hamlet again reads. Polonius crosses a step toward him and says, "Honest, my lord!" Hamlet drops the hand holding the book to his side, looks at him, remarks "Ay, sir; to be honest, as this world goes, is to be one man picked out of ten thousand," and turns away. On Polonius's reply, "That's very true, my lord," Hamlet takes up his book and "reads": "For if the sun breeds maggots in a dead dog, being a god kissing carrion – (he drops the book and looks at Polonius) Have you a daughter? . . . Let her not walk i' the sun: conception is a blessing; but as your daughter may conceive, – (he turns to go upstage, then reads a second) friend, look to't."[165] He crosses upstage right, reading.

Polonius turns toward left center and delivers his aside, then crosses upstage, speaking his line as he walks. He follows Hamlet as he comes down to the left of the chair: "What do you read, my lord?" Hamlet replies, "Words, words, words" and crosses downstage right. Polonius crosses a step right on "What is the matter, my lord?" Hamlet turns to him, bored: "Between who?" He looks at Polonius queerly. "I mean, the matter that you read, my lord." Hamlet crosses to Polonius and delivers his satirical synopsis; he pauses after "most weak hams" and concludes, "for yourself, sir, shall grow old as I am, if

Figure 26. Hamlet and Polonius (John S. O'Brien). Courtesy Billy Rose Theatre Collection, The New York Public Library for the Performing Arts.

like a crab (he indicates the movement of a crab's tail by thrusting his hand, clawlike, at Polonius, who dodges back) you could go backward."[166] He looks Polonius in the eyes for a moment (Fig. 26), then crosses right to below the chair. Polonius delivers his aside ("Though this be madness, yet there is method in't"), then turns and advances a step right: "Will you walk out of the air, my lord?"

Hamlet replies, "Into my grave," crosses a step, and leans on the chair. Polonius looks out: "Indeed, that's out of the air." He delivers his aside, resolving to "contrive the means of meeting between him and my daughter," then takes a step upstage: "My honorable lord, I will most humbly take my leave of you." He bows to Hamlet, who crosses down to right center then turns to him: "You cannot, sir, take from me any thing that I will more willingly part withal: (he turns away) except my life, except my life, except my life." He crosses right. Polonius bows: "Fare you well, my lord." Hamlet turns away; Polonius crosses to the left where he meets Rosencrantz and Guildenstern as they enter. Hamlet comments, "These tedious old fools!" and crosses right, then paces up and down, reading. Polonius addresses Rosencrantz and Guildenstern: "You go to seek the Lord Hamlet (Rosencrantz and Guildenstern bow; Hamlet throws down his book off the lower platform, right); there he is." He points to Hamlet and shakes his head. Rosencrantz replies, "God save you, sir!" Polonius exits left.[167]

Rosencrantz (crossing left to upstage) and Guildenstern (crossing left to downstage) address Hamlet. He turns and greets them cordially, crossing to left of the chair: ". . . How dost thou, Guildenstern? Ah, Rosencrantz! Good lads, how do you both?" On Guildenstern's "On fortune's cap we are not the very button," he crosses back to right center, and he takes particular delight in the bawdy exchange that follows: "Then live you about her waist, or in the middle of her favors? (smilingly)" Guildenstern, laughing, replies, "Faith, her privates we." Hamlet ripostes, "In the secret parts of fortune? O, most true; she is a strumpet. What's the news?"[168] After the ensuing lines, he crosses to the chair, leans on the back, half-sitting, and banters with them about Denmark being "a prison." He then asks them, "But, in the beaten way of friendship, what make you at Elsinore?" After Rosencrantz's reply, "To visit you, my lord; no other occasion," he comments, "Beggar that I am, I am even poor in thanks" and steps left toward them: ". . . my thanks are too dear a halfpenny."

He pauses and looks at them. "Were you not sent for? (pause) Is it your own inclining? (pause) Is it a free visitation? (pause; he looks at them) Come, deal justly with me: come, come; nay, speak."[169] He takes one step closer to them. Guildenstern, embarrassed, takes a step downstage on "What should we say, my lord?" Hamlet replies, "Why, any thing, but to the purpose. (pause) You were sent for; and there is a kind of confession in your looks, which your modesties have not craft enough to color: (pause) I know (he crosses right) the good king and queen have sent for you." He leans on the chair. Rosencrantz takes a step nearer to Guildenstern: "To what end, my lord?" "That you must teach me." Hamlet takes a step toward them and asks them to "be even and direct with me, whether you were sent for, or no?" He turns away upstage a little, but observes them sideways.[170]

Rosencrantz steps close to Guildenstern and whispers an aside: "What say you?" Hamlet, aside, comments, "Nay then, I have an eye of you – (he turns to them earnestly) If you love me, hold not off."[171] He looks steadily at Rosencrantz. Guildenstern, taking a step toward Hamlet, confesses, "My lord, we were sent for." Hamlet looks at them a moment; a slight hesitation, then a short laugh: "I will tell you why; (he is relieved; he crosses to Guildenstern and places his hand on his shoulder) so shall my anticipation prevent your discovery, and your secrecy to the king and queen moult no feather."[172]

He turns away a step right, then faces Rosencrantz and Guildenstern and sits on the back of the chair. "I have of late – but wherefore I know not – lost all my mirth . . . (he faces the audience)[173] this goodly frame, the earth, seems to me a sterile promontory . . . the air . . . appears no other thing to me than a foul and pestilent congregation of vapors." Rosencrantz and Guildenstern exchange smiles, unseen by Hamlet. He turns and looks at them an instant later.[174] He then looks out at the audience again, and in a calm neutral voice, comments, "What a piece of work is a man! how noble in reason! how infinite in faculty![175] . . . And yet, to me, what is this quintessence of dust? (he takes a step right as he speaks) man delights not me; (he turns to continue speaking but catches himself as he discovers Rosencrantz and Guildenstern smiling at each other)[176] no, nor woman neither, though by your smiling you seem to say so." Rosencrantz protests: "My lord, there was no such stuff in my thoughts." Hamlet, leaning on the chair, asks him, "Why did you laugh then, when I said 'man delights not me'?" Rosencrantz replies that if this is the case, he will take little joy in the players who are soon to arrive. Hamlet moves away from the chair, and in a dreamlike voice replies, "He that plays the king shall be welcome; his majesty shall have tribute of me."[177]

Music; an English horn from offstage left.[178] Guildenstern looks off left: "These are the players." Hamlet tells them, "Gentlemen, you are welcome to Elsinore. Your hands, come then: (he extends his hands; Rosencrantz and Guildenstern cross and take them) You are welcome: (he steps away toward the right) but (slight pause) my uncle-father and aunt-mother are deceived." He crosses back to right center. "In what, my dear lord?" asks Guildenstern. Hamlet draws them nearer to him, as though telling a secret: "I am but *mad* north-north-west: when the wind is southerly I know a hawk from a handsaw."[179] As he draws back from them Polonius speaks from off left: "Well be with you, gentlemen!" Hamlet responds "Hark you, Guildenstern (he crosses to center stage; Rosencrantz and Guildenstern cross to right center and stand at either side of him; Fig. 27); and you too: at each ear a hearer: that great baby you see there is not yet out of his swaddling clouts. I will prophesy he comes to tell me of the players; (Polonius enters from the left and crosses toward left center) mark it." He delivers his next line to Guildenstern: "You say right, sir: o' Monday morning; 'twas so indeed."

Polonius stops left center: "My lord, I have news to tell you." Hamlet, imitating Polonius's voice in a high, mocking tone, replies, "My *lord,* I have *news* to tell you."[180] He crosses to center stage. "When *Roscius* was an *actor* in *Rome,* – " Rosencrantz and Guildenstern cross up to right center above and left of the chair. Polonius announces, "The actors are come hither, my lord."

Figure 27. Hamlet with Rosencrantz (Paul Huber) and Guildenstern (Lawrence Cecil). Courtesy Billy Rose Theatre Collection, The New York Public Library for the Performing Arts.

"*Buz, buz!*" Hamlet comments to Rosencrantz and Guildenstern in a low,
drawn out tone, motioning to his head with his left hand. They smile.[181] Polonius describes the company: "The best actors in the world, either for tragedy,
comedy, history, pastoral, pastoral-comical . . . or poem unlimited." He takes
a step toward Hamlet. "Seneca cannot be too heavy . . ." Throughout Polonius's speech, Hamlet tries in vain to get in a word edgewise; afterward he lets
out a sigh of relief.[182] A pause. Hamlet looks earnestly at Polonius: "O *Jephthah, judge* of *Israel, what* a *treasure* hadst *thou!*" "What treasure had he, my
lord?" asks Polonius." Hamlet replies, "Why, (he sings the next two lines to a
plaintive tune) 'One fair daughter, and no more,/ The which he loved passing well.'" Afterwards he adds, "Am I not i' the right, *old Jephthah?*" and taps

Figure 28. Hamlet and the Players. Courtesy Billy Rose Theatre Collection, The New York Public Library for the Performing Arts.

Polonius on the chest.[183] He crosses up to left center. Polonius turns left and delivers his aside, then turns to Hamlet who, after their two-line exchange, crosses down to the right and then to right center as the Players enter.

The First Player enters left on the mainstage, followed by the Second Player and three others who form a group behind them; the First and Second Players are left center. Hamlet greets them cordially, placing his hand on the First Player's shoulder (Fig. 28): "You are *welcome,* masters; *welcome, all.*" The Players bow. "O, my old *friend!*" (upward emphasis). He steps back and addresses the First Player: "Why thy face is *valenced* since I saw thee *last* (downward emphasis); (the First Player smiles) comest thou to *beard* me in Denmark?" The First Player shakes his head. Hamlet smiles and greets the Second

Player: "What, my young lady and mistress! (the Second Player bows) . . . Pray God, your voice . . . be not cracked within the ring." The Second Player shakes his head. "Masters, you are all welcome. (all bow) . . . We'll have a speech straight: (then, quickly) come, give us a *taste* of your *quality;* (he swings the chair around so that it faces the audience) come, a passionate speech." He sits in the chair.[184]

The First Player asks, "What speech, my good lord?" and advances a step. "I heard thee speak me a speech once," Hamlet replies, "but . . . the play, I remember, pleased not the million. (First Player smiles; Hamlet smiles) 'twas caviare to the general: but it was . . . an excellent play, well digested in the scenes, set down with as much modesty as cunning." He ponders a moment, looking out, then looks at the First Player. "One speech in it I *chiefly loved:* 'twas *Aeneas'* tale to *Dido;* (the First Player nods comprehension) . . . if it *live* in your *memory* – "

The First Player bows, ponders a moment, then turns toward Hamlet and begins the speech in a grandiose manner[185] with "Anon he finds him . . . ," concluding, ". . . Pyrrhus stood,/ And like a neutral to his will and matter,/ (to Hamlet) Did nothing./ (looks out) But as we often see – " Polonius crosses downstage a step and comments to Hamlet, "This is too long." The First Player looks at Polonius, astonished. Hamlet replies to Polonius, "It shall to the barber's, with your beard. (Polonius turns and crosses to upstage left center, repulsed; Hamlet then addresses the Player) Prithee, say on: he's for a jig or a tale of bawdry, or he sleeps: (Hamlet laughs; the First Player laughs) say on: come to Hecuba." Polonius turns back toward the Player.[186]

The First Player, arms outstretched, declaims, "But who, O, who had seen the mobled queen – " Hamlet interrupts: "'The *mobled* queen?'" The First Player looks at Hamlet. Polonius comments, "That's good; 'mobled queen' is good," and crosses down to left center. The First Player looks at Polonius, then at Hamlet, who smiles. He continues his speech; on "Would have made milch the burning eyes of heaven" his voice breaks into sobs, and after his ensuing line, "And passion in the gods" he bows his head, overcome with emotion.[187]

Polonius crosses forward a step. ". . . he . . . has tears in's eyes. Prithee, no more." Pause. Hamlet comments (low, sympathetic tone) "'Tis *well;* (the First Player looks up at Hamlet) I'll have thee *speak out* the *rest* of this *soon* (low tone)." The First Player bows and takes a step upstage. Hamlet addresses Polonius: "Good my lord (Polonius crosses down below the First Player to the right of him), will you see the *players well bestowed?* . . ." Polonius agrees, and after Hamlet's ensuing speech he crosses in front of the Players: "Come, sirs." The Players bow. Hamlet addresses the others: "*Follow* him, *friends:* we'll *hear* a *play* tomorrow." Polonius exits left on the mainstage. Rosencrantz and Guildenstern bow and cross in front of the players, who bow. They go out, followed by the Second Player, the Mime Player Queen, Lucianus, and the Mime Player King.

The First Player is bowing out when Hamlet stops him: "Dost thou *hear me*, old friend" (low tone). The First Player comes on to left center. There is a long pause while Hamlet looks front and thinks, and then a sudden lowering of his brows and steeling of his glance betray the very instant when the design of using the Players to test the King flashes into his mind.[188] A pause. Hamlet looks at the First Player and asks: "Can (pause) you [/] *play* (long pause) the *Murder* (long pause) of (pause) *Gonzago?*"[189] The First Player replies, "Ay, my lord" and bows. "We'll ha't to-morrow night." The First Player again bows and Hamlet continues, slowly and thoughtfully: "You *could*, for a *need* [/], *study* a *speech* [/] of some *dozen* or *sixteen lines*, which I would *set down* and *insert in't*, could you *not?*" The First Player again replies, "Ay, my lord" and bows. "Very well," Hamlet says, and rises from the chair. "Follow that lord; (the Player bows and backs two steps left but Hamlet stops him with his next words) and look you (pause) mock him not." The First Player bows, shakes his head "no," then turns and exits left. Hamlet gazes after him for about ten seconds. He turns right then center.[190]

"Now I am *alone*."[191] Pause. Hamlet stands by the chair and begins slowly: "O, (low tone) what a *rogue* and (quicker) *peasant slave* am I! / (again slow and reflective) Is it not *monstrous* that this *player* here, / But in a *fiction*, in a *dream* (drawn out) of passion, / Could force his *soul* (drawn out) so to his own *conceit*/ That from her *working* [/] all his visage *wann'd;* / *Tears* in his eyes, *distraction* in's aspect, / A *broken* voice, and his *whole* (drawn out) *function* [/] suiting/ With *forms* to his *conceit?* and *all* for *nothing* (downward emphasis)! / For *Hecuba* (downward emphasis)! / (he pauses in thought, then:) What's *Hecu*-ba to *him*, or *he* to *Hecuba*, / That he should *weep* (drawn out) for her (downward emphasis)? What would he *do*, / Had he the *motive* and the *cue* for *passion*/ That *I* have (downward emphasis)? He would *drown* the *stage* with *tears* (drawn out) / And *cleave* (drawn out) the general ear with *horrid speech*, / Make *mad* (rising volume) the *guilty* (downward emphasis, then more softly) and *appal* the *free*, / . . . Yet *I*, / A *dull* and muddy-mettled rascal, *peak*, / Like John-a-dreams (drawn out), un*preg*nant of my *cause* (downward emphasis), / And can *say* nothing (low; downward emphasis); no (drawn out, higher), not for a *king*, / Upon whose *property* (rising volume and speed) and *most dear life* (agitated) / *A DAMN'D DEFEAT* was made (downward emphasis; pause) Am I a *coward?* / (he exclaims "aw" as though the idea was ridiculous)[192] Who calls me *villain?* (quickly, with rising volume) *breaks* my *pate* across? / *Plucks* off my *beard*, and *BLOWS* it in my *FACE?* / . . . (loud and angry) Who *DOES ME* this? / (pause) Ha! / (low and gutteral) 'Swounds, I should *take* it: for it cannot *be* (drawn out – rising volume) / But I am *pigeon-liver'd* and lack *gall* / (quickly) To make *oppression bitter*, or *ere this* / (gutteral tone) I should have *fatted* all the (rising volume) *REGION KITES/* With this [/] *SLAVE'S OFFAL:* (pause; he turns upstage and looks at the throne, then crosses to it; and then, quietly) *bloody* (drawn out), *bawdy villain!/* (upward emphasis)." He turns downstage center. "*Remorseless,* (speeding up) *treacherous, lecherous, KINDLESS* (drawn out, but still quiet) *VILLAIN!/* (and then, in a drawn-out, hysterical scream of anguish) *O VENGEANCE!*"

He rushes to the throne, center, and shakes the drape of the throne where the King sits. Long pause. When his rage ceases he turns front, one foot on the platform, one on the step, and throws down the drapery, disgusted.[193] Then, quietly, almost in a whisper: "Why, what an *ass* am I! This is (rising volume) *most brave,/* That *I,* the *son* of a *dear father* murder'd,/ *Prompted* to my *revenge* by *heaven* and *hell,/* Must, [/] like a *whore* [/],[194] (quickly) *unpack* my *heart* with *words* (drawn out),/ And *fall* a-*cursing,* like a very *drab,/* A *scullion!/* Fie upon't! foh! About (slight pause), my *BRAIN!*" (drawn out).

He strikes his head with his hand, sits in his chair, buries his head in his hands and rocks his body back and forth for about ten seconds. He then sits tensely up and looks out at the audience. Then, slowly and quietly: "Hum (an exhalation of breath), I have *heard* (slight pause) / That *guilty creatures,* sitting at a *play* (drawn out),/ Have (quicker) by the very *cunning* of the *scene/* Been struck *so* to the *soul* (drawn out; slight pause) that *presently/* They have *proclaim'd* their *malefactions;/* For *murder* (drawn out; slight pause), though it have *no tongue,* will *speak* (upward emphasis) / With *most miraculous organ.* (then, quickly) I'll *have* these *players/ Play* something like the *murder* of my *father/* Before mine *uncle:* I'll *observe* his *looks;/* I'll *TENT* him to the *QUICK:* if he but *BLENCH* (loud and gleeful),/ I *know* my *course* (downward emphasis). The *spirit* that I have *seen* (drawn out; slight pause) / *May be* the *devil;* and the *devil* hath *power* (rising emphasis) / To *assume* a *pleasing shape;* yea (low tone; drawn out), and *perhaps/* Out of my *weakness* and my *melancholy,/* As he is very *potent* with such *spirits,/* (pause) *Abuses* me to *damn* me. (slight pause) I'll have *grounds/* More *relative* than *this.* (he rises; then, in a whisper) The play, (fortissimo) *THE PLAY'S THE THING/* (pause; he steps back right a little) *WHEREIN I'LL CATCH* the *CONSCIENCE* of the *KING.*

Pause. He thinks for a moment, then takes his notebook from his blouse, writes down a few words, mutters the lines to himself, looks up, starts right, thinks a moment more, then writes again – very intensely. He finishes, then turns and exits right on the mainstage. The house curtain is lowered.[195]

The curtain calls following Act I were as follows: (1) The house curtain is raised. The King, Queen, Ophelia, and Horatio come on left on the mainstage. Laertes, Polonius, Rosencrantz, and Guildenstern come on right. The house curtain is lowered. (2) The tableau curtains come on, then the house curtain rises. The second calls are taken through the tableaus. Laertes, Ophelia, and Polonius enter. Then the King and Queen. Then Hamlet. The house curtain is lowered.[196]

First Intermission

Helen Hayes later remembered her impressions of Hamlet's scene with Rosencrantz and Guildenstern, which she recalled as usually "a mildly comic scene . . . accepted by most Hamlets as a welcome relief from the heavy drama." In Barrymore's hands, however,

> [the scene] made me cry, which was as it should have been. . . . Rosencrantz and Guildenstern had been Hamlet's close friends; they had known him well and had loved him, and yet they had been easily won over to the side that doubted him and thought him mad. There was something inexpressibly tragic in Barrymore's tortured prince, contemptuously playing the fool for a world that expected it of him.[197]

Lark Taylor recalled that during the initial run,

> Barrymore called me into his dressing room one night, and told me I was becoming a bit too colloquial in the First Player – told me to keep him "grandiose." "You do it damn well," he said, and then began to speak of Edwin Forrest and his "grandiose" manner of acting, and advised me to keep as much of that quality in the First Player as I could.[198]

Barrymore's reading of the "rogue and peasant slave" soliloquy was almost universally admired. To Charles Darnton of the *Evening World* it represented a welcome note of passion and a cry from the soul amid his restrained interpretation (17 November 1922). Barrymore later commented that here and elsewhere Hamlet experiences a "heightened intellectual intensity arising from the soul-shattering experience he had just undergone," and "reaches a height of mental excitation that, at times, deprives him of all sense of self-control."[199]

Act II

Act II, scene i. *A room in the castle.* [Temple edition III.i, 196 lines cut to 184]

The gold and black curtains behind the arch are drawn on one foot, creating a "window effect." The throne, with gold drapery, is placed right center on the lower platform. The Hamlet chair, with a gold pillow on it, is set directly below the left center break in the steps. The house curtain rises on a dark stage. Music; the lights come on during the last measure. The blue lights at the back come up on the cyclorama behind the arch; the night sky can be seen.

The King and Queen are discovered seated on the throne, the King below and right of the Queen. Guildenstern kneels right center; Rosencrantz kneels above him and to his left. Polonius stands directly above Rosencrantz. Ophelia stands on the platform, above and to the right of her father.[200]

The King and Queen question Rosencrantz and Guildenstern about what they have learned of Hamlet's condition. After telling the King and Queen about his joyous response to the Players, they rise, bow back three steps, then turn and exit left on the mainstage.[201] The King rises and gives his hand to the Queen, who also rises; both come down from the throne to stage right: "Sweet Gertrude, leave us too;/ For we have closely sent for Hamlet hither,/ That he, as 'twere by accident, may here/ Affront Ophelia:/ Her father and myself, lawful espials."[202] The Queen replies "I shall obey you." She takes a step upstage toward Ophelia and tells her she hopes her "virtues" will bring Hamlet "to his wonted way again,/ To both your honors." The King crosses to right center. After Ophelia's reply, "Madam, I wish it may," the Queen exits right.

Polonius turns to the King on "Gracious, so please you, (bows)/ We will bestow ourselves." He takes Ophelia's hand and helps her down to right center, then takes a book out of his cloak and gives it to her as he speaks. Polonius and Ophelia leaf through the book as the King delivers his aside. Polonius looks off left: "I hear him coming: let's withdraw, my lord." The King and Polonius exit right on the mainstage. Ophelia pretends to read the book, then, frightened, edges her way toward the right, looking back several times, then exits. Pause of five seconds.[203]

Hamlet enters slowly from the left on the upper platform. He is wearing an armhole cloak over his left arm. He crosses to the center of the platform, then descends the steps slowly and crosses to the right of the chair. He begins his soliloquy slowly, in a low voice: "To *be*, [/] or *not* to be (downward emphasis): *that* is the *question:*/ (he takes off his cloak, drops it on the chair, and sits; Fig. 29)[204] "*Whether* 'tis *nobler* in the *mind* (drawn out) [/] to *suffer*/ The *slings* and *arrows* of *outrageous fortune* (drawn out),/ Or to take arms against a *sea* of *troubles* (downward emphasis),/ And by *opposing* [/] *end* them (downward emphasis). [/] To *die:* [/] to *sleep* (upward emphasis);/ No more (down – almost a whisper); and *by* a *sleep* to say we *end*/ The *heart-ache* [/], and the *thousand natural shocks*/ That *flesh* is *heir* to, 'tis a *consummation* [/]/ *Devoutly* to be *wish'd* (low tone).[/] To *die* [/] (drawn out, high tone), to *sleep* (low):/ [/] To sleep: (quickly) per*chance* to *dream* (drawn out; a bitter smile, and then): *ay,* (high tone, drawn out) *there's* the *rub;* (the hurt in his eyes is reflected in his voice)/ For in that *sleep* of *death* [/] what *dreams* (drawn out) may come,/ When we

Figure 29. A pensive portrait of Barrymore in the Hamlet chair. Courtesy Billy Rose Theatre Collection, The New York Public Library for the Performing Arts.

have *shuffled off* this *mortal coil,/* Must give us *pause* . . .²⁰⁵ The *undiscover'd country* [/] from whose *bourn/* No *traveller returns, puzzles* the *will* [/],/ And *makes* us *rather* [/] *bear* those *ills* we *have/* Than *fly* to *others* that we *know* not *of?/* Thus *conscience* does make *cowards* of *us all,/* And *thus* the *native hue* of *resolution/* Is *sickled o'er* with the *pale cast* of *thought,/* And *enterprises* of great *pitch* and *moment/* With this *regard* [/] their *currents turn awry/* And *lose* the *name* of *action.* (long pause; he looks off right) *Soft* you now! (he rises to up-stage center) The *fair Ophelia!"*

Ophelia enters from the right and crosses to right center, reading as she walks, whereupon Hamlet speaks softly:²⁰⁶ "Nymph, in thy orisons/ Be all my sins remember'd." Ophelia looks up from her book: "Good my lord,/ How does your honor for this many a day?" Hamlet takes a step toward her: "I humbly thank you: well, well, well." He turns away. After her ensuing lines, Ophelia takes a beaded necklace from around her neck and offers it to Hamlet, who quickly replies, "No, not I;/ I never gave you aught." After her next speech Ophelia again offers the beads. Hamlet laughs ruefully: "Ha, ha! are you honest? . . . Are you fair? . . . the power of beauty will sooner/ transform honesty from what it is to a *bawd* (Ophelia draws back, shocked). . . . (his voice trembles to a sob) I did love [/] you [/] once."²⁰⁷ "Indeed, my lord, you made me believe so," Ophelia replies.

"You should not have believed me," Hamlet tells her quietly, turning left, "for virtue cannot so inoculate our old stock (she brings her face almost up to his and he can hardly restrain his arms from clasping themselves about her) but we shall relish of it: (ten-second pause while he looks at her intently) I loved you not."²⁰⁸ Ophelia turns her head to the front. After her line, "I was the more deceived," Hamlet crosses to her, right center; he takes her by the shoulders and turns her to him: "Get thee to a nunnery (quietly): why wouldst thou be a breeder of sinners? . . ." Throughout, his hands are held close to her body; his face is inches from hers. "What should such fellows as I do (he raises his hands slowly) crawling between heaven (a tone of longing tenderness; he raises his hands to her head; they surround her face; pause) and earth!" (he lowers his hands to her waist).²⁰⁹ Then, tenderly: "We are ar-rant knaves all; believe none of us. Go thy ways to a nunnery."

Ophelia lets her head fall on Hamlet's right breast. He looks up and groans (Fig. 30). She then tries to put her head on his left breast, but he holds her off. After looking intently at her for a moment, and then permitting his lips just to touch her hair, he wrenches himself away. He starts to exit right, but seeing the King and Polonius (offstage), he turns sharply right and looks at Ophelia, who has her head turned left and front. Pause. He thinks a mo-ment, then forces a laugh. Ophelia turns to him after a short pause. He crosses to her and takes her head in his hands. And then, quietly and gently: "Where's your father?"²¹⁰ Ophelia replies, "At home, my lord." Three-second

Figure 30. Hamlet and Ophelia (Rosalinde Fuller). Courtesy Culver Pictures.

pause. She drops her book. Hamlet starts to back away to the right, and then quickly and harshly, in a tone of angry resentment at her duplicity: "Let the doors be shut upon him, that he may play the fool no where but in's own house. Farewell." He crosses to left center and starts to exit left. Ophelia, aside, comments, "O, help him, you sweet heavens!" Hamlet stops, returns a step, and his next speeches are spoken with full knowledge of the spies. "If thou dost marry, I'll give thee this plague for thy dowry . . . Get thee to a nunnery, go: farewell." He looks off into the wings, right.[211] "Or, if thou wilt needs marry, (gasped exclamation of disgust from Ophelia) marry a fool. . . . To a nunnery, go; and quickly too. Farewell." He starts for the left exit again.[212] Ophelia, center stage, delivers her aside: "O heavenly powers, restore him!" Hamlet comes back to left center, his love for the moment turned to gall by

the discovery of the eavesdroppers.[213] "I have heard of your paintings too . . .
you jig, you amble, and you lisp, and nick-name God's creatures, and make
your wantonness your ignorance (he crosses to Ophelia and grasps her left
wrist with his right hand). Go to, I'll no more on't; it hath made me *mad.*" He
strikes his forehead with his left hand. A pause of three seconds; he clutches
Ophelia's hand.[214] "I say, we will have no more marriages: (he looks off right
toward the conspirators) those that are married already, (pause; he looks toward the throne)[215] all but one, shall live; the rest shall keep as they are."
With a sob, he takes her head in his hands, then takes her by the shoulders.
Even with his anger, his love almost conquers him; he holds her off, looks
longingly at her, then, letting go, he backs away left.[216] And then, quietly: "To
a nunnery, go." He exits left, sobbing.[217]

Pause of ten seconds, then Ophelia, center stage, begins: "O, what a noble
mind is here o'erthrown!" She crosses gradually to left center as she speaks.
At the end of her speech she is leaning on the arm of the chair, weeping.[218]
The King enters right and crosses to upstage right center, followed by Polonius, who stands below him and to his right. The King scoffs at love and madness as possible causes of Hamlet's melancholy and resolves to send him "with
speed to England." Polonius argues that the cause was "neglected love" but
agrees with his plan. On "How now, Ophelia!" he crosses to center. "You need
not tell us what Lord Hamlet said;/ We heard it all." Ophelia crosses to center stage, weeping quietly. Polonius turns to the King: "My lord, do as you
please; (bows)/ . . . To England send him, or confine him where/ Your wisdom best shall think." The King tells him, "It shall be so:/ Madness in great
ones must not unwatch'd go." The lights dim out; the house curtain falls.[219]

Barrymore's delivery of the soliloquy in this scene was frequently praised;
the *Sun* (17 November 1922) found that "He to-be-or-not-to-be'd not as one
who is speaking a famous soliloquy but as a man who is thinking and voicing
certain thoughts for the first time."

The nunnery scene was probably the most variable scene with regard to
Barrymore's stage business and emotional intensity. Taylor commented that
Barrymore "Plays all this scene very quietly" and "goes off stage without raising voice." Yet at times, he played the scene "quite roughly, even fiercely," de-
pending on the mood of the moment.[220] In addition, the blocking of this entire scene was changed early in the run, and again during the second season;
alterations are discussed in the notes. One constant, however, was the physical closeness between Hamlet and Ophelia, with its accompanying sensual
business. Gilbert Seldes noted that "A great part of the scene was played with
Ophelia almost in Hamlet's arms, and some of his bitterest taunts to her were
spoken as his hand barely was restrained from caressing her hair, and his lips
from seeking hers" (*Philadelphia Ledger,* 26 November 1922).

Lark Taylor found that in the first part of the nunnery scene, Barrymore had "moments of great beauty and pathos, but he seemed to fail utterly in one quality. He gave Ophelia no reason whatever for saying: 'Oh, help him, you sweet Heavens,' and 'Oh! Heavenly Powers, restore him!' [*sic*] seemed an entirely unnecessary line, but he gave great power and passion to his last speech in that scene – and I have heard many people say – who claim to have seen all the great Hamlets of this generation, that Barrymore's performance of this scene was the best they had ever seen."[221]

Act II, scene ii. *A hall in the castle.* [Temple edition III.ii, 417 lines cut to 219]

The gold and black curtains behind the arch remain closed one foot as in the previous scene. A small throne chair for the King is placed left center, about three feet left of the break in the steps and against them. A small throne chair for the Queen is set in the same position right center. A purple cloth is placed on the floor, extending from the break in the steps, right center, to the center of the first platform. A small stool for Ophelia is placed at the right end of the cloth. The curtain rises on a dark stage. The lights come up gradually when the curtain is up; the deep blue sky on the cyclorama remains as it was in the preceding scene.

Hamlet and the First Player enter from the left on the mainstage, speaking as they walk.[222] Hamlet is upstage right of the Player and has his upstage hand on the Player's shoulder. They cross to right center; Hamlet delivers his opening lines in a relaxed, conversational tone: "*Speak* the *speech*, I *pray* you, as I pro*noun*ced it to you, *trippingly* on the *tongue:* [/] but if you *mouth* (drawn out) it, (he stops left of center; the Player gives Hamlet a questioning look) as *many* of your *players do,* I had as lief the *town-crier* spoke my lines." The Player smiles; Hamlet smiles and walks a step or two away from him. "Nor do not saw the *air* too much with your *hand, thus;* (he makes an elaborate gesture with his hand) but use *all gently:* for in the very *torrent, tempest,* and, as I may say, *whirl-wind* of your *passion,* you must *acquire* [/] and beget a *temperance* that may give it *smoothness.*" Hamlet turns away a step or two upstage right of the Player, who replies, "I warrant your honor." He turns back to the Player: "Be not *TOO tame neither,* but let your own (places hand on Player's shoulder) [/] *discretion* [/] be your *tutor* (he steps back; then quickly): suit the *action* to the *word,* the *word* to the *action;* with this special *observance,* that you o'er*step* not the *modesty* of *nature:* for *anything* [/] so over*done* is from the *purpose* of *playing,* whose *end,* both at the *first* and *now,* was and is, to *hold,* [/] as *'twere,* the [/] *mirror* up to *nature;* to show *virtue* her own *feature, scorn* her own *image,* and the very *age* and *body* of the *time* [/] his *form* and *pressure.* Now this over*done* or come *tardy off,* (a mischievous and ironic gleam twinkles in his eyes, and his voice grows owlish with mock gravity)[223] though it make the unskillful *laugh*, cannot but make the [/] *judicious* [/] *grieve*, (Hamlet looks at the Player and says "eh?" then they both laugh; he places both hands good-naturedly on the Player's shoulders) the *censure* of the *which* [/], one must in your *allowance o'erweigh* [/] a *whole theatre* of *others. Go, make* you *ready.*" The First Player bows and exits left.[224]

Hamlet crosses to the center of the lower platform. Polonius enters stage right, followed by Rosencrantz and Guildenstern; he stops in front of the chair, and Rosencrantz and Guildenstern stand to his right. Hamlet addresses Polonius: "How now, my lord! will the king hear this piece of work?" After Polonius bows and replies, Hamlet quickly commands, "Bid the players *make haste.*" Polonius exits left; as he does so, he and Hamlet watch each other out of the corners of their eyes.[225] Hamlet addresses Rosencrantz and Guildenstern: "Will you two help to hasten them?" They agree, bow, turn, and exit left. Hamlet watches them as they exit. Then, crossing right, he calls offstage: "What ho! Horatio!" Horatio enters stage right and crosses to left of and below the chair: "Here, sweet lord, at your service." "Horatio, thou art e'en as just a man/ As e'er my conversation coped withal," Hamlet replies, in a begrudging fashion. He leans on the chair, holding Horatio aloof for the next few lines of his speech.[226] After "Give me that man/ That is not passion's slave, and I will wear him/ In my heart's core . . ./ As I *do* thee," he clasps his hand on Horatio's shoulder, then draws back with a short laugh.[227] He turns and crosses to center stage, then turns again to Horatio, who crosses to right center. A pause, then Hamlet tells him, "Something too much of this," and breaks off with half-reluctant shyness.[228] And then: "There is a play to-night before the king;/ One scene of it comes near the circumstance/ Which I have told thee of my father's death:/ (he crosses to Horatio) I prithee, when thou seest that act a-foot,/ . . . / Observe my uncle. . . ." After Horatio's reply, music is heard from offstage left. Hamlet tells Horatio, "They are coming to the play: I must be idle: (he is center stage)/ Get you a place."[229] Horatio crosses to the lower platform and stands at the right, below the steps.

The Queen, four Ladies, and two Men enter stage right on the mainstage. The Queen is wearing a large red robe, which she lets fall on her chair as she sits. One Lady stands to her right, another on the first step below her and to her right. The other two Ladies and the two Men stand on the platform behind her. The King enters from the left on the mainstage, also wearing an encompassing red robe; he is followed by two Ladies, Rosencrantz and Guildenstern, and six Men. He crosses to the right of his chair. One Lady crosses to below and left of the chair and stands on the first step; the other crosses to above and left of her on the lower platform. Rosencrantz and Guildenstern converse with these ladies; Rosencrantz stands below Guildenstern. The six

Men are grouped behind and above the King. The music quiets down and stops as the dialogue begins.[230]

The King asks, "How fares our cousin Hamlet?" and sits on his throne. Hamlet retorts, "Excellent, i' faith; of the chameleon's dish: I eat the air, promise-crammed: you cannot feed capons so." After the King's response and Hamlet's answer, Polonius enters from the left and crosses to left center.[231] Hamlet, seeing him, calls out: "My lord, you played once i' the university, you say?" Polonius crosses to the left of Hamlet and replies, "That did I, my lord, and was accounted a good actor." Hamlet murmurs "hum – " and then asks: "What did you [/] *enact?*"[232] Polonius responds, "I did enact Julius Caesar: I was killed i' the Capitol; Brutus killed me." He turns away and crosses to above and behind the King. "It was a brute part of him to kill so capital a calf there," Hamlet responds, crossing downstage right as he speaks the last few words. "Be –" He starts to speak as he turns, taking in Horatio, Rosencrantz, and Guildenstern, but stops as he sees Ophelia entering left. He pauses for about three seconds. Ophelia stops for a second, then crosses and sits on the stool on the platform. "– Be the players ready?" He crosses to the center of the lower platform on his line. Polonius crosses to the King.[233] Rosencrantz tells Hamlet, "Ay, my lord; they stay upon your patience." The Queen asks Hamlet to sit with her, but he tells her, indicating Ophelia: "No, good mother, here's metal more attractive." He crosses to the left of Ophelia.

Polonius, on the platform, addresses the King over his shoulder: "Oh, ho! Do you mark that?" Hamlet asks Ophelia, "Lady, shall I lie in your lap?" He lies down on the purple cloth to the left of Ophelia, his head toward her. She replies, "No, my lord." "I mean, my head upon your lap?" "You are merry, my lord." "Who, I?" Hamlet asks. "Ay, my lord." "O God, your only jig-maker," he replies. Then, with false gaiety, "What should a man do but be merry? for, look you, (the Queen is here smiling to the lady at her right) how cheerfully my mother looks, and my father died within 's two hours."[234] "Nay, 'tis twice two months, my lord."

After Hamlet's reply we hear music offstage left – a solo flute.[235] When the music concludes, the First Player enters at the left on the upper platform. Lights come on, striking the Player; he crosses to the center of the platform, bows, and speaks the three-line prologue, then bows again and exits. Hamlet asks, "Is this a prologue, or the posy of a ring?" Ophelia replies, "'Tis brief, my lord." Looking at the Queen, Hamlet adds, "As woman's love."[236]

The First Player enters again on the top platform and kneels left at the end of the next-to-top step below the arch. The Second Player enters at the opposite side of the platform at the same time and kneels at the right on the same step. After they have kneeled, the Mime King enters left on the top platform and crosses on the platform to left of center; the Mime Queen enters right to right of center. Both wear rich, splendid robes of stiff, gold material and stylized crowns; the Mime King has a gray beard. The mimes bow to each other (hands pressed together), then to the audience (hands down). When they assume erect positions the First Player begins his speech. The Mime King and Queen hold their hands up, palms out, even with their shoulders, and assume that position when in repose.[237]

Music is heard from offstage left and continues through the scene; it is a variation of the melody played for the prologue. The First Player, kneeling, begins his speech, chanting or intoning the lines. The mimes suit the action to the word with stylized gestures. After the First Player's speech concludes, the Second Player, also kneeling, delivers the lines of the Player Queen, intoning them in a high, rich young voice. During these and the two ensuing speeches Hamlet watches the play with interest. After the Second Player's "In second husband let me be accurst! (sharp gesture – right hand down)/ None wed the second (hands on chest) but who kill'd the first (bows head)" Hamlet looks at the Queen and delivers his aside in a low tone: "Wormwood, wormwood." The Queen looks away.[238] Again he turns his attention to the Players. After the Second Player's "If, once a widow, ever I be wife!" he laughs anxiously: "*If she should break it now!*" Everyone looks at Hamlet except the Players.[239] All look back at the play as the First Player continues. After the Mime Queen exits, turning slowly and going out stage right up the steps, the Mime King lies down at the center of the top platform. His left elbow rests on the stage; he supports his head with his left hand (Fig. 31).[240]

A buzzing of conversation is heard from the court; the music continues. Hamlet looks mischievously at the Queen, aware that the play is making her uncomfortable: "Madam, how like you this play?" The Queen replies, "The lady doth protest too much, methinks." "O, but she'll keep her word," Hamlet tells her sarcastically, with a short, nervous, almost explosive laugh.[241] "Have you heard the argument? Is there no offense in't?" the King asks nervously. "No, no, they do but jest, *poison* in jest; no offense i' the world," Hamlet replies with aggressive sarcasm. "What do you call the play?" asks the King. The music stops. Hamlet lies on the platform looking at the King. A long pause of ten to twenty seconds. The suddenly Hamlet sits up and replies: "The Mouse-trap." He pauses about five seconds before proceeding.[242] He then tells the King that the play "is the image of a murder done in Vienna" and "a knavish piece of work; but what o' that? your majesty, and we that have free souls (the King laughs good-naturedly), it touches us not . . ."[243]

Lucianus enters from the left on the top platform. He is a much exaggerated caricature of the King; his face is made up very white, with great red circles around his eyes and black lips, like a Chinese mask. His action is extremely broad. The music changes. Hamlet continues, "This is one Lucianus, nephew to the king." The First Player intones Lucianus's lines in an exaggerated manner as the Mime Lucianus performs the action. When the Mime Lu-

Figure 31. The staging of the play scene in London. Courtesy Hulton Getty Picture Collection.

cianus pours poison in the sleeping Mime King's ear, the King, greatly disturbed, looks away, but he looks directly at Hamlet when Hamlet speaks:[244] "He poisons him i' the garden for his estate." He starts to creep toward the King, then lifts himself on one arm to point accusingly:[245] "His name's Gonzago –" He leaps up center, jumps across to right of the King, leans closely over him, and speaks directly into his ear. The King becomes terror-stricken. "– the story is extant, and written in very choice Italian: you shall see anon how the murderer (the King rises, panic in his actions, and throws his cloak around him) gets the love of Gonzago's wife." The King shrieks. Hamlet jumps to the center of the first platform. The King rushes to center on the mainstage.[246]

A loud discord, then the music stops. Pandemonium. The following lines are spoken simultaneously in the confusion of the court:

QUEEN: "How fares my lord?" (rises and crosses to the King)
OPHELIA: "The King rises." (stands up)

POLONIUS: "Give o'er the play." (crosses to left center; comes down to the
  King's left)
HAMLET: What, frighted with false fire!" (wild and hysterical)[247]
KING: "Give me some light. Away!"
OTHERS: "Lights, lights, lights!"

The King rushes out left on the mainstage. Polonius, the Queen (who
leaves her robe on her chair), Ophelia, Rosencrantz, Guildenstern, and a few
courtiers follow after him. Some courtiers go off right. The First and Second
Players rise in consternation and exit right on the top platform; the Mime
Players exit left on the top platform.

Horatio crosses downstage to right center. Hamlet, wild with excitement,
runs up to the upper platform, then down again to upstage center on the first
platform, left of Horatio. He laughs hysterically. "Why, let the stricken deer
go weep (a flood of relieved tension),/ The hart ungalled play –" (an extra
Lady who stands below Horatio becomes very confused, not knowing which
way to run, and finally crosses toward the left on the mainstage; then, as
though drawn back, she crosses to below and left of Hamlet) "– For some
must watch, while some must sleep –" (the Lady screams hysterically and
runs off left) "Thus runs the world away."[248] Hamlet proclaims triumphantly,
"Would not this, sir, and a forest of feathers . . . get me a fellowship in a cry
of players, sir?" After their two-line exchange, Hamlet follows with another
verse, then crosses to Horatio and clutches his arm: "O good Horatio, I'll take
the ghost's word for a thousand pound. . . ."[249]

Polonius enters left on the mainstage. Hamlet, right center, calls "God
bless you, sir!" He makes an elaborate bow and crosses to left center, downstage right of Polonius, who tells him: "My lord, the queen would speak with
you, and presently." Hamlet looks out at the audience, pointing front: "Do
you see *yonder cloud* [/] that's almost in *shape* of a *camel?*"[250] Polonius replies,
"By the mass, and 'tis like a camel, indeed." Hamlet tells him, "Methinks it is
like a *weasel.*" Polonius indicates the shape with his finger: "It is backed like
a weasel." Hamlet speaks directly to Polonius, in a sharper voice: "Or like a
whale?" "Very like a whale," Polonius replies. "Then I will *come* to my *mother by*
and by." Hamlet crosses to Horatio for his next line: "They *fool* me to the *top*
of my *bent* (angrily)." He turns left to Polonius: "I will come *by* and *by.*" "I will
say so," Polonius replies. He bows. "'*By* and *by*' is easily said," Hamlet tells him,
and Polonius quickly exits left.

Horatio steps to the right of Hamlet and puts his hand on his arm. Hamlet places his hand on Horatio's arm and says "Good night, Horatio." Horatio replies, "Good night unto your lordship," bows, and goes out right.

Hamlet stands center: "'Tis now the very witching time of night,/ . . . now
could I drink hot blood,/ And do such bitter business as the day/ Would

quake to look on. Soft! now to my mother."[251] He starts to exit left, but then pauses and touches the chair where his mother had been sitting. The lights dim as he quickly exits left. The house curtain is lowered.

As in the nunnery scene, Hamlet's business here varied considerably in performance. Taylor felt that Barrymore failed entirely in this scene, and that he was conscious of not doing it well, trying different readings and new business "nearly every time he did it, and each time it seemed to grow worse." Critical commentary was for the most part positive, however; the *International Interpreter*, for example, praised his "powerful and restrained" performance.[252]

In his *Tribune* interview, Beauvais Fox mentioned that some of the reviewers had suggested "that Hamlet should maintain an alert surveillance of the King throughout the interior play," and noted that Barrymore "permits his eyes to follow the various sallies with Ophelia and the Queen and is himself an interested spectator of the dumb show until the crucial moment of the counterfeit murder, when he smites his eyes upon the guilt-stricken King" (14 January 1923). Barrymore commented in reply that

> Hamlet does not underestimate the astuteness of his uncle. So wise is he that he provides against betrayal by his instinctive dislike of the King. Claudius has a keen intuition of his nephew's suspicions. Obviously, a too careful scrutiny by the Prince would carry notice of the driving power of his actions and the trap would be discovered. A personality so dynamic as Hamlet's, a man of such extraordinary intellect, a mind of so many facets, requires but a flash at the King in the critical instant.

Stark Young particularly admired Barrymore's tact in the scenes with Polonius. Most actors, he wrote,

> For the applause they get play up for all it is worth Hamlet's seemingly rude wit at the old man's expense. But Mr. Barrymore gave you only Hamlet's sense of the world grown empty and life turned to rubbish in this old counselor. And, without seeming to do so he made you feel that Polonius for Hamlet stood for the kind of thing in life that had taken Ophelia from him.[253]

This scene was reblocked for the second season and new business was introduced; alterations are cited in the Notes.

The recorder scene was restored on 8 January 1923. It was retained until the second season, but was cut after opening night. The business was as follows:

Music begins off left on Hamlet's line, "Upon the talk of the poisoning?" After his "Come, some music!' Horatio exits right; Rosencrantz and Guildenstern enter left and cross to left center. Hamlet sits in the chair on "With drink, sir?" He rises and takes a step toward Rosencrantz and Guildenstern after "O wonderful son, that can so astonish a mother!" On "So I do still, by these pickers and stealers" he holds up his hand and waggles his fingers. He again sits in the chair before "Ay, sir, but 'while the grass grows' . . ." Horatio and a Player carrying a recorder enter right. Horatio crosses to right of the chair, the Player to below and right of him. After Hamlet's "O, the recorders!" Rosencrantz and Guildenstern take a couple of steps upstage. Hamlet, seeing them, jumps up, then turns to the musician as he sees the recorder. The Player gives it to him, bows out, and exits right. Hamlet crosses to the right of Rosencrantz and Guildenstern and offers them the pipe during the ensuing exchange. At the end of the scene he crosses right and pitches the pipe onto the chair. He turns and crosses right as Polonius enters left; seeing Polonius, he makes an elaborate bow.[254]

"I could interpret between you and your love" and Hamlet's command to Lucianus were restored spontaneously by Barrymore on Thursday night, 25 January 1923, and were retained during the final weeks. They were cut again during the second season. As Hamlet spoke the lines, "Begin, murderer; pox, leave thy damnable faces, and begin. Come: the croaking raven doth bellow for revenge," he beat the floor impatiently, and the court, according to Adams, looked at him "in amazement" – as was undoubtedly the case the night he restored the lines.[255]

Act II, scene iii. *A room in the castle.* [Temple edition III.iii, 98 lines cut to 47 $^1/_2$]

The tableau curtains come on during the blackout. Lights up; the baby spots focus on the heads of the curtain figures. As the lights come on the King enters through the curtains; he plays the scene in front of the tableau curtains and on the apron. He paces from right to left to right to left to right center, then reaches up to his neck, holds forth a cross on a silver chain, and begins: "O, my offense is rank, it smells to heaven . . ." On "O limed soul, that struggling to be free/ Art more engaged," he crosses to the center of the apron. After "Bow, stubborn knees, . . . All may be well," he holds the cross before him and kneels at the front of the apron, facing the audience.[256]

We see one hand parting the tableau curtains; then Hamlet enters slowly through the curtains and crosses to upstage center. He takes a few steps right, turns front, then pauses as he notices the King. He looks at him a moment, then speaks slowly and deliberately, in a low tone: "*Now* might I *do it pat,* now he is *praying;*/ And *now* I'll *do't:* (he draws his sword quickly, points it at the audience, and takes a step forward toward the King; pause) and so he *goes* to *heaven* (upward emphasis):/ And so am I *revenged* (downward emphasis). That would be *scann'd;*/ A *villain* kills my *father;* and *for that,*/ I, his *sole son,* do this *same villain* send/ To *heaven./* . . . / He *took* my *father grossly, full* of *bread,/*

Figure 32. The King at prayer scene in the 1922 New York production, with Tyrone Power as the King. Courtesy Billy Rose Theatre Collection, The New York Public Library for the Performing Arts.

With *all* his *crimes broad blown,* . . ./ And . . . am I then . . ./ To take *him* in the *purging* of his *soul,*/ (harsher tone) When he is *fit* and *season'd* for his *passage?*/ (pause) No./ (long pause; he raises his sword; his right hand grasps the pommel, his left closes around the blade below the hilt. He loosens his grasp with his right hand, then his left, then, with sinister coldness) *Up, sword,* (he raises his sword and sheaths it about one half) and know thou a more *horrid hent:* (completes sheathing of sword; Fig. 32)/ When he is *drunk asleep,* or in his *rage,*/ Or in the *incestuous pleasure* of his *bed;*/ (quick and harsh) Then *trip* him, (he raises his right hand abruptly to waist level and clenches it into a fist)[257] that his *heels* may *kick* at *heaven*/ And that his *soul* (last word drawn out; slight pause) may be as *damn'd* and *black*/ As *hell*, [/] whereto it *goes* (low tone)." He crosses back to the opening of the curtains. "My mother *stays*." He exits through the tableau curtains. The King speaks: "My words fly up, my thoughts remain below: (he rises slowly)/ Words without thoughts never to heaven go." He crosses upstage center and exits through the curtains as the lights dim out.[258] The house curtain falls.

Stark Young commented admiringly,

> It is in the scene where Hamlet catches the King praying and does not kill him . . . that the method of production employed by Mr. Hopkins and Mr. Jones is reduced . . . to its most characteristic terms. The King enters through the curtain [and] . . . kneels facing the audience. He lifts his hands and speaks to heaven. Hamlet enters through the same curtain. He debates the fitness of the time for the King's murder, decides against it, and withdraws. . . . One man is here, one is there. Here are the uplifted hands, there the sword drawn. Here, sick conscience, power, and tormented ambition; there, the torture of conflicting thoughts, the irony, the resolution. Two bodies and their relation to each other, the words, the essential drama, the eternal content of the scene. No tricks, no plausible business, no palace chapel. And no tradition.[259]

Act II, scene iv. *The Queen's closet.* [Temple edition III.iv, 217 lines cut to 143]

The tableau curtains are withdrawn during the blackout. The black curtains behind the arch come on full. A small throne chair is placed one foot to the right of the break in the steps, left center. A large three-part arras-screen featuring black and gold curtains on a wrought iron frame is placed center stage on the first platform below the steps. The house curtain rises.[260]

The Queen is discovered left center, pacing left and right above the chair. She is wearing a purple gown trimmed in gray fur. Polonius enters right and crosses to right center: "He will come straight. . . . Pray you, be round with him." The Queen replies, "I'll warrant you; fear me not. (she looks off right) Withdraw, I hear him coming."[261] Polonius crosses upstage and hides left center behind the arras.

Hamlet enters right on the mainstage and crosses to right center. He is wearing a sword. "Now, *mother,* what's the *matter?*" is spoken quickly, but with calm authority.[262] The Queen replies, "Hamlet, thou hast thy father much offended." Hamlet tells her firmly, *"Mother,* [/] *you* have my *father* [/] *much offended."* He crosses to center stage on his line *"Go, go,* you *question* with a *wicked tongue."* After a two-line exchange he moves to the Queen's right and tells her: *"No,* by the *rood, not so:*/ You are the *queen,* your *husband's brother's wife;*/

And – were it not *so* – [/] you are *my mother.*" Following the Queen's, "Nay, then, I'll set those to you that can speak," she starts right. Hamlet quickly catches her by the wrists: "*Come, come,* (quickly; he is agitated) and *sit* you *down;* (he pushes her back to the chair, and she sits)[263] You *shall* not *BUDGE;/* You go not till I *set* you up a *glass/* Where you may see the *inmost part* of you." The Queen replies, "What wilt thou do? thou wilt not murder me? (she starts up from the chair toward center stage) Help, help, ho!"

Polonius, behind the screen, calls, "What, ho! help, help, help!" Hamlet crosses up center: "*How now!* [/] A *rat?* (he draws his sword and shouts) *Dead, for a ducat* (he steps up to the screen), *dead!*" As he speaks the last word he thrusts his sword through the screen – a graceful, deliberate homicide. The Queen crosses up to right center. Polonius, behind the arras, calls, "O, I am slain!" We hear the sound of Polonius falling.[264] The Queen gasps an exclamation of horror, then crosses further upstage: "O me, what hast thou done?" Hamlet turns toward the Queen and replies quietly, "Nay, I *know not:* (pauses about five seconds) is it the *king?*"[265]

The Queen cries, "O, what a rash and bloody deed is this!" Hamlet's firm, quiet reply speaks of inward rather than outward excitation: "A *bloody deed!* almost as *bad, good mother* (crosses a step toward the Queen),/ As *kill* a *king* [/], and *marry* with his *brother.*"[266] The Queen shrinks back on her reply: "As kill a king!" Hamlet tells her in a low, quiet tone: "*Ay, lady,* [/] 'twas my *word./* (turns upstage, lifts the side of the screen, and looks at Polonius; then, languorously, with violent irony and bitter exasperation)[267] Thou *wretched, rash, intruding fool* (last word drawn out; he becomes quiet), *farewell!/* I *took* thee for thy *better.*" He sheaths his sword. The Queen wrings her hands in terror and distress. Hamlet turns, steps down from the platform, and crosses to the Queen, then to the left of the chair: "*Leave wringing* of your *hands* (agitated yet firm): *peace! sit* you *down,/* (he indicates for the Queen to sit in the chair; she crosses and sits; he crosses to her left) And let *me wring* your *heart . . .* [268] After the Queen protests his rudeness, Hamlet tells her, "Such an *act/* That *blurs* the *grace* and *blush* of *modesty . . .*" Following the Queen's response, Hamlet tells her to "*Look here,* upon *this picture,* [/] (he takes a locket on a chain from his blouse and kneels, left of the Queen) *and on this,* (he takes her locket of the King and holds both in his left hand)/ The *counterfeit presentment* of *two brothers./* (he points to his medallion with his forefinger)[269] . . . / *This was your husband.*" Then, sharply: "Look you *now,* what *follows:/* Here *is your husband;* (he points to the Queen's medallion with his forefinger; the Queen turns her head away) like a *mildew'd ear,/ Blasting* his *wholesome brother.* Have you eyes?/ . . . Ha! have you eyes? (he thrusts the medallions in front of her eyes)/[270] . . . what judgement/ Would step from this to this? (he throws the Queen's medallion down)/ . . ."[271] Hamlet rises and paces upstage center behind the Queen. She is weeping and tells him: "O Hamlet, speak no more/

Thou turn'st mine eyes into my very soul,/ And there I see such black and grained spots (sound effect: whistle, saw, and wind from off right)/ As will not leave their tinct (whistle, saw, and wind)."

Hamlet (left and above the chair) is suddenly struck by a beam of sharp greenish-white light from above – the Ghost takes possession of him. He becomes rigid, trembling, and transfixed; his eyes are wide and staring. Pause; then he speaks in a strange, deep, hoarse, measured voice like that the voice of the Ghost. His hands are stiff at his sides; the harsh light shines on his face:[272] "Nay, but to live (tenderly)/ In the rank sweat of an enseamed bed,/ Stew'd in corruption, honeying and making love/ Over the nasty sty, –"[273] The Queen, deeply agitated, tells him, "O, speak to me no more;/ These words like daggers enter in my ears . . ." Hamlet speaks slowly, his words measured, in the tones of one in a hypnotic trance:[274] "A *murderer* and a *villain;/ A slave* [/] that is not *twentieth part* the *tithe/* Of your *precedent lord . . .*" He becomes more rigid, his hands stiff and tense at his side. The Queen interjects, "No more!" "A *king* of *shreds* and *patches* –" He struggles to get out of his strange trance. The light suddenly goes off; Hamlet falls to his knees left of the Queen as though unable to support himself. As he kneels he gasps, then he shrieks wildly in terror and hysteria, as though released from the grip of his father's spirit; then, using the high head tone he used in addressing the Ghost on its first appearance: "*Save me,* and hover o'er me with your *wings,/* You *heavenly guards!*" Lights on Hamlet from the right; saw effect offstage right; he gasps heavily. He then speaks more quietly, in respectful awe: "What would your *gracious figure!*"[275] The Queen looks at Hamlet, amazed and terrified: "Alas (almost whispering), he's mad!" Hamlet looks straight and front (quietly): "Do you not *come* your *tardy son* to *chide,/* O, say!"

The Ghost speaks from behind the arras to tell Hamlet his visitation is "to whet thy almost blunted purpose." He tells him to speak to his mother. Hamlet extends his hands out to the Queen: "How is it *with* you, *lady?*" "Alas, how is't with you,/ Whereon do you look?" asks the Queen. "On *him,* on *him!* Look you how pale he glares!" The Queen looks off right: "To whom do you speak this?" Hamlet looks and points off right: "Do you see [/] *nothing there?*" The Queen looks off right: "Nothing at all; (she looks back at Hamlet) yet all that is I see." "Nor [/] did you *nothing hear?*" "No, nothing but ourselves." Hamlet tells her (dreamlike voice): "Why, *look* you *there!*" (he points off right, then crawls frantically toward the Ghost on his knees, stopping as he reaches the Queen's side)[276] "*look,* how it *steals away!/* My *father,* in his *habit* as he *lived!* (he clutches the Queen closely)/ *Look,* where he *goes,* even *now,* out at the *portal!*" The light goes out. The Queen answers him hysterically: "This is the very coinage of your brain:/ This bodiless creation ecstasy . . ." She holds Hamlet close to her. Hamlet draws back from the Queen and continues his speech in a reasonable and almost even tone:[277] "*Ecstasy!* (he looks closely into the

Figure 33. The Queen's closet scene: Hamlet and Gertrude (Blanche Yurka). Courtesy Billy Rose Theatre Collection, The New York Public Library for the Performing Arts.

Queen's eyes)/ My *pulse,* as *yours,* doth *tem*perately *keep time,*/ And makes as *healthful music:* it is not *mad*ness/ That I have *utter'd.*" He launches himself at his mother, still kneeling, and pommels the floor with his knees:[278] "*Mother,* for *love* of *grace,*/ Lay *not* that *flattering unction* to your *soul,*/ That not your *tres*pass but my *madness speaks.*" The Queen, sobbing, tells him: "O Hamlet, thou hast cleft my heart in twain." She drops her head.

Hamlet embraces her (Fig. 33) and tells her (tenderly and quietly):[279] "O, *throw away* the *worser* part of *it,*/ And *live* the *purer* [/] with the *other half.*/ Good *night:* (drawing back)." He tells her to "go not to my uncle's bed. . . . Refrain to-night,/ And that shall lend a kind of easiness/ To the next [/] absti-nence."[280] ". . . Once more, *good night:* (drawn out languorously)/ And *when* you are *desirous* to be *blest,*/ [/] I'll *blessing beg* [/] of *you* (close embrace; he buries his head in the Queen's lap).[281] For this same lord, (he looks up to Polonius's body, then rises and crosses to left center)/ I do repent:/ I will bestow him, (he turns toward the Queen) and will answer well/ The death I gave him. So, again, *good night./* (he takes her head in his hands) I must be *cruel,* only to be *kind:/* (he draws back) One word more, good lady."[282]

The Queen, still in her chair, looks out at the audience and asks "What should I do?" "I must to England: you know that?" Hamlet tells her. "Alack,/ I had forgot: 'tis so concluded on." Hamlet tells her there is a conspiracy against him but resolves to thwart it. He then looks off left: "This man shall set me packing: (he looks off left) / I'll lug the guts into the neighbor room./ Mother, good night." They embrace. Hamlet kisses her hand, and then her hair. He crosses upstage center to the screen, lifts up the screen curtain, exclaims, "Bah!" then looks at Polonius, speaking his next lines over his corpse: "*Indeed* this *counsellor/* Is now *most still,* most *secret* and most *grave,/* Who was in *life* a *foolish prating knave.*"[283] The Queen gives a long, sobbing sigh at the end of his speech, then Hamlet stoops over to pick up Polonius's body. The Queen half turns to him. He tells her, "*Good night* [/], *mother*" in a way that suggests he is asking forgiveness.[284] He drops the screen so that he is behind it. The Queen leans forward, her head in her hands. The lights dim out and the curtain falls.[285]

The curtain calls after Act II were as follows: (1) The house curtain rises: Hamlet and the Queen. (2) After the house curtain is down, the tableau curtain is brought on. The King and Horatio stand behind the tableaus. The house curtain rises, then the King, Queen, and Horatio enter through the tableaus. Then: Horatio alone, King alone, Queen alone. Then Hamlet alone. If another call: Hamlet and Queen. House curtain down.

Blanche Yurka remembered that after the second act curtain calls,

> [Barrymore] would step before the curtain to acknowledge the applause and make a speech. These speeches would begin with a courtly expression of thanks and then he would go on to recount the comments made on his performance by Paul, his Negro dresser – comments which were pungent, frank and infinitely amusing. The whole company would crowd into the front of the wings to listen. The stories were never the same and the audiences responded with laughter and delight to his informal joking. The interval over, he would retire behind the curtain. [Later] he would reappear – perfectly in key, powerful, moving – Hamlet himself, again recapturing his audience completely. It was something to see, something to have experienced.[286]

Second Intermission

Lark Taylor recalled a discussion in which Barrymore told him: "'There is an unusual thing – something that has never been done before – and not a single critic noted it.' He was referring to the incident where he acts as though the spirit of his father had taken possession of him, and was speaking to the Queen through him." The moment, Taylor commented, was "tremendously dramatic and thrilling, but I am quite certain Shakespeare had no such idea when he invented the scene. Blanche Yurka heartily disliked the way this scene was played, and spoke of it as 'Barrymore's epileptic fit.' Barrymore had considered it at length, and worked it out carefully. His attitude toward the Queen was very tender and affectionate, which I liked very much. He didn't like Hamlet saying such terrible things to his mother, and said that letting his father use him as a medium through which to speak took the curse off of the scene. 'Doing it that way makes Hamlet so much more decent,' he said – then, after a moment's patient reflection, he burst out: 'God! How I would love to talk with Shakespeare about this play!'"[287]

Much of the scene's impact resulted from the restoration of sexual passages traditionally deleted, however, and the "possession" effect hardly went unnoticed. John Corbin, writing in the *Times* (17 December 1922), found that

> As a whole the performance is cerebral rather than passionate. Even when he has killed Polonius his cry, "Is it the King?" and his wild taunt,
>
>> A bloody deed? Almost as bad, good mother,
>> As kill a King and marry with his brother!
>
> speak rather of an inward than of an outward excitation. It is only in the subsequent scene of mirroring Gertrude to her own conscience and of pleading with her against herself that emotion becomes outwardly agonized, and the result is perhaps the most tenderly impassioned and compelling passage of emotional acting in modern memory.
>
> It will not do, however, to take this as the keynote of the drama, attributing to Hamlet the Oedipus complex. Throughout Mr. Barrymore's performance, as throughout the play, chief emphasis is laid upon Hamlet's love and reverence for his father, his sense of Gertrude's guilt being incidental and subordinate. And so, at the close of this tenderly filial pleading, Hamlet's thoughts revert to Claudius –
>
>> A murderer and a villain;
>> A slave that is not twentieth part the tithe
>> Of your precedent lord –
>
> and the major motive asserts itself again in the apparition of King Hamlet. There is no darkness now to obscure the actor. A fierce light that comes as if from the invisible Ghost himself beats upon Hamlet's face, revealing the minutest play of every lineament. This is the true climax of the performance and, as it seems to me, is felt by the audience as such. For myself, certainly, it is a moment of tragic awe and passion without parallel in a lifetime of playgoing.[288]

Act III

Act III, scene i. *A room in the castle.* [Temple edition IV.v, 219 lines cut to 168]

The black curtains behind the arch come on full. A small throne chair is placed right center in the same position as it was in the play scene. The house curtain rises. The lights come on after the curtain is up. The Queen is discovered seated in the chair. She is attended by four Ladies grouped around her. Horatio is at the Queen's left and above her. A Gentlewoman stands left center.

After the Queen's exchange with the Gentlewoman, in which the Gentlewoman tells her of Ophelia's "madness," the Queen looks at Horatio who advises her, "'Twere good she were spoken with . . ." The Queen tells the Gentlewoman, "Let her come in," and the Gentlewoman exits left on the mainstage. Ophelia, a "fragile, wistful little figure, almost wraith-like," runs in from the left and crosses to upstage center.[289] She is wearing a head-wreath of flowers and a long white gown. The Gentlewoman reenters to left center. Ophelia asks, "Where is the beauteous majesty of Denmark?" The Queen (surprised) replies, "How now, Ophelia!" Ophelia crosses to a little left and above the Queen and sings: "How should I your true love know/ . . ." The Queen asks "Alas, sweet lady, what imports this song?" Ophelia's reply – like her dialogue throughout the scene – is half-spoken, half-sung. She sings another verse, crossing to left center as she sings. The King enters from the right during her song and crosses to the right of the Queen (Fig. 34). He speaks to Ophelia: "How do you, pretty lady?" She crosses to him on her reply and afterward crosses upstage to left center. She sings a bawdy verse, then crosses to left of the Queen and sings another: ". . . / Quoth she, before you tumbled me,/ You promised me to wed./ . . ." The King turns (he is close to the Queen) and asks, "How long hath she been thus?"[290]

Ophelia half-speaks, half-sings "I hope all will be well. . . . to think they should lay him i' the cold ground." She glares at the King and continues: "My brother shall know of it (bows, smiling): and so I thank you for your good counsel." She crosses to the space left of the steps on the lower platform. After "Come, my coach!" she starts up the steps: "Good night, ladies . . . (ascending) good night, good night." She exits through the black curtains behind the arch, laughing wildly.[291]

The King crosses to left center, looking after Ophelia. He tells Horatio, "Follow her close; give her good watch, I pray you." Horatio bows and exits up the steps and through the curtains. The King tells the Queen Ophelia's grief stems from her father's death; he draws a few steps closer to her. Shouts

Figure 34. Ophelia's (Fay Compton) mad scene in the 1925 London production.
Courtesy Mander & Mitchenson Collection.

are suddenly heard offstage: "Laertes King," "Choose we Laertes," "Laertes
shall be king!" They continue to grow in volume. The Queen rises and asks,
"Alack, what noise is this?" Horatio rushes on through the curtains at the top
of the stairs. The King looks at him and asks, "What is the matter?" The
Queen looks at the King anxiously during Horatio's explanation; midway
through his speech, Horatio crosses down the steps to left of the Queen. The
Queen looks off left on her ensuing lines. A loud crash is heard offstage; the
King cries, "The doors are broke."

Laertes calls from off left: "Where is this King?" He runs on from the left
to left of the King, his sword drawn: "O thou vile king,/ Give me my father!"
He thrusts his sword toward the King. The Queen rushes to Laertes's right
and places her hands on his shoulders to restrain him. After the King's first
"Let him go, Gertrude," she backs off a little but still keeps a hand on Laertes's arm; when he repeats the command she withdraws her hand and backs
off to right of the chair. After the King confirms that Polonius is dead, the

Queen crosses to left of the King, clutches his arm, and, facing Laertes, inter-jects, "But not by him." The King tells her, "Let him demand his fill," and pushes away the Queen's hand. He stands facing Laertes, listens to his de-mand for revenge, and tells him he is guiltless.[292]

We hear cries from off left (repeated three times): "Let her come in." The King turns to the sounds. Laertes asks, "How now! what noise is that?" and crosses to below and left of the steps. Ophelia appears through the black cur-tains behind the arch and comes down two steps. Laertes stares at her a mo-ment then drops his sword as he realizes who it is. The Queen sits.[293]

Ophelia stands for some time staring vacantly at Laertes, smiling and eye-ing him coquettishly. She gradually descends the stairs and approaches Laer-tes during his ensuing speech; at the end she is quite close to him. She then turns away sadly, center stage, gazes out vacantly, and sings another verse of her song, crossing to right center then center as she sings.[294] Laertes crosses slowly to left center during her song. She crosses to Laertes and sings again. Then, in pantomime, she hands him an imaginary flower: "There's rosemary (he does not take it), that's for remembrance: pray you, love, remember (she looks coyly at Laertes, then crosses left to the Gentlewoman): and there is pansies (in pantomime she gives her flowers), that's for thoughts" (she crosses slowly to the King, right center). After Laertes's line, she offers imag-inary flowers to the King – "There's fennel for you, and columbines:" – (then to the Queen) "there's rue for you: and here's some for me. . . . There's a daisy: (then, to Horatio) I would give you some violets, but they withered all when my father died: (Horatio starts to extend a hand to her, but she shrinks back) they say a' made a good end, – (she crosses to Laertes and sings) For bonnie sweet Robin is all my joy." She wanders down to center stage on Laer-tes's ensuing lines, then sings again: "His beard was as white as snow . . ." At the end of her song she tells the King and Queen, "God be wi' you." She be-comes bewildered, then with a light, crazy laugh, she runs up the stairs and through the black curtains.[295]

Laertes raises his hands to heaven: "Do you see this, O God?" He crosses to left of center below the steps and converses with the King, who takes his arm, stands close to him at his right, and tells him the matter of his father's mur-der and his sister's madness will be settled to his satisfaction. After the King's "I pray you, go with me," the King and Laertes start to cross up center. The lights dim out.

Act III, scene ii. *Another room in the castle.* [Temple edition IV.vii, 195 lines cut to 84 $^1/_2$]

The tableau curtains come on during the blackout. The lights come on grad-ually; baby spots create the halo effect on the heads of the curtain figures.

The King, followed by Laertes, enters through the curtains.[296] The King crosses to center stage; Laertes crosses to his left. The King asks Laertes for his friendship. Laertes vows revenge for the loss of his father and his sister's madness, and the King tells him: "Break not your sleeps for that." A messenger enters through the curtains with two letters from Hamlet; he kneels at the left, presents the letters, then rises, bows low, and exits through the curtains. The King reads the first letter, then looks at Laertes, who crosses a step toward the King after the King's query, "Know you the hand?" Laertes tells the King to "let him come" and pledges his allegiance. The King tells Laertes of his plan to have Hamlet die accidentally in a duel. Laertes agrees and tells the King he will poison the tip of his sword. The King replies, "Let me see," and crosses slowly to right center. After a moment he turns to Laertes: "We'll make a solemn wager on your cunnings . . ." He crosses back to Laertes (who listens intently throughout) and tells him he will prepare a poisoned drink for assurance.

The Queen is heard offstage calling, "My lord, my lord." The King backs right a step; Laertes backs left a step. The Queen enters through the curtains and tells Laertes that his sister has drowned. Laertes starts in horror; the King gives a wordless exclamation. Laertes tells the Queen he will not cry but soon breaks down weeping, holding his face in his hands. He takes a step toward the King before "Adieu, my lord," and after his concluding line he exits, sobbing, through the curtains.[297] The Queen crosses to the King, who takes her in his arms and tries to console her. He suggests that they follow Laertes. The King and Queen exit through the curtains; the lights dim out and the house curtain falls.

Act III, scene iii. *A churchyard.* [Temple edition V.i, 322 lines cut to 237]

The tableau curtains are removed during the blackout. The blue lights behind the arch project the night sky. Iron gates are placed in the arch at the top of the steps. The grave trap, center stage, is opened; it is about four feet deep and surrounded by a wall of earth and stone about one foot high. A large slab of stone, about four by six feet with "Ophelia" carved faintly in it is placed left center at the break in the steps. The house curtain rises. The lights come up gradually.[298]

Discovered: the Second Clown, standing above the grave, and the First Clown, seated on the left end of the grave with his feet hanging in the grave trap. A spade leans against the left end of the grave.[299] The Clowns discuss whether Christian burial is appropriate for suicides, and after the First Clown's "It must be 'se offendendo;' it cannot be else," he gets out of the grave, puts his shovel down, and crosses to the left of the Second Clown to deliver his mock-logical argument about drowning; he picks up the spade after

"Come, my spade," then, after the riddle about who "builds stronger than either the mason, the shipwright, or the carpenter" and the ensuing exchange, the First Clown sends his companion to "fetch me a stoup of liquor."[300] He gives the Second Clown a spank on the buttocks with his shovel and the Second Clown exits right.

The First Clown gets into the grave and starts rolling up his sleeves as he sings: "In youth, when I did love, did love . . ." Hamlet and Horatio enter from the left on the upper platform during his song; Hamlet wears a black cloak.[301] Hamlet crosses to right center on the upper platform and asks Horatio, "Has this fellow no feeling of his business that he sings at grave-making?" During Horatio's reply and the second verse of the First Clown's song, Hamlet and Horatio slowly cross down the steps to the lower platform above and right of the grave. The First Clown bends down into the grave and shovels up earth as he sings; at the end of his song he rises and lays a skull in back of the grave.[302]

Hamlet tells Horatio, "I will speak to this fellow." He crosses down to the right of the grave (Horatio at the same time crosses to his right) and addresses the First Clown: "Whose grave's this, sirrah?"[303] The first Clown answers, "Mine, sir," bends into the grave, and sings another two lines. He stands up and throws out a bone in back of the grave. Hamlet tells him, "I think it be thine indeed, for thou liest in't. . . ." After his reply, the Clown resumes digging and throws out another bone in back of the grave.[304] Hamlet asks the Clown, "What man dost thou dig it for?" The Clown looks up: "For no man, sir (resumes digging)." "What woman then?" "For none neither (digs)." "Who is to be buried in't?" The Clown straightens up: "One that was a woman, sir; but, rest her soul, she's dead." He stoops into the grave. Hamlet looks at Horatio and laughs: "How absolute the knave is! . . ." He crosses to the steps and sits above and right of the Clown: "How long hast thou been a grave-maker?"[305] The Clown straightens up, leans against the back of the grave, and tells him since "that day that our last King Hamlet o'ercame Fortinbras." Hamlet looks at Horatio, then asks the Clown: "How long is that since?" The Clown replies, " . . . it was that very day that young Hamlet was born: he that is mad, and sent into England."

Hamlet looks at Horatio, amused. He asks the Clown why Hamlet was sent into England; after the Clown's quip that "there the men are as mad as he," Hamlet and Horatio laugh. Hamlet asks the Clown, "How came he mad?" After the Clown's reply, Hamlet looks at Horatio and again they laugh. Hamlet then inquires, "How long will a man lie i' the earth ere he rot?" The Clown, after telling him "eight year or nine year . . . ," picks up the skull. Hamlet asks, "Whose was it?" The Clown holds up the skull and looks at it affectionately: "A whoreson mad fellow's it was: whose do you think it was?"[306] He looks up at Hamlet, who answers, "Nay, I know not." The Clown tells him

Figure 35. The Gravediggers' scene in London: Horatio (George Relph), Hamlet, First Clown (Ben Field), and Second Clown (Michael Martin-Harvey). Courtesy Hulton Getty Picture Collection.

"A pestilence on him for a mad rogue! (slaps skull) . . . This . . . was Yorick's skull, the king's jester." "This?" Hamlet replies, and his mood suddenly changes. "E'en that," the Clown replies (Fig. 35).

"Let me see." Hamlet holds out his hands and the Clown pitches up the skull. Hamlet catches it and sits looking at it for about six seconds before speaking. Then, with "measured and quaint melancholy":[307] "Alas, poor Yorick! (he pauses five seconds, then looks at Horatio) I knew him, Horatio: a fellow of infinite jest, of most excellent fancy: he hath borne me on his back a thousand times; and now (he raises the skull) how abhorred in my imagination it is! . . . Here hung those lips that I have kissed I know not how oft." He addresses the skull: "Where be your gibes now? . . . Not one now, to mock your own grinning? quite chop-fallen? (he holds the skull up in his right hand) . . ." He pauses five seconds at the end of his speech, then turns to Horatio. "Prithee, Horatio, tell me one thing."[308]

Horatio crosses to the right of Hamlet: "What's that, my lord?" "Dost thou think Alexander looked o' this fashion i' the earth?" Horatio replies, "E'en so." Hamlet holds up the skull and sniffs it: "And smelt so? pah!" He tosses the skull back to the First Clown, who places it above the grave. Horatio tells him, "E'en so, my lord." Hamlet comments (looking front), "To what base uses we may return, Horatio! (the Clown bends into the grave) Imperious Caesar, dead and turn'd to clay (ruthfully),/ Might stop a hole to keep the wind away."[309] He rises and crosses to the grave.

A bell starts tolling offstage. Hamlet crosses to center stage and starts; he looks off left and listens. The Clown gets out of the grave. He takes the skull and bones, lays them up on the platform, then exits right. Hamlet crosses to left of the grave, then turns to Horatio: "But soft! but soft! aside: here comes the king,/ The queen, the courtiers . . ." He crosses to behind the grave, looks into it, and shudders. He wraps his cloak around himself: "Couch we awhile, and mark."[310] The bell tolls again.

Hamlet crosses with Horatio to extreme downstage right, in the shadows; he stands left and above Horatio, screening himself with his cloak. The bell continues to toll at nine- or ten-second intervals. The funeral procession enters from the left on the mainstage. A white-robed Priest enters first and crosses to the center of the lower platform. Six women pall-bearers dressed as nuns in flowing white robes carrying the bier with the body of Ophelia (covered by a purple robe) enter next and cross to the front of the grave. Laertes, in a white robe, follows the nuns and stands above the left end of the grave. The Queen, in white, carrying flowers, enters and crosses to about four feet from the left end of the grave; the King, in white, stands to her left and a bit below her. As the procession enters the two Clowns enter right on the mainstage. The First Clown crosses to the left end of the grave, the Second Clown to the right end. The nuns place the bier directly in front of the grave, then form a straight line in front of it, their backs to the audience. They take the white pall, which is handed to them by the Clowns, and hold it to hide from the audience the moving of the body (a dummy). The Clowns lift the body into the grave, take the pall from the nuns, replace it on the bier, and exit left, carrying the bier. The nuns cross to the right, well above Hamlet and Horatio. Three stand on the lower platform, three on the mainstage to their left.[311]

The bell tolls for the last time, then Laertes speaks: "What ceremony else?" Hamlet turns to Horatio: "This is Laertes, a very noble youth: mark." Laertes repeats his question and the Priest, standing above the grave, offers his explanation. Laertes takes a step toward the Priest and asks, "Must there no more be done?" The Priest tells him, "No more . . ." and Laertes crosses upstage to behind the grave: "Lay her i' the earth. . . . A ministering angel shall my sister be,/ When thou liest howling." Hamlet, startled, exclaims: "What, the fair Ophelia!" The Queen crosses to just above the grave, strews petals into it, and says her farewell, then returns to her former position. Laertes cries out, "O, treble woe . . . Hold off the earth a while,/ Till I have caught her once more in mine arms: (he lies down above the grave and reaches into it as though touching the body, then rises to his knees and throws off his white robe) Now pile your dust upon the quick and dead . . ."[312]

Hamlet advances boldly toward the grave: "What is he whose grief/ Bears such an emphasis? . . . (he crosses to above and right of grave) This is I,/ Hamlet the Dane." He throws off his cloak. Horatio hastily retrieves it. Laertes leaps up quickly and springs at Hamlet, catching him by the throat: "The devil take thy soul!" They grapple; Hamlet gasps, ". . . Hold off thy hand." He throws Laertes to above the left end of the grave. The Queen steps to Laertes's left and holds him.[313] The King cries, "Pluck them asunder." The Queen calls, "Hamlet, Hamlet!" Horatio tosses Hamlet's cloak to the extreme right of the platform, then quickly crosses to the right of the grave and tells Hamlet, "Good my lord, be quiet." Hamlet protests that he will fight with Laertes "upon this theme/ Until my eyelids will no longer wag." "O my son, what theme?" the Queen asks. Hamlet replies, "I loved Ophelia . . ." Laertes takes a step toward Hamlet. The Queen restrains him. The King tells him, "O, he is mad, Laertes." The Queen adds: "For love of God, forbear him."

Hamlet, still intense and agitated, tells him: "'Swounds, show me what thou'lt do: (quickly)/ Woo't weep? woo't fight? . . . And, if thou prate of mountains, let them throw/ Millions of acres on us, till our ground,/ Singeing his pate against the burning zone,/ Make Ossa like a *wart*[314] Nay, an thou'lt mouth,/ (he drops into an aspirate tone, hoarse, broken with grief and with the consciousness of his words' excess) I'll rant as well as thou."[315] Horatio crosses to Hamlet, drawing him several steps to the right. "This is mere madness . . ." the Queen interjects. After she finishes, Hamlet crosses back to above the right end of the grave and addresses Laertes: ". . . What is the reason that you use me thus?/ I loved you ever: but it is no matter;/ Let Hercules himself do what he may,/ The cat will mew, (he looks at the King) and dog will have his day." Long pause. He looks longingly into the grave, his lips moving vaguely. He seems dazed. After about five seconds he turns slowly, then quietly exits right. All look after him. Silence for about three seconds.[316]

The King sends Horatio to follow him; Horatio exits, picking up Hamlet's cloak as he goes. The Queen crosses to below and right of the grave, looking after Hamlet. Laertes takes a step right. The King crosses to Laertes, who is at center stage: "Strengthen your patience in our last night's speech . . . Good Gertrude, set some watch over your son./ This grave shall have a living monument." Laertes kneels above the grave; the lights dim out and the house curtain falls.[317]

The original staging of Ophelia's burial – against a setting essentially unmodified from that used in earlier scenes – aroused a good deal of controversy and is discussed in detail in the section on the critical response to the production. The setting described here is that adopted later in the run. Barrymore's performance in this scene was, for the most part, simple and keyed low. Charles Darnton commented, however, that in the "necessary bit" of ranting with Laertes, Barrymore "proved he could do it with the best of his older predecessors" (*Evening World*, 17 November 1922).

Act III, scene iv. *A hall in the castle.* [First part of Temple edition V.ii, lines 1–235 cut to 115 lines]

The tableau curtains are brought on behind the house curtain. A small table with gold drapery is set right center near the front curtain line. The house curtain rises. The lights come up gradually. Baby spots focus on the heads of the curtain figures.

Hamlet starts his speech while offstage: "Now, the next day –" He enters through the vent in the curtains and crosses to left center, speaking as he walks; Horatio follows and crosses to right of the table: "– was our sea-fight; and what to this was sequent/ Thou know'st already."[318] After Horatio proclaims, "Why, what a king is this!" he crosses right to the front of the table and turns left; after Hamlet's ensuing line he crosses to the left of the table. Hamlet tells him he now feels justified to kill the King.

Osric, hat in hand, enters from the left on the mainstage and crosses to left center. He bows very elaborately: "Your lordship is right welcome back to Denmark." He fans himself with his hat until he speaks again.[319] Hamlet bows slightly and tells him, "I humbly thank you, sir." He turns to Horatio and asks him (aside) "Dost know this water-fly?" He sits on the edge of the table facing Osric. Horatio, laughing, replies "No, my good lord." Hamlet tells him: "Thy state is the more gracious, for 'tis a vice to know him." Osric examines a ring on his left hand while Hamlet speaks, then crosses right:[320] "Sweet lord . . . I should impart a thing to you from his majesty" (he fans himself with his hat). Hamlet tells him, "I will receive it, sir, with all diligence of spirit. Put your [/] bonnet to his right use; 'tis for the head."[321] Osric bows and continues to fan himself: "I thank your lordship, it is very hot."

After an exchange of a few lines he tells Hamlet, " . . . it is very sultry, as 'twere, – (laughs) I cannot tell how" (changes hat to his left hand). He tells Hamlet of the King's "great wager" (Hamlet motions to him to put on his hat), then describes Laertes's virtues, fanning himself with his hat (now in his right hand). Upon concluding he sighs with contentment over a thing well done.[322]

After Hamlet's reply, Horatio crosses upstage right and asks him: "Is't not possible to understand in another tongue? . . ."[323] Hamlet reclines on the table on his line, "What imports the nomination of this gentleman?" "Of Laertes?" Osric asks. Horatio laughs, crosses to right of the table, and leans on the top, delivering his aside. Hamlet and Horatio laugh softly. Hamlet and Osric discuss Laertes's "excellence" and his weapons – "rapier and dagger." Osric then reveals the details of the King's wager, which "would come to immediate trial if your lordship would vouchsafe the answer" (he bows).

Hamlet asks him, "How if I answer 'no'?" Horatio touches him warningly on the arm. After Osric's reply, Hamlet tells him: "Sir, I will walk here in the hall: if it please his majesty, it is the breathing time of day with me (he rises and takes a step toward the left): let the foils be brought . . ." He crosses upstage left after he finishes. Osric asks, "Shall I redeliver you e'en so?" Hamlet turns left: "To this effect, sir, after what flourish your nature will." Osric, after his reply, bows very low. Hamlet dismisses him; Osric sighs deeply, then exits left, fanning as he goes.

Hamlet turns to Horatio and jests about the departed courtier; he and Horatio look at each other and both laugh quietly. Hamlet crosses to the table. Horatio tells him, "You will lose this wager, my lord." Hamlet sits on the table and comments: "I do not think so; since he went into France, I have been in continual practice . . ." At the conclusion of his speech he rises and crosses to center stage; Horatio follows and stands at his right.[324] Horatio tells Hamlet to postpone the bout if he feels uneasy, but Hamlet tells him: "Not a whit; we defy augury: there is special providence in the fall of a sparrow. . . . (calmly) the readiness is all; let be." Music. Hamlet puts his arm around Horatio's shoulder; they start out center as the lights dim out.

H. T. Parker of the *Boston Transcript* (26 December 1923) commented that "In particular, is there reason to praise Mr. Stehli's disguise as Osric. Here at last was no blond, tripping, twiddling, piping fop; but a sombre 'fantastical' (as Shakespeare's day might have called him) dark of countenance, plaited locks and tones, grave, even, in his pretention [*sic*]." He added, "To cadences of Mozart must the ear go to match the serene beauty of [Barrymore's] 'The readiness is all.'"

At the time of his London production, Barrymore remarked that Hamlet "is only emotional under the greatest stress and when he is alone. He even cloaks his feelings, as when he exchanges whimsical banter with Osric after the scene at Ophelia's grave. His honesty causes his affection for Horatio, with whom he feels a great kinship. He senses ambiguity at once" (*Daily Express*, 21 February 1925).

Act III, scene v. *A hall in the castle.* [Temple edition V.ii, conclusion of scene, lines 236–414; 178 lines cut to 128]

The tableau curtains are drawn off during the blackout. The music segues into a flourish from offstage left, followed by a march for the entrance of the court. The white curtains are on full behind the arch.[325] The throne-bench is set on the lower platform left center as in the first court scene; a small throne chair for the King is set right center as in the play scene.

The lights come up gradually. Hamlet and Horatio are discovered, center stage, talking (not having left the stage from the previous scene). As the lights come on, two Servants enter from the right, carrying a table covered by gold drapery. On it are five foils, the hilts to the left, a large cup front and center, and two smaller cups on either side of it. The Servants cross and place the table near the right center break in the steps on the lower platform. They then cross downstage right center to the table used in the previous scene.

The Queen enters from the left and crosses to the throne-bench on the platform. She is wearing a large red robe (probably the same garment she had worn in the play scene), which she drapes over the back of the throne. She is followed by three Ladies and three Lords, who take places on the platform above her. As the court enters, Horatio crosses and speaks to the Queen. Hamlet remains center stage. The King enters from the right to above and right of Hamlet. He is followed by Laertes, who crosses to below and right of the King. Following Laertes comes Osric, who crosses and stands left of the table. Two Ladies cross to above the table; one stands on the platform, the other on the first step of the flight of stairs leading to the upper platform. Another Lady enters and stands on the platform directly above the chair. She is accompanied by a Lord, who stands below her and to her right. Three Lords enter; one stands on the first step, the other two on the platform to the right of the chair.[326] As soon as the court is on, the servants carry off the table used in the previous scene.

The music stops as the King speaks: "Come, Hamlet, come, and take this hand from me." Hamlet crosses toward him. Laertes crosses to the King, who takes his hand and passes it to Hamlet. As Hamlet clasps his hand warmly, the King backs to the right, above Laertes. Hamlet tells Laertes, "Give me your pardon, sir: I've done you wrong . . ." Their hands remain clasped through Laertes's response and Hamlet's answer: "I . . . will this brother's wager frankly play (hands part). Give us the foils. (he moves upstage past Horatio) Come on."

Hamlet crosses to the left of the table and selects a foil. The King crosses and sits on his chair.[327] Laertes crosses to below the table: "Come, one for me." Osric picks up the foils and crosses to below the table left of Laertes. Hamlet crosses several steps downstage center and tells Laertes, "I'll be your foil. . . ." Laertes, right center, replies, "You mock me, sir." Hamlet, left center, tells him, "No, by this hand." He feels out his blade. The King commands, "Give them the foils, young Osric. (Laertes selects a weapon from three that are offered; Osric steps back, still holding the other foils) Cousin Hamlet,/ You know the wager?" Laertes weighs his foil and tests the blade. Hamlet (crossing to left of center) replies, "*Very well,* my *lord;/* [/] Your [/] *grace* has laid the *odds* o' the *weaker side*" (laughs slightly).[328]

After the King's response, Laertes announces, "This is too heavy; let me see another." Osric crosses quickly to Laertes, who selects another foil. Osric then crosses back to the table, replaces the foils, and stands left of the table. Hamlet announces, "This *likes* me *well.* These *foils* have all a *length?*" Osric replies, "Ay, my good lord." The King tells Osric, "Set me the stoups of wine upon that table." Osric takes the large cup from the table, crosses to left of the King, kneels, and hands him the cup. Hamlet tries his foil, whipping it about and bending its point on the stage through the remainder of the King's speech: ". . . 'Now the king drinks to Hamlet.' (he drinks, then hands the cup to Osric, who is standing on the step above the King talking to a Lady) Come, begin;/ And you, the judges, bear a wary eye."[329]

Hamlet crosses to left center: "Come on, *sir.*"

Laertes moves to right of center: "Come, my lord."

They salute. They play. Hamlet taps the floor with his sword. Laertes thrusts in *seconde* at Hamlet's right leg and misses. Hamlet parries his thrust. Laertes thrusts again in *seconde* (but lower); Hamlet lifts his right foot in his parry. Laertes thrusts in *prime.* Hamlet twists his body, sidesteps, and touches Laertes in *quinte:* "*One.*" Laertes says "No." Hamlet calls, "*Judgement.*"[330]

Osric has been conversing with the lady above the King and has not seen the touch. Nevertheless he calls out, "A hit, a very palpable hit."[331] Laertes says, "Well; again." Hamlet and Laertes come to the en garde position. As their foils touch, the King speaks: "Stay; give me drink." Hamlet and Laertes return to the salute position. Osric crosses to the King with the cup. He kneels. The King takes the cup: "Hamlet, this pearl is thine (he drops a pearl in the cup); Here's to thy health. (the King pretends to drink) Give him the cup." He forces the cup to Osric, who crosses to Hamlet.

Hamlet waves him aside: "I'll *play* this *bout first;* set it *by* a *while.*" Osric crosses left and stands on the platform upstage center. "*Come.*"

They cross swords in en garde position.[332] Laertes advances twice with Hamlet retreating. Hamlet advances twice with Laertes retreating. Laertes disengages and thrusts in *prime.* Hamlet parries and ripostes in *quinte.* Laertes parries, then disengages and thrusts in *prime.* Hamlet parries with a backhand stroke and ripostes in *quarte,* Laertes parrying. Laertes thrusts in *quarte;* Hamlet parries. Laertes disengages and thrusts in *prime.* Hamlet sidesteps to the right and touches in *quinte:* "*Another hit, what say you?*"

Laertes admits, "A touch, a touch, I do confess." He crosses to above and left of the King. Hamlet crosses to Horatio, who stands below the Queen, and hands him his foil. The King comments, "Our son shall win." The Queen adds, "He's fat and scant of breath./ Here, Hamlet, take my napkin, rub thy brows (she hands her napkin to Hamlet, who takes it and crosses again to Horatio, mopping his forehead):/ The Queen carouses to thy fortune, Hamlet." She rises; Osric crosses to her with the cup. Hamlet tells her, "Good madam!" The King, startled, starts up: "Gertrude, do not drink." She tells him, "I will, my lord; I pray you, pardon me." She drinks. The King delivers his aside: "It is the poison'd cup; it is too late." The Queen offers the cup to Hamlet, who tells her: "I *dare* not *drink yet*, madam; *by* and *by*." She hands the cup back to Osric, who crosses and places it on the table; he then stands left of the table. The Queen tells Hamlet, "Come, let me wipe thy face." Hamlet, taking his foil from Horatio, crosses to the Queen and kneels below her. She wipes his brow. Laertes crosses to left of the King: "My lord, I'll hit him now." The King tells him, "I do not think't." Laertes, aside, comments, "And yet it is almost against my conscience."

Hamlet kisses the Queen's hand then crosses to left center: "Come, for the third, Laertes: you but dally . . ." Laertes replies, "Say you so? come on." They come en garde. Hamlet swings upstage center, Laertes downstage center. Laertes thrusts in *prime;* Hamlet parries. Laertes again thrusts in *prime;* Hamlet parries. Laertes thrusts high in *tierce;* Hamlet parries and their swords lock; as they draw them apart each jumps back to his original position, Hamlet left center, Laertes right of center. Laertes thrusts in *prime;* Hamlet parries. Laertes thrusts again in *prime*, touching Hamlet on the left side. Hamlet gives a short cry. As the touch is made Laertes cries, "Have at you now!" Hamlet, in parrying, has assisted the touch by bringing his foil under Laertes's; his own foil gives way under Laertes's thrust and draws against him, pointing upward.

After the touch, Laertes draws back to right center, his back to the audience; he tests his sword in an effort to appear at ease. Hamlet, laughing lightly, puts his hand to his side. As he draws it away he sees blood. He is apparently dumbfounded and looks questioningly at Horatio, then at Laertes, who avoids his eyes. Then, seeming to realize the situation, he laughs in an attempt to disarm Laertes of suspicion that he knows what has happened. He extends his foil to Laertes for the next bout.[333]

Laertes thrusts low in *prime;* Hamlet parries furiously. Laertes thrusts very low in *prime*, so that the point of his foil is on the floor. Hamlet quickly steps on the blade with his right foot, at the same time cutting Laertes's foil with his blade – causing Laertes to let go of his foil. As Laertes stoops and reaches for his weapon, Hamlet catches him by the right wrist (Fig. 36); they both come to an upright position, and Hamlet, with elaborate irony, offers Laertes

Figure 36. The duel with Laertes (Sidney Mather). Courtesy Billy Rose Theatre Collection, The New York Public Library for the Performing Arts.

his (Hamlet's) own sword, laying it over his (Hamlet's) right arm. The court expresses pleasure at Hamlet's seeming graciousness. Laertes, after a slight hesitation, takes Hamlet's foil and backs quickly to below the King. Hamlet picks up Laertes's sword and crosses slowly a step upstage left of center, at the same time running his hand slowly and sardonically along the blade and touching the tip. As he feels the point unbated he gives a violent, angry snarl, then turns and extends his foil toward Laertes, who immediately comes en garde.[334]

Hamlet, in his rage, rushes furiously at Laertes and thrusts wildly and savagely in *quinte.* Laertes parries. The King starts up and cries, "Part them; they are incensed." Hamlet draws back, disarms Laertes by whipping his foil from his hand, then runs him through in *quinte* as he cries: "*Nay, come, again.*" As the thrust is made the Queen lurches forward and is caught by the two ladies above her. Osric cries, "Look to the Queen there, ho!" and runs to the left side of Laertes. Horatio follows Hamlet as he charges across at Laertes. Immediately after the thrust, he catches Hamlet and draws him upstage center: "They bleed on both sides. How is it, my lord?" Osric supports Laertes and helps him to below and right of the table: "How is't Laertes." Laertes tells him, "Why, as a woodcock to mine own springe, Osric;/ I am justly kill'd with mine own treachery." Hamlet asks (deeply concerned, his voice tremulous), "How does the *queen?*" The King tells him, "She swounds to see them bleed." The Queen, in the arms of the two ladies, calls out, "No, no, the drink, the drink, – (she struggles half up) O, my dear Hamlet, – / The drink, the drink! I am poison'd." She sinks dead to the first platform in front of the bench, her head upstage. Her fall is lightened by the two Ladies.[335]

Hamlet shouts, "*Treachery!* [/] *seek* it *out.*" He crosses to the Queen and is about to touch her when he hears Laertes speak: "It is here, Hamlet: Hamlet, thou art slain;/ (Hamlet turns to look at Laertes, who is sitting on the steps at the right, above the King) . . . The treacherous instrument is in thy hand,/ Unbated and envenom'd: thy mother's poison'd:/ I can no more: the king, the king's to blame." The King crouches in his chair.[336]

Hamlet turns in a half-circle with his sword in his hand making an arc toward the audience and extends the sword so that it points directly at the King. He glares at the King:[337] "The *point envenom'd too!*" (firmly – downward emphasis) He strides toward the King slowly and deliberately, his sword extended at full arm's length, with ferocity and deadly intensity in his movements.[338] The King rises to below his chair. "Then, *venom* (moving slowly forward), *to thy work.*"[339] The courtiers cry, "Treason! Treason!" The King, now up, screams, "O, yet defend me, friends." Hamlet, creeping steadily forward on the King with animal fury, tells him, his voice rising, "*Here*, thou *incestuous, murderous, damned Dane,/ Drink off THIS POTION!*" He leaps at the King – a graceful, furious jump across ten feet of air – and runs him through under the left arm.[340] "*Follow my mother.*" He twists his foil as he draws it from the King's body. The King falls, his head to the right, below the chair. Hamlet gives a short cry and throws the foil on the floor. Horatio rushes to Hamlet and draws him back to right center. Laertes draws himself up on the platform.

The Lords and Ladies exit screaming and calling excitedly.[341] Osric exits left. A long pause. Horatio supports Hamlet, right center. Laertes leans upward on his elbow: "Exchange forgiveness with me, noble Hamlet (he reaches toward Hamlet):/ Mine and my father's death come not upon thee,/ Nor thine on me!" (he dies) Hamlet tells him, "*Heaven* make thee *free* of it! [/] I *follow* thee./ . . . O, I am *dead, Horatio:*/ Thou *livest;* [/] report *me* and my *cause aright/* [/] To the *unsatisfied.*" Horatio tells him, "Never believe it:/ I am more an antique Roman than a Dane: (he crosses to the table and picks up the cup from which the Queen drank; he holds it up) Here's yet some liq-uor left." He lifts it to his mouth. Hamlet catches hold of it in an attempt to restrain him: "As thou'rt a *man,/ Give* me the *cup:* [/] *let go;* by *heaven* I'll *have't.*" He finally tears the cup from Horatio and throws it down on the plat-form.[342] He collapses into Horatio's arms: "If *thou* didst *ever* hold *me* in thy *heart,/* [/] *Absent thee* [/] from *felicity* a *while* (upward emphasis),/ [/] And in this *harsh world* [/] *draw* thy *breath* in *pain,/* [/] To *tell* my *story.*" A flourish of trumpets is heard from offstage left. "What warlike noise is this?"

Osric enters from the left and tells of Fortinbras's arrival. Hamlet, center stage, tells Horatio, who is supporting him: "O, I die, Horatio;/ The potent poison quite o'er-crows my spirit:/ I cannot live to hear the news from Eng-land;/ But I do prophesy the election lights/ On Fortinbras: he has my dying voice;/ So tell him, with the occurrents, more and less,/ Which have solicit-ed. (long pause; then, in a kind of ecstasy, he rises to his toes, reaching up with his entire body, and looks out and upward for about ten or fifteen sec-onds while Horatio holds his waist) The *rest* [/] is *silence.*" He falls front, his right shoulder going down first; his jaw drops in death. As he falls Horatio catches him on his left arm and gently lowers him to the stage, his head to-ward the audience.[343] Horatio kneels above him (Osric, left, kneels as well), looking into his face: "Now cracks a noble heart. (pause) Good night, sweet prince,/ And flights of angels sing thee to thy rest!"

A flourish of trumpets is heard from off left. Horatio rises. Fortinbras and his followers (wearing chain-mail armor) enter. Two men come on at the right and left on the upper platform; they hold the white curtains back. Two more men enter through the curtains and come to the third step from the top, standing well to the side. Fortinbras enters next and comes to the center of the second step from the top. A fifth Captain comes through the curtains and stands center on the top platform. The first two men let the curtains go and stand well over on the platform.[344]

The music stops and Fortinbras speaks: "Where is this sight?" Horatio (right center at the foot of the steps and facing upward) tells him: "What is it you would see? . . . (he turns toward the front) give order that these bodies/ High on a stage be placed to the view;/ And let me speak to the yet unknow-ing world/ How these things came about." Fortinbras replies, "Let us haste to hear it. . . . Let four captains/ (he turns back and points to Hamlet; the lights start dimming) Bear Hamlet, like a soldier, to the stage . . . (four soldiers go down the steps to center stage, cross to Hamlet, and lift him to their shoul-ders as Fortinbras speaks; they slowly start to carry him up the stairs, feet first, as the lights continue to dim) and, for his passage,/ The soldiers' music and the rites of war/ Speak loudly for him." He goes up the stairs to the top plat-form, pushes the curtains aside, and points off right with his right hand: "Go, bid the soldiers shoot" (Fig. 37).

By this time the lights are very low; only the blue light through the center arch remains, seen dimly through the part in the curtains. The fifth Captain exits stage right on the top platform. As the first two Captains carrying the body reach the top platform, Fortinbras drops his right hand and music begins: a flourish of violins and trumpets. The sound of shots is heard from offstage left.[345] Horatio stands right center looking after them then crosses to the table, bows his head, and cries, his back to the audience. The Captains pause a moment on the upper platform, then bear Hamlet through the curtains. Three drum beats are heard. The house curtain falls and strikes the stage on the last beat of the drum.[346]

Wrote Alexander Woollcott,

> It lacked but twenty minutes of midnight last evening when the four tawny clad captains of Fortinbras lifted the slim, young body of the dead Prince of Denmark to their mailed shoulders, bore it slowly up the great stone steps of Elsinore and out of the brilliant, gory, earthy castle into the cool of the moonlight beyond. They stood there for an instant, they and their burden silhouetted for us as a final memory. There was a wail of trumpets in the distance, the lights faded out and the curtain fell. Thus ended an evening that will be memorable in the history of the American theater. (*Herald,* 17 November 1922)

The Critical Response

In the weeks following the opening, more than fifty reviews and critical columns appeared in the New York dailies. Many more were published in weekly and monthly magazines – an outpouring of words unprecedented in twentieth-century American criticism of a Shakespearean production. Nearly all of the commentary was positive; few superlatives were spared in praising the production and its central performance. To George Jean Nathan, the reviews read "infinitely less like dramatic criticism than like affaires d'amour."[347] Barrymore, Heywood Broun commented, "is far and away the finest Hamlet we have ever seen. He excels all others we have known in grace, fire, wit and clarity" (*World,* 17 November 1922). "This generation," declared Kenneth Macgowan, "has found its Hamlet" (*Globe,* 17 November 1922).

The key element, to most observers, was the spirit of freshness and vitality Barrymore and his production team had brought to a time-honored classic. The "anonymous" critic for *Town Topics* (almost certainly Ludwig Lewisohn of *The Nation*) commented that

> There can be no doubt . . . that the Barrymore–Jones–Hopkins production of *Hamlet* is the greatest Shakespearean production that this generation has seen in the English language. . . . The traditionalism of the stage has been

Figure 37. The Captains bear Hamlet's body from the stage in the 1925 London production. Courtesy Hulton Getty Picture Collection.

wholly discarded. An extraordinarily fresh, vivid and human imagination has re-envisaged the play. Mr. John Barrymore has, by the exercise of nothing less than genius, been able to read the play as though it were a new play to be interpreted for the first time. With a grace, a tenderness, a humanity, an eloquence that are no less consummate he renders the character and the story as spontaneously as a poem by a contemporary. I cannot overemphasize this fact. In it lies the merit and the greatness of the performance. . . . Every careful observer, with the memory of other performances in mind, will come with astonishment and delight upon passage after passage which had been and had remained mere literature to him and that now, at last, comes to life . . . The old words have been dipped into something vital and glowing. . . . This Hamlet is still Shakespeare's, but he is ours.[348]

Among the most frequently praised facets of Barrymore's performance were his intelligence, clarity, and simplicity, his "voice of most lovely quality" and "splendid sense of expressive and picturesque movement," and his "nat-

ural vein of gayety and shrewd native wit." Arthur Hornblow, writing in *Theatre Magazine*, found his impersonation to be "alive with virility and genius,"
adding that he brought "a pungency and intelligence into his portrayal un-
equalled by any of the many professional tragedians of recent years. His is a
great, beautiful and rare Hamlet. An understandable, coherent Hamlet. . . .
The American theatre may properly be proud of an actor capable of such
lofty doings."[349]

Most critics agreed with the reviewer for the *Sun* (17 November 1922),
who cited the "ease and naturalness" of Barrymore's playing. "Certainly here
is no palimpsest of all the *Hamlets* that have tottered or waddled or stalked
humorless past us in these later years, but a *Hamlet* reborn and one that, for
all its skill and graphic artfulness, is so utterly free from all that is of the stage
stagey," Woollcott wrote in his initial review (*Herald*, 17 November 1922). "Is-
suing from his lips, the very soliloquies which have so often separated out
from the rest of the play as set pieces of oratory seemed to have been spoken
for the first time last evening, seemed to have been thought for the first time
. . . seemed for once just a lonely, unhappy man's thoughts walking in the silent darkness." John Corbin found his interpretation to be "the most subdued
in modern memory," noting that "the manner, for the most part, was that of
conversation, almost colloquial, but the beauty of rhythm was never lost . . .
Very rarely did speech quicken or the voice rise to the pitch of drama, but
when this happened the effect was electric, thrilling."[350]

One recurring criticism that had haunted Barrymore for more than a decade – the accusation that he was a "personality" actor – was finally put to rest
by Ludwig Lewisohn, who commented in *The Nation* that

> Other actors can act Hamlet; he *is* Hamlet. . . . It was clear enough that hith-
> erto Mr. Barrymore never identified himself wholly with his characters. He
> always played with a touch of genius, but he played himself as Falder and
> Fedya and Richard III. Here, at last, the distance between himself and his
> creation has been eliminated. The identity of the two is complete. And be-
> cause of that identity he has been able to understand and render the text
> with a consummate freshness. . . . About Mr. Barrymore there is something
> at once fragile and burning. He is rarely obtrusive; he is rarely emphatic.
> One is haunted by that slim figure, by its wandering through a harsh and
> uncomprehended world. His voice is the voice of a thinker and poet, an
> interior voice which remains the voice of the soul even when the music of
> the verse is richly carried by it.[351]

Amid the chorus of praise, however, many critics were quick to cite deficiencies in Barrymore's portrayal. Most of their remarks seem like minor cav-
ils amid the hyperbole, yet a number of points were mentioned frequently
and bear notice. One recurring criticism was that Barrymore's Hamlet – as

was the case with his Richard III – overemphasized the cerebral aspects of his character. To George Jean Nathan, Barrymore's portrayal was "critically so precise that it is at times histrionically defective." Nathan found that his Hamlet, "like a diamond, is glittering, many coloured, hard, brilliant – but cold, intensely cold. We get from it the reflected rays of intelligence, but never – or at best rarely – the rays of heat."[352] Heywood Broun, whose positive comments on Barrymore's performance were as laudatory as any that were published, found similar deficiencies. Barrymore, he remarked, did not "sustain all the emotional values of the play. Only in a few fugitive moments did we feel sorry for Hamlet." His performance, Broun concluded, "will do everything except wring your heart" (*World*, 17 November 1922).

Walter Prichard Eaton, who more than a decade earlier had fired barbs at Barrymore's light-comedy performances, found similarly that "the complete effect of his acting . . . is far less than the haunting, tragic, wistfully terrible thing that *Hamlet* can be." Eaton granted that Barrymore's portrayal had its virtues: "slender grace and aristocratic bearing, charm, a suggestion of weakness or irresolution, tenderness, a dry humour, and beauty in melancholy," but found it lacking in "tragic power and the indescribable ability to suggest a mind broken and haunted until it dwells in the borderland of what we call sanity."[353]

These and similar comments can be seen in retrospect as a response to Barrymore's sharp departure from the familiar, Victorian conception of the character – the "Sweet Prince" and "Melancholy Dane" of tradition. Booth, Irving, Forbes-Robertson, and their less talented successors had sentimentalized Hamlet, in keeping with the artistic sensibilities of their era and its aftermath. The abrupt transition from a romantic, idealized Prince of Denmark (upon whom even the younger and more liberal critics were raised) to a more intellectual conception of Shakespeare's character – a harshly realistic young thinker capable of withering sarcasm and scorn – was jarring to many observers. Even the most favorable reviewers, such as the generally approving Charles Darnton, often ventured the opinion that Barrymore's characterization at times "seemed too mental for the good of Shakespeare's poetry" (*Evening World*, 17 November 1922).

Still, to most observers Barrymore's emphasis on the scholar-philosopher rather than the romantic side of his character ("He could well afford to let that take care of itself, or rather let it rest with his romantic appearance," wrote Darnton) was of relatively little consequence. The majority of critics who took Barrymore to task for making Hamlet "a little too sane, a little too intelligent" tempered their objections by noting moments when he revealed "the human side" of his character, the "tender and sympathetic nature." "If one does not feel the torture of a great soul encompassed by overwhelming circumstances," wrote the critic for the *New York Review*, "he at least sees the poignant suffering of a youth who is trying to puzzle out the reason for the tragic fate by which he is surrounded" (22 November 1922).[354]

Most critics found much to praise in Barrymore's vocal and verse-speaking skills ("The 'reading' of the lines was flawless – an art that was said to have been lost," commented John Corbin), yet several cited shortcomings. Stark Young, in a charge later to be leveled by a number of reviewers in London, noted that in his attempt to give a "natural" reading Barrymore occasionally allowed "phrases to fall apart in such a way that the essential musical pattern of the verse . . . is lost."[355] Walter Prichard Eaton, although commending Barrymore's "great progress in the control of his voice," found similarly that "He pumps up his emphasis on certain words, and those words are monotonously apt to be at the end of lines, or just preceding the caesural pause," adding that he had "not yet hit on the golden mean between rhythm and naturalness."[356] Heywood Broun, again citing the intellectual nature of Barrymore's portrayal, commented wryly:

> He has done marvels with his voice. In fact he has done too much. In gaining what seems to us an almost absolute precision some of the emotion and eloquence which lie in occasional imperfection is gone. Tones which rasp the ear may tear at the heart. We not only felt that Barrymore was constantly correct, but that he knew he was correct. There was at least the possibility of suspicion that his alma mater was not Wittenberg but Harvard. (*World*, 17 November 1922)

Another pervasive criticism is ironic when viewed in retrospect, for many reviewers looked upon Barrymore's portrayal as not yet a finished creation. The unstated assumption was that he would continue to revive *Hamlet* over a period of many years, decades perhaps, as had Booth, Irving, and Forbes-Robertson, all the while refining and perfecting his creation. To Stark Young, Barrymore's Hamlet was the most satisfying he had seen and boasted numerous virtues: "a beautiful presence, a profound magnetism," an absence of "theatrical faults," and a technique that was "invariably derived from the conception of the part and never allowed to run ahead of it." At the same time, however, Young saw considerable room for improvement. "This Hamlet," he wrote, ". . . must give us – and already promises . . . the suggestion of more vitality, ungovernable and deep, of more complex suffering, of not only intellectual subtlety but intellectual power as well."[357] Yet the prevailing mood was optimistic. Corbin found Barrymore's Dane to be "a truly great interpretation" and "at least potentially . . . a fit successor of the Hamlets of Forbes-Robertson and Edwin Booth," noting that "though there are heights in both character and play that are as yet unscaled, one feels always that to the artist who has accomplished so much the rest is possible" (*Times*, 17 December 1922).

Only one overwhelmingly negative review appeared in a New York daily: J. Ranken Towse's criticism in the *Post*.[358] Towse, 77 at the time and an arch-conservative, was only nine years younger than William Winter and the last of the New York critics whose opinions of *Hamlet* in performance had been formed by observation of Booth, Fechter, and Irving in their primes. Almost incredibly, Towse was unreserved in his praise for the mise-en-scène and staging. "Very seldom, if ever," he wrote, "has a great play even in the days of Irving or Beerbohm Tree, been presented with a more richly spectacular background. The stage pictures were nobly designed and gorgeously brilliant or impressively sombre in color, while every grouping has been arranged with a view to pictorial effect." Yet to Towse, Arthur Hopkins, "infected with some of the pernicious theories of Gordon Craig," had made the same errors that had made his *Macbeth* a disappointment: the play "did not harmonize" with the "finicking methods of a more artificial civilization." The chief impression conveyed by Barrymore's performance, Towse commented, was its "obvious lack of tragic power." He granted that it was "a clever, thoughtful, interesting, and fairly consistent impersonation, with an individuality all its own," but found that it "reflected only one or two of the many facets in Hamlet's manysided character" and was "marred in countless instances by misplaced or disregarded emphasis." His most vehement objections were evoked by Barrymore's repressed performance style. "In the more passionate scenes," he wrote, ". . . the lack of fire, or of anything resembling emotions of tragic intensity, robbed them of all vitality or impressiveness. . . . His tameness in some crises – as for example in the query 'Is it the King?' was indicative of an astonishing imperception." Towse grudgingly admitted that Barrymore's characterization "was not without its sympathetic appeal," but concluded that it was "the work of an attractive, earnest, and intelligent comedian laboring under a burden much too heavy for him, and as a whole was sadly ineffective." As a parting shot, he added, "As much might be said truthfully of most of his associates" (17 November 1922).

Towse's comments on Barrymore's "lack of fire" are softened somewhat when we remember that his critical judgment was grounded in the theatrical conventions of an earlier era. It is equally important, however, to bear in mind the relative youth of many of the other commentators (Broun and Macgowan were 34, Woollcott 35, Lewisohn 40, Stark Young 41 – too young to remember the Hamlets of Irving and Booth), for, given the weight of more than three centuries of accumulated stage tradition, comparisons of Barrymore with earlier interpreters of the role were inevitable. In the weeks after the opening, numerous articles appeared in the New York dailies chronicling Hamlets of the distant and recent past.[359] Columnists with long memories recalled noteworthy impersonations of the mid-to-late nineteenth century (the consensus being that Barrymore acquitted himself surprisingly well when compared to Booth, although hardly erasing his memory), and many of the younger critics took the opportunity to compare Barrymore's Dane with those of Forbes-Robertson, Sothern, Mantell, Leiber, and Hampden. In nearly all cases, comparisons were favorable.

Barrymore's portrayal, in the view of most critics, could stand shoulder to shoulder with Forbes-Robertson's Dane and was vastly superior to other Hamlets New York had seen during the first two decades of the twentieth century. Another important factor was not overlooked, for as Heywood Broun commented, "Within our time Barrymore is the only player who has made the prince young and glamorous" (*World*, 26 November 1922).

Forbes-Robertson's Hamlet was invariably mentioned with respect and affection, yet several critics felt that Barrymore, by reinterpreting his character in terms of a postwar generation in which Victorian romanticism had been supplanted by a far less idealistic view of human nature, had surpassed his esteemed interpretation. "It is with a full and vivid memory of the graciousness, the gentle pathos, the wistful beauty of Forbes-Robertson's *Hamlet*," opined Woollcott, "that we salute John Barrymore's as the most satisfying performance of the role that we have ever seen in the theater" (*Herald*, 3 December 1922). Moreover, while it was clear to most observers that Forbes-Robertson's and Barrymore's impersonations were of differing eras, at least one commentator found striking similarities in their overall approach. In a letter to the *Times* (24 December 1922), the playwright Rachel Crothers stated that

> It seems to me especially absurd to contend that Barrymore's Hamlet isn't like Forbes-Robertson's, when in reality they are so very much alike – that is, they are both read with a colloquial speech – a simplicity and naturalness. They are both played from an absolutely human standpoint, with the same basic interpretation. The manner of the older man, belonging to an older generation, is inevitably more elaborate, his gesticulation more illustrative, his grace a trifle more conspicuous and classic, for grace's sake, but the repression – the taste – the innate meaning and spirit of the two performances are to me strikingly alike – though differing much, of course, in definite execution.
>
> While Forbes-Robertson's Hamlet remains to me as something standing quite alone on the heights – above and beyond anything I had ever seen in the theatre – I now feel that John Barrymore's Hamlet is equally great, and belongs to *this* day, and, while it is necessarily still more simple and natural, because of that it loses nothing in classic dignity and nobility – and I'll wager Sir Johnston would say so himself and appreciate this young new Hamlet more deeply than any of us can.

A number of reviewers noted the fact that the Hamlets appearing on the American stage after Forbes-Robertson's retirement were rooted in an earlier conception of the character. Burns Mantle found that Barrymore was "not only the greatest American Hamlet, but the one and only American Hamlet":

> In distant competition he has Walter Hampden – but Hampden is an English actor by training and tradition. And his performance reflects both heritages. Edward Hugh Sothern is as American by training as any actor playing upon our stage, but he, too, reflects the earlier influences of his heritage, which were the influence of the English stage and the readings and traditions of his professional fathers. The Robert Bruce Mantell Hamlet is fashioned absolutely on those conventional lines from which no player in the days of this actor's early career would have dreamed of departing, the Fritz Leiber Hamlet was studied and staged in the Mantell atmosphere, and the John Kellerd Hamlet has withdrawn from the lists. . . . Here, then, is the beginning of a new order. . . . the first of a new line of Hamlets . . . the foundation for future comparisons . . . the greatest and the most fascinating of modern Hamlets. (*News*, 19 November 1922)[360]

One inescapable implication of the comparisons was that Barrymore had secured a place in the pantheon beside the acclaimed nineteenth-century interpreters of bravura Shakespeare and the legendary Shakespeareans of the more distant past: Burbage, Betterton, Garrick, Kean. This election was too abrupt, however, for one distinguished predecessor. A few months after *Hamlet* opened, "David Garrick" took the opportunity to view a performance. Soon afterward he published an open letter to Barrymore in the pages of *Vanity Fair*.[361] "Garrick"'s criticism was generally favorable, but he cautioned Barrymore that his Hamlet would need considerable refinement before it could be considered a truly great interpretation.

To soften the blow, "Garrick" admitted that he had made numerous mistakes when first attempting the part. In the early going, he confessed, he had been "irregular and vehement and pettish," and at first left out the advice to the players; he acknowledged that even after restoring this passage he spoke it "too pedantically." With the passing of time, however, he "softened and corrected" and at last perfected his conception of the part. He then took the opportunity to offer Barrymore some fraternal advice: "Sir, I erred – as I see now – and you err, in making this character and life of Hamlet too simple. . . . I made Hamlet aristocratic and fine and reduced Shakespeare's play to the thought of my century. You, Sir, have erred toward your democratic epoch. You simplify the play overmuch by making Hamlet too easy to understand; by putting him in terms too satisfactory to your public." Although generally approving of Barrymore's exchanges with Polonius and his playing of the nunnery and Queen's closet scenes, "Garrick" regarded Barrymore's portrayal as work in progress. What it needed, he told his colleague, was "the sense of a larger inner tumult" a "certain cerebral and passionate ecstasy," more "poetry and richness of soul." "Your business," he concluded, "as mine was, is to labor toward finding in your art a language suited to the finest reaches of your time."

Hopkins's Direction Criticized

Arthur Hopkins's lean, evocative staging was noticed and appreciated by the critical fraternity. To Ludwig Lewisohn, a key element of the production was its "isolation of the tragic action." The court, he observed, "is not crowded; the figures are few and pass by one another with a melancholy grace; the rhythm is grave."[362] Stark Young found that Hopkins, by stripping away the traditional embellishments of the past, had exposed the "essential and dramatic elements" of the play. "Such a production as this of Hamlet could not hope to be uniformly successful," Young concluded. "But in its best passages, without any affectation of the primitive or archaic, it achieved what primitive art can achieve: a fundamental pattern so simple and so revealing that it appeared to be mystical; and so direct and strong that it restored to the dramatic scene its primary truth and magnificence."[363]

Many details of the direction were singled out for praise; Hopkins was given credit when it was due – and occasionally when it was not. His austere groupings, Ophelia's imaginary flowers (a spontaneous decision at the second dress rehearsal), and the stylized, "Coq d' Or" staging of the play scene (for which Barrymore and Margaret Carrington were largely responsible) were often commended. Not so the spotlight Ghost, which provoked a wide variety of reactions ranging from whimsical approval ("a delightful ghost . . . of the modern Conan Doyle school," wrote one observer) to, in many cases, downright condemnation. "The Majesty of murdered Denmark," Cuthbert Wright remarked dryly, "is represented by a flood-light and a voice."[364] John Corbin objected on more practical grounds. The Ghost, he commented, "wavers fitfully against a silver-blue backdrop, some trillions of miles aloof in interstellar space, while the voice of the actor booms up-stage right, from a definite spot behind a stage wall" (*Times*, 26 November 1922).

Ironically, this effect was regarded by the critical fraternity as an original device, at least until 10 December, when Woollcott's column in the *Herald* featured a letter from William Faversham, in which the actor defended Hopkins's "innovation" and explained its continental origins.

> It isn't fair to blame Mr. Hopkins for not letting the *Ghost* appear in the flesh. He has the best traditions of Europe to go upon. In the better productions of *Hamlet*, both in Germany and Austria, the *Ghost* in the flesh has not been presented for many, many years. It has always been represented by an eery light and a voice that would represent to our imaginations the

voice of a ghost, allowing *Hamlet*'s imagination to reach across the foot-lights and stir the imagination of the audience.

Nor was Hopkins's use of this effect a first for America: Faversham had tried a similar radiance for Caesar's ghost during the 1912–13 season.[365] Much comment was devoted to the production's use of modern psychol-ogy. A number of observers noted the Oedipal ramifications of the Queen's closet scene, but many went beyond that to praise the overall psychological clarity of Hamlet's character and the production as a whole. "This Hamlet," wrote Heywood Broun (*World*, 17 November 1922), "is as modern as the most recent disciple of Freud. We learned last night, for the first time, that his trag-edy lay in the fact that he did not have the courage of his complexes." Shake-speare, wrote another critic,

> is a better expressionist than the moderns who ask for the name, and when his play is acted with an emphasis upon the powerful workings of the sub-consciousness, the effect is as of a sun upon fireworks. . . . Complexes are no more powerful now than in the seventeenth century, but the common man is more aware of them. The Freudian psychology has helped us to un-derstand *Hamlet*, that is all, and where Mr. Barrymore's company has de-parted from the plain meanings of the text in order to conform to a Freud-ian hypothesis, it is presumably Shakespeare, and not these Freudians, who has the right of it.[366]

Mention was made as well of the frank depiction of Ophelia's sexuality. "Mr. Hopkins," wrote Rachel Crothers, "has surely brought out the psychol-ogy of Ophelia's madness, the filth in the subconscious mind of an exquisite-ly pure and sensitive young girl, very strongly" (*Times*, 24 December 1922). Although the production's sexual elements were very much in keeping with the text itself and the postwar movement away from Victorian prudery, they proved too much for one playgoer, who fired off an irate letter to the *Times*. "Ophelia's filth retained, but not her blooms; Hamlet's coarseness, but not his soul. What are we coming to?" he wrote. "Sex is again emphasized in the mother scene. Here Mr. Barrymore's manner displays no disgust, though the lines are vibrant with it. He is leading up to the mother–son complex which he evidently thinks fitting to Shakespeare's words, for he fondles her again and again" (7 January 1923). Most observers found the production's sensual elements to be psychologically motivated and organic to the play rather than sensational, however, and the critical fraternity was generally approving.

Hopkins asked of his actors the same repressed, European-inspired acting style he had utilized in *Richard III* and *Macbeth*, and critical commentary, al-though divided, made it clear that this time the "natural" reading of the lines was more successful in terms of the ensemble. "Mr. Hopkins has provided a cast that will not let its various speeches stand as quotations," wrote the *Morning Telegraph* critic. "They put life and realism into every line and make the play a real human thing. Here are no bookish characters, striding hither and yon, delivering themselves of profound speeches in stilted fashion. Rather, we have a set of everyday human beings, played as we would expect human beings to be played – and, doubtless as Shakespeare himself would have them played" (17 November 1922). Many observers viewed the subdued style of playing as a welcome alternative to the exaggeration of the "rococo school," but a few expressed reservations. Maida Castellun of the *New York Call* noted that the scenes were "studiously, conscientiously underplayed," adding that in this "conversational" production "all the actors have taken their cue from the hero." She missed, however, "the soaring organ tones of Elizabethan rhetoric" and carped that the production at times suffered from "monotony, excess of method, a temperance that dangerously approaches tameness" (18 November 1922). Glenn Hughes, writing in *The Drama,* found the style to be "merely perverse and novel" and incompatible with the "romantic" nature of Shakespearean drama. Barrymore, he commented, "plays Hamlet as though thinking every instant that he must avoid tradition – as though to allow a rush of Elizabethan passion to consume him would be to prove unfaithful to the younger intellectuals."[367] The cast, lauded frequently for their speaking of the lines, was found by most critics to range from good to merely adequate; Tyrone Power's Claudius, Blanche Yurka's Gertrude, and Whitford Kane's Gravedigger were frequently cited for praise. Surprisingly little notice was given to the cuts in the text. A few critics lamented the excision of the recorder scene, but most agreed with John Corbin, who found the acting version "otherwise admirably complete" (*Times,* 17 December 1922).[368]

Altogether, Hopkins's direction and production concepts, though not without their controversial elements, were held to be a success. Rachel Crothers commented that

> as to Mr. Hopkins's concrete achievement, I think we cannot be too proud of it or too strong in our admiration. The difficulty of getting even modern commonplace lines decently and somewhat uniformly spoken as to diction and tone is almost insurmountable in the American theatre – and what he has managed to do in this alone is a great triumph. His fluid groupings and pictures and movements make one say, "I never was in Elsinore – I never hope to be there – but surely this is what it was like." (*Times,* 24 December 1922)

Jones's Scenery Criticized

With one notable exception, the Robert Edmond Jones mise-en-scène was admired and praised. The chorus of approval was led, predictably, by Kenneth

Macgowan, who commented that the "expressiveness and beauty which Jones has added by his settings, his costumes, and his lights are not to be easily estimated. They touch the highest mark in Shakespearean production in America, and, so far as I have seen it, in Europe" (*Globe,* 17 November 1922). Jones was praised for returning to a representational mode after the abstract symbolism of his designs for *Macbeth,* yet the psychological and symbolic values of his setting were not lost. The arch, according to one critic, lifted the play "into the aspect of eternity" and gave "the constant sense of the permanent and inscrutable forces against which the protagonist of the fable battles in vain."[369] The tableau curtains, commented another, were of equal symbolic impact, for their imposing row of gigantic figures, "symbols of the murdered king, whose spirit dominates the play," dwarfed the human figures on stage "almost to nothingness" and conveyed to the audience "a terrible sense of the fate in the grasp of which the hero is powerless to act."[370]

Many observers, however, found the set to be jarringly inappropriate for the graveyard scene. In an oft-repeated quip, Heywood Broun commented that "Ophelia is buried in the front parlor, which seems to us a mistake. . . . The necessity of making a graveyard of the palace is not apparent" (*World,* 18 November 1922). Even Stark Young, who found the set to be "austere and princely, lyrical and enduring" and "a visual form that is for the most part . . . inseparable from the thought of the play" commented that in the scene of Ophelia's burial it seemed "incongruous if not absurd."[371]

The only vehement detractor of Jones's overall approach was John Corbin of the *Times.* In his initial review, Corbin – an advocate of simple Elizabethan platform stagings in the manner of William Poel – commented that the set was "trivial and grotesque, encroached upon the playing space and introduced incongruities of locale quite unnecessary" (17 November 1922). He expanded upon this theme in a long article published nine days later; the major bone of contention was Jones's massive flight of steps. "Mr Jones's 'symbol' has usurped the rightful domain of the players, the area needful to the creation of any genuine dramatic effect," wrote Corbin. "One cannot play Shakespeare up and down the stairs. . . . The devitalizing effect of this huge scenic symbol is subtle as it is gross." Barrymore, he argued, was forced to play the nunnery scene "far down stage and to one side . . . huddled in a corner," and Ophelia was at best "buried in a courtyard." The actors, he concluded, were "doomed to forgo the central playing space and nibble around the edges of Mr. Jones's front stoop like mice at a cheese." Corbin found the scene of the King at prayer to be similarly disconcerting. The King, he wrote, "kneels on an apron over the orchestra pit holding his crucifix to the noses of the unfortunate folk in the front row." Hamlet then enters and speaks "in tones audible to the last row in the balcony," yet Claudius does not hear (26 November 1922).

Corbin's initial salvos sparked a lively debate, conducted in the pages of the *Times* and the *Globe*. Macgowan answered his charges in a long letter to the *Times* that defended Jones's Jessner-inspired design and was printed side by side with Corbin's response. Both concurred that the spotlight Ghost was a mistake on the part of Hopkins; little else was agreed upon. Macgowan defended the stairs by stating that Shakespeare had "used a balcony himself to get certain vertical relationships," adding that "anyone who has seen Leopold Jessner stage *Othello* and *Richard III* upon various arrangements of steps and platforms in the State Theatre in Berlin knows what fine fluidity of movement and contrast of position they give him. . . . All through Europe I saw steps used this summer with the finest effect. I should rather argue that Hopkins does not use his steps enough." The scene of the King at prayer, Macgowan wrote, was defensible on two grounds: Hamlet was speaking his thoughts in soliloquy and thus could not be heard by the King; moreover, the staging was inherently Shakespearean, as Shakespeare's theatre had employed an apron to bring the actors closer to the audience, upon which much of the action had undoubtedly occurred (10 December 1922). The debate continued for several weeks but was never ultimately resolved. Barrymore was fond of referring to the scenery simply as "Pennsylvania Station."[372]

Considerably less controversy was evoked by Jones's costumes and lighting effects. Little critical commentary was devoted to the costumes, which were mentioned only in passing, if at all, by the reviewers. The lighting effects, which again employed the cinematic techniques used in *Richard III*, were generally admired and, to one critic, made Hopkins's groupings "fade away into darkness and spring back again into sight with something like the effect which the mind uses in bringing up images" (*Evening Telegram*, 17 November 1922). Notice was taken as well of the technological advancements of the last half-century. To Walter Prichard Eaton, the costumes, lights, and setting supplied to Hamlet "a visual poetry, a subdued radiance, and a certain formal rhythm, of which Booth knew nothing."[373]

The Run

Within a few weeks of the opening, the *Herald* would note that "The exquisite young *Hamlet* of John Barrymore has captured the favor of the town to an almost passionate degree, and in the main justly" (10 December 1922). The production's artistic success was quickly reflected at the box office; *Variety* reported that the first full week drew a gross of over $19,300, and the second week took in just under $21,000, leading all nonmusical attractions.[374] Noted as well by many columnists was the fact that Hamlet attracted not just intellectuals, habitual playgoers, and Shakespeare buffs, but also a popular audience. At one packed Saturday matinee, the *Herald* reported, the audience consisted mainly of "young, very 'modern' women, making what seemed to be a first and delighted acquaintance with the masterpiece of William Shakespeare" (10 December 1922).

One critical observer, however, voiced stern objections to the populist approach. After seeing the production, John Jay Chapman, Barrymore's friend and advisor for *Richard III*, wrote to H. H. Furness Jr. in Philadelphia, informing him that

> Jack Barrymore is playing Hamlet with immense success and I would like, if possible, to get you . . . to come over for some *Thursday* or *Sat.* matinee and dine with Barrymore & me in a private room at the Century after the show. Barrymore is a man of enormous natural force and a completely charming modest fellow – positively disarming in his reverence for Shakespeare & for the learning and tradition of the subject. . . . If I had walked in off the street & seen his Hamlet without any major personal interest in it, I should have said: "It's a pure American conception – Abe Lincoln's Hamlet the slow, wise man who speaks last & is wit incarnate . . ." It is serious & personal, quiet; every sentence *put over.* It has a jazz back-ground . . . [and] other oddities done to make the public go home & say they've seen a novelty. And of course a jazz public. In order to reach the public at all he has to do what he does – and the heavy ignorant man in the audience likes it for its inescapable impact. I told him all of this and he sees it to some extent. You see he's in the grip of the times. . . . He is of course not responsible for the jazz. But *next time* he must control this part, & adopt Old Vic simplicity.

Chapman granted that Barrymore has "one or two strokes of genius" in the play, but missed "the poetic, the demonic, the hysterical." In closing, he told Furness that "it is within the scope of your general mission to know this young man. I myself adore him. He needs the society & friendship of the educated, the cultivated. If [we] could spend an evening on Hamlet with him – (which would end in hilarious pummeling of him) it would be a god send to him & help him a lot." Within a few weeks Furness attended a performance (which he later reviewed – with guarded praise – for *The Drama*); afterward he presented Barrymore with several books and with Chapman engaged the actor in "a stimulating bout anent Hamlet."[375]

More impressed, on the whole, were two young members of New York's theatrical community. After seeing the production, Eugene O'Neill wrote to Barrymore, "Your Hamlet was the very finest thing I have known in the theater – an inspiring experience for me! Discouragement with our stage becomes a rotten pose when one faces such an achievement. I was immensely elated."[376] An equally vivid impression was carried away by a 22-year-old actress. Years later, Helen Hayes remembered Barrymore's portrayal as "the finest Hamlet I've seen":

[Barrymore] had the one thing that all other actors, for me, have lacked. He wasn't acting the Prince of Denmark – he *was* a prince. He had a regal [presence] – without being stuffy, naturally, cause there was nothing ever stuffy about a Barrymore. They had the air of royalty, and he had it more than any of them. . . . You were not watching an actor trying to behave like a prince. . . . He was wonderful, in so many different lights and colors. And of course, he was so beautiful to look at.[377]

One result of the production's success was a flurry of Shakespearean activity, the like of which New York had not seen since the tercentenary festivities. "Another honorable and ancient tradition has gone all to pieces," commented the *Morning Telegraph*. "Arthur Hopkins's production of John Barrymore in *Hamlet* is proving itself a sell-out; and the legend that Shakespeare and profits are incompatable has died a highly public death. . . . [F]ollowing the opening night triumph of Mr. Barrymore as the ever-melancholy Dane, producer after producer has announced Shakespearean plans for the season" (10 December 1922).[378] A month after *Hamlet* opened, David Belasco's production of *The Merchant of Venice* made its debut and was received with politeness, even enthusiasm in some quarters; David Warfield's Shylock was generally admired. The Hopkins–Jones–Ethel Barrymore *Romeo and Juliet* that opened ten days later fared less fortunately. Hopkins had announced originally that Ethel Barrymore would appear as Rosalind, a part for which she was well suited. By early autumn, however, he had shifted his plans to the tragic sphere. The resulting production was surprisingly traditional; Jones's scenery was conservative, and little effort was made to reinterpret the play in terms of psychological values. The modern note was manifested primarily by the production's repressed acting style, which, in the view of many critics, was the play's downfall; Ethel Barrymore and her Romeo, McKay Morris, were found to be overly bland and lacking in passion. The production's failings were further emphasized less than a month later when Jane Cowl and Rollo Peters opened in the same play and won critical plaudits for their spirited, romantic interpretation. Neither the Belasco nor the Cowl productions evoked a fraction of the adulation visited upon *Hamlet,* however, leaving little doubt as to which Shakespearean production that season had made the greatest impact.

Barrymore, Hopkins, and Jones did not overlook the fact that a number of valid criticisms had been leveled against their efforts, however. Several directorial and scenic changes were made during the run in an effort to improve the production; many of these seem to have been a direct response to adverse commentary. Lark Taylor later claimed that Hopkins "apparently lost all interest in the play and us after the first night," adding that he "never came back stage, nor were there any rehearsals."[379] This is contradicted, however, by evidence from his promptbooks, which reveal that several scenes were reblocked during the run. In the first scene of the second act (Shakespeare's III.i.), for example, the initial groupings were reworked, and Barrymore's exit after the nunnery scene was changed so that he no longer "brushed by the lawful espials."[380] After seven weeks, the decision was made to restore the recorder scene. This was accomplished, according to Taylor, "with merely the briefest going over the lines in Jack's dressing-room," yet the scene "went very well, showing no lack of preparation."[381]

The Ghost scenes, another source of critical controversy, underwent changes as well. The "spotlight Ghost" was retained, but an effort was quickly made to reconcile the much-criticized disparity between the lighting effect on the backdrop and the ghostly voice emanating from the wings. This was not immediately successful, at least not to Alexander Woollcott, who quipped that "The first night [the Ghost's] speech was thick, remote and inaudible. A week later, it emerged crystal clear and neatly clipped in the manner of a lay reader intoning the service." Further adjustments were made, and two months later Woollcott reported that "a more guileful stagecraft has worked wonders with the once inert and unterrifying visitation."[382] Another response to adverse criticism came late in the run. Jones introduced an iron gate across the central arch and a large tombstone in the graveyard scene to provide a more realistic background for Ophelia's burial; she was no longer "buried in the front parlor."

Other changes were more spontaneous. To Woollcott, Barrymore's opening-night performance had "unforgettable beauty" but was at the same time "hedged with caution." That Hamlet, he wrote, "had not a free and easy stride," and "walked like a cat at night on a mantle shelf full of rare old bric-a-brac."[383] In subsequent performances, however, the reverse was often true. Whitford Kane remembered that Barrymore's constant dread was "the thought of a dull performance." To avoid becoming "stale and preachy" he would "invent new bits of business to keep the actors alive and the performance fresh."[384] The Adams and Taylor promptbooks attest to numerous departures from the opening-night blocking; the nunnery scene was acted according to the mood of the moment, and in the play scene, Taylor recalled, Barrymore "seemed to do it worse each time and was obviously dissatisfied, trying new ways at almost every performance." According to Taylor, Barrymore "became slower and more deliberate almost every performance" until he "outpaused Macready":

> Sometimes it seemed as though Barrymore would deliberately try to see how long he could make a pause. In a scene with me, when I was left alone with him after the exit of the other "Players," his pauses would frighten me. He would look at me for a long – – long time, raise his hand, open his mouth – then look at me in silence, 'til I would begin to feel panicky then he would begin to speak – long pauses between nearly every word. For ex-

ample: "Can – – – – – – – – – you – play – – – – – – – the murder – – – – – –
of – – – Gonzago?"[385]

Barrymore's spontaneity extended to the text. Taylor remembered that
one night,

> with no warning whatever, when I got my cue to speak Lucianus' speech,
> Barrymore broke in with: "I could interpret between you and your love,"
> etc., also putting in "Begin murderer – leave thy damnable faces and begin!
> Come, the croaking raven doth bellow for revenge!" [sic] He had never
> spoken these lines before, and, for a moment, I was stumped. I didn't know
> when to speak, but I managed to come in at the proper time.

The experiment evidently proved satisfying, however, for the lines were retained through the remainder of the run.[386] Almost inevitably, Barrymore
began to resort to pranks. While Whitford Kane was singing the Gravedigger's ditty, "In youth, when I did love," he would whisper to Kane that he
"ought to be in opera" and delay his entrance, forcing Kane to repeat the
song. On one occasion he painted a comic face on the dummy Kane and Cecil Clovelly had to lower into the grave. Kane and Blanche Yurka could barely contain their laughter during the scene. "'Twas rather a jolly funeral that
night," Taylor remembered, "and I wondered what the audience must have
thought of it all."[387] He could be contrite, however, when he inadvertently
caused discomfort to another actor. "I'm sorry I forgot my bally lines last
night and amputated two of your best laughs," he wrote to Kane after one
such incident. "I must have been in Patterson [sic] instead of Denmark!"[388]

Blanche Yurka later told a critic that she felt Barrymore gave "maybe three
magnificent performances all through the run, four or five that were very
good, and many that were awful."[389] Some of his worst performances were a
result of his efforts to impress visiting dignitaries. Taylor remembered that
"One night Sothern and Marlowe were in front, and Barrymore was so nervous he didn't know what to do with himself." He tried his best to play well
that night, but according to Taylor "gave the worst performance of the season." Sothern and Marlowe departed after the graveyard scene; the only comment from either, according to Taylor, was from Julia Marlowe, who said she
had never seen a company "so completely submerged."[390] On Thursday,
1 February 1923, the members of the Moscow Art Theatre (whose performances Barrymore had seen and admired) attended a matinee (Fig. 38).
Barrymore, Arthur Hopkins remembered, "was particularly anxious to impress them with the result that he played with a hysteria and extravagance
that was even exhausting to the spectator." Hopkins and Ethel Barrymore
visited him after his first scene and told him to stop pressing, but according to Hopkins, "the stampede was on, and he never got back into the cor-
ral all afternoon." (In a letter written later that day to Vladimir Nemirovich-

Figure 38. The visit of the Moscow Art Theatre, February 1923. Courtesy Billy Rose Theatre Collection, The New York Public Library for the Performing Arts.

Danchenko, Stanislavsky commented that he had found Barrymore's performance "far from ideal but very fascinating.")[391]

Barrymore told Taylor that he loved playing Hamlet and found it "one of the least taxing parts he had ever played." Comparing it to Richard III, he said: 'That bastard of a part nearly killed me. I had to work my head off to get the bloody part over. This is a cinch."[392] However, it soon became obvious to many cast members that the role was creating a physical strain. Blanche Yurka commented that Barrymore seemed unable to sustain "the entire performance at his top best. . . . It was as though his reserve of energy was limited, so that he was forced to save himself. Each night some scenes would be superbly played, others perfunctorily, and they were never the same scenes." She noticed that he seemed to be growing "very fatigued by . . . playing Hamlet eight times a week, month after month."[393] At least part of the problem arose from Barrymore's habit of chain-smoking during performances. Recalled Taylor,

One could trail him about the stage by the half-consumed cigarette butts. Sometimes he would take only two or three puffs, and throw the rest away, but nearly every time he went on the stage, he would have to fill his lungs with smoke two or three times – even if he delayed a moment or two. The result of this was that he had a wretched time with his voice before we had been playing a week, and continued to have all through the run. Paul, his mulatto valet, was kept busy with ice-bags and various other remedies, to keep his throat in condition for playing, and many a Sunday Mrs. Carrington would work with him most of the day, to get him in proper shape for Monday. He would say: "My pipes are on the bum."[394]

George Schaff, appointed by Hopkins as Barrymore's "guardian," later confided to a friend that he "always had to have a tank of oxygen in Barrymore's dressing room and that there were times he doubted that Barrymore could have completed a performance without its being administered."[395]

As the run progressed there was much speculation along Broadway as to how long Barrymore would continue in the role. Marc Connelly later recalled meeting Barrymore one day and asking him. "Everybody wants to know that," replied the actor. "What do they think this is – a tugboat race?"[396] Frank Case, the proprietor of the Algonquin, claimed to have been present in Barrymore's dressing room one day when a delegation of elderly actors, playwrights, and theatrical personages called on the actor and urged him to end his run at ninety-nine performances in memory of Booth's "record." It was as a response to their request, Case told Gene Fowler, that Barrymore decided to end his run at 101 performances.[397]

"Rumors that we were soon to close seemed absurd as we were more than selling out every performance," Lark Taylor recalled, but on Friday, 19 January 1923, the papers announced, and William Adams told the cast, that the play would close three weeks later, on 9 February. Special Tuesday matinees were added for the next three weeks in order to reach the desired 101 performances. By then, Taylor remembered, Barrymore was "tired, bored, in a highly nervous state, and wild to join his wife in Paris. He would probably have closed sooner but for his determination to beat Edwin Booth's record run." His attitude toward the cast was apologetic; he told Taylor, "God, I'm nearly crazy, I'm so worried about my kids." Michael Strange had been sending daily cablegrams from Paris urging him to join her; Barrymore's telegrams in response, Taylor remembered, were "veritable books that must have cost a small fortune."[398] Barrymore's decision forced Hopkins to refund a substantial amount of money. As one wag announced, he had become "'weary, stale' . . . but not unprofitable" – seats had been sold for many performances in advance of the closing date.[399] To console a public that was clamoring for tickets, Hopkins announced soon afterward that Barrymore had agreed to return to the role the following season. "Hopkins almost blew up when I told him I was closing," Barrymore wrote to Michael Strange, "but I looked him full in the eye and said that if we played as long as we could I would be here till God knows when and if we closed to enormous business we could get them to come again when we opened!!"[400]

The run did not conclude, however, without one last controversy. On 2 February 1923, Woollcott noted in the *Herald* that Booth's record

> has been the pride of the old folks and the passion of the statistician these many years. It is too bad that [Barrymore's] achievement should be thus conspicuously underscored. To play past the hundred performance mark and then stop short while the crowds are still coming gives the unfortunate effect of thumbing an impish nose at a great memory. Yet we cannot agree with the suggestion that it would be a more graceful gesture to halt the engagement at the ninety-ninth performance. That, we think, would be just a trifle too gracious. It may be annoying at have Barrymore even seem to thumb his nose at Mr. Booth. It would be intolerable to have him be condescending to him – in the manner of one letting a friend win at chess.

Barrymore immediately composed a response, printed by the *Herald* two days later, in which he took the opportunity to "clear up a matter that has evidently created some comment and given rise to various surmises which up to date have been wide of the mark." He claimed that he "intended playing Hamlet up to the first of March, but illness in my family, who are abroad, makes it imperative that I shorten the engagement and sail February 10," adding, "I do not in sincerity believe there is any human being alive who has a deeper reverence for the isolated grandeur and the perennially beautiful and touching figure of Edwin Booth than I have," and concluding that "I do not think one plays Hamlet to make or break records, as it is too noble a vehicle. . . ." It seems likely, however, that this statement contained a good deal of public posturing designed to save face; there is no indication in Barrymore's letters to Michael Strange of illness in the family, and the allure of ending the run on a record-setting note must have seemed irresistible.

The final performance had been sold out for several weeks in advance. On Friday, 9 February, the announcement was made that standing room would be offered beginning at 7:30. When that hour arrived the box-office line stretched nearly a block. Within a few minutes all available tickets were sold, and nearly a thousand people were turned away. After the second act Barrymore made a brief speech of thanks; the final curtain fell at midnight, by which time stars from other theatres had joined the rows of standees.[401] Afterward, Barrymore bid farewell to the members of the company. "He looked haggard and weary when we said good-bye," Taylor later remembered. "The stress of so many performances a week had left its mark and he was beginning to show signs of the notorious temper, but to me he was always gracious, kindly and courteous, and that season of *Hamlet* is one of my happiest memories of the theater."[402] Barrymore went directly from the theatre to the West Side Docks. At 2:30 A.M. he boarded the Cunard liner *Majestic;* the following morning he sailed for Europe, where he would spend the next seven months.

Second Season and Tour

On 6 September 1923, Hopkins announced to the press that Barrymore would return to the stage in November "for a four weeks' engagement" in *Hamlet* (ultimately shortened to three), followed by a brief tour of the principal cities (Fig. 39). Negotiations were then under way, he added, "to present Mr. Barrymore in *Hamlet* in London next spring." Eight days later, Barrymore returned to New York on the *Mauritania,* looking healthy and relaxed, according to one dockside reporter. Within a few days he departed for California, where he was scheduled to film *Beau Brummel,* an adaptation of Richard Mansfield's popular stage vehicle.[403]

By early November Barrymore's work on the film was nearly completed, and Hopkins summoned his company to begin preparations for the second season. Rehearsals commenced at the Plymouth at 11 A.M. on Monday, 5 November, with William Adams reading Barrymore's lines in his absence. There were numerous changes in the cast. Tyrone Power had another engagement, and Frederick Lewis had rejoined the Sothern and Marlowe company. During early rehearsals, Lark Taylor remembered, Blanche Yurka was temporarily unavailable, and her part was read by Winifred Salisbury, who had taken over the part of the "Gentlewoman"; a "Mr. Fitzgerald" read Polonius (a change necessitated after John S. O'Brien, suffering from cancer, committed suicide) and was later replaced by Moffat Johnstone; Kenneth Hunter took over the role of the King.[404]

The most noteworthy change occurring during the second-season rehearsal period was Hopkins's decision to feature a visible Ghost in Shakespeare's I.v. In an official announcement, he maintained that "this restoration of the actor to view has nothing to do with adherence to tradition," adding that he now desired to "convey the struggle of a spirit to come in contact with a living person, and the corresponding struggle of the person, Hamlet, feeling the presence of the spirit, to communicate with it."[405] Another change was necessitated by the tour: Scenes taking place on the apron during the first season were reblocked due to the technical difficulties of constructing an apron in the various theatres in which the production would appear. There were other changes as well, including more than a dozen cuts and stets to the text. These are documented in detail in William Adams's promptbook, which he used to conduct second-season rehearsals. Most alterations were relatively minor, involving only a few lines. The Queen's speech following Ophelia's

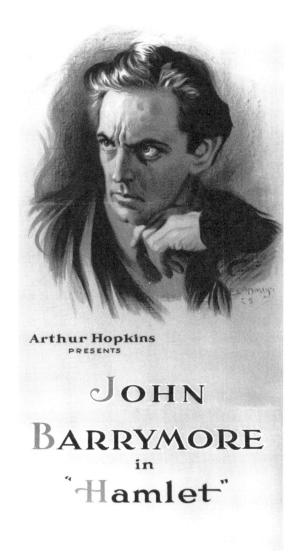

Figure 39. Poster for the second season of *Hamlet,* November 1923. Courtesy Billy Rose Theatre Collection, The New York Public Library for the Performing Arts.

mad scene was restored in its entirety, however, and the recorder scene, inserted late in the first season, was retained.[406]

To house his revival, Hopkins rented the Manhattan Opera House on 34th Street, which boasted a seating capacity of over three thousand – more than three times that of the Harris. Barrymore arrived in New York on Saturday morning, 24 November, and rehearsed with the company for the next two days. "Got here on a Saturday . . . and began rehearsing madly with the new people," he wrote to Michael Strange. "Saturday afternoon and night and Sunday and Sunday night: and the Ghost was all wrong and [I] had to sit up till six in the morning Sunday night with Jones fixing it properly."[407]

Opening night was scheduled for Monday, 26 November, with tickets priced from $3.30 to 55 cents for evening performances and $2.75 to 55 cents for matinees. That evening, according to the *World,* Barrymore was greeted by a crowded auditorium, which "accorded him an ovation, shrill whistles and cheers mingling with a swell of applause to proclaim that here was something which deserved to be described as a triumphal return" (27 November 1923). At the end of the first act, the audience "demanded his appearance before them and kept him there bowing and smiling, wearily, for many minutes" (*Tribune,* 27 November 1923).

Reviews in the New York papers the next day and thereafter tended to be brief. The production was by then taken for granted by the critics, who devoted only a fraction of the column space to the revival that they had to the premiere. Most agreed, however, that Barrymore's performance had improved since the initial season. "It is a pity that we all overdrew our generous accounts in the National Bank of Adjectives when this performance was new to New York a year ago," wrote Woollcott in the *Herald* (1 December 1923). "For now it is a better performance, richer, more fused, more mellow. . . . Now we have both the profound thought and the troubled heart, and something has given the blending smoothness." The critics were unanimous in their approval of the physical appearance of the Ghost, represented in the revival by the familiar slim figure in silver armor and long white whiskers. Kenneth Hunter's Claudius and Moffatt Johnston's Polonius were deemed worthy additions to the cast.

As was the case with the first-season reviews, however, the bulk of the praise was devoted to Barrymore's performance, which, according to the *Evening Telegram,* had "grown in power and in poise" (8 December 1923). "Possibly no more intelligent reading of *Hamlet* was ever done," wrote the *Sun and Globe* (27 November 1923). "Certainly it would have pleased Shakespeare to watch John Barrymore play his greatest role." Several columnists made mention of the fact that Barrymore's was the third Hamlet to appear in New York that season, but clearly there was no competition. Sothern's repertory appearance in the role at the end of October had been greeted with scarcely a critical mention, and Sir John Martin-Harvey's Dane, which had opened a week earlier, was assailed for its "oratorical method" and "vocal monotony." Noted as well was the fact that Barrymore presented "an ideal figure of Hamlet, youthful and princely, so unlike certain elderly gentlemen who have essayed the role."[408]

For the next three weeks, Hamlet played to near-capacity houses at most performances.[409] The production drew more than $20,000 the first week, exceeded $25,000 the second week, and the final week grossed more than $30,000.[410] On 15 December, Barrymore played his final Hamlet in New York, and the next week began his first trip into the provinces in five years.[411] The first week was divided between New Haven and Hartford. Barrymore commuted back to New York every evening. According to Taylor, he hurried through the play to make his train, "shortening the performance almost an hour, to its great improvement."[412]

The company spent Christmas week in Boston, where they appeared at the Boston Opera House and grossed nearly $34,000. Barrymore was no longer able to commute, and the production regained its former length; the critical praise continued, although one reviewer complained that the "slowness of pace in action and long pauses between lines" were disturbing.[413]

One interested observer at the Wednesday matinee was a 20-year-old Harvard sophomore who had spent the previous semester in G. L. Kittredge's Shakespeare course, which was devoted entirely that term to a line-by-line analysis of *Hamlet*. Years later, Elliot Norton, who subsequently became dean of the Boston drama critics, looked back upon Barrymore's performance. "It was enormously exciting," he recalled. "The first great Hamlet I had seen. I had seen some of the touring Hamlets – Walter Hampden and people like that – but nothing like this." He was impressed by the "absolute clarity in his diction," adding "you heard and understood every word." Throughout, Barrymore "seemed to be possessed . . . a demented man carried along by the rush of words and by his emotions and passions." To Norton, the most thrilling moment in the performance was Barrymore's "almost balletic" leap at the King. "I remember at the time it seemed definitely that he had actually killed the King, he was so carried away at that point," he recalled. Still, one moment in the play convinced Norton that Barrymore was able to "control himself in the most extraordinary way." During the play scene, while watching the King and Laertes intently, he glanced at Horatio and asked him, in an undertone, "I wonder what the audience would think if I should say Hollywood now instead of wormwood." "I had the feeling I wasn't hearing this, I was so caught up in the action," Norton remembered, for "at that point [Barrymore] was almost insanely concentrated on what he was doing and what he was watching. And a moment later . . . he said, 'Wormwood, wormwood,' in such a way again that you feel he was entirely caught up in the action."[414]

The tour proceeded to Philadelphia, where Barrymore, according to Taylor, "acted like a spoiled child, pretending to forget lines, and making silly speeches to the audience, referring to Philadelphia as his dear old hometown." "I was born here you know," he announced to one audience. "My grandmother told me if I ever became a great actor I could play in Philadelphia. I don't know whether I'm a great actor or not, but my God! – It's good to play here."[415] Among those in attendance that week was a 17-year-old University of Pennsylvania student, Louis M. Simon, who later became a stage manager for Arthur Hopkins, and was for many years thereafter public relations director of the Actors Fund of America. "My over-all impression," he recalled years later, "was that I was witnessing one of the greatest and most thrilling theatre experiences that could be imagined. . . . Barrymore's towering performance along with the Jones/Hopkins concept of staging Shakespeare [made an] overwhelming impression on me." As was the case with many observers, an eccentricity of Barrymore's portrayal remained vivid many years later:

> At the performance I saw, he was suffering from a drippy head cold which kept him constantly reaching for a handkerchief stuffed in his doublet. But he was so convincing that the audience simply accepted the fact that Hamlet – as any other human being – was not immune to the common cold. In fact at one point where Hamlet reaches for the locket containing [his father's] "likeness," he pulled out the handkerchief instead, uttered a not-very-sotto-voce "God damn it!", stuffed the hanky back in his bosom, drew out the locket . . . and proceeded with Shakespeare's lines as if nothing untoward had happened.[416]

Originally the tour had been planned to extend into March, with a stop in Detroit and a four-week run in Chicago, but within a few weeks it became clear to Hopkins and the company that Barrymore was again wearying of the role. On 2 January a closing notice was posted on the call board, informing the cast that *Hamlet* would play its final performance in Cleveland on 26 January. Soon afterward, Hopkins made a public announcement, citing "the physical strain of playing this role, as he does, eight times a week," as the reason for his star's withdrawal.[417] The tour proceeded to Washington, where President and Mrs. Coolidge attended the opening-night performance. Coolidge invited Barrymore and Hopkins to visit the White House the next day, where he admitted that he had seen only two Hamlets, the other being E. H. Sothern's. Asked by Barrymore which he preferred, the president responded after a moment, "Well, Mr. Sothern's clothes were prettier than yours." Soon afterward, Margaret Carrington paid a visit to the company. She told Taylor that she was upset and indignant over the closing and was "going to use all her influence to prevent it."[418] Barrymore, however, paid little heed. "Thank *God* there are only two more weeks of it and then I go to bed on the boat," he wrote to Michael Strange. By then, too, he was determined to play Hamlet in London and had booked passage for 2 February. A cabled invitation from the Shakespeare Memorial Committee to go to England that spring and play Hamlet had only firmed his resolve.[419]

In Pittsburgh the following week, Barrymore seemed weary and petulant; he began to voice suspicions that the other actors in the company were trying to upstage him. "You were doing something with your bean," he told Taylor after one performance. On 21 January, the production opened its final week at the Hanna Theatre in Cleveland, where Hopkins's brother William was City Manager. Opening night was packed, despite a raging blizzard, and Barrymore, Taylor remembered, gave "a truly great performance." In his curtain speech after the second act, he told the audience, "I'm glad to be in Arthur Hopkins' home town. He's a perfect peach. Like the banker who seduced the lady, he made me what I am today." After considerable applause he concluded, "I am always closing up on Arthur, like an oyster to a hungry man."[420]

"Of all the mimes and antics now strutting among us," wrote William F. McDermott in the *Plain Dealer,* only Barrymore "has that eccentric, evasive lightning spark that men call genius" (22 January 1924). The eccentricity as well as the lightning was much in evidence that final week. Taylor recalled,

> One night, after playing dice all the night before, our unpredictable star ran across the stage to the King and went through all the motions of a crap game. Later, as we walked on for a scene, he asked me, quite audibly, to come to a party he was giving the next night. He interrupted the dialogue in the Graveyard to invite the grave-diggers. Thus were most of the cast asked, the audience hearing each invitation.

On 26 January, Barrymore gave what would prove to be his final performance of Hamlet in America. A closing night party was held at the Hollenden Hotel, where each of the women in the company found a $100 bill under her plate, along with a note of apology from Barrymore for closing so suddenly. "When we said good-bye he held my hand tightly, saying, 'For God's sake fix it up with Arthur so you can go to London with me in April. Don't take anything that you can't get out of,'" Taylor remembered.[421] The next day Barrymore returned to New York, confident that a British *Hamlet* featuring members of his American cast could be swiftly and easily arranged.

4

The London *Hamlet*, 1925

There he was, the amazing Jack Barrymore, on stage at the Haymarket.
Everything about him was exciting. He was athletic, he had charisma and,
to my young mind, he played the part to perfection.

– Laurence Olivier[1]

JOHN BARRYMORE'S 1925 PRODUCTION of *Hamlet* at the Haymarket Theatre, London, has often been regarded as little more than a footnote to the acclaimed New York production; yet his equally successful London *Hamlet* stands as a theatrical landmark in its own right. In England, Barrymore served for the only time in his career as producer and director as well as star. In order to mount his production he was forced to overcome numerous obstacles, most notably the formidable commercialism and anti-Shakespearean bias that had dominated West End theatre for more than a decade following the outbreak of the First World War. His success as an actor-manager paved the way for the return of West End Shakespeare as a commercially viable, glamorous theatrical event in the tradition of Irving and Tree.

The production proved, in particular, a seminal influence on the directing styles of E. Harcourt Williams and Margaret Webster, two members of the cast who became prominent directors of Shakespeare during the ensuing decade. Moreover, Barrymore's ground-breaking interpretation of Shakespeare's character was to serve in England, as it had in America, as a revolutionary bridge between the genteel, beautifully spoken "Sweet Prince" of Victorian tradition and the harsher, more psychological "modern man" favored by subsequent twentieth-century Hamlets – including Laurence Olivier and John Gielgud, both of whom saw and admired Barrymore's production.

During the final weeks of his American tour, Barrymore had resolved to accept what he considered to be the ultimate challenge. "Now I began to dream of real accomplishment," he remembered years later. "To me, the greatest height that an actor could reach was to play *Hamlet* successfully in London – Shakespeare's own country."[2] Barrymore was aware that Edwin Booth, whose New York "record" he had broken, had added to his prestige by playing Shakespeare in London, and the more recent British engagements of Sothern and Marlowe and James K. Hackett might well have encouraged him.

A crucial setback came, however, as Barrymore prepared for his journey. He had attempted to persuade Arthur Hopkins to reprise his role as producer and director in London, but Hopkins, after making preliminary inquiries, gave a polite yet firm refusal. He did not feel that there was anything but loss to be encountered, a prominent English newspaper publisher having told him: "If Barrymore has the audacity to come to London in *Hamlet* they'll kill him."[3] Barrymore was stung by Hopkins's response, but vowed to produce and direct the production himself if necessary. His disappointment was soon assuaged when Hopkins promised the loan of William Adams, George Schaff, and the Robert Edmond Jones sets and costumes.

Barrymore departed for London on 2 February 1924 with the aim of finding a theatre and raising production capital. His plan was to begin rehearsals in April with a company that would include many members of his American cast.[4] In London, he sought assistance from his friend Sir Gerald Du Maurier, who made inquiries about a venue for the production. "Still in the thick of getting a theatre – Du Maurier is helping me and his manager – I hope to God they are on the level but he will surely put through *something* for himself," he wrote to Michael Strange in Paris in early March. "I am trying to get His Majesty's Theatre which is far and away the best for us."[5]

The attempt to lease His Majesty's quickly fell through, and soon afterward, Barrymore joined forces with Constance Collier, his costar in *Peter Ibbetson*, who had agreed to play Gertrude (Fig. 40). Together they made the rounds in search of a theatre and financial backing. Their initial efforts were, however, unsuccessful. British theatre was still dominated by the flimsy comedies and melodramas of the First World War and its aftermath, and West End managers were reluctant to gamble on a commercial Shakespearean production. An American star only heightened the potential risks. Recent attempts at West End Shakespeare had not been particularly successful, the managers reminded them. Shakespeare, they argued, was the domain of the Old Vic, which enjoyed loyal audiences and minimal commercial pressures.[6] A similarly disappointing response came from the Shakespeare Memorial Committee, whose limited resources precluded the possibility of sponsoring a major commercial revival in London. They could offer only encouragement and the possibility of a Stratford production if Barrymore failed in his attempts to present *Hamlet* in the West End.

Nevertheless, Barrymore persisted. At one point he persuaded Basil Dean, the newly appointed joint managing director of Drury Lane, to ask his theatre's directors if they would sponsor the production. Barrymore "was without resources or organization of any kind," Dean remembered, and the suggestion that Drury Lane should finance *Hamlet* "enraged the board." Constance Collier recalled that Barrymore often did little to further his own quest. His mercurial personality and brash, confident style of presenting his proposal tended to shock the conservative managers. Barrymore later confessed that he felt ill at ease in the role of theatrical businessman; he was always relieved when the conversation in the managers' offices could turn away from theatre rental to subjects like hunting and fishing.[7] In late April or early May, he wrote to Michael Strange: "If everything I do from every angle does not materialize in my getting a theatre this spring and it is pretty late – I will do it in the autumn. It is a very definite *fight*. I see that and one must expect one disappointment after another but if one has the firm intention it cannot be deterred."[8] Soon afterward, he joined Michael Strange in France, where he remained through the summer.

Barrymore returned to America in September 1924. He was discouraged by his lack of success, but failure to obtain a theatre had only strengthened his resolve to present *Hamlet* before a London audience. "It was a consuming ambition," he remembered. "I *had* to do it."[9] In early November he returned to London, renting James McNeill Whistler's former residence at No. 2 Cheyne Walk in Chelsea. There he joined Michael Strange and their 3-year-old daughter Diana, and he continued to search for a theatre and financial backing.

The Cast

In December, although he was still without a theatre, Barrymore took a daring step. On the advice of Constance Collier, he cast the principal roles with English actors – Malcolm Keen as the King, Herbert Waring as Polonius, and Courtenay Thorpe as the Ghost – and began rehearsing them individually and in small groups. Fay Compton, a young English actress who had met Barrymore the previous summer in France, later remembered that

> Constance Collier . . . took me over to see him and said, "Jack, you've got to have this girl to play Ophelia." And Jack took a look at me and said, "Oh yeah? Very well, then. We'll have a look at her." Then I went to see him in London, and he said to me "I don't think you know anything about Shakespeare, do you?" And I said, "Well, no, I've only played Perdita at school." He said, "Very well, then. I'll teach you. I'll take a fortnight to teach you before we start rehearsing." And bless be, if he didn't come to my little house in Trevor Square and teach me – literally teach me – for a fortnight, until he got me as perfect as he could get me. It was a wonderful experience. I don't know any other actor-manager would have bothered, but he did.[10]

Figure 40. Hamlet and Gertrude (Constance Collier). Courtesy Hulton Getty Picture Collection.

Negotiations for a venue continued while Barrymore worked with his principals.[11] Fay Compton later remembered the air of uncertainty surrounding these rehearsals: "Though the cast was arranged, the scenery and costumes on their way from New York, every preliminary to rehearsals looked to," it seemed that Barrymore "was not going to be able to get a theatre in which to produce the play! We all lived through a very trying period when negotiations for practically every theatre in London were entered into, only to be abandoned for some reason or another." But time was not wasted. "Day after day he rehearsed the Ophelia scenes with me," Fay Compton continued, "always fired with an enthusiasm that in itself was an inspiration to anyone working with him, full of ideas, full of encouragement, and unsparing in his efforts to help me perfect, as far as I was capable, my attempt to mirror Ophelia's sad story."[12]

Constance Collier, aware of Barrymore's difficulties in dealing with the managers, finally decided to take matters into her own hands. "I persuaded Jack to let me do most of the negotiations," she recalled. She talked to Frederick Harrison, lessee and manager of the Haymarket Theatre, "and I got the contracts drawn up before Jack met that very conservative and dignified gentleman. He had a production coming on, but there was an intervening period of six weeks and he was glad to get his rent paid."[13]

Soon afterward, Barrymore formed a partnership with the English producer William Foss, who was to oversee the financial details of the production and share equally in any profits. The contracts were signed on 24 January 1925.[14] Barrymore was elated to be able to present Hamlet at the Haymarket, where his father had enjoyed a successful run as visiting American leading man in the Bancrofts' company forty years earlier. He invested $25,000 of his own money in the production, half the initial cost, and the other half of the money was raised in London.[15]

With most of the principals well advanced in their parts, the next step was the casting of the secondary characters and walk-ons. News of Barrymore's Broadway successes in Shakespeare and his fame as a star of the silent screen had preceded him: His London *Hamlet* promised to be an extraordinary occasion. All the young and aspiring actors in London were eager to join the *Hamlet* company, but in the end Barrymore engaged a number of actors from the current show at the Haymarket, James M. Barrie's *A Kiss for Cinderella*. Harding Steerman (Priest), Stanley Roberts (Messenger), Roy Travers (Bernardo), and Alison Leggatt (Court Lady and understudy for Ophelia) were cast in open auditions. "We all regarded him with bated breath," Alison Leggatt recalled. "The very great John Barrymore. He had a great glamour about him, a glamour no one else had."[16]

At least one member of the cast was enlisted from Barrymore's London circle of theatrical friends. Margaret Webster, 19 at the time, was offered the small part of "A Gentlewoman" after Barrymore came to dinner to renew his friendship with her parents, Ben Webster and May Whitty, old family friends from his English schooldays.[17] The only members of the American cast retained were Burnel Lundbec and Vadim Uraneff, who played the Mime Player King and Lucianus.

Rehearsals

Full rehearsals began in late January 1925. Barrymore had chosen to retain much of the staging and interpretation worked out for the American production, so his primary challenge as a director was to weld his British company into a unified ensemble.[18] He was assisted in his directorial duties by Margaret Carrington, who had come from America at his request to advise on matters of voice and interpretation.[19] Barrymore had been alarmed to find that a number of company members spoke Shakespearean verse in the cadenced, musical style of an earlier day, and it was Carrington who helped them achieve a more natural effect. E. Harcourt Williams, cast as the First Player, remembered one such session:

> One day Mrs. Carrington said to me: "Why do you assume that particular voice when you are speaking Shakespeare? Do you do anything else besides Shakespeare?" I replied that I sometimes told stories to children. "Tell me one then." And I began, thoroughly amazed, to tell her Hans Andersen's "Tinder Box." "But that's your real voice," she exclaimed. "That's the voice you ought to use in Shakespeare." A flash of lightning could hardly have shown me more.[20]

Members of the English cast began to realize that they were to be part of an extraordinary production. Margaret Webster remembered that Barrymore "did not unmask his full fire at rehearsals, but the glittering, lithe, demonic quality shone through like flashing steel." His approach to the character "made all the other Hamlets seem stodgy by comparison."[21]

The opening night was set for Thursday, 19 February 1925. Advance bookings were considerable, with tickets ranging in price from £4 16s and £3 13s for boxes to 1s 2d for the gallery. As rehearsals progressed, Barrymore told Malcolm Watson of the *Daily Telegraph* how he felt about his impending production: "Pretty much as Sydney Carton probably felt when he set his foot on the lowest step leading to the scaffold." Nevertheless, he confided that his nervousness was tempered with a sense of satisfaction that he was to realize one of his "most cherished ambitions" by "appearing in a Shakespearean play before a London audience."[22]

Margaret Webster recalled that despite his legendary temper, Barrymore's behavior during most of the rehearsal period was "impeccable, all dignity and charm." There was one outburst, however, during the only full-company rehearsal prior to opening. The cast had been instructed by Barrymore and stage manager William Adams (who had supervised rehearsals of the secondary characters and walk-ons) to begin whispering as they took their places on the set. However, their initial attempt at Act I, scene ii, did not satisfy the director:

> "No, no, NO!" With a piercing yell Barrymore leaped from his chair and confronted us. "It won't do at all – not at all!" We were paralyzed. He ran his hands through his hair as if in desperation. "Don't you understand – when the curtain goes up it's dark – BLACK!" (Subdued murmurs of "Yes, Mr. Barrymore.") "They can't see you." ("No, Mr. Barrymore." "But you're

all whispering . . ." ("We know – we did – we were . . .") "But it was the wrong kind of whispering. You've got to make the audience understand right away that this is a very LECHEROUS Court!" Silence. . . . We did it again. We did it a lot of times. Finally, lechery triumphed and we went on with the scene.[23]

Afterward, the company gathered onstage for notes and comments. Barrymore, exhausted by his duties, nevertheless made a point of singling out each member of the cast for special praise. "Miss Compton, yours will be the most enchanting and most adorable Ophelia since that of Ellen Terry. . . . My dear Constance. I can't tell you how magnificent you are. . . . Laertes, you were a flaming ball of fire tonight . . . particularly in the duel scenes where, without any apparent effort at self-protection, you seem always to be in the right place." At the conclusion of his speech, the mood was lightened by a frequent visitor to rehearsals: Peter, the Haymarket's resident tomcat, who emerged, as if on cue, onto the stage. "As for you, my dear fellow," Barrymore commented, reaching down to stroke him, "you are going to make a hell of a hit in one of my soliloquies."[24]

As the opening night approached, London newspapers and magazines began to herald the event with considerable anticipation. One commentator noted that Barrymore's appearance at the Haymarket "was looked forward to with an eager expectancy for the like of which one must go back to the old Lyceum first nights when Irving was in his prime," adding that "The occasion was widely heralded – and that without any puffing – as the event of the year."[25]

Tickets for opening night had been sold out for weeks in advance. Even so, the London correspondent for the *New York Sun* cabled that the "gallery gods, as if sensing the approach of a memorable event, formed an interminable queue on the sidewalks of the Haymarket" (20 February 1925). The stalls and boxes were packed with celebrities, including the Earl and Countess of Oxford and Asquith, Princess Bibesco, Arnold Bennett, Henry Arthur Jones, John Masefield, A. A. Milne, and Somerset Maugham. The London theatrical establishment was represented by Sir Squire Bancroft, Madge Kendall, Ben Webster and May Whitty, Mary Anderson, Gerald Du Maurier, and Lilian Braithwaite. Dame Nellie Melba attended and sent Barrymore a laurel wreath. George Bernard Shaw sat in the stalls, "looking quite American in tortoise shell glasses [and] commenting animatedly between the acts";[26] he attended the performance as a guest of Barrymore's wife, Michael Strange.

A few minutes before the house lights went down, Barrymore addressed his fellow actors, many of whom were gathered onstage as the Haymarket filled to capacity:

I powdered the beads of sweat off the forehead and sauntered on to the stage smoking a cigarette. I wanted to put up a bluff of casualness to the other members of the company. . . . I understood that they were apprehensive and I appreciated their reason for being so. There had only been time for one full dress rehearsal with the scenery, and it was complicated for persons not accustomed to it. . . . I did the best I could to encourage them. I think this is the best performance I have ever given. No other make-believe that I have accomplished has been so authentic, I am sure, as my simulated calmness that night.[27]

Soon afterward, the curtain rose on the Robert Edmond Jones set. As the first scene progressed, Barrymore took his place in the wings, chain-smoking in an attempt to calm his nerves. "Then came my own first scene," he remembered years later. "I threw my cigarette away and on the darkened stage I sat waiting for the curtain to go up."[28]

Almost four hours later, the final curtain was rung down. The *Sun* correspondent cabled on 20 February 1925 that there had been "eight curtain calls after the first act, almost as many more after the second and so much commotion at the end of the performance – which came after the stroke of midnight – that Barrymore, visibly and doubtless truly moved, was brought before the curtain for a graceful and ingratiating curtain speech." "I had felt a natural diffidence amounting to a positive terror in playing Hamlet before you, but that feeling has been greatly allayed by your kindness and appreciation," commented the triumphant actor. After words of praise for his supporting cast and the Haymarket, which he called "the foremost theatre in the world," he concluded, "It's a great thing that Denmark, England and America can blend so well."

Critical Response and Aftermath

Reviews the next day and soon afterward were overwhelmingly favorable. Although none of the London critics found Barrymore superior to Irving and Forbes-Robertson, many were favorable in their comparisons.[29] James Agate, writing in the *Sunday Times,* noted that Barrymore's Hamlet (Fig. 41) drew "fewer tears" than Forbes-Robertson's, but on the whole he declared it "nearer to Shakespeare's whole creation than any other I have seen." He went on to describe Barrymore's qualifications for the role:

First a handsome face, intellectual as to the brow. . . . Next an agreeable voice, touching nobility here and there, but lacking the organ-note and in emotion running too easily to the head-notes of the tenor. Add the purest diction, perfect enunciation, and unexampled clarity. Now note a slim figure and the general illusion of princeliness and youth. All these are informed – and here is the key – by intellectual capacity of a rare order and analytical power of extreme cogency.

Like many of his colleagues, Agate found that the main flaw in Barrymore's performance lay in his verse speaking. "How, with such gifts, does Shakespeare's poetry fare?" he asked. "A trifle ill is the answer." Barrymore, he commented, "attempts to get power by sudden gusts, choosing a single word for an explosion. Sometimes the choice is quite arbitrary . . . the words, being perfunctory, are robbed of their just splendour" (22 February 1925).

Other critics, echoing their American counterparts, carped at the fact that Barrymore's performance, while dynamic and startlingly clear, seemed to favor intellect rather than emotion. "He suffers, he reasons, he lets you see what he means, but you do not weep for him," wrote the reviewer for *The Queen*.[30] A. B. Walkley, the veteran critic for the *Times*, commented similarly that Barrymore "appeals to your judgement, not to your nerves," but found on the whole that "he successfully appeals, for every moment of his work is of the highest interest" (20 February 1925).

Duly noted was the fact that the genteel, melancholy Dane of Forbes-Robertson and Martin-Harvey had been supplanted by a harsher, more psychological interpretation of Shakespeare's character. As in America, the "Sweet Prince" of Victorian tradition was often missed, but both Agate and Walkley were generally approving of the "new" way of viewing Shakespeare's character. "You have but to scratch the god," Agate commented, "and the demon instantly appears" (*Sunday Times*, 22 February 1925).

A number of reviewers with long memories compared Barrymore's Hamlet favorably with that of Edwin Booth. Barrymore's speech, like Booth's, was praised for its lack of an American accent. "It was a pleasure to hear verse spoken with such precision and without any accent, either of America, Oxford or Kensington," commented the *Daily News* critic. "It was just Anglo–Saxon English" (20 February 1925). Hesketh Pearson noted an additional wrinkle: Barrymore had replaced the customary artificial, elocutionary speech of nineteenth- and early-twentieth-century Shakespearean productions with a more natural method of pronunciation. "He pronounces 'my' and 'mine' as they should be pronounced, not as "'me' and 'min,'" noted Pearson, adding: "That alone was worth crossing the Atlantic for."[31]

Many commentators praised the athleticism and vitality Barrymore brought to the role. Walkley noted that Barrymore demonstrated "a bodily agility that would do no discredit to Mr. Douglas Fairbanks. (See him gyrate like a top in the play scene! See him take a running jump at the King at the end!)" Barrymore's staging was singled out for praise as well. Lennox Robinson commented admiringly that "Acting is not his only gift; he is a great producer [i.e., director]. Every piece of grouping and movement was beautiful,

Figure 41. A portrait of Barrymore at the time of the London production. Courtesy Hulton Getty Picture Collection.

and there were moments in the production I shall never forget and never want to – the second scene in the first act [was] astonishingly pictorial in the Edwin Abbey manner" (*Sunday Observer,* 1 March 1925). Jones's unit setting, as novel in London as it had been in America, was almost universally admired.[32]

All in all, the critics seemed to agree with the reviewer for *The Bookman,* who wrote that "One cannot fail to recognize in this production an historic event."[33] Although talented Hamlets had appeared on the London stage in the years since Forbes-Robertson's 1913 farewell performance, most notably Ernest Milton and Ion Swinley, they clearly lacked the glamour, charisma, and popular appeal of Barrymore's portrayal. His revolutionary use of modern psychology, his conversational approach to the text, his athleticism and personal magnetism had combined to create a stunning theatrical success.[34]

One notice, however, was to depress Barrymore through the remainder of his run, and indeed, throughout his entire career. In later years he would often refer to this minority view as "A haymaker at the Haymarket." This most scathing criticism of *Hamlet* came in a typewritten letter that George Bernard Shaw wrote to Barrymore on 22 February 1925. Although he quibbled at the use of the Oedipus complex as a motivating factor, Shaw's main objection came not to Barrymore's interpretation but rather to the cuts made in the play:

My dear Mr Barrymore,

I have to thank you for inviting me – and in such kind terms too – to your first performance of Hamlet in London; and I am glad you had no reason to complain of your reception, or, on the whole, of your press. Everyone felt that the occasion was one of extraordinary interest; and as far as your personality was concerned they were not disappointed.

I doubt, however, whether you have been able to follow the course of Shakespearean production in England during the last fifteen years or so enough to realize the audacity of your handling of the play. When I last saw it performed at Stratford-on-Avon, practically the entire play was given in three hours and three quarters, with one interval of ten minutes; and it made the time pass without the least tedium though the cast was not in any way remarkable. On Thursday last you played five minutes longer with the play cut to ribbons, even to the breath-bereaving extremity of cutting out the recorders, which is rather like playing King John without little Arthur.

You saved, say, an hour and a half on Shakespear by the cutting, and filled it up with an interpolated drama of your own in dumb show. This was a pretty daring thing to do. In modern shop plays, without characters or anything but the commonest dialogue, the actor has to supply everything but the mere story, getting in the psychology between the lines, and presenting in his own person the fascinating hero whom the author has been unable to create. He is not substituting something of his own for something of the author's: he is filling up a void and doing the author's work for him. And the author ought to be extremely obliged to him.

But to try this method on Shakespear is to is to take on an appalling responsibility and put up a staggering pretension. Shakespear, with all his shortcomings, was a very great playwright; and the actor who undertakes to improve his plays undertakes thereby to excel to an extraordinary degree in two professions in both of which the highest success is extremely rare. Shakespear himself, though by no means a modest man, did not pretend to be able to play Hamlet as well as write it: he was content to do a recitation in the dark as the ghost. But you have ventured not only to act Hamlet but to discard about a third of Shakespear's script and substitute stuff of your own, and that, too, without the help of dialogue. Instead of giving what is called a reading of Hamlet, you say, in effect, "I am not going to read Hamlet at all: I am going to leave it out. But see what I give you in exchange!"

Such an enterprise must justify itself by its effect on the public. You discard the recorders as hackneyed back chat, and the scene with the king after the death of Polonius, with such speeches as "How all occasions do inform against me!" as obsolete junk, and offer instead a demonstration of that very modern discovery called the Oedipus complex, thereby adding a really incestuous motive on Hamlet's part to the merely conventional incest of a marriage (now legal in England) with a deceased husband's brother. You change Hamlet and Ophelia into Romeo and Juliet. As producer, you allow Laertes and Ophelia to hug each other as lovers instead of lecturing and squabbling like hectoring big brother and little sister: another complex!

Now your success in this must depend on whether the play invented by Barrymore on the Shakespear foundation is as gripping as the Shakespear play, and whether your dumb show can hold an audience as a straightforward reading of Shakespear's rhetoric can. I await the decision with interest.

My own opinion is, of course, that of an author. I write plays that play for three hours and a half even with instantaneous changes and only one short interval. There is no time for silences or pauses: the actor must play on the line and not between the lines, and must do nine tenths of his acting with his voice. Hamlet – Shakespear's Hamlet – can be done from end to end in four hours in that way; and it never flags nor bores. Done in any other way Shakespear is the worst of bores, because he has to be chopped into a mere cold stew. I prefer my way. I wish you would try it, and concentrate on acting rather than on authorship, at which, believe me, Shakespear can write your head off. But that may be vicarious professional jealousy on my part.

I did not dare to say all this to Mrs Barrymore on the night. It was chilly enough for her without a coat in the stalls without any cold water from

yours perhaps too candidly,
G. Bernard Shaw.[35]

Shaw's view of Barrymore's text was predictable in light of his previously published comments on the subject.[36] These represented only one side of an ongoing debate, yet they served to underscore the fact that the practice of textual restoration pioneered by Forbes-Robertson, Poel, and Barker had established itself more strongly in London than it had in New York. More than half a dozen British commentators took Barrymore to task for his much-abridged acting version, and their critiques were often sternly worded.[37] William Poel, for example, saw the production twice and thought Barrymore the most interesting English-speaking Hamlet he had seen, superior to Irving or Forbes-Robertson. Although he admired the way Barrymore "talked his part all the way through and got the other actors to do the same," he remarked that "the version he acts should not be called Shakespeare's *Hamlet,* but scenes from *Hamlet.*"[38]

Shaw's comments also struck at the heart of Barrymore's dramatic technique, and here again he was echoed by many of the London critics. The pauses and pantomime Barrymore employed had been utilized successfully by Irving and Fechter half a century earlier and represented a departure from the cadenced delivery used subsequently by Forbes-Robertson and his less talented contemporaries, Martin-Harvey and Tree. At the same time, however, they were contrary to the more recent trend toward rapid verse speaking championed by Poel and Barker. These devices went a long way toward furthering the "natural" illusion Barrymore sought and served to clarify his reading, yet many critics, agreeing with Shaw, felt that Barrymore carried them to extremes at the expense of Shakespeare's text. "Mr. Barrymore spoke deliberately, he showed you each idea in the making, like a slow-motion picture," Herbert Farjeon commented, concluding that "I think it was due to the tardiness of Mr. Barrymore's utterance that in a performance lasting nearly four hours we got . . . so little of the play" (*Weekly Westminster,* 28 February 1925; *Sphere,* 7 March 1925). Similarly, the critic for *The Stage* complained that Barrymore's performance suffered from "an excess of detail – not merely in the matter of pauses, but in lifting of the eyebrows frequently, or in suiting the action to the word too closely (as by fingering the cheek when it is mentioned) and so forth" (26 February 1925).[39]

Although most observers embraced the "new" Hamlet, many of the younger members of Britain's theatrical profession, schooled in the rapid verse speaking of Poel and Barker, voiced objections to Barrymore's "psychological" interpretation. Gwen Ffrangcon-Davies, one of England's leading Shakespearean actresses, was in the audience one night after concluding her appearance as Titania in Basil Dean's production of *A Midsummer Night's Dream* at Drury Lane, and years later she recalled her disappointment in Barrymore's portrayal:

> Frankly, I found that it was much too motivated by his work in the cinema which in those days, as you know, was very old fashioned – you know, the dreadful pauses and so on. . . . The production was very good, indeed, but Barrymore's Hamlet was not for me, the definitive Hamlet at all. He was a very personable beautiful actor . . . but I was not carried away by him. It was a very stylized performance, I thought.

Aware that hers was a minority view, she nevertheless took exception to Barrymore's depiction of the role. "It was greatly praised," she later remembered. "Oh, lord, yes, and all the critics went to town about it, and so on. But for me, I wouldn't count him as one of the great Hamlets that I've seen. I

came away with the memory that I found it a rather 'theatrical' performance."[40]

A similar impression was formed by a 23-year-old amateur actor whose days
were spent as a clerk for the Chappell music-publishing company. Maurice
Evans remembered years later that for him the chief attraction of Barrymore's Hamlet was the West End debut of his friend and fellow amateur, Margaret Webster. He emerged unimpressed with Barrymore's interpretation. "It
was an indifferent production, really," remembered Evans. "He had one wonderful scene where he crawled around on all fours, up the stairs [I.v] . . . that
was about it." Evans granted that the 43-year-old Barrymore had "a very sensitive appearance" and looked "ideal" in the part, but much preferred Ion
Swinley's Hamlet, which he had seen the previous year at the Old Vic. "Swinley was a trained classical actor," he commented. Barrymore, on the other
hand, was jarring in his nontraditional manner of speaking verse. Although
Barrymore "looked marvellous," he "lacked a certain thing about speaking
Shakespeare."[41]

A number of young actors were more than willing to forgive Barrymore's
sins against iambic pentameter, however, many citing the fresh, dynamic qualities he brought to the role. In the audience one afternoon for a matinee performance was a 20-year-old actor who had made his first significant Shakespearean appearance the previous year as Romeo to Gwen Ffrangcon-Davies's
Juliet. Years later, Sir John Gielgud noted his admiration for Barrymore's interpretation: "In personality and person he was greatly distinguished, and
very sardonic and amusing in a way, sort of dregs humor, which I thought
was very good for Hamlet. . . . He had tremendous drive and power, and a
romantic sensibility which was very rare." Gielgud remembered the stunning
impact of Barrymore's success before conservative and demanding West End
audiences, which had shown little hospitality to Shakespearean productions
during the previous decade:

> Everybody was very impressed. But of course it was very unusual a Shake-
> speare performance should suddenly take the town by storm as it did. Be-
> tween the end of Herbert Tree's reign [and Barrymore's appearance]
> there was very little Shakespeare done in the West End of London, and it
> was very extraordinary that Barrymore should come from America, with his
> scenery, but with an English cast, and make a great success.[42]

One of Barrymore's greatest admirers during the run of *Hamlet* was a 17-
year-old scholarship student at Elsie Fogerty's Central School of Speech
Training and Dramatic Art. Years later, Sir Laurence Olivier paid tribute to
Barrymore's interpretation:

> Although he was American, his English speech was perfect. He was astound-
> ing. He had everything going for him, including startling good looks. . . . It

seemed to me that he breathed life into the character, which, since Irving, had descended into arias and false inflections – all very beautiful and poetic, but castrated. Barrymore put back the balls.[43]

The excitement and controversy generated by Barrymore's production assured full houses, and the production was quickly sold out for its scheduled six weeks and a three-week extension. Encouraged by his reception, Barrymore settled in for the run. As in America, however, his performance was by no means predictable. During one matinee, attended by the young Canadian actor Raymond Massey, Barrymore, annoyed by a persistent cougher sitting in the stalls, silenced his tormentor in a novel manner. In the middle of his "rogue and peasant slave" soliloquy he fixed his gaze on the offender and, without breaking rhythmic stride, interpolated his own line: "Bark! Bark! Bark on! Thou phlegm beclotted cur!" It was, Massey testified, "a heroic moment that rocked London."[44]

Hamlet's stage business could be equally unpredictable. Barrymore was not averse to trying new business when the mood struck him, as it often did; in the graveyard scene, he would frequently engage in "'hawking and spitting,' very audible jokes, and scathing imitations of the other actors, the audience or both" in an effort to break the serious demeanor of his fellow actors.[45]

The passion and energy Barrymore brought to the role became the stuff of theatrical legend. Constance Collier recalled that the part of Laertes required several changes of personnel.

> Boys used to come in so proud and happy they had been chosen [for the role]. Little did they know what was in store for them. When the graveyard scene came, Jack would fight violently. . . . They would bear it patiently for a time, quite bewildered as to what had happened to them, thinking it was their own clumsiness, that the blows they had received were accidental, but not at all: Jack fought Laertes with the greatest realism. . . . He hated the actors who played the part. In the end they had to give up and send in their notices and retire – covered in scars, and then another bright, young-faced actor, full of enthusiasm, would take their place![46]

According to Margaret Webster, the actors playing Laertes wisely took to wearing hockey pads under their costumes. At one performance this protection was inadequate, however, when Barrymore, having thoroughly stabbed Laertes, who had already fallen into Osric's arms, felt a need to administer a coup de grace; he abruptly leaped forward and slashed his dying adversary across his unpadded behind.[47]

Barrymore's passionate, unpredictable onstage behavior extended to the other actors as well. "We never knew what 'state of health,' should we say, he

Figure 42. Hamlet and Ophelia (Fay Compton). Courtesy Hulton Getty Picture Collection.

would be in," commented Fay Compton, who recalled one particular night's nunnery scene (Fig. 42):

> On I went and said to him, "How does your honor for this many a day?" And he said, "Well, I thank thee. Well, well, *well.*" [Slap] And that was a sock on my face, and I was sent into the prompt corner! So I remained there and played the nunnery scene there. I couldn't see him until after the mad scene, so I went to see him then, and I knocked on the door and I said, "Jack, can I come in," and he said, "Oh, come in," and I said, "I don't take anything from you, Jack, but you really must not hit me on the stage." And he looked at me and he said, "I'm terribly sorry, Fay, but you looked so goddamned pure."[48]

Onstage unpredictability did not lessen Miss Compton's admiration for her leading man, however. As was the case with other company members, she was aware that a sense of humor and adventure were prerequisites to working with the mercurial star; she maintained a personal fondness for Barrymore in spite of his eccentricities and lack of discipline.

The adulation Barrymore received from audiences and members of the cast was in sharp contrast to the situation he found at home. Nights spent at Cheyne Walk were often punctuated by violent quarrels with Michael Strange. After one particularly tempestuous episode, Barrymore and his wife agreed to a final separation. He moved from Cheyne Walk to the Ritz Hotel, and she returned to New York with the children shortly thereafter.[49]

Barrymore assuaged any grief he might have felt at the breakup of his marriage by plunging into an exhausting whirlpool of social occasions with the same energy and passion he revealed onstage. He spent numerous evenings at the Garrick, Savage, and American clubs, which had presented him with honorary memberships, while the Gallery First Nighters Club, the Garrick, the English-Speaking Union, the Dramatic Circle, the Old Players, and the Lyceum gave luncheons and dinners in his honor. Relishing his triumph and his acceptance by the English theatregoing public, he rarely refused an invitation.[50]

On 23 March, the Prince of Wales occupied the Royal Box at the Haymarket. After the play, the prince received Barrymore, commenting that although he did not enjoy serious plays as a rule, he had enjoyed Barrymore's rendering very much. In subsequent weeks, Barrymore and the future Edward VIII spent many evenings together at parties and private clubs. When the prince wondered how Barrymore could play an exhausting role eight times a week and still have the energy for what seemed to be an endless round of social occasions, Barrymore replied: "My simple recipe is fervor and champagne." This comment was clearly no exaggeration, as Margaret Webster testified. "To fortify himself against the strain of playing Hamlet eight times a week," she remembered, "he would drink champagne steadily all through the performance whenever he was not actually on the stage. A dresser would wait for him in the wings, glass in hand, whenever he made an exit. By the last scene he was apt to be a little excited."[51]

Eventually the strain began to show. Arnold Bennett noted in his diary that Barrymore, following one performance of *Hamlet*, arrived at a dinner party given by Lady Colfax after one o' clock in the morning. He "seemed to be partly exhausted and partly intoxicated."[52] John Gielgud saw Barrymore speak at a dinner given by the Old Players soon afterward. "He looked absolutely terrible, with enormous pouches under his eyes," recalled Sir John. "I was amazed . . . because on the stage he looked very beautiful."[53] The performance on Thursday 9 April had to be canceled on account of throat trouble, and a special matinee was added the following Monday.[54]

The final performance of *Hamlet* was scheduled for Saturday, 18 April. Although Barrymore could easily have attracted full houses for months to come, many of the cast members had already contracted for other plays. In addition, Frederick Harrison was contractually obligated to open his next production within a specified period of time or his option would lapse. Money was no longer an issue: Barrymore's financial gamble had paid off handsomely. He had recouped his original investment and made a ten-thousand-dollar profit.[55] However, after nine weeks of performing Hamlet and cutting a wide social swirl, he was physically exhausted and again weary of the role. Constance Collier recalled that

> By this time that strange resentment of any part he played too long had overtaken him, and he hated the very sight of the stage and the lines he had to speak. . . . He gave so much of himself and with every performance he died a little, I think . . . it seemed a chip off his life. He was really obsessed on the stage and not a bit of the offstage Jack existed! Acting had the most extraordinary physical effect on him.[56]

At his final performance, Barrymore, after praising the members of his supporting company and the Haymarket staff, thanked company, staff, and audience for "the most happy, significant and enchanting experience I have ever had since I have been in the theatre." He took his final bow amid cries of "Come back" from the appreciative audience.

After a week in the country, Barrymore returned to London and made plans to depart for America, where he was scheduled to begin a new film in June.[57] Offers to play Hamlet in Paris and Berlin had been graciously declined, although he hinted that a return to England, and perhaps Continental productions as well, were in his future plans. His final days in London were spent, in part, composing letters of thanks to his English friends and associates. To James Agate he wrote:

> I am sailing to the patchouli'd environs of Hollywood on Thursday [30 April] to engage in commerce by painting my profile one odd color after another, and before I go I want merely to send you a line to thank you for your kindness to me during these, my first significant days in England. I am sorry I could not have seen more of you between labor, luncheons, exhaustion and fatuous public utterances; it has been slightly difficult for me to function as a human being, which in spite of being an actor I still insist on as part of my birthright as a fisherman. I shall be back in a few months, and before I begin painting my nose again, could not we get together and ascertain definitely if Chateau Yquem is what it used to be?
>
> Good-bye and many thanks. It has all been great fun, and I shall never forget it.[58]

On 30 April, Barrymore sailed for New York on the *Olympic*. He complained of exhaustion to dockside reporters, but at the same time he felt enormous pride in his success. His audacity, unflagging determination, and a year of relentless effort had paid off in a production that would linger in the memories of English playgoers for decades to come. Years later, A. E. Wilson summed up the impact of Barrymore's performance, calling his London Hamlet "a rich and electrifying experience not likely to be forgotten. Here was a lithe and handsome prince, graceful in form who, in spite of certain curious mannerisms, impressed one by his perfect enunciation – there was not a trace of American accent in his stage speech – as well as by the intellectual and poetic force of his acting."[59]

A decade later, at the height of his Hollywood fame, Barrymore looked back fondly on his London *Hamlet* – a production he would term "the theatrical achievement of which I am proudest." "The important thing," he wrote, "was that John Barrymore, once a wild, irresponsible, no-good comedian, had pulled himself together, had worked so hard and so conscientiously and so effectively that London praised his performance of *Hamlet!* The most critical Shakespeare audiences on earth had applauded John Barrymore's *Hamlet!* God, what satisfaction!"[60] That others were satisfied as well there can be no doubt. As Laurence Olivier eloquently put it: "When he was on stage, the sun came out."[61]

PART THREE

AFTERMATH

5

Shakespeare in Hollywood, 1925–1942

One must sorrow that a man of such genius should be a drunken clown.
– Title card from *The Beloved Rogue* (1927)

IN THE YEARS BETWEEN 1925 and his death in 1942, John Barrymore's acting was confined mainly to motion pictures. In Hollywood, he found no Ned Sheldon, Robert Edmond Jones, or Arthur Hopkins to guide him. Instead, he discovered an industry dominated mainly by a small group of men whose attitudes and motivations were strikingly similar to those held by the Theatrical Trust. In many ways Jack Warner and Louis B. Mayer were in direct line of descent from A. L. Erlanger and Charles Frohman. Their philosophies of entertainment were of a kind: Commerce, rather than art, was the guiding principle; personalities and their carefully chosen vehicles sold tickets.

During this same period, much of which encompassed the so-called Golden Age of Hollywood, the theatre was feeling the full impact of the revolution that took place during the teens and early 1920s. The late 1920s and 1930s saw a flowering of "serious drama" unprecedented in the history of the American stage. Playwrights such as Robert E. Sherwood, Maxwell Anderson, Elmer Rice, Eugene O'Neill, Clifford Odets, and Thornton Wilder contributed to a Renaissance of American drama; there were more than a dozen Shaw productions; *Hamlet* was the most frequently revived play on the Broadway stage.[1] The Hollywood moguls, however, geared their efforts mainly to mass audiences and vehicles that would "play on the road." Like their Syndicate forebears, they kept the heartland supplied with a steady diet of popularly conceived comedies, musicals, costume dramas, and melodramas, and they similarly viewed Shakespeare as a prestige, "highbrow" attraction with limited public appeal.

Little wonder, then, that Barrymore's defection to motion pictures aroused a good deal of negative comment from the intellectual and artistic communities that had rejoiced at his Richard III and his Hamlet. Many observers felt that Barrymore had a moral duty to rededicate his energies to the "high art" of the stage. Barrymore, however, felt no such obligation. Those who had worked with him during the period of his ascent to the status of America's preeminent tragedian lamented his abdication; yet at the same time they found ample motivation for his decision to devote his talents elsewhere. According to Arthur Hopkins,

> He loved to create, but once that had been accomplished, he was like an artist who could not bear to look again upon a finished painting, or a writer who was nauseated by a glimpse of some past creation. . . . He was in no sense what the theater knows as a trouper, what his forebears had been, what his uncle John and sister Ethel were. The creative part of the theater he loved. Its repetition was unbearable.

Hopkins believed the lack of further challenges to be an equally significant factor: "After *Hamlet* – what? He faced the Alexandrian dilemma. What new world was there to be conquered?"[2]

The answer, of course, lay in motion pictures. Barrymore had reached the pinnacle of success in the theatrical arena and by 1925 he clearly felt the desire to move on to a new form of expression and saw the means to do so. The rise of motion pictures had in many ways made obsolete the performance tradition of Shakespearean crusaders carrying the Bard to every corner of the land. For Edwin Booth, the New York season and provincial touring had been matters of economic necessity. Barrymore, however, had the option of practicing his craft in a medium that required considerably less time and effort and offered far greater financial rewards. But a principal allure for the actor, beyond money and a lightened workload, was the opportunity to create a wide gallery of characterizations without the wearying repetition demanded by the theatre. "Once the character was photographed," remarked Arthur Hopkins, "he was free."[3]

Even after his defection to Hollywood, however, Barrymore had no intention of abandoning the theatre or Shakespeare entirely. Three times during the next dozen years he devised plans to revive *Hamlet* onstage on the West Coast, and three times during the same period he devoted time and effort toward making a sound film of the play. All of these efforts failed. Barrymore's seventeen-year tenure in Hollywood also featured three successful attempts at Shakespeare. A soliloquy from his version of *Richard III* was featured in the 1929 Warner Brothers revue *The Show of Shows;* in 1936, he played Mercutio in the MGM film of *Romeo and Juliet;* and the following year he appeared in a series of six Shakespearean radio broadcasts for NBC.

In many ways, however, the cinematic and recorded evidence is a mixed blessing. By the time of *Romeo and Juliet* and the radio broadcasts, Barrymore's skills had eroded; the performances preserved for posterity offer only tantalizing hints of the virtuosity he had brought to his stage portrayals a decade earlier. Along with his mythic accomplishments came mythic intemperance: heavy drinking, reckless spending, a mercurial disregard for his personal well-being, hubristic excesses that led ultimately to a long period of decline.

The annals of the stage are filled, of course, with similar stories. George Frederick Cooke, Edmund Kean, and Junius Brutus Booth each experienced a comparable, though less alarming, decline due to hard living and alcohol, which eroded their skills and shortened their lives. Barrymore's last years were in many ways unprecedented, however, for he ended his career not by struggling gallantly on with the traditional Shakespearean repertory, but instead by parodying his former greatness in an ill-starred stageplay, in several films, and on the radio.

It is not my intention here to delve into the psychological reasons for Barrymore's epic self-destructiveness, a complex issue and one for which there are no easy answers. Nor do I intend to discuss in detail the majority of his films except those that bear directly upon Shakespeare; most have been adequately documented elsewhere.[4] Rather, my purpose is simply to examine his post-1925 associations with Shakespeare, successful and unsuccessful (to which little attention has heretofore been paid), and to situate these efforts within the dual contexts of his career and of American theatre–film culture. These efforts are in many ways revealing, for they reflect not only the manner in which Shakespeare came to be regarded in American culture in general during the twentieth century, but also the ways in which Shakespearean drama made the journey from the "high" art of the stage to the "popular" art of the cinema and an audience of millions.

The Golden Years: 1925–1934

On 6 May 1925, Barrymore, fresh from his triumphant *Hamlet* at the Haymarket, arrived in New York on the *Olympic*. Soon afterward he departed for Los Angeles, where he was to begin work on the first film on his new Warner Brothers agreement. His contract specified a salary of $76,250 per picture and included numerous perquisites: a suite at the Ambassador Hotel, a chauffeured limousine, star billing and promotion in keeping with his standing, reputation, and prestige, and the prerogative to approve his own scripts and costars.[5] For his first film he elected to play Captain Ahab in an adaptation of *Moby-Dick*, retitled *The Sea Beast*. As a concession to public and studio taste, the scenario, by Bess Meredyth, added a love interest, played by the 19-year-old actress Dolores Costello, whom Barrymore spied one day on the Warner lot, and with whom he soon became romantically involved.

Soon after the completion of his initial film for Warner Brothers in October 1925, Barrymore began to consider a return to the London stage. He had confided to the British critic Chance Newton that he longed to try his luck in England as Iago or Richard III; William Foss, coproducer of the London *Hamlet,* was eager for his appearance in the latter role. In late November 1925, however, Barrymore cabled his London attorneys to inform Foss and his partners that "Production and costumes Richard Third destroyed by fire must work here till March twentieth would be a gigantic labor and great expense making London in time also doctor doubts if my physical condition will permit it as I am terribly overtired from intensive work . . ."[6]

The loss of the costumes and scenery and the demands of film work may merely have presented a convenient excuse, however; Barrymore's published comments during this period almost invariably reflect no immediate desire to return to the stage.[7] Instead, he turned his attention to his next Warner Brothers epic: *Don Juan,* in which he played both the noted rake and, in a prologue, his father. While in the process of filming, Barrymore was contacted frequently by Foss with proposals for a spring season at the Haymarket, on which they held a joint option. By 26 March 1926, however, Foss seemed resigned to the fact that the Haymarket season would be impossible. He then wrote to Barrymore asking him to do a new version of the Paolo and Francesca legend in October. Six weeks later, however, on 12 May, he was curtly informed through Barrymore's London attorneys that the option on the Haymarket had lapsed.[8]

Barrymore's decision might well have been influenced by a new film technology that was rapidly making its presence known. On 6 August 1926 *Don Juan* premiered in New York. Promotional material stressed the 191 kisses Barrymore bestowed in the course of the film and his "Great Lover" image, but the chief attraction, to many observers, was the new Vitaphone sound system that accompanied the film. The short subjects preceding *Don Juan* included an address by the industry-appointed movie "czar" Will Hays and musical shorts featuring opera singers, a violinist, a novelty guitarist, and an orchestra; the film itself featured a synchronized score and sound effects. "The future of this new contrivance is boundless," remarked Mordaunt Hall, the *Times* film critic, who noted almost in passing that Barrymore leaped through the feature in a "captivating manner" (7 August 1926).

Don Juan proved a popular success, but a number of Barrymore's friends and admirers continued to stress what they considered to be his moral obligation to return to the theatre. Johnston Forbes-Robertson, with whom he exchanged autobiographies, pleaded, "By this time you will have made a fortune at the moving picture business . . . give it up and come back to the stage." Norman Bel Geddes urged him to do a new American play; David Belasco inquired as to his availability for a production; William Foss wired with an offer of a twelve-week London season commencing in February, suggesting a month of *Richard III,* a month of *Hamlet,* then a third play, mentioning the possibility of His Majesty's Theatre. All were politely refused. On 11 December 1926 Barrymore wired Foss: "Terribly sorry not free for one year possibly longer assure you would otherwise be very happy to renew old association with you." To his friend Gerald Du Maurier he wrote, "God knows when I can come to England again as I seem to have sold my kidneys for a mess of celuloid."[9]

Through 1926 and early 1927 Barrymore concentrated almost exclusively on silent films. *Don Juan* was followed by *When a Man Loves,* an adaptation of *Manon Lescaut,* in which Barrymore costarred with Dolores Costello. His Warner Brothers contract completed, he signed for three films with United Artists; the first was *The Beloved Rogue,* in which he played the fifteenth-century French poet and adventurer Francois Villon.

During this period Barrymore enjoyed unprecedented prosperity and spent lavishly on material acquisitions: He bought King Vidor's Tower Road mansion, a ninety-three-foot schooner, a library of rare books, and dozens of exotic animals and birds. In an effort to sort out his chaotic finances he engaged Henry Hotchener, a tax lawyer, as his manager. His romance with Dolores Costello flourished; his film work gave him creative freedom and freedom from the repetition that had discouraged him on the stage. Still, he could hardly have been unaware of the sharp and growing condemnation of his films by the intellectual community that only a few years earlier had embraced his rise as America's premier tragedian. Stark Young complained that

> Since the *Hamlet* we have had the sex appeal movies. . . . Of these moving pictures of Mr. Barrymore's last years, these puzzled people, looking at them and wondering afterward, can only observe that they are rotten, vulgar, empty, in bad taste, dishonest, noisome with a silly and unwholesome exhibitionism, and odious with a kind of stale and degenerate studio adolescence. Their appeal is cheap, cynical and specious. The only possible virtue in Mr. Barrymore's progress, as these films show him, is a certain advance in athletics; he is more agile, he leaps, rides and hops to a better showing, an advance encouraged no doubt by the competition with Mr. Douglas Fairbanks' appeal. . . . Artistically, the only thing we could say about Mr. Barrymore's performances is that he brings to them remnants of his tricks and mannerisms that stiffen them slightly and perhaps convey the sense of acting to a public that has seen but little of it. . . . The little measure of its superiority over most movie acting, in sophistication and technical expertness, is only another way of saying how low Mr. Barrymore has fallen.[10]

Barrymore was undoubtedly stung by the critical condemnation of his film work. A decade earlier, he had found himself in a similar position; he had recognized the lack of artistic merit in his stage and film vehicles of the time and had responded by doing *Justice*. After two years of devoting his energies exclusively to silent films, his thoughts took a similar turn. Soon afterward he began to contemplate an ambitious return to the stage and to Shakespeare, encouraged (and perhaps spurred to competition as well) by his brother Lionel's success in an eight-week Los Angeles revival of *The Copperhead*.

On 18 March 1927, Barrymore wrote to his British representative about the possibility of bringing over the *Hamlet* costumes and scenery stored in London. A number of occurrences soon afterward encouraged his plan. He began reading soliloquies at public events. On 22 April, he delivered a radio broadcast of speeches from *Hamlet* and *Richard III* under the auspices of the Shakespeare Foundation to benefit a fund to rebuild the burned-down theatre at Stratford-upon-Avon; on 27 June, he recited a speech from *Hamlet* at a benefit for ex–baseball star Mike Donlin at Philharmonic Auditorium in Los Angeles.[11] In July, Robert Edmond Jones visited Barrymore and further encouraged his ambitions. A few days later Jones wrote,

> I was awfully excited to hear that you will come back some day. You can do anything you want in any way you want to do it. There is nobody else in that position in the theatre today. There is Arthur, and Margaret, and me, and all the big roles that have ever been written. It is a great happiness to me to have something like this to look forward to.[12]

After completing *Tempest*, a romantic melodrama set against the background of the Russian Revolution, Barrymore turned his full attention to his proposed Shakespearean revival. By early February 1928, a plan to produce *Hamlet* had been set in motion. Barrymore's first step was to attempt to reassemble his London production team. He wrote to George Schaff in New York to obtain technical information, at the same time inquiring about William Adams's availability. Soon afterward, the *Hamlet* costumes and scenery arrived in Los Angeles. For the next few months, Barrymore's efforts remained focused on his revival. He took his manager to the Hollywood Bowl to test the acoustics; in early April he journeyed to New York to confer with Schaff on production details. A few days later the revival was announced to the press.[13]

By late June, arrangements had been made to give *Hamlet* first at the Greek Theatre at Berkeley under the sponsorship of the University of California, and then at the Hollywood Bowl for the week of 10 September. On 7 July Schaff forwarded the salary and expense list for the 1922 production; Barrymore sent several telegrams to William Adams in New York attempting to enlist his services. Soon afterward he turned his attention to casting the play. "The movies are invading Shakespeare," proclaimed one newspaper columnist on 23 July 1928, noting that the veteran film actors Montagu Love and

Alec B. Francis had been chosen as the King and Polonius. Around the same time, Barrymore wrote to Ned Sheldon in New York, telling him, "I am concentrating entirely on *The Dane in the Bowl,* which I will produce early in September. . . . These sylvan interludes may be the precursor of better things."[14]

In August, however, after six months of planning, the production was canceled abruptly and without explanation. Here, as elsewhere, there are no easy answers for the abandonment of a project in which Barrymore had invested considerable time and effort. The unavailability of William Adams, whose organizational skills would have been invaluable, may have played a part. A more crucial issue, however, was probably the narrow window in time slotted for the production. Barrymore had agreed to make an additional film for United Artists for $150,000 and was scheduled to begin work on *Eternal Love* the week of 17 September, two days after the last scheduled *Hamlet* performance. The studio's investment in the film (and Barrymore's own enormous salary) precluded the possibility of delaying the stage revival if additional preparation time was needed. There were also the demands of Barrymore's personal life. While preparing for *Hamlet,* he was hammering out the details of his divorce from Michael Strange, which became final on 18 August; at the same time he was making plans to marry Dolores Costello. After six weeks on location in Canada making what proved to be his final silent film, he returned to Hollywood, where on 24 November 1928 he entered into his third marriage.

Another significant variable may also have come into play: the advent of talking motion pictures. By the time *Eternal Love* was completed, technology had progressed beyond synchronized sound tracks and most Hollywood studios had accepted sound as the wave of the future. Actors with trained voices found their services highly in demand. Barrymore immediately recognized the opportunities the new medium presented. "Will you try to think of some more movies for me, ones where the talking device might possibly be used," he wrote to Ned Sheldon. "It seems to be coming in, and apparently now is the time for me to make a killing in it."[15] The desire to revive *Hamlet* might well have seemed secondary to the financial opportunity presented by Barrymore's new contract at Warner Brothers, a five-picture deal stipulating a salary of $150,000 per film and a share of the profits.

Warner Brothers soon provided Barrymore with his first opportunity to present Shakespeare to the filmgoing public. The coming of sound had sparked a Hollywood trend: To showcase their stable of actors and prove to the public that they could speak, sing, and maintain their charisma in the new medium, most studios set plans in motion for lavish cinema variety shows. The first to debut was MGM's *Hollywood Revue,* now best remembered for introducing "Singin' in the Rain." At the time of its premiere, however, on 13 April 1929, the highlight, to many observers, was Norma Shearer and John

Gilbert's appearance in the balcony scene from *Romeo and Juliet*. This scene was first played "straight," and then, after Lionel Barrymore, who was then an MGM director, yelled "cut" and read a telegram from the studio protesting that modern audiences wouldn't understand the language, was given a "jazzed up" treatment with modern, colloquial paraphrasing.

After completing *General Crack*, a costume melodrama set in eighteenth-century Austria (released in December 1929), Barrymore was quickly enlisted for his studio's response to the trend-setting *Hollywood Revue*. Warner Brothers, trying to outdo the competition, budgeted *The Show of Shows* at $800,000 and billed their production as a "Super-revue" featuring "77 stars," "1,000 Hollywood beauties," and "everything from Shakespeare to super-jazz."[16] Of its 124 minutes, 103 were filmed in color; its stars included Frank Fay, Beatrice Lillie, Richard Barthelmess, Dolores and Helene Costello, Myrna Loy, Douglas Fairbanks Jr., and Rin Tin Tin. Barrymore's contribution, a response to the Shearer–Gilbert balcony scene, was a brief scene adapted from his stage version of *Richard III*, for which he was paid a special fee of $25,000. In August 1929, he went before the cameras for his initial film sequence as a Shakespearean, appearing first in street clothes to introduce the scene. Viewed today, the sequence proves strikingly effective. After a slow fade, the camera fades in again on a mound of bodies. E. J. Ratcliffe and Anthony Bushell enter first as York and Edward and deliver a few lines from *3 Henry VI*, I.i; then Barrymore, as Gloucester, enters, carrying the severed head of the Duke of Somerset (Fig. 43). After a brief exchange the others exit, and Barrymore delivers an abridged version of Gloucester's soliloquy from *3 Henry VI*, III.ii (*"Would* [they] were *wasted, marrow, bones* and *all"*). His reading is often broad and stagy, his gestures and expressions exaggerated by cinematic standards, yet his characterization is powerful, displaying bravura force.

The Show of Shows was presented to New York in a gala premiere on 20 November 1929. Barrymore's appearance as Gloucester was fifteenth on the bill, preceded by a ballad, "Your Love Is All I Crave," sung by Frank Fay and Harry Akst, and followed by a musical episode featuring "10 Specialty Dancing Teams," "350 Chorus Beauties," and "150 Colored Entertainers." The program notes left little doubt as to which segment was expected to prove the highlight, however, promoting Barrymore as "the greatest living actor" and "America's supreme dramatic artist on both stage and screen." The premiere generated excitement in the same degree as Barrymore's debut as Hamlet seven years earlier. Crowds surged around the theatre for the entire evening, and the *Times* reported that "the instant Mr. Barrymore, clad in every-day clothes, appeared upon the screen and announced that he was going to do this Shakespearean passage, the audience, before he uttered a word, whispered one to another, 'It's John Barrymore.'" His brother, Lionel, added the

Figure 43. Barrymore as Richard III in the 1929 Warner Brothers film *The Show of Shows.* Courtesy James Kotsilibas-Davis collection.

reviewer, "has been heard in pictures on several occasions, but this was the first time John's voice has come from the shadows" (21 November 1929).

Critical comments the next day were as laudatory as any visited upon Barrymore's stage performance of Gloucester nine years earlier. To Richard Watts Jr. of the *Herald Tribune,* the *Richard III* sequence proved the most "impressive and significant feature" of a film otherwise marked by "a wild extravaganza of cinema opulence, Tin Pan music and chorus dancing." Barrymore, he commented, "plays the scene . . . so vividly and beautifully as to suggest miraculous things that might be achieved in the filming of an entire Shakespearean drama" (21 November 1929). Equally impressed was Jack Warner, who was present at the premiere and the next day wired Barrymore: "Dear

John *Show of Shows* opened last night and truthfully never saw an audience go for anything like they went for your soliloquy . . . Papers are agog seems they forgot everyone else and only thought of a guy named Barrymore . . . This is just as expected and should be."[17]

By the spring of 1930, *General Crack* had been released to modest success, and Barrymore had completed *The Man from Blankley's,* in which he utilized his long-neglected skills as a farceur by playing Lord Strathpeffer, a mild-mannered beetle collector who wanders into the wrong house and is mistaken for a dinner guest hired for the evening. A sound version of *Moby-Dick* was then in production. As the film neared completion, Barrymore's thoughts turned once again to *Hamlet,* this time on a more ambitious scale. He began to envision a stage revival in the Hollywood Bowl, to be followed by a sound film of the play produced as the fourth film under his Warner Brothers contract.

Jack Warner was open to the idea and had, in fact, signed Barrymore to his initial contract after seeing his Broadway *Hamlet* seven years earlier. Barrymore and his manager complicated the issue, however, by telling the studio chief that another company was interested in filming *Hamlet* as well. On 25 March 1930, Warner wrote to Barrymore, expressing surprise that Hotchener would approach him and tell him about the rival offer when his Warner Brothers contract had nearly a year to go. Barrymore replied in a letter dated the next day, in which he stated that he regretted that Warner had made the question of producing *Hamlet* "a personal matter when it was only a business one" and remarked,

It is true, as Hotchener said, that I have had an offer of more money; so it was natural that the matter be brought to your attention at this time. I simply requested Hotchener to go to you and say that as *Hamlet* would require an enormously greater amount of time, labor, and detailed attention on my part than an average play (which you yourself admitted to Hotchener), I thought I was entitled to get more money for it.

Shakespearean plays are my specialty: I have given long years to producing and acting them, with very great financial success both here and abroad. From this experience I know that to put them on properly for talking pictures would require a tremendous amount of time and work – very much greater than for any other type of production. I do not think this could be reasonably expected of me under my present contract, and when Hotchener told me of the other offer, entailing more money for this production, I naturally arranged that he should see you or Darryl [Zanuck] as your representative, as he is mine, to discuss the arrangements. . . . I particularly want you to understand that I would very much prefer to do *Hamlet* with you, if you will meet my terms, which must be reasonable or such offers would not have come from other sources; and I think that you, Darryl, and myself could make something great out of it together.

There was never any question of my *breaking* my present contract with you, but only of *modifying* it, and it seems to me that, considering the especial knowledge and experience I have with this play, and the attitude of the public towards my association with it all over the world (and particularly the success in England, which was so widely advertised in this country because it was the only time an American actor had ever accomplished it), and considering the extra labor and concentration it would require from me, an additional $50,000 and 5% more of the gross are not unreasonable in view of the tremendous possibilities of this picture and the fact that we both realize that it is undoubtedly my "ace in the hole."[18]

Plans for the stage and film *Hamlet* continued, despite the difference in opinion. On 8 April 1930, a daughter, Dolores Ethel Mae, was born to Dolores Costello, and soon afterward Barrymore, confident of success, began dreaming out the production. He and Henry Hotchener paid a $500 deposit to the Hollywood Bowl Association to reserve dates for the stage revival, and came up with the idea of engaging "a cast of experienced Shakespearean actors who could do the play first for the stage, and then for the 'movies' without the necessity for the many weeks of selecting a cast and then rehearsing it that are usually necessary."[19]

On 6 June 1930, Hotchener departed for England on Barrymore's behest. His mission was to approach the Stratford-upon-Avon company regarding the possibility of supporting Barrymore in his stage and film productions. For several months he negotiated with the company management, but even with the promise of significant financial rewards to the actors and their theatre, his efforts proved a failure. On 21 August Barrymore's London representative wrote to Hotchener, stating that the company's director had decided that "the company cannot play with any star artist" as it was "under the control of the Governors of the Shakespeare Memorial Theatre" and produced Shakespeare plays "on an agreed book, which is intended to give the best representation of Shakespeare's works without any question of bringing one or other character into prominence." He stated, however, that "he would give any assistance he could to Mr. Barrymore if he wished to engage an English Company to produce a 'Talkie' film of one of Shakespeare's plays."[20]

There is no evidence, however, that the matter was pursued any further. Like Barrymore's attempt at *Hamlet* two years earlier, the plan for a revival and film of the play was ultimately abandoned. Again, there are no easy explanations for its failure. Financial reasons and Hollywood's disdain for Shakespeare did not necessarily preclude the project. Warner Brothers was not averse to an occasional "prestige" film, and in fact had achieved considerable success with George Arliss's *Disraeli* the previous year. Barrymore's acclaimed excerpt from *Richard III* was fresh in the public and studio mind and would have been a strong selling point in his favor. Had he and his manager not quibbled over money, had he been willing to forgo part of his salary in exchange for a percentage of the profits, the film might well have been made. To produce *Hamlet* in London, he had taken a pay cut and gambled his own money, yet there is no indication that he was willing to take a similar step to capture his performance on film. In all probability the main issue did not involve other commitments or the demands of his personal life, but rather a growing ambivalence toward the project after months of planning and effort had again come to naught; or he may, in fact, have feared comparison to his New York and London achievements in the role. By early autumn, the proposed stage–film *Hamlet* had been set aside. Instead, Barrymore appeared in *Svengali*, an adaptation of Herbert Tree's stage success *Trilby*, followed by *The Mad Genius*, a similar, though far inferior vehicle. After its release, Warner Brothers, discouraged by the modest financial return on its five-film investment, declined to renew Barrymore's contract at its former terms.

Barrymore then proceeded to sign a nonexclusive agreement with MGM, and for three years there were no thoughts – or at least no practical plans – for *Hamlet*. He worked steadily during this period, and many of the films in which he appeared were among the finest offered by Hollywood at the time. His first MGM film was *Arsène Lupin*, released in 1931, in which he costarred with his brother Lionel, followed the next year by *Grand Hotel* (featuring an all-star cast including Lionel, Greta Garbo, and Joan Crawford), *A Bill of Divorcement* (with Katharine Hepburn), *State's Attorney*, and *Rasputin and the Empress*, in which all three Barrymores costarred for the first time. The year 1933 saw the release of *Topaze, Long Lost Father* (in which Barrymore appeared opposite Helen Chandler, who had played one of the little princes in *Richard III*), *Reunion in Vienna, Dinner at Eight, Night Flight* (his last film with Lionel at MGM), and *Counsellor at Law*. In 1934, *Twentieth Century* was released, in which Barrymore played a madcap Broadway producer-director opposite Carole Lombard, a characterization that many consider to be his finest contribution to film.[21]

Gene Fowler later reported that Barrymore's total income for the nine years he devoted almost exclusively to motion pictures was $2,634,500. During this period he enjoyed economic and domestic comfort; on 4 June 1932, a son, John Barrymore Jr., was born, in many ways completing what, on the surface at least, appeared to be an idyllic period in the actor's life.[22] The entreaties to return to the stage continued, yet all were refused. Theresa Helburn asked Barrymore to do a season with the Theatre Guild; Burns Mantle published an open letter urging his return to Broadway. Barrymore's response was simply, "I can't give up $175,000 a year and an easy life to take a sentimental journey for the stage. Hell, I'd be a fool to do that."[23] Even the pleas of Margaret Carrington were ignored. "I went to Hollywood to ask him to come back to the theatre," she remembered; but when she climbed the hill to his house and saw how he lived in the sunshine, saw his collection of tropical birds and fish, his library of rare volumes, his wife and "two beautiful children," her heart sank. "I knew I had come on a lost cause," she recalled. She pleaded with him to return to New York and build a Barrymore Theatre where at least one of the Barrymores could act, believing that they could have perpetuated the "theatre of elegance and distinction established by their forebears." Barrymore, however, would have none of it.[24]

During this same period, however, there were numerous foreshadowings of the collapse to come. As early as 1930, Barrymore had experienced a severe gastric hemorrhage, yet he continued to drink heavily. On 30 October 1933, he was called to Universal to retake a scene for *Counsellor at Law* and suddenly found himself unable to remember the short scene he was required to play. After numerous takes the shooting was called to a halt. He was able to complete his scene the next day, but his memory loss disturbed him and began recurring time and again.[25]

Perhaps as a response to this incident and to the impending cancellation of his MGM contract (word of which quickly spread among the film community), Barrymore, in the autumn of 1933, again began to contemplate a return to more artistic endeavors. Announcements were made that he was considering an appearance as Hamlet opposite Lillian Gish's Ophelia the following summer at Central City, Colorado, under the direction of Robert Edmond Jones, and that he would revive the play at the Hollywood Bowl with Helen Chandler. With Kenneth Macgowan, by then a film producer at RKO, he entered into negotiations with Bernard Shaw for a film version of *The Devil's Disciple*.[26] At the same time, Macgowan, one of the few producers in Hollywood with leanings toward "intellectual" drama, made arrangements to film a screen test for a technicolor film of *Hamlet*.

On 8 December 1933, Barrymore's MGM contract was abrogated "by mutual consent." That same day, RKO forwarded a memorandum of agreement to film two scenes from *Hamlet*, which, if successful, would lead to a full-length film to be financed by John Hay Whitney, the multimillionaire chairman of Pioneer Pictures/Selznick International. Filming commenced three days later, with Robert Edmond Jones directing and Margaret Carrington (by then married to Jones after the death of her first husband) again coaching Barrymore for the role. The screen test, a copy of which is preserved in the film library of the Museum of Modern Art, features abridged versions of Hamlet's first encounter with the Ghost (I.iv) and the scene of the King at prayer (III.iii); both retain the blocking of the New York stage production. The result, viewed today, is impressive. Barrymore's readings are powerful and subtle, and his voice retains a crisp, youthful timbre. When seen in long and medium shots he is strikingly effective; only in closeup are his 51 years apparent.[27]

That evening, however, Barrymore attempted to recite the "O, all you host of heaven" soliloquy for Jones, Margaret Carrington, and Henry Hotchener, and again his memory failed.[28] He was haunted by his inability to remember lines he had spoken hundreds of times and began to voice reservations about reprising the role, yet plans for the film continued. On 26 December, Macgowan wrote to Barrymore, reporting that

> I have just had a letter from E. H. Griffith, who saw the HAMLET tests with Whitney in New York. I have not heard from Whitney or anyone else in New York. [Griffith] says:
> "I think Whitney has pretty definitely made up his mind that HAMLET is important but that it is too necessarily an experiment for his first picture. He said he thought it would be alright for the second. Helen Hayes and I ran into him the other night at 'Twenty One' and we discussed it at great length. I even got Helen to agree to play Ophelia in the hope of selling him (she actually means it, too) but I think he is afraid of it. As for me, I found Barrymore's performance electrifying. Nobody in the world can read verse the way he can, for my money. Robert Loraine probably reads better in a classic manner but lacks the emotion and the humanizing, modernistic understandability. The guy is simply immense! He gives you chills and fever. I told Whitney I would get the money for the production if he went in on the color end of it and that we would let RKO release it if they wanted to. He seemed interested in that but still desired to think about it and suggested that I might appear before his associates, in his company, and state what we thought about HAMLET, which I would be glad to do.

Macgowan added in closing that "Frank O' Heron would like us to do HAMLET with you in black and white, in case Whitney and the company decided against color."[29]

Like Barrymore's earlier attempt at filming *Hamlet*, however, the project was ultimately shelved. Barrymore's age and appearance in closeups may have been a contributing factor. Financial considerations doubtless played an important role as well; Whitney and his partners clearly regarded the proposed film as an artistically valid yet economically risky proposition. Even if Whitney and his associates had been willing to gamble, however, the events that soon took place virtually negated the possibility that Barrymore's Hamlet would be preserved on film.

Transition: 1934–6

In retrospect, it is easy to see a clear line of demarcation between Barrymore's early work in Hollywood and his later period, when years of drinking and hard living had the cumulative effect of depriving him of his ability to act with subtlety and control. The loss of control extended to his private life as well; his name became associated more with tabloid headlines than artistic triumphs. Brooks Atkinson, longtime drama critic of the *New York Times,* appropriately compared Barrymore to Icarus of Greek legend, who soared upon wings crafted by his father Daedelus but plunged to earth when he ignored his father's instructions and flew too close to the sun.[30] A glance back upon Barrymore's "rapid, unexpected ascent" reveals many Daedelus figures: Edward Sheldon, Arthur Hopkins, Robert Edmond Jones, Margaret Carrington. By the same token, it is easy to see the golden allure of Hollywood and the disregard of the entreaties to return to the stage as the keys to his downfall. However, the analogy, although appropriate, carries only so far, for the seeds of Barrymore's descent were sown not by Hollywood but rather from within. By the mid-1930s, the wax on his wings had begun to melt, and his rapid plunge to earth had commenced.

On 8 April 1934, the future still looked promising. Barrymore read the Ghost scene (playing both roles) and two scenes from the soon to be released *Twentieth Century* on a *Hall of Fame* radio program. Plans were underway for a stage revival of *Hamlet,* and a film version of the play was still a possibility. A month later, on 8 May, he reported to RKO to begin work on *Hat, Coat and Glove,* a murder mystery produced by Kenneth Macgowan. The director, Worthington Miner, later remembered that Barrymore's scene that day required him simply to walk into a department store in Budapest and purchase the three articles named in the film's title. Barrymore found himself unable to remember his lines, however, or even the name of his character despite numerous takes, and it was decided to postpone shooting until the next day. The following morning, the results were no better. Miner tried the scene several times but "each time [Barrymore's] desperation became more intense and more painful," he remembered. Barrymore was sent home, and the company shot around him for several days. When he returned, however, he discovered that his mysterious memory loss had persisted. Barrymore exploded in frustration at Miner and Kenneth Macgowan, and soon afterward they decided reluctantly to replace him with Ricardo Cortez.[31]

According to Dolores Costello, Barrymore had been "drinking steadily for two years," was quickly becoming a "hopeless alcoholic," and was at the same time exhausted from making nine films in rapid succession during the same period.[32] The result, on 14 May, was a mental and physical breakdown that necessitated weeks of hospitalization. He was haunted at the time by his father's collapse three decades earlier and feared syphilis as the cause. Tests proved negative, however, and doctors attributed his memory loss and physical problems to the cumulative effects of overwork and his prodigious drinking.[33] Plans for a revival of *Hamlet* were abandoned, and Barrymore attempted a cruise on his yacht with his wife and children in an effort to recover his health. The cruise proved disastrous, however, and in its aftermath Barrymore fled from his wife and Beverly Hills on 28 August 1934.

A few weeks later, Barrymore arrived in London, where on 20 September 1934 he signed a contract for $60,000 for six weeks' work with Alexander Korda's London Film Productions. Within days it was announced that the film would be *Hamlet*. Privately, however, Barrymore was beginning to feel reluctant to challenge his own legend. He told Henry Hotchener,

> I wonder if I am up to doing *Hamlet?* Thousands here remember me in it at the Haymarket. They would be sure to see the film. And if I'm not as good as I was at the Haymarket, it will be just too bad. The flattening out that Bernard Shaw gave me ten years ago would be nothing to what he'd do this time. He'd have me beheaded in the Tower of London.

Barrymore examined his edema-swollen ankles and 52-year-old features in the mirror. He tested his memory, finding it perfect with the soliloquies, yet he found himself unable to remember the Ghost scene. "It looks as if *Hamlet* is out," he told his manager.[34]

In October, Barrymore journeyed to Italy; the next month he went on to India, where he remained until January 1935. He then decided abruptly to cancel his contract with Korda and return to America. On 31 January he arrived in New York, where a month later he became gravely ill in a hotel room and was again hospitalized.

During this period of confinement Barrymore was visited by a stagestruck 19-year-old Hunter College sophomore, Elaine Jacobs, who gained entry to his room by inventing a story that she had been asked to interview a celebrity for a journalism class assignment. Barrymore, ill and vulnerable, was smitten by his new acquaintance and soon began paying court to Jacobs and her mother. Within a few months he had moved into the Jacobs apartment on Riverside Drive, a fact that, when discovered by the press, resulted in sensational tabloid headlines. The headlines continued over the next few months; Barrymore spent lavishly on his new paramour (dubbed "Lily Maid of Ask-a-Lot" by one wag); they had much-publicized quarrels, became engaged, broke the engagement. The tabloid onslaught reached its peak after 19 September, when Barrymore, convinced the relationship was over, departed by train for California. An editor, sensing a good story, hired an airplane for Elaine Jacobs (who had by then taken to calling herself "Elaine Barrie") to pursue Barrymore across the country. In Kansas City she made a public appeal on the radio for Barrymore to come back. The result was a new flurry of headlines as "Ariel" pursued her "Caliban" (as they were dubbed by the press) across the country.

The Caliban and Ariel affair marked a radical change in the way that Barrymore was perceived by the public. He was, of course, by no means the first actor to become romantically involved with a woman many years his junior, nor was he the first eminent Shakespearean to become embroiled in romantic scandal.[35] It may be argued, however, that Barrymore never completely recovered from the media frenzy that accompanied his every move during this period. Prior to 1935 he was regarded as charmingly eccentric, a romantic hell-raiser, a "manly" drinker – an image parodied astutely by George S. Kaufman and Edna Ferber in their 1927 play *The Royal Family;* yet at the same time he was heralded as "America's supreme dramatic artist," the foremost actor of his generation, a man whose colorful escapades only enhanced his legend. He emerged from the Caliban and Ariel headlines, however, with a new image: the aging satyr, the has-been alcoholic, the much-married ham. The flamboyance and charming eccentricities of the teens and twenties began to seem far less endearing.

Had Barrymore retained the skills of earlier years and made efforts to maintain a consistent and dignified public posture, the impact of his highly publicized activities might well have been minimized; but he did not, and he could not. Although he handled his adversity with aplomb and a sense of humor, the circumstances in which he found himself during the mid-to-late 1930s contributed to a profound loss of self-respect. His numerous stays in hospitals and sanitariums, moreover, were temporary respites at best from his dependence on alcohol. In a way, Barrymore's efforts during this phase of his life may be viewed as heroic, for he continued to practice his craft as best he could, in part to honor his monumental debts. This same period, however, saw a sharp decline in the quality of his vehicles and his performances therein.

Decline: 1936–42

To realize the extent to which Barrymore's skills had diminished, one need only compare his performance in the December 1933 *Hamlet* screen test to his next film characterization: Mercutio in MGM's *Romeo and Juliet*. To Barrymore, the opportunity to end his two-year exile from the motion picture cameras in a Shakespearean role must surely have seemed fortuitous, yet the performance captured by the cameras beginning in early 1936 reveals an actor whose consummate abilities had been ravaged.

That the opportunity arose at all was the result of a unique set of circumstances. *Romeo and Juliet* was to be only the third full-length Hollywood attempt at Shakespeare during the sound era, and was, like *The Show of Shows*, a direct response to another studio's effort.[36] Norma Shearer had longed to attempt a full-length version of the play since her 1929 balcony scene with John Gilbert. After hearing of Warner Brothers' plan to film *A Midsummer Night's Dream*, she persuaded her husband, Irving Thalberg, MGM's head of

production, to approach Louis B. Mayer. The studio chief initially opposed
the idea. Eddie Mannix, Thalberg's assistant at the time, later remembered
that Mayer

> was ready to have an apoplectic fit when Irving sprang *that* one on him. . . .
> Irving tried to tell him that Jack Warner was producing *A Midsummer Night's
> Dream* over at Warner's, but [Mayer] only snapped: "If Jack wants to make
> a fool of himself messing with Max Reinhardt and that Shakespeare high-
> falutin' stuff, that's *his* funeral! Why should we run Jack a race to bankrupt-
> cy court? Hell, the film would cost a couple of million!" Irving mollified
> him slightly by stating his estimated cost at $900,000. Furthermore it would
> be good for prestige.[37]

Eventually, the go-ahead was given. George Cukor, the film's director, later remembered that a guiding principle during preproduction was that the
play "had to be rendered clear for the general public."[38] The script, adapted
by Talbot Jennings, transformed Shakespeare's verse into prose and cut approximately one-quarter of the text to ensure a reasonable running time;
many (though not all) of the bawdy passages were deleted by order of the
Hays Office. Fidelity to Shakespeare's words was maintained scrupulously,
however – a result, no doubt, of a much-repeated quip arising from the 1929
Douglas Fairbanks–Mary Pickford *Taming of the Shrew,* which was credited to
William Shakespeare, with "additional dialogue by Sam Taylor."[39] The Cornell University scholar William Strunk was engaged as literary advisor, Agnes
de Mille was hired as choreographer, and Oliver Messel was brought over
from England to design and supervise the sets and costumes. The emphasis
was on elaborate production values and pageantry to a degree that Herbert
Tree surely would have approved. George Cukor later remembered that "The
feeling at MGM was: let's show them we can put on the dog with the best of
'em."[40]

Norma Shearer, whose Shakespearean experience was confined to her
brief scene in *Hollywood Revue,* studied with Constance Collier, and later, at
Barrymore's urging, with Margaret Carrington. Several actors were considered for Romeo. Fredric March was offered the part but declined; the role
was eventually accepted by the 43-year-old Leslie Howard. Barrymore was an
obvious choice for Mercutio, at least in theory; his Shakespearean accomplishments and his prestige value still lingered on in the film community.
Even so, Louis B. Mayer had reservations. Barrymore's unreliability, memory
loss, and alcohol-related illnesses were cause for concern. Nevertheless, Thalberg and Cukor were confident of his abilities and were willing to gamble on
him, particularly after he agreed to make a filmed test of Mercutio (with Reginald Denny, who had appeared with Barrymore in *Richard III* and the *Hamlet* screen test, reading Romeo, Juliet, and the remainder of the roles) and

proved he could remember his lines. Even so, Thalberg and Cukor were aware of the difficulties he might present and took steps to prevent potential disruptions. Elaine Barrie was barred from the set, and Barrymore was installed in a sanitarium for alcoholics across the street from the studio, euphemistically known as "Kelley's Rest Home."

Once filming began, however, it was apparent to those involved with the production that Barrymore was a much-changed man. Basil Rathbone, the film's Tybalt, later remembered that

> At fifty-four . . . John was too old for the role; he was very unsure of himself, up to his ears in trouble with young Elaine Barrie, and he was drinking and unreliable on the set. . . . It was so sad to see him in such a state – the greatest Shakespearean stage actor of his time, who had forgotten more about acting than most people around him would ever know.[41]

Margaret Carrington was brought out to Hollywood to help nurse him through the role. On the set one day, she tried to distract his attention by suggesting that he read the Queen Mab speech with an Irish accent. Barrymore "pounced upon the suggestion and read the speech without the slightest hesitation. The words poured from his lips with brilliance. And what tempo! It was a tour de force. His theatre instincts were afire again." When Cukor heard the speech, he was "amazed at the change" in Barrymore, but he decided reluctantly against using the accent in the film. Carrington's kindness, skill, and patience helped Barrymore enormously, although on one occasion she was heard to remark sarcastically, "If drink would only kill the Barrymores then we could all have a peaceful life."[42]

Eventually, Thalberg and Cukor's worst fears came true when Barrymore's clandestine drinking and general instability began to cause costly delays. On the morning that filming was scheduled for the scene after the Capulets' ball, all went well until Barrymore came to Mercutio's line, "He heareth not, he moveth not, he stirreth not." At that point, he felt compelled to substitute his own final phrase: "he pisseth not." Basil Rathbone, though not in the scene, had come to the set that day to observe the filming. He later remembered that Cukor walked over to Barrymore and pleaded with him to say the line correctly. Barrymore agreed and additional takes were attempted, yet each time he repeated his scatological reading. Finally, Thalberg was called to the set and pleaded with Barrymore to speak the line as written. "Very well," Barrymore replied. "Just once I will say it that thou mayest see how it stinketh." He delivered the line correctly – just once – and the completed take was used in the final version of the film.[43]

Soon afterward, Mayer and Thalberg, weary of Barrymore's shenanigans and worried that he would be unable to complete the project, decided to have him replaced, offering the role to William Powell. The actor refused, however, telling them that Barrymore had been kind to him when Powell had had a supporting role in the silent *Sherlock Holmes* fifteen years earlier. Cukor and Norma Shearer personally interceded with Mayer after Barrymore had been absent for several days, reminding him that Barrymore had made money for the studio in the past, and that firing him would be devastating to his brother, Lionel, a loyal company man whose wife was experiencing severe health problems at the time.[44] Perhaps because he feared further humiliation, Barrymore summoned enough discipline to complete his scenes. "He was a *miracle* at times like that," recalled Reginald Denny. "He somehow pulled himself together and was his old, great self, for as long as the camera held him."[45]

Romeo and Juliet completed shooting on 7 May 1936 and was released little more than three months later. Almost predictably, it was regarded in many quarters not as entertainment but rather as a cultural event, "Hollywood's admission ticket to the rare pasturelands of art itself."[46] The production values and Norma Shearer and Leslie Howard's performances were generally admired. Barrymore's contribution, however, evoked sharply divided opinions (Fig. 44). To a number of reviewers he could still do no wrong. The critic for the *Washington Times* (1 September 1936) found the performance to be "the greatest acting John Barrymore has given to the screen art," adding, "This is the kind of a Mercutio that Shakespeare wrote and it is the kind that John Barrymore acts . . . with all the radiant understanding that made him the greatest of Hamlets." Other reviewers, however, enough to constitute a small majority, found Barrymore's impersonation to be surprisingly inadequate. Elliot Norton, an admirer of Barrymore's Hamlet a dozen years earlier, termed his performance "a disappointment," commenting that "there is certainly no reason why he should not play the role magnificently. But he overplays it so badly as to become almost embarrassing" (*Boston Post,* 6 September 1936). "The actor whose performances of *Hamlet* and *Richard III* are treasured memories of theatregoers throws his reputation as an interpreter of Shakespeare into the discard with his slapstick playing," carped the *Philadelphia Inquirer–Public Ledger* (31 August 1936).[47]

These and similar comments were the first overwhelmingly negative response Barrymore had received as a Shakespearean. In the past he had made films perfunctorily, without caring about the result; he had engaged in drunken escapades that delayed shooting; he had been subject to sharp critical disapproval of his performances and vehicles. At the same time, however, he had still been capable of brilliant, subtle characterizations, even when the role and the script had been less than ideal. *Romeo and Juliet,* on the other hand, gave the first indication to the public and the critical fraternity that his skills had taken a sharp downslide.

Figure 44. An MGM publicity photo of Barrymore as Mercutio in *Romeo and Juliet* (1936). Courtesy James Kotsilibas-Davis collection.

Barrymore's declining abilities were emphasized further a mere two months after the film's release, when the first significant challenge arose to his Shakespearean legacy in New York. On 8 October 1936, John Gielgud opened at the Empire Theatre in *Hamlet* and was received in many quarters with an enthusiasm rivaling that which had greeted Barrymore's appearance in the role fourteen years earlier. Barrymore graciously sent Gielgud a congratulatory telegram, yet he was doubtless aware of the symbolic impact when Gielgud eclipsed his "record" and went on to play a total of 132 performances. "I was a bridge between two periods," he told a young friend and admirer, "and my period has passed."[48]

At the same time, word spread quickly about the problems Barrymore had presented on the set of *Romeo and Juliet*. In the fourteen months following its completion, he made only one film: *Maytime*, in which played a supporting role and was third on the bill to Nelson Eddy and Jeanette MacDonald. This period was, by all accounts, personally tumultuous. In October 1936 his divorce from Dolores Costello was finalized; on 8 November, he and Elaine Barrie were married in Yuma, Arizona; New Years Day, 1937, found him again in Kelley's Rest Home after a public quarrel with his fourth wife; on 12 January 1937 he collapsed on the *Maytime* set; three days later he was served with divorce papers; on 16 February he filed for bankruptcy protection from his creditors.[49]

By that time, producers were understandably reluctant to offer him roles, given his health, marital, and drinking problems and his reputation for unprofessional behavior. Barrymore was aware of the damage to his career, of the chaos that surrounded his personal life and finances; yet he refused to be crushed. In early March he began to contemplate a phoenixlike rise. Perhaps from a need for self-assurance, or in an effort to salvage his faded prestige, or simply because no other professional alternative was available, he gathered himself together and resolved to make yet another attempt at *Hamlet* in the Hollywood Bowl.

Through a mutual friend, he heard about the 28-year-old actor and director Robert Breen, who had played an acclaimed Hamlet several years earlier and was then in charge of the Chicago unit of the Federal Theatre Project. Soon afterward, he invited Breen to the West Coast to direct his production.[50] Barrymore assured the director that the Caliban and Ariel saga was "over – deader than a doornail." He was undiscouraged by his age (he was 55 at the time); the vast dimensions of the Bowl, he felt, would be enough to create the necessary illusion. For several months, Breen and Barrymore rehearsed the part and hammered out production concepts. Barrymore, Breen remembered, consumed gallons of coffee and always seemed to be in good humor; at the time he was under the charge of a male nurse who rarely left his side and forbade him to drink. Breen admired Barrymore's ability and was delighted at his readings, despite an occasional tendency to be florid, which Breen attempted to eliminate as they were working. Barrymore's memory of the lines was near-perfect, Breen remembered, and he could learn and remember anything he wanted to. Breen got Duncan Whiteside to design a setting for the production with multiple levels and steps (although Lee Simonson was at the same time lobbying for him to use the experimental set he had designed four years earlier).[51] Partial funding was pledged by the West Coast concert impresario L. E. Behymer, and tentative dates were reserved at the Bowl.

Barrymore was aware of the impact of his negative publicity on potential audiences ("They're going to come expecting me to fall into the orchestra," he told Breen), yet the director was confident of his ability to give a consummate performance. The first announcement of the production came on 29 May, when the *Hollywood Reporter* wrote that "John Barrymore has been signed for a revival of *Hamlet*, to be staged here at the Hollywood Bowl about September 13," with negotiations under way for a nationwide tour to follow. Soon afterward, Breen's wife, Wilva Davis, journeyed to the West Coast to visit her husband. The day she arrived, however, the reconciliation Breen had feared came to pass: Barrymore accepted a call from Elaine Barrie, from whom he had been legally divorced in April. "You wouldn't believe how the man melted, crumbled," Wilva Davis remembered. In the days that followed, Barrymore pressured Breen to agree to his ex-wife as Ophelia, which the director rejected emphatically. Plans for the production began to unravel. On 6 June, it was announced in the *Times* that "Mr. Barrymore advises that the Hollywood Bowl show 'of necessity has been postponed' because of 'prior motion-picture commitments which developed sooner than I had anticipated.'" But he added that "this should in no way affect a mid-season national tour which possibly I will do." By that point, however, it seemed likely to those connected with the project that little or nothing would come of the months of preparation they had invested. On 13 June, Lee Simonson composed a letter of consolation to Breen's wife. "My dear Miss Davis," he wrote. "John did a Barrymore. It isn't his first. He closed Hopkins's *Hamlet* years ago with $40,000 in advance sales at the B.O. Tell Mr. Breen I'm almost as disappointed as he is."[52]

The immediate reason for the production's postponement was probably the sudden opportunity that arose for Barrymore to return to Shakespeare in a far less risky medium. On 6 June 1937, the *Times* announced that CBS had planned a summer series of eight Shakespearean radio plays featuring leading artists of stage and screen, including Leslie Howard in *Much Ado about Nothing*, Walter Huston in *Henry IV, Part I*, and Edward G. Robinson in *The Taming of the Shrew*. Within a few days, Barrymore was approached by NBC and agreed to star in a rival series of broadcasts for $2,000 per episode, to be aired also on Monday night, in an overlapping time slot, in direct competition with the CBS programs (Fig. 45).[53]

On 21 June 1937 the series began with a forty-five-minute version of *Hamlet*, which was broadcast from NBC's Los Angeles studios. Barrymore doubled as Hamlet and the Ghost; the cast included the veteran English actor Brandon Hurst as the King and Hans Conried as Laertes. Barrymore's voice is noticeably darker, his readings wearier and less subtle than in the screen test produced three and a half years earlier, yet he manages a forceful performance. *Variety* praised his interpretation, but carped that the abridged text made the story difficult to understand for those unfamiliar with the play. The critic lamented the absence of Ophelia and found Hamlet's duel with Laertes mystifying "since it's never explained even who Laertes is, or why he permits the King to cajole him into starting the fight" (23 June 1937).

Hamlet was followed on 28 June by *Richard III*, with Elaine Barrie (with whom Barrymore had been reconciled publicly after the *Hamlet* broadcast) as Lady Anne. To modern ears Barrymore's readings often seem exaggerated, florid, yet *Variety* praised his performance as "Juicy roast beef – not ham – of the tradition that was." The critic added that Elaine Barrie was "not a hopeless trouper," noting that "She may be a one-emotion actress, but, boys, she can handle scorn" (30 June 1937).

King Lear was scheduled the following week, but at the beginning of the 5 July broadcast it was announced that Barrymore had selected *Macbeth* for performance instead. A recording of the broadcast makes it obvious that at times that he is merely reading the lines, yet his darker, more mature voice seems appropriate to the character, and he projects a powerful affinity with the Thane. Elaine Barrie's Riverside Drive accent and odd pronunciation as Lady Macbeth are a distinct liability, however, and the *Variety* critic did not greet the production with the approval he had visited upon earlier efforts. "Sans costumes, sans scenery, lacking the opportunity to set the mood, the tug-o'-war between original text, theatrical tradition and the bald, cold limited scope of radio tends to defeat even as astute a Shakespearean spouter as John Barrymore," he commented (7 July 1937).

At the conclusion of *Macbeth,* Barrymore invited the radio audience to tune in the following week for *The Tempest,* "featuring that seemingly heavily publicized couple, Caliban and Ariel." His duties for the 12 July broadcast included doubling as Caliban (in a bizarre, strangled voice) and Prospero. Walter Brennan appeared as Stephano, Robert Warwick (Montague in the MGM *Romeo and Juliet*) was featured as Alonso, and Elaine Barrie's lack of Shakespearean vocal skill as Miranda and Ariel was again apparent.

That same evening the rival CBS series premiered with Burgess Meredith as Hamlet. By this time *Variety* chose to ignore the Barrymore series entirely and devoted much of its review of the CBS series's debut to an analysis of audience taste and the networks' motivation for presenting Shakespeare to a radio audience. "It's a pretty good bet that the nation as a whole would trade in John Barrymore and Burgess Meredith combined for Jack Benny's version of *Hamlet,*" the critic commented, adding, "It's also pretty clear that neither Columbia nor NBC is thinking of listeners, but of that vague value known as 'Prestige.'" He predicted that the series would result in "scrapbooks full of publicity, tie-ups with English teachers . . . comments from stuffed shirts, and a flurry of admiration which will possibly be followed by a sudden jolting real-

Figure 45. Barrymore broadcasting his "Streamlined Shakespeare" radio series for NBC, 1937. Courtesy James Kotsilibas-Davis collection.

ization that only in summer, when it doesn't interfere with biz, would the networks indulge in such artistic capers" (14 July 1937).

The Barrymore series concluded with two additional broadcasts. On 19 July he doubled as a gruff, drunken Sir Toby Belch and an over-the-top Malvolio in *Twelfth Night,* followed the next week by a broad, flamboyant Petruchio in *The Taming of the Shrew,* in both of which he clearly relished the opportunity to play Shakespearean comedy.

After completing his radio duties, and perhaps encouraged by the response, Barrymore continued to contemplate a Hollywood Bowl *Hamlet* and tour. In July 1937 he wrote to his attorney: "I am plugging away at the play – devising effects for it, etc. . . . The Bowl dimension has possibilities that would be unforgettable. They have never been properly utilized in drama there. I'll just sit tight, and try not to go screwy." He was worried, however, that "some other ham [might] beat me to it" and pledged his attorney to secrecy.[54] "Robert [Breen] was hoping against hope to salvage it," his wife later remembered, but the project was soon set aside for good.

One reason for its abandonment may have been the motion picture opportunities that arose after the Shakespearean radio broadcasts. Barrymore's NBC series served to restore a good deal of his prestige, and his sobriety and reliability while working for the network assured a number of producers that he was, in fact, employable. For the next two years he worked steadily, rising from the ashes of his shattered reputation, although the decline in quality from his earlier film work, in terms of both his vehicles and his performances, is apparent more often than not. He was reduced to supporting roles, often in B pictures, yet he worked earnestly and to the best of his ability to keep himself active and to honor his debts. He had difficulty memorizing lines and required his dialogue to be written on blackboards just out of camera range; directors and fellow actors were generally sympathetic, however. He settled into a quiet domestic life (relatively speaking), and managed to avoid much of the unfavorable publicity that had plagued him for several years. The year 1937 saw the release of *Bulldog Drummond Comes Back, Night Club Scandal, Bulldog Drummond's Revenge,* and *True Confession* (with Carole Lombard); the following year Barrymore was featured in *Romance in the Dark, Bulldog Drummond's Peril,* and *Marie Antoinette,* a big-budget MGM feature starring Norma Shearer, in which he essayed the small yet crucial role of Louis XV. Robert Morley, who played his grandson, Louis XVI, later remembered that Barrymore was largely on the wagon and behaved professionally throughout the filming, yet at the same time he "didn't seem to care about much."[55] *Spawn of the North* (in which he was billed fifth) and *Hold that Coed* (a college comedy in which he played a madcap politician) followed soon afterward.

In 1939 Barrymore essayed what would prove to be his last serious role: an ex–Harvard scholar reduced by alcoholism to a night watchman's job in RKO's *The Great Man Votes.* The director, 27-year-old Garson Kanin, sold Barrymore on the role and later devised an ingenious stratagem to bolster his professionalism and self-esteem. "It struck me that . . . he had lost a certain amount of respect for himself," Kanin remembered, and accordingly, he conceived a plan to have the entire cast and crew restore his sense of dignity by addressing him as "Mr. Barrymore" throughout the filming. The actor responded to Kanin's able direction and the atmosphere on the set with a subtle, affecting performance.[56] That same year also saw the release of *Midnight,* a Parisian comedy starring Don Ameche and Claudette Colbert, in which Barrymore's wife essayed a small role, her only significant screen appearance.

Claudette Colbert later remembered that Barrymore seemed to require his blackboards only as a "security blanket," adding, "I never caught him looking at [them] once." Yet the completed film reveals two traits that often typified Barrymore's later performances: weariness and exaggeration. At one point he engages in flamboyant eye-rolling for the camera, a device John Drew had used for his exits thirty years earlier, delighting the Empire Theatre balcony, but jarringly inappropriate to the intimacy of film.[57]

By the time of *Midnight*'s release, however, there had been another development that would accelerate Icarus' plunge to earth. During the late thirties, Barrymore, while devoting himself almost exclusively to motion pictures, had remained an active theatregoer. He saw Maurice Evans's *Richard II* (which he admired) and *Hamlet* (which he concluded had "no balls"), both directed by his London *Hamlet* colleague Margaret Webster; he and his fourth wife saw and admired the Lunts, whom they had quixotic hopes of emulating. Encouraged by his wife and buoyed by her theatrical ambitions, Barrymore began reading scripts with a view to returning to the stage. Among the plays submitted for his consideration was *My Dear Children,* a featherweight farce by a pair of novice playwrights, Catherine Turney and Jerry Horwin, which had been making the rounds of producers without success. Its protagonist, Alan Manville, was similar in many ways to the John Barrymore of tabloid headlines: a much-married, over-the-hill Shakespearean who had taken refuge in a chateau in the Swiss Alps, where he is visited by his three daughters (all named for Shakespearean heroines) and their suitors.

From the first, Barrymore realized that the play was a flimsy, exploitative vehicle, and one can only speculate on his reasons for considering it. As was the case with *Clair de Lune* nearly two decades earlier, he was sympathetic to his wife's artistic ambitions and was eager to give her a public hearing; like Michael Strange, Elaine exerted a good deal of influence.[58] Both rather innocently envisioned the play as a warmup for better things; it would be followed, in their grand scheme, by a Broadway production of *Macbeth*. Barrymore was also eager to honor his numerous debts, toward which an ample part of his salary would be deducted. It is likely that he was stimulated, as well, by a genuine affection for the theatre he had long neglected, and by the challenge of returning to the stage after fourteen years, even with the problems of memorization it presented. He was not averse to poking fun at his public persona and in this instance, seems to have taken a perverse delight in doing so.

Many of his friends found it distressing that Barrymore sought to return to a medium he had once graced in a featherweight vehicle that exploited his tarnished image. Barrymore visited Ned Sheldon and read him the script, also discussing his ambition to play Macbeth. In a letter dictated soon afterward, Sheldon replied that

You were very nice to listen so patiently to my criticism of *My Dear Children.*
I know just how it feels when one is enthusiastic about something to run
point-blank into disagreement. But I know, too, that you wanted me to be
honest and tell you exactly how it struck me. . . . Of course, my opinion is
only that of one man, and I hope you will get others. I think that Charlie
MacArthur, Ben Hecht, Arthur Hopkins, Robert Sherwood, Robert E.
Jones, and Sidney Howard would be glad to give their disinterested, sympathetic, and valuable advice. While you are at it, ask them what they think of
Macbeth and whether they cannot suggest another classic. To my mind there
are three points against *Macbeth* – against it, I mean, as your first production. These points are (1) the fact that *Macbeth* has never been a popular
play in America, no matter who played it; (2) the fact that no actor ever
made a great personal success or really hit the bull's-eye as *Macbeth;* and
(3) the danger, which Elaine was quick to recognize, of making her first
New York appearance in such a tremendously exacting part.[59]

As had been the case with *Clair de Lune,* however, Barrymore chose to ignore the advice of his trusted associates and proceeded with plans to appear
in *My Dear Children,* with his wife Elaine playing one of his daughters. He approached Arthur Hopkins about producing and directing the play, but Hopkins wisely declined. Eventually, the producing team of Richard Aldrich and
Richard Meyers, confident of financial success with Barrymore in the lead (although surely aware of the exploitative nature of the vehicle), agreed to finance the production and engaged Otto Preminger as director.

At the dress rehearsal, it was apparent to one observer that Barrymore was
still capable of theatrical magic. Dr. Benjamin Shalett, a New York physician,
later remembered that at the beginning of the third act, he "left the prop-
dresser where he had been leaning. He walked to an unpainted, rough prop-
bench and sat down. With his cigarette dangling from his fingers, slouched
on the prop bench, he suddenly went into Hamlet's ['To be, or not to be'] soliloquy," a few lines of which were inserted into the play. As he began, Shallet
recalled, "it seemed that some invisible switch was thrown which cleared the
stage of makeshift props and the scene was suddenly set for *Hamlet,* Act III,
scene I. So magical was the art of this man." But then "suddenly and cruelly
it was over. Barrymore was mouthing again the drivel of *My Dear Children.*"[60]

On 24 March 1939, the production opened at Princeton's McCarter Theatre with Albert Einstein and numerous New York first-nighters in the audience. Barrymore stuck to the script until, forgetting a line and unable to hear
the prompter, he called out, "Just a little louder, darling. I couldn't hear you."
After the final curtain he was greeted by a five-minute ovation, to which he
responded, "I can scarely tell you, not having heard that beautiful sound for
more than fifteen years [*sic*], how deeply it affects me. It's pure music to my
ears."[61]

The play then set off on a tour consisting mainly of one- and two-night stands. As the tour progressed through the South and Midwest, however, Barrymore soon came to resent the play and his fourth wife. Again there were much-publicized quarrels with Elaine Barrie; Barrymore showed up in an inebriated state and made unprintable comments at a luncheon in Omaha scheduled to promote the play. He improvised on the script whenever his memory failed or the impulse arose, and on at least one occasion resorted to four-letter words.[62] After further marital tumult, Elaine Barrie agreed to be replaced and left the tour in St. Louis.

On 8 May 1939 the production limped into in Chicago, the scene of Barrymore's successful early appearances in *A Stubborn Cinderella* and *A Thief for a Night*. The play was scheduled originally for a two-week run, yet it soon became a phenomenon unprecedented in the annals of the American stage. For eight months, *My Dear Children* drew capacity crowds, but many in the audience came not to see a play, but rather a figure whose unpredictable behavior was the chief allure. Many of Barrymore's interpolations in *My Dear Children* emerged as genuine improvements on the flimsy script (and were later included in the published edition). Had he confined himself to in-character improvisations, they might have seemed only one more eccentricity in his ample catalogue. Barrymore felt compelled, however, to enliven the proceedings further by stepping out of character to make numerous references to his personal life. When the play required him to drink a glass of prop whiskey, he would often comment, "God! I wish that was real." Loud noises outside the theatre invariably inspired the quip, "My God! My wife's in town." Equally alarming were his frequent greetings of latecomers with "Where the hell have you been," his habit of stopping the show to address friends in the audience, and his inability to refrain from profanity whenever the urge arose[63] – and as himself rather than as a character in a play. The result, on many occasions, was a grotesque, unpredictable circus.

Ned Sheldon, blind and bedridden in New York, was kept abreast of the situation. On 18 July 1939 he wrote to Barrymore:

> Why not close the play, return to Hollywood . . . and make some money? I realize your interest in the theatre and sympathize with it, as you well know, but I see no use in continuing to play *My Dear Children* when so much has to be taken out of your salary that you are losing money. . . . Do a few pictures, Jack, at the best salary obtainable, get some of these immediate debts cleared up, and then come back to the theatre with another play and without obstacles.
>
> You telegraphed me about *Macbeth*, asking what I thought. As you know, it is my favorite play. But I doubt very much if next season is the right time to produce it. . . . I understand how you feel about the play, and it might be a fine idea to do it sometime on the heels of a real success. In other words,

when you are in a position to indulge yourself and take a chance. But you are not in this position now, and should go after something where the money is more or less sure. At present that means pictures. Later on when your decks are cleared and your financial sky is blue, then is the time to consider a *Macbeth* production. Also I doubt very much if you are in physical shape to play such an exacting role eight times a week. You asked me what I thought, and there it is.[64]

Barrymore again ignored Sheldon's advice, however, despite ill health; at one point he collapsed and was hospitalized, yet he returned to *My Dear Children* within a week. Lloyd Lewis, writing about the production a few months later in the *New York Times,* termed it "a peep-show, a spiritual strip-tease with [Barrymore] as a sort of Gypsy Rose John." Barrymore, he commented, "realizes that his Hamlet days are done and that he is henceforth an exhibition, not a great actor." When his lines required him to mention the days when he was a great Hamlet, he smirked and "all but thrust out his tongue" (10 September 1939). Robert Breen, who had worked with Barrymore on *Hamlet* two years earlier, attended a performance and later told his wife that he found it "impossible to describe how awful and cheap it was." He went backstage after the performance but later wished he had not. Barrymore burst into tears when he saw the young director and begged him, "Can you get me out of this?" "We'll see," Breen replied, but Barrymore, with an air of resignation, told him, "I know. It's too late."

After closing in Chicago, the play again toured briefly; a New York engagement was then scheduled to commence on 31 January 1940 at the Belasco. Brooks Atkinson, the *Times* drama critic, remembered that on opening night, the 44th Street block where the theatre was located "was filled with a silent crowd of curiosity-seekers who looked as if they hoped to be present at the final degradation of Icarus. . . . The crowds that watched the tumbrels pass in the French Revolution could not have been more pitiless or morbid." In the lobby, Atkinson recalled, theatregoers jostled one another and "squeezed by the ticket taker as if they were going to a notorious peepshow." Finally, the curtain went up, and after a brief expository scene, Barrymore made his entrance in a raffish fur coat, "ravaged and jaunty, weary and sardonic, ill and sprightly." Atkinson was "shocked by what seventeen years of revelry had done to the greatest romantic actor we ever had"[65] (Fig. 46).

Barrymore was greeted by a wave of applause from an assembly that included Constance Collier, Jack Warner, and Tyrone Power III. That evening he stuck to the script, for the most part, although he dropped a chance remark about his brother Lionel and included a reference, by then de rigueur, to his drinking habits. Reviews the next day and soon afterward tended to be harsh. "It is unnecessary to criticize Mr. Barrymore's acting, for all this can hardly be summed up as acting," commented the *World–Telegram.* "He de-

Figure 46. Barrymore and his fourth wife, Elaine Barrie, in *My Dear Children.* Courtesy Photofest.

liberately cut great slices of ham into the performance, chewing scenery and mouthing round phrases in the exaggerated manner of the pretentious Shakespearean actors of the dead past. It was a burlesque" (1 February 1940). "To what depths the old star system can descend when not checked by good taste and respect for theatre is tragically demonstrated by John Barrymore's appearance in *My Dear Children,*" admonished the *Theatre Arts* critic. "A footling farce of no merit, it is transformed by an actor who should be the honor and pride of the American theatre into a piece of first-class exhibitionism. It is impossible to review as a play."[66]

The only encouraging comments came from Brooks Atkinson in the *Times* (1 February 1940):

[Barrymore] is still the most gifted actor in this country . . . he has the personal magnetism that electrifies a play and an audience at the same time
and takes instant command of a whole theatre. In contrast with the Barrymore who dominated the theatre by memorable works twenty years ago, he
is a ravaged figure now. But the fact remains that he can still act like a man
whom the gods have generously endowed and like a man who knows the art
and the business of stage expression. . . .

If Mr. Barrymore were a ham, this trashy story and his appearance in it
might be a pathetic ordeal for his old admirers. But he is a wit. He plays it
with an alert sense of mischief. . . . Although he has recklessly played the
fool for a number of years, he is nobody's fool in *My Dear Children*, but a superbly gifted actor on a tired holiday.

The headlines continued. Within a few days of the opening Barrymore
collapsed and was again hospitalized; several performances were canceled,
but the actor rallied and soon rejoined the company. Two weeks into the run
Elaine Barrie took over her old role. Soon afterward Barrymore permitted a
Pathé News cameraman to film him in his dressing room. "The gentlemen
from the newsreel have informed me that they wish to see the Barrymore
pro-feel," he commented, looking ill and frail. "That is, as much of it as is
left."[67] Yet he found the strength to continue. During the four months of the
run, he began improvising freely once again; ultimately his appearance in
My Dear Children generated nearly as many critical columns as his Hamlet
eighteen years earlier. Brooks Atkinson continued to voice his support, but
he was alone in doing so. Commented the *World–Telegram,*

All this is no service to the theater that the Barrymores profess to love so
well. On the contrary, it is an open invitation and appeal to the public not
to come and see a good play or an artistic performance, but to see the humiliation of a fallen idol and the abasement of a once magnificent talent.
. . . The humor of Mr. Barrymore's improvisations is completely lost in the
pathos and tragedy of the situation. It is Belasco running a flea circus, or
Bernhardt in three-a-day vaudeville. (10 February 1940)[68]

Barrymore was still capable of reminding audiences of his former greatness,
as was the case when he spoke his nightly excerpt from "To be or not to be"
or when he recited the "rogue and peasant slave" soliloquy at several charitable events during the run. The rest of the time, however, he paraded himself
as the Has-Been Ham, a constant reminder to his old friends and admirers of
how far he had fallen.[69]

During the run, Barrymore received an offer to film *My Dear Children* for
$150,000; yet perhaps because he again found himself bankrupt after paying
off his first series of debts, he ultimately accepted $50,000 more to appear in
The Great Profile, a more strikingly exploitative vehicle, for Twentieth Century–Fox. (The film had been intended originally as a vehicle for Adolphe Men-

jou, who had parodied Barrymore in the 1936 film *Sing, Baby, Sing.*) *My Dear Children* played its final performance on 18 May, and two weeks later Barrymore reported to the Fox lot. As the alcoholic, has-been Shakespearean "Evans Garrick," he parodied his exploits in connection with *My Dear Children* and drank his way through the filming.[70] The *Times* critic noted that *The Great Profile* opened in New York as the lower half of a double bill and commented that "As a play it is a feeble thing, hardly matching the spectacular public accounts of his amours." He concluded that "In the Winter of his discontent Mr. Barrymore is selling his talent at cut-rate" (18 October 1940).

The self-parody continued on coast-to-coast radio broadcasts. Barrymore became a fixture on Rudy Vallee's "Sealtest Hour," where the jokes invariably centered on his drinking, marital problems, and has-been status. Lionel Barrymore later defended his brother's compulsive desire to keep working, attributing it to a sense of obligation to his debts:

> There were sincere persons, old friends among them, who turned away under the understandable conviction that he had sold out the last sacred cup on the altar, his self-respect, his art. He did it simply to get tax money. It was all he could do. He used a tarnished and broken tool in its extremity, in this willful, tongue-and-cheek impersonation of an old tragedian, but he used it like a master. He was utterly conscious of what he was doing and why it was necessary to do it.[71]

While working in radio, Barrymore continued to appear in whatever films were offered. The year 1941 saw the release of *The Invisible Woman*, in which he portrayed an eccentric inventor, and *World Premiere*, in which he caricatured a megalomaniacal film producer. Neither was of much artistic merit, yet both offered the actor an opportunity to portray a character other than a caricature of himself, for which he undoubtedly was grateful.

Almost incredibly, he continued to contemplate a revival of *Macbeth*, this time in the Hollywood Bowl. In the spring of 1941, Barrymore approached Judith Anderson, who had played Lady Macbeth opposite Laurence Olivier's Thane at the Old Vic four years earlier, with an offer to reprise her role. Dame Judith later remembered that he seemed inebriated at the time, and she thought the project impossible until Barrymore launched into soliloquies from *Hamlet* and other Shakespearean plays. He recited them beautifully, she remembered, and for those brief moments he became a different person, absolutely transcendent; yet the project never went any further.[72] It seems equally quixotic that film producers continued to consider the actor for serious roles. Bette Davis was eager to have him appear as Sheridan Whiteside in *The Man Who Came to Dinner.* He agreed to a screen test, but it was obvious to those viewing the result that he was far too ill and weary to attempt the part.

In the summer of 1941, Barrymore began work on what would prove his final film: *Playmates,* costarring the bandleader Kay Kaiser. His character was called "John Barrymore," and he was required only to play himself; his role was that of an over-the-hill Shakespearean whose only chance of landing a radio contract and getting himself out of debt is to appear at a Shakespeare festival with Kaiser. He gives an excerpt from the "To be or not to be" soliloquy affectingly and is treated with dignity and respect by Kaiser and his band, yet the film features predictable jibes at his has-been status and financial woes, and he often appears tired and frail.

In retrospect, he could hardly have attempted a more ironic exit, for the film attempts to find comedy in the juxtaposition of two seemingly incongruous elements: Shakespeare and big-band music. Two decades earlier, Barrymore's personal glamour and fresh, spontaneous approach to Richard III and Hamlet had drawn broad audiences, many of whom were witnessing a Shakespeare play for the first time. *Playmates,* however, emphasizes the seemingly unbridgeable gap between "high" and "popular" culture. The audiences for Shakespeare and popular music are separate and distinct, the film good-naturedly suggests, and never the twain shall meet. Moreover, although Barrymore gives a subdued reading to the "To be or not to be" soliloquy, much of the rest of his performance is awash in deliberate affectation and floridity – the antitheses of his trenchant Shakespearean portrayals on Broadway two decades earlier. One need only consider the dozens of comments that had greeted his Richard III and Hamlet as a welcome change from the rhetorical speech and scenery chewing of the "old school" to appreciate the tragic irony of much of his final film. The repression and subtle power that had distinguished his Shakespearean performances of the twenties and his films of the early thirties give way – in many cases deliberately but in some cases not – to exaggeration, self-parody, the exploding consonants and flamboyant excesses of an old-school ham.

The *Times* responded to *Playmates* in the moralistic tone that had become all too common in reviews of Barrymore's later work. "It may be amusing to some people to witness the spectacle of John Barrymore making a buffoon of himself on the screen, but this spectator for one fails to see the humor of it," wrote their critic (26 December 1941). The *Herald Tribune,* more generously, found Barrymore "exceedingly funny at times in playing himself" and concluded, "*Playmates* isn't the best picture to come along, but it is definitely not the worst" (26 December 1941).

Barrymore continued to work steadily on the Rudy Vallee radio program, where at times, amid the buffoonery, he was granted the opportunity to present Shakespearean scenes for their dramatic value. At the end of one broadcast he delivered an abridged "Now is the winter of our discontent" soliloquy from *Richard III,* followed by the scene with Clarence, opposite his brother,

Lionel. On 29 January 1942 Vallee featured Barrymore and his 20-year-old daughter Diana (by then a veteran of two Broadway shows and under contract to Universal Studios) in the balcony scene from *Romeo and Juliet.* "Don't use that made-actress voice," he remarked to his daughter during rehearsals:

> Let me tell you something about Shakespeare. The only reason I thought I was successful at it was because I played it as if Shakespeare had written the play for me. The part had never been acted before. Now you think the same way. This isn't a classic. . . . There's no precedent to follow. The first time these lines will have been read before an audience will be when you read them on the show.[73]

On 5 March, Barrymore, along with Lionel and Diana, appeared as Brutus, Caesar, and Calpurnia in an excerpt from *Julius Caesar.* The *Times* commented soon afterward that

> Occasionally . . . Mr. Barrymore does give his radio public a flash of what he once was. But it is only a flash, and in its own fashion it is as morbid as the jokes. Occasionally, too, he reminds you that he was a first-rate light comedian in the days before *Justice.* . . . But there is very little in the Vallee program with which even a first-rate comedian could do much. (22 March 1942)

Less than two months later, on 19 May 1942, Barrymore attended a rehearsal in which the writers had inserted a line from *Romeo and Juliet* that had nothing to do with what came before or afterward: "Soft! What light through yonder window breaks?" It proved the last line he ever spoke as an actor. Soon afterward he swayed and began to collapse, and Vallee caught him to prevent him from falling. "I guess this is one time I miss my cue," he said faintly.[74] He was taken to Hollywood Presbyterian Hospital, where he was diagnosed with bronchial pneumonia, hardening of the arteries, hemorrhaging ulcers, and cirrhosis of the liver. For ten days he faded and rallied, drifting in and out of consciousness until 29 May, when at 10:20 P.M. he died in his sleep.[75]

Commentaries appearing over the next few days almost invariably lamented the dissipation of his talents. On 31 May, James Agate wrote in his diary: "The tragic thing is when a man of genius throws his genius away. . . . In my view a man of genius should hold his genius as precious as his life. I can never forgive Kean for dying at the age of forty-six. Barrymore could have been as great an actor as Talma, and was not."[76] That same day, an anonymous editorial writer in the *New York Herald Tribune* offered a more charitable view:

> The moralists . . . could prove that he never achieved more than one-tenth of the fine things of which he was capable. . . . They said it was "sad" that in his latter years he had become a "caricature" of a once magnificent figure. But none of this was news to Barrymore, nor did he allow it to disturb him

unduly. . . . Here was an actor. Was ever there a better in America? Tens of
thousands of playgoers will swear that his virtuosity was unsurpassed anywhere, and they may be right. . . . No matter what he touched, he gave it a
manner and a dash. He was born to be an actor, and when he conscientiously set himself to a task he could blend his genius with a thoroughly
sound and intelligent craftsmanship.

Soon afterward, Arthur Hopkins delivered a tribute to Barrymore in a
nationwide radio address. Like most observers, he acknowledged the abdication and decline; yet he preferred to recall "the period of Barrymore's flowering, a period in which the theatre of our time reached its highest expression
and raised him to the stratosphere reached only by Booth and Irving." He
concluded simply, "Long will he live as the artist, who above all others, exalt-
ed the theatre of his time, the actor who touched immortality and made it visible to grateful mortals."[77]

Epilogue

He charted new areas of expression that remain open for others to explore. Where man has been, man will go again. Areas once visited do not remain content with neglect. . . .

There are liberators of the spirit.

In our theatre time John Barrymore was the greatest of these. The liberator not only frees his own time, he frees succeeding time.

– Arthur Hopkins[1]

THE INFLUENCE OF BARRYMORE and his production team on the ways in which the bravura repertory was acted and produced in the English language was lasting and profound. Writing in 1928 of *Richard III* and *Hamlet*, Rex Smith commented in *Theatre Magazine* that "It is to be doubted that Barrymore realizes the influence such courageous translations of classic characters will have on the theatre of the future."[2] Even then, contemporary observers recognized that the precedents set by these revivals would resonate far beyond their historical moment. Indeed, the perspective of time now enables the Barrymore revivals to be viewed in a new light: as an axis between nineteenth- and twentieth-century values and a seminal influence upon modern performances and productions.

To realize the impact of Barrymore's portrayals one need only examine some of the noteworthy performances that followed in their wake, particularly during the 1930s, when the methods he introduced provided a wellspring for subsequent interpreters. Laurence Olivier freely acknowledged the influence of Barrymore's impersonation on his 1937 Hamlet at the Old Vic and on his film of 1947, admitting "I admired Barrymore and used much of his Hamlet in mine."[3] Olivier borrowed liberally from Barrymore's stage business; his *Hamlet* film incorporated a variation on Barrymore's athletic leap at the King and the image of the four Captains pausing a moment as they carry Hamlet's lifeless body up a massive flight of stairs. More significantly, Olivier retained the Oedipal ramifications of the Queen's closet scene, both on the stage and in his film. Like Barrymore, he did not follow a strictly Freudian party line, yet he consulted with the eminent Freudian analyst Ernest Jones prior to his stage and film productions and utilized many of his suggestions, giving further impetus to a trend that began with Barrymore's portrayal.

In this he was by no means alone. The 1931 Raymond Massey–Norman Bel Geddes *Hamlet* featured a protagonist who recited the Ghost's lines while a dimly lit figure stood mutely by, as if the apparition's presence had emerged from his own subconscious. The 1936 John Gielgud–Guthrie McClintic *Hamlet* in New York, like the Barrymore–Hopkins–Jones production fourteen years earlier, stressed Ophelia's transition from sexual repression to the opposite extreme. Soon afterward, Gielgud wrote that "psychoanalysis would nowadays seem to be so generally understood that any modern audience accepts [Ophelia's bawdiness] as the result of repression." (Interestingly, Gielgud also utilized a "nonphysical" Ghost in 1936 and in the 1964 production of *Hamlet* he directed starring Richard Burton.)[4] By 1990, the tendency to view Ophelia's transformation and Hamlet's relationship with the Queen in the context of the characters' sexuality – a subject of controversy in the Barrymore and Olivier productions – had become accepted as a producible interpretation to such a degree that Franco Zeffirelli's inclusion of these elements in his film of the play elicited scarcely a critical mention.

Equally important to the future were the performance methods Barrymore initiated with his *Richard III* and *Hamlet*. In order to understand fully the impact of his new and more "natural" style, one must recall something of the conventions that typified Shakespearean performance during the late nineteenth and early twentieth centuries. Recordings of Johnston Forbes-Robertson, Herbert Beerbohm Tree, E. H. Sothern, and their contemporaries are revealing. Although Forbes-Robertson displays a rich tonal variety (and Tree and Sothern a lack thereof), there is a striking common quality to their speech: an elevated, poetic formalism reflecting late-nineteenth-century manners and aesthetic ideals. It was doubtless this same quality that led William Poel to despair in 1913 that "our actors who excel in modern plays by the truth and force of their presentation of life . . . in Shakespeare make use of an elocution that no human being was ever known to indulge in."[5] Forbes-Robertson possessed the ability to make his impersonations seem simultaneously poetic and real, yet the majority of his contemporaries and successors lacked his skill, contributing to a widespread awareness of the gap between "realistic" and "Shakespearean" acting.

Barrymore's "colloquial" verse speaking introduced to the stage the vocal manner of a postwar gentleman – a point of demarcation from what E. Harcourt Williams, echoing Poel's protest and Margaret Carrington's teachings, later termed the "absurd convention of the Shakespearean voice." As an ex-

ample of the older method he cited specifically the Victorian practice of substituting "me" and "min" for "my" and "mine" – a tendency Barrymore had
been praised in London for eliminating.[6] In casting aside the "tragic elevation" and elocutionary formality of Victorian Shakespeare and its aftermath,
Barrymore initiated an approach that was much in evidence in the performances of subsequent Shakespearean interpreters during the twenties, thirties, and beyond. To one critic, Raymond Massey's Hamlet seemed to be
"thinking and speaking in prose" (*Sun*, 6 November 1931); John Gielgud was
praised for speaking verse "with the quick spontaneity of a modern man"
(*Times*, 9 October 1936).

The restrained bearing and gestures Barrymore brought to Shakespeare –
the sense of "modern men who live by their woes in narrow rooms," as Ludwig Lewisohn succinctly put it – marked a similar turning point in interpretive technique. Williams recalled that the habit had been to "speak Shakespeare to a windmill of waving arms, in the vain hope that some kind of
'period' was being achieved thereby."[7] While his comments doubtless reflect
observation of actors of less than first-rank status, references to Booth making "statues on the stage" and Forbes-Robertson's "conspicuous grace" are
reminders that physical as well as vocal stylization was a convention of Victorian performance. Like his more "natural" delivery, Barrymore's repressed,
modern physicality was much in evidence in the portrayals of subsequent interpreters. Brooks Atkinson praised Maurice Evans for abandoning "the posturing . . . tradition has imposed upon Hamlets" (*Times*, 13 October 1938),
yet he was surely aware that this method had originated fourteen years earlier with Barrymore's performance.

The "realistic" elements Barrymore introduced in his characterizations –
the vocal and physical modernity, the sexuality and psychological method of
interpretation – heralded the dawn of a new age in the theatre. Through
much of the Victorian era and beyond, the tendency had been for Shakespeare's characters to be presented in "an ideal manner, as far removed
as possible from the plane of actual life." When Barrymore began preparations for *Richard III* and *Hamlet* the plays were still grounded in nineteenth-
century interpretive tradition, yet his decision, with the encouragement of
Arthur Hopkins and Margaret Carrington, to treat the plays as "works newly written" proved enormously successful. Elements of his technique would
extend through the portrayals of Gielgud, Olivier, and Evans to the performances later in the century of Richard Burton, David Warner, and Nicol Wil-
liamson. Gielgud's initial Hamlet in 1930 and Evans's first New York appearance in the role in 1938 were directed, respectively, by Barrymore company
alumni E. Harcourt Williams and Margaret Webster, whose notions of Shakespearean interpretation were clearly influenced by Barrymore's characterization. This, and Olivier's frank acknowledgment of emulating Barrymore

when he first played the role in 1937, provide a direct link between Barrymore and the three most notable English Hamlets of the ensuing decade.

The innovative methods introduced by Barrymore's artistic associates also
served as touchstones for a generation and beyond and were to be much imitated in years to come. Although Arthur Hopkins wrote two years after *Hamlet* that "a little of Craig goes a long way," *Richard III* and *Hamlet* were among
the first important English-language productions of Shakespearean tragedy
to utilize effectively his aesthetic principles, tempered with the influence of
Reinhardt's more practical sensibilities. Hopkins's spare, repressed stagings –
a noteworthy shift from the ornate mountings of late-nineteenth- and early-
twentieth-century tradition – proved the wave of the future. Though David
Belasco's picturesque revival of *The Merchant of Venice* opened a month after
Hamlet, it was perhaps the last important production of the traditional repertory to offer playgoers the vital motion and crowds of extras that had typified
staging in the Duke of Saxe-Meiningen–Augustin Daly tradition. Robert Edmond Jones's designs similarly helped to create a new Anglo–American tradition of Shakespearean investiture. Norman Bel Geddes's Jones-influenced
arrangement of stairs, levels, and platforms in his 1931 *Hamlet* with Raymond
Massey would be praised for its "brooding symbolism" (*Sun*, 6 November
1931), and the 1934 Motley settings for John Gielgud's *Hamlet* at the New
Theatre in London and Jo Mielziner's set for Gielgud's 1936 New York revival featured a comparable arrangement of stairs and platforms. Permanent,
symbolic settings for the plays, modified only by easily moved set pieces necessary to suggest the locale of individual scenes, rapidly became an accepted
convention of English-language productions of the tragedies, one that per-
sists in the present day.[8]

The pioneering efforts of Barrymore, Hopkins, and Jones established a
stimulating point of connection for post-1920 audiences. It is important to
remember, of course, that one of the chief complaints of A. C. Wheeler in
1890 and of the anonymous commentator for the *New York Times* in 1909 was
that Shakespeare did not speak to an age, that his characters revealed no
phase of "the life that people know." Barrymore's portrayals expressed the
new doubts of post-1918 audiences; his harshly realistic characterizations –
a radical departure from Victorian idealism – captured the emerging spirit
of an era. By reinterpreting the plays in light of postwar aesthetic values and
modern psychological theory, and by refusing to view them as revered classics as they were often regarded, Barrymore and his associates narrowed the
gap between Shakespeare and ordinary playgoers and, in doing so, looked
forward to the impulse to "contemporize" the plays that became a keynote
of later twentieth-century practice. This impulse, of course, has often resulted in excess and directorial distortion for the sake of novelty; modern prac-

titioners might learn an important lesson by remembering that Barrymore, Hopkins, and Jones attempted to make themselves "servants of the play."

In a sense, one can only lament the fact that Barrymore chose to abdicate his position as the leading classical actor of the English-speaking stage: It is easy to imagine his success as Othello, Iago, Lear. Looking back on the years of their collaboration, Arthur Hopkins recalled that they had dreamed of a repertory that would one day tour the world. *Richard III* was to be followed by productions of *Hamlet, Cyrano, Faust, Peer Gynt,* and *Richard II;* of these, only *Hamlet* was done. Barrymore was doubtless discouraged by the repetition a classical repertory would have demanded, and, perhaps too selfishly, felt little obligation to his audiences or his abilities. Those who had worked with him were aware, however, that the psychic intensity and athleticism of his best performances – the same qualities that could galvanize audiences – resulted in considerable fatigue and took a toll on his strength and enthusiasm. They were aware, too, that he received little gratification from even his most acclaimed characterizations once he had created a role. As he wrote to Michael Strange in October 1922, a month before he opened in *Hamlet:* "There really is something about [acting in the theatre] that goes against my grain and makes me unhappy. . . . Getting it *on* – developing every angle of it . . . the creative element has for me interest and vitality enough. . . . But after it is *done – born* – the repetition of it lays around my soul like a damp web."[9] In retrospect, his failure to continue with the proposed repertory and his abandonment of the theatre for Hollywood seemed almost inevitable. Like the Hamlet of Goethe's "costly vase" passage quoted in his memoirs, a great deed had been "laid upon a soul unequal to the performance of it."

Ultimately, however, Barrymore's decision to devote his skills to another mode of artistic expression, like Barker's abandonment of directing to apply his energies to literature and lecturing, must be respected. "That he would have had an unparalleled career there was no doubt, and he knew it," Hopkins observed. "He did not forsake undreamed-of realms. His renunciation was with full knowledge of what he was leaving." He found himself temperamentally unsuited for the role of Shakespearean crusader and doubtless realized that the tradition of actor-managers barnstorming the land with a classical repertory was a vanishing institution. Walter Hampden and Fritz Leiber carried on the tradition a few years longer, but it was perhaps no coincidence that they devoted much of their post-1930 careers to films. Moreover, as Laurence Olivier commented perceptively: "I'm sure that if Beverly Hills had been around for Burbage, Garrick, Kean and Irving, they would have boarded a fast ship to the New World before breakfast."[10]

Certainly Barrymore's work is subject to limitation: He devoted only a relatively brief period of his career to Shakespeare and attempted only two of

the great roles. Booth and Irving, and in a later generation, Olivier and Gielgud, performed virtually every important Shakespearean role time and again
over the course of their lifetimes. Still, as Arthur Hopkins observed, "High
achievement is not measured by length of duration. . . . Nothing subsequent
to his great creative era could destroy his rich period of realization."[11] His
characterizations proved anew to a generation of theatregoers that Shakespeare's tragic protagonists could be vital, dangerous, and exciting. His intellectual approach to Richard and Hamlet captured the spirit of postwar ration-
alism, and although it reflected but one possible interpretation of these
characters it proved persuasive to contemporary critics. His portrayals liberated the bravura repertory from the constraints of Victorian tradition, and,
like the impersonations of Garrick and Kean, impressed upon some of the
most sophisticated observers of an age that something extraordinarily fresh
and dynamic had burst upon the realm of Shakespearean performance. Although his brilliance, like Kean's, could be coupled with erraticism and self-
destructive urges, most contemporary observers likely would have agreed
with Alexander Woollcott, who found him to be a Shakespearean "of such
qualities of mind and mask as life gives sparingly a few times in a hundred
years" (*Herald*, 4 December 1922).

   In evaluating Barrymore as a tragedian one must conclude that he was, in
fact, a great actor of Shakespeare as well as an important transitional figure
in the history of the Shakespearean stage. Arriving in New York after his triumphant Hamlet at the Haymarket in London, he proclaimed to dockside
reporters, with the confident modesty of an actor who has made his mark:
"Most [English critics] compared me to Sir Henry Irving. They all said Irving
was better" (*World*, 7 May 1925). Yet the record shows that comparisons were
generally favorable when contemporary critics seeking to appraise his performances recalled the immortals of the recent past. One measure of his accomplishment, to audiences of his time and beyond, was his ability to match
the impact of his acclaimed predecessors while reinterpreting classic roles
with an innovative artistry that redefined those characters for the postwar
generation. As the historian Lloyd Morris observed, "To playgoers who had
seen him in his great roles, the vivid memory of his performances furnished
a criterion. Like Booth before him, he survived as a standard, a challenge to
all aspirants, and more than a decade was to pass before a direct comparison
with him was invited."[12]

   Indeed, like the eminent Shakespeareans of the Victorian and Edwardian
era, Barrymore created standards of performance that were to be evoked
time and again in comparisons with subsequent aspirants to Shakespearean
distinction. George Jean Nathan, writing in 1943 about George Coulouris's
Richard III, took the actor to task for offering a broad, externalized characterization like that of Robert B. Mantell; Fritz Leiber's Richard had "foxiness"

but was similarly dependent on Shakespearean tricks; Walter Hampden was a "college professor" who lectured rather than playing the part. Only Barrymore had captured "the evil fascination, the workable hypocrisy, the pragmatic irony, the human being within the shell of viciousness, and the possibility of future rulership that in sum convincingly constitutes the character."[13] John Gielgud's 1936 Hamlet at the Empire Theatre was greeted by many observers as the first portrayal of the role in New York since Barrymore's to merit similar accolades. A number of commentators felt that Gielgud's interpretation was equally worthy of the pantheon, yet Barrymore's Dane was by no means overshadowed, and a number of American critics took the opportunity to champion his interpretation. "My standard of excellence in a characterization of Hamlet is frankly Mr. Barrymore," wrote Richard Watts Jr. "His was to my mind not only the finest portrayal of the role that I have ever seen but was also the most magnificent piece of acting within my memory" (*Herald Tribune,* 9 October 1936).

Recalling the actor's work years later, Robert Edmond Jones commented that Barrymore was "seldom given credit for his very unusual intelligence. He was not wise, perhaps, but his mind was swift as the flight of a falcon." Barrymore was capable of profoundly moving moments of introspection. "I have always felt that Barrymore was at his best – that he said more to an audience . . . when he was alone on a great stage, in the midst of great spaces, a man alone with destiny," Jones remembered. At the same time, he could reveal his extraordinary personal presence in electrifying flashes. "As I look back on the various parts he played," Jones remarked, "it seems to me that they all shared a shrinking quality, a holding back, a kind of hesitation . . . one sensed the fastidious aristocratic delicacy, the rapier-like finesse. When I think of Jack the image of a rapier is always in my mind, a shrinking and then a flashing attack." He was, Jones concluded, "a miraculous being, a presence all fire and dream."[14] Like Kean a century earlier, he startled the theatrical world with the vitality and force of his impersonations; he spoke for modernism as Kean had spoken for Romanticism, and exemplified the cultural and theatrical foment of a rapidly changing era.

Modern actors and practitioners might learn a good deal from the examples set by Barrymore and his production team. "We were all three – Barrymore, Hopkins, Jones – theatre-minded and forward-looking and daring," wrote Robert Edmond Jones. The idealistic vision with which they approached their work is seldom echoed today. "We dreamed and it was done," Jones remembered. "Nothing seemed too high, too far. Nothing seemed unattainable."[15] It is important to remember, as well, that although Barrymore reached a level of status and skill attained among American Shakespeareans only by Edwin Booth, a decade earlier he had been merely a clever comedian with limited ability and ambition. His reinvention of himself as an actor was the product of resolve and exhaustive labor to develop a technique that would raise his skills to a higher artistic level. The result was a personal metamorphosis undreamed of by critics who a decade earlier had "flourished the usual theatrical measuring stick of 'personal limitations.'" From "the young good-for-nothing who gayly and facetiously wins out in *The Fortune Hunter*" and "*Anatol* of the lively Parisian adventures" he rose to become an artist of winged imagination who at his best, wrote Richard Watts Jr., "made acting seem something so memorable and important that it belonged in the cultural heritage of all of us lucky enough to have encountered it."[16] Not the least of his accomplishments was the fact that his efforts, along with those of his artistic confreres, helped to reinvent the Shakespearean theatre of his time and of time to come.

APPENDIXES

The Casts

Information on the casts has been gathered from a number of sources including *Who's Who in the Theatre; Who Was Who in the Theatre;* obituaries in *Variety* and the *New York Times; New York Times* theatre and film reviews; J. P. Wearing's *The London Stage: A Calendar of Plays and Players,* 7 vols. (Metuchen, N.J.: Scarecrow Press, 1976–93); clipping files at Lincoln Center and the Theatre Museum, London; and the American and British branches of Actors Equity.

I. *Richard III:* 6 March–31 March 1920

The cast for *Richard III* was as follows:

King Henry VI	Arthur Row
Queen Margaret	Rosalind Ivan
Edward, Prince of Wales (their son)	Burford Hampden
Duke of York	Marshall Vincent
Duchess of York	Mrs. Thomas Wise

Their Sons

Edward (afterwards King Edward IV)	Reginald Denny
George (afterwards Duke of Clarence)	E. J. Ballantine
Richard (afterwards Duke of Gloucester and Richard III)	John Barrymore

Sons of Edward IV

Edward	Mary Hughes
Richard	Helen Chandler
Children of Clarence	Helen Chandler
	Lois Bartlett
Earl of Warwick	Walter Ringham
Duke of Buckingham	Leslie Palmer
Duke of Norfolk	Robert Whitehouse
Earl of Derby	George De Winter
Lord Hastings	Lewis Sealy

Cardinal Bourchier	Montague Rutherford
Earl of Westmoreland	Robert Whitehouse
Lord Clifford	Stanley Warmington
Lord Rivers	William J. Keighley
Lord Grey	Denis Auburn
Sir James Tyrell	John M. Troughton
Sir Richard Ratcliff	Montague Rutherford
Sir William Catesby	Stanley Warmington
Sir James Blount	Malcolm Barrett
Sir William Brackenbury	William J. Keighley
The Lord Mayor of London	Isadore Marcil
First Murderer	Tracy Barrow
Second Murderer	Cecil Clovelly
Richmond	Raymond Bloomer
Queen Elizabeth (wife of Edward IV)	Evelyn Walsh Hall
Lady Anne (daughter-in-law to Henry VI)	Helen Robbins

Of the cast members, many later vanished into obscurity, disappearing entirely from the annals of the stage. Some continued their careers as journeymen; a few achieved distinction.

Arthur Row (1878–1961) continued to act, mainly in small parts, until the late 1950s. He appeared in Orson Welles's 1937 *Julius Caesar,* the national touring company of *A Streetcar Named Desire,* and the Broadway production of *Inherit the Wind.* In 1955 he published a biography of Sarah Bernhardt, *Sarah the Divine;* he had been Bernhardt's press agent during one of her last American tours.

The Queen Margaret, Rosalind Ivan (1881–1959) was born in England; she played Nerissa to the Shylock of Henry Irving and the Portia of Ellen Terry during their 1901–2 American tour and subsequent Lyceum season. By 1920 she was an established veteran; she enjoyed a long stage career and later achieved distinction in a number of films, including *The Suspect, The Corn Is Green,* and *Johnny Belinda.*

Burford Hampden (b. 1899; fl. 1911–35), who played Edward, Prince of Wales, was also a native of England. He began his career as a child, appearing as Puck in Herbert Tree's 1911 revival of *A Midsummer Night's Dream,* and made his Broadway debut later that year in *The Blue Bird.* In 1921 he appeared as Donalbain in the Hopkins–Jones–Lionel Barrymore *Macbeth.* He remained active in the American theatre until the mid-1930s.

Marshall Vincent, the Duke of York (fl. 1915–28), was born in England, began his career there, and made his New York debut in 1915 in *Sherlock Holmes.* He later became a Broadway journeyman, appearing steadily until 1928.

The anachronistically billed Mrs. Thomas Wise (fl. 1894–1929), who played the Duchess of York, was, in fact, Gertrude Whitty, the sister of May Whitty, and had known Barrymore since his childhood. She married Barrymore's friend and costar in *Uncle Sam,* Thomas A. Wise, and enjoyed a long career in America and England, mainly in comedy.

Reginald Denny (1891–1967), who played King Edward IV, was also English-born; he later achieved distinction in Hollywood, appearing in more than eighty films. He played Benvolio to Barrymore's Mercutio in the 1936 MGM film of *Romeo and Juliet* and also appeared with Barrymore in *Sherlock Holmes*, the 1933 screen test for *Hamlet*, and three films in the *Bulldog Drummond* series.

The Clarence, E. J. Ballantine (c. 1878–1968) and the Second Murderer, Cecil Clovelly (c. 1890–1965) were Hopkins regulars. Ballantine, who trained at Herbert Tree's Academy of Dramatic Art, appeared in *Redemption* and *The Jest;* he later played Malcolm in the Hopkins *Macbeth* and Marcellus in the Barrymore–Hopkins–Jones *Hamlet*. Clovelly acted with Barrymore in *Justice, Peter Ibbetson,* and *The Jest* and appeared as the Second Gravedigger in *Hamlet*.

The Irish-born Lewis Sealy (1850–1931), who played Lord Hastings, was a versatile character actor with numerous credits in London and New York. So too was the English-born Stanley Warmington (1884–1941), who doubled Lord Clifford and Sir William Catesby; his credits included a year with Tree at His Majesty's, a Barker–Vedrenne season at the Court, and Lewis Waller's production of *Henry V.*

Walter Ringham (fl. 1906–27), who played the Earl of Warwick, and Montague Rutherford (1877–1927), who doubled as Cardinal Bourchier and Sir Richard Ratcliff, were English-born veterans of the Forbes-Robertson company and appeared with the actor for several seasons in *Hamlet, Othello,* and *The Merchant of Venice*. Rutherford appeared as Rosencrantz and the Priest in Forbes-Robertson's 1913 film of *Hamlet*.

John M. Troughton (fl. 1920–35), who played Tyrell, made his Broadway debut in *Richard III*. He made a number of subsequent Broadway appearances, usually in light comedy.

Tracy Barrow (1865–1935), the First Murderer, was an English-born character actor who came to America in 1907 to appear in *The New York Idea* and later became a mainstay of Mrs. Fiske's company.

William J. Keighley (1889–1984), who doubled Lord Rivers and Sir William Brackenbury, was born in Philadelphia; at 16 he joined Ben Greet's American touring company, appearing in ten Shakespeare plays. He later became a Broadway journeyman; his appearances included Paris to Ethel Barrymore's Juliet. In the mid-1920s he turned to directing with fortuitous results. After nearly a decade of directing stage productions in New York, London, and Los Angeles, he became a prolific and highly successful motion picture director. He directed more than thirty films between 1933 and 1953, mostly for Warner Brothers, including *The Prince and the Pauper, The Fighting 69th,* and *The Man Who Came to Dinner.*

The Buckingham, Leslie Palmer (fl. 1903–32) turned to acting after fifteen years in the British navy. During the 1903–4 and 1904–5 seasons he was a member of Sir Henry Irving's company; he later joined John Martin-Harvey's company. His first Broadway appearance came in 1913, his last in 1929; he appeared in several films in the early 1930s.

Raymond Bloomer (fl. 1911–27), who played Richmond, made his Broadway debut in 1911; a year after *Richard III* he played Macduff to Lionel Barrymore's Macbeth and later appeared in several silent films, the last of which appeared in 1927.

Evelyn Walsh Hall, the Queen Elizabeth (fl. 1912–32), was born in England and appeared in several London productions between 1912 and 1919. She made her Broadway debut in *Richard III*, made a few more Broadway appearances during the 1920s, and acted in a number of films between 1927 and 1932.

Helen Robbins, the Lady Anne (fl. 1918–24), was a young actress whose prior experience consisted mainly of a series of productions in 1918 and 1919 with the Greenwich Village Players, a "little theatre" group. She played Lady Macduff in Hopkins's production of *Macbeth*. Ellean in Ethel Barrymore's 1924 revival of *The Second Mrs. Tanqueray* was her last Broadway appearance.

Isadore Marcil, the Lord Mayor (fl. 1913–33) was a journeyman who appeared in a dozen Broadway plays over the course of two decades; Malcolm Barrett (fl. 1920–6), who played Sir James Blount, later appeared in Hopkins's 1926 revival of *The Jest;* Denis Auburn, the Lord Grey (fl. 1920–3), appeared with Sothern and Marlowe in their 1923 *Cymbeline;* Robert Whitehouse (fl. 1919–20), who doubled as Norfolk and Westmoreland, made his second and final Broadway appearance in *Richard III;* the production marked the only Broadway appearance of George De Winter, who played the Earl of Derby.

Notable among the three children in the production was Helen Chandler (1909–65), who played one of the little princes. She made her debut in Hopkins's 1918 production of *Penrod,* appeared as "The Boy" in the Hopkins *Macbeth,* and in 1925 played Ophelia opposite Basil Sydney's Hamlet in the New York modern-dress production. She subsequently enjoyed a distinguished career on Broadway and in Hollywood. In 1934 she appeared with Barrymore in the film version of *Long Lost Father.* Lois Bartlett (fl. 1917–21) had appeared with Barrymore two years earlier in *Redemption;* Mary Hughes (fl. 1920–1) later appeared in the Hopkins–Jones–Lionel Barrymore *Macbeth.*

There were two stage managers. The first was William Seymour (1855–1933), who began his career as a callboy at Booth's theatre, appeared as the Actress in Booth's 1870 production of *Hamlet,* and later became a noted stage manager (serving a long tour of duty with Charles Frohman) and director. He became ill during rehearsals and was replaced by Arthur Hurley (c. 1876–1941), a Hopkins veteran who had stage-managed *The Jest* and later directed film shorts for Warners and Fox and several plays on Broadway.

II. *Hamlet:* 16 November 1922 – 9 February 1923

The opening-night cast was as follows:

Francisco	John Clark
Bernardo	Lark Taylor
Horatio	Frederick Lewis
Marcellus	E. J. Ballantine
Ghost of Hamlet's Father	Reginald Pole

Hamlet	John Barrymore
Claudius	Tyrone Power
Gertrude	Blanche Yurka
Polonius	John S. O'Brien
Laertes	Sidney Mather
Ophelia	Rosalinde Fuller
Rosencrantz	Paul Huber
Guildenstern	Lawrence Cecil
First Player	Lark Taylor
Player King	Burnel Lundbec
Second Player	Norman Hearn
Player Queen	Richard Skinner
Lucianus	Vadim Uraneff
A Gentlewoman	Stephanie D'Este
King's Messenger	Frank Boyd
First Gravedigger	Whitford Kane
Second Gravedigger	Cecil Clovelly
A Priest	Reginald Pole
Osric	Edgar Stehli
Fortinbras	Lowden Adams

The Francisco, John Clark, and the King's Messenger, Frank Boyd, were in fact both Boyd Clarke (c. 1895–1957), who doubled as Francisco (as John Boyd) and Rosencrantz during the second season and tour. Clarke (or Clark, as he sometimes spelled it) was born in Rochester, New York, and joined Forbes-Robertson's touring company as a young man. He made his Broadway debut in *The Weavers* in 1915; the following year he appeared in the tercentenary production of *The Tempest*. After service in World War I he joined the Sothern and Marlowe company for their 1919–20 comeback season, playing Guildenstern, Valentine in *Twelfth Night*, and a servant to Petruchio. His last Broadway appearance came in 1925; he later returned to Rochester, where he was active in community theatre.

Lark Taylor (1881–1946), who played Bernardo, the First Player, and Fortinbras, made several Broadway appearances after *Hamlet*, the last in 1930; he later made his home in Nashville, where he founded a "little theatre" group and worked as a radio announcer.

Frederick Lewis, the Horatio (1873–1946), made his stage debut in Savannah, Georgia in 1891. He came to New York six years later and in 1903 played Orlando opposite Henrietta Crosman's Rosalind. In the autumn of 1905 he joined the Sothern and Marlowe company, playing Mercutio, Don Pedro, Horatio, and Macduff; he remained with the company (and with Sothern and Marlowe individually) until their 1914 retirement. In 1919 he rejoined the company when Sothern and Marlowe made their comeback; after their final farewell he made a number of Broadway appearances and toured with his own Shakespearean company.

Reginald Pole (fl. 1910–39; d. 1960), who spoke the voice of the Ghost and played the Priest, was the nephew of William Poel and retained the original family spelling of his name. In 1910 he directed his first Shakespeare production at Cambridge in association with the poet Rupert Brooke, with whom he founded the Marlowe Dramatic Society. He subsequently produced and directed a number of Shakespeare, Ibsen, and Greek plays in England. He directed several special matinee performances in New York, including *The Idiot* (1922) and *King Lear* (1923), in which he played the title role. His last Broadway appearance came in 1939 in *The Possessed,* and he later toured the country as a lecturer.

The Claudius, Tyrone Power (1869–1931), was the grandson of the popular nineteenth-century Irish actor and the father of the film actor of the same name. He made his stage debut in Florida in 1886; between 1890 and 1898 he worked principally with Daly's Company in New York, appearing as Frederick in *As You Like It,* Antonio in *Much Ado About Nothing,* and Caliban in *The Tempest.* He appeared with Tree in America and in London, toured with Maurice Barrymore and Mrs. Fiske in *Becky Sharp,* and spent a season as a member of Irving's company. In 1912 he played an acclaimed Brutus in William Faversham's production of *Julius Caesar,* and subsequently mounted his own production in which he played Mark Antony. He reprised his Brutus in the 1918 Shakespeare Playhouse production and made numerous Broadway appearances and several silent films during the 1920s.

Blanche Yurka (1887–1974), who played Gertrude, was born in Bohemia; she was brought to the United States as a child and raised in Minnesota. She came to New York to study singing, worked with David Belasco in several productions, and subsequently made numerous Broadway appearances. During the 1920s she was seen in New York in *Man and the Masses, The Wild Duck, Lysistrata, Hedda Gabler,* and many more. She worked steadily on Broadway for nearly sixty years; her last New York appearance came in the title role of a 1970 revival of *The Madwoman of Chaillot.* Her film performances include a memorable Madame Defarge in *A Tale of Two Cities.*

The Polonius, John S. O'Brien (c. 1885–1923), began his stage career in the early 1900s. He toured with Ben Greet's company, made his Broadway debut in 1915, and the following year appeared with Barrymore in *Justice.* In 1919 he won critical praise for his Seward in John Drinkwater's *Abraham Lincoln.* Suffering from cancer, he committed suicide in June 1923.

Sidney Mather (1876–1925), the Laertes, spent much of his career with the Sothern and Marlowe company. He first appeared with Sothern in 1901 in *If I Were King* and joined Sothern and Marlowe for their initial season three years later. His roles included Laertes, Tybalt, Banquo, and Sebastian in *Twelfth Night.* He toured with Richard Mansfield during the 1905–6 season, appearing in *Richard III;* his last New York appearance was in *Tea for Three,* a vaudeville act, at the Palace in 1925.

The Ophelia, Rosalinde Fuller (1892–1982) was born in England; she began her career as a teenaged singer of British ballads and toured successfully with her sisters in Great Britain and America. In 1919 she returned to the United States to try her luck as an actress and appeared in several musicals. After *Hamlet,* she made a number of Broadway appearances to 1936; she subsequently devoted much of her career to touring with her one-woman show of songs and skits.

Paul Huber (c. 1896–1981), the Rosencrantz, was a native of Wilkes-Barre, Pennsylvania; he graduated from Dartmouth, made his Broadway debut in 1920 with William Powell in *Spanish Love,* and made many subsequent Broadway appearances to 1964.

The Guildenstern, Lawrence Cecil (fl. c. 1895–1932), was born in London; he made his stage debut at age 10 as a page in a revival of George Rignold's *Henry V.* He later joined Frank Benson's company and worked with Tree at His Majesty's. After serving in the First World War he came to America and made his Broadway debut as the Sergeant and the Second Murderer in the 1921 Lionel Barrymore *Macbeth.* He subsequently appeared in a number of Shakespearean roles in New York including Laertes, Macduff, Cassio, and Cassius for the Fritz Leiber Repertory Company.

Frank Norman Hearn Jr. (c. 1907–32), the Second Player, was born in Brighton, England. He was brought to the United States as a child and at the age of 9 appeared in vaudeville; his legitimate stage debut came in 1919 when he played the juvenile in *Wake Up, Jonathan* with Mrs. Fiske. Later Broadway appearances included *The Buccaneer* (1925) and *The Shannons of Broadway* (1928). He died at 24 of a lung infection brought on by tonsillitis.

The Player King, Burnel Lundbec (fl. 1922–5) made his only Broadway appearances in *Hamlet;* he was one of only two members of the New York cast to appear in Barrymore's 1925 London production.

The Player Queen, Richard Skinner (1900–71), was a young Harvard graduate; he made his Broadway debut in *Hamlet.* He later appeared on Broadway in *The Taming of the Shrew* and helped to organize the Jitney Players, a long-lived touring company, in 1925. He subsequently enjoyed a distinguished career as a company manager in summer theatres and on Broadway.

Vadim Uraneff (fl. 1920–39), who played Lucianus, was born in Russia and was at one time assistant stage director of the Imperial Theatre in Petrograd. He made his Broadway debut in *Musk* in 1920, which he also directed, and subsequently acted in and directed a number of productions in New York during the 1920s and 1930s. He later appeared in Barrymore's London production of *Hamlet* and in several silent films, including Barrymore's 1926 *The Sea Beast.*

The First Gravedigger, Whitford Kane (1881–1956), was born in Ireland; he made his debut in Belfast in 1903 and subsequently toured in Shakespearean repertory. His first London appearance came at the Duke of York's as O'Cleary in *Justice* (1910). In 1912 he journeyed to America, where he appeared in more than fifty Broadway productions over the next four decades. He played the First Gravedigger for twenty-three Hamlets (and nearly twice that number of Ophelias), including Walter Hampden and Maurice Evans.

Edgar Stehli (1884–1973), the Osric, was born in France and raised in Zurich. He received Bachelor's and Master's degrees from Cornell. His debut in stock came in 1908; his Broadway debut came eight years later. He worked

steadily on Broadway for fifty years, including stints with the Provincetown
Players and the Theatre Guild. He also worked extensively in radio and television.

The opening-night Fortinbras was Lowden Adams (fl. 1917–32), who had
appeared with Barrymore in *Peter Ibbetson*. Evidence indicates that he was awarded this thirteen-line role in the final scene on short notice; the *New York Herald*
(1 November 1922) announced that Alexander Giglio had been cast in the
part, and it was he who read the role during early rehearsals. Hopkins grew dissatisfied with Adams's reading as well, and Fortinbras was taken over by Lark
Taylor on 18 November 1922, two days after the opening.

The Gentlewoman, Stephanie D'Este, made her only Broadway appearance
in *Hamlet*.

In addition to the speaking roles, twenty extras were employed: six Court
Ladies (one of whom doubled as understudy for Ophelia), and fourteen sol-
dier/attendants, one of whom served as assistant stage manager.

The stage manager, William P. Adams (1887–1972) – a distant cousin of the
actress Maude Adams – graduated from the College of Music in Cincinnati; in
1912 he joined the Sothern and Marlowe company as stage manager, remaining on and off for a decade. He was later a drama coach at Yale, acted in a number of plays on Broadway, including *Damn Yankees*, and served as president of
AFTRA.

The incidental music was composed by Robert Russell Bennett (1894–
1981), who went on to enjoy a distinguished career as a symphonic composer
and Broadway arranger. He orchestrated many of George Gershwin's symphonic compositions and more than two hundred Broadway scores, including
those for *Showboat* and *Oklahoma!* His score was conducted by Maurice Nitke (fl.
1917–27), a Warsaw-born violinist and composer who also provided music for
Peter Ibbetson, *Redemption*, and *The Jest*.

IIa: Hamlet Salary List and Expenses

On 7 July 1928, George Schaff, at Barrymore's request, sent the actor a list of
cast salaries and expenses for the 1922–3 New York production of *Hamlet*,
which Barrymore intended to use to estimate expenses in connection with his
planned production of *Hamlet* in the Hollywood Bowl. I have corrected
Schaff's occasional misspellings and incorrect or incomplete assignment of
roles. One note of explanation is appropriate: Barrymore, in addition to his
salary, received half the profits of the production, as had been his arrangement with Hopkins since *Redemption*. The cast salaries and other production
expenses for the 1922–3 season were as follows:

John Barrymore	$1,000	
John Clark	40	Francisco, Messenger
Lark Taylor	200	Bernardo, 1st Player, Fortinbras
Frederick Lewis	200	Horatio
E. J. Ballantine	125	Marcellus
Reginald Pole	200	Ghost, Priest

Tyrone Power	635	King
Blanche Yurka	300	Queen
John O'Brien	150	Polonius
Sidney Mather	300	Laertes
Rosalinde Fuller	175	Ophelia
Paul Huber	125	Rosencrantz
Lawrence Cecil	100	Guildenstern
Burnel Lundbec	60	Mime Player King
Frank Hearn	60	Second Player
Richard Skinner	60	Mime Player Queen
Vadim Uraneff	75	Gonzago
Whitford Kane	150	Gravedigger
Cecil Clovelly	75	2nd Gravedigger
Edgar Stehli	150	Osric
Stephanie D'Este	30	Gentlewoman and Court Lady
Miss [Alice] Keating	40	Court Lady and Understudy
5 Court Ladies	130	
Mr. Smithborne	45	Extra Man and Assistant Stage Manager
13 Extra Men @ 20	260	
C. Lebrecht	67	Assistant Electrician
Mrs. [Lulu] Fralick	50	Wardrobe Mistress
William Adams	125	Stage Manager
Robert Russell Bennett	50	Composed Music
John Milton	50	Understudy
Manager	140	
Agent	150	
	5,317	

First Week Statement – *Hamlet*

Railroad Fares	480
Advertising (Newspapers)	300
Hauling	300
Lamp Operator	48
Props	40
Telegrams & Postage	10
Agent's Expense Account	25
Printing (Heralds and Lithographs)	75
Salaries (as per attached itemized list)	5,317
Crew	315
Musicians	830
	7,740

Extra expenses, impossible to estimate, as follows: stagehands, musicians, electric current and other expenses.

IIb. Hamlet Second Season and Tour: 26 November 1923 –
26 January 1924

Second season cast changes were as follows:

Boyd Clarke, who doubled Francisco and the King's Messenger during the first season, replaced Paul Huber as Rosencrantz; he retained the role of Francisco, billing himself this time as John Boyd.

John Connery (c. 1876–1950), the Marcellus, was a veteran of the Robert B. Mantell company and had appeared in Mantell's *Richard III* when he returned to New York in 1904. He played Seyton in James K. Hackett's 1924 *Macbeth;* his last New York appearance came in 1933.

J. Colvil Dunn (fl. 1919–45), the Horatio, had been a member of the Sothern and Marlowe company for their 1919–20 comeback season; in 1924 he appeared with Ethel Barrymore in *The Second Mrs. Tanqueray.* He acted on Broadway in fourteen plays in all; his last appearance came in 1945 in *The Hasty Heart.*

Kenneth Hunter (1882–1961), who took over the role of the King, was born in South Africa; he made his Broadway debut in 1911 and a year later appeared in William Faversham's production of *Julius Caesar.* In 1922 he acted in the Hopkins–Jones–Ethel Barrymore *Romeo and Juliet;* he later played Gratiano and Claudius in *The Merchant of Venice* and *Hamlet* with Ethel Barrymore and Walter Hampden. He appeared in a number of films between 1938 and 1942, including *The Adventures of Robin Hood* and *The Moon and Sixpence.*

Several actors were tried for Polonius, a change necessitated by John S. O'Brien's suicide. The role was eventually awarded to the Edinburgh-born veteran Moffatt Johnston (1886–1935), who had appeared in numerous productions for the Theatre Guild, including *R.U.R., Back to Methusaleh,* and *The Devil's Disciple.* In 1924 he played Macduff to Hackett's *Macbeth.*

Russell Morrison (c. 1884–1956), the Second Gravedigger, made his Broadway debut in 1916 in Hopkins's production of *The Happy Ending;* he made more than two dozen Broadway appearances during his career, including the 1923 American premiere of *Six Characters in Search of an Author* and the 1955 revival.

The role of the King's Messenger was assumed by H. Charlson Smith (fl. 1919–24), who had appeared in *The Jest.* The other new members of the cast were Jose Ruiz (Mime Player Queen) and Winifred Salisbury (A Gentlewoman); their only Broadway appearances came in Barrymore's 1923–4 *Hamlet.*

III. The Cast of the London *Hamlet:* 19 February 1925 –
18 April 1925

The cast of the London *Hamlet* was as follows:

Claudius	Malcolm Keen
Hamlet	John Barrymore
Polonius	Herbert Waring
Horatio	George Relph

Laertes	Ian Fleming
Rosencrantz	Jevan Brandon-Thomas
Guildenstern	Michael Hogan
Osric	Frederick Cooper
A Priest	Harding Steerman
A Messenger	Stanley Roberts
A Gentleman	Edmund Gordon
Bernardo	Roy Travers
Marcellus	John Michael
Francisco	A. G. Poulton
Player King	E. Harcourt Williams
Player Queen	Arnold Bowen
[Mime] Player King	Burnel Lundbec
[Mime] Player Queen	Byam Shaw
The Poisoner	Vadim Uraneff
First Gravedigger	Ben Field
Second Gravedigger	Michael Martin-Harvey
Fortinbras	Shayle Gardner
Ghost	Courtenay Thorpe
Gertrude	Constance Collier
Ophelia	Fay Compton
Gentlewoman	Peggy Webster

The Claudius, Malcolm Keen (1887–1970), made his first stage appearance in 1902, walking on at His Majesty's in Herbert Tree's production of *Ulysses;* he subsequently achieved distinction in numerous West End and Broadway performances and also appeared in many films. He reprised his Claudius in the West End in 1930 and 1931 and appeared in the same role in John Gielgud's 1936 New York *Hamlet,* in which he also read the lines of the Ghost.

Herbert Waring, the Polonius (1857–1932), made his stage debut in 1877; between 1883 and 1888 he was a member of the Hare and Kendall company at the St. James's, after which he toured a season in America as Mary Anderson's leading man. The following year he played Torvald in the first English production of *A Doll's House.* He later played Iago to Forbes-Robertson's Othello and worked steadily in the West End until 1928.

Horatio was played by George Relph (1888–1960), who made his first appearance on the London stage in 1909. He enjoyed a distinguished career in classical and commercial drama and later played Clarence and Buckingham opposite Laurence Olivier's Richard III. He also appeared with Olivier in *Peer Gynt, Oedipus Rex,* and *The Critic.*

The opening-night Laertes was Ian Fleming (1888–1969), who was born in Australia; he made his provincial debut in 1904 and his London debut eleven years later. He made several dozen post-*Hamlet* appearances in the West End, mainly in comedy and melodrama. He was replaced during the run by Nigel Clarke (1895–1976), who made his debut in 1920 with Frank Benson's company, remaining for four years; he later became a mainstay of Donald Wolfit's company, where he appeared in a number of Shakespearean roles.

Jevan Brandon-Thomas, the Rosencrantz (1898–1977), was the son of the playwright Brandon Thomas. After service in the First World War he made his debut as Jack Chesney in *Charley's Aunt*. He later toured with Ben Greet's company, ran repertory companies at Edinburgh and Glasgow, and made a number of West End appearances.

Michael Hogan (b. 1898; fl. 1914–68), who doubled as Guildenstern and Marcellus, billing himself in the latter role as John Michael, trained at the Royal Academy of Dramatic Art. He made his debut in 1914, walking on in *A Midsummer Night's Dream*, and subsequently worked steadily in the West End, on Broadway, in films, and on the radio for more than fifty years.

The Osric, Frederick Cooper (1890–1945), made his stage debut in 1910; he appeared numerous times in the West End and on tour to 1935. He was featured in more than half a dozen Shaw revivals and created the role of Mr. Prior in *Outward Bound*.

Harding Steerman (fl. 1908–36), who played the Priest, was a journeyman who worked steadily as an actor and stage manager for nearly thirty years.

Stanley Roberts, the King's Messenger (fl. 1906–25), worked mainly in the provinces; he made three West End appearances, the last of which came in *Hamlet*.

Edmund Gordon, the Gentleman (fl. 1924–9), made a total of eight West End appearances in the mid-to-late 1920s, mainly in light comedy.

Roy Travers, the Bernardo (fl. 1924–7), made his stage debut as a child in *The Blue Bird* in 1909; he made five West End appearances during the mid-1920s.

Francisco was played by A. G. Poulton (b. 1867; fl. 1893–1932), a veteran actor who had appeared as Launce and Mr. Burgess, respectively, in Barker's 1904 productions of *Two Gentlemen of Verona* and *Candida* at the Court; he worked steadily in London until the early 1930s.

E. Harcourt Williams, the Player King (1880–1957) made his debut in Belfast in 1898 with Frank Benson's company, with whom he remained for five years. In 1911 and 1912 he appeared in the West End premieres of Shaw's *Fanny's First Play* and Barker's *The Voysey Inheritance*. Between 1929 and 1934 he was director of the Old Vic, where he produced and directed more than fifty productions. He later appeared with John Gielgud in *Richard II* and the Casson–Barker *King Lear*, and with Laurence Olivier in the stage and film versions of *Richard III* and the film of *Henry V*.

Arnold Bowen, the Second Player, made his only West End appearance in *Hamlet*.

The Mime Player Queen, billed as "Byam Shaw," was in all likelihood Glen Byam Shaw (1904–86), the son of the noted painter J. Byam Shaw. Although mysteriously he did not list *Hamlet* among his credits in *Who's Who* entries, no other actor of that name was active in London at the time. After a provincial apprenticeship he made his West End debut in *Hamlet;* four months later he appeared in *The Cherry Orchard* at the Lyric, Hammersmith. He continued to act through the early 1940s, appearing as Laertes in John Gielgud's 1934 *Hamlet*, Benvolio in the Olivier–Gielgud *Romeo and Juliet*, and Horatio in Gielgud's 1939 *Hamlet*. After service in the Second World War he turned to directing, serving as codirector (and later director) at the Shakespeare Memorial Theatre at Stratford-upon-Avon, where his productions included Olivier's *Macbeth*, Michael Redgrave's *Hamlet*, and Charles Laughton's *King Lear*. He later directed in the West End and served as director of Sadler's Wells and the English Opera.

Ben Field, the First Gravedigger (c. 1878–1939), made his debut in 1897. In 1905 he supported Tree in *An Enemy of the People* at His Majesty's, and he later appeared with Tree in revivals of *The Merchant of Venice*, *Twelfth Night*, and *Julius Caesar*. His last West End appearance came in 1934 when he reprised his First Gravedigger to John Gielgud's Hamlet at the New Theatre.

The Second Gravedigger, Michael Martin-Harvey (fl. 1925–54; d. 1975), was the son of Sir John Martin-Harvey. He appeared in several West End productions during the mid-1920s and made eleven film appearances between 1924 and 1954, usually in eccentric character parts.

The Fortinbras, Shayle Gardner (1890–1945), was born in New Zealand; he studied for the stage at the Royal Academy of Dramatic Art and made his debut at His Majesty's in 1913 in *Joseph and His Brethren*. He worked steadily for the next thirty years, mainly in the West End; in 1924 he created the part of Robert de Beaudricourt in Shaw's *Saint Joan*.

The Ghost was played by Courtenay Thorpe (fl. 1885–1926). As a young man he went to America, where he established himself as a matinee idol and appeared in several Ibsen plays. He later returned to England; during the mid-1890s he appeared in several British Ibsen premieres with the Independent Theatre. In 1897 his Ghost in the Independent Theatre production of *Hamlet* was praised by Bernard Shaw; five years later he joined Forbes-Robertson's company to play the same role. His last West End appearance came in 1926 when he reprised his Ghost opposite Russell Thorndike's *Hamlet*.

Constance Collier, the Gertrude (1878–1955), made her debut at the age of 3 as Peaseblossom in a revival of *A Midsummer Night's Dream*. As a teenager she became one of the Gaiety Girls; in 1901 she was engaged by Beerbohm Tree for His Majesty's and remained under his management for six years. In 1916 she appeared with both Tree and Thomas A. Wise in New York tercentenary productions of *The Merry Wives of Windsor*; the following year she costarred with Barrymore in *Peter Ibbetson*. She remained active on the stage until the early 1940s and also appeared in many films, including *Dinner at Eight* and *Stage Door*.

The Ophelia, Fay Compton (1894–1978), was born into a distinguished theatrical family. She made her first stage appearance in 1911 in *The Follies;* her 1920 performance in *Mary Rose* was critically acclaimed. For nearly half a century thereafter she worked steadily in the West End, at the Old Vic, and on Broadway. In 1939 she appeared as Ophelia opposite John Gielgud's Hamlet. The following year she played Regan in the Casson–Barker *King Lear*, and she later played Gertrude to Richard Burton's Hamlet at the Old Vic. Her film performances include a memorable Emilia in Orson Welles's *Othello*.

Margaret Webster (1905–72), the Gentlewoman, went on to enjoy a distinguished career as an actress-director. She made numerous appearances in the West End and played a wide variety of Shakespearean roles at the Old Vic during the 1929–30 season. Her many credits as a director include American productions of *Richard II* and *Hamlet* with Maurice Evans and Paul Robeson's 1943 *Othello*, in which she also played Emilia.

Notable among the Court Ladies is Alison Leggatt (1904–90), who also understudied Ophelia. She won the gold medal at Elsie Fogerty's Central School of Speech Training and Dramatic Art in 1924 and made her West End debut later that year. She worked steadily on the stage and in films for the next fifty years, creating roles in Noel Coward's *Cavalcade* and *Tonight at 8:30* and John Osborne's *Epitaph for George Dillon*.

The Texts

I: The Text of *Richard III*

The acting text for *Richard III* underwent numerous drafts, revisions, and alterations between the summer of 1919 and the first full week of performances. No copy of the opening-night text or subsequent alterations is known to survive. Edward Sheldon's draft promptbook in the Harvard Theatre Collection represents an early version of the text and probably dates from the fall or early winter of 1919; later documentation of the performance version reveals that much of its structure remained intact. The arrangement of the scenes was as follows:

ACT I

Scene i. London. The Parliament House. [From *3 Henry VI*, I.i]
Scene ii. York's Castle. [I.ii; concluding with Richard's soliloquy from III.ii]
Scene iii. The same. [II.i]
Scene iv. Field of Battle. [A hybrid scene, arranged from V.ii, II.iii, II.iv, II.v, IV.vi, IV.viii, V.v, and II.vi]

ACT II

Scene i. London. A cell in the Tower. [*3 Henry VI*, V.vi]
Scene ii. Before the Tower. [*Richard III*, I.i and I.ii]
Scene iii. The palace. [I.iii]
Scene iv. The same. [II.i and II.ii]

ACT III

Scene i. Before the Tower. [III.i]
Scene ii. The Palace. [III.vii]
Scene iii. Before the Tower. [IV.i]
Scene iv. Parliament House. [IV.ii and IV.iii]

ACT IV

Scene i. Before the Tower. [IV. iv]
Scene ii. Bosworth Field. [from V.iii]

Scene iii. Richard's Camp. [from V.iii]
Scene iv. The battlefield. [V.iv and V.v]

Review evidence indicates that there were numerous changes in the text before opening night. There were two notable structural alterations. The first was the rearrangement of the text into a three-act version, with the order of scenes, taken from the opening-night program, as follows:

ACT I

Scene i.   Throne Room.
Scene ii.   York's Castle.
Scene iii. The same.
Scene iv.   Tewkesberry [*sic*].
Scene v.   A cell in the Tower of London.
Scene vi.   Outside the Tower.

ACT II

Scene i.   Throne Room.
Scene ii.   A cell in the Tower.
Scene iii. Throne Room.
Scene iv.   Outside the Tower.
Scene v.   The same.

ACT III

Scene i.   Throne Room.
Scene ii.   Outside the Tower.
Scene iii. Richmond's Camp.
Scene iv.   Richard's Tent.
Scene v.   Bosworth.

The opening-night version contained the addition of one major scene: the murder of Clarence, omitted in the draft promptbook (*Richard III,* I.iv; II.ii in the Sheldon adaptation). In all likelihood there was one scene deleted as well: the brief scene with Queen Elizabeth, the Duchess of York, and Lady Anne (Shakespeare's IV.i; III.iii in the Sheldon draft), where Elizabeth attempts to visit her young sons and Anne laments that she must go to be crowned as Richard's queen. There is evidence that suggests this was the case. To be included, it would had to have come either at the end of Act II or the beginning of Act III. Barrymore's grasping of an imaginary scepter at the close of Sheldon's II.v was in all probability the signal for the act curtain. An anonymous editorial in the *Globe* (8 March 1920), moreover, listed this scene as having been deleted. This brief commentary (possibly the work of Kenneth Macgowan), noted that the scenes omitted from *Richard III* were "if memory holds, scenes 3 and 4 from Act II, scenes 2, 3, 4, 5, and 6 from Act III, scenes 1 and 5 from Act IV, and scenes 1 and 2 from Act V." This account is otherwise correct, suggesting that the scene was indeed deleted.

Discrepancies between the draft promptbook and the opening-night text can in many cases be reconciled through the frequent citation of scenes and passages from the play in reviews of the production. The scene of Clarence's murder, omitted in the draft, is mentioned frequently, for example, as is the inclusion of "Now is the winter of our discontent," similarly absent in the draft, but referred to in numerous critical sources. The review in the 8 March 1920 *Evening Telegram* attests to the fact that among the additions to the soliloquy from *3 Henry VI*, III.ii were the lines where "Richard compares himself favorably with Nestor, Ulysses, Sinon, 'Proteus for advantages' and 'the murderous Machiavel,'" omitted in the draft.

There are numerous inconsistencies. The most complete description of the six scenes from *3 Henry VI* was published in the 8 March 1920 *Journal of Commerce*. This account states: "The first [scene] shows the agreement between Henry and the Duke of York that the latter shall succeed Henry on the throne. Then Richard induces his father, the Duke, to break his oath to wait for Henry's death. Queen Margaret and her son refuse to abide by Henry's weak surrender. Tewkesbury follows, when Richard stabs the Prince of Wales and is created Duke of Gloucester, and then a scene in the Tower when Gloucester murders the aged Henry VI." This, however, is misleading in a sense: Arthur Row's account mentions specifically that his business with Margaret and his son came "at the end of my first scene." The third scene on opening night (later deleted) may have differed from the version in the draft, but probably centered on Richard (the 8 March 1920 *Sun* notes that he welcomes the news of his father's death, as in the Sheldon promptbook) and featured an account, rather than a depiction, of Margaret and the Prince of Wales. The fourth scene, at Tewkesbury, may not have included all of the material from Sheldon's draft, yet the review evidence (for example, the 8 March *Journal of Commerce*) indicates that much of this was retained.

Lesser inconsistencies include the fact that the draft promptbook (and Barrymore's subsequent recordings) begin Richard's first soliloquy "Would they were wasted" rather than "Would he" as in Shakespeare's version; Burns Mantle, in the 9 March *Evening Mail*, mentions the use of the "little known but helpful soliloquy beginning 'Would he (Edward IV) were wasted, marrow, bones and all . . .'" He may have been referring to a published edition of the play, however; the review in the *Sun* implies that the order of events in Sheldon's draft was retained, and that this soliloquy came in the second scene when Edward was still Earl of March. Mantle concludes the line "the golden time I hope for," whereas both the promptbook and published text conclude "look for." Similarly, Louis V. De Foe, in the 14 March 1920 *World*, commented that "The splendor of the episodes of the court reaches its climax in the second act when Richard, seated beside Queen Anne, is revealed at the summit of his evil career." In all likelihood, this is either an error or reflects a shifting of this scene from the third to the second act after opening night; the 10 March *New York Clipper* notes that "The pageantry of the performance . . . reached its height in the throne room of Richard seated with Anne at his side." The opening-night program lists the two final scenes of the second act (Richard's exchange with the little princes and the proffer of the crown) as taking place "Outside the Tower." The third act begins in the throne room; this scene, in the draft, begins with the coronation.

The extensive cuts made after the four-hour opening-night performance were mentioned in the 9 March 1920 *New York Times* and other newspapers. Most of these, with the exception of the elimination of the third scene, at York's Castle, are not now recoverable.

II: The Text of *Hamlet*

The following are the cuts to the performance text for the Barrymore–Hopkins–Jones *Hamlet;* all line numberings refer to the 1919 Temple edition.

ACT I

The text of I.i:

The cuts were lines 60–63; 70–127a (the story of Fortinbras and the Norwegian war and Horatio's lines following the ghost's reentry); 133–146; and 149b–157 (the legend of the cock crow). Lines 127b–132 (Horatio's lines after the reentry of the ghost) were transposed to after 51 (the Ghost's first "exit").

The text of I.ii:

The cuts to this scene are traditional and come mainly from the King's lines. They are lines 17–41 (the King's discussion of Fortinbras and the dispatching of Voltimand and Cornelius); 46–49a (part of the King's address to Laertes); 81 (Hamlet's line about the "dejected havior of the visage"); and 95–106a (part of the King's admonition to Hamlet to avoid excessive mourning). Lines 11–13 of the King's opening speech were cut in rehearsal but restored prior to the opening. Line 81 is not cut in Barrymore's studybook, as it is in Adams and Taylor; given his general carelessness with the cuts, their word is more reliable. Adams notes an extra "your loves" in line 254.

The text of I.iii:

Lines 10–14a, 15–18, 23–28, and 36–44 were cut from Laertes's advice to Ophelia. A notable retention, however, was his warning of the loss of honor if "your chaste treasure open/ To his unmaster'd importunity" (31–32), which was cut by Hampden, Sothern, and Forbes-Robertson for the sake of propriety. The remainder of the cuts were as follows: 73–74, 94–97, 103–109, 115b–123a, and 127b–131a. Two lines were cut from Polonius's advice to Laertes, and the rest, with the exception of Ophelia's rejoinder to her father (103), were deleted from his wordy lecturing to his daughter.

The text of I.iv:

The ghost scenes were played continuously, and are grouped as one scene in Adams's promptbook. Cut in I.iv were 21–38a (Hamlet's lengthy discourse on

Danish drinking habits); 58–62; 73 and 74b–78a (the latter part of Horatio's warning to Hamlet). In I.v the deletions, taken entirely from the Ghost's speeches, were 27a and 28b; 32–34a ("Lethe wharf"); 47–54 ("O Hamlet, what a falling off was there"); 64b–73 (the description of the working of the poison); and 77–78. Notable among the retentions was the Ghost's "So lust, though to a radiant angel link'd,/ Will sate itself in a celestial bed" (55–56). Retained as well were the mildly disrespectful epithets with which Hamlet addresses the Ghost ("old mole," etc.), which were cut in many nineteenth-century productions.

The text of I.v:

The entire Polonius–Reynaldo scene (1–73a) was deleted. Lines 105–106, 114–117a, and 118–120 were cut from Polonius's exchange with Ophelia. Her full description of Hamlet "with his doublet all unbraced,/ No hat upon his head, his stockings foul'd" (ll. 78–79) was retained.

The text of I.vi:

Approximately one-third of this lengthy scene was deleted. The cuts were 11–14 (the King's address to Rosencrantz and Guildenstern); 21b–26a (the Queen's address to Rosencrantz and Guildenstern); 36b–37, 40–43a, 51–55, and 58–104 (the Norwegian subplot, Voltimand and Cornelius, and Polonius's "Brevity is the soul of wit" speech); 129b–139 (Polonius's "And" at the beginning of line 140 was changed to "To"); 157–159a; 164b–167a; 263–277 (Hamlet, Rosencrantz, and Guildenstern's discussion of dreams); 297b–298; 333b–385 (the Players' background); 388b–393a; 402–404; 433–439; 440b–441; 461b–467a; 470b–489 (Hamlet's recitation of "The rugged Pyrrhus"); 505b–519 (the end of the First Player's speech); 533–535; 549b–551; 557b–558a; 571b–575. Lines 428 and 429 were inverted. An extra "The play!" was added to line 633.

There is some confusion surrounding the "rogue and peasant slave" soliloquy. Taylor 2 (his rehearsal studybook) makes no cuts whatsoever. The Adams typescript does not include lines 591–592 ("Confound the ignorant, and amaze indeed/ The very faculties of eyes and ears") and 601a ("Tweaks me by the nose?"). These lines may have been deleted by Barrymore late in the first season and were probably later restored. Taylor 4 (his overall record) deletes line 600, "Plucks off my beard and blows it in my face?" and changes "whore" to "bawd" in line 614. Compounding matters, Taylor 1 makes no deletions, nor does the Barrymore studybook; Taylor 2 deletes line 600 but leaves "whore." The "beard" line may have been a second-season deletion. The replacement of "whore" with "bawd," not noted elsewhere, may have been made for the 1923–4 road tour. Certainly this was unnecessary in New York. Among the notable retentions in this scene was the bawdy "secret parts of fortune" exchange, traditionally cut for reasons of propriety in nineteenth- and early-twentieth-century productions. Forbes-Robertson excluded it, as did Hampden and Sothern in their 1919–20 promptbooks.

ACT II

The text of II.i:

The cuts were as follows: two and a half lines of Hamlet's soliloquy (72b–74; "the law's delay,/ The insolence of office, and the spurns/ That patient merit of the unworthy takes"); and the King's lines 179–183a. The King's lines 33–37a were originally cut but were restored during the first season.

The text of II.ii:

The play scene was subject to a number of textual revisions during the first season and the second season and tour. The opening-night cuts were as follows: 9b–16 and 32b–50a (from Hamlet's advice to the Players; here given to the First Player only, of course); 65–67 and 73b–76a from Hamlet's speech to Horatio; 122–128 (the bawdy "country matters" exchange with Ophelia); 141a–145 ("the hobby-horse is forgot"); the entire dumb show; 146–158; 167–168, 173–178, 185–186, 192–193 and 200–223 from the speeches of the First and Second Players; 256–265 (Hamlet's "I could interpret between you and your love," his bawdy reference to "a groaning to take off my edge," and his command to Lucianus to begin); 288 (from Hamlet's postplay speech to Horatio); 302–389 (the recorder scene) and 405b ("Leave me, friends"); and 411–417 (from the "witching time of night" soliloquy). The two lines of Hamlet and Horatio's farewell at the end of the scene were interpolated.

The recorder scene was restored briefly at the end of the first season and for opening night of the second and is discussed in the section following II.ii, as is Barrymore's restoration of "I could interpret between you and your love" and Hamlet's "Begin, murderer" command to Lucianus.

The promptbooks contain a number of discrepancies. Adams's typescript does not include lines 282–296. The "stricken deer" verse is inserted separately in pen but the ensuing lines are not included. Taylor 3 cuts only the "fellowship in a cry of players" line. Taylor 4 leaves "with two provincial roses on my razed shoes" in; it is cut elsewhere in Taylor. Hamlet's final speech in this scene is given in several different versions. Taylor 1, 2, and 4 end the scene on line 410: "Soft! now to my mother"; 411–417 are cut. Taylor 3 (second season) includes 413–415. Adams has Hamlet begin the speech on line 410, concluding with 411 and 413–415. Taylor 2 probably represents the opening-night version; Adams probably represents the speech as it stood at the end of the first season. The discrepancies make it likely that this speech had cuts and stets during the run as well.

The text of II.iii:

The King–Rosencrantz exchange, Polonius's news that Hamlet is going to his mother's closet, and his subsequent pledge to hide behind the arras (1–35) were cut. 46b–51a and 57–64a were cut from the King's speech of repentance. 91–92 and 96 were cut from Hamlet's speech over the King at prayer.

The text of II.iv:

The cuts were as follows: 6 (Hamlet's offstage calling to his mother); 32b–33; 45b–51a; 71b–76a; 78–81; 85b–88a; 107–108 and 114 (from the Hamlet–Ghost exchange); 117–124a (from the Queen's comments during the visitation); 126–130; 142b–144a and 147–155 (from Hamlet's "ecstasy" speech); 161–165a; 173b–175 (Hamlet's comment that heaven is punishing him with the death of Polonius); 179; 181–199 (Hamlet's sarcastic speech to the Queen in which he tells her not to follow his advice); 204a–205b. A notable retention was 91b–94a, although the lines were spoken while in the throes of the "ghostly possession." Hampden and Sothern, for example, retained only half this passage, cutting "Stew'd in corruption, honeying and making love/ Over the nasty sty." Sothern altered the sexually explicit "enseamed" in the preceding line to "incestuous." Forbes-Robertson omitted this passage entirely.

The text of III.i:

The first four scenes of Shakespeare's fourth act – IV.i (the King and Queen's discussion of Polonius's murder); IV.ii (Hamlet's scene with Rosencrantz and Guildenstern, ending "Hide fox, and all after"); IV.iii (the bantering about Polonius's body); and IV.iv (Fortinbras and the "How all occasions" soliloquy) were cut. IV.iii was cut during the last week of rehearsal; the third act began originally with the King's "Now, Hamlet, where's Polonius?"

The cuts to III.i were 11–13 (from the Gentlewoman's speech); 17–20 (the Queen's aside); 33–35 and 37–39 (Ophelia's "Larded with sweet flowers" song); 79b–96a (from the King's speech before Laertes's entrance); 97; 103–105; 112b–115a (Laertes's instructions to his men); 133b–135a; 138–139a; 146–148; 161–163; 174; 190–195 (the first verse of Ophelia's final song); 206–212a (from the King's speech to Laertes after Ophelia's exit); 214–215 (from Laertes's reply). An actress spoke the lines of "A Gentleman"; Horatio was assigned the lines of "Another Gentleman." The notable retentions were those of Ophelia's bawdiest songs (48–55 and 59–66), cut for reasons of propriety in most nineteenth- and early-twentieth-century productions. These were cut in Forbes-Robertson's 1914 promptbook and Sothern's 1919–20 acting version. Hampden cut them as well in his promptbook made the latter season; they were later restored.

The text of III.ii:

The cuts were extensive and as follows: 3–24, 27–29a, 30a–35, 37, 40–41a, 51, 59, 63–64a, 69b–71, 74b–82a, 84–95, 101b–103a, 108–130a, 149b–155, 166–185. The Queen's offstage "My lord, my lord" was interpolated. Lines 166–184a (Laertes's query and the Queen's long account of Ophelia's death) were restored for the second season.

The text of III.iii:

The cuts were as follows: 26–32a, 33–42 (excepting "Come, my spade" [32b] from the Gravediggers' exchange); 77–78; 83–126a (Hamlet's and Horatio's comments on the Gravedigger at work and a verse of his song); the end of 149 ("By")–153 (to "galls his kibe"); 224–235 ("the noble dust of Alexander"); 283–286a and the "Gentlemen" at the end of 287; 299 ("woo't drink up eisel? eat a crocodile?"); 321–322.

The text of III.iv:

The first part of Shakespeare's V.ii was played as a separate scene. The cuts were as follows: 1–52a (Hamlet's tale of the battle at sea); 58b–62a; 68b–70; 75–80a; 87a–90; 108–109 and "faith" from 110; 121–123 and "him" from 124; 128–130; 154–171 (the wager of horses and carriages against swords); 193– 218 (Hamlet's comments on Osric and the exchange with "A Lord"); 234b–235a ("Let be" is retained). Lines 117–120 and 124–127 (Hamlet's reply to Osric's description of Laertes and Osric's next lines) are not included in Adams and were probably cut during the first season.

The text of III.v:

The cuts were as follows: lines 241b–250 (Hamlet's explanation to Laertes that his actions were the result of "madness"); 279–281 and 286–288 (from the King's speech prior to the duel); 322 (Hamlet's "O villainy! Ho! Let the door be lock'd!"); 328b–330a and 338b–339 (from Laertes's dying explanation); 344a and 345–349a ("this fell sergeant, death"); 349b was changed to "O, I am dead, Horatio"; 355–356 ("What a wounded name . . ."); 372; 378b–385 (the First Ambassador–Horatio exchange); 391b–397a (Horatio's lines); 400–406a and 412–413 (from Horatio and Fortinbras's final speeches). Lines 279–281 are included in Taylor 1 and 4 but cut elsewhere.

Notes

Preface

1. The biographical studies of Barrymore and his family are as follows: Alma Power-Waters, *John Barrymore: The Legend and the Man* (New York: Julian Messner, 1941); Gene Fowler, *Good Night, Sweet Prince* (New York: Viking, 1944); Hollis Alpert, *The Barrymores* (New York: Dial Press, 1964); James Kotsilibas-Davis, *Great Times Good Times: The Odyssey of Maurice Barrymore* (Garden City, N.Y.: Doubleday, 1977); John Kobler, *Damned in Paradise: The Life of John Barrymore* (New York: Atheneum, 1977); Kotsilibas-Davis, *The Barrymores: The Royal Family in Hollywood* (New York: Crown, 1981); and Margot Peters, *The House of Barrymore* (New York: Knopf, 1990). Martin F. Norden's *John Barrymore: A Bio-Bibliography* (Westport, Conn.: Greenwood, 1995), although primarily a bibliographic resource, contains a biographical essay. With the exception of *Great Times Good Times*, which covers a period extending only to 1905, all of these biographies make some mention of *Richard III* and *Hamlet;* usually they devote only a few pages to these productions, however. In addition, there are half a dozen Drew–Barrymore family autobiographies: Louisa Lane Drew, *Autobiographical Sketch of Mrs. John Drew* (New York: Scribner's, 1899); John Drew, *My Years on the Stage* (New York: Dutton, 1922); John Barrymore, *Confessions of an Actor* (Indianapolis: Bobbs–Merrill, 1926); idem, *We Three* (New York: Saalfield, 1935); Lionel Barrymore, with Cameron Shipp, *We Barrymores* (New York: Appleton–Century–Crofts, 1951); and Ethel Barrymore, *Memories* (New York: Harper & Brothers, 1955). All are valuable as firsthand recollections, yet like many theatrical autobiographies they reflect the tendency of actors to reinvent themselves for public consumption. Chapters dealing with Barrymore's *Richard III* and *Hamlet* are included in Scott Colley, *Richard's Himself Again* (Westport, Conn.: Greenwood, 1992), and John A. Mills, *Hamlet on Stage: The Great Tradition* (Westport, Conn.: Greenwood, 1984). These are discussed in the notes to Chapters 2 and 3, as are a number of pertinent unpublished doctoral dissertations.

Prologue

1. See, for example, the 20 February 1925 *Westminster Gazette*, the 21 February 1925 *Daily Graphic*, the 22 February 1925 *Empire News*, and the 21 February 1925 *Birmingham Post*.

2. For accounts of America's cultural history during the pre– and post–First World War era, I am indebted to Ann Douglas, *Terrible Honesty: Mongrel Manhattan in the*

1920s (New York: Farrar, Straus & Giroux, 1995); Henry F. May, *The End of American Innocence* (New York: Knopf, 1959); Malcolm Cowley, ed., *Fitzgerald and the Jazz Age* (New York: Scribner's, 1966); Adele Heller and Lois Rudnick, eds., *1915, The Cultural Moment* (New Brunswick: Rutgers University Press, 1991); Warren I. Susman, *Culture as History* (New York: Pantheon, 1973); Paul A. Carter, *Another Part of the Twenties* (New York: Columbia University Press, 1977); and Edward Wagenknecht, *American Profile, 1900–1909* (Amherst: University of Massachusetts Press, 1982).

3. "If this young fellow": Percy Fitzgerald, *Life of David Garrick* (London: Simpkin, Marshall, Hamilton, Kent & Co., 1899), 53. See also Thomas Davies, *Memoirs of the Life of David Garrick* (Boston: Walls & Lilly, 1818), 46. "We wish we had": William Hazlitt, *Complete Works*, ed. P. P. Howe, 21 vols. (New York: AMS Press, 1967), V: 345.

4. *Nation* (6 December 1922), 646; *Sketch* (4 March 1925), 418.

5. The literature on Booth and Irving is too vast to list more than a representative sampling here. For Booth, see, for example, William Winter, *Life and Art of Edwin Booth* (New York: MacMillan, 1893); Edwina Booth Grossman, *Edwin Booth: Recollections by His Daughter and Letters to Her and Her Friends* (New York: Century, 1894); Katherine Goodale, *Behind the Scenes with Edwin Booth* (Boston: Houghton Mifflin, 1931); Richard Lockridge, *Darling of Misfortune: Edwin Booth, 1833–1893* (New York: Century, 1932); Stanley Kimmel, *The Mad Booths of Maryland*, rev. ed. (New York: Dover, 1969); Eleanor Ruggles, *Prince of Players* (New York: W. W. Norton, 1953); Charles H. Shattuck, *The Hamlet of Edwin Booth* (Urbana: University of Illinois Press, 1969); Daniel J. Watermeier, *Between Actor and Critic: Selected Letters of Edwin Booth and William Winter* (Princeton: Princeton University Press, 1971); idem, *Edwin Booth's Performances: The Mary Isabella Stone Commentaries* (Ann Arbor: UMI, 1990); and L. Terry Oggel, *Edwin Booth: A Bio-Bibliography* (Westport, Conn.: Greenwood, 1992). For Irving see Bram Stoker, *Personal Reminiscences of Henry Irving*, 2 vols. (New York: MacMillan, 1906); Austin Brereton, *The Life of Henry Irving*, 2 vols. (New York: Longman, 1908); Gordon Craig, *Henry Irving* (New York: Longmans Green, 1930); H. A. Saintsbury and Ceil Palmer, eds., *We Saw Him Act* (London: Hurst & Blackett, 1930); Laurence Irving, *Henry Irving: The Actor and His World* (New York: MacMillan, 1952); and Alan Hughes, *Henry Irving, Shakespearean* (Cambridge: Cambridge University Press, 1981). For Mansfield see Richard Wilstach, *Richard Mansfield: The Man and the Actor* (New York: Scribner's, 1908) and William Winter, *Life and Art of Richard Mansfield*, 2 vols. (New York: Moffat, Yard, 1910). For Forbes-Robertson see his autobiography, *A Player under Three Reigns* (Boston: Little, Brown, 1925). I have also relied upon William Winter, *Shakespeare on the Stage*, 3 vols. (New York: Moffat, Yard, 1911–16); J. Ranken Towse, *Sixty Years of the Theatre* (New York: Funk & Wagnalls, 1916); Garff B. Wilson, *A History of American Acting* (Bloomington: Indiana University Press, 1966); and Charles H. Shattuck, *Shakespeare on the American Stage*, 2 vols. (Washington, D.C.: Folger, 1976/1987).

6. Winter's quote is from his review of Booth's *Hamlet* in the 26 October 1875 *New-York Tribune*. "With which he was most identified": Charles H. Shattuck, "Edwin Booth's *Hamlet*: A New Promptbook," *Harvard Library Bulletin* (January 1967), 20–40 (at 20). I am indebted to Shattuck's accounts of Booth (see n. 5) for much of the discussion of Booth in this section.

7. Gene Fowler, in *Good Night, Sweet Prince*, 194, includes a colorful Barrymore anecdote in which the actor claimed to have seen Irving's Richard III in London in the

company of his sister. Irving's 1896–7 revival would have been the only opportunity for Barrymore to have seen him in this role; it played for one performance on 19 December 1896 and thirty-four additional performances between 27 February and 7 April 1897. School records reveal that Barrymore was at Georgetown Preparatory School in Rockville, Maryland, at the time, and Ethel Barrymore was then on tour in *Rosemary*. It is likely, however, that Barrymore witnessed Irving's Shylock, which played frequently in the repertory during the spring of 1898 while Ethel was a member of the Lyceum company (although she did not act in *The Merchant of Venice*); John was in London at the time. Barrymore's praise of Irving is from the 22 January 1925 *Daily Telegraph* (London). In a survey published in the 13 April 1940 *Billboard* he listed Irving as his favorite actor.

8. Barrymore's claim to have seen Mansfield's Richard III (*Good Night, Sweet Prince*, 194), unlike his claim to have seen Irving's impersonation, is within the realm of possibility. Mansfield featured the play in his repertory when he appeared at the Lafayette Square Opera House in Washington during the 1896–7 season, while Barrymore was a student at Georgetown; he also performed Richard III in New York and on tour during the 1904–5 and 1905–6 seasons, when Barrymore might easily have seen him in the role.

9. Hesketh Pearson, *The Last Actor-Managers* (London: White Lion, 1950), 1; Bernard Shaw, *Our Theatre in the Nineties*, 3 vols. (London: Constable, 1932), III: 206; Carol Jones Carlisle, *Shakespeare in the Greenroom* (Chapel Hill: University of North Carolina Press, 1969), 79. See also William A. Armstrong, "Bernard Shaw and Forbes-Robertson's *Hamlet*," *Shakespeare Quarterly* 15 (Winter 1964), 27–31. Here, Armstrong demonstrates that Shaw advised Forbes-Robertson closely when he was preparing for the role and, in fact, practically directed him. Shaw's glowing notice of Forbes-Robertson's portrayal and his sharp disapproval of Barrymore's "between the lines" business twenty-eight years later can best be understood in light of his view that Forbes-Robertson's "on the line and to the line" method was the "correct" way to play the role. Shaw's criticism of Barrymore's cuts to the text, which I discuss at length in Chapter 4, is ironic, however; Forbes-Robertson restored the final appearance of Fortinbras (most acting texts to that time ended on "The rest is silence") but acted a version of the play from which more than a thousand lines – including sexual references and such harshnesses as "I'll lug the guts" – had been deleted.

10. *Daily Telegraph* (London) (22 January 1925).

11. For a more detailed account see Lawrence W. Levine, *Highbrow/Lowbrow* (Cambridge, Mass.: Harvard University Press, 1988). I am indebted to Levine's initial essay in this volume, "William Shakespeare in America," for much of the material in this discussion.

12. A. A. Lipscomb, "Uses of Shakespeare off the Stage," *Harper's New Monthly Magazine* (August 1882), 431–8.

13. A. C. Wheeler, "The Extinction of Shakespeare," *The Arena* 1 (March 1890), 423–31.

14. Mansfield, to be fair, introduced American playgoers to Shaw's *Arms and the Man* and *The Devil's Disciple* during the 1894–5 and 1897–8 seasons, played Rostand's *Cyrano* during the season of 1898–9, produced Ibsen's *Peer Gynt* in 1907, and acted in a number of other "literary" dramas; yet he balanced such "prestige" attractions with more frequent performances of *Dr. Jekyll and Mr. Hyde, A Parisian Romance, Don Juan*, and *Beau Brummel*, to name only a few. In addition to his *Richard III* revivals, discussed earlier, Mansfield revived his Shylock, first seen in 1893,

during the 1897–8, 1904–5, and 1905–6 seasons; his *Henry V* and *Julius Caesar*, produced during the 1900–1 and 1902–3 seasons, respectively, were not revived. Irving's non-Shakespearean repertory for his American tours during these years consisted almost exclusively of costume melodrama: *The Bells, Waterloo, Louis XI*, Tennyson's *Becket*, and several more. For Mansfield's repertory see Winter, *Life and Art*, II: 269–97; for Irving's American repertory see Stoker, *Personal Reminiscences*.

15. For the practitioners discussed in this section I have relied on a number of sources, of which the following represent a partial listing. For Poel see Robert Speaight, *William Poel and the Elizabethan Revival* (London: Heineman, 1954) and Rinda F. Lundstrom, *William Poel's Hamlets* (Ann Arbor: UMI, 1984); for Craig and Appia, in addition to their own published writings, see Christopher Innes, *Edward Gordon Craig* (New York: Cambridge University Press, 1983); Laurence Senelick, *Gordon Craig's Moscow Hamlet* (Westport, Conn.: Greenwood, 1982); and Richard Beacham, *Adolphe Appia* (New York: Cambridge University Press, 1987); for Reinhardt see Huntly Carter, *The Theatre of Max Reinhardt* (New York: Mitchell Kennerley, 1913); Oliver M. Sayler, ed., *Max Reinhardt and His Theatre* (New York: Brentano's, 1924); and J. L. Styan, *Max Reinhardt* (New York: Cambridge University Press, 1982); for Barker see C. B. Purdom, *Harley Granville Barker* (Cambridge, Mass.; Harvard University Press, 1956); Elmer Salenius, *Harley Granville Barker* (Boston: Twayne, 1982); Christine Dymkowski, *Harley Granville Barker: Preface to Modern Shakespeare* (Washington, D.C.: Folger, 1986); and Dennis Kennedy, *Granville Barker and the Dream of Theatre* (New York: Cambridge University Press, 1985). A good overview of the developments of this period is provided in J. L. Styan, *The Shakespeare Revolution* (New York: Cambridge University Press, 1977).

16. For a detailed listing of Reinhardt's productions during this period see Styan, *Max Reinhardt*, 131–40.

17. *Saturday Review* (23 November 1912), 637–8.

18. *New York Times* (19 March 1905).

19. Little has been published to date on the actors discussed in this section. For Sothern and Marlowe see E. H. Sothern, *The Melancholy Tale of "Me": My Remembrances* (New York: Scribner's, 1916); C. E. Russell, *Julia Marlowe, Her Life and Art* (New York: Appleton, 1926); E. H. Sothern, *Julia Marlowe's Story*, ed. Fairfax Downey (New York: Rinehart, 1954); and Patti S. Derrick, "Julia Marlowe: An Actress Caught between Traditions," *Theatre Survey* 32 (May 1991), 85–105. For Mantell see C. J. Bulliet, *Robert Mantell's Romance* (Boston: Luce, 1918) and Attilio Favorini, "'Richard's Himself Again!': Robert Mantell's Shakespearean Debut in New York City," *Educational Theatre Journal* 24 (December 1972), 402–14. I am also indebted to Charles H. Shattuck's discussions of Sothern and Marlowe and Mantell in *Shakespeare on the American Stage*, II: 244–90, 225–43. For Hampden see Gene J. Parola, "Walter Hampden's Career as Actor-Manager" (Ph.D. diss.: Dept. of Theatre, Indiana University, 1970) and Eugene M. Laurent, "Walter Hampden: Actor-Manager" (Ph.D. diss.: Dept. of Theatre, University of Illinois at Urbana–Champaign, 1969).

20. *New York Times* (18 September 1900). See also the 18 September 1900 *New York American* and the 2 October 1900 *Boston Transcript*.

21. Edward Fales Coward, "Shakespeare Spells Ruin No Longer," *Theatre Magazine* (December 1919), 364.

22. Lloyd Morris, *Curtain Time* (New York: Random House, 1953), 287.

23. *Town & Country* (1 April 1920), 40. For a more detailed account of the decline

in public favor to which Sothern and Marlowe were subject in their later years see Derrick, "Julia Marlowe."

24. Sothern, *Julia Marlowe's Story*, 216–17.
25. G. C. D. Odell, *Shakespeare from Betterton to Irving*. 2 vols. (New York: Scribner's 1920), II: 468–9.
26. Ibid., II: 469.
27. *Literary Digest* (14 December 1918), 29.
28. Ada Patterson, "Shakespeare Made Smart," *Theatre Magazine* (March 1919), 154.
29. Ibid.
30. Ibid.
31. *Denver Post* (26 November 1922); see also Clayton Hamilton's comments in his "Seen on the Stage" column in *Vogue* (1 May 1920), 80, 162, 164, 166, 170 (at 162).
32. Brooks Atkinson, *Broadway*, rev. ed. (New York: Macmillan, 1974), 385. See also Alexander Woollcott's comments in the 20 April 1921 *New York Times*.
33. Coward, "Shakespeare Spells Ruin No Longer," 364.
34. Hopkins did not see a Shakespearean production during his visit to the Deutsches Theater in the summer of 1913, yet he was surely aware of Reinhardt's methods. Jones, on the other hand, witnessed a number of Reinhardt's Shakespearean revivals while he was a backstage observer at the Deutsches Theater during the 1913–14 season; both visits are discussed in Chapter 1.

Chapter 1. The Education of an Actor, 1882–1919

1. John Barrymore, "What Is a Juvenile Lead?" *Theatre Magazine* (June 1914), 304, 317 (at 317).
2. John Barrymore, "The Prevailing Mode in Acting," *The Spotlight* (12 August 1910).
3. "Mercutio or Benedick or Petruchio": *Rochester Democrat and Chronicle* (10 March 1912); "the young vagabond": Alexander Woollcott, "The Two Barrymores," *Everybody's Magazine* (June 1920), 31; "a clever player": Keene Sumner, "The Hidden Talents of 'Jack' Barrymore," *American Magazine* (June 1919), 36–7, 149–50, 153–4 (at 37).
4. "Resourceful mind": Woollcott, "Two Barrymores"; "vehicles designed to present": Brooks Atkinson, *Broadway*, rev. ed. (New York: Macmillan, 1974), 21; "the easiest means": *Rochester Democrat and Chronicle* (10 March 1912).
5. O. B. Bunce, "Mr. Booth's Hamlet," *Appleton's Journal* (20 and 27 November 1875), 657–9, 689–91. For a similarly mixed notice see the 30 October 1875 *Spirit of the Times*.
6. The appearances of the Lanes opposite Macready are documented in playbills from the Theatre Royal, Bristol, at the British Library. On 11 April 1821, for example, Thomas Lane appeared with the tragedian as the Second Witch in *Macbeth* with Eliza Lane among the "chorus of singing witches," a traditional interpolation at the time. On 13 April of that year Thomas Lane played the Duke of Norfolk to Macready's Richard III; on 9 January 1824 he played Osric to Macready's Hamlet and also supported Macready in *Othello* and *King John* during this same engagement. For Louisa Lane Drew see her *Autobiographical Sketch of Mrs. John Drew* (New York: Scribner's, 1899), where she discusses her appearances opposite Macready, Forrest, and the elder Booth; she acted with all three at the Park Theatre in New York in the early 1840s and played Shakespearean heroines opposite Edwin and John Wilkes Booth at the Arch Street Theatre in Philadelphia during the early

1860s. See also Claire Noreen Barnes, "Actress of All Work: A Survey of the Performance Career of Louisa Lane Drew" (Ph.D. diss.: Dept. of Theatre, Tufts University, 1986). Little has been written on John Drew Sr.; the most detailed account published to date is in Montrose J. Moses, *Famous Actor Families in America* (New York: Crowell, 1906), 175–9.

7. The family Bible is the Theatre Collection, Philadelphia Free Library. There is controversy surrounding the birthdates of Barrymore and his sister and brother; see Margot Peters, *The House of Barrymore* (New York: Knopf, 1990), 9. A copy of Barrymore's birth certificate (University of Colorado at Boulder, Special Collections; hereafter abbreviated as UCB/SC), obtained by Gene Fowler much after the fact, lists Barrymore's birthdate as 14 February; Barrymore listed 15 February in American and English school records, however, and this date is more likely.

8. Louisa Drew, unidentified newspaper interview, Harvard Theatre Collection [San Francisco, 1896].

9. Alma Power-Waters, *John Barrymore: The Legend and the Man* (New York: Julian Messner, 1941), 13.

10. Charles A. Freeman, "Little Jack Barrymore," *Screen Book Magazine* (June 1931), 21, 98–9. Freeman dates Barrymore's year at Mount Pleasant Military Academy as beginning in September 1895, but this conflicts with records at Georgetown, which show him entering the latter institution in October 1895; Barrymore probably entered Mount Pleasant in September 1894.

11. For Barrymore's seduction by his stepmother see Gene Fowler, *Good Night, Sweet Prince* (New York: Viking, 1944), 89–90. I am grateful to Jon Reynolds, Georgetown University Archivist, for providing copies of Barrymore's Georgetown records, including the excerpt from the Prefect of Discipline's diary.

12. I am indebted to F. R. Miles and Stephen Chaplin, archivists at King's College School and the Slade School, for providing detailed records of Barrymore's English school days, only a small portion of which I could utilize here. For Ethel Barrymore's Lyceum season see Peters, *House of Barrymore*, 49–52; for Maurice Barrymore's Haymarket seasons see James Kotsilibas-Davis, *Great Times Good Times: The Odyssey of Maurice Barrymore* (Garden City, N.Y.: Doubleday, 1977), 214–42. None of these seasons involved Shakespearean roles.

13. Barrymore's appearance with his father in Cincinnati is mentioned in the 14 October 1900 *Cincinnati Enquirer* and the 27 October 1900 *Dramatic Mirror;* mysteriously, he again appeared with his father in *A Man of the World* in Springfield, Massachusetts, commencing on 14 January 1901, and in Worcester, Massachusetts, beginning on 21 January – two months after he went to work for the *Evening Journal.*

14. Fowler, *Good Night, Sweet Prince*, 104.

15. *New York Herald* (17 May 1925); John Barrymore, *Confessions of an Actor* (Indianapolis: Bobbs–Merrill, 1926), unpaginated.

16. "A certain adaptability": Barrymore, *Confessions;* this same source contains Barrymore's recollections of his weeks with the Rankin–O'Neil troupe. His decision to leave the company was a wise one in retrospect; in early December the company's props and costumes were attached by W. S. Cleveland, and Nance O'Neil turned to vaudeville to recoup her fortunes. See Locke Scrapbook 371 (Nance O'Neil), Billy Rose Theatre Collection, The New York Public Library for the Performing Arts at Lincoln Center (hereafter Lincoln Center).

17. Fowler, *Good Night, Sweet Prince*, 117.

18. For Barrymore's irresponsibility in these years see ibid., 116–21; Fowler's state-

ments that Barrymore missed the opening night of *The Dictator* in New York and was drunk for his London opening in the same play are contradicted by review evidence, however. See also Ethel Barrymore, *Memories* (New York: Harper & Brothers, 1955), 149; Peters, *House of Barrymore*, 104, 551; and Hollis Alpert, *The Barrymores* (New York: Dial Press, 1964), 130. During this period Barrymore performed in small roles at two Actors Fund benefits: On 13 May 1904, he appeared at the Knickerbocker in *Yvette;* on 26 January 1906 he appeared at the Broadway Theatre in *Miss Civilization.*

19. Charles Frohman papers, Manuscript Division, New York Public Library (hereafter MS Div., NYPL).

20. "A deep, serious, psychological character": John Barrymore, "Blame It on the Queen," *American Magazine* (March 1933), 20–3, 114–19 (at 116).

21. Charles Frohman papers, MS Div., NYPL; "very bad" is from Hayman's 9 April 1907 letter to Frohman. Hayman's letters of 15 and 22 February attest that Barrymore was slated to appear with his sister in Galsworthy's *The Silver Box* on Broadway, but his "illness" and the play's short run prevented it. The Thaw trial received extensive coverage in the press. On 20 March the prosecutor asked for a special hearing on Thaw's sanity, which convened five days later. With principal testimony complete, Barrymore undoubtedly felt it safe to return to New York. The trial ended in a hung jury on 12 April; Thaw was later retried and found guilty. See Evelyn Nesbit, *Prodigal Days* (New York: Julian Messner, 1934) and Gerald Langford, *The Murder of Stanford White* (Indianapolis: Bobbs–Merrill, 1962).

22. Daniel Frohman had had his eye on Barrymore for several months, with a number of projects under discussion; see Hayman's 18 January 1907 letter to Charles Frohman and his 8 February 1907 letter to Ethel Barrymore, Charles Frohman papers, MS Div., NYPL.

23. Marie V. Wilde's account of Barrymore's antics and Drew's response appeared in the 10 December 1922 *New York Herald.*

24. For positive comments on Barrymore's performance, see, for example, the 17 March 1908 *New York Herald* and *New York Times.* See also Alf Hayman's 16 March 1908 letter to Charles Frohman, Charles Frohman papers, MS Div., NYPL.

25. Barrymore, "The Prevailing Mode in Acting."

26. Quoted in Clara Morris, "The Dressing Room Reception Where I First Met Ellen Terry and Mrs. John Drew," *McClure's* (December 1903), 210.

27. Walter Prichard Eaton, "Personality and the Player," *Collier's* (22 October 1910), 17, 34.

28. Katherine Harris, by all accounts a capable supporting actress, appeared onstage with Barrymore in *The Fortune Hunter* (tour), *Uncle Sam, Half a Husband, On the Quiet, The Affairs of Anatol, A Thief for a Night, Believe Me Xantippe, The Yellow Ticket* (midrun replacement), and *Kick-In.* She also appeared with her husband in the films *Nearly a King* and *The Lost Bridegroom.*

29. For Sheldon see Eric Wollencott Barnes, *The Man Who Lived Twice* (New York: Scribner's, 1956) and Loren K. Ruff, *Edward Sheldon* (Boston: Twayne, 1982).

30. Travis Bogard and Jackson R. Bryer, eds., *Selected Letters of Eugene O'Neill* (New Haven: Yale University Press, 1988), 199.

31. In January and February 1912 Barrymore appeared opposite his sister on Broadway in J. M. Barrie's *A Slice of Life;* he then began rehearsals for *Half a Husband* under the direction of Arnold Daly, which played in several upstate New York cities before closing on the road. That summer he appeared in stock at the Belasco Theatre in Los Angeles in *On the Quiet, The Honor of the Family,* and *The Man from Home.*

32. Barrymore's scheduled appearance in *Anatol* was announced on May 1912, six months after he had begun working with Sheldon, and it is possible that Sheldon helped to steer him toward Ames; see, for example, the brief article in the 15 May 1912 *Toledo Blade* wryly headlined "Is It a Promotion?" In May 1913, Barrymore and his wife appeared briefly in vaudeville in a scene from *Anatol;* see John Barrymore, "Lionel, Ethel and I: King, Queen and Jack," *American Magazine* (February 1933), 11–15, 70, 72, 74 (at 74).

33. Barrymore opened in *A Thief for a Night* – a "melodramatic comedy" adapted by P. G. Wodehouse from one of his novels – at McVicker's Theatre in Chicago on 30 March 1913; the show had a six-week run. *Believe Me, Xantippe* was the prizewinning play in a contest sponsored by the Boston manager John Craig; its author, Frederick Ballard, had studied with George Pierce Baker. The union of play and player might well have been brokered by Sheldon who, despite his artistic leanings, recognized Barrymore's need for vehicles. Earlier in the year he had offered Barrymore the male lead in *Romance* opposite Doris Keane, which went on to become his greatest commercial success. Barrymore declined, however, thinking himself wrong for the part of a clergyman.

34. Regarding Barrymore's boozy shenanigans during the run of *The Yellow Ticket* see Fowler, *Good Night, Sweet Prince*, 146–7, and Lloyd Morris, *Curtain Time* (New York: Random House, 1953), 316. For further evidence of his desire to prove himself as an actor during this period, see Barrymore, "What Is a Juvenile Lead?" 304, 317.

35. For a more detailed account of Barrymore's Italian sojourn see Barnes, *Man Who Lived Twice*, 100–1, and Fowler, *Good Night, Sweet Prince*, 147–52.

36. Sumner, "Hidden Talents," 37. See also Al H. Woods, "Why I Believe in Deciding Things Quickly," *American Magazine* (March 1918), 74.

37. *The Lonely Heart* was announced as Barrymore's next project several times between 1914 and 1917. It finally received a production in Baltimore in 1920 with Basil Sydney in the leading role and proved a failure; see Barnes, *Man Who Lived Twice*, 145–6. Interestingly, Barrymore expressed a desire to play the lead in Shaw's *Androcles and the Lion*, produced by Barker as part of his repertory season at Wallack's; see the 21 February 1915 *New York Times*.

38. For a more detailed discussion of the Lubin films see Spencer M. Berger, "The Search for John Barrymore," *American Screen Classic* (November–December 1981), 8–11, 13; see also Joseph Garton, *The Film Acting of John Barrymore* (New York: Arno Press, 1982), 54–7, and Peters, *House of Barrymore*, 556–7.

39. Barrymore, *Confessions*.

40. "Completely responsible": Fowler, *Good Night, Sweet Prince,* 149. For Lionel Barrymore's comments on Sheldon's influence see Lionel Barrymore, with Cameron Shipp, *We Barrymores* (New York: Appleton–Century–Crofts, 1951), 158–9; for Woollcott's comments see his "Two Barrymores"; for Hopkins's comments see Arthur Hopkins, *Reference Point* (New York: Samuel French, 1948), 104–5, 113; "His determination": ibid., 105.

41. Ben Iden Payne, *A Life in a Wooden O* (New Haven: Yale University Press, 1977), 128–9.

42. Clayton Hamilton, "Seen on the Stage," *Vogue* (1 May 1920), 80, 162, 164, 166, 170 (at 162). Whitford Kane attests to Barrymore drinking Bevo during the *Justice* period in *Are We All Met?* (London: Elkin, Mathews & Marrot, 1931), 190; Ashton Stevens, in *Actorviews* (Chicago: Covici–McGee, 1923), 62, and Constance Collier, in an unpublished essay on Barrymore's acting (UCB/SC), 9, testify to the fact that he refrained from drinking through the end of the *Peter Ibbetson* tour.

43. Woollcott's comments are from his 23 April 1916 column; see also his columns in the 9 and 16 April *New York Times* and his article, "John Barrymore Arrives – A Great Man," *Everybody's Magazine* (June 1916), 122–4. For Barrymore's reaction to his success see Helen Ten Broeck, "From Comedy to Tragedy," *Theatre Magazine* (July 1916), 23, 38.

44. Cathleen Nesbitt, *A Little Love & Good Company* (Owings Mills, Md.: Stemmer House, 1977), 93.

45. Kane, *Are We All Met?* 189–90.

46. Collier, unpublished essay, 17.

47. For a more detailed account of Barrymore's irresponsibility on the *Ibbetson* tour see Peters, *House of Barrymore*, 170–2, and Fowler, *Good Night, Sweet Prince*, 169–71. "Jack came into my dressing room": Collier, unpublished essay, 17.

48. Hopkins discusses his career in his *Reference Point* and *To a Lonely Boy* (Garden City, N.Y.: Doubleday, 1937); he discusses his theoretical approach to directing in *How's Your Second Act?* (New York: Samuel French, 1918). See also Delmar J. Hansen, "The Directing Theory and Practice of Arthur Hopkins" (Ph.D. diss.: Dept. of Theatre, University of Iowa, 1961) and Bruce R. Halverson, "Arthur Hopkins: A Theatrical Biography" (Ph.D. diss.: Dept. of Theatre, University of Washington, 1971).

49. Hopkins, *To a Lonely Boy*, 151.

50. For Jones see Ralph Pendleton, ed., *The Theatre of Robert Edmond Jones* (Middletown, Conn.: Wesleyan University Press, 1958); Dana Sue McDermott, "A Theatre of Dreams: Robert Edmond Jones' Theatrical Vision and Creative Process" (Ph.D. diss.: Dept. of Theatre, University of California at Berkeley, 1979); Eugene R. Black, "Robert Edmond Jones: Poetic Artist of the New Stagecraft" (Ph.D. diss.: Dept. of Theatre, University of Wisconsin at Madison, 1955); and McDermott, "The Apprenticeship of Robert Edmond Jones," *Theatre Survey* 29 (November 1988), 193–212, and "Creativity in the Theatre," *Theatre Journal* (May 1984), 213–30.

51. Robert Edmond Jones, *The Dramatic Imagination* (New York: Duell, Sloan & Pearce, 1941), 26.

52. A minor mystery surrounds Barrymore's initial meeting with Hopkins. The producer later recalled the exchange as occurring at a time when Barrymore was scheduled to tour in *Peter Ibbetson*, which would have been the autumn of 1917. See, for example, Hopkins, *Reference Point*, 103, and *To a Lonely Boy*, 167; see also Fowler, *Good Night, Sweet Prince*, 180. Barrymore, however, was announced as "to be seen in an English version of Tolstoi's *The Living Corpse*" in the March 1917 edition of *Theatre Magazine*. *A Successful Calamity* opened on 5 February 1917 at the Booth Theatre and was transferred that autumn to the Plymouth. The *Theatre Magazine* announcement may have referred to Sheldon's adaptation, but it is possible that the initial Barrymore–Hopkins meeting took place in February. Hopkins discusses the "brief and nebulous preliminaries" in *Reference Point*, 103; see also Fowler, *Good Night Sweet Prince*, 179.

53. Barrymore's financial terms for *Redemption* are discussed in Ward Morehouse, *Matinee Tomorrow* (New York: Whittlesey House, 1949), 170; Hopkins discusses his arrangement with Barrymore in *To a Lonely Boy*, 167–8, and in Fowler, *Good Night, Sweet Prince*, 180–1.

54. Barrymore and Michael Strange both mention the latter's work in adapting *The Living Corpse* (with no mention of Sheldon), Barrymore in *Confessions* and Strange in *Who Tells Me True* (New York: Scribner's, 1940), 156–7. Sheldon's first version

of the play (*The Man Who Was Dead*) is in the U.S. Copyright Office with a copyright date of 27 October 1916. A comparison of Sheldon's draft and the performance text is revealing; many of the lines are identical or strikingly similar. Given Michael Strange's difficulties in writing dialogue (discussed in Chapter 3) and Sheldon's skill, experience, and subsequent textual collaborations with Hopkins and Barrymore, it seems likely that much of the acting version was Sheldon's handiwork. In "The Two Barrymores," Alexander Woollcott credits Sheldon with having worked on all four of Barrymore's post-*Justice* scripts (*Peter Ibbetson, Redemption, The Jest,* and *Richard III*); Woollcott was in a position to know. Hopkins's comments on rehearsals are from Fowler, *Good Night, Sweet Prince,* 181, and his own *Reference Point,* 107–8.

55. Barrymore's performance in *Redemption* evoked a wide spectrum of critical response. Francis Hackett's review appeared in the *New Republic* (19 October 1918), 349. Corbin's comments are from his 6 October 1918 column in the *New York Times;* the "male Bernhardt" quote is from an unidentified review in a New York daily, John Barrymore Scrapbook [call no. MWEZ n.c. 23,125], Lincoln Center. Another unidentified review in the same source states that "His technical equipment for so complex a role is still limited. There is an irritating monotony to his speech at times . . . but his intellectual grasp of the character is absolute." In his 6 October column, Corbin also commented on Barrymore's vocal limitations, but on the whole he admired his performance. His comments on Hopkins's and Jones's contributions are from his 4 October 1918 review in the *Times.*

56. Robert Edmond Jones, unpublished notes, Wesleyan University.

57. John Barrymore, letter to Robert Hosea, n.d. [1919]; Lincoln Center.

58. "Sensational successes of the decade": *New York Times* (10 April 1919); "remarkable for its grace and imagination": *Sun* (10 April 1919); "the enthralling quality": *New York American* (10 April 1919).

59. "Sufficient variety of modulation": *Boston Transcript* (10 May 1919); "monotonous sameness": *New York Herald* (10 April 1919). For similar comments on Barrymore's vocal monotony in *The Jest,* see the *New Republic* (10 May 1919), 55. "Insignificant compared with": *World* (10 April 1919); "No play we can remember": *New York Tribune* (10 April 1919).

60. *New Republic* (10 May 1919), 55. See also John Corbin's comments in the 27 April 1919 *New York Times.*

61. *New York Times* (27 April 1919); *Chicago Tribune* (20 April 1919); *New York Times* (28 September 1919).

Chapter 2. *Richard III,* 1920

1. Little has been written on Barrymore's production of *Richard III.* A brief account with some stage business is provided by Scott Colley in *Richard's Himself Again* (Westport, Conn.: Greenwood, 1992), 151–8, based mainly on Harvard Theatre Collection newspaper clippings. Larry D. Clark's article, "John Barrymore's Richard III," in *Theatre History Studies* 4 (1984), 31–7, views the production in light of the 1919–20 Broadway season and offers a short discussion of the critical response. Aubrey Berg devotes a chapter of his dissertation, "Collaborators: Arthur Hopkins, Robert Edmond Jones, and the Barrymores" (University of Illinois at Urbana–Champaign, 1979), to *Richard III,* summarizing a sampling of review evidence and material in Fowler's and Kobler's biographies. The biographies mentioned in

note 1 to the Preface all feature a few pages on the production, but these segments consist mainly of anecdotes and a brief sampling of criticism. The production is mentioned in many standard histories of the theatre and books on Shakespearean production, but these offer little by way of detail. See, for example, Robert Speaight, *Shakespeare on the Stage* (Boston: Little, Brown, 1973), 168, 171, and Bernard Grebanier, *Then Came Each Actor* (New York: David McKay, 1975), 436.

2. "Storming the fortresses": *Morning Telegraph* (8 March 1920); "intellectual, stealthy, crafty": *World* (8 March 1920): "amazing triumph": *Evening World* (8 March 1920).

3. *Theatre Arts Anthology* (New York: Theatre Arts Books, 1950), 386.

4. Robert Edmond Jones, unpublished notes, Wesleyan University.

5. John Barrymore, "Blame It on the Queen," *American Magazine* (March 1933), 20–3, 114–19 (at 117); he includes a similar account in *Confessions of an Actor* (Indianapolis: Bobbs–Merrill, 1926), unpaginated.

6. Clayton Hamilton, "Seen on the Stage," *Vogue* (1 May 1920), 80, 162, 164, 166, 170 (at 162); "in the spring of 1919" is from his slightly altered notice in his book of the same title (New York: Henry Holt, 1920), 41. Barrymore also mentions that "friends had wanted me to do Hamlet first" in *Confessions*. See also Barrymore's comments in the 1939 serial autobiography issued by the North American Newspaper Alliance, published, for example, in the 12, 19, and 26 February 1939 *Hartford Courant*. Here he states: "At first there was some discussion as to whether it would be best to do *Hamlet* first. I considered this the harder role and *Richard III* a step up to it. Therefore Richard became preparation for Hamlet."

7. Barrymore, *Confessions*.

8. *World Magazine* (13 June 1920).

9. Jones, Wesleyan notes.

10. Arthur Hopkins, *To a Lonely Boy* (Garden City, N.Y.: Doubleday, 1937), 199–200.

11. Sigmund Freud, "Some Character-Types Met with in Psycho-Analytic Work," trans. E. C. Mayne, in *The Complete Psychological Works of Sigmund Freud*, 24 vols., ed. James Strachey (London: Hogarth Press, 1957), XIV (1914–16): 311–15. The essay was originally published (in German) in the last issue of *Imago* for the year 1916.

12. Ibid., 315.

13. Hopkins, *To a Lonely Boy*, 7–8.

14. Sheldon received no credit on the playbill as adaptor; his contribution was widely known in the theatrical and journalistic communities, however, and many reviewers acknowledged his role as textual arranger. See, for example, the 8 March 1920 *New York Globe*, *Town Topics* (11 March 1920), and Hamilton, "Seen on the Stage," 164. Barrymore's letters to Michael Strange sent from Santa Barbara during the summer of 1919 (Lincoln Center), reveal that Sheldon, also in California, was seriously ill at the time; he probably accomplished little that summer. However, the many sources crediting him as adaptor make it likely that he had recovered sufficiently by the fall and early winter to work further on his adaptation, though it seems probable that Hopkins, with Barrymore's assistance, made additional revisions prior to and during rehearsals; Sheldon was still in California at that time.

15. The abridged version of Richard's soliloquy from *3 Henry IV*, III.ii, was later lengthened; the most obvious addition would be the inclusion of the opening soliloquy from Shakespeare's *Richard III*, which came toward the end of the first act. In Sheldon's draft, not a single line of "Now is the winter of our discontent" was retained. For a more detailed discussion of the draft promptbook and acting text of *Richard III*, see Appendix B. All subsequent line numberings refer to the Temple

editions of *3 Henry VI* and *Richard III*. These were originally published in 1895 by J. M. Dent (London) and E. P. Dutton (New York) and were issued in many later editions. The texts used by Sheldon in preparing his adaptation are unknown; the Temple *Hamlet* was used for the 1922 Hopkins–Jones–Barrymore production, however, and I have employed the Temple editions in this chapter for the sake of regularity. For Cibber's adaptation, see Christopher Spencer, ed., *Five Restoration Adaptations of Shakespeare* (Urbana: University of Illinois Press, 1965), 275–344.

16. Sheldon's alteration of the text to clarify "obscure" passages had recent precedent; for similar changes see William Winter's adaptation for Edwin Booth's 1877 acting edition in *The Shakespearean Plays of Edwin Booth*, 2 vols. [repr. ed.] (Philadelphia: Penn Publishing Co., 1908), II.

17. Arthur William Row, "Barrymore Legend," unpublished essay, Arthur William Row papers, MS Div., NYPL, 21. Several versions of this essay exist, each with slight variations; additional drafts are at Lincoln Center.

18. "Jack's chief handicap": Gene Fowler, *Good Night, Sweet Prince* (New York: Viking, 1944), 190; "I went out into the woods": Barrymore, "Blame It on the Queen," 117.

19. Fowler, *Good Night, Sweet Prince*, 190.

20. Row, "Barrymore Legend," 21. Row also states, in his review of Fowler's *Good Night, Sweet Prince* in *Sign Post* (24 February 1944), that Barrymore studied with three voice and diction teachers. He cites Margaret Carrington in "Barrymore Legend" but does not identify either of the previous teachers.

21. Information on Margaret Carrington and the Huston family was provided in part during a series of in-person and telephone interviews with Margaret Carrington's niece, Margaret Huston Walters, held between January 1990 and June 1992. I am also indebted to articles and obituaries at Lincoln Center and the Metro Toronto Central Reference Library; to articles in the *New York Times*, the *Toronto Globe*, the *Toronto Sun*, and *Toronto Saturday Night*; and to Robert Edmond Jones's 29 December 1942 letter to Gene Fowler (UCB/SC), which contains valuable biographical information about Margaret Carrington. See also Stark Young, "Distinction and Theatre," *New Republic* (24 August 1942), 227–8.

22. Jones quotes: 29 December 1942 letter to Gene Fowler.

23. Margaret Carrington, unpublished essay on John Barrymore's acting, Wesleyan University. Carrington's "notes" on her collaboration with Barrymore survive in three complete essay versions, several incomplete versions, and a number of fragments. Two of these complete manuscripts are in the Robert Edmond Jones papers at Wesleyan collected by Ralph Pendleton in connection with his book *The Theatre of Robert Edmond Jones* (Middletown, Conn.: Wesleyan University Press, 1958). References to Barrymore's marital difficulties make it likely that they were written during the late 1930s or early 1940s, when Barrymore was embroiled in much-publicized squabbles with his fourth wife. These complete drafts are eleven typewritten pages in length, but since they are near-duplicates and it is difficult to differentiate here between drafts, I refer to them subsequently simply as "Wesleyan drafts." The fragments of Carrington's essay, more than twenty in all, range from a paragraph to three pages; three bear the titles "John Barrymore" or "The John Barrymore I Know." Most of these are also at Wesleyan University; as they are similar to the complete drafts, I have not quoted from them here. Several of the fragmentary versions contain emendations by Jones or are entirely in his hand. It is likely that these essays and notes were a collaboration, with Jones revising much

of Carrington's language; they were married at the time. A few similar fragments are in the Robert Edmond Jones papers at the Harvard Theatre Collection. When a quotation is from one of Jones's many notes about Barrymore at Wesleyan (in all of which he is clearly the sole author) I have so indicated.

Inexplicably, the Wesleyan drafts contain little mention of Carrington's work with Barrymore on *Hamlet*. A more detailed account of their collaboration on this production is provided in another complete version of Carrington's essay, "The John Barrymore I Knew," in the Gene Fowler papers at the University of Colorado (UCB/SC). This copy is Fowler's transcription of notes sent by Jones after Margaret Carrington's death in 1942. The Fowler manuscript, eight pages in length, is reprinted in full in Martin F. Norden, *John Barrymore: A Bio-Bibliography* (Westport, Conn.: Greenwood, 1995), 293–6. Norden errs, however, in identifying this manuscript as "an early draft," and he was apparently unaware of the existence of the additional drafts at Wesleyan, or of the collaborative nature of these essays. A reference to Barrymore's film *The Great Profile* makes it possible to date the Fowler MS as having been written after October 1940, when that film was released.

24. Barrymore, "Blame It on the Queen," 117. For similar comments on Carrington's use of this technique see E. Harcourt Williams, *Four Years at the Old Vic: 1929–1933* (London: Putnam, 1935), 20–1.

25. Carrington, Wesleyan drafts.

26. "It is common knowledge": Wesleyan drafts; "I had hoped": "John Barrymore I Knew," 2–3.

27. "Humility, patience and concentration": "John Barrymore I Knew," 5; "intonations": Barrymore, *Confessions;* "learned to speak": idem, "Blame It on the Queen," 117.

28. Carrington, Wesleyan drafts.

29. "John Barrymore I Knew," 1, 3.

30. Ibid., 7–8.

31. Carrington, Wesleyan drafts.

32. Hopkins, *To a Lonely Boy*, 200–1. The myth is repeated, for example, in John Kobler, *Damned in Paradise: The Life of John Barrymore* (New York: Atheneum, 1977), 153, and Margot Peters, *The House of Barrymore* (New York: Knopf, 1990), 197.

33. Arthur Hopkins, *Reference Point* (New York: Samuel French, 1948), 59–62.

34. Row, "Barrymore Legend," 21–2.

35. The beginning of rehearsals was announced in the 3 February 1920 *New York Sun*, with 26 February given as the date of the opening. They had originally been scheduled to begin a week earlier, but Barrymore's bout with the grippe (perhaps merely an excuse to disguise the need for additional preparation and casting time) delayed their start. The original opening date, scheduled for the week of 15 February, was announced in the *Morning Telegraph* (18 January 1920) and other newspapers. Arthur Row's contract for *Richard III* (MS Div., NYPL) was not signed until 16 February, however. Among its provisions is one that states, "The actor, if required, shall give four weeks rehearsal without pay." It is possible that the first two weeks featured preliminary rehearsals with a partial cast, but there may also have been delays in the contract signing. Hopkins's comments on the first rehearsal are from *To a Lonely Boy*, 200.

36. Hopkins, *To a Lonely Boy*, 201.

37. Arthur Feinsod, *The Simple Stage* (Westport, Conn.: Greenwood, 1992), 154.

38. Hopkins, *Reference Point*, 69.

39. Arthur William Row, draft letter, n.d., box 8, folder 3, MS Div., NYPL.
40. William Keighley, unpublished autobiographical essay, William Keighley scrap-
    book, Lincoln Center, 9.
41. Row, "Barrymore Legend," 21, 23. At times, however, Barrymore's patience grew
    thin. Mrs. Thomas Wise, the production's Duchess of York (in private life Gertrude
    Whitty, sister of Dame May), later remembered that at one rehearsal Barrymore
    grew increasingly frustrated at the Queen Margaret, Rosalind Ivan, and finally ex-
    ploded with a loud "Chr-ist" that ground the proceedings to a halt. Interview with
    Alexander Clark, 1 August 1991.
42. Fowler, *Good Night, Sweet Prince*, 194. The "stones in his shoe" account was related
    to the author by Barrymore's grandson, Antony Fairbanks, in a telephone conver-
    sation in July 1990; he had heard this story from his grandmother, Dolores Cos-
    tello – Barrymore's third wife, whom he had married in 1928. In all likelihood it
    predates the account Fowler attributed to Barrymore by at least a decade.
43. Keighley, autobiographical essay, 9.
44. Row, "Barrymore Legend," 23.
45. Details of Jones's settings and costumes, both in these sections and in the recon-
    struction, are based upon his sketches for the *Richard III* costumes at the Harry
    Ransom Humanities Research Center, University of Texas at Austin, additional
    costume sketches at the Harvard Theatre Collection, newspaper descriptions,
    and Francis Bruguiere's production photographs at Lincoln Center, the Museum
    of the City of New York, and other archives. Four of Jones's sketches for the set
    are reproduced in *Theatre Arts* 4 (April 1920), 129–32.
46. Feinsod, *Simple Stage*, 153.
47. Arthur Row attests to the lowering of the house curtain between Sheldon's I.v and
    I.vi in "Barrymore Legend," 25; this interval required a change of scene and a
    major change of costume for Barrymore, from armor to tunic and hose. There is
    no documentation for the use of the house curtain to mask other scene changes
    but Woollcott's reference to "more than a dozen illusion-dispelling intervals" sug-
    gests that this was the case. If the house curtain was used between I.v and I.vi, it
    was surely used elsewhere. See also the reconstruction of *Hamlet* in Chapter 3,
    where there is ample documentation for the lowering of the house curtain for
    most scene changes. "Episodic panorama": *Theatre Magazine* (April 1920), 310.
48. *Current Opinion* (April 1920), 499.
49. See Eric Wollencott Barnes, *The Man Who Lived Twice* (New York: Scribner's, 1956),
    114–18.
50. *Town Topics* (11 March 1920), 14.
51. The soliloquy from *3 Henry VI*, III.ii was released as a 78-rpm record by RCA Vic-
    tor in 1928; another version of this soliloquy was filmed for the 1929 Warner
    Brothers cinematic revue *The Show of Shows*. In June 1937, Barrymore performed
    an abridged version of *Richard III* as part of NBC's "Streamlined Shakespeare" se-
    ries; a copy is at the Museum of Television & Radio. The broadcast was later re-
    leased commercially in further abridged form by Audio Rarities. Both the film and
    the broadcast are discussed in Chapter 5. The Hammerstein Collection of Re-
    corded Sound, Lincoln Center, owns a copy of Barrymore's private recordings. A
    1941 radio show with Rudy Vallee, later released commercially, contains a much-
    abridged "Now is the winter of our discontent" and the scene with Clarence.
52. Row, review of *Good Night, Sweet Prince*, in *Sign Post* (24 February 1944); Carring-
    ton, Wesleyan drafts.
53. *Variety* (12 March 1920).

54. Telephone interview with Maurice Valency, 3 April 1989.

55. Barrymore's entrance following "slightly behind" his brother's: interviews with Alexander Clark, 28 February 1990 and 1 August 1991. The *Morning Telegraph* (8 March 1920) noted that he entered "almost immediately." Barrymore's costume: production photo, Lincoln Center. "Swaggering insolence": *New York American* (8 March 1920); "canvas bag": interviews with Alexander Clark.

56. Line reading: *Show of Shows*.

57. Row, "Barrymore Legend," 22–3.

58. Ibid., 28–9.

59. Soliloquy: RCA Victor recording; *Show of Shows*; 1937 radio broadcast. Concluding gesture: *Show of Shows*.

60. "Weird, uncanny": Row, "Barrymore Legend," 28; flings hand away: ibid., 25.

61. Line readings: private recording.

62. *Nation* (27 March 1920), 403.

63. Row, "Barrymore Legend," 25.

64. *Hartford Courant* (14 March 1920).

65. *New York Herald* (8 March 1920); *Christian Science Monitor* (16 March 1920). Line reading after Clarence's exit: Vallee program. As the "winter of our discontent" soliloquy delivered on this same program is oddly cut, with seemingly every other line omitted, I have not included it here.

66. "Six gentlemen . . . one remains": William Seymour, "Some Richards I Have Seen," *Theatre Magazine* (June 1920), 565. Jones's costume sketch specifies eight mourners; Seymour, writing after the fact, is more reliable. An anonymous manuscript sketch for a biography of Arthur Hopkins, in the Arthur Hopkins papers at Lincoln Center, notes that " the supernumeraries . . . are banished to outer darkness." These papers were uncataloged at the time this book went to press; I am grateful to Senior Archivist Mary Ellen Rogan for providing me with access.

67. *New York Tribune* (14 March 1920); *Daily News* (27 March 1943); *Evening Mail* (9 March 1920).

68. Directly to the audience: Carrington, "John Barrymore I Knew," 8; "Sneering cynicism": *New York Tribune* (14 March 1920); "Full height of success": *Brooklyn Times* (9 March 1920); line readings: radio broadcast.

69. "In bodily shape": Row, "Barrymore Legend," 24; "ironic laughter": *New York Post* (8 March 1920).

70. Hamilton, "Seen on the Stage," 166.

71. The Queen's quiet tones: *Sun–Herald* (8 March 1920).

72. Fox Pollen, "Shakespeare and Benelli," *Arts and Decoration* (April 1920), 397.

73. "Swift baiting": *Nation* (27 March 1920), 403.

74. *World* (14 March 1920).

75. *Evening Mail* (9 March 1920).

76. *Billboard* (27 March 1920); *Town & Country* (1 April 1920), 40. Richard's position center stage: interview with Alexander Clark, 1 August 1991. The use of a real horse in this scene aroused a good deal of comment; see, for example, the 4 April 1920 *New York Tribune*.

77. Line reading: radio broadcast; "converses": *Christian Science Monitor* (16 March 1920).

78. Radio broadcast.

79. Barrymore's concluding business: Hamilton, "Seen on the Stage," 166; *World* (14 March 1920); *New York Post* (8 March 1920).

80. Hamilton, "Seen on the Stage," 166.

81. "Audacious initial plunge": *New York Commercial* (8 March 1920); see also *Variety* (12 March 1920). Barrymore's curtain speech between the second and third acts may seem odd to modern audiences, but it was hardly unprecedented. Taking bows and making speeches between acts was a popular custom during the nineteenth and early twentieth centuries; see, for example, the account of the bows between acts in *Hamlet* in Chapter 3, based on promptbook records. The entrance of other members of the Drew–Barrymore family was described in many newspaper reviews; John Drew was then appearing in *The Cat Bird* at Maxine Elliot's; Ethel Barrymore was in *Déclassée* at the Empire; Lionel Barrymore was in *The Letter of the Law* at the Criterion.

82. *World* (14 March 1920); *Billboard* (27 March 1920); *Evening Telegram* (8 March 1920).

83. "A disintegration of the spirit:" *Nation* (27 March 1920), 403. "Meditating the death of the princes": *Town & Country* (1 April 1920), 40.

84. Interview with Alexander Clark, 28 February 1990; radio broadcast.

85. *World* (8 March 1920); radio broadcast.

86. *New York Times* (8 March 1920).

87. *New York Post* (8 March 1920); radio broadcast.

88. In the 4 April 1920 *Philadelphia Public Ledger*, Gilbert Seldes noted a scene in which there were "no actors at all" – merely the silver-lined coronation robe, which was illuminated as it lay on the throne. It is possible that this device was used at the beginning of the third act but more likely that it was used at the end of III.i; as I have been unable to determine with certainty the point at which this was done, I have not included it in the reconstruction.

89. *Evening Telegram* (8 March 1920).

90. *Sun–Herald* (8 March 1920).

91. *World* (8 March 1920).

92. See also the 14 March 1920 *Pittsburgh Post.*

93. *Sun–Herald* (8 March 1920).

94. *Christian Science Monitor* (16 March 1920). Firm and direct: radio broadcast.

95. *New York Tribune* (8 March 1920).

96. *Sun–Herald* (8 March 1920).

97. *New York American* (8 March 1920).

98. Line readings: private recording; radio broadcast.

99. *New York American* (8 March 1920); *New York Tribune* (8 March 1920).

100. *World* (8 March 1920); *Sun–Herald* (8 March 1920); radio broadcast.

101. *Springfield Union* (11 April 1920); *World* (8 March 1920). Much comment was devoted to Barrymore's "amazing stage fall" (*New York Tribune*, 8 March 1920); he landed, according to the *Springfield Union*, with a crash "which fairly shook the theatre." The critic added that "At many a performance . . . he was as distinctly knocked out by his fall as a beaten prize-fighter. On one or two occasions it was necessary for him to be carried to his dressing room." "Hands clutch the air": *Call* (14 April 1920). See also Power-Waters, *John Barrymore*, 100.

102. *Current Opinion* (April 1920), 499.

103. Walter Prichard Eaton, *The Actor's Heritage* (Freeport, N.Y.: Books for Libraries Presses, 1970 [repr. ed; orig. pub. 1924]), 270, 272.

104. See also *Town & Country* (1 April 1920), 40. Lawrence Reamer, writing in the *Sun–Herald* (14 March 1920) found that Barrymore was "free from all the disturbing mannerisms characteristic of his recent predecessors. He is neither grotesque in movement nor hollow in voice as Henry Irving was, nor does he suffer from the

feebleness of utterance and the lackadaisical manner which often interfered with the enjoyment of Beerbohm Tree's efforts. Richard Mansfield's muscle bound movements were never free in spite of the physical force he was always able to suggest in body and voice. Never, indeed, was an aspirant to the honors of Shakespeare freer from physical traits of a disturbing nature than Mr. Barrymore."

105. *Life* (18 March 1920), 510.

106. See also 19 March 1920 editions of the *Pittsburgh Post* and the *Hartford Courant*.

107. *New Republic* (24 March 1920), 122.

108. *Town & Country* (1 April 1920), 40.

109. *Nation* (27 March 1920), 404. For similar criticism see *Town Topics* (11 March 1920) – the author is probably Lewisohn – and Lewisohn's "A Note on Acting" in *Nation* (17 November 1920), 569–70.

110. Hamilton, "Seen on the Stage," 166.

111. Barrymore, "Blame It on the Queen," 118. For positive comments, see, for example, the 8 March 1920 editions of the *New York Globe*, *New York American*, and *Commercial* and the 13 March *Dramatic Mirror*. For negative comments see the 8 March *World*, whose critic complained that Barrymore's "manner of speech was somewhat dry, and his voice lacked vigor and volume" but remarked that "his reading of Shakespeare's verse was singularly pure and clear."

112. Hamilton, "Seen on the Stage," 166.

113. See, for example, Marie Lennards's comments in *Billboard* (27 March 1920); the cast, she commented, "seemed to have keyed their voices to Mr. Barrymore's quiet and suppressed tones, but they lacked his singular purity and clearness." See also Pollen, "Shakespeare and Benelli," 448; Pollen comments that "All the contributing characters speak in what is practically a monotone, and with mask-like faces."

114. Seymour, "Some Richards I Have Seen," 502. See also *Life* (18 March 1920), 510.

115. *Nation* (27 March 1920), 403. See also the *New Republic* (24 March 1920), 122, and Kenneth Macgowan's comments in *Theatre Arts* 4 (April 1920), 104.

116. *Town & Country* (1 April 1920), 40.

117. *Variety* (19 March 1920).

118. *Town & Country* (1 April 1920), 40.

119. Row, "Barrymore Legend," 24; Hopkins, *To a Lonely Boy*, 201.

120. Barrymore, *Confessions*; Fowler, *Good Night, Sweet Prince*, 194.

121. Interview with Alexander Clark, 28 February 1990.

122. Fowler, *Good Night, Sweet Prince*, 178–9. See also Marc Connelly, *Voices Offstage* (New York: Holt, Rinehart & Winston, 1968), 237, where Connelly comments: "I know that back in the twenties everyone who saw it judged John Barrymore's *Hamlet* to be unforgettable. Great though it was, I found his *Richard III* even more impressive. Barrymore's sinister, half-mad hunchback became incandescent as he gleefully anticipated his conquest of the Lady Anne. The genius of the actor contrived a slight but inspired alteration of Shakespeare's: 'Was ever woman in this humour wooed? Was ever woman in this humour won?' The change to 'Never was woman in this manner wooed; never was woman in this manner won' heightened the deviltry in Richard's gloating."

123. Keighley, autobiographical essay, 9.

124. *Variety* (26 March 1920). Hopkins announced to the press that playing seven performances a week would enable Barrymore to conserve his strength and continue in the role for three weeks longer than he might under ordinary circumstances – an optimistic prediction that proved ironic in retrospect.

125. *Variety* (16 April 1920).
126. Keighley, autobiographical essay, 10.
127. *Springfield Union* (14 April 1920).
128. Strange, *Who Tells Me True*, 208.
129. Carrington, "John Barrymore I Knew," 3.
130. Robert Edmond Jones, unpublished essay on John Barrymore, Harvard Theatre Collection.
131. Barrymore's routine at Muldoon's was described in the *New York American* (25 April 1920) and elsewhere; see, for example, Barrymore's comments in the *World Magazine* (13 June 1920).
132. Letter to John Jay Chapman, 13 April 1920, Houghton Library, Harvard. According to one biographer of Chapman, he was observing Barrymore closely in 1919 and 1920; see Richard B. Hovey, *John Jay Chapman – An American Mind* (New York: Columbia University Press, 1959), 264. Chapman's views on *Richard III* were published in his essay collection, *A Glance Toward Shakespeare* (Boston: Atlantic Monthly Press, 1922), 27–32. "This play," wrote Chapman, "is a rattling melodrama . . . boisterous and stagy, – almost an extravaganza, – and would be intolerable but for the wonderful godlike humor that pervades it."
133. Row, "Barrymore Legend," 25–6.

Chapter 3. Hamlet, 1922–1924

1. *Nation* (6 December 1922), 648.
2. Arthur Hopkins, letter to Gene Fowler [c. October 1942], UCB/SC. An abridged version of this statement was published in Gene Fowler, *Good Night, Sweet Prince* (New York: Viking, 1944), 208.
3. *Evening Mail* (18 November 1922).
4. *New York Globe* (30 October 1920); *New York Times* (2 November 1920).
5. For a detailed account of Jones's work on this production see Dana Sue McDermott, "The Void in *Macbeth*," *Themes in Drama* 4 (1982), 113–25.
6. *New York Times* (6 February and 13 February 1921).
7. *Theatre Arts* 5 (April 1921), 92. Only a few positive reviews were published; see, for example, the 25 February 1921 edition of *Variety*. See also Smith Ely Jelliffe's comments, quoted in *Current Opinion* (April 1921), 495–6.
8. For Hopkins and Jones's contributions see Robert Benchley's review in *Life* (10 March 1921), 352. Here Benchley writes: "The Hopkins method, as nearly as can be ascertained, was to eliminate all non-essential things from the stage and the acting, leaving Shakespeare in the essence. Unfortunately they left the eliminator on too long, and not even Shakespeare was left." "You did everything": Gene Fowler, *Minutes of the Last Meeting* (New York: Viking, 1954), 63.
9. Barrymore's letter to Alexander Woollcott in defense of his wife's play is at the Houghton Library, Harvard. Excerpts appear in Fowler, *Good Night, Sweet Prince*, 200–1. See also Barrymore's comments in his *Confessions of an Actor* (Indianapolis: Bobbs–Merrill, 1926), unpaginated. In May 1921, while appearing in *Clair de Lune*, Barrymore walked on as Romeo in two performances of the annual Equity Show; his appearance was part of a costume parade in which a number of actors dressed as Shakespearean characters and were announced by Nance O'Neil. During the day he filmed interior scenes for *The Lotus Eater*. On 8 May 1921, the *New York Times* announced that the film was practically finished; it was released in November 1921.

10. John Barrymore, "Blame It on the Queen," *American Magazine* (March 1933), 20–3, 114–19 (at 118).
11. See, for example, Michael Strange's account in *Who Tells Me True* (New York: Scribner's, 1940), 175–85, and John Kobler, *Damned in Paradise: The Life of John Barrymore* (New York: Atheneum, 1977), 167. Both accounts are much after the fact. Barrymore, after returning from England, spent several months in the Bahamas during the late winter and spring of 1922; a number of his letters to Michael Strange from this period (they were separated between September 1921 and June 1922) are at Lincoln Center. He returned to New York in mid-May, and it is likely that his journeys to French Lick and White Sulphur Springs and his meeting with Hopkins occurred soon afterward.
12. Ethel Barrymore, *Memories* (New York: Harper & Brothers, 1955), 247.
13. Barrymore, *Confessions*.
14. Hopkins, letter to Gene Fowler [c. October 1942], UCB/SC. See also Barrymore's account in "Blame It on the Queen," 118.
15. *New York Times* (17 and 21 March 1920).
16. Margaret Carrington, "The John Barrymore I Knew," 3, UCB/SC.
17. There is no evidence to indicate directly that Hopkins cut the play before June 1922. See, however, his account in Chapter 2 of textual preparations for *Richard III*; it seems unlikely that Barrymore began his formal study of the play with an uncut text, and it is probable that tentative cuts – the bulk of the fourth act, for example – had been made by this time. In "John Barrymore I Knew," 3, Margaret Carrington remembered that Barrymore "came out to our farm in Connecticut about the end of June." Michael Strange's sailing on the *Mauritania* was mentioned in the 26 June 1922 *New York Times* and other newspapers. The decision for her to spend the summer of preparation away from Barrymore may have been a conscious one, and was, in any case, a wise one, given their tumultuous history.
18. Margaret Huston Walters's recollections of the summer of 1922 were shared in a series of in-person and telephone interviews held between January 1990 and June 1992. I am grateful to Margaret Walters as well, for her many letters about her aunt and her methods of voice training, and for providing me with two unpublished essays she wrote about her aunt and Barrymore. All subsequent quotations, unless otherwise specified, are from the interviews.
19. Carrington, "John Barrymore I Knew," 4, 6.
20. Margaret Huston Walters, "My Aunt Margaret," unpublished essay, author's collection.
21. Carrington, "John Barrymore I Knew," 5. Among the visitors that summer, Margaret Walters recalled, were Arthur Hopkins (who came up to check on Barrymore's progress), Ethel Barrymore, and the actress Peggy Wood, at the time a candidate for Ophelia. See Alexander Woollcott's 17 December 1922 column in the *New York Herald* and Barrymore's 17 October 1922 letter to Michael Strange, Lincoln Center.
22. The studybook was presented to The Players by Robert Edmond Jones after Margaret Carrington's death in 1942. Significant notations made by Barrymore are cited in the notes to the reconstruction of *Hamlet* in performance. See also Barrymore's letter to Michael Strange, n.d. [October 1923] in which he writes, eight months after his first New York season in *Hamlet:* "I see now clearly why I need & have needed Margaret. She . . . [helps me to avoid] a certain kind of bunkum . . . to formulate devices for making it all seem like the real thing."

23. The date of Barrymore's return to New York is unknown. It seems likely, however, that he had concluded his work in Connecticut by the time of Hopkins's announcement of the production on 7 September (see, for example, the 8 September *New York Times*); he was almost certainly in New York by 10 September when Michael Strange arrived from Europe on the *Adriatic*. "His ideas frightened Jack": Fowler, *Good Night, Sweet Prince*, 206. "We argued for four days": Barrymore, "Blame It on the Queen," 118. See also Barrymore's 18 October 1922 to Michael Strange, where he writes: "[I have] just come from the theatre where the company came for the first time. Jones has just left. I brought him back here to dinner to talk to him about how I wanted the play done. It is pretty hard to pierce the precious structure of his head with the lurid vitality – some of that play needs."

24. *The Interpretation of Dreams* was published in 1900 and translated into English in 1913; Part I, which includes a discussion of *Hamlet*, is available in Freud, *The Complete Psychological Works of Sigmund Freud*, 24 vols., ed. James Strachey (London: Hogarth Press, 1957), IV (1900). The *Hamlet* remarks are at 263–6. Ernest Jones's article appeared in the January 1910 issue of the *American Journal of Psychology*; an expanded, book-length version, *Hamlet and Oedipus*, was later published (New York: W. W. Norton, 1949).

25. Fowler, *Good Night, Sweet Prince*, 213–14, 210–11.

26. Will Fowler, *The Young Man from Denver* (New York: Doubleday, 1962), 205–6.

27. Ibid., 208. Hollis Alpert later interviewed Dr. Hyman in connection with *The Barrymores* (New York: Dial Press, 1964); his comments are on pp. 227–8. Hyman claimed that Barrymore saw Dr. Pearce Bailey (1865–1922) "once or twice." Bailey died in February 1922, however, and Barrymore certainly did not consult him during the preparatory period for *Hamlet*. Barrymore may have consulted with Edwin Zabriskie (1874–1959), who practiced neurology and psychiatry in the New York area, but there is no evidence to indicate this other than Hyman's statement.

28. Arthur and Barbara Gelb, *O'Neill* (New York: Harper & Brothers, 1962), 565. Jelliffe (1866–1945) was a pioneering New York analyst who combined Freudian, Jungian, and Adlerian theory; for a more complete discussion of his career see John C. Burnham, *Jelliffe: American Psychiatrist and Physician* (Chicago: University of Chicago Press, 1983); Helena Jelliffe Goldschmidt's recollections of her father advising on Ophelia's mad song are on p. 151. Helena had also appeared in the 1921 Hopkins–Jones–Lionel Barrymore *Macbeth*. It seems well within the realm of possibility, even likely, that Barrymore consulted Jelliffe, as Jelliffe had taken an interest in the actor five years earlier; his analyses of Peter Ibbetson, Fedya, and Giannetto appeared in the 3 September 1917 and 18 January and 4 October 1919 editions of the *New York Medical Journal*.

29. "Fascinated with Freud" is from Blanche Yurka's comments in the anonymous manuscript sketch for a biography of Arthur Hopkins, Lincoln Center. "That bastard": Fowler, *Young Man from Denver*, 210, and Kobler, *Damned in Paradise*, 180.

30. Kobler, *Damned in Paradise*, 174.

31. In "Blame It on the Queen," 118, Barrymore mentions that he worked with Margaret Carrington a total of four months; it seems likely, however, that he did not devote his full attention to the production until 7 October, when Michael Strange again sailed for Europe. He spent the following weekend with Carrington at Denbigh; see his 8 and 9 October letters to Michael Strange, Lincoln Center.

32. Whitford Kane, *Are We All Met?* (London: Elkin, Mathews & Marrot, 1931), 224, 226.

33. Lark Taylor, "With Hey Ho!" unpublished autobiography, Vanderbilt University Special Collections, 331.
34. John F. Otis Jr., "The Barrymore *Hamlet:* 1922–1925," (Ph.D. diss.: Dept. of Theatre, University of Illinois, 1968), 24.
35. Taylor, "With Hey Ho!" 331.
36. Letter to Michael Strange, Lincoln Center. Barrymore also states that "Peggy Wood cannot play Ophelia as her manager Savage will not let her off" and he adds that "Tyrone Power thank God is going to play the King – if he is toned down he may be great." In this same letter he states that Eva Le Gallienne was also a candidate for Ophelia and mentions that "I had a long talk to Miss Helburn the Theatre Guild woman about her but she is under contract with Shubert for *Lilliom* all season. . . . God knows *who* we are going to get for [the Queen] – perhaps Violet Cooper. Everything seems to point toward her now." It is likely that Rosalinde Fuller and Blanche Yurka were formally awarded their roles the next day. See also Barrymore's 11 October 1922 letter to Michael Strange, in which he discusses going to the theatre with Carrington and Jones to see Louis Calvert, at the time a candidate for the King.
37. Blanche Yurka, *Bohemian Girl* (Athens: Ohio University Press, 1970), 96–7.
38. The 18 October date for the start of rehearsals is noted in the unpaginated early pages of Lark Taylor's rehearsal studybook and in Barrymore's 18 October 1922 letter to Michael Strange; the scheduled times are in Otis, "Barrymore *Hamlet,*" 25–6. In *Bohemian Girl*, 98, Blanche Yurka states that preliminary rehearsals without Barrymore went on for "over a week," but in all likelihood she was thinking of second-season rehearsals when Barrymore was completing a film in Hollywood; she mentions that Barrymore arrived "from the coast." Taylor's comments are from "With Hey Ho!" 332, and "My Season with John Barrymore in Hamlet" (unpublished essay, Vanderbilt University Special Collections), 1.
39. Taylor, "With Hey Ho!" 332.
40. Taylor, "My Season," 1.
41. Taylor, "With Hey Ho!" 333.
42. Kane, *Are We All Met?* 227–8.
43. Yurka, *Bohemian Girl*, 98–9.
44. Taylor, "With Hey Ho!" 335.
45. Yurka, *Bohemian Girl*, 98.
46. Taylor, "My Season," 3.
47. Ibid., 2–3.
48. Ibid., 3.
49. The cutting of IV.iii during the last week of rehearsals is noted in Taylor's first-season studybook, 116; in his 8 October letter to Michael Strange, Barrymore commented that "A great deal of the play that is cut out usually I have a lurking desire to put *back*. The pungent gross vitality of the scene about the worms and the body of Polonius for instance." The staging of the fight scene is discussed in Taylor, "My Season," 4.
50. Taylor, "With Hey Ho!" 333; "My Season," 2.
51. Taylor, "With Hey Ho!" 336.
52. Kane, *Are We All Met?* 229–33.
53. Taylor "My Season," 4.
54. Yurka, *Bohemian Girl*, 99.
55. Ethel Barrymore, *Memories*, 247–8.

56. An account of their journey, with text by Macgowan and sketches by Jones, was published later that year as *Continental Stagecraft* (New York: Harcourt Brace, 1922).

57. Ibid., 130–1. In Germany, Jessner's signature motif had already spread to other directors, most notably Jürgen Fehling, who utilized *Jessnertreppen* in his production of Ernst Toller's *Masse-Mensch* at the Berlin Volksbühne. See ibid., 150–5.

58. The approximate dimensions of the set are noted in scale drawings made by Lark Taylor, which he included in three of his promptbooks. The apron was eliminated for the second season and tour.

59. *Variety* (24 November 1922). Interestingly, Jones's design for the tableau curtain figures resembles one of Barrymore's early drawings; see the photographic section following p. 442 in James Kotsilibas-Davis, *Great Times Good Times: The Odyssey of Maurice Barrymore* (Garden City, N.Y.: Doubleday, 1977).

60. Kane, *Are We All Met?* 229–33.

61. Louis M. Simon, "The Stagehand B'way Producers Regarded as an Artistic Partner," *Variety* (10 June 1981).

62. A detailed light plot is included in the unpaginated early pages of William Adams's stage manager's promptbook and was copied by Taylor into his own promptbooks. See also Francis Bruguiere, "The Camera and the Scene," *Theatre Arts Anthology* (New York: Theatre Arts Books, 1950), 400–2. Bruguiere comments, "In the production of *Hamlet* there were continually shifting moods of color through the different scenes."

63. See, for example, the 10 December 1922 *New York Herald*.

64. The Adams promptbook includes a complete property list, copied by Taylor into his own promptbooks.

65. Kane, *Are We All Met?* 233–4.

66. Taylor, "With Hey Ho!" 335–6; "My Season," 3. For details of the costumes I have drawn upon production photographs by Francis Bruguiere at Lincoln Center, the Museum of the City of New York, and elsewhere; additional details are provided by self-portraits in costume by Cecil Clovelly, E. J. Ballantine, and Frank Hearn in Lark Taylor's second-season promptbook. I have also drawn upon Sasha's photographs of the 1925 London production for a few details; more than forty of these are in the Hulton Getty Picture Collection in London.

67. Taylor, "With Hey Ho!" 336.

68. Ibid.; "My Season," 4.

69. See, for example, *The Bookman* (January 1923), 665.

70. *Evening Mail* (18 November 1922); see also *Evening Telegram* (8 December 1923).

71. *New York Globe* (22 November 1922).

72. See also Taylor's account of Barrymore's speech in "My Season," 5.

73. Arthur Hopkins, *To a Lonely Boy* (Garden City, N.Y.: Doubleday, 1937), 231.

74. Jones's drawings for the set were published in *Theatre Arts* 7 (January 1923), 43–6, and *Theatre Magazine* (January 1923), 22.

75. In 1925 Barrymore recorded "To be, or not to be" for Famous Records; in 1928 he recorded the "rogue and peasant slave" soliloquy for RCA Victor; private recordings made on acetate disks feature two readings of Hamlet's advice to the Players (Lincoln Center). Barrymore's 1937 radio broadcast of *Hamlet* for NBC's "Streamlined Shakespeare" series is at the Museum of Radio & Television. This was released, in abridged form, as a commercial recording in several versions; Audio Rarities 2280/2281 also includes a recording of the "To be, or not to be" soliloquy, which was not spoken on the radio broadcast. Gryphon 900 (Lincoln Center) contains another version of "To be, or not to be."

76. A copy of the screen test is in the Film Division, Museum of Modern Art.
77. Taylor, "My Season," 16.
78. All HAM numbers mentioned subsequently refer to Charles H. Shattuck, *The Shakespeare Promptbooks* (Urbana: University of Illinois Press, 1965). Adams's promptbook, donated to Lincoln Center after the publication of this work, is not listed.
79. HAM 154 in Shattuck; HAM 30 in the Folger catalogue; henceforth referred to as Taylor 1. On 10 February 1923, Taylor wrote on one of the unpaginated final pages: "I've marked on this book for several months – and have the satisfaction of knowing that not another copy of [the] original cuts and markings – as per rehearsals and first performance – exists – or can ever be made. – Even Barrymore himself possesses no copy – and wants to go over my copy with me some day – but we didn't do it."
80. HAM 155, henceforth referred to as Taylor 2.
81. HAM 156; HAM 31 in the Folger catalogue; henceforth referred to as Taylor 3.
82. HAM 157; henceforth referred to as Taylor 4.
83. Henceforth referred to as Adams. Another copy of this text may have been used as Barrymore's second-season studybook, and the typescript may have been prepared for this purpose. In at least half a dozen instances, stage directions refer to Hamlet as "you," although on a few occasions other characters are referred to as "you" as well. Barrymore's studybook at The Players contains incomplete cuts to the part of Hamlet and to many of the scenes in which he does not appear; it would have been of limited use in jogging his memory for the second season. The Adams promptbook is paginated by scene and is subsequently cited in this manner.
84. HAM 158. Henceforth referred to as Studybook.
85. Archer's "On Cutting Shakespeare" was published in *Fortnightly Review* (June 1919), 965–73; Shaw's response, "On Cutting Shakespear," is in the August 1919 issue, 215–18. Shaw concluded that "There are a thousand most sensible reasons for cutting not only Shakespear's plays, but all plays, all symphonies, all operas, all epics, and all pictures which are too large for the dining-room. And there is absolutely no reason on earth for not cutting them except the design of the author, who was probably too conceited to be a good judge of his own work."
86. Hampden, for example, deleted references to Ophelia's "chaste treasure" (I.iii), the Ghost's mention of "lewdness" and "lust" (I.v), the "secret parts of fortune" exchange, and most of the other sexual references, as did Sothern and Forbes-Robertson. For Hampden I have used his 1919 promptbook of *Hamlet* (probably utilized until 1924) at The Players. For Sothern I relied upon William Adams's stage manager's promptbook at Lincoln Center, prepared for the 1919–20 season; for Forbes-Robertson I have used the 1914 promptbook at the Huntington Library. Forbes-Robertson, in keeping with Victorian moral values and his "genteel" approach, deleted not only the sexual references but also such harshnesses as "Now might I do it pat" and "I'll lug the guts." Significant Hopkins–Barrymore restorations are discussed in Appendix B. All line references there and elsewhere are to the Temple *Hamlet*, the edition used by the cast. This edition, edited by Israel Gollancz, was first published in 1895 by J. M. Dent (London) and E. P. Dutton (New York). It subsequently had more than a dozen printings; Barrymore and the cast used the 1919 edition.
87. For comments by Barrymore about his character similar to those in the *New York Tribune* interview, see the 27 January 1924 *Cleveland Plain Dealer* and Barrymore's 8 October 1922 letter to Michael Strange. Here he writes: "He has *many* sides –

great profundity – vision beauty and crystalline sanity – and in the face of evil or 'bunkum' a virile justly sardonic – clearly grossness – an *arrow-like* quality – direct and certain – almost careless it is so sure – it is only with *himself* he is ever uncertain. He *knows* too much he *thinks* too deeply too *truly* – he is too highly sensitised too genuinely intellectual to be *conclusive*."

88. Line cuts for the various incarnations of this production are specified in section II of Appendix B.

There have been several previous attempts at reconstruction. The only published narrative account of stage business to date has been in John A. Mills, *Hamlet on Stage: The Great Tradition* (Westport, Conn.: Greenwood, 1984), 189–207. Mills utilized two of Taylor's promptbooks and offers a brief yet effective hybrid of the main business of Barrymore's New York and London *Hamlet*s. Marvin Rosenberg, in *The Masks of Hamlet* (Newark: University of Delaware Press, 1992), includes some of Barrymore's stage business in his scene-by-scene account of noteworthy stage interpretations. Four unpublished doctoral dissertations have featured accounts of the production along with attempts to document stage business. David N. Davis used the Folger promptbooks in "The Hamlets of Edwin Booth, John Barrymore, and Christopher Plummer" (Wayne State University, 1968); he provides a slightly more detailed account than is available in Mills. John F. Otis Jr. attempted a fuller reconstruction in "The Barrymore *Hamlet:* 1922–1925"; Aubrey Berg's "Collaborators: Arthur Hopkins, Robert Edmond Jones, and the Barrymores" (University of Illinois at Urbana–Champaign, 1979) focuses on the collaborative process, although some stage business is included. Of these, the most detailed account of stage business is in Otis, who used all four Taylor promptbooks and interviewed William P. Adams, Blanche Yurka, and other members of the *Hamlet* company. Otis's account preserves perhaps a dozen readings – particularly in the first court scene – that might otherwise have been lost. However, he apparently did not have access to Adams's promptbook, with its wealth of documentation, and some of the information communicated orally by Adams forty-five years after the fact was erroneous and is contradicted by other sources. Adams stated, for example, that Blanche Yurka was the first actor cast and that the recorder scene was played for only one performance and then cut. Daniel Ronald Kroll's "Hamlet from Edwin Booth to Laurence Olivier: Some Changing Interpretations Reflecting Changes in Culture and in the Tastes of Audiences" (Columbia University, 1959) devotes minimal space to stage business, but situates Barrymore's performance in the context of other major nineteenth- and twentieth-century actors of the role. The post-1940 biographies of Barrymore and his family discussed in n. 1 to the Preface feature discussions of *Hamlet* but for the most part confine themselves to anecdotes and a sampling of criticism; stage business is largely ignored.

89. Taylor 1 and 3, 1, contain the opening music, also recorded in the unpaginated early pages of Taylor 4. The initial business is from Taylor 3 and 4, 1, and Adams I.i, 1. "Fearful and anxious": Taylor, "With Hey Ho!" 334.

90. Taylor 4, 1.

91. Ibid., 2.

92. *Daily News* (17 November 1922). It is possible, however, that this may have referred to I.iv; no mention is made of this effect in the Adams light plot.

93. Taylor 3, 3.

94. Horatio's lines here are transposed from later in the scene; see Appendix B. Adams, I.i, 3, places "Stay! speak, speak" at the end of Horatio's speech; Taylor, in all four promptbooks, places this at the beginning.

95. No sound effect for the cock crow is specified in any of the promptbooks; it was probably not used during the first season. Apparently it was tried during second-season rehearsals and perhaps in performance; Adams I.i, 3, contains a note in pen – "cock crow" – but it is crossed out. Lines 70–127a were cut; see Appendix B.

96. Taylor 3, 7.

97. *World* (18 November 1922). Heywood Broun found that "The effect is one of the most beautiful we have ever seen in the theatre."

98. Taylor 3, 8, notes that there was "a long wait after [the first] scene – during which time the audience is seated. Frequently Barrymore would take this time to dress – and the wait would sometimes be for 10 minutes – one night it was 20 minutes."

99. Lights up during the last measure of curtain music: Taylor 3 and 4, 8; Adams, I.ii, 1; Taylor 3, 8, includes the music. Whispered conversation: Margaret Webster, *The Same Only Different* (London: Gollancz, 1969), 300–1; idem, *Shakespeare Today* (London: J. M. Dent, 1957), 107.

100. Tense: Webster, *Shakespeare Today*, 107; "a thing entirely apart": *International Interpreter* (16 December 1922), 1165. Hamlet's initial pose is taken from a 1925 Sasha photo at the Hulton Getty Picture Collection (see Fig. 24). The Queen is standing in the photo, but is seated in American promptbook records of the production; the positions of the other principal characters were the same. The *Daily News* (London) described Hamlet as "listless with grief" when first seen (20 February 1925). Taylor 2, 9, features a drawing of two thrones with the King downstage left of the Queen; this represents the earliest blocking, changed during the run. The later arrangement is used here. "Amorous groups": John Gielgud, "The Hamlet Tradition," in Rosamond Gilder, *John Gielgud's Hamlet* (New York: Oxford University Press, 1937), 37. Costumes: *Evening Telegram* (17 November 1922) and *Daily News* (17 November 1922).

101. *International Interpreter* (16 December 1922), 1165; *Evening Telegram* (17 November 1922).

102. Adams, I.ii, 1; Taylor 4, 8.

103. Taylor 4, 10; Adams has him rise at his exit.

104. Taylor 1 and 3, 10–11.

105. "Taciturn and cryptic": *International Interpreter* (16 December 1922), 1165. Pause after "Ay, Madam": Otis, "Barrymore *Hamlet*," 69.

106. Emphases and rising tone: Studybook, 13; "quickly": Otis, "Barrymore *Hamlet*," 70.

107. Emphasis on "good mother": Otis, "Barrymore *Hamlet*," 70; fingers cloak: *New Statesman* (7 March 1925), 626, and *Boston Transcript* (26 December 1923).

108. "Shapes": studybook, 13; emphasis on "seem," and slowness: Otis, "Barrymore *Hamlet*," 70; the slight pauses are noted in Adams, I.ii, 2. Emphasis on "But I have that . . . ," Studybook, 13. A letter to the *New York Times* (7 January 1923) noted that, at least once, Barrymore interpolated "are" in "These but the trappings. . . ."

109. Taylor 3, 11–12; Adams, I.ii, 2.

110. "Long pause" and "looks at the Queen and then looks away": Taylor 3, 13. Adams I.ii, 3 notes that music was used here during the second season; the Taylor promptbooks do not include a music cue.

111. *New York Review* (18 November 1922); Otis, "Barrymore *Hamlet*," 70–1.

112. Marked "up" in Studybook, 15.

113. *New York Review* (22 November 1922); *Evening Telegram* (17 November 1922).

114. *International Interpreter* (16 December 1922), 1165; James Agate, *Ego 7* (London: George G. Harrap, 1945), 265. Studybook, 15, notes "gesture" after "uses of this world."

115. Otis, "Barrymore *Hamlet*," 71.

116. *New Republic* (6 December 1922), 45.

117. "Drawn out": Otis, "Barrymore *Hamlet*," 71. Firmer and more regular: *International Interpreter* (16 December 1922), 1165; Studybook, 15, notes "Surprise."

118. Emphasis on "dexterity": Adams, I.ii, 3. Pause: Taylor 4, 14.

119. Readings to the end of the scene, except where noted, are from the 1937 radio broadcast. "Boyish comrade": *Morning Telegraph* (17 November 1922). Clasps Horatio's shoulders: Taylor 3 and 4, 14.

120. "Jovially": Taylor 2, 17. Emphasis on second "thrift": Studybook, 16. Pauses and emphasis on "coldly": Adams, I.ii, 4.

121. Taylor, "With Hey Ho!" 345.

122. Taylor 4, 17.

123. Intently: Taylor 3, 17; pause: Taylor 3, 17, and Adams, I.ii, 6. Astonished: *New York Globe* (13 December 1922).

124. Adams, I.ii, 7.

125. "High" and "breath": Studybook, 21. Blocking and glaring at throne: Adams I.ii. 7. The glaring at the throne was a second-season innovation, noted by Adams in pen; Barrymore's exit in Taylor 1, 2, and 3 is R; Taylor 4 says L. The *Westminster Gazette* (20 February 1925) noted Barrymore's "occasional tendency to break up concluding lines into triplets such as 'all the earth – o'erwhelm them – to men's eyes.'" This reading is retained in the 1937 radio broadcast.

126. Webster, *Same Only Different*, 300–1, and *Shakespeare Today*, 107. The London production, directed by Barrymore, used a variation on the American staging. Adams I.ii, 1, has every character except Hamlet looking toward the throne as the scene begins; the critic for the *Evening Telegram* (17 November 1922) noted that the stage is "slowly and silently flooded with light."

127. The business in this scene is from Adams, I.iii, 1–3, and Taylor 1, 3, and 4, 19–24. "In a more gentle manner": Adams, I.iii, 3.

128. Taylor, "My Season," 8. See also Stark Young's positive comments in the *New Republic* (6 December 1922), 45; for a negative view of O'Brien's characterization see John Corbin's review in the *New York Times* (17 November 1922).

129. Line readings: *Hamlet* screen test and 1937 radio broadcast.

130. Expression: Taylor 1, 3, and 4, 25. However, see also H. H. Furness Jr.'s comments in *The Drama* (March 1923), 207–8, 230 (at 207); Furness found that "Barrymore shows terror or fear rather than a wondering maze of awe at such a sight." The *Daily News* (London) noted that he was "almost speechless with terror" at the Ghost's first appearance (20 February 1925). Face brilliantly lighted: unidentified Boston review, Harvard Theatre Collection (25 December 1923). Cloak slips off his shoulders: Adams I.iv, 1; screen test. Studybook, 29, notes "attack high" before "Angels and ministers of grace defend us!"

131. Clasps hands; reaches for sword: screen test.

132. Furness found that on this line there was no "manifestation of actual fear; it is the questioning of one who doubts the identity of this vision." *The Drama* (March 1923), 207. See also *The Spectator* (28 February 1925), 319, which noted that there was "no emphasis on 'life' or 'pin.'" This contradicts the emphases in the screen test and recordings.

133. Taylor 3, 27.

134. Robert Speaight, *William Poel and the Elizabethan Revival* (London: Heineman, 1954), 27. Poel, according to Speaight, had seen Salvini use this business and de-

scribed it to his nephew, Reginald Pole, who played the Ghost in New York and on tour. Pole shared this business with Barrymore, who adopted it in his own performance.

135. Adams I.iv, 2; screen test. The business with the sword had also been used by Booth; see Charles H. Shattuck, *The Hamlet of Edwin Booth* (Urbana: University of Illinois Press, 1969), 145–7.

136. Adams, I.iv, 2–3.

137. Ibid., I.iv, 3, and light plot.

138. Adams, light plot; Taylor 1, 28. During the second season, the Ghost appeared onstage as the familiar armor-clad figure; a short light was used on the Ghost, who stood below and left of the steps.

139. Adams's light plot notes that during the second season the light on the Ghost dimmed out on "fretful porpentine" and then another light for the Ghost, striking on the lower platform, came on slowly, reaching full on "List, list, O list."

140. This, according to Margaret Carrington, was a crucial moment of transition for Hamlet's character; her comments are quoted in the "Summer of Preparation" section of this chapter. However, see also Barrymore's comments on his uncertainty as to the vision's identity following the reconstruction of I.iv, where he contradicts Carrington's statement.

141. Adams, I.iv, 3–4.

142. This was cut for the second season, when the Ghost backed out slowly left and exited.

143. "Well nigh invisible": *New York Times* (17 December 1922). Studybook, 36, contains the notation, "sincerely (pitifully)" next to this speech. The readings are from the 1937 radio broadcast. For a slight variation on the initial business of the soliloquy see A. C. Sprague, *The Stage Business in Shakespeare's Plays: A Postscript*, repr. ed. (Folcroft, Pa.: Folcroft Press, 1969), 16. Sprague recalls Barrymore beginning the "host of heaven" speech gazing upward, yet Taylor 1 and 2 have him falling face down.

144. Kane, *Are We All Met?* 231. *Punch* (25 February 1925), 218, noted the "unexpectedly vociferous vehemence of 'O most pernicious woman! O villain! villain!'"

145. *Shadowland* (February 1923), 38.

146. Ibid.; Bernard Grebanier, *The Heart of Hamlet* (New York: Crowell, 1960), 144. Emphasis on "all": Adams, I.iv, 6.

147. Adams, I.iv, 6.

148. Taylor 3, 34.

149. *New York Times* (17 December 1922).

150. *New Statesman* (7 March 1925), 627.

151. Otis, "Barrymore *Hamlet*," 86; William Adams was the source.

152. Emphasis on "I": Studybook, 41; this same page also contains the notation "sadly again" next to this speech.

153. Adams, I.iv, 7.

154. A letter to the *New York Globe* (13 December 1922) complained that Hamlet held his bosom friend, Horatio, at arm's length, said to him, "Nay, let's go in together," and then went in alone. Barrymore wrote "boyishly" in his studybook next to this speech; this may refer to the last line.

155. Fowler, *Good Night, Sweet Prince*, 210–11.

156. Taylor 3, 44, notes that during the second season, when the apron was eliminated, this scene was played well downstage on the mainstage.

157. Adams I.v, 1; this was the blocking at the end of the first season. Taylor's prompt-books are contradictory and suggest that several changes were made. Taylor 1 says Ophelia is discovered LC; Taylor 2 (the opening-night blocking) says she enters C and crosses to the apron; Taylor 3 (second season) says she is discovered RC well downstage; Taylor 4 says she is discovered LC on the apron.

158. Adams, I.v, 1.

159. Ibid., I.v, 2; Taylor 3, 45. Taylor 1 and 4 state that he holds the curtains for her and follows her out.

160. No music is specified in any of the Taylor promptbooks. Adams I.vi, 1 includes a music cue but does not specify instruments. The trumpet and drum flourish is like-ly, given its use in introducing other court scenes.

161. Adams, I.vi, 1; Taylor 4, 46, says that the King and Queen are seated on a bench up on the first platform, C; this was first-season blocking. Taylor's diagram on the same page contradicts this, and his diagram in Taylor 3 shows two chairs; this rep-resents a second-season change.

162. Taylor 3, 47–8.

163. Adams, I.vi, 2.

164. Ibid., I.vi, 4; Taylor 4, 53.

165. Adams, I.vi, 4; Taylor 1, 3, and 4, 53.

166. Adams, I.vi, 4; Taylor 3, 54.

167. Taylor 3, 55; Adams, I.vi, 4.

168. Taylor 3, 55, says that he leans on the chair here; Adams and Taylor 4 place this two lines later; Taylor 2, 58–9 (the rehearsal blocking) places this eight lines later.

169. Adams, I.vi, 6.

170. Taylor 3, 57.

171. Taylor 4, 57.

172. Adams, I.vi, 6.

173. Taylor 4, 57; Adams, I.vi, 6.

174. "Exchange smiles": Adams, I.vi, 6. "Turns and looks at them": Taylor 4, 58. Study-book, 61, contains the note, "to look at them."

175. Studybook, 61, contains the note, "Here look out but not interpret."

176. Taylor 3, 58, notes that "For a time Barrymore used to laugh quite gaily at this point – and balance himself on the back of his chair. – It was one innovation of his season that seemed meaningless – and he soon stopped doing it."

177. Studybook, 61.

178. The music is in Taylor 1 and 4, 60, and Taylor 3, 58.

179. Adams, I.vi, 7; emphasis on "mad": Studybook, 64.

180. Line readings: radio broadcast.

181. Taylor 3 and 4, 61.

182. Taylor 3, 61, notes that this business "crept in" but was not done during the sec-ond season and "is not good."

183. Taylor 3, 62, notes that during the second season Hamlet "Half-intoned it – 'Twas more effective sung." Taps Polonius on the chest: Adams, I.vi, 8.

184. Adams, I.vi, 8. Along with much other business in the scene, this was variable; Tay-lor 4, for example, has him sitting on "but it was never acted."

185. Taylor, "My Season," 13.

186. Adams, I.vi, 9; Taylor 3 and 4, 64–5.

187. Taylor 4, 65; Adams, I.vi, 9.

188. Taylor 4, 66; *Evening Mail* (17 November 1922).

189. Taylor, "My Season," 11.
190. Taylor 4, 66.
191. Line readings: RCA Victor recording and radio broadcast.
192. Adams, I.vi, 11.
193. Ibid.
194. Slight pauses: *New Republic* (6 December 1922), 45.
195. Adams, I.vi, 11; correction in pen. Originally, and during the second season, Hamlet exited R (Taylor 1 and 3, 68); at the end of the first season the curtain fell as Hamlet sat in the chair writing madly (Adams, I.vi, 11).
196. The curtain call is in the unnumbered early pages in Adams.
197. Helen Hayes, "Helen Hayes Picks the 10 Most Memorable Stage Performances," *Colliers* (22 September 1951), 20–1, 80–1 (at 20).
198. Taylor, "My Season," 13.
199. *Daily Telegraph* (London), 22 January 1925.
200. Adams, II.i, 1. Taylor 3 contains a note that the blocking of this scene was "changed . . . early last season – and retained." The blocking described in the text is the second arrangement. The original first-season blocking had the King and Queen on twin thrones on the first platform, L; Hamlet's chair was C on the mainstage; Rosencrantz and Guildenstern knelt parallel to each other SL front, facing the King; Polonius (R) and Ophelia (L) stood at the base of the step leading to the first platform. Taylor 3 includes diagrams of both arrangements. Contradictions between Adams and Taylor 3 and 4 make it likely that the scene was further reblocked during the second season.
201. Adams II.i, 1, says they exit R, as was probably done after the first-season alterations; all four Taylor promptbooks say they exit L.
202. Lines 33–37a of the King's speech were restored for the second season. Adams II.i, 2, notes this in pen, as does Taylor 2, 76.
203. Adams II.i, 2, contains a second-season change in pen – she crosses quickly to C, looking off L, then exits R. The pause is in Taylor 3, 75.
204. Hamlet's entrance for "To be, or not to be" was done in several different ways. Adams and Taylor 2 have him entering from the mainstage; Taylor 3 and 4, 75, note that he entered from L on the top platform, crossed to C, then went down the stairs to RC and slowly crossed LC to the chair. Taylor 1 says he enters through the curtains, C, on the top platform. Adams is the only source that mentions the cloak. All four Taylor promptbooks have Hamlet sitting in the chair after his first line; Adams has him sit after "Whether 'tis nobler in the mind." The business of sitting during the soliloquy was hardly novel and had been used by Booth in 1870; see Shattuck, *Hamlet of Edwin Booth*, 187–8. Line readings of the soliloquy are from Famous Records, Audio Rarities 2280, and Gryphon 900. Barrymore's studybook has the notation "high" next to the beginning of this speech; this is contradicted by his recordings.
205. Bitter smile and high inflection on "Ay": Herman Weinberg, "John Barrymore: Profile of a Royal Performer," in Danny Peary, ed., *Closeups* (New York: Workman Press, 1978), 93–4. Desmond MacCarthy noted that Barrymore gave a "gust of unnecessary emphasis at the words 'bare bodkin.'" *New Statesman* (7 March 1925), 626. This passage is not included in Barrymore's recordings of the soliloquy. See also the *Sunday Express* (22 February 1925) which commented that "in . . . 'his quietus made with a bare bodkin,' the last word was shot out fortissimo, as if it were a clarion summons to the distinguished Director of Public Prosecutions."

206. *Philadelphia Ledger* (22 November 1922).
207. Adams, II.i, 4; *New Statesman* (7 March 1925), 626. The emphasis on "bawd" is from Adams. Pauses in "I did love you once": *Manchester City News* (11 April 1925).
208. *International Interpreter* (16 December 1922), 1165, 1167; Taylor 3, 77.
209. See James Agate's 22 February 1925 review in the *Sunday Times* (London), and *New Statesman* (7 March 1925), 626. The Temple edition, Adams, and Agate say "heaven and earth"; Desmond MacCarthy, in *New Statesman*, says "earth and heaven," either an error or a reversal by Barrymore at the performance he attended.
210. Adams II.i, 4; *International Interpreter* (16 December 1922), 1167. Taylor 4, 78, notes that the original business after "Go thy ways to a nunnery" was as follows: "Looking over Ophelia's head he sees Polonius and the King off R, crosses to R, then turns and looks at Ophelia." Taylor comments that "This business was changed – Hamlet goes to R – sees Polonius and King off R – gives gasp of pain and anger – looks at Ophelia – who avoids his look and will not meet his eye – crosses back to Ophelia and stands quite close to her – speaks calmly and gently. Sometimes he would be quite rough and fierce." See also John Corbin's description of Hamlet's "simulated frenzy" in the 26 November 1922 *New York Times*. Taylor 2, 81, notes than in the original blocking Hamlet held her arms on "Where's your father?"
211. Hamlet's tone of angry resentment is described by Furness in *The Drama* (March 1923), 208; he notes that later, "with great effort, he restrains himself from clasping her in his arms." Taylor 1 and 2 say that Hamlet crosses R as he starts to exit; this represents the earliest blocking. Chance Newton, writing in the *Referee* (22 February 1925), commented that "the distracted prince's supposed love for [Ophelia] broke forth in a very touching manner. The sudden revulsion on finding the poor, love-lorn damsel lying to him (by order) was a thrilling dramatic stroke." Adams, II.i, 4, notes that during the second season Ophelia crossed to Hamlet but backed R and upstage a step before "O, help him, you sweet heavens!" Furness (op. cit., 208) noted that "The next speeches bidding her go to a nunnery, and his denunciation are spoken as though with a backward glance at the two spies, meaning 'Do you want madness? You shall have your money's worth then!'" A letter to the *New York Times*, published on 7 January 1923, notes that Hamlet "looks into the wings three distinct times." Taylor cites only one instance, Adams none; the other times may have come here and following the next "Farewell."
212. Adams, II.i, 4; Taylor 1 and 4, 78, say backs away R.
213. *International Interpreter* (16 December 1922), 1167.
214. Emphasis on "mad": Studybook, 82; strikes forehead: Adams II.i, 5. Taylor 3, 78, notes the three-second pause and clutching Ophelia's hand.
215. Looks toward conspirators: Taylor 3, 78. Looks toward throne: Adams II.i, 5, written in pen for the second season.
216. Adams II.i, 5. See also Furness's comments in *The Drama* (March 1923), 208.
217. Originally the exit was R; Taylor 4, 79, explains that "about the 8th week this exit was changed." John Corbin, writing in the *New York Times* (26 November 1922), noted the problem of the original exit R where he "brushes by the spies, as if they had ceased to be." *The Spectator* (28 February 1925), noted that "His final 'to a nunnery go' sounds upon the poor lady's perplexity almost as a discreet recommendation to one legal way out of a scandal. She would hardly have believed him in earnest."
218. Ten-second pause and gradual cross: Taylor 3, 79. Adams II.i, 5 notes that during the second season she crossed to the chair and sat on "quite, quite down!"

219. Taylor 3 and 4 have Polonius crossing to C on "How now, Ophelia!" Adams II.i, 5, says that Ophelia crosses to the King and Polonius before this line; during the second season she rose from the chair and looked toward them. Ophelia's cross to C weeping quietly is from Adams II.i, 5. Polonius's turn and bow is from Taylor 3, 80. Adams II.i, 6, notes that during the second season Ophelia sank into her chair after the King's last line. Taylor 3, 80, has the scene ending with the King, followed by Polonius and Ophelia, exiting R as the lights dim out.

220. Taylor 3, 78–9.

221. Taylor, "My Season," 11.

222. The advice to the Player is included on the radio broadcast and in two fuller versions on Barrymore's private recordings. In all of these Barrymore's "colloquial" approach is apparent. The stage business is from Adams II.ii,. 1, and Taylor 1, 3, and 4, 80–1. Subsequent line readings are from the radio broadcast.

223. *New York Herald* (4 December 1922).

224. The 7 January 1923 letter to the *New York Times* found another example of paraphrasing here, complaining that "he substitutes 'values more than' for 'must in your allowance o'erweigh.'"

225. Adams II.ii, 2.

226. *New York Times* (7 January 1923). A 13 December 1922 letter to the *New York Globe* noted that he pronounced "rev-e-nue" instead of the traditional "re-ven-ue."

227. Adams II.ii, 2. Lines 68–73b are cut in Adams but in elsewhere; they are cut and restored in Taylor 2. Emphasis on "do": Otis, "Barrymore *Hamlet*," 122.

228. Blocking and clasps hand on Horatio's shoulder: Taylor 3, 83. Draws back with a short laugh: Adams II.ii, 2. Breaks off with half-reluctant shyness: *New Statesman* (7 March 1925), 626. However, see also the 7 January 1923 letter to the *New York Times*; its author found that the speech was delivered with "get-it-over-with condescension."

229. Taylor 2, 88, notes that he sat on the steps here in the original blocking.

230. Adams II.ii, 2–3.

231. During the second season Hamlet was seated on the steps for these lines and rose when calling Polonius; Adams II.ii, 3.

232. Adams II.ii, 3.

233. Ibid.; Taylor 4, 84.

234. Lies on purple cloth: Taylor 3, 85; Taylor 2 has this business two lines later, Adams after "you are merry, my lord." Taylor 3, 85, contains a note after this line that "On some occasions Barrymore would clutch Ophelia's hand – leaving his head on her lap – glaring at the Queen. Usually he wouldn't touch Ophelia." Queen smiles to a lady to her R: Adams II.ii, 4.

235. The music is in Taylor 1, 85, and Taylor 3 and 4, 86; it is the same as for the first entry of the Players. Taylor 1 and 4 say flute; Adams II.ii, 4 says oboe or English horn.

236. This business was changed during the first season; the Player spoke over the music when it was half-finished; it concluded at the same time as his speech. Taylor 4, 85; Adams II.ii, 4. "Looking at the Queen": Adams II.ii, 4.

237. The blocking for the play within a play is from Taylor 1, 3, and 4, 85–91, and Adams, II.ii, 4–6. A more detailed description of the mime players' actions is in Adams, written in pen for the second season. Taylor provides no description of these actions.

238. Taylor 3 and 4, 88.

239. Emphasis: Studybook, 94. Laughs anxiously: Adams, II.ii, 5.

240. Taylor 3 and 4, 89.
241. Barrymore, letter to Michael Strange, n.d. [1922–3], box 2, folder 14, Lincoln Center. Here he comments that when Hamlet "is laying [*sic*] on the floor in the play scene . . . he looks mischievously at the Queen because the play he has arranged is making her so uncomfortable." The business almost certainly occurred here. In *The Drama* (March 1923), 208, Furness adds the details of his response to "the lady doth protest."
242. The *Times* (London) noted that Barrymore was "aggressively sarcastic in his remarks on *The Mousetrap* to the King" (20 February 1925). Pauses: Taylor 3 and 4, 90. This business was an innovation that came in January 1924, during the last month of the tour. During the first season Hamlet spoke his line, "The Mousetrap," almost immediately. As even Taylor agreed that it was an effective bit of business, I have included it in the narrative. Emphasis on "poison": Studybook, 95.
243. Adams, II.ii, 5.
244. Description of Lucianus: Taylor 4, 90. King's response to Lucianus: Adams II.ii, 6.
245. Adams II.ii, 6; *International Interpreter* (16 December 1922), 1167. Neither Adams nor Taylor note the lifting on one arm and pointing, which is captured in a 1922 Bruguiere photograph (see the part-title pages of the present volume). The *International Interpreter* notes its presence in the staging but not its place; in all likelihood it came here.
246. Taylor 4, 91; this was new business for the second season. Barrymore may have delivered all or much of this speech during the first season while pointing at the King.
247. "Wild and hysterical": Furness in *The Drama* (March 1923), 208; the remainder of the business is from Adams II.ii, 6, and Taylor 4, 91.
248. "A flood of relieved tension": *International Interpreter* (16 December 1922), 1167. The business with the Court Lady, which is from Adams, II.ii, 6 $^1/_2$ B, was second-season business and later cut. See also the 26 December 1923 *Boston Transcript*.
249. The second verse and Horatio's reply are cut in Adams, retained elsewhere. In all likelihood this was a second-season change.
250. Readings: radio broadcast.
251. These lines are cut in Adams; the speech begins "Soft."
252. Taylor, "My Season," 11; *International Interpreter* (16 December 1922), 1167.
253. *New Republic* (6 December 1922), 46.
254. The business is from Adams, II.ii, 8–9; a few details are from Taylor 1, 92–5.
255. Taylor 2, 95–6; Taylor 4, 90. The business is from Adams, II.ii, 6 $^1/_2$; this sheet was inserted into the promptbook and represents second-season business. The line in the reconstruction is from the Temple edition; in Adams it reads: "Pox, murderer, leave thy damnable faces and begin./ Come; the croaking raven doth bellow for revenge."
256. Taylor 4, 96, says lights up gradually – King discovered C; Taylor 2, 105, says he paces R to L to R. The business here is from the screen test and from Adams; line readings are from the screen test. This scene was played on the mainstage during the second season and tour.
257. The business is from the screen test; Adams says he completes the sheathing of his sword on "kick." "Sinister coldness": *Evening Mail* (17 November 1922).
258. Taylor 4, 100, has the scene ending in a blackout with the King onstage.
259. *New Republic* (6 December 1922), 46. See also the 17 November 1922 *Evening Mail* and Barrymore's comments on the cuts to this scene in his 14 January 1923 *New York Tribune* interview.

260. Adams says gold curtains; all four Taylor promptbooks say black. The arras was approximately twelve feet high and sixteen feet wide; see Jones's drawing in *Theatre Magazine* (January 1923), 22.

261. Queen looks off R: Adams, II.iv, 1; later in the first season she looked off L, where Hamlet made his entrance; all Taylor promptbooks say R.

262. Word emphasis, except where noted: radio broadcast.

263. Adams, II.iv, 1.

264. Ibid., II.iv, 2; *New York Tribune* (17 November 1922). *The Bookman* (April 1925) noted a "long interval between Polonius's cry from the arras and Hamlet's running him through." This is contradicted by Adams's promptbook.

265. *New York Post* (17 November 1922); Taylor 3, 101. See also the 17 December 1922 *New York Times*.

266. *New York Times* (17 December 1922).

267. *The Freeman* (3 January 1923), 401.

268. Adams, II.iv, 2, has her sit on "sit you down"; all four Taylor promptbooks have her sitting on "What have I done?"

269. *New York Times* (7 January 1923).

270. Adams, II.iv, 3.

271. Taylor 4, 103.

272. Adams, II.iv, 3; Taylor 1, 3, and 4, 104; Taylor, "My Season," 9; *New York Times* (17 December 1922). Taylor 3 and 4 note that in Cleveland, the last week of the second season, a picture of Reginald Pole as the Ghost was made and projected on Hamlet to convey the impression of the Ghost taking possession.

273. Taylor 2, 112.

274. Furness, in *The Drama* (March 1923), 208.

275. Adams II.iv, 3–4; Taylor 1, 3 and 4, 104; Furness, in *The Drama* (March 1923), 208.

276. Adams II.iv, 4; *New Republic* (6 December 1922), 45.

277. *New Republic* (6 December 1922), 45.

278. Agate, *Ego* 7, 265.

279. *International Interpreter* (16 December 1922), 1167.

280. Pause: Adams, II.iv, 5.

281. Ibid., II.iv, 5.

282. Ibid., II.iv, 5; Taylor 1 and 3, 107.

283. Taylor 3, 109.

284. *Spectator* (28 February 1925), 319.

285. Adams, II.iv, 5–6, does not have him rise until "Mother, good night." Taylor 3, 109, says that the lights dim out as the Queen starts off R.

286. The curtain calls are from Adams; unpaginated early pages. Individual calls were cut for the second season. Blanche Yurka's account of the curtain speeches is in *Bohemian Girl*, 102.

287. Taylor, "My Season," 9.

288. See also J. Ranken Towse's comments in the 17 November 1922 *New York Post*. Stark Young found that the climax of the play came a scene earlier; see comments in the *New Republic* (6 December 1922), 46. Corbin's remarks notwithstanding, a number of observers did find Oedipal connotations in Hamlet's close embraces with his mother. Heywood Broun, for example, noted that "Barrymore's most original contribution to the role probably lies in his amplification of the unconscious motives of the Prince. He plays the closet episode with the Queen exactly as if it were a love scene. Nor did this seem fantastic to us. Shakespeare was a better Freudian than almost any of the moderns because he did not know the lingo. He

merely set down the facts" (*World*, 17 November 1922). For additional commentary see the section on the critical response to the production.

289. Taylor, "My Season," 3.

290. Adams III.i, 1; Taylor 1, 3, and 4, 122–4.

291. Adams III.i, 2; Taylor 1, 3, and 4, 124–5.

292. Adams III.i, 3–4; Taylor 1, 3, and 4, 125–7.

293. Adams III.i, 4.

294. Gradually descends and approaches; coquettishly: Taylor 4, 128. Gazes out vacantly: Taylor 3, 129. A copy of the music for Ophelia's song is at the Museum of the City of New York.

295. Adams III.i, 5, and Taylor 3 and 4 say she "goes up steps to top platform." In Taylor 1 and 2 she merely exits C. No mention is made of the precarious backward exit Fay Compton made in London, noted there by many critics. See, for example, the 28 February 1925 *Spectator* and the 26 February 1925 *Stage*.

296. Adams III.ii, 1. Taylor 1 and 3, 132, say they are discovered; the business is from Adams, III.ii, 1–3, and Taylor, 1, 3, and 4, 132–40.

297. Adams III.ii, 3.

298. The scenery for the graveyard scene was changed during the run. Originally, the white curtains were brought on behind the arch and the scene was played on a bare stage, as noted in Taylor 4, 145. There was a good deal of negative criticism, however (discussed in the section on the critical response to the set), which no doubt convinced Hopkins and Jones that changes were necessary. On Thursday, 1 February 1923, iron gates topped with a cross were placed in the archway, a large slab of "granite" for Ophelia's grave was placed at the break in the steps LC, and the grave was surrounded by earth and stone. Taylor contradicts himself on the date these changes were initiated. Taylor 2, 150, says it was the Tuesday, 30 January matinee; Taylor 4, 144, notes that the changes were made two days later, "in honor of the visit of the Moscow Art Players, I suppose." The latter date seems likely. The arrangement given here is the second one. In both cases, the burial was held at night. The descriptions are from Adams III.iii, 1, and Taylor 3, 144. Adams's property plot notes that a second stone placed three feet R of the grave was used the second season.

299. Adams III.iii, 1; Taylor 1 says spade in hand.

300. During the initial season, Cecil Clovelly, who played the Second Clown, was arrested for bootlegging and was forced to miss a matinee. His arrest was publicized in the metropolitan dailies. According to Taylor, he was released from custody in time for the evening performance, and that night, when Whitford Kane, as the First Clown, told him, "'fetch me a stoup of liquor,'" the audience yelled, and later, when Barrymore came on, he [Barrymore] guyed through his entire scene, completely demoralizing everyone." "My Season," 15.

301. The business here is from Adams, III.iii, 1–2; originally Hamlet and Horatio entered through the curtains, then crossed L on the top platform. The second season they entered through the gate, as in Taylor 3, 147.

302. The second season the Gravedigger was given no earth for the grave, so he pretended to spade up earth, and according to Taylor "grumbled every performance because he had no earth – nor bones for the scene." Taylor 3, 147.

303. At one point Hamlet sat on the steps here rather than several lines later (crossed out in Taylor 4, 149), or on the stone during the second season (crossed out in Adams, III.iii, 2).

304. Taylor 1, 3, and 4, 149; Adams has the Clown toss up the bone after "rest her soul, she's dead."
305. Adams, III.iii, 3. During the second season he sat on the stone.
306. Looks at Horatio, amused: Taylor 3, 150. Clown looks at skull "affectionately": Taylor 3, 151.
307. Looks at skull for six seconds before speaking: Taylor 3, 151."Quaint and measured melancholy": *New Statesman* (7 March 1925), 626.
308. Taylor 3, 152, notes that during the second season Hamlet held the skull down in both hands on "quite chop-fallen." Adams, III.iii, 4, has him rise to above the R side of the grave after "how abhorred in my imagination it is." This is crossed out, and was probably done briefly at the end of the first season.
309. *New Statesman* (7 March 1925), 626.
310. Adams, III.iii, 5.
311. Ibid.; Taylor 3, 153 (second season), says 3 R and 3 L of the grave.
312. Adams, III.iii, 6.
313. Ibid., III.iii, 6–7.
314. *New York Globe* (13 December 1922).
315. *New Republic* (6 December 1922), 45–6.
316. Taylor 3, 156.
317. Adams, III.iii, 6–7.
318. Taylor 3, 158, notes that the second season they entered R on the mainstage.
319. Adams, III.iv, 1.
320. Taylor 1, 3, and 4, 160.
321. Adams, III.iv, 1.
322. Ibid., III.iv, 2.
323. Hamlet's much-abridged speech about Laertes, as well as Osric's reply here, were cut the second season; Adams, III.iv, 2, notes in pen that Horatio pauses a moment for Osric's laughs.
324. Adams, III.iv, 3; Taylor 1, 3, and 4 do not have him sitting here; Taylor 2 has him rising at the beginning of his final speech.
325. Adams's curtain plot notes in pen that the second season the gold curtains were drawn on two feet.
326. Adams, III.v, 1 and 1a.
327. Ibid., III.v, 1. Taylor 2 and 4 have the King sitting four lines later on, "Give them the foils." Taylor 1 and 3 have him sitting after he places Laertes's hand in Hamlet's.
328. Readings: radio broadcast.
329. Adams, III.v, 2; Taylor 4, 166.
330. Adams and Taylor 1, 3, and 4 contain detailed accounts of Hamlet's duel with Laertes. There are a number of discrepancies, however. When one of the combatants thrust in *prime* in Adams, for example, Taylor often says *carte* [*quarte*]. Where there are differences I have generally gone with Adams, with the exception of the second bout, where Taylor provides a more complete description.
331. Adams, III.v, 3.
332. The en garde position is not specified in either Adams or Taylor, but seems likely, given the ensuing descriptions.
333. Adams, III.v, 4.
334. Ibid., III.v, 5; see also Grebanier, *Heart of Hamlet*, 243–4.
335. Adams, III.v, 5; Taylor 1, 3, and 4, 168–9.

336. Adams, III.v, 5–6; Taylor 1, 3, and 4, 169.
337. Adams, III.v, 6, notes that the second season the King threw a rock down on the chair (presumably, a sound effect) and rose, his arm stricken.
338. *Evening Mail* (17 November 1922).
339. Adams, III.v, 6, notes that during the first season the King held his cloak away from his left arm, "which must be well away from body." This was crossed out for the second season, when the King stood on his chair.
340. *Commercial Advertiser* (26 November 1922); *Vogue* (15 January 1923), 55.
341. Adams, III.v, 6.
342. Ibid., III.v, 7, notes that during the second season Hamlet finally tears the cup away and throws it on the table.
343. Ibid.; *New York Tribune* (17 November 1922).
344. Adams, III.v, 7. At the first performance, Fortinbras entered L on the mainstage followed by four captains. This was changed after opening night; subsequently the four captains entered C on the top platform through the curtains and took positions up and down the steps on either side at the end. Fortinbras entered C at the trumpet flourish. The fifth captain was added later during the first season and was eliminated the second season.
345. Taylor 3, 172; the music is in Taylor 3, 172, and Taylor 1, 173.
346. Adams, III.v, 8.
347. *Smart Set* (January 1923), 136.
348. *Town Topics* (23 November 1923), 13. The notice is signed with the pseudonym "The Highbrow," but on a number of major points (for example, comparing Jones's Romanesque arch to the "sky-piercing windows" in Reinhardt's *Macbeth*) and in much of its language it is similar to Lewisohn's review in *The Nation* (6 December 1922).
349. "Intelligence": see, for example, the 17 November 1922 *New York Herald* and *Evening World* and *Town & Country* (15 December 1922), 38. "Clarity": *New York Times* (17 December 1922); see also the 17 December 1922 *Daily News*. "Simplicity": *World* (17 November 1922); see also the *New York Times* (17 November 1922) and *The Drama* (March 1923), 207. "Voice" and "movement": *Shadowland* (February 1923), 38. "Shrewd native wit": *New York Times* (17 November 1922); see also *Town & Country* (15 December 1922), 38, and Heywood Broun's comments in the *World* (17 November 1922): "There was great artistry . . . in the manner in which Barrymore flicked out the wit of Hamlet. Here was no class day orator in the manner of Walter Hampden, but a young man who might have had a lot of fun in the world if the time had not been out of joint." Arthur Hornblow's comments are from *Theatre Magazine* (January 1923), 21.
350. *New York Times* (17 December and 17 November 1922). See also the 22 November *New York Review*.
351. *Nation* (6 December 1922), 646; 648.
352. *Smart Set* (January 1923), 137.
353. *Freeman* (10 January 1923), 424.
354. See also the 17 November 1922 *Evening Mail*.
355. *New Republic* (6 December 1922), 45.
356. *Freeman* (10 January 1923), 424.
357. *New Republic* (6 December 1922), 45. See also the *New York Globe* (17 November 1922), the *New York Call* (18 November 1922), and *Variety* (24 November 1922). Barrymore's response to Young's criticism was that "The *New Republic* man seems slightly hair splitting. It is rather like talking about the boot laces of the Grenadiers

in a mural painting. But he is right possibly about one thing they seem to want *acting* instead of actually what a person would really *do* in life." Letter to Michael Strange, n.d. [1922–3], Lincoln Center.

358. The only other negative review I have found is in UCB/SC, n.p., n.d.; it is almost certainly from an out-of-town paper and was written soon after the opening. The author's virulence makes Towse's response seem mild in comparison. He or she writes, for example, that "The beauty, the drama and the sense of the play have been slaughtered to appease the impertinent idiosyncracies of Mr. Jones, the insensate conceit of Mr. Barrymore and the piffling pretense of Mr. Hopkins."

359. See, for example, Sasqui Smith, "Hamlets He Has Known," in the 26 November 1922 *World*, Joseph I. C. Clarke, "Broadway Shakespearean Revival Brings to Mind the Great Actors of the Past Who Played the Prince," in the 10 December 1922 *New York Herald*, and "Hamlets of Last 50 Years Reviewed by W. A. Brady" in the 15 December 1922 *New York Globe*.

360. Over a dozen critics and columnists took the opportunity to compare Barrymore with his predecessors. Kenneth Macgowan commented that "Forbes-Robertson's Hamlet . . . has stood as the best of the twentieth century, here as well as in England. The Hamlets of the pedestrian Sothern, the heavy Mantell, the vital, but immature Leiber, stand nowhere beside it. Only Walter Hampden has given us any hint of an impersonation to be compared with Forbes-Robertson's. Now at last comes a Hamlet that definitely overtops every performance of the part in English since Booth died"; *Vogue* (15 January 1923), 54–5. "Set beside this performance," wrote William McDermott of the *Cleveland Plain Dealer*, "Forbes-Robertson's prince seems like an elderly statesman, E. H. Sothern's like a Shakespearean scholar speaking lines and Walter Hampden's like a fiery but elocutionary and tricky actor. Barrymore . . . plays Hamlet as simply and naturally as if *Hamlet* were not a sacred legend but a new piece by Somerset Maugham. So enacted the play takes on new values, a directness, a simplicity and a power to excite and interest." Undated clipping, Lincoln Center. See also Alexander Woollcott's comments in the 17 November 1922 *New York Herald*, where he remarks: "One who has seen all the *Hamlets* given in this country in the last twenty-five years must give over the very front of his report to the conviction that this new one is the finest of them all."

361. Stark Young, "David Garrick to John Barrymore," in his *Glamour* (Freeport, N.Y.: Books for Libraries Press, 1971) [repr. ed.; orig. pub. 1925], 128–36. This is a slightly revised version of Young's article, which appeared originally in *Vanity Fair* (February 1923), 55, 80.

362. *Nation* (6 December 1922), 646.

363. *New Republic* (6 December 1922), 46.

364. *New York Evening Journal* (17 November 1922); *Freeman* (3 January 1923), 401.

365. Faversham claimed that he eliminated this effect after Tyrone Power, his Brutus, protested, but restored it when Power left the company. However, see also Power's response in the 17 December 1922 *New York Herald*; Power denied that this was the case and added that he had used an "eerie light" for the ghost in his own production of the play. The use of a light for the Ghost in *Hamlet* was by no means universal in Germany and Austria, though; see, for example, the photo of Reinhardt's 1919–20 production in *Theatre Arts* 4 (April 1920), 168, which features the familiar armor-clad figure.

366. "Hamlet, Expressionist," Harvard Theatre Collection clipping, n.p., n.d. See also the 25 November 1922 *Baltimore Sun*.

367. Glenn Hughes, "Repressed Acting and Shakespeare," *The Drama* (March 1923), 211.

368. *Variety* (24 November 1922) found that "The text is of the fullest – several scenes that commonly are elided here are given in full." For dissenting views see H. H. Furness Jr.'s comments in *The Drama* (March 1923), 208, Towse's comments in the *New York Post* (17 November 1922), and Gilbert Seldes's comments in the 26 November 1922 *Philadelphia Ledger*. "Much was cut out of the play, necessarily," Seldes wrote, "and naturally of that a great deal was missed." Most of the critics had short memories in this respect; Hampden's substantially fuller acting version was given no significant mention.

369. *Town Topics* (23 November 1922), 13.

370. Patrick Kearney, "Symbolism and the New Hamlet," *Vanity Fair* (January 1923), 41, 98 (at 98).

371. *New Republic* (6 December 1922), 46; see also Young's revised version of his initial review in *Immortal Shadows* (repr. ed.; New York: Octagon Books, 1973), as well as the 17 November 1922 *Sun*.

372. See, for example, Macgowan's 17 December 1922 letter to the *New York Times*, and his 28 December 1922 column in the *New York Globe*. For a more detailed account of the debate and a retrospective view of the set's impact, see Daniel Krempel and James H. Clay, "'New Stagecraft' Forty Years After: The Hopkins–Jones *Hamlet*," *Western Speech* 29 (Fall 1965): 201–10. Barrymore's description of the set as "Pennsylvania Station" is from Taylor, "My Season," 5.

373. *Freeman* (10 January 1923), 425. See also *Evening Telegram* (8 December 1923).

374. *Variety* (1 and 8 December 1922).

375. John Jay Chapman, letter to H. H. Furness Jr., 24 November 1922, Special Collections, University of Pennsylvania. See also Chapman's letters to Barrymore in the Michael Strange correspondence, Lincoln Center. On 11 December 1922 Chapman wrote after again seeing *Hamlet*: "It seemed to me that I'm right about everything. It was a finer performance – more subtle, more rapid, more fluid." The next day he wrote to invite Barrymore to have lunch with him and Walter Hampden: "Sooner or later – & I don't see why it should not be tomorrow – you & Hampden will act Othello & Iago, changing on alternate nights & there will be something to see on our stage. . . . Both of you are big natures & entirely above jealousy." Barrymore's 31 December 1922 telegram to Furness mentions the "stimulating bout" and is also in the Special Collections, University of Pennsylvania.

376. Louis Sheaffer, *O'Neill: Son and Artist* (Boston: Little, Brown, 1973), 176.

377. Telephone interview with Helen Hayes, 25 July 1989.

378. More than a dozen Shakespearean productions were announced that season; see, for example, the *New York Clipper* (29 November 1922) and *Variety* (1 December 1922). Of these (in addition to revivals discussed in the text), only *As You Like It* (with Marjorie Rambeau) and a production of *The Comedy of Errors* were mounted; Walter Hampden wisely came in with *Cyrano de Bergerac*. The Lincoln Center newspaper review clipping book for the 1922–3 season contains a representative sampling of criticism of the Belasco *Merchant of Venice* and the rival productions of *Romeo and Juliet*; the Hopkins–Jones–Ethel Barrymore version closed on 28 January; the Cowl production played for 160 performances.

379. Taylor, "With Hey Ho!" 344.

380. Taylor 3, 72, notes the reworking of this scene.

381. Taylor, "With Hey Ho!" 344. Taylor 4, 92, notes that the recorder scene was first performed on 8 January 1923. It was retained for the remainder of the season and

for rehearsals and opening night of the second season, and is included in Adams's promptbook; it was not, as Adams later claimed (Otis, "Barrymore *Hamlet*," 52), tried for one performance then eliminated.

382. *New York Herald* (3 December 1922 and 2 February 1923).

383. *New York Herald* (2 February 1923); see also Kenneth Macgowan's comments in *Theatre Arts* 7 (April 1923), 79.

384. Kane, *Are We All Met?* 237.

385. Nunnery and play scenes: Taylor, "With Hey Ho!" 345. Here, Taylor also notes that Tyrone Power, sensing Barrymore's difficulty with the play scene, made suggestions and told him about the effect Irving had made with the line, "What, frighted with false fire?" Yet according to Taylor, Barrymore took little notice. Pauses: Taylor, "My Season," 10–11.

386. Taylor, "My Season," 13.

387. Kane, *Are We All Met?* 237–8; Taylor, "My Season," 8–9.

388. Kane, *Are We All Met?* 235.

389. Telephone interview with Elliot Norton, 29 March 1989. See also Richard Watts Jr.'s comments in the 7 June 1942 *New York Herald Tribune*. Here Watts writes: "I think I saw him something like five times in 'Hamlet' and I recall that three times it seemed to me the most stirring performance I have ever encountered, and twice it was obvious that he was merely going through the words and the motions."

390. Taylor, "My Season," 10; "With Hey Ho!" 344.

391. Hopkins, *To a Lonely Boy*, 231–2. Ethel Barrymore claimed that after her visit "he relaxed and was his great self again" (*Memories*, 248); Taylor thought the performance "was one of the best he ever gave" ("With Hey Ho!" 348–9). Kenneth Macgowan reported that Barrymore "played with a hot-spirited vigor which recognized and exploited to the fullest the mad quality of Hamlet's speech in the first half of the drama. It was wild and beautiful. But toward the end the fervor had grown monotonous and weak, and he played the graveyard scene as tamely as ever, and only summoned up strength to keep his magnificent murder of the king upon the plane it had reached on the first night." *Theatre Arts* 7 (April 1923), 97. After the performance, Stanislavsky and the rest of the company made their way backstage; an awkward silence, Hopkins remembered, was broken by Olga Knipper, who asked Barrymore, "Do you really do this eight times a week?" (*To a Lonely Boy*, 232). See also Taylor's accounts of the backstage visit in "With Hey Ho!" 332, "My Season," 14, and the unpaginated final pages of Taylor 2. Stanislavsky's letter is quoted in Laurence Senelick, *Gordon Craig's Moscow Hamlet* (Westport, Conn.: Greenwood, 1982), 187.

392. Taylor, "My Season," 7. For similar comments see Barrymore's undated letter to Michael Strange, n.d. [1922–3, box 2, folder 14], Lincoln Center. Here he writes: "Hamlet doesn't make [me] one millionth as tired as Richard III as he is so simple & human & real and has no fictitious emotions or silly pyrotechnical balderdashes!"

393. Yurka, *Bohemian Girl*, 100.

394. Taylor, "My Season," 6–7. See also Barrymore's undated letter to Michael Strange [box 2, folder 13], Lincoln Center. in which he writes: "Last week we broke the record of the theatre since it was built and the houses are always sold out and for the last four or five performances your own father [i.e., Barrymore] has been playing under the strain of having his poor voice go completely back on him which anyone can tell her [i.e., Strange] is the most nerve wracking and maddening thing in the world."

395. Louis M. Simon, letter to the author, 18 August 1990.
396. Alan Churchill, *The Theatrical Twenties* (New York: McGraw–Hill, 1975), 58.
397. "Delegation of elderly actors": Fowler, *Good Night, Sweet Prince*, 217.
398. "Rumors that we were soon to close": Taylor, "With Hey Ho!" 350; the *New York Times* published Hopkins's announcement on 20 January 1923. In his 25 December 1922 letter to Michael Strange, Barrymore wrote that he was planning to close *Hamlet* by the end of February or the first of March; he ultimately closed three weeks sooner. "Highly nervous state": Taylor, "With Hey Ho!" 351–2. Mysteriously, the lengthy cables to which Taylor refers have not survived in the Barrymore–Strange correspondence at Lincoln Center, although there are many letters from this period. However, in an undated letter to Michael Strange [box 3, folder 1, c. 1923] Barrymore writes that he has been sending her cables every four days; these, too, have not survived.
399. *Toledo Blade*, n.d. [February 1923], Locke Scrapbook 41, Lincoln Center.
400. "Hopkins almost blew up": letter to Michael Strange, n.d. [box 2, folder 17; c. January 1923], Lincoln Center.
401. *New York Times* (10 February 1923).
402. Taylor, "With Hey Ho!" 352.
403. Hopkins announcement: *Evening Telegram* (7 September 1923). Healthy and relaxed: *New York Herald* (15 September 1923). On 9 February 1923, the day before his departure for Europe, Barrymore signed a contract with Warner Brothers; *Beau Brummel* was announced at the time, as was a screen adaptation of Sacha Guitry's *Deburau*. Both projects were to be made under the supervision of David Belasco (*New York Tribune*, 16 February 1923). *Deburau* was never filmed, and Belasco did not participate in the making of *Beau Brummel*. For an account of Barrymore's activities during the making of *Beau Brummel* see Mary Astor, *My Story* (Garden City, N.Y.: Doubleday, 1959), 68–78. Astor discusses her romantic involvement with Barrymore during the filming, *Hamlet* second season, and tour. In an undated letter to Michael Strange [c. September 1923], Barrymore wrote to his wife in Paris of his plans for the second season: "He is going to break the glad news to Arthur Hopkins tonight – that his own season is going to be terribly short." In another letter to Michael Strange, probably written in October, he wrote, "He opens in *Hamlet* on November 26th and sails for his own mother's lap on *January 15th* so help him God!"
404. Taylor's comments on second-season rehearsals are in the unpaginated early pages of Taylor 2. For more information on second-season cast changes, see section II.b of Appendix A.
405. *New York Times* (25 November 1923).
406. The second-season cuts in Adams are as follows (scene numberings refer to the Adams promptbook): I.i, 50, 174b-175; I.ii, 11–13 (from the King's initial speech; these lines were cut originally but restored the first season), 44–45; I.iii, 22, 54–55; I.iv, 44–45a, 55–57; I.v, 101, 103–104 (the latter lines were apparently restored the first season); I.vi, 5b–7a, 8b–9, 16, 26b–34, 125–128, 301; II.i, 33–34, 174–177a; III.i, 41a, 144b–155; III.ii, 189b–190; III.v, 255b–260, 270, 298b ("He's fat and scant of breath"). In III.ii, 167–184b (the Queen's description of Ophelia's drowning) was restored. The alterations continued after the opening. On Tuesday, 27 November, the cast was called to the theatre at 7 P.M. and the recorder scene was cut, perhaps in an effort to reduce the running time. Taylor notes this in the unpaginated early pages in Taylor 2.
407. Letter to Michael Strange, n.d. [November 1923], Lincoln Center.

408. The only dissenting review of the second-season production appeared in the *New York Post* (27 November 1923). It is signed "N." (and is almost certainly not Towse); the critic "found much to respect and not a little to admire" but concluded that Barrymore's portrayal "does not reach the plane of the great Hamlets of the past, nor of the greatest Hamlet of to-day – Mr. Walter Hampden." For another dissenting view of the second-season production by a young student of literature, see Stephen Hannigan's unpublished 7 December 1923 essay, which is pasted into a *Hamlet* scrapbook [call no. MWEZ n. c. 4439] at Lincoln Center. For the Hamlet "competition," see, for example, the 27 November 1923 review in the *Evening Telegram*. For Martin-Harvey, see the 20 November 1923 comments in the *New York Times* and the *New York Tribune*, but see also Taylor 2; on one of the unnumbered pages at the beginning, Taylor notes that Barrymore expressed admiration for Martin-Harvey's interpretation. "Certain elderly gentlemen": *Evening Telegram* (8 December 1923).

409. Among the interested observers during the second season was Sgt. Stuart De Witt of the West 30th Street police station, who on 13 December was assigned to observe a performance after his superiors received a complaint that the play was immoral. Queried during an intermission, De Witt commented that he had found nothing untoward and expressed admiration for the production and Barrymore's performance (*New York Times*, 14 December 1923).

410. *Daily News* (12 December 1923).

411. The tour dates were as follows: 17–19 December, New Haven; 20–22 December, Hartford; 24–29 December, Boston; 31 December–5 January, Philadelphia; 7–12 January, Washington; 14–19 January, Pittsburgh; 21–26 January, Cleveland. The unnumbered early pages of Taylor 2 contain a preliminary itinerary that was subsequently changed.

412. Taylor, "With Hey Ho!" 358. Barrymore's rapid performances and subsequent commute were occasioned in part by his desire to see Mary Astor, who was in New York at the time.

413. *New York Times* (6 January 1924); Taylor, "With Hey Ho!" 358–9. During the Boston run, Barrymore was sketched by John Singer Sargent. He was pleased enough with the result to have duplicates made for presentation to the company. The comment regarding Barrymore's "Slowness of pace" is from an unidentified Boston review, Harvard Theatre Collection (25 December 1923).

414. Telephone interview with Elliot Norton, 29 March 1989.

415. Taylor, "With Hey Ho!" 359; the curtain speech is set down in an unpaginated early page of Taylor 3.

416. Louis M. Simon, letter to the author, 18 August 1990.

417. Closing notice: Taylor, "With Hey Ho!" 359. Hopkins announcement: *New York Review* (12 January 1924). In an undated letter to Michael Strange [box 2, folder 14; probably early to mid-December 1923], he mentions that he had grown weary of the role and planned to sail for Europe between 16 January and 2 February. Here he writes:

"He simply cannot *bear it*. The absurd repetition of an utterly exhausting part for *what* in the name of God. . . . It is all . . . so utterly against his centre that to keep it up is sheer *madness* when there are other ways of making a living. Only the meanest thing happened when he got back here – he found Hopkins had signed contracts for fourteen weeks which almost drove me off my nut – and your own father raised hell – and he has a divine idea that came to him last night when he was playing this damned interminable Scandinavian Po!

"First we decided to play ten weeks more or less tentatively as he said the company all expected it to. So what he is going to do is to figure out just how much money the company would make in ten weeks and how much Hopkins would too on an average and out of what he makes give the equivalent amount to Hopkins and the company after say six weeks. He has looked up the sailings and on either the Cunard or White Star lines there is no fast or good boat between January the sixteenth and February second. I am going to do my damndest to sail on January sixteenth. . . . It means I will not make any money practically out of the engagement but I will surely get some from the movie and it is being fair to the company & Hopkins."

It is unlikely, however, that Barrymore's financial offer was accepted; the second season and tour ultimately played for a total of nine weeks.

418. Coolidge visit: Alma Power-Waters, *John Barrymore: The Legend and the Man* (New York: Julian Messner, 1941), 119. In "With Hey Ho!" 361, Taylor noted that "Hopkins was with us for opening night in Washington, but seemed depressed and unhappy, with little to say." He added that on the night President Coolidge attended, Barrymore, "in a bad mood, gave one of his worst performances." By the end of the week he was "more agreeable." Carrington's visit: Taylor, "With Hey Ho!" 361. See also Barrymore's letter to Michael Strange, postmarked 13 January 1924 (Lincoln Center). Here he writes: "I met the President who is like a rather canny grocer in a one night stand."

419. "Only two more weeks of it": 13 January 1924 letter to Michael Strange. Barrymore's cabled invitation from the Shakespeare Memorial Committee, signed by Sir Frank Meyer Bart, chairman, arrived on 11 January 1924. This prompted a press release from Hopkins, and the cable was mentioned the next day in most of the New York dailies. The *New York Herald* (12 January 1924) noted that Hopkins "will conclude negotiations immediately for a London theater in which to present him."

420. "You were doing something" and Cleveland curtain speech: Taylor, "With Hey Ho!" 362.

421. Ibid., 362–4.

Chapter 4. The London *Hamlet*, 1925

1. Laurence Olivier, *On Acting* (New York: Simon & Schuster, 1986), 60.

2. John Barrymore, "Blame It on the Queen," *American Magazine* (March 1933), 20–3, 114–19 (at 118). For more than four years, Barrymore had been interested in appearing in London; at various times it had been announced that he would be seen there in *The Jest*, and in *Richard III* and *Redemption* in repertory. See, for example, the 24 January 1920 issue of *Variety*. His plan to go to London to play Hamlet probably originated during the spring of 1923; an undated letter to Michael Strange posted from London during that period states, "I went to meet Gerald [Du Maurier] . . . who said he would phone Grossmith again about 'His Majesty's' . . . I am getting kind of *scared* of playing Hamlet before these people in a way. . . ." In another undated letter [November 1923] written prior to second-season rehearsals, he told Michael Strange: "I am going to rehearse Hamlet only *two* days – and weed out the company for England as we go along."

3. Barrymore, "Blame It on the Queen," 118.

4. Taylor, "With Hey Ho!" 363–4.

5. Letter to Michael Strange, n.d. [postmarked 7 March 1924], Lincoln Center.

6. John Barrymore, *Confessions of an Actor* (Indianapolis: Bobbs–Merrill, 1926), un-paginated. The last *Hamlet* in the West End had been Ion Swinley's brief appearance in repertory with the Old Vic company in 1924; five years earlier, John Martin-Harvey and Frank Benson had starred in productions during the 1919–20 season. Ernest Milton had played an acclaimed Hamlet at the Old Vic during the 1918–19, 1922–3, and 1924–5 seasons. See J. C. Trewin, *Shakespeare on the English Stage, 1900–1964* (London: Barrie & Rockliff, 1964), 264–6, 287–8.

7. "Without resources": Basil Dean, *Seven Ages* (London: Hutchinson, 1970), 231. Often did little to further his own quest: Constance Collier, unpublished essay on Barrymore's acting (UCB/SC), 7. Ill at ease in the role of theatrical businessman: Barrymore, *Confessions*. Among the theatres Barrymore attempted to rent during this period was the Palace. In an undated letter to Michael Strange [c. April 1924] he wrote: "[T]he Palace was available for 600 pound a week. The situation is that Cochran has no money to go in on sharing terms or any other basis but rental. There is a distinct feeling here all around which C. Collier is wise enough to see – to *keep me out*." Arthur Hopkins was advising Barrymore at the time and had cabled Barrymore from New York, but he was not directly involved in raising funds or securing a theatre.

8. Letter to Michael Strange, n.d. [c. April/May 1924], Lincoln Center. Here he also states that "I wired Hopkins I had no intention of ever playing in America again unless I played here first."

9. Barrymore, "Blame It on the Queen," 118.

10. Fay Compton, BBC Radio interview, 1 May 1968; BBC Sound Archive, London.

11. On 9 January 1925 it was announced that the production would take place at The Prince's Theatre in the West End; see, for example, the *New York American, World*, and *Mirror* for this date. The London correspondent for Universal Services cabled, however, that The Prince's had long been considered an unfortunate house, as it had been the scene of many failures. Shakespeare in the heart of London, he added, was not a paying proposition, and Barrymore had "refused to heed the advice of well-meaning friends" and intended to appear in England "under what are generally considered discouraging conditions." A final agreement was never reached, and the plan to present *Hamlet* at The Prince's was set aside.

12. Fay Compton, *Rosemary* (London: Alston Rivers Ltd., 1926), 226–7.

13. Collier, unpublished essay, 7. On 24 January 1925, Barrymore presented Harrison with a check for £3,300 to cover six weeks rent at £550 per week. This sum represented a tidy profit for Harrison, whose lease stipulated a weekly rent of £167 10s 6p. Production account books, Haymarket Theatre Archive, London.

14. A copy of Barrymore's contract is at UCB/SC. It specifies a salary of £200 per week (later reduced to £150) plus half the net profits. Barrymore also took an option for a special season at the Haymarket of eight to twelve weeks the following year, to commence between 5 April and 3 May 1926.

15. Barrymore, *Confessions*.

16. Interview with Alison Leggatt, 12 August 1988.

17. Margaret Webster, *The Same Only Different* (London: Gollancz, 1969), 297–9.

18. The main difference between the American and British productions, according to Barrymore, lay in his interpretation of his role. To one interviewer he commented that "I am playing Hamlet in London less emotionally, on purpose, than I used to do it in America. One learns a great deal about the character by not playing it for awhile. My conception of the part will probably go on changing till I am nine-

ty, when I shall feel that I know at last how to play it" *Daily Express* (21 February 1925). Barrymore used a modified version of the Ghost as per the second season in America, utilizing a subtle radiance at first and then having the actor appear on-stage in Shakespeare's I.v; Hamlet's face in this scene was illuminated by a shaft of light. In the play scene he lay lengthwise on the second stair, with his face turned sideways to the King. Ophelia's backward exit may have been a new device as well. The Second Clown was played as a bare-chested boy with a Cockney accent. New scenery for the graveyard scene was designed by Norman Wilkinson: Three enormous candles were placed behind the arch, and iron railings were set at the back. In an interview in the 26 February 1925 *Morning Post*, Barrymore noted that he had introduced "some scenery suggesting trees" in this scene, but commented that they were dimly lit and unnoticeable on opening night. In addition, many characters wore costumes that differed from those in the American production; see, for example, the Queen's costume in Fig. 33 (New York) and Fig. 40 (London).

19. Barrymore may also have sought advice on the staging and performances from Arthur Hopkins and Johnston Forbes-Robertson. The *World* (9 January 1925) announced that Hopkins was scheduled to sail for London on 27 January; he almost certainly sat in on some of the rehearsals and was present on opening night. In *Shakespeare – Hit or Miss?* (London: Sidgwick & Jackson, 1991), 33, Sir John Gielgud reports that he was told that Forbes-Robertson "came to one of the rehearsals, presumably to tender his advice to Barrymore."

20. E. Harcourt Williams, *Four Years at the Old Vic: 1929–1933* (London: Putnam, 1935), 20–1.

21. Webster, *Same Only Different*, 301.

22. *Daily Telegraph* (22 January 1925).

23. Webster, *Same Only Different*, 300–1.

24. Barrymore, *Confessions;* Compton, *Rosemary*, 228–9.

25. *Morning Post* (20 February 1925). The London correspondent for the *New York Post* (20 February 1925) reported that Barrymore rehearsed until 5 o'clock in the morning on the day before the opening, then "went at it again in the late afternoon to make the performance as polished as possible."

26. *New York Herald* (20 February 1925).

27. Barrymore, *Confessions.*

28. Ibid.

29. See comments in 20 February 1925 editions of *The Star* and the *Daily Telegraph.*

30. "A New Hamlet," *The Queen* (25 February 1925), 8.

31. Hesketh Pearson, "Hamlet," *Theatre World* (March 1925), 33.

32. Agate proclaimed the set to be "the most beautiful thing I have ever seen on any stage" (*Sunday Times*, 22 February 1925); see also Herbert Farjeon's comments in *The Sphere* (7 March 1925), 272. For dissenting views see the 28 February 1925 *Spectator* and the 26 February 1925 *Stage.*

33. *Bookman* (April 1925), 68.

34. See also *Daily News* (20 February 1925).

35. Bernard Shaw, letter to John Barrymore, 22 February 1925. Manuscript Division, Boston University Library.

36. For a notice that is virtually the opposite of Shaw's comments to Barrymore, see his 2 October 1897 review of Forbes-Robertson's Hamlet in Bernard Shaw, *Our Theatre in the Nineties*, 3 vols. (London: Constable, 1932), III: 200–7. Shaw praised

Forbes-Robertson for restoring a good deal of Shakespeare's text and noted that he "does not utter half a line; then stop to act; and go on with another half line; then stop to act again, with the clock running away from Shakespear's chances all the time. He plays as Shakespear should be played, on the line and to the line, with the utterance and acting simultaneous, inseparable and in fact identical." See also Shaw's 1919 essay, "On Cutting Shakespear," *Fortnightly Review* (August 1919), 215–18.

37. Shaw was far from alone in decrying the cuts in the play. See, for example, Hesketh Pearson, "Hamlet," *Theatre World* (March 1925), 33, and the *Weekly Westminster* (28 February 1925).

38. Robert Speaight, *William Poel and the Elizabethan Revival* (London: Heineman, 1954), 27–8.

39. Poel, for example, found that the pauses grew tiresome from repetition and exaggeration. Speaight, *William Poel*, 28. See also the *Daily Mail* (20 February 1925).

40. Telephone interview with Gwen Ffrangcon-Davies, 15 August 1988. See also Dame Peggy Ashcroft's remarks in *Shakespeare Survey* 40 (1987), 12, 16, and Gordon Crosse's manuscript diary for March 1925 in the Shakespeare Library, Birmingham Central Library. Crosse admired the staging but voiced strident objections to Barrymore's "appalling slowness of speech and movement," "long pauses between sentences," and cut text.

41. Telephone interview with Maurice Evans, 17 December 1988.

42. Telephone interview with Sir John Gielgud, 7 September 1988.

43. Olivier, *On Acting*, 60–1.

44. Raymond Massey, *A Hundred Different Lives* (Toronto: McClelland & Stewart, 1979), 286.

45. Webster, *Same Only Different*, 301. See also George Pleydell Bancroft, *Stage and Bar* (London: Faber & Faber, 1939), 272.

46. Collier, unpublished essay, 9–10.

47. Webster, *Same Only Different*, 302.

48. Fay Compton, BBC Radio interview, 26 September 1962 [recorded 5 June 1962], BBC Sound Archive, London.

49. Strange, *Who Tells Me True*, 214–16.

50. John Kobler, *Damned in Paradise: The Life of John Barrymore* (New York: Atheneum, 1977), 200.

51. Alma Power-Waters, *John Barrymore: The Legend and the Man* (New York: Julian Messner, 1941), 137; *New York Times* (7 May 1925); Webster, *Same Only Different*, 301–2.

52. Arnold Bennett, diaries, vol. 26, entry for 21 March 1925. Berg Collection, NYPL.

53. Telephone interview with Sir John Gielgud, 7 September 1988.

54. Arnold Bennett, diaries, vol. 26, entry for 10 April 1925.

55. Barrymore, *Confessions*.

56. Collier, unpublished essay, 8.

57. On 12 March 1925, the *New York Evening Journal* announced that Barrymore, while in London, had signed a long-term contract with Warner Brothers for a series of special productions, to commence in June. Legal correspondence concerning his contract is at UCB/SC.

58. James Agate, *Ego* (London: Hamish Hamilton, 1935), 109–10.

59. A. E. Wilson, *Playgoer's Pilgrimage* (London: Stanley Paul, [1948]), 189–90.

60. Barrymore, "Blame It on the Queen," 118.

61. Olivier, *On Acting*, 61.

Chapter 5. Shakespeare in Hollywood, 1925–1942

1. Francis Teague, "Hamlet in the Thirties," *Theatre Survey* 26 (May 1985), 63–79 (at 63).
2. "He loved to create": Arthur Hopkins, *To a Lonely Boy* (Garden City, N.Y.: Doubleday, 1937), 230; "Alexandrian dilemma": idem, *Reference Point* (New York: Samuel French, 1948), 121.
3. "Once the character": Arthur Hopkins, radio address prior to a broadcast of *Redemption*, UCB/SC [c. 1942–3]. There are many published statements in which Barrymore discussed his reasons for leaving the stage. See, for example, his comments in his *Confessions of an Actor* (Indianapolis: Bobbs–Merrill, 1926), unpaginated, where he states: "Not even the promise of great returns . . . can force me to cart myself, Hamlet and a lot of scenery around wherever they will let me. . . . I am no trouper." Barrymore's 30 May 1942 obituary in the *New York Herald Tribune* quotes him as saying, "The stage? I'm never going back. It's work. Why should I go back. In pictures I can loaf." See also Barrymore, "Blame It on the Queen," *American Magazine* (March 1933), 20–3, 114–19 (at 119), in which he states that following the London *Hamlet*, it seemed that "from that point there was no place to go but back"; Alma Power-Waters, *John Barrymore: The Legend and the Man* (New York: Julian Messner, 1941), 142, where he is quoted as saying, "The most important thing that the screen offers, as against the stage, is [a] lack of repetition – the continual playing of a part, which is so ruinous to an actor, is entirely eliminated"; and James Kotsilibas-Davis, *The Barrymores: The Royal Family in Hollywood* (New York: Crown, 1981), 44, where he is quoted on the eve of his departure for Hollywood in 1925: "An actor is in hard luck because everything he does should be better than the thing he did before. There is no resting and no going back. I can't get hold of what I want for New York, and I'm not satisfied with giving a second-rate performance." He was more succinct with his sister, commenting, "I can't go farting around the country playing King Lear for the rest of my life." Kotsilibas-Davis, *Barrymores*, 44.
4. For a more detailed discussion of Barrymore's film work see Kotsilibas-Davis, *Barrymores;* Joseph Garton, *The Film Acting of John Barrymore* (New York: Arno Press, 1982); Margot Peters, *The House of Barrymore* (New York: Knopf, 1990); and Martin F. Norden's *John Barrymore: A Bio-Bibliography* (Westport, Conn.: Greenwood, 1995).
5. The *New York Times* (7 May 1925) quoted Barrymore, upon his arrival, as saying, "I intend to go to Berlin in the Fall and produce *Hamlet* in German, if they will let me." He had, in fact, received offers to play Hamlet in Berlin and Paris; both were ultimately declined. The terms of Barrymore's contract are detailed in a 7 July 1925 letter to Barrymore from his attorney, UCB/SC.
6. A transcript of Barrymore's cable is contained in a 1 December 1925 letter from his London attorneys, UCB/SC.
7. See, for example, "Hamlet in Hollywood," pt. I, *Ladies Home Journal* (June 1927), 6–7, 59, 61–2, and pt. II (June 1927), 17, 184, 86; and "Up Against It in Hollywood," *Ladies Home Journal* (January 1928) 15, 76, 79.
8. Letter to William Foss, 12 May 1926, UCB/SC.
9. Johnston Forbes-Robertson, letter to John Barrymore, 16 June 1926; William Foss, telegram to Barrymore, 7 December 1926; John Barrymore, telegram to William Foss, 11 December 1926, telegram to David Belasco, 26 April 1927, and telegram to Gerald Du Maurier, 7 September 1926. UCB/SC.

10. *New Republic* (14 September 1927), 98–9. See also Barrymore, "Blame It on the Queen," 119.

11. Barrymore's 18 March 1927 cable to his London attorneys and documentation of his 22 April radio broadcast and 27 June speech at the Donlin benefit are at UCB/SC. Another factor might well have influenced Barrymore's desire to return to the stage; after the Donlin benefit, he journeyed to San Francisco to be at the bedside of John Drew, who had taken ill while touring in *Trelawny of the Wells*. He remained until 9 July when the valiant old trouper, a man of the theatre to the last, died at 73.

12. Robert Edmond Jones, letter to John Barrymore, n.d. [July 1927], UCB/SC.

13. Copies of Barrymore's correspondence with George Schaff and William Adams are at UCB/SC. On 21 February 1928, Schaff sent the lighting equipment list to Barrymore but added that William Adams was "pretty well tied up." Testing the acoustics: Gene Fowler, *Good Night, Sweet Prince* (New York: Viking, 1944), 300. The production was announced in a 10 April 1928 clipping at the Academy of Motion Picture Arts and Sciences, n.p.: "John Barrymore in *Hamlet* in the Hollywood Bowl, it was announced yesterday. Costumes and scenery used in the London production have arrived in Hollywood for the local showing, and Barrymore himself is in New York conferring with the master electrician who officiated abroad and in New York." See also the 6 May *New York Times*. On 13 June 1928, the *Times* reported that "Regardless of his activities in the new field [motion pictures], it is understood that Barrymore will carry out his plan to give *Hamlet* in the Hollywood Bowl and the Greek Theater at Berkeley in the late summer." On 10 April, Barrymore signed a contract with RCA Victor for a commercial recording of soliloquies from *Richard III* and *Hamlet* (see Chapter 2, n. 51; Chapter 3, n. 75); his contract and subsequent royalty statements are at UCB/SC. On 29 March 1928, Barrymore delivered a soliloquy from *Hamlet* as part of a nationwide radio broadcast made by United Artists stars, designed largely to promote the advent of talking pictures.

14. A 23 June 1928 telegram from Henry Hotchener to John Considine, a United Artists executive, states: "Arranged to give Hamlet first at Berkeley, then at the Hollywood Bowl for week beginning September 10. Barrymore can begin picture week beginning September 17." On 12 July Barrymore wrote to Considine: "I am concentrating on *Hamlet*, which is an extremely intensive and intricate proposition to bring to a successful conclusion, which I intend to do"; UCB/SC. Barrymore wired William Adams in New York on 10, 16, and 24 July 1928; on 7 July 1928 he signed his new contract with Warner Brothers, stipulating that he have "The star part in five (5) photoplays," the first to commence on 1 April 1929 and the fifth on 10 January 1931; he was to receive $150,000 and 10 percent of the gross receipts of each picture, and was advanced the sum of $50,000 per film; UCB/SC. The casting of Montagu Love and Alec B. Francis is noted in a 23 July 1928 clipping, Academy of Motion Picture Arts and Sciences, n.p. Barrymore's letter to Sheldon is quoted in Eric Wollencott Barnes, *The Man Who Lived Twice* (New York: Scribner's, 1956), 234.

15. Barnes, *Man Who Lived Twice*, 237.

16. This and the subsequent program quote are from a copy of the *Show of Shows* program at the Academy of Motion Picture Arts and Sciences; Paramount and Fox later followed suit with similar cinematic revues.

17. Jack Warner, 21 November 1929 telegram to John Barrymore, UCB/SC.

18. Warner's 25 March 1930 letter to Barrymore and Barrymore's 26 March reply are at UCB/SC, as is a letter dispatched by Warner the next day, in which he stated "Rather than go into a long correspondence, I prefer waiting until you have finished *Moby Dick,* and you and I will then have a talk in general on the contents of my letter as well as yours."

19. The $500 deposit and the proposal to engage a cast for both stage and film productions of *Hamlet* are mentioned in Henry Hotchener's 23 February 1932 letter to the Internal Revenue Service and other correspondence, UCB/SC.

20. The response of the Stratford company to the Barrymore–Hotchener proposal is detailed in a 21 August 1930 letter to Hotchener from Barrymore's London attorneys; UCB/SC. On 11 November 1930, Hotchener belatedly replied to this letter, stating that "As the whole idea of Mr. Barrymore's doing a 'talkie' of a Shakespearean play is very nebulous (his next two pictures are already chosen and are not Shakespearean), there would be no advantage in meeting [the director] at this time. In fact, there are so many distinguished English actors now in Hollywood, that I think we shall have no trouble in getting a cast if and when the time comes."

21. *Arsène Lupin, Grand Hotel, Rasputin and the Empress, Reunion in Vienna, Dinner at Eight,* and *Night Flight* were MGM releases; *State's Attorney, A Bill of Divorcement, Topaze,* and *Long Lost Father* were released by RKO; *Counsellor at Law* and *Twentieth Century* were produced by Universal and Columbia, respectively. Barrymore later attributed his staying power in the cinema to his demand for a variety of roles, much in evidence during this period; his statement is cited in his 30 May 1942 obituary in the *New York Herald Tribune.*

22. Fowler's account of Barrymore's 1925–34 earnings is at UCB/SC; the total includes radio and print article fees. Ironically, his golden period in Hollywood spanned precisely the same length of time as had elapsed between the opening night of *Justice* and the final performance of *Hamlet* in London: nine years. The aura of domestic happiness and tranquillity was promoted by Barrymore in "My Son John," *American Magazine* (May 1933), 58–61, 78, 80, 82. During this same period, however, Barrymore's third marriage was beginning to disintegrate due to his pathological jealousy, reckless spending, and increasing dependence on alcohol. See John Kobler, *Damned in Paradise: The Life of John Barrymore* (New York: Atheneum, 1977), 285–8.

23. Theresa Helburn's 12 and 14 April 1932 wires are at UCB/SC. Burns Mantle quoted Barrymore in the 11 February 1940 *Daily News;* his open letter had been published years earlier.

24. Margaret Carrington, "The John Barrymore I Knew," 6–7, UCB/SC.

25. Gastric hemorrhage: Fowler, *Good Night, Sweet Prince,* 335; *Counsellor at Law* retakes: ibid., 345–9.

26. The Central City *Hamlet* is cited in an unidentified 11 September 1933 clipping, James Kotsilibas-Davis collection; the Hollywood Bowl project with Helen Chandler is cited in Peters, *House of Barrymore,* 599. The UCB/SC has much correspondence concerning negotiations for *The Devil's Disciple;* for published excerpts see Fowler, *Good Night, Sweet Prince,* 350–2. On 1 November 1933, Macgowan wrote to Barrymore: "Bernard Shaw has stood pat on his price for *The Devil's Disciple* . . . will talk *Hamlet* in a week or two"; UCB/SC.

27. The screen test (identified as Test No. 7) features a translucent figure as the Ghost; Reginald Denny and Donald Crisp lend their skills as Horatio and Marcellus. The actors who play the Ghost and Claudius are not identified.

28. Fowler, *Good Night, Sweet Prince*, 353–4; the source was probably Henry Hotchener's shorthand diary, wherein he kept a record of Barrymore's activities over a ten-year period, for which Fowler paid a substantial fee. This is not, however, in the UCB/SC with the other material Fowler gathered, and was in all likelihood reclaimed by Hotchener after Fowler completed his biography.

29. Kenneth Macgowan, 26 December 1933 letter to John Barrymore, UCB/SC.

30. Brooks Atkinson, *Broadway*, rev. ed. (New York: Macmillan, 1974), 145.

31. See Miner's account in *The Directors Guild of America Oral History Series, vol. 2: Worthington Miner* (Metuchen, N.J.: Scarecrow Press, 1985), 109–12.

32. Hollis Alpert, *The Barrymores* (New York: Dial Press, 1964), 335.

33. Fowler, *Good Night, Sweet Prince*, 355–7.

34. Ibid., 366–7. On 18 September 1934 the BBC wrote to Barrymore inviting him to broadcast a scene from *Hamlet* with Fay Compton; the broadcast was never made (UCB/SC). The proposed *Hamlet* film was also announced in the 22 September 1934 *Daily Telegraph*.

35. See, for example, the account of *Cox* v. *Kean* in Giles Playfair's *Kean* (rev. ed. London: Columbus, 1988), 236–48, and Richard Moody, *Edwin Forrest: First Star of the American Stage* (New York: Knopf, 1960), 299–324.

36. The first Shakespearean film to feature sound, the Douglas Fairbanks–Mary Pickford *Taming of the Shrew*, premiered in New York on 29 November 1929, little more than a week after *The Show of Shows* made its debut. Both principals were partners in United Artists, the producing organization, and felt confident that their star drawing power and the novelty of the "talkies" would be enough to overcome the public's aversion to Shakespeare. Even so, exhibitors, worried that a "highbrow" production would be box-office poison, were assured that the film would be strongly promoted as "a comedy." See Alexander Walker, *The Shattered Silents* (London: Elm Tree Books, 1978), 150. The next Shakespearean film to emerge from Hollywood, the 1935 Max Reinhardt—William Dieterle *A Midsummer Night's Dream*, was equally dependent on star power and comedy and featured James Cagney as Bottom, Joe E. Brown as Flute, and Mickey Rooney as Puck. (Reinhardt had at one point suggested Barrymore for Oberon.) It was regarded similarly by its studio as a "prestige" vehicle, and was heralded by Warner Brothers and the press as a "cultural event" rather than as entertainment. See Lawrence W. Levine, *Highbrow/Lowbrow* (Cambridge, Mass.: Harvard University Press, 1988), 52–3.

37. Quoted in Lawrence J. Quirk, *Norma: The Story of Norma Shearer* (New York: St. Martin's Press, 1988), 170–1. Mayer knew his audience; the film lost money, reportedly nine hundred thousand to one million dollars. See ibid., 171, and Carlos Clarens, *George Cukor* (London: Secker & Warburg, 1976), 144.

38. Quoted in Clarens, *George Cukor*, 144.

39. The screenplay was published, along with essays by many of the principals, as *Romeo and Juliet by William Shakespeare: A Motion Picture Edition* (New York: Random House, 1936). See also Barrymore's brief essay on the character of Mercutio, 243–4.

40. Quirk, *Norma*, 174.

41. Ibid., 172.

42. "Irish accent": Margaret Carrington, unpublished essay on John Barrymore's acting, Wesleyan University; "If only drink": Alpert, *Barrymores*, 346.

43. Basil Rathbone, *In and Out of Character* (Garden City, N.Y.: Doubleday, 1962), 134–5.

44. Quirk, *Norma*, 174; see also Gene D. Phillips, *George Cukor* (Boston: Twayne, 1982), 42–3.
45. Quirk, *Norma*, 173.
46. *New Republic* (2 September 1936), 104.
47. For additional positive comments, see, for example, the 31 August 1936 *New York World–Telegram*, the 9 September 1936 *Boston Traveller*, the 6 September 1936 *Pittsburgh Press* ("a grand, bravura characterization"), the 31 August 1936 *Philadelphia Evening Public Ledger*, the 21 August 1936 *New York American*, the 31 August 1936 *Boston Post*, and the 23 August 1936 *New York Herald Tribune*. For sharply negative comments see the 2 September 1936 *New Republic*, the 10 September 1936 *New York Post* (John Mason Brown found the character to be "violently overplayed"), the 18 October 1936 *Sunday Times* (London), and the 23 August 1936 *Brooklyn Eagle* ("An embarrassing exhibition. The delivery is entirely of the boards and very old boards at that").
48. Barrymore's telegram to Gielgud is quoted in Peters, *House of Barrymore*, 392–3; Barrymore's statement was made to Philip Rhodes, a young friend and admirer, and is quoted in ibid., 446. After *Romeo and Juliet*, Thalberg and Cukor were eager for Barrymore to play Baron de Varville in *Camille*, but they soon realized he was in no shape to do so, much to Cukor's regret.
49. The tumult Barrymore experienced during this period is amply documented in materials at the UCB/SC and clippings at the Academy of Motion Picture Arts and Sciences.
50. The account of the 1937 Hollywood Bowl *Hamlet* and Robert Breen's subsequent visit to *My Dear Children* is based on a series of interviews with Wilva Davis Breen held between May 1989 and January 1992; I am grateful, as well, for her written recollections of that time.
51. Simonson's 1933 set designs for *Hamlet* are reproduced in Lee Simonson, *Part of a Lifetime: Drawings and Designs 1919–1940* (New York: Duell, Sloan & Pearce, 1943), 68–70.
52. Lee Simonson, 13 June 1937 letter to Wilva Davis Breen, Federal Theatre Archive, George Mason University. Elaine Barrie's interlocutory decree was dimissed two months later in August 1937; she was granted a second interlocutory decree on 27 November 1940, and the divorce became final the next year.
53. *Variety* (23 June 1937) reported on the networks' competition and Barrymore's salary. The NBC broadcasts were scheduled from 9:30 to 10:15 P.M. EST on the NBC Blue Network; the CBS series ran from 9 to 10 P.M. Like *Romeo and Juliet*, the NBC broadcasts were conceived as an imitative response to a rival's Shakespearean effort and were designed primarily to gain prestige. An NBC press release issued on 14 June puffed that the series would "mark a historic turning point in the history of radio drama" and boasted of NBC's "eight years of experience in offering Shakespeare's plays to the radio public," during which time "seventy programs of all the best known Shakespearean dramas" had been presented. Barrymore was quoted as saying, "If Shakespeare, in his grave, could see the dignity and reverence with which his comedies have been treated, his bones would rattle like dice. . . . I feel that he wanted them played the way we intend to play them." At the beginning of the 12 July broadcast, Barrymore, in keeping with the "prestige" nature of the event, read a telegram from the president of a national women's organization praising the series as "a forward step in education entertainment." The press release is at Lincoln Center; all six broadcasts are in the collection of the Museum of Television & Radio.

54. A transcript of Barrymore's letter is in the UCB/SC; it is quoted, in part, in Fowler, *Good Night, Sweet Prince*, 416–17.
55. Interview with Robert Morley, 14 August 1989.
56. For a more detailed account see Garson Kanin, *Hollywood* (New York: Viking, 1974), 23–55. Interestingly, two years earlier Kanin had directed *Hitch Your Wagon!*, a short-lived Broadway play that parodied Barrymore's romantic escapades with Elaine Barrie.
57. Telephone interview with Claudette Colbert, 11 May 1989.
58. "The production was Elaine's idea, and even she didn't think too highly about it," Charles MacArthur later remembered. "She explained rather blandly that it would serve to introduce her to New York, and prepare the way for a production of *Macbeth* later in the season, when she would appear as Lady Macbeth." Quoted in Fowler, *Good Night, Sweet Prince*, 424. Elaine Barrie's lack of artistic taste and judgment and willingness to consider exploitative material was much in evidence a year earlier; during a separation from Barrymore she appeared in a lurid two-reeler, *How to Undress in Front of Your Husband*. She may have influenced her husband, but the decision to proceed was undoubtedly his own.
59. Quoted in Barnes, *Man Who Lived Twice*, 239–40.
60. Dr. Benjamin Shalett, 27 March 1939 letter to Gene Fowler, UCB/SC.
61. Catherine Turney and Jerry Horwin, *My Dear Children* (New York: Random House, 1940), vii; *New York Times* (25 May 1939).
62. See Otto Preminger's account in his autobiography, *Preminger* (Garden City, N.Y.: Doubleday, 1977), 58; see also Alpert, *Barrymores*, 352.
63. Turney and Horwin, *My Dear Children*, 10, 154, vii. See also Douglas Fairbanks Jr.'s account in *The Salad Days* (New York: Doubleday, 1988), 333–5.
64. Quoted in Barnes, *Man Who Lived Twice*, 240–2.
65. "Silent crowd": Atkinson, *Broadway*, 153. "Squeezed by the ticket taker": Atkinson, introduction to Power-Waters, *John Barrymore*, xii–xiii.
66. For an account of Barrymore's opening-night departures from the script, see Brooks Atkinson's 1 February 1940 review in the *New York Times*. Grist for the tabloids was provided when an unemployed actor in green tights bounded onstage during Barrymore's curtain call, and by Barrymore's postplay reconciliation with his fourth wife. For a more detailed account, see Fowler, *Good Night, Sweet Prince*, 438–9. Review quote: *Theatre Arts* 24 (April 1940), 234–5. See also the 1 February 1940 *Daily News*.
67. The Pathé newsreel was included in the John Barrymore episode of the television series *Biography*; author's collection.
68. See also Burns Mantle's comments in the 11 February 1940 *Daily News*. "Never in the history of the native theatre has there been such a day-to-day ballyhoo trailing an actor," he wrote. "The whole thing is pretty cheap, and is getting tiresome."
69. Barrymore recited the "rogue and peasant slave" soliloquy at the Associated Actors and Artists Ball at the Waldorf Astoria on 21 April 1940, and also at the Shakespeare Club of New York's fiftieth anniversary celebration at the National Arts Club. See the 22 April 1940 *New York Times* and Gabriel Fallon, "One Man's Hamlet," *Irish Monthly* (May 1948), 232–3.
70. Barrymore again declared bankruptcy on 5 June 1940, when he stated to the court that he owed $110,000 to creditors and was in default of $200,000 in back payments to his wives; he was at the time filming *The Great Profile*. The nature of the material undoubtedly seemed secondary to the opportunity to earn $200,000 for a month's work before the cameras.

71. Lionel Barrymore, with Cameron Shipp, *We Barrymores* (New York: Appleton–Century–Crofts, 1951), 277; see also Gene Fowler, *Minutes of the Last Meeting* (New York: Viking, 1954), 190.

72. Telephone interview with Dame Judith Anderson, 5 October 1991; James Kotsilibas-Davis, telephone interview with Dame Judith Anderson, July 1991; see also Fowler, *Minutes of the Last Meeting*, 82-3; and J. P. McEvoy, "Barrymore – Clown Prince of Denmark," *Stage* (January 1941), 27-8.

73. Diana Barrymore and Gerold Frank, *Too Much Too Soon* (New York: Henry Holt, 1957), 182.

74. Vallee program rehearsal tape (19 May 1942), Museum of Television & Radio; Kobler, *Damned in Paradise*, 360-1; Lionel Barrymore, *We Barrymores*, 278. Kobler's account has Barrymore reading three lines from *Romeo and Juliet;* the rehearsal tape has only one.

75. Fowler, *Good Night, Sweet Prince*, 463-8.

76. James Agate, *Ego 5* (London: George G. Harrap, 1942), 232-3.

77. Hopkins, radio address prior to a broadcast of *Redemption*, UCB/SC, n.d. [c. 1942-3].

Epilogue

1. Arthur Hopkins, *Reference Point* (New York: Samuel French, 1948), 122-3.

2. Rex Smith, "John Barrymore: An Amazing Personality," *Theatre Magazine* (April 1928), 23, 70, 72 (at 23).

3. A wellspring for subsequent interpreters: see Francis Teague, "Hamlet in the Thirties," *Theatre Survey* 26 (May 1985), 63-79 (at 66-8). "I admired Barrymore": Laurence Olivier, *On Acting* (New York: Simon & Schuster, 1986), 98. See also John Kobler, *Damned in Paradise: The Life of John Barrymore* (New York: Atheneum, 1977), 200, where Olivier is quoted as saying: "He was stunning, so exciting, his voice, his high jumps. I modeled my Hamlet on his, and people said, 'Why is Larry always leaping about?'. . . I must have been the most gymnastic Hamlet anyone has seen – not more than Barrymore, I suppose. I emulated him."

4. Rosamond Gilder, *John Gielgud's Hamlet* (New York: Oxford University Press, 1937), 46. The voice of the Ghost in Gielgud's 1936 revival again boomed from the wings while a shadowy figure was seen onstage; the part was spoken by Malcolm Keen, who had played Claudius in Barrymore's London production. When Gielgud directed Burton in 1964, a similar effect was used; the Ghost was represented by a shadow on the back wall and the voice, this time recorded, was Gielgud's.

5. William Poel, *Shakespeare in the Theatre* (London: Sidgwick & Jackson, 1913), 57-8.

6. E. Harcourt Williams, *Four Years at the Old Vic: 1929-1933* (London: Putnam, 1935), 17-18. Barrymore's elimination of "me" and "min" was praised by Hesketh Pearson in *Theatre World* (March 1925), 33. See also Olivier, *On Acting*, 61-2. Olivier acknowledged that his method of delivery owed a good deal to Barrymore, and commented that "Some critics knocked him for his way of speaking verse, as indeed, was to happen to me in later years. They were wrong; I know they were wrong. He had a way of choosing a word and then exploding it in a moment of passion. Perhaps you did not always agree with the choice, but it was constantly riveting. He would vary his pace, but never gabble, was always understandable. . . . For my money he really seemed to understand Hamlet."

7. Lewisohn's comments: *Nation* (6 December 1922), 646. See also J. Ranken Towse's comments in the 8 March 1920 *New York Post* and Clayton Hamilton's remarks in

Vogue (1 May 1920), 166, regarding Barrymore's "repressed" movement and gesture as Richard III in comparison to the broad, "Shakespearean" physicality of Mansfield and Mantell. "A windmill of waving arms": Williams, *Four Years at the Old Vic*, 16–17.

8. "A little of Craig": Oliver M. Sayler, ed., *Max Reinhardt and His Theatre* (New York: Brentano's, 1924), 339. For a dissenting view on the influence of Jones's Craig-inspired designs, see Daniel Krempel and James H. Clay, "'New Stagecraft' Forty Years After: The Hopkins–Jones *Hamlet*," *Western Speech* 29 (Fall 1965): 201–10. Here the authors argue that Jones's designs for *Hamlet* were a logical extension of the pictorial tradition of staging in evidence since the Renaissance and conclude that most modern productions adhere to something like the Poel method. Krempel and Clay cite the Guthrie Theatre in Minneapolis and the theatres at Stratford, Ontario, and Chichester as examples of Poel's influence, which they find to be prevalent, yet they overlook a good deal of evidence regarding the subsequent use of symbolic unit settings and hybrid methods.

9. A repertory that would one day tour the world: Arthur Hopkins, *To a Lonely Boy* (Garden City, N.Y.: Doubleday, 1937), 202; "The creative element": letter to Michael Strange, 11 October 1922, Lincoln Center.

10. "That he would have had an unparalleled career": Hopkins, *To a Lonely Boy*, 230. "If Beverly Hills had been around": Olivier, *On Acting*, 62.

11. Hopkins, *Reference Point*, 122.

12. Lloyd Morris, *Curtain Time* (New York: Random House, 1953), 323.

13. George Jean Nathan, review of *Richard III* (26 March 1943) in *Theatre Book of the Year, 1942–1943* (New York: Knopf, 1943), 263–5. See also Burns Mantle's review of the same production in the 27 March 1943 *Daily News*.

14. "Swift as the flight of a falcon" and "a man alone with destiny": Robert Edmond Jones, unpublished notes, Wesleyan University; "a shrinking quality": idem, unpublished essay on John Barrymore, Harvard Theatre Collection.

15. "We were all three": Jones, Wesleyan notes; "We dreamed and it was done": Jones, Harvard essay.

16. *New York Herald Tribune* (7 June 1942).

Selected Bibliography

Books

Agate, James. *Ego*. London: Hamish Hamilton, 1935.
    Ego 5. London: George G. Harrap, 1942.
    Ego 7. London: George G. Harrap, 1945.
Alpert, Hollis. *The Barrymores*. New York: Dial Press, 1964.
Astor, Mary. *My Story*. Garden City, N.Y.: Doubleday, 1959.
Atkinson, Brooks. *Broadway*. Rev. ed. New York: Macmillan, 1974.
Barnes, Eric Wollencott. *The Man Who Lived Twice*. New York: Scribner's, 1956.
Barrymore, Diana, and Gerold Frank. *Too Much Too Soon*. New York: Henry Holt, 1957.
Barrymore, Elaine, and Sandford Doty. *All My Sins Remembered*. New York: Appleton–Century, 1964.
Barrymore, Ethel. *Memories*. New York: Harper & Brothers, 1955.
Barrymore, John. *Confessions of an Actor*. Indianapolis: Bobbs–Merrill, 1926.
    We Three: Lionel, Ethel, John. New York: Saalfield, 1935.
Barrymore, Lionel, with Cameron Shipp. *We Barrymores*. New York: Appleton–Century–Crofts, 1951.
Bulliet, C. J. *Robert Mantell's Romance*. Boston: Luce, 1918.
Burnham, John C. *Jelliffe: American Psychiatrist and Physician*. Chicago: University of Chicago Press, 1983.
Cheney, Sheldon. *The Art Theatre*. Rev. ed. New York: Knopf, 1925.
Churchill, Alan. *The Great White Way*. New York: Dutton, 1962.
    The Theatrical Twenties. New York: McGraw–Hill, 1975.
Clarens, Carlos. *George Cukor*. London: Secker & Warburg, 1976.
Cohen-Stratyner, Barbara Naomi, ed. *Performing Arts Resources 13: The Drews and the Barrymores*. New York: Theatre Library Association, 1988.
Coleman, Marian Moore. *Fair Rosalind*. Cheshire, Conn.: Cherry Hill Books, 1969.
Colley, Scott. *Richard's Himself Again*. Westport, Conn.: Greenwood, 1992.
Collier, Constance. *Harlequinade*. London: John Lane, 1929.
Compton, Fay. *Rosemary*. London: Alston Rivers, 1926.
Connelly, Marc. *Voices Offstage*. New York: Holt, Rinehart & Winston, 1968.
Crosse, Gordon. *Shakespearean Playgoing: 1890–1952*. London: A. R. Mowbray, 1953.
Dean, Basil. *Seven Ages*. London: Hutchinson, 1970.
Douglas, Ann. *Terrible Honesty: Mongrel Manhattan in the 1920s*. New York: Farrar, Straus & Giroux, 1995.

Drew, John. *My Years on the Stage*. New York: Dutton, 1922.

Drew, Louisa Lane. *Autobiographical Sketch of Mrs. John Drew*. New York: Scribner's, 1899.

Feinsod, Arthur. *The Simple Stage*. Westport, Conn.: Greenwood, 1992.

Forbes-Robertson, Johnston. *A Player under Three Reigns*. Boston: Little, Brown, 1925.

Fowler, Gene. *Good Night, Sweet Prince*. New York: Viking, 1944.

    Minutes of the Last Meeting. New York: Viking, 1954.

Fowler, Will. *The Young Man from Denver*. New York: Doubleday, 1962.

Freud, Sigmund. *Complete Psychological Works of Sigmund Freud*, ed. James Strachey. London: Hogarth Press, 1957.

Garton, Joseph. *The Film Acting of John Barrymore*. New York: Arno Press, 1982.

Gelb, Arthur, and Barbara Gelb. *O'Neill*. New York: Harper & Brothers, 1962.

Gielgud, John. *Gielgud: An Actor and His Time*. New York: Clarkson N. Potter, 1979.

    Shakespeare – Hit or Miss? London: Sidgwick & Jackson, 1991.

    Stage Directions. London: Heinemann, 1963.

Gilder, Rosamond. *John Gielgud's Hamlet*. New York: Oxford University Press, 1937.

Grebanier, Bernard. *The Heart of Hamlet*. New York: Crowell, 1960.

    Then Came Each Actor. New York: David McKay, 1975.

Hammond, Percy. *But – Is It Art*. Garden City, N.Y.: Doubleday, Page & Co., 1927.

Heller, Adele, and Lois Rudnick, eds. *1915, The Cultural Moment*. New Brunswick, N.J.: Rutgers University Press, 1991.

Hewitt, Barnard. *Theatre U.S.A.* New York: McGraw–Hill, 1959.

Hopkins, Arthur. *How's Your Second Act?* New York: Samuel French, 1918.

    Reference Point. New York: Samuel French, 1948.

    To a Lonely Boy. Garden City, N.Y.: Doubleday, 1937.

Hughes, Alan. *Henry Irving, Shakespearean*. Cambridge: Cambridge University Press, 1981.

Jones, Ernest. *Hamlet and Oedipus*. New York: W. W. Norton, 1949.

Jones, Robert Edmond. *The Dramatic Imagination*. New York: Duell, Sloan & Pearce, 1941.

Kane, Whitford. *Are We All Met?* London: Elkin, Mathews & Marrot, 1931.

Kanin, Garson. *Hollywood*. New York: Viking, 1974.

Kobler, John. *Damned in Paradise: The Life of John Barrymore*. New York: Atheneum, 1977.

Kotsilibas-Davis, James. *Great Times Good Times: The Odyssey of Maurice Barrymore*. Garden City, N.Y.: Doubleday, 1977.

    The Barrymores: The Royal Family in Hollywood. New York: Crown, 1981.

Levine, Lawrence W. *Highbrow/Lowbrow*. Cambridge: Harvard University Press, 1988.

Macgowan, Kenneth, and Robert Edmond Jones. *Continental Stagecraft*. New York: Harcourt Brace, 1922.

Mangan, Richard, ed. *John Gielgud's Notes from the Gods*. London: Nick Hern, 1995.

Marcosson, Issac F. and Daniel Frohman. *Charles Frohman: Manager and Man*. New York: Harper & Brothers, 1916.

Massey, Raymond. *A Hundred Different Lives*. Toronto: McClelland & Stewart, 1979.

May, Henry F. *The End of American Innocence*. New York: Knopf, 1959.

Mills, John A. *Hamlet on Stage: The Great Tradition*. Westport, Conn.: Greenwood, 1985.

Morehouse, Ward. *Matinee Tomorrow*. New York: Whittlesey House, 1949.

Morris, Lloyd. *Curtain Time*. New York: Random House, 1953.

Moses, Montrose J. *Famous Actor Families in America*. New York: Crowell, 1906.

Nesbitt, Cathleen. *A Little Love & Good Company*. Owings Mills, Md.: Stemmer House, 1977.

Norden, Martin F. *John Barrymore: A Bio-Bibliography.* Westport, Conn.: Greenwood, 1995.

Odell, G. C. D. *Shakespeare from Betterton to Irving.* 2 vols. New York: Scribner's, 1920.

Olivier, Laurence. *On Acting.* New York: Simon & Schuster, 1986.

Patterson, Michael. *The Revolution in German Theatre: 1900–1933.* London: Routledge & Kegan Paul, 1981.

Payne, Ben Iden. *A Life in a Wooden O.* New Haven: Yale University Press, 1977.

Pendleton, Ralph, ed. *The Theatre of Robert Edmond Jones.* Middletown, Conn.: Wesleyan University Press, 1958.

Peters, Margot. *The House of Barrymore.* New York: Knopf, 1990.

Phillips, Gene D. *George Cukor.* Boston: Twayne, 1982.

Power-Waters, Alma. *John Barrymore: The Legend and the Man.* New York: Julian Messner, 1941.

Preminger, Otto. *Preminger.* Garden City, N.Y.: Doubleday, 1977.

Quirk, Lawrence. *Norma: The Story of Norma Shearer.* New York: St. Martin's Press, 1988.

Rathbone, Basil. *In and Out of Character.* Garden City, N.Y.: Doubleday, 1962.

Rosenberg, Marvin. *The Masks of Hamlet.* Newark: University of Delaware Press, 1992.

Ruff, Loren. *Edward Sheldon.* Boston: Twayne, 1982.

Sayler, Oliver M., ed. *Max Reinhardt and His Theatre.* New York: Brentano's, 1924.

Shattuck, Charles H. *The Hamlet of Edwin Booth.* Urbana: University of Illinois Press, 1969.

Shakespeare on the American Stage. 2 vols. Washington, D.C.: Folger, 1976/1987.

The Shakespeare Promptbooks. Urbana: University of Illinois Press, 1965.

Sheaffer, Louis. *O'Neill: Son and Artist.* Boston: Little, Brown, 1973.

Simon, Henry W. *The Teaching of Shakespeare in American Schools and Colleges.* New York: Scribner's, 1932.

Sothern, E. H. *Julia Marlowe's Story.* ed. Fairfax Downey. New York: Rinehart, 1954.

The Melancholy Tale of "Me": My Remembrances. New York: Scribner's, 1916.

Speaight, Robert. *Shakespeare on the Stage.* Boston: Little, Brown, 1973.

William Poel and the Elizabethan Revival. London: Heinemann, 1954.

Stevens, Ashton. *Actorviews.* Chicago: Covici–McGee, 1923.

Strange, Michael. *Who Tells Me True.* New York: Scribner's, 1940.

Styan, J. L. *Max Reinhardt.* New York: Cambridge University Press, 1982.

The Shakespeare Revolution. New York: Cambridge University Press, 1977.

Trewin, J. C. *Shakespeare on the English Stage: 1900–1964.* London: Barrie & Rockliff, 1964.

Wagenknecht, Edward. *American Profile, 1900–1909.* Amherst: University of Massachusetts Press, 1982.

Walker, Alexander. *The Shattered Silents.* London: Elm Tree Books, 1978.

Webster, Margaret. *The Same Only Different.* London: Gollancz, 1969.

Shakespeare Today. London: J. M. Dent, 1957.

Willett, John. *Expressionism.* New York: McGraw–Hill, 1970.

Williams, E. Harcourt. *Four Years at the Old Vic: 1929–1933.* London: Putnam, 1935.

Wilson, A. E. *Playgoer's Pilgrimage.* London: Stanley Paul [1948].

Wilson, Garff B. *A History of American Acting.* Bloomington: Indiana University Press, 1966.

Wilstach, Paul. *Richard Mansfield: The Man and the Actor.* New York: Scribner's, 1908.

Winter, William. *Life and Art of Richard Mansfield.* 2 vols. New York: Moffat, Yard, 1910.

Yurka, Blanche. *Bohemian Girl.* Athens: Ohio University Press, 1970.

Articles

Barrymore, John. "The Prevailing Mode in Acting." *The Spotlight* (12 August 1910).
  "Those Incredible Barrymores." *American Magazine* (February 1933), 11–15, 70, 72,
  74; (March 1933), 20–3, 114–19; (April 1933), 26–9, 77–8; (May 1933), 58–61,
  78, 80, 82.
"What Is a Juvenile Lead?" *Theatre Magazine* (June 1914), 304, 317.
Browne, E. Martin. "English Hamlets of the Twentieth Century." *Shakespeare Survey* 9
  (1956), 16–23.
Clark, Larry D. "John Barrymore's Richard III." *Theatre History Studies* 4 (1984), 31–7.
Derrick, Patti S. "Julia Marlowe: An Actress Caught between Traditions." *Theatre Survey*
  32 (May 1991), 85–105.
Fallon, Gabriel. "One Man's Hamlet." *Irish Monthly* (May 1948), 228–33.
Favorini, Attilio. "'Richard's Himself Again': Robert Mantell's Shakespearean Debut in
  New York City." *Educational Theatre Journal* 24 (December 1972), 402–14.
Gabriel, Gilbert W. "John Barrymore as Hamlet: How the Actor Progressed Toward
  Shakespearean Roles." *World's Work* (September 1925), 498–501.
Kearney, Patrick. "Symbolism and the New Hamlet." *Vanity Fair* (January 1923), 41, 98.
Krempel, Daniel, and James H. Clay. "'New Stagecraft' Forty Years After: The Hop-
  kins–Jones *Hamlet*." *Western Speech* 29 (Fall 1965), 201–10.
Hayes, Helen. "Helen Hayes Picks the Ten Most Memorable Stage Performances." *Col-
  lier's* (22 September 1951), 20–1, 80–1.
Hughes, Glenn. "Repressed Acting and Shakespeare." *The Drama* (March 1923), 211.
Lipscomb, A. A. "Uses of Shakespeare off the Stage." *Harper's New Monthly Magazine*
  (August 1882), 431–8.
McDermott, Dana Sue. "The Apprenticeship of Robert Edmond Jones." *Theatre Survey*
  29 (November 1988), 193–212.
"The Void in *Macbeth*." *Themes in Drama* 4 (1982), 113–25.
McEvoy, J. P. "Barrymore – Clown Prince of Denmark." *Stage* (January 1941), 27–8.
Morrison, Michael A. "John Barrymore's 'Hamlet' at the Haymarket Theatre, 1925."
  New Theatre Quarterly 27 (August 1991), 246–60.
Patterson, Ada. "Shakespeare Made Smart." *Theatre Magazine* (March 1919), 154.
Row, Arthur William. "'Why I Do Not Play Long Seasons': Being an Interview with John
  Barrymore." *Professional Bulletin, Stage and Screen* (July 1926), 6.
Seymour, William D. "Some Richards I Have Seen." *Theatre Magazine* (June 1920), 502,
  565.
Sumner, Keene. "The Hidden Talents of 'Jack' Barrymore." *American Magazine* (June
  1919), 36–7, 149–52.
Teague, Francis. "Hamlet in the Thirties." *Theatre Survey* 26 (May 1985), 63–79.
Ten Broeck, Helen. "From Comedy to Tragedy." *Theatre Magazine* (July 1916), 23, 38.
Wheeler. A. C. "The Extinction of Shakespeare." *The Arena* 1 (March 1890), 423–31.
Woollcott, Alexander. "John Barrymore Arrives – A Great Man." *Everybody's Magazine*
  (June 1916), 122–4.
"The Two Barrymores." *Everybody's Magazine* (June 1920), 31.

Dissertations

Berg, Aubrey. "Collaborators: Arthur Hopkins, Robert Edmond Jones, and the Barrymores." Ph.D. diss.: Dept. of Theatre, University of Illinois at Urbana–Champaign,
  1979.

Davis, David N. "The Hamlets of Edwin Booth, John Barrymore, and Christopher Plummer." Ph.D. diss.: Dept. of Theatre, Wayne State University, 1968.

Kroll, Daniel R. "Hamlet from Edwin Booth to Laurence Olivier: Some Changing Interpretations Reflecting Changes in Culture and in the Tastes of Audiences." Ph.D. diss.: Dept. of English, Columbia University, 1959.

Otis, John F., Jr. "The Barrymore *Hamlet:* 1922–1925." Ph.D. diss.: Dept. of Theatre, University of Illinois, 1968.?

Promptbooks

Adams, William. Second season promptbook for *Hamlet* [1923]. Lincoln Center.

Promptbook for the Sothern and Marlowe *Hamlet,* 1919. Lincoln Center.

Barrymore, John. Studybook for *Hamlet* [1922–23]. Hampden–Booth Library, The Players.

Forbes-Robertson, Johnston. Promptbook for *Hamlet* [1914]. Huntington Library.

Hampden, Walter. Promptbook for *Hamlet* [1919]. Hampden–Booth Library, The Players.

Mansfield, Richard. Promptbook for *Richard III* [pub. ed., 1889]. Harvard Theatre Collection.

Sheldon, Edward. Draft promptbook for *Richard III* [1919]. Harvard Theatre Collection.

Taylor, John Lark. Promptbook for the Barrymore–Hopkins–Jones *Hamlet.* 1922. Vanderbilt University, Special Collections.

Promptbook for the Barrymore–Hopkins–Jones *Hamlet.* January 1924. Vanderbilt University, Special Collections.

Promptbook for the Barrymore–Hopkins–Jones *Hamlet.* 1922–3. Folger Shakespeare Library.

Promptbook for the Barrymore–Hopkins–Jones *Hamlet.* 1923–4. Folger Shakespeare Library.

Unpublished Sources

Barrymore, John. Letter to John Jay Chapman, 13 April 1920. Houghton Library, Harvard.

Letters to Michael Strange, 1917–25. Lincoln Center.

Letter to Robert Hosea, n.d. [1919]. Lincoln Center.

Letter to Jack Warner, 26 March 1930. University of Colorado at Boulder, Special Collections.

Bennett, Arnold. Diaries, vol. 26 [1925]. Berg Collection, New York Public Library.

Carrington, Margaret. Unpublished essays and notes on John Barrymore. Wesleyan University; also University of Colorado at Boulder, Special Collections.

Chapman, John Jay. Letter to H. H. Furness Jr., 24 November 1922. University of Pennsylvania, Special Collections.

Collier, Constance. Unpublished essay on John Barrymore's acting. University of Colorado at Boulder, Special Collections.

Crosse, Gordon. Manuscript diary for March 1925. Shakespeare Library, Birmingham Public Library.

Frohman, Charles. Business correspondence. Manuscript Division, New York Public Library.

Hopkins, Arthur. Papers, 1918–1950. Lincoln Center.

Jones, Robert Edmond. Letter to John Barrymore [July 1927]. University of Colorado at Boulder, Special Collections.

Unpublished essay on John Barrymore. Harvard Theatre Collection.

Unpublished notes. Wesleyan University.

Keighley, William. Unpublished autobiographical essay. Lincoln Center.

Macgowan, Kenneth. Letter to John Barrymore, 26 December 1933. University of Colorado at Boulder, Special Collections.

Row, Arthur William. "Barrymore Legend." Manuscript Division, New York Public Library; also Lincoln Center.

Shaw, Bernard. Letter to John Barrymore, 22 February 1925. Manuscript Division, Boston University.

Simonson, Lee. Letter to Wilva Davis Breen, 13 June 1937. Federal Theatre Archive, George Mason University.

Taylor, John Lark. "My Season with John Barrymore in *Hamlet*." Unpublished essay, Vanderbilt University, Special Collections.

"With Hey Ho!" Unpublished autobiography, Vanderbilt University, Special Collections.

Index

Index